PRACTICAL

Linux

M. Drew Streib

Michael Turner

John Ray

Bill Ball, et al.

Contents
at a Glance

que®

A Division of Macmillan USA
201 West 103rd Street
Indianapolis, Indiana 46290

Introduc...

I Linux Ba...
1 Introducin...
2 Entering C...
3 Navigating ...
4 Using Text E...
5 Printing Files ...

II Configuring Your System
6 Configuring Your Environment 99
7 Working with Hard Drives 113
8 Adding Tape and Zip Drives 129
9 Enabling a PC Card Device 137
10 Adding a Pointing Device 147
11 Configuring a Modem and Fax Service 153

III The X Window System
12 Running and Configuring X 169
13 Using a Window Manager 189
14 Performing Common X Operations 197
15 Using Graphics and Multimedia Tools 215

IV Connecting to Your Internet Service Provider
16 Connecting to Your Internet Service Provider 249
17 Using Electronic Mail 265
18 Using FTP 283
19 Using Web Browsers 295
20 Using telnet and Internet Relay Chat 309

V System Administration
21 Basic Shell Programming 321
22 Using Basic Programming Tools 339
23 Using Boot Managers 351
24 Managing Users and Groups 361
25 Managing Scheduling Services 389
26 Managing Network Connections 405
27 Managing Daemons 431
28 Managing the File System 453
29 Managing Applications 481
30 System Maintenance 503
31 Managing the Kernel 527

VI Appendixes
A Resources 579
B Using Linux HOWTO Documents 585
C Top 50 Linux Commands and Utilities 597
D Glossary 621

Index 643

i

Practical Linux

Copyright © 2000 by Que Corporation

International Standard Book Number: 0-7897-2251-8

Library of Congress Catalog Card Number: 99-068220

Printed in the United States of America

First Printing: June, 2000

02 01 00   4 3 2 1

Trademarks

Warning and Disclaimer

Acquisitions Editor
Gretchen Ganser

Development Editor
Hugh Vandivier

Technical Editor
Kurt Wall

Managing Editor
Matt Purcell

Project Editor
Pamela Woolf

Copy Editor
Michael Dietsch

Indexers
Eric Schroeder
Kevin Kent

Proofreader
Benjamin Berg

Team Coordinator
Cindy Teeters

Interior Designer
Anne Jones

Cover Designer
Rader Design

Copywriter
Eric Borgert

Layout Technicians
Tim Osborn
Mark Walchle

Contents

Introduction 1

I Linux Basics

1 Introducing the Shell 5

Welcome to Linux 6

What Is a Shell? 7

Logging in to Linux 8
  Creating a User Account at the Command Line 9
  Creating a User Account in X11 with the usercfg Command 9
  Changing Your Password 11
  Running Commands as the Root Operator 11
  Using Virtual Consoles 12

Logging Out of Linux 13
  Rebooting Linux 13
  Shutting Down Linux 13

Getting Help 14
  Getting Help with the man Command 14
  Getting Help in X11 with the xman Client 15
  Getting Help with the info Command 15
  Getting Help with the GNOME Help Browser 16
  Getting Help Using the KDE Help Browser 17
  Getting Help with the whatis Command 17
  Getting Help with the apropos Command 18

2 Entering Commands 19

Entering Commands at the Shell Command Line 20
  Case Sensitivity 20
  Editing the Command Line 20

Saving Keystrokes with Shell History 21
Using the Tab Key to Complete Commands 21
Entering Multiple Commands 22
Breaking Long Command Lines 22
Entering Commands in GNOME 23
Entering Commands in KDE 23

Creating Shell Commands 24
  Using the >, >>, and < Redirection Operators 24
  Redirecting Error Output by the Numbers 26
  Using Pipes to Build Commands 26
  Running Programs in the Background 27
  Creating Shell Commands with autoexpect 28

Controlling Programs 29
  Using Job Control 29
  Using the ps and kill Commands 30

Using Wildcards 31
  Building Regular Expressions 31

Selecting a Shell 32
  Changing Shells with the chsh Command 33

3 Navigating the Linux File System 35

Printing the Current Working Directory 36

Changing Directories with the cd Command 36

Listing Directories 37
  Listing Directories and Files with the ls Command 38
  Echoing Directory Contents with the echo Command 39

Viewing Text Files 39
  Viewing Text Files with the cat Command 40
  Viewing Text Files with the less and more Pager Commands 41

Creating Files and Directories **43**
  Using touch to Create and Update Files and Directories **43**
  Creating Directories with the mkdir Command **43**

Copying Files and Directories **44**
  Copying Files with the cp Command **44**
  Copying Directories with the cp Command **44**

Moving and Renaming Files and Directories **45**
  Moving and Renaming Files and Directories with the mv Command **45**

Creating Symbolic Links **46**
  Linking Files with the ln Command **46**
  Linking Directories with the ln Command **48**

Deleting Files and Directories **49**
  Deleting Files with the rm Command **49**
  Deleting Directories with the rmdir Command **49**
  Deleting Directories with the rm Command **50**

Finding Files and Directories **50**
  Finding Files with the find Command **50**
  Finding Files and Directories with the locate Command **51**
  Finding Programs and Manual Pages with the whereis Command and the which Command **52**

Using the GNOME gmc Client **52**
  Creating Directories Using the GNOME gmc Client **53**
  Copying, Moving, and Renaming Files and Directories Using the GNOME gmc Client **54**
  Creating Symbolic Links Using the GNOME gmc Client **54**

Deleting Files and Directories using the GNOME gmc Client **54**
  Searching for Files with GNOME's Search Tool **55**

Using the KDE File Manager kfm **55**
  Creating Directories Using KDE's kfm **56**
  Copying Files and Directories Using kfm **56**
  Moving and Renaming Files and Directories and Creating Symlinks Using kfm **57**
  Deleting Files and Using KDE's Trash Can **57**
  Searching the File System with KDE's kfind Client **57**

Searching Text Files **58**
  Using the grep Command **58**
  Using the egrep Command **60**
  Using the fgrep Command **60**
  Using the strings Command **61**
  Using the egrep and fgrep Commands **61**

4 Using Text Editors 63

Selecting an Editor **64**
  Commercial Linux Word Processors **64**
  Using Screen Editors **67**
  Using Stream Editors **75**

Using Linux Dictionaries **77**
  Getting the web2 Dictionary **77**
  Dictionaries: Rolling Your Own **78**
  Spell Checking with the ispell Command **78**
  Using Internet Dictionaries with the dict Clients **79**

Saving Paper with the mpage Command **79**

Creating Formatted Documents **80**
  Using Text-Formatting Filter Commands **80**
  Using Text-Processing Systems **82**

5 Printing Files **87**

Adding Printers **88**
Checking Your Printer **88**
Adding a Local Printer by Editing
/etc/printcap **90**

Configuring Printers for WordPerfect for
Linux **91**

Spooling Files to Your Printer **92**
Printing Files at the Command Line **93**
Listing the Print Queue **93**

Controlling Printers and Print Jobs **93**
Reordering Print Jobs **95**
Stopping Print Jobs **95**
Sending Faxes with the lpr Command **95**

II Configuring Your System

6 Configuring Your Environment **99**

Displaying Environment Variables with the
printenv Command **100**
Displaying Environment Variables with the
env Command **102**
Setting an Environment Variable on the
Command Line **102**
Deleting an Environment Variable from the
Command Line **103**
Setting Command PATHs **104**

Customizing Your Login **105**
Customizing Your Command-Line
Prompt **106**

Creating Aliases **108**

Using the linuxconf Utility **109**

7 Working with Hard Drives **113**

Determining the Volume Device and
Partition **114**
Hard Drive Devices **115**

Choosing a File System **118**

Adding a Hard Drive **119**
Identifying Hard Drives and Devices **119**

Partitioning a Hard Drive with the fdisk
Command **120**

Manipulating Partitions with the sfdisk
Command **123**

Mounting a Hard Drive or Other
Device **124**

Mounting and Unmounting Remote NFS
Hard Drives **126**

Mounting File Systems with linuxconf **126**

8 Adding Tape and Zip Drives **129**

Adding a Tape Drive **130**
Installing a Tape Drive **130**
Using the mt Command **131**

Adding a Zip Drive **132**
Before Installing a Zip Drive **133**
Ejecting, Password-Protecting, and Read-
Write–Protecting Zip Disks **134**

9 Enabling a PC Card Device **137**

Enabling PCMCIA Services **138**
Determining Your PCMCIA Controller **139**

Using the cardmgr Command **141**
Listing Your PC Card and Drivers **141**
Disabling cardmgr Command Event
Notification **142**

Using the cardctl Command   *142*
  Obtaining the Status of PC Cards   143
  Listing Your PC Card Configuration   143
  Inserting a PC Card   144
  Ejecting a PC Card   144
  *Suspending and Restoring PC Card
  Power   145*

10 Adding a Pointing Device   147

Adding a Mouse   *148*
  Using and Configuring gpm   148
  Configuring a Synaptics Touchpad   149

Installing a Joystick   *151*
  Configuring a Joystick   152

11 Configuring a Modem and Fax Service   153

Selecting a Modem for Linux   *154*
  *Using the dmesg Command to Check Serial
  Port Status   154*
  *Testing Your Modem with the echo
  Command   155*

Creating the /dev/modem Device   *156*
  *Creating /dev/modem with the ln
  Command   156*
  *Getting Serial Port Information with the set-
  serial Command   156*

Enabling Dial-In Service   *157*
  Configuring Linux for Dial-in Service   157
  *Configuring Linux for Dial-in PPP
  Service   160*

Configuring Fax Service   *161*
  Configuring the fax Shell Script   162
  Testing Your Fax Configuration   163
  *Sending a Fax Using the fax Shell
  Script   164*
  Setting Up to Wait for Incoming Faxes   164

  *Checking the Status of Incoming or Outgoing
  Faxes   164*
  Viewing Received Faxes   164
  Printing a Received Fax   165
  Deleting a Received Fax   165

III **The X Window System**

12 Running and Configuring X   169

Configuring XFree86 with XF86Setup   *170*

Configuring Xfree86 with
XConfigurator   *170*
  Configuring Your Graphics Card   170

Starting X11   *171*
  Using the startx Command   171
  Using Virtual Consoles with X   172
  Starting Multiple X Sessions   172

Stopping X   *173*

System and X Session Control with Display
Managers   *173*
  Logging In with xdm   173
  Customizing the xdm Banner Screens   176

Customizing the .xinitrc Startup Script   *178*

Customizing Your Workspace   *179*
  Setting a Screen Saver   179
  Setting the Background Desktop Color   182
  *Setting the Background Desktop
  Pattern   182*
  Using a Desktop Wallpaper   182
  Setting the Mouse Pointer   184
  Configuring the Mouse   185
  Configuring Terminal Windows   186

Using X11 Resources   *187*

13 Using a Window Manager 189

Window Managers and Desktop Environments **190**

Selecting an X11 Window Manager **190**
The K Desktop Environment and kwm **191**
Enlightenment **192**
Window Maker **193**

Starting a Window Manager **193**
Starting KDE **194**
Starting Enlightenment/GNOME **194**
Starting Window Maker **195**

14 Performing Common X Operations 197

Using X11 Toolkit Command-Line Options **198**
Using Geometry Settings to Set Window Size **198**
Setting Foreground and Background Colors **199**

Moving, Resizing, and Managing Windows **200**
Specifying an X11 Window Title **200**
Minimizing, Maximizing, or Closing Windows **201**

Viewing X11 Fonts **202**
Viewing X11 Fonts with the xfontsel Client **203**

Using the xfd Client to View Font Character Maps **203**

Copying and Pasting Text **206**
Using the xcutsel Client to Copy Text **206**
Copying Text with the xclipboard Client **207**

Capturing Windows and the Desktop **208**
Using xwd to Capture Windows **208**
Using xwud to Display Window Dumps **209**

Using the xloadimage Client to View Captures **210**
Capturing and Viewing Screens with the xv Client **210**
Using the xmag Client to Capture Magnified Images **212**

15 Using Graphics and Multimedia Tools 215

Selecting a Graphics Program **216**
Using the GIMP Client **216**
Using ImageMagick **224**

Translating or Converting Graphics **229**
Using the pbm, ppm, and pnm Utilities **233**

Previewing Graphics and PostScript Documents **234**
Using the gv PostScript Previewer **234**
Using Adobe Acrobat **237**

Playing Music CDs **240**

Watching and Listening to Internet TV and Radio **243**
Using RealPlayer **244**

Playing Animations and Movies with the xanim Client **245**

IV Connecting to Your Internet Service Provider

16 Connecting to Your Internet Service Provider 249

Configuring a PPP Connection **250**
Checking Your Serial Port and Modem **251**
Checking Your Linux Kernel and File System for PPP Support **251**

Configuring PPP for Your ISP **253**

Configuring Your PPP Connection
Scripts *254*
    Editing the ppp-on Connection Script *254*

Configuring PPP with kppp *255*

Starting a PPP Connection *257*
    *Starting a PPP Connection Using the minicom
    Program* *257*
    *Starting a PPP Connection with the ppp-on
    Script* *258*
    Starting a PPP Connection with kppp *258*
    Closing Your PPP Connection *258*

Checking Your PPP Connection *259*
    *Checking PPP Connections with the ifconfig
    Command* *259*
    *Getting PPP Statistics with the pppstats
    Command* *260*
    Getting PPP Statistics with kpppload *260*
    *Testing PPP Connection Speed with the ping
    Command* *260*
    *Getting PPP Interface Information with the
    route Command* *261*
    *Troubleshooting PPP Connections with Your
    System Log* *261*

17 Using Electronic Mail **265**

Retrieving Electronic Mail *266*
    Using fetchmail *266*

Selecting a Mail Program *269*
    Using mail *269*
    Using pine *271*
    *Using Netscape Messenger to Create, Send,
    and Read Mail* *274*

Managing Electronic Mail *280*
    Configuring procmail to Filter Mail *281*

18 Using FTP **283**
    Using ftp to Download Files *286*
    Using ftp Help Commands *291*

Using the ncftp Command *292*
    Downloading with the ncftp Command *292*

Using Netscape to Download Files *293*

19 Using Web Browsers **295**
    Configuring the Lynx Browser *298*

Using Netscape Communicator *300*
    *Downloading and Installing Netscape
    Communicator* *300*
    Working with Netscape Communicator *303*

20 Using telnet and Internet Relay Chat **309**

Using the telnet Command *310*
    Connecting to Other Computers *310*
    *Downloading Files During telnet
    Sessions* *313*

Chatting with Internet Relay Chat *314*
    Starting an irc Session *314*

V System Administration

21 Basic Shell Programming **321**

What Shell Scripts Are Used For *322*

Writing Shell Programs *323*
    Good Programming Practice *323*
    A Sample Program *323*

Using Shell Variables *327*
    Using Variables in Scripts *328*
    A Sample Script *328*

Using Shell Constructs *332*
    *Conditional Constructs: The if
    Statement* *333*
    Repeating Commands with while *336*
    Repeating Commands with for *336*

Writing Shell Functions *336*
    A Simple Shell Function *337*
    Using a Library *338*

22 Using Basic Programming Tools **339**

Recompiling Code *340*

Compiling Programs with gcc *340*

Linking Programs with the ld Linker *341*

Building Programs with the make Command *342*
  A Sample Program *343*
  make Options *344*
  A Sample Program: the make Command *345*
  A Sample Program *345*

Specifying Different Makefiles *347*

Getting Started Quickly with New Programs *347*

Specifying Different Makefiles *349*

Building X11 Makefiles with the xmkmf Script *349*

23 Using Boot Managers **351**

How Linux Boots: LILO/LOADLIN *352*

Configuring LILO *352*
  Changing the Default Boot *354*
  Passing Kernel Parameters *354*
  Booting to a Specific Run Level *355*

Using LOADLIN *356*
  Booting from DOS to Linux *356*
  Setting Up LOADLIN *357*
  Passing Kernel Parameters with LOADLIN *359*

24 Managing Users and Groups **361**

Users, Groups, and Their Relation to the System *362*

Using the usercfg Tool *363*
  Adding a User with usercfg *365*
  View/Edit Users *367*
  Locking a User *368*
  Unlocking a User *369*
  Removing a User *370*
  Adding a Group *371*
  Editing an Existing Group *373*
  Removing a Group *373*
  Finishing Up with usercfg *373*

Adding, Editing, and Deleting Users Using the Command Line *373*
  Adding Users with useradd *374*
  Modifying Users with the usermod Command *374*
  Deleting Users with the userdel Command *375*

Adding, Editing, and Deleting Groups *376*
  Adding Groups with the groupadd Command *376*
  Modifying Groups with the groupmod Command *376*
  Deleting Groups with the groupdel Command *376*

Changing User and Group Ownership *377*
  Managing Groups with gpasswd *377*
  Using the chgrp Command *378*

Changing File Ownership and Permissions *378*
  Using the chown Command *378*
  Using the chmod Command *379*

Advanced Concepts: Password Authentication Module *382*
  Improving System Security Using PAM *382*

25 Managing Scheduling Services **389**

Configuring inittab and rc Files *390*
  The inittab File *391*
  The rc Files *394*

Configuring crontab Scheduling
Service *395*
  Enabling crontab Service 396
  crontab Entries 396
  *Allowing and Preventing Access to the crontab
  Service 399*

Configuring the at Command Service *400*
  Enabling at Command Service 400
  *Common Problems with the at
  Command 401*
  *Allowing and Preventing Access to the at
  Command Service 403*

26 **Managing Network Connections 405**

Configuring Network Connections
Manually *406*
  Configuring the Loopback Interface 406
  Configuring an Ethernet Card 407
  Setting a Default Route 408
  *Configuring Hostname and DNS
  Information 409*
  *Using DHCP to Configure Your Network
  Settings 411*

Configuring Network Connections with
linuxconf *411*
  Using the Network Configuration Tool 412
  *Setting the Hostname and the Domain
  Name 413*
  Setting the Name Servers 413
  Adding a PPP Interface 413
  Adding a SLIP Interface 416

Adding a PLIP Interface *418*

Adding an Ethernet Interface *420*
  Setting Up a Router 421
  Connecting Two Linux Systems 423
  *Connecting a Mac OS Machine to a Linux
  System 423*
  *Connecting a Windows Machine to a Linux
  System 424*

Enabling the Network File System
Service *425*

Enabling Dial-In Service *427*
  Setting Up the PPP Options Files 427
  Configuring Getty Devices 428

27 **Managing Daemons 431**

Editing and Creating Run Levels *434*

Editing inittab *435*

Using chkconfig *436*
  Listing Services by Using chkconfig 436
  Removing a Service by Using chkconfig 437
  Adding a Service by Using chkconfig 437
  Resetting Service Information 437

Editing Startup and Shutdown Scripts *438*
  A Sample init Script 438
  init Script Checklist 440

Customizing the Login Greeting *441*
  *Customizing the Login Greeting for Network
  Connections 442*

Enabling and Customizing the MOTD *443*

Using the tksysv Tool *443*
  Adding a Service with tksysv 444
  Using ksysv 446
  *Starting and Stopping Network
  Services 447*

Using the ntsysv Tool *448*

Enabling FTP Access *448*

Enabling a Web Server *450*
  Configuring the Apache Web Server 451

28 Managing the File System 453

Mounting and Unmounting File
Systems *454*
   Using the usermount Command 454
   *Formatting a Floppy Using the kfloppy
   Command 456*
   Using the mount Command 457

Setting Up New File Systems *461*
   Starting linuxconf 462
   linuxconf 466
   Editing /etc/fstab Manually 467

Creating New File Systems *469*
   *How to Organize Your File System
   Tree 472*

Repairing File Systems *473*

Disaster Recovery *476*
   What's Vital and What Isn't? 476
   When to Back Up 477
   What to Do with the Backups 478
   Reviewing Your Backup Strategy 478
   Coping with Disaster 478

29 Managing Applications 481

Package Management with rpm *482*
   *The rpm Command's Major Modes and
   Common Options 482*
   Installing Packages 483
   Upgrading Packages 486
   Uninstalling Packages 486
   Querying Packages 488
   Verifying Packages 491
   *Using KDE's kPackage System to Manage
   RPMs 493*
   Installing and Using the xrpm Client 496

Converting Between Different Package
Methods *500*

30 System Maintenance 503

Performing System Backups *504*
   *Compressing and Decompressing Files and
   Directories 504*
   *Compressed Archiving with the tar
   Command 505*
   *Using find to Locate Files for tar
   Backups 509*
   Using taper for Backups 513
   Backing Up with Floppy Disks 517
   Backing Up with Removable Drives 518

Performing File System Maintenance *521*
   Deleting Unnecessary Files 521
   Undeleting Files 522

Maximizing Disk Space *523*
   Performing System Cleanups 523
   *Compressing Unused Documents and
   Directories 526*

31 Managing the Kernel 527

Adding a Module to the Kernel
Configuration *528*

Editing the Linux Kernel Configuration
Files *531*
   Configuring Your Sound Card 532
   Plug and Play Devices 534

Managing Modules *535*
   Installing Modules 535
   Listing Loaded Modules 535
   Creating Module Dependencies 536
   Enabling Modules at Boot Time 537

Managing Processes *538*
   Using the /proc Directory Information 539
   Viewing the System Load Average 540
   *Viewing Processes with the top
   Command 540*

Viewing Processes with the ps
Command **542**
Using the kill and killall Commands and
Process IDs **543**

Recompiling the Kernel **545**
Installing the New Kernel Source **545**
Before Configuring the Kernel **546**
Using make config **547**
Using make xconfig **562**
Building and Installing the Kernel **570**
Installing the Kernel **573**

VI **Appendixes**

A Resources 579

Usenet Resources **580**

World Wide Web Resources **581**

B Using Linux HOWTO Documents 585

C Top 50 Linux Commands and Utilities 597

General Guidelines **598**

The List **599**
  & **599**
  adduser **599**
  alias **599**
  apropos **600**
  banner **600**
  bg **601**
  bind **601**
  cat **601**
  cd **602**
  chgrp **602**
  chmod **602**
  chown **603**

chroot **604**
cp **604**
dd **604**
userdel **604**
env **605**
fc **605**
fg **605**
file **606**
find **606**
ftp **607**
grep **607**
groff **607**
gzip **607**
gunzip **608**
halt **608**
hostname **608**
kill **608**
killall **608**
less **608**
locate **609**
login **609**
logout **609**
lpc **609**
lpd **609**
lpq **610**
lpr **610**
ls **610**
make **611**
man **611**
mesg **611**
mkdir **612**
mkfs **612**
mkswap **612**
more **612**
mount **612**
mv **613**
netstat **613**
passwd **614**
ps **614**

pwd *614*
rm *614*
rmdir *615*
set *615*
shutdown *615*
su *615*
swapoff *616*
swapon *616*
tail *616*
talk *616*
tar *616*
telnet *616*
top *617*
umount *617*

unalias *617*
unzip *617*
wall *617*
who *617*
write *618*
xhost *618*
xmkmf *618*
xset *618*
zip *619*

Summary *619*

D Glossary 621

Index 643

About the Authors

M. Drew Streib is a senior programmer specializing in Web applications for VA Linux Systems (http://www.valinux.com), the system administrator for Linux International (http://li.org), and a senior programmer for SourceForge (http://sourceforge.net). He also contributes to many open-source projects in his free time. Drew programs in several languages but now spends most of his time in PHP, C, and Perl.

When **Michael Turner** was ten years old, his father bought an Apple II. Since then, not even his fianceé has managed to drag him away from behind a monitor. He currently works for VA Linux Systems where his business card reads "Geek." Michael lives in Silicon Valley, California with his fianceé, his cat, a few pet reptiles, and a home LAN that puts many corporations to shame.

Michael discovered Linux and the open source movement in 1995 when he was looking for a cheap and reliable OS for his company's firewall. Five years have passed and he's proud to say that he and his fianceé run Linux on every computer and server in the house.

John Ray is an award-winning Web application developer and network programmer for The Ohio State University. He holds a computer engineering degree from OSU and oversees network operations for one of its colleges. There, he implemented a campus-wide database for maintaining TCP/IP information for a wide range of networked computers. For the past five years, John has used Linux exclusively for his programming efforts and has championed its use for projects inside and outside the University. He provides customized Linux and UNIX-based TCP/IP programming solutions to businesses nationwide. His other publications include *Sams Teach Yourself Linux in 10 Minutes*, *Special Edition Using Red Hat Linux*, *Special Edition Using TCP/IP*, and *Linux Maximum Security*.

Bill Ball is the author of a half-dozen best-selling books about Linux: *Sams Teach Yourself Linux in 24 Hours*, Que's *Using Linux*, Sams' *Red Hat Linux 6 Unleashed*, Sams' *How to Use Linux*, and Sams' *Linux Unleashed, Fourth Edition*. He is a technical writer, editor, and magazine journalist and has been working with computers for the past 20 years. He first started working with Linux, beginning with kernel version .99, after moving from BSD4.3 Machten for the Apple Macintosh. He has published articles in magazines such as *Computer Shopper* and *MacTech Magazine* and first started editing books for Que in 1986. An avid fly-fisherman, he builds bamboo fly rods and fishes on the nearby Potomac River when he's not driving his vintage MG sports car. Bill is a member of the Northern Virginia Linux Users Group (NOVALUG), and lives in the Shirlington area of Arlington County, Virginia.

Tony Guntharp is a site manager of `http://coldstorage.org` for VA Linux Systems.

Jan Walter is a Senior Systems Architect for the Adrenaline Group in Washington, D.C. He formerly consulted in the Vancouver, Canada area. His work in Vancouver included work with Internet e-commerce systems as well as support of smaller clients using Windows NT, OS/2, and of course Linux.

Steve Shah is a systems administrator at the Center for Environmental Research and Technology at the University of California, Riverside. He received his B.S. in computer science with a minor in creative writing, and is currently working on his M.S. in computer science there as well. Occasionally, Steve leaves his console to pursue analog activities such as deejaying and spending time with his better half, Heidi.

Sriranga Veeraraghavan works in the area of network management at Cisco Systems, Inc. He enjoys developing software using Java, C, Perl, and Shell for both Linux and Solaris. His pastimes include playing Marathon and debugging routing problems in his heterogeneous network at home. Sriranga graduated from the University of California at Berkeley in 1997 with an engineering degree and is pursuing further studies at Stanford University. His most recent book is *Sams Teach Yourself Shell Programming in 24 Hours*.

Tad Bohlsen is currently the technology manager for a nonprofit organization, and also a consultant on technology issues. In the past he has served as a UNIX system administrator and shell script developer, and worked with companies such as Juno Online Services and HBO.

David Pitts has co-written more than a half-dozen books covering Linux, UNIX, and CGI programming in Perl. He is an author, consultant, systems administrator, programmer, instructor, Web developer, and Christian. David can be reached at `dpitts@mk.net`. His Web page, `http://www.dpitts.com`, contains more information about him. Currently, David lives in Sacramento, California with his first wife, Dana; her beautiful teen-aged cousin, Ashley; and their invisible cat, Spot. David's favorite quote comes from Saint Francis of Assisi: "Preach the Gospel, and, if necessary, use words."

Dedication

M. Drew Streib:

To Dan, Patti, and Dave, who have always supported me.

Michael Turner:

I would like to thank Amy, whose support helped make the deadlines possible.

introduction

Linux has enjoyed incredible growth as an operating system in the past few years. Years of refinement have helped it to grow out of a niche market and into the mainstream. You can now find Linux in mission-critical servers and on home desktops. Taking the time to learn about Linux will help increase your productivity and will enhance your overall computer experience.

This book is designed for all Linux users, from Linux newcomers to seasoned system administrators. New users will want to start at the beginning and follow the tutorial-style nature of the book. More experienced users will get more out of the later book chapters. The entire book makes an excellent reference manual for common (and some not-so-common) tasks.

Rather than choose a specific distribution for *Practical Linux*, we have chosen to be as distribution neutral as possible. Plenty of excellent programs are available that span all major distributions. Learning these tools ensures that you will never be locked into one company's version of Linux. We should note, however, that some of the tasks in this book can also be accomplished with distribution-specific tools, often times more easily than with standard programs. You should learn and use these tools if they make you more productive, realizing that they might not be available in another Linux distribution.

We wrote this book in a task-oriented fashion, explaining the steps required to complete each task. Learning by example can be very easy and is often the best way to understand computer skills. *Practical Linux* is organized in a manner that makes it a good reference.

Part I, "Linux Basics," introduces you to Linux, explains initial setup and use of common command-line functions and familiarizes you with the operating system.

Part II, "Configuring Your System," guides you through more advanced system setup, focusing on system hardware and peripheral devices.

Part III, "The X Window System," explains X Window, the graphical environment for Linux, including setup, configuration, and use.

Part IV, "Connecting to Your Internet Service Provider," connects you to the Internet, helping you set up your ISP connection and explaining many network programs available in Linux.

Part V, "System Administration," contains advanced system setup information including user management, shell programming, and system optimization.

I hope that you get as much out of Linux as I have. Open source software has shown that it can succeed in the commercial market. After you learn the basics of Linux, I would encourage you to give something back to the open source community. Programmers can of course contribute source code, but non-programmers can also play an important role by telling authors about the bugs they find, writing documentation, or simply telling others about what open source products work well.

Enjoy this book and best wishes with your Linux experience.

part

I

LINUX BASICS

Introducing the Shell   5   1

Entering Commands   19   2

Navigating the Linux File System   35   3

Using Text Editors   63   4

Printing Files   87   5

Introducing the Shell

Welcome to Linux ●

What is a shell? ●

Logging in to Linux ●

Logging out of Linux ●

Getting help ●

> **What is Linux?**
>
> Linux is the kernel, or core, of a UNIX-like computer operating system. Linux, written by Linus Torvalds, was first released over the Internet in 1991. Since then, Linux has exploded in popularity, maturing with each new version and bug fix. When you install and use Linux, you're installing and using a *distribution*, or collection of associated programs bundled with the Linux kernel. There are a number of popular Linux distributions, including Red Hat Linux, Slackware, Debian, Caldera, Mandrake, TurboLinux, and S.u.S.E. Each distribution has a different installation method and is bundled with different software maintenance tools.

Welcome to Linux

Congratulations on choosing and using Linux, today's newest, most popular, flexible, and powerful free computer operating system. Hang on, because you're riding along the crest of a rising tidal wave of new users, as Linux spreads around the globe. While governments and corporations publicly battle one another over commercial software issues, Linux has been steadily gaining worldwide acceptance and respect as a viable alternative computer operating system. Linux quietly sidesteps the restrictions that hold commercial software hostage in the marketplace in a number of ways:

- Linux is distributed under the terms of the Free Software Foundation's General Public License, or GPL. This license preserves software copyrights, but ensures distribution of programs with source code.
- Linux is distributed over the Internet, and is easy to download, upgrade, and share.
- Programmers all over the world create, distribute, and maintain programs for Linux, and much of this software is also distributed under the GPL.

Linux continues to evolve, and major improvements to the last several versions make using, installing, and maintaining this operating system easier than ever. With Linux's increasing popularity, kernel bug fixes and new versions of free software appear every day on more and more Internet servers. New features of the latest versions of the Linux kernel and distributions include the following:

- Support for dynamic code-module loading and unloading. If a printer or sound card is needed, the appropriate code module is loaded from a disk and then released after use as appropriate.
- Increased support for a wide variety of devices such as sound cards, scanners, hard disks, tape drives, printers, digital cameras, and joysticks.
- Increasingly easier installation, configuration, and system maintenance with dozens of different GUI (graphical user interface) programs, many of which surpass commercial software peers in convenience and ease of use.

What does *open source* mean anyway?

The Linux operating system belongs to a genre of software called *free* or *open source*. Open-source software operates on a simple concept: Software must be accompanied with the source code that makes it work. Open-source software is synonymous with the term *free software*. In this case, *free* refers to freedom (as in "free speech" not "free beer").

Shipping source code with software allows users to easily make changes, run bug fixes, install patches, and make improvements to make the software work better. As a result, software evolves quickly and efficiently. Open-source software taps into the brain power of developers all over the world, rather than just a few who work for any one company. Patches and bug fixes seem to appear overnight rather than years later.

The open-source movement has been growing over the past 15–20 years and has now gained enough momentum to pose a serious threat to corporate giants in the software industry. Products such as Linux, the GIMP (an image-manipulation package), and GNU Emacs are testaments that the free software model works.

For more information about open-source software, check the Web sites `http://www.gnu.org` and `http://www.opensource.org`, or read Eric Raymond's essay, "The Cathedral and the Bazaar" (which you can find at `http://www.tuxedo.org/~esr/writings/cathedral-bazaar/`).

There are now versions of Linux for Intel-based PCs, the Apple PowerMacintosh, Digital's Alpha PCs, and Sun SPARC-compatibles. Each version of Linux comes with complete source code, so you can customize, correct bugs, or recompile the operating system.

SEE ALSO

➤ *To learn how to rebuild the Linux kernel, see page 527.*

➤ *To learn how to manage kernel modules, see page 535.*

What Is a Shell?

This chapter, which introduces you to Linux, assumes that you've just booted Linux for the first time after installation. The *shell* is a program started after you log in to Linux that provides a command-line interface between you and the Linux kernel. Typed commands are interpreted by the shell and sent to the *kernel*, which in turn opens, closes, reads, and writes files. There are a number of shells for Linux; the default shell for most distributions, however, is called bash and is found under the /bin directory. The shell's internal commands and functions can also be used to write programs.

SEE ALSO

➤ *To learn how to write shell programs, see page 323.*

➤ *To learn about how to use the shell, see page 20.*

Logging in to Linux

When you sit down at your Linux terminal, the first thing you should see is a login prompt. Linux was written with your computer's security in mind. Each user should have her own account and appropriate access privileges. When you log in, keep in mind that the computer attempts to match your username and password to the ones it has on file. Spelling and punctuation count, so be sure to pick a username and password you will remember!

Working from the login and password prompt at a text console interface

1. After you boot Linux for the first time, you'll see login and password prompts on your display. To access Linux, type root at the login prompt and press Enter.

   ```
   localhost login: root
   Password:
   ```

2. At the password prompt, type the password you chose when you installed Linux.

3. After you press the Enter key, the screen will clear, and you'll be presented with a command line:

   ```
   #
   ```

Some Linux configurations present you with a graphical login rather than a command-line prompt. After entering your username and password, you will boot directly into X (the Linux windowing system). If this happens and you'd prefer to use the command line, you can simply press Ctrl+Alt+F2. To escape back to X, press Ctrl+Alt+F7.

SEE ALSO

➤ *For more information about X, see page 189.*

➤ *To learn about virtual consoles, go to page 12.*

Although you can manually edit system files to create, add, edit, or delete users and user information, Linux comes with several command-line and graphical interface tools that make the job a lot easier. The first thing you should do after booting Linux following installation is to create your own user account.

Starting to work with Linux

1. Create a username for yourself or others. Optionally, enter user account information.

2. Create a password for yourself or new users.

3. Exit or log out of Linux.

4. Log in to Linux with your new username and password.

Running as root can be dangerous!

Before you start using Linux, you should create a username and password for yourself instead of running as the root operator all the time. Log in as the root operator only when you need to upgrade Linux, add or partition a new hard drive, perform system maintenance or recovery, or run root-only tools. As the root operator, you can create or destroy any file in any directory in your system. Improperly specified unconditional file deletions using wildcards or inadvertent file and directory copying will not only wipe out entire directories, but can also impact any other mounted file systems on the machine, such as Windows. Always keep a backup of important files!

Creating a User Account at the Command Line

When you first log in to Linux, you will probably be logged in as the root operator. A few distributions, such as Debian and OpenLinux, give you the option to create a user account during installation. Nevertheless, part of effectively administering a Linux box includes managing user accounts.

Create a username foryourself with the `useradd` command, found under the `/usr/sbin` directory, like so:

```
# useradd mike
```

The `useradd` command creates a user entry in a file called `passwd`, under the `/etc` directory. This entry lists the user's name and password, along with a home directory and default shell:

```
mike:x:501:501:Michael Smith:/home/mike:/bin/bash
```

Some versions of `useradd` ask you for details about the user, such as the user's full name and password. Other versions leave this extra information blank and expect you to fill it in later.

Creating a User Account in X11 with the *usercfg* Command

If you're running the X Window System, the `linuxconf` utility in its graphical form will provide an easy way to add or modify user accounts. If you have `linuxconf` installed, you might have an icon available to launch it, or you can type the following in a terminal window:

```
# linuxconf
```

The `linuxconf` utility provides an easy way to control the configuration of your system. For more information about using the `linuxconf` utility, see "Using the `linuxconf` Utility" in Chapter 6, "Configuring Your Environment." If you select User Accounts, Normal, User Accounts from the command tree on the left, you are

9

presented with a list of current users. Now click the Add button and you'll see a form similar to Figure 1.1.

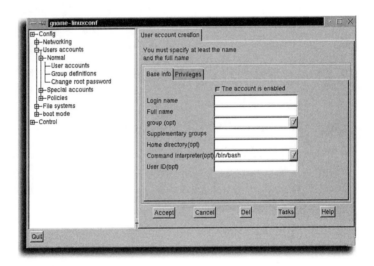

FIGURE 1.1
The `linuxconf` add user utility provides an intuitive GUI for managing user accounts. This is an example of the GNOME version. There are several other versions of `linuxconf`, so don't panic if yours looks a little different. See Chapter 6 for more information.

To create a User Account

1. Fill in the user's login name and full name. You can fill in the other information in the form if you want, or let `linuxconf` provide default answers.

2. Click the `Accept` button.

3. Now choose a password for the user account.

4. Retype the password to make sure you didn't make a typing error.

5. Click the Quit button when you are finished creating accounts to close that tab in `linuxconf`.

SEE ALSO

➤ *To learn how to start the X Window System, see page 171.*

➤ *To learn more about the* `linuxconf` *utility, see page 109.*

Changing Your Password

As a user, you can change your own password, or as the root operator, you can change the password for any user on your system. To change a password, use the passwd command, as follows:

```
$ passwd
(current> UNIX password:
New UNIX password:
Retype new UNIX password:
passwd: all authentication tokens updated successfully
```

If you are logged in as the root user, you can set the password for another account by using passwd followed by the username, like so:

```
# passwd amy
```

The passwd command, found under the /usr/bin directory, prompts for a new password, and then asks you to type it again to verify the change. If the password you've chosen is too easy to guess, the system might not allow you to change it. If this happens, try choosing a password that would not be similar to any word in the dictionary. After you make the change, the /etc/passwd entry reflects the password as an encrypted string like so:

```
mike:Qzq/xNwYPy0OU:501:501:Michael Smith:/home/mike:/bin/bash
```

On some systems, the encrypted string might appear, instead, in the file /etc/shadow. If you are using shadow passwords, the encrypted string will appear as an *x* in /etc/passwd, like so:

```
mike:x:501:501:Michael Smith:/home/mike:/bin/bash
```

SEE ALSO

➤ *To learn more about passwords, see page 382.*

Running Commands as the Root Operator

After you've logged in under your new username, you're just like any other user, with one important exception: You know the root password. From now on, whenever you have to accomplish important system tasks or run programs as root, you don't have to exit Linux and log back in as the root operator. Instead, you can use the su, or superuser, command to temporarily become the root user. The su command can be used by itself or with the -c (command) option to run a program:

```
$ whoami
amy
$ su
```

```
Password:
# whoami
root
# exit
$ su -c 'useradd michael'
Password:
$
```

In this example, the whoami command, found under the /usr/bin directory, reports on who you are. The su command prompts for a password before allowing you to become the root operator.

After you run root commands, use the shell's exit command to return to your original shell and identity. When the su command is used with the -c option, the specified root command, enclosed in quotes, is run and you're immediately returned to your shell. Always use caution when running commands as the root operator.

Using Virtual Consoles

Linux also allows you to log in multiple times, and as different users, through the use of virtual consoles. *Virtual consoles* offer a way to run two or more shells at the same time. Virtual consoles are handy when you want to run two or more programs simultaneously, or if you must have a root shell open at all times.

Linux allows you to open at least six virtual consoles at once. When you start Linux, the login prompt is presented at virtual console number 1. You select virtual consoles by pressing the Alt keys along with a Function key (from F1 to F6).

Use a virtual console after starting Linux

1. Type your username at the login prompt, and then press Enter.

2. Type your password, and then press Enter.

3. At any point, you can press the F2, F3, F4, F5, or F6 function key to start using a new virtual console. A new login prompt will appear.

4. Repeat the login process using your username, the root operator username, or another username.

To switch back to your first, or initial, login shell, hold down the Alt key and press the F1 function key. Switch between virtual consoles by using the appropriate Alt+function-key combination.

Logging Out of Linux

After you create a new user account and a new user's password, log out of Linux by using the either the `logout` or `exit` command, as follows:

```
$ exit
```

```
$ logout
```

After you enter either of these commands, the display will clear, and the Linux login prompt will be redisplayed.

Rebooting Linux

To reboot your system, always use the `shutdown` command, which is found under the `/sbin` directory. Just powering off your computer can cause severe disk errors, and is an unsafe practice. I cannot stress enough the importance of properly shutting down your system. You must be the root operator or use the `su` command to use the `shutdown` command.

The `shutdown` command takes several command-line options. For example, using the `-r`, or *reboot*, option followed by the word `now` will reboot your system immediately:

```
# shutdown -r now
```

Many systems are configured to treat the Ctrl+Alt+Del combination the same as if you had typed the above command as root.

Shutting Down Linux

The `shutdown` command's `-h`, or *halt*, option shuts down Linux. As with the `-r` option, a time (in seconds) or the word `now` can be used to specify when you want Linux to shut down. Using the following command will enable you to shut down your system immediately:

```
# shutdown -h now
```

Reboot: Controlling the Vulcan nerve pinch: Ctrl+Alt+Del

You can reboot your system using the Ctrl+Alt+Del key combination. To restrict this keystroke combination for use only by the root operator, create a file called `shutdown.allow` under the `/etc` directory. This improves security when you're running Linux as a server or if you're worried about someone inadvertently restarting your system. For more details, see the `shutdown` command's manual page.

Getting Help

Linux distributions include documentation about nearly all the programs, commands, and files installed on your hard drive. Each distribution also comes with a number of commands and programs designed to help you learn about your system. These commands are discussed in the following sections.

Getting Help with the *man* Command

The man command is used to display help, or documentation called *manual pages*, about a command, file, or other Linux function. To read a manual page, specify a program name on the command line. To learn about the man command, follow it with the word man, like so:

```
$ man man
```

The man pages are displayed using an application called less. Manual pages (sometimes called *man pages*) are text files written using a special format. To read about the format of these pages, use the man command's section option to read the man manual page under the /usr/man/man7 directory, as follows:

```
$ man 7 man
```

SEE ALSO

➤ *For more information about navigating through* less, *see page 41.*

Manual pages and documentation are located under the /usr/man directory in several sections organized by task or type. Table 1.1 lists these different sections.

Table 1.1 Manual Page Sections

Section	Type of Documentation
1	Commands (general programs)
2	System calls (kernel functions)
3	Library calls (programming functions)
4	Special files (/dev directory files)
5	File formats (/etc/passwd and others)
6	Games
7	Macro packages (man page formats, and so on)
8	System management (root operator utilities)
9	Kernel routines (kernel source routines)

Getting Help in X11 with the *xman* Client

To read manual pages while using the X Window System, simply start the xman client from the command line of the terminal window:

```
$ xman &
```

Figure 1.2 shows a man page viewed within the X Window System.

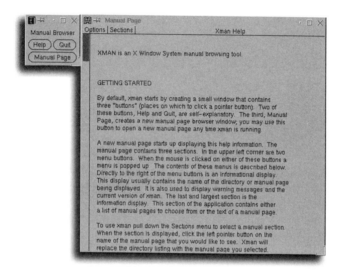

FIGURE 1.2
The xman X11 client displays manual pages in a scrolling window.

Getting Help with the *info* Command

Some commands might be documented in a format readable with the info command. The info utility is a robust browser for finding detailed information on a topic. To start using info, type the info command with no arguments:

```
$ info
```

The introductory page that appears mentions that pressing the h key will give you a tutorial on navigating and using the info system. The first time you use info you should go through the tutorial to get a feel for info's powerful features. Table 1.2 shows the basic navigation key bindings for info. After you've become comfortable with the info system, you can jump straight to the topic you're interested in by following the info command with a keyword:

```
$ info man
```

Table 1.2 Basic Navigation Keys for Info

Description	Key
Go to the next page	n
Go to the previous page	p
Scroll down a page	space
Scroll up a page	delete
Return to the top of the page	b
Select a link	Enter

Getting Help with the GNOME Help Browser

 If you are using the GNOME Desktop Environment, you can use the GNOME help browser to view man pages, info pages, or the GNOME user guide and documentation. Start the Help Browser by clicking Help System in the GNOME main menu, by clicking the help system icon on the panel, or from the command line in a terminal window (see Figure 1.3):

```
$ gnome-help-browser &
```

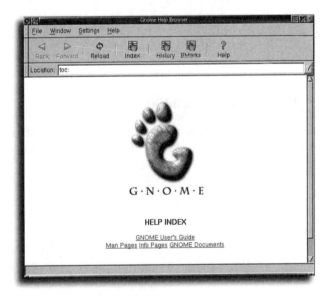

FIGURE 1.3
The GNOME Help Browser provides a simple way to get information about your system.

The Help Browser functions much like a Web browser. As seen in Figure 1.3, links on the index page will take you to the sections you choose. For example, clicking the link Man Pages brings you to a list of documentation provided by the man command.

Getting Help Using the KDE Help Browser

 The K Desktop Environment (KDE) Help Browser looks and works like a Web browser (see Figure 1.4). You can access documentation about the KDE workspace and applications by clicking the underlined links. KDE's help browser provides the same information you would find in the man or info pages, plus other KDE-specific tips and documentation.

FIGURE 1.4
The KDE Help Browser gives you a graphical view of system documentation. Navigate much as you would in a Web browser.

Getting Help with the *whatis* Command

Use the whatis command if you're unsure about what a program does. Using this command prints a short synopsis of each specified command. For example, issuing the command # whatis cal returns the following result:

```
cal (1)            - displays a calendar
```

The synopsis of the specified command is extracted from the command's manual page and is located in a database called whatis. The whatis database, located under the /usr/man directory, is built each day by a crontab script run each week by the makewhatis.cron script in the /etc/cron.weekly directory. This script runs the make-whatis command, found under the /usr/sbin directory. If you find that whatis doesn't work the first time, you might need to manually run makewhatis.

Getting Help with the *apropos* Command

The apropos command uses the whatis database to display all related matches of the command's name. Use this command to find related commands or actions for programs installed on your system. For example, issuing the command

```
# apropos bell
```

returns the following result:

```
beep, flash (3)       - Curses bell and screen flash routines
bell (n)              - Rings a display's bell
```

If you do not have apropos installed on your system, you can use the man command's -K option; however, this is a slow way to search for the information because the man command must search through each manual page in each manual page section.

Entering Commands

Entering commands at the shell
command line

Creating shell commands

Controlling programs

Using wildcards

Selecting a shell

Entering Commands at the Shell Command Line

Using Linux means using a command line. Even if you always run the X Window System, you'll need to know how to use the shell at one time or another. By under-standing how the shell interprets your keystrokes, you'll learn how to work faster and more efficiently when you enter commands.

Case Sensitivity

All shells for Linux are case sensitive. (Actually, Linux is always case sensitive, not just shells.) This means filenames must be specified exactly as they exist, using uppercase, mixed-case, or lowercase letters and characters. Filenames can be as much as 256 characters long, and can contain many different types of characters. For example, the following are valid (but not necessarily good) sample filenames:

```
a_long-filename+a-long=extension
averylongfilenamethatistoolongformostfilenames
pAymEoRyOuWiLlnEvErsEeyOurCaTaGain
a file

a[file]
file:name
 filename
file.txt
file2.txt.extension
~@#^
```

Reserved characters, or characters not to be used in filenames, include the following:

```
" , ' * & ) ( | ! ` ? \ / < > ;
```

Note that it is possible to create a filename with a leading space, an embedded space, or that consists entirely of spaces. Nevertheless, this is not a good practice; it could cause problems later on, especially if you need to manipulate a list of filenames or you want to delete a file.

SEE ALSO

➤ *To learn how to delete files and directories, see page 49.*

Editing the Command Line

Whether you can edit text entered at the command line depends on the shell being used. The default Linux shell, `bash`, supports command-line editing. The basic edit-ing commands are listed in Table 2.1, and are entered either by pressing special keys on your keyboard or by using a Ctrl+key combination. Occasionally, keyboard mappings might be a little different. Check the distribution documentation if standard key mappings don't seem to work for you.

Table 2.1 *bash* Shell Command-Line Editing Keys

Action	Key or Keystroke Combination
Move forward one character	right cursor, Ctrl+F
Move forward one word	Alt+F
Move backward one character	left cursor, Ctrl+B
Move backward one word	Alt+B
Move to beginning of line	Ctrl+A
Move to end of line	Ctrl+E
Delete next character	Ctrl+D
Delete next word	Alt+D
Delete to end of line	Ctrl+K
Delete to beginning of line	Ctrl+U

Saving Keystrokes with Shell History

If your shell supports command-line history, you can scroll through previously entered commands. The default shell, bash, saves the last 1,000 command lines in a file called .bash_history in your home directory. To quickly reenter a command line, use the up or down cursor keys to scroll through the list.

SEE ALSO

➤ *To increase or decrease the number of command histories for* bash, *see page 102.*

Using the Tab Key to Complete Commands

Another feature of the bash shell is command completion. To quickly type or find the name of a command or all commands with similar spellings, type the first few letters of a command's name, and then press the Tab key on your keyboard. For example, type the following:

$da

Pressing the Tab key results as follows:

`$date`

If you enter enough unique letters of a program's name, the shell will complete the program's name for you. If you enter only the first few letters, you'll have to press Tab twice in succession. For example, type the following:

`$ pi`

Then press the Tab key twice in succession for results similar to this:

```
pi1toppm    pic    pick    picttoppm    pilot    ping
pi3topbm    pic2tpic    pico    pidof    pine
```

The shell will print all commands that could be a completion of the letters you typed.

Entering Multiple Commands

To enter several commands on a single command line, use the semicolon (;), like so:

`$ ls ; cat file.txt`

This runs the `ls` (list directory) command, followed by the display of the file, `file.txt`, by the `cat` (concatenate) command.

SEE ALSO

➤ *To learn how to create, copy, or delete directories, see Chapter 3, "Navigating the Linux File System."*

Breaking Long Command Lines

Although most shells automatically wrap long command lines when you reach the end of a line, you can use the backslash character (\) with the semicolon to type multiple commands, or single commands on separate lines:

```
$ ls /tmp ;\
>ls /boot ;\
>ls /var/log/uucp
```

The shell automatically prints the > character to show that a long command is being entered. Using the backslash makes complex command lines easier to read.

Entering Commands in GNOME

 When working in X11, you can keep a terminal emulator open if you are entering many shell commands. There are times, however, when you might want to just run a single quick command. GNOME provides some additional command tools for this or other special situations.

The GNOME panel menu provides an option called Run Command. Selecting this will launch a dialog box like the one in Figure 2.1. Using this client, you can type in any command, just as you would at a shell prompt. Because the client disappears as soon as the command is run, it is best used for commands where you are opening a standalone program, rather than asking for output that would be displayed as text immediately following your command. For example, use grun to open Emacs or xcalc, but not to ping another computer or run ls on a directory.

FIGURE 2.1
The GNOME Run Program utility keeps a list of recently entered commands, which you can access from the drop-down menu.

Besides the text input field, grun provides two other ways to enter commands. You can use the drop-down menu to select from a command history. You can also use the Browse option to select a program from the directory tree.

Another quick command tool can be invoked from the command line by typing grun. This will evoke a single text field (without the *browse* or down arrow options). You can type the command you want to run in the text field and press Enter. This is a particularly useful method of opening an application which you do not intend to close when you exit your terminal session.

Entering Commands in KDE

 KDE also provides a quick command entry utility. Press Alt+F2 to bring up KDE's Command widget and type whatever you'd like to run. As with the GNOME grun utility, you won't want to use commands whose text output (standard output) you want to see.

Creating Shell Commands

The shell recognizes a number of special characters on the command line. This section shows how to use these characters to do the following:

- Send a program's output to a file.
- Have a program read text from a file.
- Append a program's output to a file.
- Run a program in the background.

Using the >, >>, and < Redirection Operators

Shell redirection operators are used to direct a program's input and output. The shell can be used to feed a program input from another application, from the command line, or even from another file. These operators are used to copy, create, or overwrite files; to build reports; or to create databases.

The cat (short for concatenate) command is used to print one or more files to your display. When used with the >, known as the *standard output redirection operator*, the cat command will copy a file by sending its output to another file:

```
$ cat report.txt >newreport.txt
```

This is called *redirecting the standard output*. Through use of redirection, the output of the cat command is sent to a specified file in the current directory.

You can also combine the cat command and shell command-line redirection as a method to quickly create and enter text in a file.

Quick text entry

1. Use the cat command along with output redirection on the command line to send all typed input from the keyboard directly to a text file:

```
$ cat >myfile.txt
>This is a line of text.
>This is the second line of text.
>This is the last line of text.
```

2. When you've finished typing your text, press Ctrl+D to enter an end-of-file mark:

```
>[EOF]
```

3. To check your text, use the `cat` command:

```
$ cat myfile.txt
This is a line of text.
This is the second line of text.
This is the last line of text.
```

The < (standard input) redirection operator feeds information to a program as follows:

```
$ cat <report.txt
```

Here, the `cat` command reads the contents of the file `report.txt` and sends its contents to your display. To build a largerreport, use the >> append operator to add output to existing files like so:

```
$ cat <report.txt >>newreport.txt
```

If the file `newreport.txt` does not exist, it will be created. If the file exists, the contents of the file `report.txt` will be appended to the end of the file `newreport.txt`.

A more obscure redirection operator is the <<, known as the *here operator*. Use this operator to tell the shell when to stop reading input:

```
$ cat <<end
> this is
> the
> end
this is
the
$
```

When the shell reads the specified word following the << operator, it stops reading input. In this case, the `cat` command echoes all entered input until the word `end` is specified, and then properly echoes to the display.

Output redirection can be dangerous!

Indiscriminately redirecting the output of programs can cause you to lose data because any existing file with the same name as the one on the command line will be overwritten. Make sure you do not redirect output to an existing file. A safer approach is to use the >> (append redirection) operator to append output. That way, the worst thing that can happen is that data will be appended to the existing file. This is another good reason why you shouldn't run Linux as the root operator. You can overwrite any file on your system, including important configuration files and even the kernel.

Redirecting Error Output by the Numbers

The standard input and output have assigned file numbers in the shell. The standard input uses the number 0, and the standard output uses the number 1. Another type of output is *standard error*, and its number is 2.

Most commands for Linux report errors using the standard error output, and send the error message to your display as follows:

```
$ cat report.txt >newreport.txt
cat: report.txt: No such file or directory
```

By properly redirecting a program's output, you can build a log of any errors. Specify that the standard error output is always sent and appended to a file like so:

```
$ cat report.txt >newreport.txt 2>>errors.log
$ cat errors.log
cat: report.txt: No such file or directory
```

Because the error output has been redirected to a file, no error message is printed on the display. Although the file newreport.txt will be empty, the file errors.log will contain a list of errors.

Using Pipes to Build Commands

The vertical bar (or *pipe*) character (|) is called the *pipe operator*, and is used to send output from one command to the input on another. Use input and output redirection with pipes to quickly build custom commands.

Pipes can save time and effort, and work with many commands found under Linux. In order for you to be able to use a command in a pipe, the program must be able to read the standard input and write to the standard output. Such programs are also called *filters*.

SEE ALSO

➤ *To learn more about text processing filters, see page 80.*

Pipes range from simple to complex, and are used for many purposes. The following are some examples of how pipes can be used:

```
$ cat report.txt | wc -l >number_of_lines.txt
```

The preceding example counts the numbers of lines in a file and generates a report.

```
$ find / | wc -l >number_of_files.txt
```

This command line counts the number of files on your system, starting at the / or root directory.

```
$ find / | sort | uniq -d >duplicate_filenames.txt
```

This example generates a report of your system's duplicate files (files with the same name).

```
$ strings /usr/lib/ispell/american.hash | sort | tee uppercase.dict |
\ tr A-Z a-z >lowercase.dict
```

This example extracts a list of words from the system's dictionary by using the `strings` command and the output is sorted. The `tee` command is then used to save a copy of the dictionary, still in its original, uppercase form, while the output is converted to lowercase by the `tr` command, and then saved in lowercase. This creates two different dictionaries: one containing uppercase words, and the other containing lowercase words.

Not all programs work the same way

Not all commands for Linux read from the standard input and write to the standard output. Make sure to read a program's manual page before using the program to build important or complex pipes. See the section "Using Pipes to Build Commands" for more information.

Running Programs in the Background

Use an ampersand (&) to start and run a program in the background. Although you can use a virtual console to run other programs at the same time, background programs can be started quite easily from a single terminal or command line.

You'll use background processes quite often if you use the X Window System. Most X11 clients do not offer a terminal window or command line, so it is necessary to run the client in the background to free your terminal for further input like so:

```
$ xcalc &
$
```

This command starts the X11 `xcalc` (calculator) client, leaving your terminal free for other command lines.

SEE ALSO
➤ *To learn more about using X11 clients, see page 169.*

Creating Shell Commands with *autoexpect*

The scripting language, `expect`, can be used to create a script that automates tasks normally requiring user input. The `expect` scripts will look for screen output matching a pattern you've specified and generate a response as if you'd typed it at the keyboard. For example, if logging in to your ISP requires you to enter a username and password, you might consider creating a script that looks for the prompt `username:` and types `michael` as a response. The intricacies of writing an `expect` script are beyond the scope of this book, but the `autoexpect` utility can automate the process of creating simple scripts. The `autoexpect` program, when run, records what you type along with the prompts you received, and creates an `expect` script based on it.

```
$autoexpect
autoexpect started, file is script.exp
$ftp ftp.us.kernel.org
Connected to ftp.us.kernel.org.
220
Name (ftp.us.kernel.org:michael): anonymous
331 Anonymous login ok, send your complete e-mail address as password.
Password:
230 Anonymous access granted, restrictions apply.
Remote system type is UNIX.
Using binary mode to transfer files.
ftp> cd /pub/linux/kernel/v2.2
250 CWD command successful.
ftp> ls
200 PORT command successful.
150 Opening ASCII mode data connection for file list.
-r--r--r--   1 merlin    merlin           0 Aug 26 00:45 LATEST-IS-2.2.12
-r--r--r--   1 merlin    merlin          27 Jan 26  1999 README
-r--r--r--   1 merlin    merlin    10592549 Jan 26  1999 linux-2.2.0.tar.bz2
-r--r--r--   1 merlin    merlin         344 Jan 26  1999 linux-2.2.0.tar.bz2.sign
-r--r--r--   1 merlin    merlin    13080195 Jan 26  1999 linux-2.2.0.tar.gz
...
-r--r--r--   1 merlin    merlin       32992 May 13 23:54 patch-2.2.9.gz
-r--r--r--   1 merlin    merlin         344 May 13 23:54 patch-2.2.9.gz.sign
226 Transfer complete.
ftp> exit
221 Goodbye.
$exit
exit
```

```
autoexpect done, file is script.exp
$
```

This example creates a script that uses ftp to look for a new kernel release. The output has been edited to conserve space.

---

autoexpect records every keystroke

While `autoexpect` runs, it records every keystroke that you type. This includes backspaces, deletes, and arrow keys.

It also requires that the information that you tell it to expect be exactly what it receives. For instance, if you set up an `expect` script to log in to an FTP server, and the server presents a different message of the day or time-date stamp every time you log in, `autoexpect` will not work. It relies on having the same output every time it runs.

Controlling Programs

Most (but not all) shells support some form of control over background processes. Important features include the following:

- Listing current background programs
- Pausing running programs
- Stopping running processes
- Bringing to the foreground programs sent to the background

Controlling background programs is called *job control*.

Using Job Control

Use job control to manage multiple running programs. You can start programs in the background from the bash shell command line with the & operator, or you can suspend a program by pressing Ctrl+z. The shell will respond by printing a job number, followed by a process number of the program:

```
$ sc &
[1] 2689
```

Running programs sent to the background with Ctrl+z will disappear, and the shell will print a job number like so:

```
[2]+ Stopped     sc
```

Many programs or several instances of a single program can be started, suspended, or run. To obtain a list of currently running programs, use the bash shell's jobs command:

```
$ jobs
[2]   Stopped                    sc
[3]-  Stopped (tty output)       pico report.txt
[4]+  Stopped                    xcalc
```

The jobs command prints each program's job number along with the command line used to start the program. To selectively bring back a program, use the fg (foreground) command followed by the job number, as follows:

```
$ fg 3
```

This example would return the pico text editor to your display. If you would rather have a suspended program resume in the background, use bg instead of fg:

```
$ bg 4
[4]+ xcalc &
$
```

Notice that the shell automatically adds the & as if you had typed it originally.

Using the *ps* and *kill* Commands

All system processes are assigned a unique process number by the Linux kernel. To see the process numbers of currently running programs, use the ps (process status) command. (To save space, not all processes running on the author's machine at the time of writing are listed here.) This listing shows that the su command is running with a process number of 1658:

```
$ ps
...
 1658  p0 S    0:00 su
 1659  p0 S    0:00 bash
 2713  p0 T    0:00 pico report.txt
 2714  p0 T    0:00 pico newreport.txt
...
```

You can stop programs by specifying the process number along with the kill command as follows:

```
$ kill -9 2714
[4]+  Killed                     pico newreport.txt
```

SEE ALSO

➤ *To learn more about controlling processes and other background programs, see page 538.*

Stopping programs by killing a process by using a process number is an often inconvenient way to stop background programs. Use the `kill` command, followed by the percent sign (%) and the job number or command name, to stop a program like so:

```
$ kill %3
[3]+  Terminated              pico report.txt
$ kill %pico
[3]+  Terminated              pico report.txt
```

Halting programs by job number or name should be used instead of killing processes because you can all too easily enter a wrong process number, and inadvertently bring your system toa halt.

Using Wildcards

Wildcards are used on the shell command line to specify files by name or extension. Shells for Linux offer sophisticated forms of wildcards that you can use to perform complex pattern matching. Creating complex wildcards is called building regular expressions.

Building Regular Expressions

Regular expressions are wildcard patterns, built using a special command-line syntax. This syntax uses a number of special characters, some of which are listed in Table 2.2.

Table 2.2 Common Regular Expressions and Characters

Expression	Action
*	Match all characters
?	Match a single character
[a–z]	Match a range of characters
[0123]	Match a range of characters
\?	Match the ? character
\)	Match the) character
^abc	Match pattern abc at the beginning of lines
$abc	Match pattern abc at the end of lines

SEE ALSO

➤ *For more information about using regular expressions with search programs such as* grep, *see page 58.*

Use the asterisk (*) to find all matches for leading or trailing patterns:

```
$ ls *.txt
```

The order of characters in pattern expressions is important. To find characters normally interpreted by the shell as having special meaning, use the backslash (\) as an *escape character* to "escape" the pattern:

```
$  ls *\?*
```

This command lists all files with a ? in the filename.

More regular expressions

Regular expressions are documented in the bash shell, ed, and grep command manual pages. See these pages for additional approaches and characters used to build complex patterns.

Selecting a Shell

A number of different shells work with Linux, and each has its own features, capabilities, and limitations. Table 2.3 lists shells normally installed on many Linux systems.

Table 2.3 Common Shells for Linux

Name	Description
ash	A small shell
bash	The default Linux shell
pdksh	Public-domain version ksh shell
tcsh	Compatible version of csh shell
zsh	Compatible ksh, csh, and sh shell with some extra features

Acceptable system shells are listed in a file called shells under the /etc directory:

```
/bin/bash
/bin/bsh
/bin/sh
/bin/ash
/bin/bsh
/bin/tcsh
```

```
/bin/csh
/bin/ksh
/bin/zsh
/usr/bin/pine
```

Some of the shells listed in this file are not actual programs installed on your system, but are symbolic links to existing shells.

SEE ALSO
➤ *To learn about shell programming, see page 321.*
➤ *To learn more about creating or using symbolic links, see page 46.*

Also note that the last entry in the /etc/shells file contains the pathname for the pine email program. As the root operator, you can add programs to the /etc/shells list, and then restrict a user to running only one or a menu of certain programs after logging in.

Changing Shells with the *chsh* Command

To change the shell run after you log in to Linux, use the chsh (change shell) command, found under the /usr/bin directory. You can use the chsh command by itself on the command line or with the -s (shell) option:

```
$ chsh
Changing shell for bball.
Password:
New shell [/bin/bash]: /bin/zsh
Shell changed.

$ chsh -s /bin/bash
Password:
Shell changed.
```

The full pathname, or directory to the desired shell or program, must be provided. Using the previous listing of entries in the /etc/shell file, the root operator can also restrict users to running a single program, such as the pine email command:

```
# chsh -s /usr/bin/pine heather
Changing shell for heather.
Shell changed.
```

When user heather logs in, the pine mailer will run. After quitting the program, heather will be logged out. This is a handy way to restrict users, such as children, to certain types of Linux programs.

To see a list of acceptable shells for your system, use chsh's -1 (list) option:

```
# chsh -1
/bin/bash
/bin/bsh
/bin/sh
/bin/ash
/bin/bsh
/bin/tcsh
/bin/csh
/bin/ksh
/bin/zsh
/usr/bin/pine
```

chapter

3

Navigating the Linux File System

Printing the current working directory ●

Changing directories with the cd command ●

Listing directories ●

Viewing text files ●

Creating files and directories ●

Copying files and directories ●

Moving and renaming files and directories ●

Creating symbolic links ●

Deleting files and directories ●

Finding files and directories ●

Using the GNOME gmc client ●

Using the KDE file manager kfm ●

Searching text files ●

You should know where you are or where you're going when you work with Linux. This section shows you how to navigate your directories at the console or through a terminal window, the GNOME desktop, and the K Desktop Environment (KDE) in X.

Printing the Current Working Directory

Use the pwd (print working directory) command to print the current, or present, working directory (that is, the directory where you are at that moment):

```
$ pwd
/home/michael
```

A binary version of the pwd command can be found under the /bin directory, but nearly all shells have a built-in pwd command.

The built-in pwd command is documented in each shell's manual pages; or, from a bash command line, type help pwd.

Changing Directories with the *cd* Command

Use the cd (change directory) command to navigate through the Linux file system's directories. Use this command with a directory specification or pathname to move to a specified directory. This command is built in to each Linux shell, and can also be used as a shortcut to quickly move back to your home directory.

```
$ pwd
/home/michael
$ cd /usr/bin
$ pwd
/usr/bin
$ cd
/home/michael
```

If you enter the cd command by itself, you'll return to your home directory (specified in the $HOME environment variable). Move up to the next directory by entering two periods and a forward slash (../) with the cd command, like so:

```
$ pwd
/home/michael
$ cd ../
$ pwd
/home
```

SEE ALSO

➤ *To learn more about shell environment variables, see page 99.*

The two periods represent the parent directory. Using a single period represents the current directory, but is not useful for navigating the directory structure. A hyphen, however, can be used as a quick navigation tool:

```
$ pwd
/home/michael
$ cd /usr/local/bin
$ cd -
$ pwd
/home/michael
```

Use a hyphen with the cd command to quickly navigate between the two most recently visited directories (in the previous example, I navigated from my home directory to the /usr/local/bin directory and then back to my home directory). Use the tab key on the command line to change directories without typing a full path-name:

```
$ cd /usr/loc[tab]
returns
$ cd /usr/local/
```

Use this approach to save typing and time when navigating to known directories. When you press the tab key, it will complete the directory or filename if it finds only one option that matches what you've typed. If it finds none or more than one match, the terminal will beep. Pressing tab again yields a list of possible matches (if there are any).

```
$ cd /usr/l[tab]
lib     libexec     local
$ cd /usr/l
```

Listing Directories

Listing the contents of directories, like navigating through your system, is a basic skill you should quickly master. The following sections describe several directory listing programs that are usually included with most Linux distributions.

Listing Directories and Files with the *ls* Command

Use the ls (list directory) command to list the contents of one or several directories. This command has more than 40 different command-line options that can be combined to format listings. Wildcards can be used to specify certain files or directories. To list the contents of the /usr/local/ directory, type the following:

```
$ ls /usr/local/
bin       etc      info     lib      qt       src
doc       games    lesstif  man      sbin
```

By default, the ls command lists the contents of directories in columns, sorted vertically. You can use different command-line options and wildcards to view directory contents in different formats. For example, the -F (classify) option identifies directories and executable files by appending a forward slash (/) and asterisk (*) to file or directory names:

```
$ ls  -F /usr/local/lib/*
/usr/local/lib/cddb:
eb104910
/usr/local/lib/saytime:
saytime.sh*  sounds/
```

Table 3.1 lists some common command-line options that you can use to view directory contents in different formats.

Table 3.1 Common *ls* Command-Line Options

Flag	Description
-d	List directory names, not directory contents
-l	Long format listing (includes file size, dates, permissions, and so on)
-m	List filenames separated by commas
-x	Sort filenames in columns horizontally
-a	List all files (including those beginning with .)
-A	List all files, but not . and ..
-C	Sort files in columns vertically
-F	Identify directories, links, and executables
-R	List directory contents recursively
-S	Sort files by size
--color	Use color to identify files

SEE ALSO

➤ *To create* ls *command aliases with useful options such as* -lA, *see page 37.*

Changing file and directory listing colors

You can use ls --color to easily distinguish file types in a directory listing by color. For instance, by default all the subdirectories will be blue, executables will be green, text files will be white. If you plan to make an alias for this, it's preferable to use ls --color=auto which will only colorize output sent to your screen (and not confuse programs you are piping output to). To learn how to customize which colors are used for certain files, see the info or man page on dircolors.

SEE ALSO

➤ *For more information on creating aliases see page 108.*

The ls command is documented in its manual page. You should also check out the manual pages for related directory listing commands, such as dir, vdir, lsattr, tree, and dircolors.

Echoing Directory Contents with the *echo* Command

The echo command can also be used to list the contents of directories. This command, built in to each shell, is also a program found under the /bin directory. In order to list directories and files, specify a wildcard on the command line like so:

```
$ echo /*
/bin /boot /dev /etc /home /lib /lost+found
/mnt /opt /proc /root /sbin /tmp /usr /var
```

Here's another example:

```
$ echo /mnt/z*
/mnt/zip /mnt/zipln
```

The echo command prints all matching filenames in alphabetical order, but does not format the listing in columns. Use the ls command for formatted listings.

Viewing Text Files

Linux distributions come with a number of text-viewing programs. The following sections discuss several of these programs, such as the cat command and interactive viewers (called *pagers*), that you can use to view text files without running a text editor.

Viewing Text Files with the *cat* Command

Use the cat (concatenate) command to print the contents of files to your console display or terminal window. This command is best used to print short files to your display because long files will scroll too fast for you to read.

```
$ cat /etc/issue
Red Hat Linux release 5.0 (Hurricane)
Kernel 2.0.31 on an i586
```

Use the cat command's -n (line-numbering) option to have file listings automatically numbered:

```
$ cat -n /etc/issue
    1
    2  Red Hat Linux release 5.0 (Hurricane)
    3  Kernel 2.0.31 on an i586
    4
```

Display multiple files either by listing the names on the command line or by using a wildcard. Use output redirection operators, such as > or >>, to create, copy, overwrite, or append a single file or multiple files. For example, the following command line combines the contents of file1.txt and file2.txt, and creates file3.txt:

```
$ cat file1.txt file2.txt >file3.txt
```

The next line appends the contents of file1.txt onto file2.txt:

```
$ cat file1.txt >>file2.txt
```

Finally, the following command line takes the contents of file2.txt and either creates or overwrites file1.txt:

```
$ cat file2.txt >file1.txt
```

By redirecting keyboard input to a file, the cat command can be used as a quick text editor:

```
$ cat > friends.txt
Michael
Cynthia
Lisa
Mark
```

The cat command reads characters from the keyboard until Ctrl+D (the end-of-text character) is typed. The cat command will print any type of file, including non–human-readable files like program binaries. If you accidentally cat a binary file, you can stop cat by using the Ctrl+C key sequence. catting a binary file can have unpredictable results, such as scrambling your terminal characters. For this reason, you should really avoid doing this by using the file command to find out what sort of file it is that you want to cat:

```
$ file /bin/gunzip
/bin/gunzip: ELF 32-bit LSB executable, Intel 80386, version 1,
➥dynamically linked (uses shared libs), stripped
$ file bookmarks.html
bookmarks.html: exported SGML document text
$ cat bookmarks.html
```

For more details about using the cat and file command, see their manual pages.

SEE ALSO

➤ *For more information about the* file *command, refer to Appendix C, "Top 50 Linux Commands and Utilities," page 597.*

➤ *For information about using redirection operators, see page 24.*

➤ *To change file ownership permissions, see page 378.*

Viewing Text Files with the *less* and *more* Pager Commands

Pager commands such as more and less are used to interactively read text files. Most users will prefer to read files by using the less command, which has more features than the more pager. Both more and less are used with a filename on the command line, and both accept wildcards to read multiple files. Following are a few examples:

```
$ less friends.txt
Michael
Cynthia
Lisa
Mark
friends.txt (END)
```

Because the less command is designed to let the user scroll through multiple pages of a file, it stops printing the contents of the file to your display at the end of the screen rather than the end of a file. To move down line by line, press the down-arrow key. You can press the spacebar to move down an entire screen or press b to move back up a screen. To move up line by line, press the up-arrow key. Use P to scroll up screen by screen. To quit, press q. Use / to search for words or strings. See the man page on less for more details.

The less command not only accepts multiple filenames and wildcards, but can also be used with input and output redirection operators. The more and less programs are similar, but the less pager has many additional features, including the following:

- Using cursor keys to scroll through documents
- Horizontal scrolling for wide documents
- Jumping to document bookmarks
- Keyboard command customization
- Sophisticated searching of multiple documents

The `more` command will automatically quit when it reaches the end of the file. (Remember, the `less` command requires that you type q.) The `more` command will only allow you to move forward through the file, whereas the `less` pager allows you to move both forward and backward.

The `less` pager is usually the default manual page reader, although this option can changed by defining a `$PAGER` shell environment string. Check out Table 3.2 for some `less` pager commands.

Table 3.2 Common *less* Pager Commands

Action	more	less
Forward one line	Enter or s	Enter, e, j, or cursor down
Backward one line		y, k, or cursor up
Forward one screen	Space, z, or f	Space, z, or f
Backward one screen	b	b
Help	h or ?	h
Previous file	:p	:p
Next file	:n	:n
Search str	/	/
Quit	q	q

SEE ALSO
➤ *For information on setting environment variables, see page 102.*

Custom keys, or key bindings, for the `less` command can be defined and created in a binary file called `.less` in your home directory. Use the `lesskey` command to read or create this file. See the `lesskey` manual page for more information.

Creating Files and Directories

Creating files and directories is an integral part of organizing your data while using Linux. The following sections show you how to create files and directories, so you can later copy, move, and organize your information.

Using *touch* to Create and Update Files and Directories

The touch command is used to create or update files and directories. Use touch with a new filename to create a file, or use an existing filename to update the file's access and modification times. For example, the following command line uses touch to create three files:

```
$ touch file1 file2 file3
```

Use ls -l to check the modification time of a file, like this:

```
$ ls -l *.txt
-rw-rw-r-- 1 michael   users   12 Jan 25 12:38 friends.txt
```

In the following lines, the touch command is used to update the friends.txt file's access and modification time to be four days more recent:

```
$ touch friends.txt
$ ls -l *.txt
-rw-rw-r-- 1 michael   users   12 Jan 29 16:14 friends.txt
```

The touch command is useful to quickly create files, and can be used by other programs during system-management tasks (such as backups). For more information, see the touch manual page.

Creating Directories with the *mkdir* Command

The mkdir (make directory) command is used to create directories. Use mkdir with a directory name on the command line. For example, the following command line creates a directory called homework:

```
$ mkdir homework
```

mkdir can also be used to quickly create a hierarchy of directories. Use the -p (parent) command-line option to create each directory required in the structure (existing directories will not be overwritten):

```
$ mkdir -p homework/compsci/linux/kernal_hacking/
```

Copying Files and Directories

The ability to quickly and efficiently copy files and directories is important when using Linux. The following sections show you how to copy single or multiple files and directories.

Copying Files with the *cp* Command

The cp (copy) command is used to copy files. Use the original filename followed by a new filename on the command line to copy a single file:

```
$ cp notes notes.old
```

Use wildcards to copy multiple files to a new location:

```
$ cp *jpg vacation_pics/
```

Use the cp command with caution. Unless you use the -i (interactive) command-line option, the cp command overwrites existing files without prompting you first. When you use the -i option, the cp command prompts for a y or n:

```
$ cp -i notes.old notes
cp: overwrite `notes'? y
```

An even better approach is to use the -b (backup) option with the cp command. To create a backup of any files that can be overwritten, try the following:

```
$ cp -bi notes.old notes
cp: overwrite `notes'? y
$ ls note*
notes.old notes notes~
```

Notice that each backup file has a tilde (~) appended to its name.

Copying Directories with the *cp* Command

The -P (parent) command-line option, along with the -R (recursive) command-line option, not only copies files within one directory to another directory, but also any directories inside. For example, each of the following command lines copy the directory current and any files or directories within to the lastweek directory:

```
$ cp -PR current lastweek
$ cp -R current lastweek
$ cp -R current lastweek
```

The cp command has nearly 40 command-line options. For details, see the cp manual page.

Moving and Renaming Files and Directories

Moving and renaming files and directories, like file navigation and copying, is a basic skill you'll need when organizing information within Linux. The following sections demonstrate how to use the mv command to move and rename files and directories.

Moving and Renaming Files and Directories with the *mv* Command

The mv (move) command is used to move or rename files and directories. To rename a file or directory, specify the old filename and the new filename on the command line (unlike the cp command, mv does not leave a copy of the original file or directory):

```
$ mv error.log error.log.oct99
```

Use the mv command with caution. You can easily overwrite existing files unless you use the -i (interactive) command-line option. When you use the -i option, the mv command asks for permission to overwrite an existing file, like this:

```
$ mv -i error.log error.log.oct99
mv: replace `error.log.oct99'? y
```

A safer way to use the mv command is with the -b (backup) option. When combined with the -i option, the mv -b command asks for permission to overwrite a file, and also creates a backup, like this:

```
$ mv -bi error.log error.log.oct99
mv: replace `error.log.oct99'? y
$ ls err*
error.log.oct99 error.log.oct99~
```

If you use the -b (backup) option, the mv command creates a backup of the file being overwritten. The original file remains, with a tilde (~) appended to its filename.

The mv command will move files from one directory to another using either of the following methods. mv will only move files (not directories) from one file system to another.

SEE ALSO

➤ *For more information about managing file systems, see Chapter 28.*

```
$ mv error.log /1999_errorlogs/
$ mv error.log /1999_errorlogs/error.log.oct99
```

Using the mv command, you can move entire directories. If the destination directory does not exist, mv renames the directory:

```
$ ls -F
school/    science/
$ mv school homework
$ ls -F
homework/    science/
```

If the destination directory exists, the entire directory is moved inside the destination directory.

```
$ ls -F
homework/    science/
$ ls -F homework
compsci/    biology/
$ mv science homework
$ ls -F
homework/
$ ls -F homework
science/  compsci/  biology/
```

Creating Symbolic Links

Symbolic links are convenient shortcuts used to link existing files or directories to files or directories with more convenient locations or names. By default, a number of symbolic links are created when Linux is installed:

- Various shells listed under the /bin directory, such as bsh, csh, and sh, are actually symbolic links to other shells, such as bash or tcsh.
- The computer's modem device can be a link to /dev/modem instead of /dev/cua1 or /dev/ttyS1.
- The ex and vi editors are links to the vim text editor.

Linking Files with the *ln* Command

There are times when you find that it is convenient to have more than one path to the same file. Say that you want to easily be able to execute an application from anywhere, without typing the entire path to the file. You might create a link from /usr/local/bin to the file's executable.

SEE ALSO
➤ *For information about environment variables, see page 102.*

There are two kinds of links in the Linux world: hard links and soft links. They have similar effects but are two very different beasts.

Soft Links

A *soft link* is a very small file that you create in a directory. The sole content of this file is the path to the file you are linking it to. So if you create a soft link from /home/michael/foo to /usr/local/bin/foo, you could execute the file, /usr/local/bin/foo, and it would behave as if you were executing /home/michael/foo. However, the file in /usr/local/bin/ would be nothing but a set of instructions pointing the shell to the file in /home/michael. Think of it as call forwarding for your shell! Also, keep in mind that if you delete the original file, your soft link will point at nothing and will be totally useless. (Just like if you forward all your calls to your cellular phone but then turn the cell phone off, your calls will have nowhere to go and the call forwarding will be useless.)

Soft links will work across networked file systems, mounted devices, other file systems, and directories.

To create a soft link, use the ln command with the -s (symbolic link) command-line option, with the original filename followed by the name of the desired link:

```
$ ln -s graphicwithalongname.xcf graphic.xcf
$ ls -l
-rw-rw-r--   1 michael    users   16821 Feb 10 15:22
➥graphicwithalongname.xcf
lrwxrwxrwx   1 michael    users       4 Feb 10 15:22
➥graphic.xcf-> graphicwithalongname.xcf
```

Notice that if you type ls -l, the directory listing for the soft link reflects the file to which it points.

Hard Links

Hard links work a bit differently than soft links. Let's return to the call forwarding analogy. If a soft link is like call forwarding for a phone number, a hard link would be like having multiple phone numbers that point to the same phone.

Every file on your computer is written to a physical spot on your hard drive. That spot is called an inode and inodes each have a number. When you type ls for a directory listing, you are really looking at an index that tells the file system which inode corresponds to each file. If you type `ls -i`, you will see a directory listing with the inode numbers:

```
$ ls -i
1091611 saved-messages   1091701 sent-mail   1091610
➥sent-mail-jun-1999
```

When you create a hard link, you are just creating another directory listing to point to the same inode. You can create as many hard links on the system to a single file as you would like without taking up any more disk space. If you delete the original file, the second remains because you have not deleted the inode to which it points. The only way you can delete any file on the file system is by deleting all the hard links to that file. If you make changes to the original file, all the links will reflect that change (because they are all pointing to the same inode).

Hard links do not work across networked file systems, partitions, mounted devices, or any other file system. They also do not work for directories. You can only create a hard link to a file on the same disk and partition as the original.

Use the `ln` command (without the `-s` option) to create a hard link:

```
$ ln graphicwithalongname.xcf newgraphic.xcf
$ ls -l file*
-rw-rw-r--   2 michael     users      16821 Feb 10 15:22
➥graphicwithalongname.xcf
lrwxrwxrwx   1 michael     users          4 Feb 10 15:22
➥graphic.xcf -> graphicwithalongname.xcf
-rw-rw-r--   2 michael     users      16821 Feb 10 15:22
➥newgraphic.xcf
$ ls -i
 45146 graphicwithalongname.xcf     45146 newgraphic.xcf
```

Notice that both the files in the example above have the same inode number.

Linking Directories with the *ln* Command

The `ln -s` command can also be used to create links to often-used directories. (Note you cannot hard link directories.)

```
$ ln -s /var/http/html/   /home/amy/website
```

Now, instead of having to type a long pathname when moving files, you can use the following instead:

```
$ mv *jpg website/
```

Deleting Files and Directories

Removing files and directories is another common task when using Linux and should be performed with care. Deleted files and directories are irrevocably lost. This is a great reason to always maintain backups of important files or directories.

Deleting Files with the *rm* Command

The `rm` (remove) command is used to delete files and directories. You delete files by including a single filename or several filenames on the command line, like so:

```
$ rm sentmailJune1998 sentmailJuly1998 sentmailAugust1998
```

Use wildcards to delete multiple files:

```
$ rm *1998
```

The `rm` command with the `-r` (recursive) can also be used to delete files within a specified directory. If you attempt to delete a directory without this option, the `rm` command complains and quits. The `-i` (interactive) option elicits a prompt before deleting each file in the directory. This option is set up to be automatically included with `rm` on many machines. Conversely, the `-f` (force) option specifies that you do not want to be prompted for each file in the directory. It also suppresses error messages and warnings (so use it with caution). See the following example:

```
$ rm -ri sentmail/
rm: descend directory `sentmail'? y
rm: remove `sentmail/sentmailJune1998'? y
rm: remove `sentmail/sentmailJuly1998'? y
rm: remove `sentmail/sentmailAugust1998'? y
rm: remove directory `sentmail'? Y
```

Deleting Directories with the *rmdir* Command

You can remove directories by using the `rmdir` command.

```
$ rmdir homework/compsci/linux/kernal_hacking
$ rmdir homework/compsci
rmdir: homework/compsci: Directory not empty
```

However, if any files or directories exist below the specified directory, you must move or delete those first.

Deleting Directories with the *rm* Command

The rm command can be used like the rmdir command to remove directories, but you must use the -r (recursive) option in conjunction with the -f (force) option to do so. This combination of options removes files and directories without asking for confirmation. Here is an example:

```
$ rm -rf homework
```

Using the rm command while root can be dangerous

The rm command, used with the -fr (recursive and force) options, is especially dangerous to use if you're running as the root operator. A single command line can wipe out your system. Use the -fr option with caution; this unconditional delete destroys all files and directories in its path. Avoid using this option while logged in as the root operator unless you're absolutely certain of the files and directories you want to delete.

Finding Files and Directories

Although navigating your disk's directories and listing directory contents can be helpful for finding needed files, Linux comes with several search utilities that will work much faster. The following sections demonstrate how to use several of these commands to quickly and efficiently find files or directories.

Finding Files with the *find* Command

The find command is used to search all mounted file systems for the name or partial name of a file or directory. This powerful command can be used to do much more than simply find files. To search for files or directories, specify a search path and search pattern on the command line, like so:

```
$ find /usr -name *emacs -xdev
```

As shown in the following, this search of the /usr directory for the emacs editor and other files locates the emacs program and its manual page. But be warned! Searching a file system, especially in a network environment with remotely mounted file systems, can take a *long* time. The -xdev option specifies that you only want to search your local machine. I should also note that -xdev will not search across other file systems that you have mounted on your local machine:

```
/usr/bin/emacs
/usr/bin/xemacs
```

```
/usr/lib/emacs
/usr/share/emacs
```

The find command reports files by type, date, time, size, or search pattern. Use the -atime command-line option to find new or little-used programs. The -type f flag lets find know that the type of item you are searching for is a file (as opposed to a directory, symlink, device, and so on). For example, the following command line locates programs accessed in the last 100 days:

```
$ find /usr/bin -type f -atime +100 -print
```

The next command line locates programs that are one or fewer days old:

```
$ find /usr/bin -type f -atime -1 -print
```

To search by size, use the -size option, followed by a number in blocks (512 bytes), bytes, or kilobytes (1024 bytes). For example, the following command locates all programs in the /usr/bin directory that are larger than 500,000 bytes:

```
$ find /usr/bin -type f -size +500k -print
```

Use the -exec option to act on found files. For example, the following command line deletes all core dumps found in your Linux file system. Without the -xdev option, Linux system managers can use this approach to also clean up other file systems.

```
$ find / -name core -xdev -exec rm `{}' `;'
```

This command line works by starting a search at the /, or root directory. The find command descends through all your directories, looking for any file that is named core. If a file is found, the rm command is used to delete the file.

For more details about the find command's many different options and search specifications, see its manual page.

SEE ALSO

➤ *For information about using* find *for system administration tasks, see page 503.*

Finding Files and Directories with the *locate* Command

Use the locate command to quickly locate files or directories on your system. This program works very quickly because it uses a database of filenames instead of searching your hard drives, as the find program does. Wildcards can be used to either expand or narrow a search. For example, to look for any icons of the emacs text editor, use the locate command like this:

```
$ locate *icon*emacs*
/usr/share/icons/emacs_3d.xpm
/usr/share/icons/lemacs.xpm
/usr/share/icons/xemacs.xpm
```

The `locate` command searches a database called `locatedb`. This database is created with the `updatedb` command. The format of the `locatedb` database is documented in the `locatedb` manual page. System managers generally use the `cron` daemon and an `updatedb` `crontab` entry to keep the `locate` command's database current and accurate.

SEE ALSO

➤ *For details about using the* `cron` *daemon and* `crontab` *file, see page 396.*

Finding Programs and Manual Pages with the *whereis* Command and the *which* Command

The `whereis` command is used to list the locations of program binaries, related files, and manual pages. Use this command to verify manual pages and to determine the pathnames of programs or their source files. For example, type the following:

```
$ whereis vi
```

This command yields the following result:

```
vi: /bin/vi    /usr/man/man1/vi.1
```

The `whereis` command works a lot faster than the `find` command because the paths searched are built into the program. To search only for manual pages, use the `-m` option. Use the `-b` option for binary searches and the `-s` option to search for sources.

The `which` command is more rudimentary than the `whereis` command but is also designed to help you locate a file or application. The `which` command simply checks to see whether the program specified is located anywhere within your path. It prints to screen the first instance it finds and then stops, as in the following example:

```
$ which vi
/bin/vi
```

SEE ALSO

➤ *For more information about your path and environment variables, see page 102.*

Using the GNOME *gmc* Client

The GNOME Desktop Environment, which runs with the X Window System, is packaged with a file management application known as the GNOME Midnight Commander, or `gmc`. `gmc` is based on an older application called The Midnight Commander. The GNOME version includes an easy-to-use graphical interface which wasn't included in the original.

To launch gmc, select File Manager from the GNOME panel menu, or run the gmc command as follows:

```
$ gmc &
```

This will bring up a window like the one shown in Figure 3.1.

SEE ALSO

➤ *For details on starting and using X, see Part III, "The X Window System," starting on page 167.*

➤ *To learn more about GNOME, see the section, "Starting Enlightenment/Gnome," on page 194.*

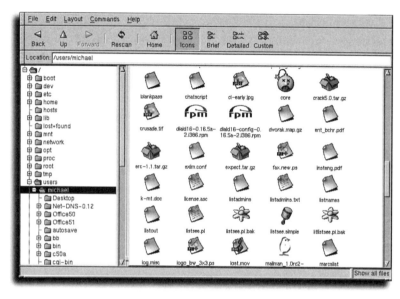

FIGURE 3.1
The GNOME Midnight Commander provides an easy visual interface to the file system. It is also responsible for your GNOME desktop icons.

Creating Directories Using the GNOME *gmc* Client

When you open gmc, you will find a graphical representation of your directory tree on the left; on the right, you will see the contents of the directory that is highlighted on the left.

To create a new directory, start by selecting File from the menu at the top. Then move down the menu to New and follow the arrow to the right. The submenu that pops up will contain a selection for Directory. This brings up a dialog box where you can enter the name of the directory you want to create. This can either be a subdirectory under the directory highlighted on the left side of gmc, or a complete path name.

An easier method is to select the parent directory on the left and then right-click in the white space around the directory contents on the right. Select New Directory from the pop-up menu. Fill in the dialog box as mentioned earlier.

Copying, Moving, and Renaming Files and Directories Using the GNOME *gmc* Client

To copy a file with gmc, right-click the file or directory you want to duplicate. The Copy dialog box pops up with a list of options for copying your file. Under the Destination tab, there is a text field where you can type the path where you want to copy the file. You can also select the Browse option to browse the directory tree for the exact location. The other tab in this dialog box is entitled Advanced Options and allows you to copy directories recursively, preserve symlinks, follow links, and preserve file attributes.

Moving a file or directory with gmc is easy. Grab the file or directory with your mouse and drop it in the directory where you want to put it. Or if you prefer, you can highlight the file or directory and select Move from the File menu. The third choice is to right-click the file or directory and select Move from the pop-up menu.

To rename a file or directory, right-click the file or directory from the right pane of the window. Now select Properties from the pop-up menu and you will see the Properties dialog box. Under the Statistics tab is a field marked File Name. Change the filename in the text field and click OK.

Creating Symbolic Links Using the GNOME *gmc* Client

When you right-click a file or directory in gmc, one option on the pop-up menu is Symlink. Selecting this option will present you with a dialog box where you can type the name and path of the symlink you'd like to create. The symlink will point at the file you selected.

SEE ALSO
➤ *For a fuller explanation of symlinks, see page 46.*

Deleting Files and Directories using the GNOME *gmc* Client

Deleting a file or directory in gmc can be done by selecting the file or directory in the right pane and choosing Delete from the pop-up menu. If you choose to delete a directory that isn't empty, you'll see a dialog box asking whether you want to delete everything in it first. If you are deleting multiple directories at once, you can make your answer apply to all the remaining directories as well.

Searching for Files with GNOME's Search Tool

The GNOME Search Tool provides another way to locate files in the directory tree. It can be launched from the Utilities section of the GNOME panel menu or from the command line like this:

```
$ gsearchtool &
```

After typing in the directory to start find in, you can add or remove search criteria as seen in Figure 3.2.

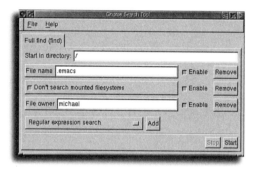

FIGURE 3.2
You can search for files using complex search dialogs with gsearchtool by entering criteria in text fields and selecting options in drop-down boxes. Each time you click the Add button, gsearchtool will add more fields.

Using the KDE File Manager *kfm*

If you use the K Desktop Environment with the X Window System, you will have access to the K File Manager. Despite its name, kfm is actually a Web browser (see Figure 3.3). However, it has been tailored with functions that make it useful for manipulating files and directories. Like its GNOME counterpart, it is also the program that manages your desktop icons. You can bring up the kfm client by selecting Home Directory from the K menu or by selecting the home directory icon on the panel. You can navigate to different directories by clicking on folder icons (or the up arrow as needed) or by typing a file path in the Location: box.

SEE ALSO

➤ *For details on starting and using X, see Part III, "The X Window System," starting on page 167.*

➤ *To learn more about GNOME, see the section, "Starting Enlightenment/Gnome," on page 194.*

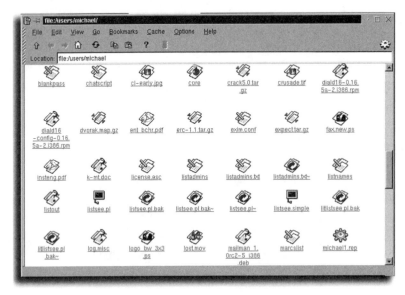

FIGURE 3.3
Although kfm is typically used for manipulating files on your hard drive, you can also use it to surf the Web. Just type the URL in the Location box.

Creating Directories Using KDE's *kfm*

There are a couple of simple ways to create directories using kfm. The first approach is to right-click the white space around the files. When you see the pop-up menu, select New, and then choose Folder from the submenu. In the dialog box, type the name of the directory you want to create. You can type the entire path if you choose. There is a second way to create new directories in kfm. Open the File drop-down menu from the top of the window. Select New from the menu and Folder from the submenu. Then, just type the folder name in the dialog box.

Copying Files and Directories Using *kfm*

Copying files and directories with kfm can be done quickly and easily. kfm uses the X11 clipboard for copying files. Just highlight the file or directory you want to copy by clicking once on the file's icon. To copy to the clipboard, either right-click and select Copy from the menu, select Copy from the drop-down Edit menu, or use the Ctrl+c key binding. Next, use kfm to navigate to the desired location. Now click once in the white space and choose Paste from the right-click menu or the drop-down Edit menu, or use the Ctrl+v key binding. Note that if you try to copy a file into the same directory as the original, kfm prompts you to rename the file or choose a new location.

kfm also allows you to copy files by dragging them and dropping them into the folder where you want them. If the folder you want to drop the file into isn't visible, you can open a second kfm and point it to the right folder before dragging. When you drop the file, kfm asks you whether you'd like to copy, move, or link the file you're manipulating. After you make your selection, kfm copies, moves, or links the file as directed.

Moving and Renaming Files and Directories and Creating Symlinks Using *kfm*

Moving files or directories and creating symlinks in kfm is as easy as dragging the original and dropping it where you want to move or symlink it. As mentioned in the previous section, when you drop the file you will be presented with a pop-up menu asking whether you want to move, copy, or symlink the file.

SEE ALSO

➤ *For a fuller explanation of symlinks, see page 46.*

Deleting Files and Using KDE's Trash Can

When you right-click a file in kfm, one of the options on the pop-up menu is Delete. You can use this option to delete a file you no longer want; a slightly safer method, however, might be to select Move to Trash, which just relocates your unwanted file to a special area. You can also move a file to the trash can by highlighting it in kfm and either pressing Ctrl+x or selecting Edit, Move to Trash. This way, if you need to recover a file you moved to the trash can, you can click the trash can icon on your desktop, which opens kfm to your trash directory. There you can open or move your previously trashed files. When you are really sure that you no longer want any of the files in your trash can, you can right-click the trash can icon and select Empty Trash Bin from the pop-up menu, which will permanently delete from your system all files in your trash can.

Searching the File System with KDE's *kfind* Client

To search for a particular file in the directory tree, you can use the kfind client, either by selecting Find Files from the K menu, or from the command line:

```
$ kfind &
```

The resulting dialog box allows you to input the name of the file you are searching for, what directory to start looking in, and whether you want to recursively scan the subdirectories. If this isn't detailed enough for your search, select the Date Modified tab to narrow your search by when the file was created or last modified. Finally the Advanced tab allows you to specify the type of file, its size, or text it contains. When all your data about the file is entered, click the Start Search icon, select the File menu and the Start Search option, or press Ctrl+f. kfind will expand its dialog box to include its results at the bottom, as seen in Figure 3.4.

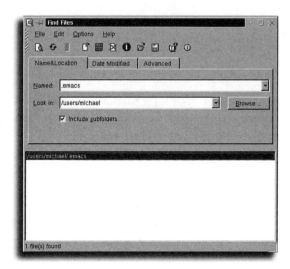

FIGURE 3.4
The various tabs in the kfind dialog box let you narrow down your search by many different criteria.

Searching Text Files

Linux also comes with a number of programs that you can use to search files. Some of these commands use regular expressions (introduced in Chapter 2, "Entering Commands"), while others, such as the strings command, offer limited search capabilities.

Using the *grep* Command

The grep command is part of a family of commands: grep, fgrep, and egrep. These commands are closely related, but have different capabilities in the type of expressions or wildcards that can be used on the command line. For example, to look for any occurrence of the word *hacker* in the file cathedral-bazaar.txt:

```
$ grep -n hacker cathedral-bazaar.txt
278:  happy extreme, is that a lot of users are hackers too.
➥Because source
279:  code is available, they can be effective hackers.  This can be
...
1269:  That being the case, it's doubly important that open-source
➥hackers
1416:  the hacker culture mirrors the organization of its software,
➥and vice-
```

The grep command returns matches for simple words as patterns on the command line. The -n (number) command-line option prints the line number of the matching line in which the pattern is found. The grep command, by default, recognizes and uses only basic regular expressions. If you want to use extended regular expressions, use egrep.

```
$ grep '\(gp' /etc/info-dir
grep: Unmatched ( or \(
```

Each grep command reads the standard input and writes to the standard output. However, search patterns can also be placed in a text file and used with the -f (file) option. The -f option tells grep to obtain matches from a file. The -n option specifies that grep should print the line numbers where it finds the matches. In this example you have a file that contains the words you want to search for:

```
$ cat searchfile
esr
Web
$ grep -n -f searchfile cathedral-bazaar.txt
180:  Linus Torvalds <http://www.tuxedo.org/~esr/faqs/linus>, for
➥example,
1033:  birth of the World Wide Web, and that Linux left its infancy
➥during
1178:  <http://www.tuxedo.org/~esr/writings/magic-cauldron/>.
1456:  Linux.  The paper is accessible on the World Wide Web at
1477:  available on the Web at  <http://www.agorics.com/
➥agorpapers.html>.
1640:  invent Emacs or the World Wide Web or the Internet itself by
➥chasing
1785:  $Id: cathedral-bazaar.sgml,v 1.46 1999/08/08 02:21:32
➥esr Exp $
```

The grep command has more than 20 different command-line options and can be used to emulate the fgrep or egrep commands with the -F and -E options. For details about these programs, see the grep manual page, or use the GNU info program to read the info pages.

SEE ALSO

➤ *To learn how to use regular expressions, see page 31.*

➤ *To learn more about shell scripts, see page 321.*

➤ *To learn how to compress or decompress files, see page 504.*

Using the *egrep* Command

The egrep command uses extended regular expressions (introduced in Chapter 2) for pattern matching, but also handles regular searches like grep and fgrep:

```
# egrep -n tee /etc/info-dir
92:* tee: (sh-utils)tee invocation.   Redirect to multiple files.
```

The difference between egrep and the other grep commands becomes apparent when regular expressions are used:

```
# egrep '\(gp' /etc/info-dir
* gpm: (gpm).                 Text-mode mouse library.
```

The egrep program returns a match, whereas fgrep reports nothing, and grep reports an error. Apostrophes (') are used to protect expressions from being interpreted by the shell.

The egrep command reads the standard input and writes to the standard output. Search patterns can be placed in a text file and used with the -f (file) option.

Using the *fgrep* Command

The fgrep command uses fixed strings for searching. Patterns and files are specified on the command line like so:

```
# fgrep -n tee /etc/info-dir
92:* tee: (sh-utils)tee invocation.   Redirect to multiple files.
```

As illustrated by the following, the fgrep command does not recognize regular expressions:

```
# fgrep '\(gp' /etc/info-dir
```

Because the `fgrep` command does not recognize expressions other than simple wild-cards, no match is reported. Like the other `grep` commands, `fgrep` can use search patterns placed in a text file and used with the `-f` (file) option:

```
# cat > search.txt
gpm
[EOT]
# fgrep -f search.txt /etc/info-dir
* gpm: (gpm).              Text-mode mouse library.
```

Using the *strings* Command

Use the `strings` command to extract strings from binary files. This can be useful for peeking inside programs or for finding information inside commands. Combine the output of the `strings` command with other searching programs by using pipes. For example, the following command line reports on the copyright information of each program under the `/usr/bin` directory:

```
# find /usr/bin | xargs strings -f | fgrep Copyright | less
```

Without the `-f` (report files) option, the `strings` command does not insert the searched file's name in the output fed to the `fgrep` command.

SEE ALSO

➤ *To learn how to use regular expressions, see page 31.*

➤ *To learn more about shell scripts, see page 321.*

➤ *To learn how to compress or decompress files, see page 504.*

➤ *For details on using pipes, see page 26.*

Using the *egrep* and *fgrep* Commands

The `egrep` command uses extended regular expressions for pattern matching, but also handles simple searches like `grep` and `fgrep`:

```
$ egrep -n Id cathedral-bazaar.txt
304:  fluid and very user-driven.  Ideas and prototype modes
➥were often
1785:  $Id: cathedral-bazaar.sgml,v 1.46 1999/08/08 02:21:32
➥esr Exp $
```

Here you have used `egrep`, just like `grep`, to search for lines that contain the charac-ters *Id*. The difference between `egrep` and the other `grep` commands becomes appar-ent when regular expressions are used:

```
$ egrep -n Id[a-z]+ cathedral-bazaar.txt
304:  fluid and very user-driven.  Ideas and prototype modes were
➥often
$ grep -n Id[a-z]+ cathedral-bazaar.txt
$ fgrep -n Id[a-z]+ cathedral-bazaar.txt
$
```

This time you searched for the characters *Id* immediately followed by one or more lowercase letters. The egrep program returns a match. grep returns nothing because the + you used means match one or more of the preceding patterns (any character between *a* and *z* in this case). This construct is recognized only when using extended regular expressions. fgrep reports nothing because it looks only for what you've literally typed (fixed strings), and not regular expressions. Single quotes (') can be used if you need to protect expressions and patterns from being interpreted by the shell.

```
$ fgrep -n '*' cathedral-bazaar.txt
788:  the data stream as little as possible - and *never* throw away
```

---

zgrep: searching compressed files

A related program called zgrep can be used to search compressed text files by using regular expressions. This program, a shell script, uses the grep or egrep program, along with the gzip command to decompress and search files on-the-fly.

---

chapter

4

Using Text Editors

Selecting an editor •

Using Linux dictionaries •

Saving paper with the mpage •
command

Creating formatted documents •

Text editors are important tools for Linux users. At one time or another, you'll need to use a text editor to configure your system. Although Linux continues to mature with each release, not every system-administration tool has point-and-click convenience. To use Linux efficiently and productively, you should choose a text editor best suited to your needs and preferences.

Selecting an Editor

Many Linux distributions come with more than 20 text editors, if you count all the variations. Some editors can emulate others, and many also come with special versions for the X Window System. This section covers some basic information about the more common text editors.

Text editors are sometimes thought of as word processors, or interactive, screen-oriented programs used to open or create text files; to enter or change text; and then to print or save text files. Text editors used for word processing usually support cursor movement through a file and are screen-oriented. Some editors, such as those for X11, also have pull-down menus and other convenient user interfaces.

You can also perform text editing with non-interactive programs, such as text filters or stream editors (discussed later in this chapter).

Commercial Linux Word Processors

Few users realize that they have a surprising number of choices when considering word processing for Linux. Many of these software packages (such as the WordPerfect word processor shown in Figure 4.1, from `http://www.corel.com`) require the X Window System, and many require the X11 Motif software libraries. If you're interested in trying some of these programs, see the `Commercial-HOWTO` under the `/usr/doc` directory, or check out the following Web sites:

`http://linux.corel.com/linux8/index.htm`

`http://www.abisource.com`

`http://www.redhat.com/appindex/OfficeApps/`

`http://www.suse.com/`

`http://www.applix.com`

`http://www.sun.com/staroffice/`

SEE ALSO

➤ *To learn more about the X Window System, see page 169.*

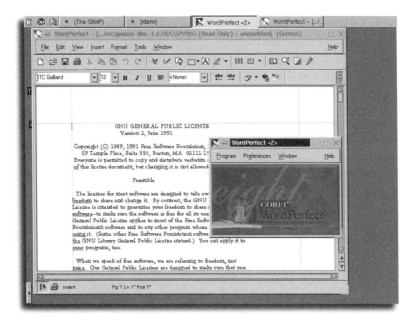

FIGURE 4.1
The WordPerfect word processing program for Linux typically uses the X Window System, although there is also a version of WordPerfect available for character terminals.

Starting WordPerfect for Linux

WordPerfect has a long-standing reputation as a full-featured word processor available for many platforms. Corel will allow users to download and install WordPerfect for Linux for free as long as it's for personal use only (see http://linux.corel.com for details).You can start WordPerfect either from your desktop panel's application menu or from the command line:

```
$ xwp &
```

SEE ALSO

➤ *For more information about using WordPerfect, see Que's Special Edition Using Corel WordPerfect 8 for Linux.*

WordPerfect will start up with two windows open. One is the control panel for all your open WordPerfect documents; the other is a blank document ready for your input.

Starting Applix Words

The Applixware office suite is published by Applix Inc. (http://www.applix.com) and provides many common office tools for many operating systems, including Linux.

Applixware for Linux can be found at `http://www.applix.com/applixware/linux/main.cfm`. When you have Applix installed, you can select Applix from your Applications menu or type `applix` at the command line:

```
$ applix &
```

This will invoke the Applix menu window. From the five icons listed, you can select the type of document you want to open. See Figure 4.2. The icon on the far left, which looks like a piece of paper, will allow you to open a new text document.

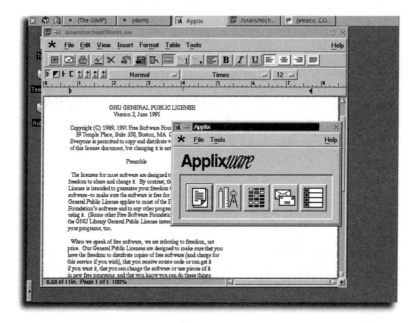

FIGURE 4.2
The Applix word processor is very simple. Use the help file to guide you through document creating and editing.

Starting StarOffice Star Writer

StarOffice is a intuitive and comprehensive office suite. StarOffice has recently been acquired by Sun Microsystems and can be downloaded and used for free. See `http://www.sun.com/staroffice/` for more details. After it has been installed on your system, you can get to StarOffice a few ways. The easiest is to select it from the Applications menu in your X desktop. You can also type the following at the command line:

```
$ soffice &
```

StarOffice installations will not always place the `soffice` command in your environment path. You might want to create a symlink to it in /usr/local/bin.

When StarOffice starts, it will give you a window with several options. See Figure 4.3. Select the option which best fits the document type that you'd like to create. StarOffice has extensive help files to answer any further questions you might have.

SEE ALSO

➤ *For a fuller explanation of symlinks, see page 46.*

➤ *For more information about using StarOffice, see Special Edition Using StarOffice by Michael Koch and Sarah Murray, with Werner Roth (ISBN: 0-7897-1993-2).*

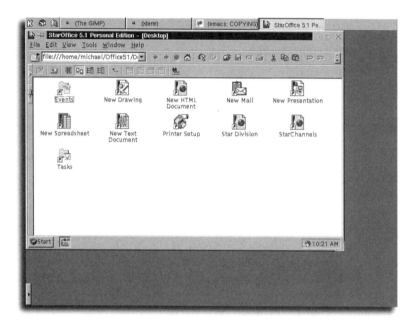

FIGURE 4.3
The StarOffice desktop area contains shortcuts to open new documents of various types. You can also create shortcuts to your most used documents on the desktop. See the help section for more details.

Using Screen Editors

Screen editors are easy to use, and are usually the preferred tools for programmers, writers, and casual users. Some Linux screen editors work only with the X Window System, while others work from the console or X11. Some important features to look for when choosing a screen editor include the following:

- Support for cursor keys to navigate through a file
- Easily remembered control keys or easy-to-use menus
- The capability to print files
- Crash protection for work in progress, such as automatic backups
- Support for spell-checking of documents
- Easy-to-use search-and-replace features to make changes in a file
- The capability to cut and paste of blocks of text
- The capability to turn word wrap or paragraph justification on or off
- Good documentation, or built-in help

Using the *emacs* Environment

The emacs text editor is among the most popular text editors. It is undoubtedly the most feature rich, although it is probably not the easiest to use for the novice. emacs is short for *editing macros*. Originally developed by Richard Stallman, this program is much, much more than a text editor. emacs can be used as a programming environment and Linux shell; also, emacs contains a Lisp language interpreter, sends email, browses Web sites, reads Usenet news, supports calendar and diary functions, and even plays games! emacs supports multiple modes to support specialized functions.

The emacs editor is distributed by the Free Software Foundation under the GPL (General Public License) as part of the GNU project. Depending on your installation, emacs can take up quite a lot of disk space (35MB or more); however you can significantly minimize this by choosing to install fewer options.

emacs does auto-saves. This is particularly useful in the event of a lockup or system problem. Automatically saved files are named the same as the original file but with a hash (#) before and after the filename. When you restart emacs and open the file you were editing when you were interrupted, you will be asked if you want to load the automatically saved version. Emacs also creates a backup by default of any file you edit, with a tilde (~) appended to the end.

emacs has nearly two dozen different command-line options, but it is easy to start. To open or create a text file, run emacs on the command line, followed the by the name of a new or existing file, like this:

```
$ emacs textfile
```

If you're using the X Window System, emacs creates or opens your file and displays its main window as shown in Figure 4.4. Note that the X11 version of emacs supports menus and the mouse.

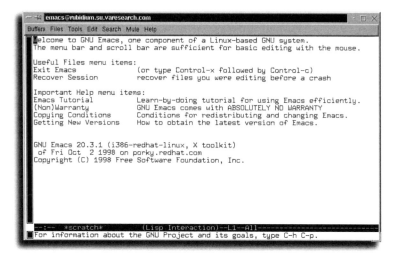

FIGURE 4.4
The emacs editor in the X Window System supports menus and the mouse.

To run emacs inside the window of an X11 terminal rather than in its own window, use the -nw (*no window*) option, like this:

```
$ emacs -nw textfile
```

Note

The Xemacs text editor is the cousin to emacs with a focus on operating well within a graphical user interface (GUI). Although each editor runs in either X or text mode, Xemacs is designed to look nicer and run better in X. Both editors are similar but it's important to keep in mind that they are not the same. The development team for Xemacs seems to share political differences with Richard Stallman, the original creator of emacs, which is why these two groups maintain separate packages. I'll leave it up to the users to try them both out and decide which one they prefer.

This runs emacs and opens your file. Learning emacs can take some time, but its built-in tutorial will get you started. If you're new to emacs, using this tutorial is essential.

Starting the *emacs* tutorial

1. Start emacs from the console or the command line of an X11 terminal window:
   ```
   $ emacs
   ```

2. Hold down the Ctrl key, and press H. You see a prompt at the bottom of the screen:
   ```
   C-h (Type ? for further options)-
   ```

3. Press T, and emacs starts its tutorial.

emacs can take some time to learn. You might find it easier to start with the X11 version, which uses menus. Table 4.1 lists the basic keystrokes you need in order to get started creating and editing files. emacs makes heavy use of a key called Meta that doesn't really exist on PC keyboards, so the Alt key is usually used in its place. Keep in mind that some distributions might map your keys differently so if these key bindings don't work, check your documentation. If your distribution doesn't provide a reasonable default, you can also use the Esc key instead of the Alt or Meta keys in emacs. See the emacs manual page for details.

Table 4.1 Basic *emacs* Commands

Action	Key Command(s)
Move the cursor backward one character	Ctrl+B or left arrow
Move the cursor down one line	Ctrl+N or down arrow
Move the cursor forward one character	Ctrl+F or right arrow
Move the cursor up one line	Ctrl+P or up arrow
Delete the current character	Ctrl+D or Del
Delete the current line	Ctrl+K
Delete the current word	Alt+D
Go to the beginning of the file	Alt+<
Go to the end of the current line	Ctrl+E
Go to the end of the file	Alt+>
Go to the beginning of the current line	Ctrl+A
Open a file	Ctrl+X, Ctrl+F
Page down one screen	Ctrl+V
Page up one screen	Alt+V
Quit emacs	Ctrl+X, Ctrl+C
Save the current file	Ctrl+X, Ctrl+S
Save the file as	Ctrl+X Ctrl+W
Show help	Ctrl+H
Start the tutorial	Ctrl+H T
Undo the last operation	Ctrl+_

Documentation for emacs can be found in the emacs man pages, the info pages, or at http://www.gnu.org.

Features of the *vi* and *vim* Editors

vim and vi are likely the most commonly used text editors in the UNIX world. It is useful to learn at least the basics of editing with vi or vim because you can be sure that some version of it will be installed on any Linux machine you encounter. Additionally, if you ever experience system problems, vi is one of the few applications that will still run when few other things are working correctly.

The vim editor is compatible with the original vi editor, which was an enhancement to the early line-oriented editor, ed. vim also comes in an X11 version called gvim, which supports multiple scrolling windows and menus.

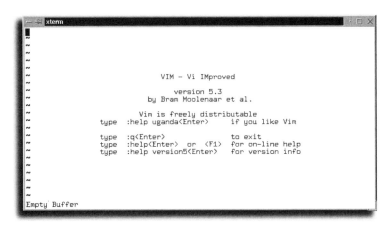

FIGURE 4.5
Although a bit cumbersome to the novice, the vim text editor is among the most commonly used and reliable editors available.

The vim editor has 23 command-line options, which are documented in its manual page. This editor features built-in help, split-screen windows, block moves, command-line editing, horizontal scrolling, cut-and-paste, and word wrap for word processing.

The X11 version of the vim editor, gvim, features split-scrollable windows, custom colors, window sizes, scrollbars, syntax highlighting, and menus you can customize.

Using vim might seem a bit unintuitive to the novice, but once you master a few commands, you will find that you can quickly and effectively edit text and write code with this powerful editor. It is important to understand that there are two basic modes for using vim: insert mode and command mode. You can toggle between these modes by using the i and Esc keys; i for *insert*, and Esc for *command*. Below is a list of other important vim key bindings. All of these should be used in the command mode.

Table 4.2 Basic *vim* Commands

Action	Key Command(s)
Move the cursor backward one character	h or left arrow
Move the cursor down one line	j or down arrow
Move the cursor forward one character	l or right arrow
Move the cursor up one line	k or up arrow
Delete the current character	x or Del
Delete the current line	dd
Delete the current word	dw
Go to the beginning of the file	1G
Go to the end of the current line	$
Go to the end of the file	G
Go to the beginning of the current line	^
Open a file	vi *filename*
Search through a file for a string	/
Quit vim, abandoning all changes	:q!
Save the current file	:w
Show help	:help
Insert text	i
Undo the last operation	u

Editing Text with the *pico* Editor

The pico editor is part of the pine electronic mail program's software package. Though it lacks many advanced features found in emacs or vi, it is an easy-to-use editor. This no-nonsense program is compact, reliable, and efficient (you don't have to use pine in order to edit files with pico). pico even supports your mouse when used with the -m command-line option, like this:

```
$ pico -m homework
```

`pico` opens your file, as shown in Figure 4.6. If you're running the X Window System, click one of the commands at the bottom of the screen to progress.

FIGURE 4.6
The `pico` editor is an simple, compact, and efficient text editor.

`pico` also protects your work in progress in the unfortunate event of a system crash (a rare event for Linux users), and saves your work with your original file's name with the extension `.save`. If you were working on an original file, the saved file is called `pico.save`.

Table 4.3 lists many of the common commands you can use when editing text.

Table 4.3 Basic *pico* Commands

Action	Key Command(s)
Move the cursor backward one character	Ctrl+B
Move the cursor down one line	Ctrl+N
Move the cursor forward one character	Ctrl+F
Move the cursor up one line	Ctrl+P
Delete the current character	Ctrl+D
Delete (cut) the current line	Ctrl+K
Display the cursor position	Ctrl+C
Go to the end of the current line	Ctrl+E
Go to the beginning of the current line	Ctrl+A
Insert a file	Ctrl+R
Justify the current paragraph	Ctrl+J

continues...

Table 4.3 Continued	
Action	Key Command(s)
Page down one screen	Ctrl+V
Page up one screen	Ctrl+Y
Paste text or unjustify	Ctrl+U
Quit pico	Ctrl+X
Search for text	Ctrl+W
Start the spelling check	Ctrl+T
Save the file as	Ctrl+O
Show help	Ctrl+G

Features of the *joe* Editor

The joe editor software package includes fivedifferent editors: jmacs, joe, jpico, jstar, and rjoe. The jmacs version uses many commands similar to the emacs editor. The jpico version emulates the pico text editor. If you remember using the WordStar word-processing program, the jstar editor will be familiar. The rjoe editor edits only files specified on the command line.

Edit .joerc (in your home directory) to change joe's help menus, display, and keyboard commands.

Read the joe manual page for details about using and configuring each version, or use joe's built-in help (accessed by pressing Ctrl+k, followed by the h key).

Features of the *jed* Editor

The jed editor, like vim and emacs, comes in a version for the console and a version for the X Window System (xjed). To configure the jed editor, copy the file jed.rc to your home directory with the name .jedrc. (Note that you might need to type whereis jed to verify the path of the jed.rc file.)

The jed editor has built-in help (you can access it by pressing Esc, the ?, and then h). Read the jed documentation and the jed manual page for more information.

Defining a Default Text Editor

You might want to set your user profile up so that you have a default editor. This will ensure that any application that invokes the edit command and recognizes the EDITOR environment variable will give you the editor of your choice.

1. If you are using the bash shell, move to your home directory and open your `.profile` file the editor of your choice. (In the example, I use `vi`.)

```
$ cd /home/amy
$ vi .profile
```

2. Set the `EDITOR` variable to the name of the editor you want to use by inserting the following lines (use the `i` command to insert with `vi`):

```
EDITOR=vi
export EDITOR
```

3. Save the file and exit (by typing `:wq` if you're using `vi`).

4. This will take effect next time you log in.

If you use a shell other than *bash*, you will want to read the documentation regarding changing environment variables in your shell.

SEE ALSO

➤ *To learn more about shell environment variables, see page 102.*

Using Stream Editors

Using your shell's standard input and standard output is another way to edit text. This practice, called *redirection* (using the < or > operators), also uses shell pipelines (with the | operator) to change streams of text. Specialized programs, such as `sed`, are designed to accept redirection and piped text, and are called *stream editors*.

SEE ALSO

➤ *To learn how to use the shell redirection and pipe operators, see page 24.*

Search and Replace Operations with the *sed* Editor

Use `sed` (stream editor) to quickly edit text from the command line. The `sed` editor has more than two dozen commands, and also uses regular expressions (similar to those of the `egrep` command).

SEE ALSO

➤ `egrep` *is discussed in the section titled "Searching for Text Files" in Chapter 3 on page 58.*

The `sed` command can be used to quickly make global changes in a text document without loading a word processor or text editor. For example, if the unfortunate miscreant in the following text is not Mr. Price, but his wife, the phrase `Mr.` would need to be changed to `Mrs.`:

```
As stated in our previous discussion, Mr. Price has not responded to our
complaints, and has not returned our overtures aimed at resolving this credit
problem. Mr. Price knows that we have attempted to make contact, but has
spurned our requests for resolution, even after foreclosure on the property
in question. Mr. Price's whereabouts remain unknown, but was last seen on St.
John's Island.
```

Use the sed's s (substitute) command to find each instance of the string Mr. and replace it with Mrs. Place a g (for global) at the end of the search and replace string to specify that you want *all* instances of the word *Mr.* replaced. Omitting the g would tell sed to only replace the first occurrence that it finds.

```
$ sed s/Mr./Mrs./g <notice.txt
As stated in our previous discussion, Mrs. Price has not responded to our
complaints, and has not returned our overtures aimed at resolving this credit
problem. Mrs. Price knows that we have attempted to make contact, but has
spurned our requests for resolution, even after foreclosure on the property in
question. Mrs. Price's whereabouts remain unknown, but was last seen on St.
John's Island.
```

Note that each instance of Mr. has been changed to Mrs., and that the sed command echoes the input back to your display, but does not save this output to the file. To create a new file, use the > redirection operator:

```
$ sed s/Mr./Mrs./g <notice.txt >correctnotice.txt
```

Entering the sed command's -f (script file) command-line option followed by the name of a script file feeds sed a list of changes to perform on a text file.

Using a *sed* script file

1. To make numerous, regular changes to text files, use an editing script with the sed command. For example, using your favorite text editor, create a file called personnel.txt, and enter a paragraph like this:

   ```
   Heretofore, all employees must report in by telephone, in accordance with
   the personnel guide book. Pursuant to the guide book, this and other
   regulations are applicable to all employees, and all employees must
   utilize the guide book. A new employee must also acquire or procure the
   guide book as a draft implementation, or the company will terminate the
   employee's position.
   ```

2. Save the file, and then create a script file with the name grammar.sed. Enter a list of sed commands, like these:

   ```
   s/utilize/use/
   s/procure/get/
   s/acquire/buy/
   s/draft implementation/draft/
   ```

```
s/Heretofore/From now on/
s/in accordance with/according to/
s/thereto/to/
s/Pursuant/According/
s/are applicable/apply/
s/terminate/end/
```

3. Save the file, and exit your text editor. Using the sed command's -f option followed by the name of your script file, use the shell redirection operator to feed the original text file into the sed command, like this:

```
$ sed -f grammar.sed <personnel.txt
From now on, all employees must report in by telephone, according to the
personnel guide book. According to the guide book, this and other
regulations apply to all employees, and all employees must use the guide
book. A new employee must also buy or get the guide book as a draft, or the
company will end the employee's position.
```

4. The sed command has replaced each word or phrase with the simpler replacement—almost like a grammar-checking program. Experiment with your own scripts to check punctuation or writing style.

Using Linux Dictionaries

Correct spelling is an important part of writing and word processing, and spelling errors can be embarrassing. Most Linux distributions come with several tools to check spelling or look up words in the system dictionary, usually found under the /usr/dict directory (type whereis linux.words at the command prompt to verify this).

The default system dictionary, words (which could be a symbolic link to the file linux.words under the /usr/dict directory), contains more than 45,000 correctly spelled words in an alphabetical list.

Getting the *web2* Dictionary

Not satisfied with 45,000 words? You can get another dictionary, web2, which contains an alphabetized list of more than 234,000 words. The web2 dictionary is usually accompanied by a dictionary of proper names, containing more than 1,300 names, and a word-phrase hyphenation dictionary, called web2a, which contains more than 75,000 phrases.

To get these files, browse to the following URL:

```
ftp://ftp.digital.com/pub/BSD/net2/share/dict
```

Dictionaries: Rolling Your Own

Don't want to use the standard system dictionary? Need to build your own dictionaries containing specialized words for the medical or legal fields? Try using a combination of text filters and shell pipe operators to build your own, with a command line like this:

```
$ find *.txt | xargs cat | tr ' ' '\n'| sort | uniq >mydict.txt
```

This command line uses the `find` command to pipe the names of all files in the current directory to the `xargs` command. The `xargs` command takes each of the filenames that find matches and runs them through the `cat` command, which then uses the `tr` command to translate each space between words to a carriage return, building a single list of words. This list of words is then sorted with the `sort` command, and any duplicate words are removed with the `uniq` command. The result wont be perfect, but you'll have a dictionary list of all the words in your documents.

SEE ALSO

➤ *To learn more about the* `find` *command, see page 50.*

Spell Checking with the *ispell* Command

Most Linux distributions come with the interactive spelling program `ispell`. Use this program alone or with your text editor to correct spelling mistakes. Most editors included with Linux distributions can use this program.

Using *ispell* to check spelling

1. Use the `ispell` command followed by a filename to check spelling interactively, like this:

   ```
   $ ispell document.txt
   ```

2. If no misspelled words are found, `ispell` returns you to the command line. If there are misspellings, the first misspelled word is displayed at the top of your screen, along with the filename. The misspelled word is displayed in context, and a numbered list of suggested replacements is shown, followed by a command-line prompt at the bottom of the screen.

   Here's how the `ispell` code looks in action:

   ```
   personall              File: document.txt

   Heretofore, all employees must report in by telephone, in accordance with
   the personall guidebook. Pursuant to the guide book, this and other

    0: personal
    1: personally
   ```

```
    2: personals
    3: person all
    4: person-all


[SP] <number> R)epl A)ccept I)nsert L)ookup U)ncap Q)uit e(X)it or ?
➥for help
```

3. Correct the misspelled word by typing the number of the suggested replacement word, or press R to type your own replacement. The `ispell` command responds with the following prompt:

```
Replace with:

personall
regurlations
```

The `ispell` command prints a list of misspelled words found in your document. The `ispell` software package also includes utilities to build new `ispell` dictionaries. For details, read the `ispell` manual pages.

Using Internet Dictionaries with the *dict* Clients

If you are looking for the definition of a word rather than its spelling, the `dict`, `gdict`, and `kdict` clients grab a definition from dictionaries on the Internet. Simply type `dict` followed by the word you want defined. Many distributions do not install these clients by default. `dict` can be downloaded at `http://www.dict.org/`. `gdict` can be downloaded at `http://www.psilord.com/code/gdict/`. Finally, `kdict` can be downloaded at `http://www.rhrk.uni-kl.de/~gebauerc/kdict/`.

```
$ dict gnu
DEFINITION 0
gnu \'n(y)u:\ n or gnu or gnus [modif. of Bushman nqu] pl  : any of several
    large African antelopes (genera Connochaetes and XGorgon) with a head like
    that of an ox, short mane, long tail, and horns in both sexes that curve
    downward and outward
```

If you are using GNOME or KDE under the X Window System, you might have a GUI tool (`gdict` or `kdict` respectively) that allows you to type your word into a box and receive your answer in the text field at the bottom.

Saving Paper with the *mpage* Command

Years ago, computer industry wags fatuously predicted that word processing would lead to paperless offices. But as many of us have woefully realized, this revolution has instead lead to the demise of erasable bond and correction fluid, and a perverse *increase* in the use of paper (we had a laser printer in our former office named *tree-eater*).

If you're a serious Linux user, and if you're serious about saving paper, you should not only recycle, but also use the mpage command to print at least two pages on a single sheet of paper. The mpage command, followed by a number, will print 1, 2, 4, or 8 pages of text on a single sheet of paper. For example, to print two pages on a single sheet, use the -2 option followed by the -P option, like so:

```
$ mpage -2 -o massivedocument.txt -P
```

This mpage command creates a PostScript file from your document, and sends the output through your printer. If you have installed your printer correctly, you'll get a nice printout (at least on laser or inkjet printers) of two side-by-side pages on each sheet of paper. Using the -o command prevents the printing of a line border around your text.

SEE ALSO

➤ *For more information on setting up your printer for Linux, see page 87.*

The mpage command also prints odd- or even-numbered pages, prints page headers, uses different fonts or margins, supports duplex printing, and even reverses a print document by starting at the document's end. See the mpage manual page for more information.

Creating Formatted Documents

Text editors can do basic formatting of text, such as limiting the number of characters or words per line and justifying paragraphs. But to add page numbering, sophisticated indenting, or multiple columns and fonts, you must use a formatting or typesetting system. Text formatting utilities, such as the pr or fmt commands, areusually small text utilities that add headers, footers, margins, and page numbers, usually through command-line options. *Typesetting* systems, such as groff or TeX, offer a bewildering array of commands that you must insert in your documents before processing.

Using Text-Formatting Filter Commands

Use text-formatting filter programs if you don't want to learn the complicated formatting commands of typesetting systems. Text filters change the output of your documents with several simple command-line options. Use a text-formatting program to quickly format your documents.

Formatting with the *pr* Command

The `pr` command has nearly 20 different command-line options to format documents. For example, to print a document with a page header containing the time and
the phrase *Committee Report* and using a left margin of 10 characters, use the `pr` command like so:

```
$ pr +2 -h "Committee Report" -o 10 <report.txt | lpr
```

Because the preceding command uses the + operator followed by a page number, `pr`
starts numbering pages on page 2. The `-h` option tells it to print the header
"Committee Report" at the top of each page. By using the `-o 10` flag, you specify
that you want a left margin of 10 pixels. Next, you use < `report.txt` to tell `pr` that
`report.txt` is the file you want to feed it; and finally, you pipe it through `lpr` to print
the output. The `pr` program also formats text into columns via the `-COLUMN`
command-line option. For example, to print the system dictionary in three columns
per page, use the `pr` command like this (obviously, I haven't shown the entire output):

```
$ pr -3 /usr/dict/words
98-03-15 16:36                    web2                    Page    1
A                    Abaris              abbotnullius
a                    abarthrosis             abbotship
aa                   abarticular            abbreviate
aal                  abarticulation        abbreviately
aalii                abas                  abbreviation
aam                  abase                 abbreviator
```

See the `pr` manual page for more options, such as `-l 1`, which can be used to remove
the page header from the output.

Formatting with the *fmt* Command

Use the `fmt` command along with the `pr` command to change the width of your text
documents. Use the `fmt` command to format text into the line width you specify, and
then send the text through the `pr` command for additional formatting. For example,
to format the *Cathedral and the Bazaar* paper by Eric Raymond, use the `fmt -w`
(width) option followed by a line width (in numbers of characters), and then pipe the
output to the `pr` command using the `-o` (margin) option followed by a margin (in
numbers of characters), like so:

```
$ fmt -w 40 <cathedral-bazaar.txt | pr -o 15
99-09-30 19:22                                    Page    1
                    The Cathedral and the Bazaar by
                    Eric S. Raymond $Date: 1999/08/08
                    02:21:32 $
```

```
                     I anatomize a successful open-source
                     project, fetchmail, that was run as
                     a deliberate test of some surprising
                     theories about software engineering
                     suggested by the history of Linux.
                     I discuss these theories in terms
                     of two fundamentally different
                     development styles, the ``cathedral''
                     model of most of the commercial
                     world versus the ``bazaar'' model
                     of the Linux world.  I show that
                     these models derive from opposing
                     assumptions about the nature of the
                     software-debugging task.
```

Obviously, I have not shown all the output here; nonetheless, you should see that this is a convenient way to format text from the command line.

Using Text-Processing Systems

Typesetting documents using text-processing systems, such as groff or TeX, is usually a three-step process:

1. Use a text editor to create a document. In the text, insert typesetting commands.
2. Process the document through the typesetting program, which then produces a formatted document.
3. Preview the document, checking for errors, or send the document to a printer.

The following sections discuss the formatting of text with the groff and TeX systems.

Formatting Text with the *groff* Formatter

The GNU groff typesetting system uses special formatting commands, called *macros*, to format documents. The man macro set is used to format your system's manual pages. For example, to format and display the contents of the cat manual page, you can use any of the following three command lines (each does the same thing):

```
$ man cat

$ nroff -man /usr/man/man1/cat.1 | less

$ groff -Tascii -man /usr/man/man1/cat.1 | less
```

These examples assume that you have installed the man pages for cat on your machine and that your man pages have not been precompressed. Notice that you use the -T option to specify that you want the output to be presented in ASCII format. The -man option tells groff to format the page like a man page. Try this example without the -man flag. You'll see that the same information is presented but with no formatting whatsoever.

You can see the groff man macros if you use the cat command to print the cat manual page, like this:

```
$ cat /usr/man/man1/cat.1
.TH CAT 1 "GNU Text Utilities" "FSF" \" -*- nroff -*-
.SH NAME
cat \- concatenate files and print on the standard output
.SH SYNOPSIS
.B cat
[\-benstuvAET] [\-\-number] [\-\-number-nonblank] [\-\-squeeze-blank]
[\-\-show-nonprinting] [\-\-show-ends] [\-\-show-tabs] [\-\-show-all]
[\-\-help] [\-\-version]
[file...]
.SH DESCRIPTION
```

I have not reproduced the entire contents of the cat.1 manual page, but if you compare the output from the man, nroff, or groff commands to the original form of the cat manual page, you should see that the man macros, represented by *dot* commands (such as .TH and .SH) cause special formatting. These dot commands and other manual page macros are documented in the man.7 manual page under the /usr/man/man7 directory.

There are several other sets of typesetting macros for the groff formatting system. When you use these macros in a text document, you must specify the macro set used on the groff command line, like so:

```
$ groff -Tascii -mm mydocument.txt
```

In the example above, the -m option tells groff to check for a macro named *m* and run the document through the *m* macro.

Documentation for these macros is located in various groff-related manual pages. Table 4.4 lists some common groff macros from the mm manuscript macro set.

Table 4.4 Common *groff* Macros for *mm* Manuscript Macros

Purpose	Macro Name
Center justify	.ds C
End text box	.b2
Justification off	.sa 0
Justification on	.sa 1
Line fill off	.ds N
Line fill on	.ds F
New paragraph with *x* indent	.p x
No indents	.ds L
Right justify	.ds R
Start bold text	.b
Start text box	.b1
Use columns	.mc
Use one column	.1c
Use two columns	.2c

If you don't want to use a macro set, try some common groff commands, listed in Table 4.5. The macros in Table 4.4 are specific to the mm macro set. The commands in Table 4.5 work globally with groff.

Table 4.5 Common *groff* Typesetting Commands

Purpose	Command
Begin new page	.bp
Begin new paragraph	.pp
Center next *x* lines	.ce x
Center text *x*	.ce x
Insert (space) *n* inches down	.sp ni
Insert *n* inches down	.sv ni
Set font bold	.ft B
Set font Roman	.ft R

Purpose	Command
Set line spacing to *n*	`.ls n`
Temporary indent *n* inches	`.ti ni`
Turn off line fill	`.nf`
Turn on centering	`.ce`
Turn on indenting *n* inches	`.in ni`
Turn on line fill	`.fi`
Underline next *n* lines	`.ul n`

Use the `groff -T` command-line option followed by an output format specifier to create different document formats, such as PostScript, TeX `dvi`, text, HP printer-control language, or PCL. Preview your documents before printing, and see the `groff` manual pages for more information about thistypesetting system.

Formatting Text with *TeX*

The `TeX` typesetting system is a formidable collection of programs, fonts, and other utilities. This sophisticated system includes more than 65 programs, along with related support files such as libraries, macros, and documentation. A typical `TeX` installation requires nearly 50MB of hard-drive space for the system files, macros, and fonts. Using TeX can be a complex process and often produces lots of screen output, so be warned!

The `TeX` typesetting system uses formatting commands inserted in text files, a process similar to `groff`'s system. To see how `TeX` uses its macros, try processing a sample file, such as `samples.tex`, which is found under the `TeX` directories.

Processing a sample *TeX* file

1. Use the `latex` command to typeset the `samples.tex` file. This process can take up to a minute on some Linux systems. The `latex` command uses special `TeX` macros to format documents. Latex is not installed by default on many systems, so if you need to download a copy, you can go to `http://metalab.unc.edu/pub/packages/TeX/macros/latex/`. Use this command followed by the name of the `TeX` source document to create a text `.dvi` file, like this example (note that `samples.tex` might be in a different location on your system. See your documentation for details.):

   ```
   $ latex  /usr/lib/texmf/texmf/doc/generic/pstricks/samples.tex
   ```

2. Convert the resulting .dvi file, samples.dvi, to PostScript by using the dvips command. Use the -f command to read the file from the standard input, and redirect the output to a PostScript file:

```
$ dvips -f <samples.dvi >samples.ps
```

3. Preview the PostScript document using the gv (Ghost View) PostScript previewer:

```
$ gv samples.ps
```

4. To print the document, click the File menu and select the Print Document option, or use the lpr command followed by the -P printer option, like this:

```
$ lpr -Plp samples.ps
```

TeX can produce complex diagrams and documents, but it takes some effort on your part to learn the system. Read the TeX and related manual pages, look at the TeX info files, and browse the TeX documentation. The package includes an easy-to-navigate HTML-formatted manual and FAQ.

Saving time previewing *dvi* documents

Previewing TeX dvi documents can take several minutes, and is very system-intensive. The best way to preview TeX dvi documents is to convert the file to PostScript with the dvips command, and then to use the gv PostScript previewer, like so:

```
$ dvips -f < mytexdoc.dvi >_mytexdoc.ps
$ gv mytextdoc.ps
```

Printing Files

Adding printers •

Configuring printers for WordPerfect
for Linux •

Spooling files to your printer •

Controlling printers and print jobs •

Adding Printers

If you did not set up a printer when you installed Linux, or if you want to add a different printer to your system, you can do so in at least two ways (both of which are discussed in this chapter):

- Manually
- By using the Red Hat Linux `printtool` command for the X Window System

Printers are described under Linux as character-mode devices. The most common of these devices are parallel-port printers and are listed under the `/dev` directory, with names similar to `lp`. Here's a sample listing of parallel-port printers:

```
# ls /dev/lp*
/dev/lp0 /dev/lp1 /dev/lp2
```

You should find at least three parallel printer devices listed under the `/dev` directory.

SEE ALSO

➤ *To learn more about the X Window System, see page 169.*

Tip

If the startup messages scroll by too quickly, wait for Linux to boot, log on, and then pipe the output of the **dmesg** command through the `less` pager:

```
# dmesg | less
```

Checking Your Printer

There are many ways to ensure that a printer you created when you installed Linux is working.

Checking an installed printer

1. Watch the startup messages while Linux is booting; look for a line specifying a found printer device, such as this:
   ```
   lp1 at 0x0378, (polling)
   ```

   This line indicates that Linux found a parallel port device that uses the `/dev/lp1` device.

2. Print a directory listing by sending the output of the `ls` command directly to your printer, or the found device, with a command line similar to the following:
   ```
   # ls >/dev/lp1
   ```

Your printer should activate and print a list of the current directory.

3. If your printer does nothing (make sure it is plugged in and turned on), you can try looking at the contents of the devices file under the proc directory by issuing the following command:

```
# cat /proc/devices
```

The devices file lists all active devices for your system. Look for the lp device under the list of character devices. The device is listed like this:

```
Character devices:
  1 mem
  2 pty
  3 ttyp
  4 ttyp
  5 cua
  6 lp
  7 vcs
 10 misc
 14 sound
127 pcmcia
```

4. Ensure that parallel printing is available, either as a loadable code module (lp.o) under the /lib/modules/*kernel-version*/misc directory or as code that is compiled into your kernel. Use the lsmod command to look for the lp module in kernel memory, like this:

```
# lsmod
Module          Pages   Used by
lp     2    1 (autoclean)
serial_cs    1    0
fixed_cs    1    0
ds     2    [serial_cs fixed_cs]    4
i82365    4    2
pcmcia_core    8    [serial_cs fixed_cs ds i82365]  5
vfat    3    1 (autoclean)
```

5. If you cannot detect a printer, or if you don't see the lp module, read the Printing-HOWTO, found in your documentation directory for details about installing a printer.

SEE ALSO

➤ *To learn more about using redirection operators and pipes in the shell, see page 24.*

➤ *To learn more about Linux modules, see page 535.*

> **Using a serial printer**
>
> Serial printers are serial devices with names similar to your serial or modem ports, such as `/dev/ttyS0`. For information about serial ports or serial printer cables, see the Serial-HOWTO in your systems documentation directory. To learn all the details about setting up a serial printer, see the Printing-HOWTO. Be sure to set your serial port and printer to the same speed. To learn how, read the `setserial` command manual page.

Adding a Local Printer by Editing */etc/printcap*

You can add a printer by entering a printer capability definition in the system printer capability database, `printcap`. This file is found under the `/etc` directory, and is a text file that can be changed only by the root operator.

The format, commands, and syntax to use when creating a printer entry in the `/etc/printcap` file are found in the `printcap` manual page. There are more than 40 different commands, but you can quickly create a printer with only the `mx` (maximum size of spooled files) and `sd` (spool directory) commands.

Configuring a simple printer

1. To create a printer called `mylp` for the `/dev/lp1` device, open the `/etc/printcap` file with your preferred text editor. The `sd` option tells the Linux printing daemon, `lpd`, where to temporarily place printed (spooled) files. The `mx` command, used with a value of `0`, places no limit on the size of spooled files. Type an entry such as this:

    ```
    mylp:\
            :sd=/var/spool/lpd/mylp:\
            :mx#0:\
            :lp=/dev/lp1:
    ```

2. Save the entry, and then create the printer's spool directory by using the `mkdir` command:

    ```
    # mkdir /var/spool/lpd/mylp
    ```

3. Make sure the directory `lp` has the correct group ownership and permissions by using the `chgrp` and `chmod` commands, as follows:

    ```
    # chgrp lp /var/spool/lpd/mylp
    # chmod 755 /var/spool/lpd/mylp
    ```

4. Test the printer entry with the `lpr` (line printer command) using the `-P` option to specify your newly created printer:

    ```
    # lpr -Pmylp test.txt
    ```

5. Your printer should activate and print the test document.

SEE ALSO

➤ *For more information about changing permissions and ownerships by using the* chown *and* chgrp *commands, see page 378.*

➤ *To learn more about creating directories, see page 43.*

> **Tip**
>
> You might see a "staircase" effect in the printout. This is a common occurrence, indicating that your printer is not completely returning to the beginning of a line before printing another line. Although you can try to set your printer to insert a return after a linefeed, the best solution is to use a printer filter.

SEE ALSO

➤ *For information about other ways to save disk space, see page 523.*

Configuring Printers for WordPerfect for Linux

Rather than using the system printer settings, WordPerfect 8 installs its own printer drivers and works from its own settings. The easiest way to add a printer to WordPerfect for Linux is to do so while installing WordPerfect. When you run the installation script, WordPerfect asks you to select your printers from a list. Scroll through the list to select your printer. Highlight it and click Add. Next it asks you to assign your printer to a device. Select your printer from the list of installed printers and click Assign. You should receive a pop-up box with a list of devices (most users should select lpr). Then click OK.

If you've already installed WordPerfect, and you want to change or add printers, select the File menu and then select Print (or press F5). This spawns the Print dialog box where you can select the printer you want to print to by clicking the Select button. In the next box, you can double-check that the printer you want to install isn't already there. If it's not, click the Printer Create/Edit button at the bottom-right of the dialog box. This brings up the Printer Create/Edit dialog box, shown in Figure 5.1, in which you need to click the Add button. The Add Printer Driver dialog box lists all the available drivers that come with WordPerfect. You can select your printer from this list. If the driver is not listed here, click the file icon at the top right. Now you can look through your entire directory structure for the printer driver. If you don't have it on your hard drive, you need to download it from the printer manufacturer's Web site.

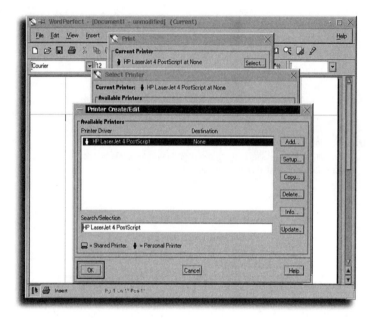

FIGURE 5.1
The Printer Create/Edit dialog box.

WordPerfect 8 includes an extensive list of printer drivers that come with the package. You can easily find and install your printer of choice.

After you select the correct printer, you are returned to the Printer Create/Edit dialog box. Use the Setup option to configure the printer properly. Be sure to specify a destination using the Destination button. Now click OK.

Spooling Files to Your Printer

Linux uses a modified printing system inherited from the Berkeley Software Distribution (BSD) UNIX operating system. This system is called *line-printer spooling*. Linux starts printing services by running lpd, the line printer daemon, after you boot. This daemon runs in the background, and waits for program or command-line print requests.

Documents are printed with the lpr command. To print a text document, use the lpr command along with the -P (printer) option to select a desired printer, like this:

```
$ lpr -Pmylp mydocument
```

The printer name used with the -P option will be the name of a printer you've defined in your printcap file.

```
# lpr -Pmylp /usr/share/ghostscript/3.33/examples/tiger.ps
```

Linux printing automatically recognizes and prints text and PostScript documents and graphics. (If you have a color printer, you can print color PostScript documents and graphics.)

Printing Files at the Command Line

Spooled documents are sent to a directory with the name of your printer, under the /var/spool/lpd directory. The lpr command, like many Linux programs, can also be used as a filter to print the output of other programs. For example, to quickly print a calendar for a year, pipe the output of the cal (calendar) command through the lpr command, like this:

```
# cal 2000 | lpr
```

A 12-month calendar for the year 2000 will be printed on the default printer. Use this approach to print manual pages or other documents on your printer.

Listing the Print Queue

After you print several documents using the lpr command, use the lpq (line-printer queue) command to see a list of documents waiting to be printed:

```
# lpq
lp is ready and printing
Rank      Owner   Job    Files                   Total Size
active    bball   13     (standard input)        1972 bytes
```

The lpq command will report on the status of your printer and spooled documents.

Controlling Printers and Print Jobs

Printers and the order of print jobs can be controlled with the lpc (line-printer control) command. The lpc command has 14 built-in commands, but, as shown in Table 5.1, only the root operator can use every command. Each command can be used on the command line when you start lpc, and some commands require the name of a printer. For example, suppose you're the root operator and want to stop printing. If you simply use stop the lpc command will complain and quit:

```
# lpc stop
Usage: stop {all | printer}
```

To stop a particular printer, specify the command followed by the printer's name, like this:

```
# lpc stop mylp
mylp:
        printing disabled
```

The lpc command will echo the printer's name, followed by a message verifying that printing is stopped for that printer.

Table 5.1   Line Printer Control Program Commands

Command	Any User	Root Only	Action
abort		x	Stops the lpd daemon and disables printing
clean		x	Removes files from printer queue
disable		x	Turns off a printer's queue
down	x		Stops lpd and disables printer
enable		x	Turns on spooling
exit	x		Quits lpc
help	x		Help on commands
quit	x		Quits lpc
restart		x	Restarts spooling daemon
start		x	Enables printing, starts spooling daemon
status	x		Status of daemon and queue
stop		x	Stops spooling after current job, then disables printing
topq		x	Puts printer job at top of queue
up		x	Enables printers and restarts spooling

Use the status command to get the status of all printers, or if used with a printer's name, to report on the status of a particular printer, like this:

```
# lpc status
mylp:
        queuing is enabled
        printing is enabled
        no entries
        no daemon present
```

Reordering Print Jobs

The `lpc` command can also be used to move print jobs or spooled files to the top of the print queue. In order to see the waiting jobs, use the `lpq` command, as follows:

```
# lpq
mylp is ready and printing
Rank      Owner    Job   Files              Total Size
active    bball    13    (standard input)   1972 bytes
active    michael  14    (standard input)   4058 bytes
active    amy      15    (standard input)   20103 bytes
```

Root operators can use the `topq` command followed by a job number or user's name (as reported by the `lpq` command) to specify that a certain job is to be printed next:

```
# lpc topq 14
```

This command line will move `michael`'s job to the top of the printer queue for the printer `mylp`.

Stopping Print Jobs

To stop a print job, first use the `lprm` command to see the list of jobs waiting to be printed. Then use the `lprm` command followed by a job number:

```
# lprm 13
```

This command line will stop job 13. As root operator, you can also stop all the print jobs for a particular user at a particular printer by using the `lprm` command followed by the `-P` option (the printer's name) and the user's name, like this:

```
# lprm -Pmylp bball
```

This command line will stop all print jobs sent to the printer `mylp` by the user `bball`.

Sending Faxes with the *lpr* Command

The `lpr` command can also be used to send faxes if you've installed and configured fax service, as outlined in Chapter 11, "Configuring a Modem and Fax Service," in the section titled "Configuring Fax Service." You must first make sure that fax service using the `efax` software package is working properly.

Using *lpr* and *efax* to send faxes

1. Log on as root operator.
2. Using your preferred text editor, open the `/etc/printcap` database.

3. Create a fax printer entry by typing the following:

```
fax:\
        :lp=/dev/null:\
        :sd=/var/spool/fax:\
        :if=/usr/bin/faxlpr:
```

4. Create a link called `faxlpr` to the fax command with the `ln` command like this:

```
# ln /usr/bin/fax /usr/bin/faxlpr
```

5. Create a directory called `/var/spool/fax` with the `mkdir` command, like this:

```
# mkdir /var/spool/fax
```

6. Use the `chmod` commands to give the fax directory the correct permissions, as follows:

```
# chmod 770 /var/spool/fax
```

7. To send a fax, use the `-P` (printer) and `-J` (job number) options to specify the fax printer and the outgoing fax number, like this:

```
# lpr -Pfax -J 16505551212 myfax.txt
```

This will send the text document, `myfax.txt`, to the fax number specified on the `lpr` command line.

SEE ALSO

➤ *For more information about setting up fax service, see page 161.*

part

II

CONFIGURING YOUR SYSTEM

Configuring Your Environment 99   6

Working with Hard Drives 113   7

Adding Tape and Zip Drives 129   8

Enabling a PC Card Device 137   9

Adding a Pointing Device 147   10

Configuring a Modem and Fax Service 153   11

chapter

6

Configuring Your Environment

Displaying environment variables with
the printenv command •

Customizing your login •

Creating aliases •

Using the linuxconf utility •

The shell specified in your /etc/passwd entry runs after you log in to Linux. Your shell then loads several files located in different directories on your system. These files, called *resource*, *profile*, or *login* files, are located in your home directory and the /etc directory. For the default Linux shell, bash, these files include the following:

- /etc/profile—Contains systemwide environment settings. This is the first file the shell looks for when you log in. This file sets environment variables such as the path for every user on the system.

- .bash_profile, .bash_login, or .profile—These files exist in your home directory and contain environment settings local to your account. Your shell looks for these files in the order they are listed here. If it does not find .bash_profile, it looks for .bash_login. If it doesn't find .bash_login, it looks for .profile. These files are virtually the same and set environmental variables specific only to the user (such as their path).

- /etc/bashrc—Contains systemwide aliases. The shell looks here before looking at .bashrc. The information in this file applies to all the users on the system.

- .bashrc—In your home directory, contains aliases local to your account. Changing a .bashrc file effects only the user who owns the file. This sets aliases specific to the user.

- .bash_history—A list of recently entered commands.

The profile files contain *environment variables*, which are definitions of values the shell or other programs recognize after you log in. The bash shell recognizes more than 50 different environment variables, and you can also define many of your own.

Displaying Environment Variables with the *printenv* Command

Use the printenv command, found under the /usr/bin directory, to print the value of a particular variable, or a list of currently defined environment variables, like so:

```
$ printenv SHELL
/bin/bash
$ printenv
USERNAME=
ENV=/home/bball/.bashrc
BROWSER=/usr/local/bin/netscape
HISTSIZE=1000
HOSTNAME=localhost.localdomain
```

```
LOGNAME=bball
HISTFILESIZE=1000
MAIL=/var/spool/mail/bball
HOSTTYPE=i386
PATH=/usr/local/bin:/bin:/usr/bin:.:/usr/sbin:/sbin:/usr/X11R6/bin:
\/usr/local/bin:/usr/bin/mh:/home/bball/bin
HOME=/root
SHELL=/bin/bash
USER=bball
HOSTDISPLAY=localhost.localdomain:0.0
DISPLAY=:0.0
OSTYPE=Linux
NNTPSERVER=news.staffnet.com
SHLVL=5
EDITOR=/usr/bin/pico
```

Not all the environment variables listed here will be present on your system. Many systems have different values (such as USER, ENV, or HOSTNAME). Some commonly defined environment variables are listed in Table 6.1.

Table 6.1 Common *bash* and User Environment Variables

Variable	Description
EDITOR	Default system editor
HISTSIZE	The number of command lines to remember
HOME	Home directory for the current user
HOSTTYPE	The system architecture in use
LOGNAME	Name of the current user
MAIL	The directory to check for incoming mail
OSTYPE	The operating system in use
PATH	Paths to search for commands
PS1	Definition of the command-line prompt
PS2	Character used in the secondary command-line prompt
SHELL	Name of the shell currently in use
SHLVL	The number of shells currently running
TERM	The type of terminal in use
USER	Name of the current user

Displaying Environment Variables with the *env* Command

You can also use the env command, to print a list of your currently defined environment variables, as follows:

```
$ env
```

Unlike the printenv command, env will only display all your environment variables, and not the value of just a single variable.

Setting an Environment Variable on the Command Line

What method you use to set an environment variable from the command line depends on the shell being used. The bash shell requires the use of the built-in export command. Environment variables are traditionally named using uppercase letters, although this is not required. Creating a variable on the command line using bash takes the following form:

```
$ VARIABLE_NAME='value'; export VARIABLE_NAME
```

Although you can also shorten this to the form:

```
$ export VARIABLE_NAME='value'
```

Creating the *EDITOR* environment variable

1. To create or set an environment variable defining a default text editor (used by many system-administration utilities), export the variable with a command line such as the following:
   ```
   $ EDITOR='/usr/bin/emacs'; export EDITOR
   ```

2. This command line creates the environment variable EDITOR. To verify the EDITOR variable, use the printenv command like so:
   ```
   $ printenv EDITOR
   /usr/bin/emacs
   ```

The tcsh shell requires the built-in setenv command to define a variable:

```
> setenv VARIABLE_NAME=value
```

Defining a variable using the ksh shell requires its built-in export command:

```
$ export VARIABLE_NAME=value
```

A more convenient way to set environment variables from the command line of any shell is to use the env command:

```
$ env VARIABLE_NAME=value
```

Temporary environment variables

Environment variables set from the command line are only temporary. Although this approach might be useful for testing just-installed software or for entering password keys to run protected software, these variables last only as long as you're logged in or running a particular terminal. To make this change effective for each login, add the definition to the proper shell initialization or resource file. See the later section "Customizing Your Login" for more information.

Environment variables are traditionally named using uppercase letters, although this is not required. The tcsh shell requires the built-in setenv command to define a variable:

```
# setenv VARIABLE_NAME=value
```

Defining a variable using the ksh shell requires its built-in export command:

```
# export VARIABLE_NAME=value
```

A more convenient way to set environment variables from the command line of any shell is to use the env command:

```
# env VARIABLE_NAME=value
```

Deleting an Environment Variable from the Command Line

You cannot delete an environment variable in the current shell unless you know the proper shell command to use. Knowing how to do this is important if you need to create variables to test temporarily installed software.

To delete a variable using bash, use the built-in unset command:

```
$ unset VARIABLE_NAME
```

To delete the variable using the tcsh shell, use its built-in unsetenv command:

```
> unsetenv VARIABLE_NAME
```

The ksh shell, like bash, requires the built-in unset command:

```
$ unset VARIABLE_NAME
```

The env command, along with its -u (unset) command-line variable, can be used with any shell to delete an environment variable:

```
$ env -u VARIABLE_NAME
```

Setting Command *PATH*s

One of the most important environment variables is the PATH variable. PATH defines the directory or directories where the shell can find executable programs. If the PATH variable is not properly set, you must type the complete directory to the name of a program to run the command.

For example, if you're not logged in as the root operator but you want to run the fuser command to find existing processes used by a program, the shell reports that the command is not found, as shown in the following:

```
$ fuser bash
bash: fuser: command not found
```

However, you know the command exists on your system because the whereis command reports the fuser pathname, as shown here:

```
# whereis fuser
fuser: /usr/sbin/fuser /usr/man/man1/fuser.1
```

Although you can run the fuser command by typing its complete pathname, a much better approach is to add the /usr/sbin directory to your shell's PATH environment variable. To do this temporarily, use the env command, like so:

```
$ env PATH=$PATH:/usr/sbin
$ fuser /bin/bash
/bin/bash:    244e   342e   361e   362e   579e   582m   1187m   1277e   1893e
```

Notice that instead of typing out the entire current value of PATH before tacking /usr/sbin on the end, you can refer to the current value of the variable by placing a $ in front of its name.

SEE ALSO

➤ *To learn how to control processes, see page 538.*

➤ *To learn more about using the* whereis *command, see page 52.*

➤ *To learn more about using environment variable, see page 327.*

To add the new directory to your PATH environment variable, and to make this change effective for each time you log in, add the path to the file .bash_profile or .profile in your home directory.

Adding a path to *.profile*

1. Open .profile in your favorite text editor and find the PATH definition, which will look similar to the following line:
   ```
   PATH=$PATH:$HOME/bin
   ```

2. Change the PATH definition line to be similar to the following:

```
PATH=$PATH:$HOME/bin:/usr/sbin
```

Note that multiple entries are separated with a colon (:).

SEE ALSO

➤ *To learn more about text editors for Linux, see Chapter 4, "Using Text Editors."*

3. To enable this change for all current or future users, make sure you're logged in as the root operator, and make the change to the PATH definition line in thefile profile under the /etc directory:

```
PATH=$PATH:/usr/X11R6/bin:/usr/local/bin:/usr/sbin
```

Warning: Be careful when editing your PATH

Make changes to your **PATH** variable carefully. If you make a mistake, the shell won't know where to find commands. Copy any existing **PATH** definitions and then cautiously make your changes, especially if you edit the systemwide **PATH** definition in /etc/profile as the root operator.

Customizing Your Login

Changes made to shell variables in the .bashrc and profile files under the /etc directory affect all users and are systemwide. Individual users can make changes, or local definitions, to the .bashrc and .profile under their home directories. Local environment variables are defined in .profile like so:

```
# .profile

# Get the aliases and functions
if [ -f ~/.bashrc ]; then
        . ~/.bashrc
fi

# User-specific environment and startup programs

PATH=$PATH:$HOME/bin
ENV=$HOME/.bashrc
USERNAME=""

export USERNAME ENV PATH
```

Lines beginning with a pound sign (#) are comments and are ignored by the shell. When you log in, the bash shell uses this program to first look for a file called .bashrc in your home directory, and then sets some basic environment variables. The .bashrc file in your home directory contains alias definitions (see the section "Creating Aliases," later in this chapter, for more information), as shown in the following:

```
# .bashrc

# User-specific aliases and functions

# Source global definitions
if [ -f /etc/bashrc ]; then
        . /etc/bashrc
fi
```

Both files are read by your shell after you log in, and can be edited to add custom definitions.

Customizing Your Command-Line Prompt

The default bash shell prompt variable, PS1, is defined in /etc/profile. The prompt definition uses special characters recognized by the bash shell, as shown here:

```
PS1="[\u@\h \W]\\$ "
```

In this example, the \u is replaced by your username; the \h is replaced by your machine's name; the \W is replaced with the name of the directory you are currently in; and the \\$ is printed as a $ unless you are root, in which case it is a #.

```
[michael@brain stuff]$
```

Copy this line to your .profile, and then edit the string to define your own prompt. Don't forget to add PS1 to the export line in .profile:

```
export USERNAME ENV PATH PS1
```

Table 6.2 lists the prompt characters recognized by bash.

Table 6.2 *bash* Shell Prompt Characters

Character	Definition
\!	Print the history number of command
\#	Display the number of this command

Character	Definition
\$	Print a # if you're root or $ otherwise
\W	Print the base name of the current working directory
\[	Begin sequence of non-printing characters
\\	Print a backslash
\]	End sequence of non-printing characters
\d	Use the date in prompt
\h	Use the computer's hostname in the prompt
\n	Print a newline in the prompt
\nnn	Character of octal number nnn
\s	Print the name of the shell
\t	Print the time
\u	Print the current user's name
\w	Show the current working directory

Test different prompts from the command line by using the bash shell's export command, like so:

```
$  PS1='\d \t: '  ;export PS1
Wed Feb 11 16:53:32:
```

Use terminal escape codes to create different character effects, such as highlighting, in your prompt, as in the following:

```
$ PS1="[\033[4m\u\033[0m@\033[4m\h\033[0m]:";export PS1
```

This definition highlights your name (\u) and the hostname (\h) of your computer at the prompt of your console or an X11 xterm terminal window. In an X11 terminal window, the name and hostname will be underlined (see the sidebar "Terminal definitions," later in this chapter).

SEE ALSO

➤ *To learn more about your computer's hostname, see page 405.*

➤ *To learn more about the X Window System, see page 169.*

➤ *To learn how to use X11 terminals, see page 186.*

➤ *To learn more about customizing your prompt, see the Bash Prompt HOWTO.*

> **Terminal definitions**
>
> Different terminals, such as X11's xterm and rxvt or the Linux console, have different capabilities and respond differently to escape sequences. The terminal definitions for your system are defined in the terminal capability database, called `termcap`, found under the `/etc` directory, and additional definitions are found in numerous subdirectories under the `/usr/lib/terminfo` directory. Do not edit or change the `termcap` file unless you are absolutely sure about what you're doing; incorrect entries can render your screen useless (make a backup copy first). Documentation for the `termcap` entries can be found in the `/etc/termcap` file, and in the `terminfo` and `termcap` manual pages.

Creating Aliases

Aliases are redefinitions of commands, usually in shortened form. Systemwide alias definitions are entered by the root operator in the `bashrc` file under the `/etc` directory, but you can define your own in your `.bashrc` file. Several of these aliases are especially useful:

```
alias cp='cp -i'
alias mv='mv -i'
alias rm='rm -i'
alias ls='ls --color=auto'
```

In this example you are redefining the default action of the `cp`, `mv`, and `rm` commands to use interactive querying, which provides a measure of safety when copying, deleting, moving, or renaming files. Aliases can also be used to craft new commands or variations of often-used commands and command-line options, such as redefining `ls` to use color by default.

In a more detailed example you display the current month's calendar in a small, floating window (although the ical X11 client can be used, the calendar is much larger). Here you create an alias by combining the `cal`, or calendar command, and the X11 xmessage client.

Creating a GUI calendar alias

1. Using your favorite text editor, open the file `.bashrc` in your home directory, and add the following line:
```
alias xcal='cal | xmessage -file -'&'
```

2. Name the alias `xcal`. This alias uses the `cal` command's output piped through the X11 xmessage client. The ampersand background operator (&) will run the program in the background automatically.

3. To use the xcal alias right away without the need to log out and then log back in, use the bash shell's built-in source command, and then try the xcal alias like so:

```
# source .bashrc
# xcal
```

SEE ALSO

➤ *To learn more about the* cp, rm, *and* mv *commands, see Chapter 3, "Navigating the Linux File System."*

➤ *To learn more about X11 clients, see page 169.*

Using the *linuxconf* Utility

The linuxconf utility is an attempt to provide a consistent front end to the many configuration files in Linux. Part of the goal of linuxconf is not only to be able to make changes to your Linux configuration, but also to make those changes active, restarting daemons if necessary. Flexibility and configurability is achieved through the use of modules. Each module allows configuration of a particular aspect, such as mounting hard drives, configuring the Apache Web server, or administering user accounts. It has over thirty modules available and more are being written all the time. linuxconf is designed to be usable in a variety of situations and so it has a variety of user interfaces. The four basic interfaces to linuxconf include command-line, text-based menus, graphical menus under the X Window System (with or without GNOME), and the Web. To use linuxconf from the command line, try the following:

```
# linuxconf --status
List of things required to activate current configuration
    Executing: /etc/rc.d/rc3.d/S10network reload
    Executing: /etc/rc.d/rc3.d/S85gpm start
```

This shows a list of what needs to be done to bring the system up-to-date or what changes have been made but not activated. The menu-based uses of linuxconf present you with a list of modules that are installed. Figure 6.1 shows a text-based menu, whereas Figures 6.2 and 6.3 show possible appearances in X, and finally Figure 6.4 shows the Web-based interface. Selecting a module to configure brings up a dialog box where you can enter, or change, the information relevant to that function. Some interfaces allow you to have more than one of these dialog boxes open at a time, whereas others make you close one to open another. Either way, when you close, you'll be asked whether you want to make your changes active, see what would need to be restarted to make the changes active, or just quit.

CHAPTER 6 Configuring Your Environment

FIGURE 6.1
The text-based configuration of linuxconf gives you menu based control of your Linux installation when the X Window System is not functioning or not installed.

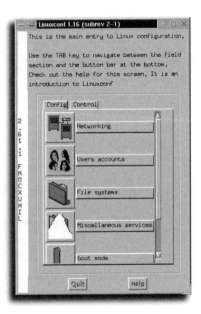

FIGURE 6.2
The GUI-based interface of linuxconf is probably most used on systems running X. It provides an easy point-and-click interface to configuring your system.

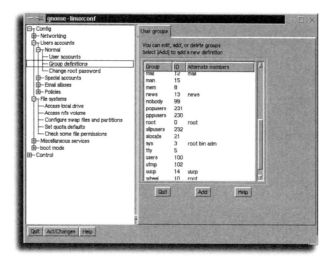

FIGURE 6.3

If you happen to be running the GNOME desktop environment under X, your GUI probably looks more like this. In addition to fitting nicely into the GNOME environment, this version also allows multiple dialog box tabs on the right side, while browsing a tree of modules on the left.

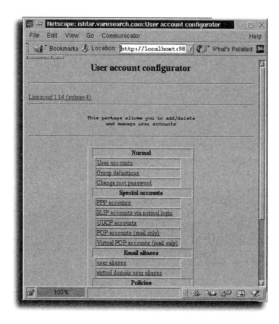

FIGURE 6.4

The Web-based interface can be accessed from any Web browser and is very useful if you need to administer as system remotely.

Be careful with automated configuration tools

The `linuxconf` utility can be very useful for changing the configuration of your system. The modular design means new pieces can be easily added to the system, but watch out because new modules might not be as fully tested as older ones. Be sure to watch closely when using new modules so you don't accidentally mess up the subsystem they're configuring. Preview changes before making them active, and when in doubt, read the man or info pages for that system.

chapter

7

Working with Hard Drives

Determining the volume device and partition ●

Choosing a file system ●

Adding a hard drive ●

Partitioning a hard drive with the fdisk command ●

Manipulating partitions with the sfdisk command ●

Mounting a hard drive or other device ●

Mounting and unmounting remote NFS hard drives ●

Mounting file systems with linuxconf ●

Determining the Volume Device and Partition

After installing Linux (follow the instructions in Appendix A) you should at least know a little about the hard drive installed on your system. You should also know about the `fdisk` command (some distributions' installation scripts might include a proprietary tool instead of `fdisk`) because you created a *partition* on an existing *volume*, or hard drive, to make room for the kernel and software included with your Linux distribution. You might have installed Linux entirely in a single partition, or created several additional partitions to hold different parts of the Linux *file system*, or directory structure.

Linux supports a variety of file systems. Its native file system format is the `ext2fs`. If your Linux system shares a hard drive with DOS or Windows, your system will likely also use the `msdos`, or `vfat` file system on your hard drive. Table 7.1 lists the file systems recognized by the `mount` command for Linux, which is used to attach a disk device to a specific Linux directory, or *mount point*.

Table 7.1 File Systems Recognized by *mount*

Type	Name
affs	Amiga file system
coherent	Coherent UNIX file system
extfs	Extended file system, successor to the minix file system for Linux (outdated)
ext2fs	The current native Linux, or second extended, file system
hpfs	OS/2 file system (read-only)
iso9660	CD-ROM file system (read-only)
minix	The original Linux file system (no longer used)
msdos	DOS file system
nfs	Sun Microsystems' network file system
proc	Linux Process Information file system
romfs	Read-only memory file system (for embedded systems)
smbfs	Session message block (network) file system
swap	The swap file system used by Linux to temporarily store memory
sysv	UNIX system V file system
ufs	BSD, Digital UNIX file system
umsdos	File system to support coexistent DOS and Linux files

Type	Name
vfat	Windows file system
xenix	Xenix file system

SEE ALSO

➤ *For more information about the Linux kernel and loading modules, see page 535.*

Many of these you might never use; however, it's helpful to know which ones have support built into (or loadable by) your kernel.

Determining your kernel file system support

1. To find out what file systems are currently supported by your kernel, use the cat command to see the contents of the file systems file under the /proc directory, like this:

```
#  cat /proc/filesystems
    ext2
            ext2
    msdos
nodev   proc
    vfat
    iso9660
```

This example shows that the kernel is currently supporting the ext2, msdos, vfat, proc, and iso9660 file systems. Your system might have a DOS or Windows file system mounted, and an actively mounted CD-ROM.

2. Support for different file systems might come from support compiled into your Linux kernel, or through loadable kernel modules under the /lib/modules/ *kernel-version*/fs directory. To see the types of file system support modules available for your version of Linux, use the ls command to look in your module directory:

```
# ls /lib/modules/2*/fs
autofs.o  hpfs.o    minix.o   nfs.o     sysv.o    _umsdos.o  xiafs.o
ext.o     isofs.o   ncpfs.o   smbfs.o   ufs.o     vfat.o
```

The ls command lists all modules under the fs (file system) module directory.

Hard Drive Devices

Hard drive devices are found under the /dev directory, which contains more than 1,400 device names for many different devices (such as serial or printer ports, mice, scanners, sound cards, tape drives, CD-ROM drives, and hard drives). Table 7.2 lists some common devices and device names used as data storage, and explains partition numbers when associated with a storage device.

SEE ALSO

➤ For more information about adding other devices (such as a mouse) to your system, see page 147.

Table 7.2 Common Storage Device Examples

Device name	Type of Media, Volume, or Partition
/dev/hda	The first IDE drive
/dev/hda2	The second partition on the first IDE drive (/dev/hda) volume
/dev/hdc	The third IDE drive
/dev/hdd1	The first partition on the fourth IDE drive
/dev/sda	The first SCSI drive
/dev/sda4	The fourth partition on the /dev/sda volume

SEE ALSO

➤ To learn more about managing the Linux file system table, see page 461.

Your system's current hard drives are listed in the fstab (file system table), found under the /etc/ directory. The /etc/fstab file is a map to the storage devices used by Linux for native Linux files, or for mounting of other file systems, and provides directions to the mount command about where and how to mount each specified device.

Use the cat command to look at your system's fstab, like this:

```
$ cat /etc/fstab
/dev/hda6      /                ext2     defaults        1 1
/dev/hda5      swap             swap     defaults        0 0
/dev/fd0       /mnt/floppy      ext2     noauto          0 0
/dev/cdrom     /mnt/cdrom       iso9660 user,noauto,dev,exec,ro,suid 0 0
none           /proc            proc     defaults        0 0
/dev/hde1      /mnt/flash       vfat     user,noauto,dev,exec,suid    0 0
/dev/sda4      /mnt/zip         vfat     user,noauto,dev,exec,suid    0 0
/dev/sda4      /mnt/zipext2     ext2     user,noauto,dev,exec,suid    0 0
/dev/hda1      /mnt/dos         vfat     user,noauto,dev,exec,suid    0 0
```

This file system table shows (starting from the left column) the device, where the device can be found if mounted (the mount point), the type of file system, and several mounting options for each device. Note that there are two entries for the same device, /dev/sda4, but that each has a different file system specified in the table. This is because the /dev/sda4 device is a removable SCSI drive that is manually mounted at different times with *media*, or disks, containing different file systems.

Use the df (free disk space) command to see the amount of free space left on any currently mounted devices:

```
# df
File system     1024-blocks  Used Available Capacity Mounted on
/dev/hda6          1443464  985613   383263    72%    /
/dev/hde1            14580   10956     3624    75%    /mnt/flash
/dev/hdc            596900  596900        0   100%    /mnt/cdrom
/dev/hda1           511744  419136    92608    82%    /mnt/dos
/dev/sda4            98078   23176    74902    24%    /mnt/zip
```

The -h option to df presents a more human readable format, converting large numbers of bytes into their megabyte or gigabyte equivalents.

The df command shows reveals the following information:

- The root Linux partition on /dev/hda6, mounted at the / directory
- A small storage drive on /dev/hde1, mounted at the /mnt/flash directory
- A CD-ROM at /dev/hdc, mounted at the /mnt/cdrom directory
- A partition at /dev/hda1, mounted at the /mnt/dos directory
- A hard drive on /dev/sda4, mounted at the /mnt/zip directory

Although the df command is handy for determining how much room can be left on your storage devices, you must use the mount command if you want to know what file system exists for each device. Use the mount command with its -v (verbose) option:

```
# mount -v
/dev/hda6 on / type ext2 (rw)
/dev/hde1 on /mnt/flash type vfat (rw)
/dev/hdc on /mnt/cdrom type iso9660 (ro)
/dev/sda4 on /mnt/zip type vfat (rw)
/dev/hda1 on /mnt/dos type vfat (rw)
```

The mount command reports the following:

- Any mounted devices
- Where the device is mounted in your Linux file system or directory structure
- The file system used on the device
- Whether you can read and write (rw), or read only (ro) from the device

SEE ALSO

➤ *For information about other ways to mount file systems, see page 454.*

File system support does not mean formatting

Although Linux supports many different types of file systems to allow reading and writing of files, you might still need to use another operating system to format a new hard drive with a non-Linux file system. Linux does not come with disk-formatting utilities for most other file systems (except DOS; see the `mtools` manual page for more information).

Choosing a File System

When you add a hard drive to your system and want to use Linux and DOS or Windows, use the `ext2` and `msdos` or `vfat` file systems. Although you can use the `msdos` file system for a DOS partition, you should use the `vfat` file system for a Windows 95 partition so you can use larger partitions and get long-filename support. If you mount a `vfat` partition under a Linux directory, the `ls` command shows the proper long filenames like this:

```
# ls /mnt/dos/windows/*.bmp
/mnt/dos/windows/Black Thatch.bmp    /mnt/dos/windows/Pinstripe.bmp
/mnt/dos/windows/Blue Rivets.bmp     /mnt/dos/windows/Red Blocks.bmp
/mnt/dos/windows/Bubbles.bmp         /mnt/dos/windows/Sandstone.bmp
/mnt/dos/windows/Carved Stone.bmp    /mnt/dos/windows/Setup.bmp
/mnt/dos/windows/Circles.bmp         /mnt/dos/windows/Stitches.bmp
/mnt/dos/windows/Clouds.bmp          /mnt/dos/windows/Straw Mat.bmp
/mnt/dos/windows/Forest.bmp          /mnt/dos/windows/Tiles.bmp
/mnt/dos/windows/Gold Weave.bmp      /mnt/dos/windows/Triangles.bmp
/mnt/dos/windows/Houndstooth.bmp     /mnt/dos/windows/Waves.bmp
/mnt/dos/windows/Metal Links.bmp
```

A DOS partition does not support long filenames, so if you use an `msdos` file system, mount it, and then copy files from your Linux file system to the DOS partition, the `ls` command would show files from the previous example like this:

```
# ls /mnt/dos/windows/*.bmp
/mnt/dos/windows/blackt~1.bmp    /mnt/dos/windows/pinstr~1.bmp
/mnt/dos/windows/blueri~1.bmp    /mnt/dos/windows/redblo~1.bmp
/mnt/dos/windows/bubbles.bmp     /mnt/dos/windows/sandst~1.bmp
/mnt/dos/windows/carved~1.bmp    /mnt/dos/windows/setup.bmp
/mnt/dos/windows/circles.bmp     /mnt/dos/windows/stitches.bmp
/mnt/dos/windows/clouds.bmp      /mnt/dos/windows/strawm~1.bmp
/mnt/dos/windows/forest.bmp      /mnt/dos/windows/tiles.bmp
/mnt/dos/windows/goldwe~1.bmp    /mnt/dos/windows/triang~1.bmp
```

```
/mnt/dos/windows/hounds~1.bmp    /mnt/dos/windows/waves.bmp
/mnt/dos/windows/metall~1.bmp
```

If you add a hard drive to Linux or repartition an existing drive, you can use any file system you want as long as the `fdisk` and `mount` commands support the file system. If you're going to use the new storage only for Linux, use the `ext2` file system; if you want to share files between Linux and Windows, stick with `vfat`. You need to make sure that `vfat` is supported in your kernel or available as a loadable module. Windows recognizes the `vfat` partition, but not one formatted to use `ext2`. This is even more important when using removable devices such as flash cards or Zip drives.

Adding a Hard Drive

Linux comes with several programs that you'll need when adding a hard drive. For configuring, formatting, and mounting storage devices for Linux you can use the `fdisk`, `mke2fs`, and `mount` commands.

Install your drive properly

Before configuring a drive for Linux, follow your computer manufacturer's instructions for properly installing the hardware. Make sure that all cables are correctly connected and that any switch configurations are made to match the drive to your existing system. If you've installed a SCSI drive, make sure that all cables are firmly attached and that the SCSI chain is properly terminated.

Identifying Hard Drives and Devices

The entries in your `/dev` directory will depend on the type of hard drive you have installed. Most hard drives come in one of two varieties: IDE or SCSI. IDE hard drives appear on your system in the form `/dev/hdX`, where `X` represents an a for the first drive, a b for the second, and so on For example, you might have your main hard drive on `/dev/hda` and your CD-ROM drive on `/dev/hdc`. SCSI devices (which can include scanners, tape drives, and other devices) are represented as `/dev/sdX`, where again the `X` is a letter representing which SCSI device is being referred to. A partition on the hard drive will be noted by a number at the end of the hard drive device. For example, the first partition on your second SCSI device would be `/dev/sdb1`.

Partitioning a Hard Drive with the *fdisk* Command

Use the fdisk command to prepare a new hard drive with one or more partitions. fdisk is not the most intuitive Linux command but it can be used to quickly prepare a hard drive for use.

Don't overwrite the partition you're running on

If you need to repartition a hard drive that's already in use, be sure to unmount it first. If it is ever necessary to repartition the hard drive you have / mounted on, you should boot into single user mode first.

SEE ALSO

➤ *For more information on run levels, see page 355.*

1. Log in as the root operator. Use the fdisk command to prepare and partition a hard drive by specifying the drive's device name on the command line:

```
# fdisk /dev/sda
Command (m for help): m
```

2. fdisk prints a prompt after recognizing your device. Press M for a list of fdisk commands. The program responds like this:

```
Command action
   a   toggle a bootable flag
   b   edit bsd disklabel
   c   toggle the dos compatibility flag
   d   delete a partition
   l   list known partition types
   m   print this menu
   n   add a new partition
   p   print the partition table
   q   quit without saving changes
   t   change a partition's system id
   u   change display/entry units
   v   verify the partition table
   w   write table to disk and exit
   x   extra functionality (experts only)
```

3. Press N to add a new partition table. The fdisk program responds as follows:

```
Command (m for help): n
Command action
   e   extended
   p   primary partition (1-4)
```

4. You're only going to use one primary partition on this drive, so press P for a primary partition. The fdisk program responds as follows:

```
p
Partition number (1-4):
```

5. Type the number 1, and press Enter. The `fdisk` responds with the following:

```
Partition number (1-4): 1
First cylinder (1-96):
```

6. Note that this is a small hard drive (smaller than 100MB), as indicated by the small number of cylinders. Type the number 1 and press Enter. The `fdisk` command then asks for the ending cylinder number for the partition:

```
First cylinder (1-96): 1
Last cylinder or +size or +seism or +sizeK ([1]-96):
```

7. Type 96, and press Enter (if you'd entered 50, you'd still have 46 cylinders on the device and could create a new partition to run from cylinder 51 to 96, about half the storage capacity of the drive) .

```
Last cylinder or +size or +sizeM or +sizeK ([1]-96): 96
```

8. Press P to print the partition table:

```
Command (m for help): p
Disk /dev/sda: 64 heads, 32 sectors, 96 cylinders
Units = cylinders of 2048 * 512 bytes

     Device Boot   Begin    Start     End    Blocks   Id  System
/dev/sda1                1        1      96     98288   83  Linux native
Command (m for help):
```

9. To change the partition's type, press T.

```
Command (m for help): t
```

10. `fdisk` asks for the partition to change. Type 1.

```
Partition number (1-4): 1
```

11. `fdisk` asks for a hex code, representing a type of file system. To see the types of file systems you can use, press L, and `fdisk` prints a list like this:

```
Hex code (type L to list codes): L

 0   Empty          9   AIX bootable    75  PC/IX         b7  BSDI fs
 1   DOS 12-bit FAT a   OS/2 Boot Manag 80  Old MINIX     b8  BSDI swap
 2   XENIX root     b   Win95 FAT32     81  Linux/MINIX   c7  Syrinx
 3   XENIX usr      40  Venix 80286     82  Linux swap    db  CP/M
 4   DOS 16-bit <32M 51 Novell?         83  Linux native  e1  DOS access
 5   Extended       52  Microport       93  Amoeba        e3  DOS R/O
 6   DOS 16-bit >=32 63 GNU HURD        94  Amoeba BBT    f2  DOS
secondary
 7   OS/2 HPFS      64  Novell Netware  a5  BSD/386       ff  BBT
 8   AIX            65  Novell Netware
Hex code (type L to list codes):
```

12. To use the new partition for Linux, type the number 83 and press Enter:

```
Hex code (type L to list codes): 83
Changed system type of partition 1 to 83 (Linux native)
```

```
Command (m for help): p

Disk /dev/sda: 64 heads, 32 sectors, 96 cylinders
Units = cylinders of 2048 * 512 bytes

    Device Boot    Begin    Start     End   Blocks   Id  System
/dev/sda1             1        1      96    98288   83  Linux native
Command (m for help):
```

13. fdisk prints a short message, informing you of the new file system type. Use the p command to confirm this, and use the w command to save your changes and exit. The fdisk command prints the following short message and then quits:

```
Command (m for help): w
The partition table has been altered!

Calling ioctl() to re-read partition table.
Synching disks.

WARNING: If you have created or modified any DOS 6.x
partitions, please see the fdisk manual page for _additional information.
```

After partitioning a drive and specifying a file system, you still must format the drive. To format the drive for use by Linux, use the mke2fs command. This command has several command-line options; the most important is -c, which you use to check for any bad blocks during formatting. To format this chapter's sample drive, use the mke2fs command with -c option, followed by the device name, like so:

```
# mke2fs  mke2fs -c /dev/sda4
mke2fs 1.10, 24-Apr-97 for EXT2 FS 0.5b, 95/08/09
Linux ext2 file system format
File system label=
24576 inodes, 98288 blocks
4914 blocks (5.00%) reserved for the super user
First data block=1
Block size=1024 (log=0)
Fragment size=1024 (log=0)
12 block groups
8192 blocks per group, 8192 fragments per group
2048 inodes per group
Superblock backups stored on blocks:
        8193, 16385, 24577, 32769, 40961, 49153, 57345,
        65537, 73729, 81921, 90113
Checking for bad blocks (read-only test):  2240/    98288
```

The `mke2fs` command starts checking your drive before formatting (which can take at least several minutes), and then formats your drive:

```
Writing inode tables: done
Writing superblocks and file system accounting information: done
```

Hidden space on Linux drives?

Note that by default (and for safety reasons) the `mke2fs` command reserves 5% of a drive's space for use by the root operator. This allows processes running as root to continue writing logs and other necessary files after users have filled all the publicly available space. Because of this, a 1GB hard drive might have nearly 50MB of free drive space available, even though disk utilities such as `df` report that the drive is nearly full. To use all available space on a Linux `ext2` file system, use `mke2fs  -m` followed by the number `0` when formatting a drive. Use this option with care.

Manipulating Partitions with the *sfdisk* Command

You can also manipulate your hard drive partitions from the command line (or within scripts) using the `sfdisk` command. As an example to list all the partitions on your system, type the following:

```
# sfdisk -l
```

The resulting output displays onscreen:

```
/dev/sda1          0+    15    16-   128488+  82  Linux swap
/dev/sda2     *    16   260    245  1967962+  83  Linux native
/dev/sda3          0     -      0         0   0  Empty
/dev/sda4          0     -      0         0   0  Empty
```

If you ever need the size of a partition you can use `sfdisk` with the `-s` option followed by the partition. If you don't give it a partition name, it will tell you the size of all the partitions.

```
# sfdisk -s
/dev/hda:   6342840
total: 6342840 blocks
```

`sfdisk` can also be used to make changes to the partition table of your hard drive. Because of the command line nature of `sfdisk`, this comes in useful for automated scripts (such as the installation scripts, for example) but isdangerous for manual use. A menu-driven partition, such as `fdisk` mentioned earlier, is a better choice for making changes to your hard drive by hand.

Mounting a Hard Drive or Other Device

After partitioning and formatting a new drive, you must mount the drive. To mount a new drive, you must have a mount point, know the drive's file system type, and know the drive's device name.

Mounting a newly partitioned and formatted drive

1. Log in as the root operator. Use `mkdir` to create a mount point for the new drive, like this:

   ```
   # mkdir /mnt/zipext2
   ```

2. Use the `mount` command, and specify the type of file system using the `-t` option, the device name, and the mount point:

   ```
   # mount -t ext2 /dev/sda4 /mnt/zipext2
   ```

3. Use the `df` command to verify that the new drive has been mounted:

   ```
   # df
   File system       1024-blocks  Used  Available Capacity Mounted on
   /dev/hda6          1443464 1011187   357689      74%    /
   /dev/sda4            95167      13    90240       0%    /mnt/zipext2
   ```

4. To unmount the drive, use the `umount` command followed by the mounting point:

   ```
   # umount /mnt/zipext2
   ```

The final step in installing a new drive is to make an entry in the file system table. This will ensure that the device is available the next time you boot Linux, and simplifies the job of mounting the file system. For example, with a proper `fstab` entry, mounting the sample hard drive would be as simple as the following:

```
# mount /mnt/zipext2
```

Getting clues from boot messages

If you install a new hard drive and boot Linux, carefully examine your system's boot messages. If the screen scrolls by too quickly for you to read, use the **dmesg** command after you boot and log in to Linux to list the boot-up messages. Linux should recognize any new devices attached to interfaces supported by your kernel.

Although you can use a GUI tool (such as the `linuxconf` utility) to make changes to your system, you can also manually edit the `/etc/fstab` file using a text editor. Be warned! Make a copy of this file before proceeding, and have an emergency boot disk handy. If you screw up `fstab`, you might not be able to boot properly or mount your Linux file system.

Adding an entry to the sample drive

1. To add an entry to the sample drive, log in as the root operator. Use your favorite text editor to edit `fstab`:

   `# vi /etc/fstab`

2. Add a line to the file, specifying the device name, the mount point, the file system type, and mounting options:

   `/dev/sda4      /mnt/zipext2     ext2    user,noauto,dev,exec,suid 0 0`

3. These mounting options specify that the drive will not be automatically mounted when Linux boots but will allow anyone to mount or unmount the drive. To have the drive automatically mounted, and to restrict unmounting or mounting to the root operator only, use an entry like the following:

   `/dev/sda4      /mnt/zipext2     ext2    defaults 0 0`

Table 7.3 lists common mounting options that you can use in a file system table entry. For complete details, see the `mount` command's manual page.

Table 7.3   Common Mounting Options in */etc/fstab*

Option	Keyword
Allow programs to run from device	exec
Allow users to mount the device	user
Device must be specified to mount	noauto
Do not allow programs to run from device	noexec
Do not allow users to mount the device	nouser
Mount automatically at boot	auto
Mount the device read-only	ro
Mount the device read-write	rw

SEE ALSO

➤ *For more information about choosing a text editor, see page 63.*

Mounting and Unmounting Remote NFS Hard Drives

The network file system, or NFS, was developed by Sun Microsystems to allow file systems to be transparently mounted across a local area network. This means that a hard drive on another computer can be mounted as if it were local to your computer. NFS is an invaluable tool for sharing data between users or in a networked environment, allowing a single file server be responsible for all users' data.

Mounting a file system exported from an NFS server is as easy as mounting a local hard drive partition, and the syntax is almost identical. In your mount command or fstab entry, replace the hard drive partition name with the hostname of the NFS server (or its IP address), a colon, and the path to the directory you want:

```
# mount homeserver:/home/michael /mnt
```

This example mounts the directory /home/michael on a server named homeserver as /mnt on my local machine. You can unmount this with the umount command just like any other file system. The same example as an entry in my /etc/fstab might look like this:

```
# cat /etc/fstab
# <file system>       <mount point>    <type>  <options>        <dump> <pass>
/dev/cdrom            /mnt/cdrom       auto    noauto,unhide,user  0      0
/dev/fd0              /mnt/floppy      auto    noauto,user         0      0
proc                  /proc            proc    defaults            0      0
/dev/sda2             /                ext2    defaults            1      1
/dev/sda1             none             swap    defaults            0      0
homeserver:/home/michael /mnt          nfs     rw                  0      0
```

Mounting File Systems with *linuxconf*

If you are using the linuxconf program as described in Chapter 6, "Configuring Your Environment," you can visually make adjustments to your /etc/fstab or mount a file system. Under the File Systems section you will notice separate modules for Access Local Drive or Access NFS Volume. Choosing either option brings up the Volume Specification tab, shown in Figure 7.1, where you can enter the details of the file system you want to mount. The new file system will now be in your fstab and will be mounted when you activate your changes in linuxconf.

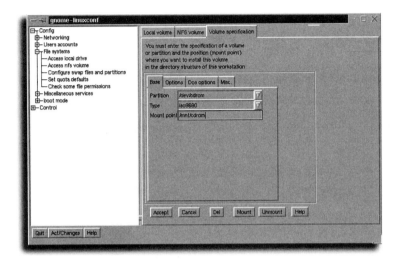

FIGURE 7.1
The linuxconf tool also allows you to change options on file systems you already have in your /etc/fstab.

SEE ALSO

➤ *For more information about* linuxconf, *see page 109.*

8

Adding Tape and Zip Drives

Adding a tape drive

Adding a Zip drive

This chapter describes how to install and use a tape and Iomega Zip drive with Linux. Tape drives and removable drives are often used for system backups and archiving of important software. Removable drives can also be used to store a Linux file system.

SEE ALSO

➤ *To learn how to back up your system, see page 476.*

Adding a Tape Drive

Numerous tape drives are supported by Linux through the `ftape` and `st` tape modules. The `ftape` module is a device driver used to support floppy-controller tape drives or removable backup devices, whereas the `st` module supports SCSI tape devices. Both modules are automatically loaded and unloaded by the `kmod` system daemon when needed during tape operation.

Generally speaking, although nearly all SCSI and floppy-controller tape drives should work with modern Linux kernels, version 2.0 and up, many high-speed or parallel-port tapes might not. Check the Hardware-HOWTO or Ftape-HOWTO pages to see whether your tape drive and interface are supported. The Linux HOWTO pages are typically installed under `/usr/doc` or `/usr/share/doc`. Check your distribution to verify that the HOWTO docs are available or for more information about where they have been installed.

Installing a Tape Drive

SCSI tape drives are either attached directly to an installed SCSI adapter or added to the current SCSI device chain. Make sure that a free device number is used, and that the SCSI chain is properly terminated. The devices used to support SCSI tape drives are found under the `/dev` directory and begin with the letters `st` or `nst`:

```
/dev/st0   /dev/st1   /dev/st2   /dev/st3
/dev/st4   /dev/st5   /dev/st6   /dev/st7
/dev/nst0  /dev/nst1  /dev/nst2  /dev/nst3
/dev/nst4  /dev/nst5  /dev/nst6  /dev/nst7
```

There are two types of tape drive devices:

- Rewinding—Rewinding devices automatically rewind after tape operation.
- Nonrewinding—Devices with names starting with `n` are nonrewinding tape devices and will not rewind after tape operation.

For more information about these SCSI tape devices, see the `st` manual page.

Floppy-controller tape drives are attached to the spare floppy controller port. You cannot use your floppy drive when using a floppy tape drive. The devices used to support tape drives are found under the /dev directory and have the letters ft in their filenames:

```
/dev/nrft0  /dev/nrft2  /dev/rft0  /dev/rft2
/dev/nrft1  /dev/nrft3  /dev/rft1  /dev/rft3
```

Creating a tape drive device symbolic link

1. Choose the device names, such as /dev/st0 or /dev/rft0, that match your SCSI or floppy tape drive.

2. As the root operator, use the ln command to create symbolic links for your devices, like so:

```
# ln -s /dev/nrft0 /dev/nftape
# ln -s /dev/rft0 /dev/ftape
```

This command creates easily remembered names of your tape drive.

Using the *mt* Command

The mt (magnetic tape) command is used to control tapes in your tape drive. These operations include the following:

- Rewinding the tape
- Retensioning the tape
- Erasing the tape
- More than two dozen SCSI-specific tape operations

The mt command can also be used by backup scripts, such as taper, or other backup utilities, such as the tar or cpio commands, to archive Linux directories and files. The mt command has several different command-line options, but is usually used with the -f option to specify the tape device followed by a command:

```
# mt -f /dev/nftape command
```

Tape drives, unlike other file systems, are not mounted or unmounted for read or write operation.

SEE ALSO

➤ *To learn more about mounting file systems and using the* mount *command, see page 124.*
➤ *To learn how to use the* tar *and* cpio *commands, see page 505.*

Retensioning Tapes

When a tape sits unused for a time, the tension, or tightness of the tape around its reel, will change. The general consensus among Linux tape users is that it is a good idea to retension new tapes before use. Tapes should be retensioned before use to take up any existing slack, and to make sure the tape conforms to your tape drive's tension strength. This will help to reduce the risk of errors during backups. To retension a tape, insert the tape into the tape drive and then use the mt command with the nonrewinding tape drive device and the retension command:

```
# mt -f /dev/nftape retension
```

The mt command also accepts reten as a shortcut for retension.

Rewinding Tapes

Although some tape drives automatically rewind inserted tapes, you might occasionally need to rewind a tape yourself, especially if a backup operation has been halted by software or operator intervention. To rewind a tape, use the mt command with the nonrewinding tape drive device and the rewind command:

```
# mt -f /dev/nftape rewind
```

Preparing Tapes for Linux Backups

Before using a formatted tape for backups, you must generally use the mt command to erase the tape and prepare it for Linux. To erase a tape, use the mt command with the nonrewinding tape drive device and the erase command:

```
# mt -f /dev/nftape erase
```

Adding a Zip Drive

There are many different versions of the Zip drive. Most styles of Zip drive are supported under Linux but some, such as the USB version, are still waiting for Linux drivers to be developed. Check the Zip Drive Mini-HOWTO for information on drivers for your model.

The Zip drive is an affordable alternative to removable hard drives, although the current hardware and format limits disk capacity to a little less than 250MB of storage. If you need a larger removable drive, consider other drives from Iomega or Syquest. Support exists for the SCSI version of the Zip drive because it is treated like any other SCSI disk (check the Hardware-HOWTO page to see whether your SCSI adapter is supported). The parallel-port Zip drive is also supported if you either recompile the kernel or use a loadable software module. The Zip-plus and Zip250 require a different loadable module, and the ATAPI version uses the standard ATAPI driver as if it were a large floppy drive.

For more information about Iomega Zip drives, use your favorite Web browser to visit the following site:

```
http://www.iomega.com
```

SEE ALSO

➤ *For details about recompiling the Linux kernel, see page 545.*

➤ *For details about using modules with the Linux kernel, see page 535.*

Installing Linux on a Zip disk

For details about how to install Linux on a Zip disk, read John Wiggins' mini-HOWTO called *Installing Linux on a Zip Disk*. This document outlines the basic steps required to set up, format, and mount a Zip disk for use as a root file system. This procedure requires, among other things, crafting a custom kernel with SCSI support and the **ppa** driver, creating a boot disk, and selecting various packages to build a file system small enough to fit on a Zip disk.

Before Installing a Zip Drive

Although most Linux distributions come with the required drivers and file-system utilities to support Zip drives, you must ensure the following before installation:

- For most Zip drives, the kernel must have SCSI support either compiled in or available as loadable modules.

- Parallel-port drives will require that parallel printer support is not compiled into the Linux kernel, but instead should be available as a loadable module. The **ppa** driver needs to be loaded prior to the printer's **lp** module.

- A copy of Grant Guenther's Zip Drive Mini-HOWTO page should be on hand. This document contains technical details of kernel configuration and driver customization and provides pointers to the latest drivers. Use this to find installation specifics that match your version of the Zip drive. Check your distribution's documentation to see where HOWTOs might be installed on your system. For the most up to date collection of HOWTOs, point your Web browser at the Linux Documentation Project: `http://www.linuxdoc.org`.

SEE ALSO

➤ *To install a hard drive, see page 119.*

> **File systems: Use *vfat* for Windows**
>
> Linux users with a Windows partition will probably want to use the `vfat` file system type for DOS-formatted Zip disks. You'll benefit by being able to use 32-character filenames either for Linux or Windows files copied to the Zip disk.

Ejecting, Password-Protecting, and Read-Write–Protecting Zip Disks

Use the `ziptool` command to take advantage of some of the unique features of the Zip drive, such as read-write protection or password protection. Other features of `ziptool` include the following:

- Eject an unmounted Zip disk.
- Report on read-write protection of an unmounted Zip disk.
- Toggle read-write protection of a unmounted Zip disk.
- Enable or disable password protection of an unmounted, write-enabled Zip disk.

For a copy of the `ziptool` program, check your distribution or browse the following Web site:

```
http://www.novia.net/~segura/ziptool/
```

There were once many different Zip drive utilities that went by the name `ziptool`. Be sure to check the man page or other documentation for your version if it differs from what I discuss here. To use `ziptool`, specify one of the options followed by the device volume name (`/dev/sda`), not the device partition name (`/dev/sda4`).

Ejecting a Zip disk

1. Unmount the Zip disk by using the `umount` command followed by the pathname of the Zip disk's mount point:
   ```
   # umount /mnt/zip
   ```

2. To eject the disk, use `ziptool`'s `-e` (eject) option:
   ```
   # ziptool -e /dev/sda
   ```

   Use this `ziptool` option to physically eject a Zip disk.

Password-protecting a Zip disk

1. Password-protecting a Zip disk requires that a disk be inserted into the Zip drive but not mounted. If the drive is mounted, first unmount the disk with the `umount` command.

2. To check on the status of the disk, and to get a report on the password or read-write status, use ziptool's -s (status) option:

```
# ziptool -s /dev/sda
ziptool: medium is not protected.
```

3. To password-protect and enable read-only protection of a Zip disk, use the -rp option, like so:

```
# ziptool -rp /dev/sda
Password: mypasswd
ziptool: medium is password write-protected.
```

To delete password protection and enable writing to the disk, use the -rw (read-write) option:

```
# ziptool -rw /dev/sda
Password: mypasswd
ziptool: medium is not protected.
```

Remember your Zip disk's password

If you forget the password when you protect a Zip disk with `ziptool`, the disk will have to be reformatted before it can be used again for storage (otherwise, it makes a nice, but expensive, coaster for your coffee table).

Read-write protecting a Zip disk

1. To make the Zip disk write-protected, use the -ro (read-only) option:

```
# ziptool -ro /dev/sda
ziptool: medium is write-protected.
```

2. To toggle the read-write protection, use the ziptool command with the -rw option:

```
# ziptool -rw /dev/sda
ziptool: medium is not protected.
```

Enabling a PC Card Device

Enabling PCMCIA Services   ●

Using the `cardmgr` Command   ●

Using the `cardctl` Command   ●

Enabling PCMCIA Services

Newer Linux kernels with support for loadable and unloadable code modules have made life a lot easier for laptop users with special devices such as PCMCIA, or PC cards. Fortunately, Linux supports many of these devices through the kmod and cardmgr daemons (started at bootup), which automatically load and unload needed modules as devices are inserted or ejected.

To use PC cards or services with Linux, you should install the pcmcia package. Check your distribution's documentation for details on installing a package.

SEE ALSO

➤ *To learn more about the Linux kernel and module control, see page 535.*

➤ *See page 483 to learn more about installing packages.*

This package installs the following:

- The pcmcia configuration files and database, usually under the /etc/pcmcia directory
- A directory containing loadable PC card modules, usually under the /lib/modules/*kernel-version* directory
- Specialized startup scripts used to load the PC card drivers
- Several different PC card programs
- Various documentation files and manual pages

Some of the PC cards supported by the cardmgr daemon include the following:

- Ethernet/Fast Ethernet cards
- Token-ring adapters
- Wireless network adapters
- Modems
- Memory cards
- SCSI interface adapters
- ATA/IDE CD-ROM interface adapters
- Multifunction cards, such as LAN/modem cards
- ATA/IDE drive cards
- Miscellaneous cards, such as GPS (Global Positioning Service) cards

SEE ALSO

➤ *To learn more about Linux and using serial ports and modems, see page 154.*

➤ *To learn about Linux networking services, see page 405.*

Will my PC card work with Linux?

To determine whether Linux supports your PC card, read the file **SUPPORTED.CARDS** in the pcmcia documentation directory. If you don't see your card listed, try it anyway! Many cards are supported even though they are not listed; even if your card is not recognized at startup, you might be able to configure it to work. Some older laptops might not work with some newer "cardbus" style PC cards. Check your laptop's documentation for details.

Details about configuring unrecognized cards are found in the **PCMCIA-HOWTO** page (probably) found under the **/usr/share/doc/HOWTO** directory. For the latest version of the **PCMCIA-HOWTO**, a Linux PCMCIA programmer's guide, or a list of the latest supported PC cards, browse David Hinds's Web pages at the following address:

```
http://pcmcia.sourceforge.org
```

Determining Your PCMCIA Controller

In order to set up Linux for PC card service, first determine both the number of slots available for PC cards and the type of PC card controller installed on your computer. Use the probe command, to report the number of slots:

```
# probe
PCI bridge probe: Cirrus PD6729 found, 2 sockets.
```

Use the probe command's -m command-line option to find the type of controller chip used in your computer:

```
# probe -m
i82365
```

The type of controller chip should be either cic or i82365. This information will be used to configure the cardmgr daemon.

Enabling PC card service

1. To enable PC card services for Linux, make sure you're logged in as the root operator. You will also need to find out where your distribution stores its PCMCIA configuration info. In some cases it might actually be in the start up scripts; in others it might be a separate file.

2. Open the `pcmcia config` file using your favorite text editor. Enter the words `PCMCIA=yes` (if they are not already there) along with the type of PC card controller (`PCIC`) used in your computer (either `i82365` or `tcic`; see the `probe -m` output, above):

   ```
   PCMCIA=yes
   PCIC=i82365
   PCIC_OPTS=
   CORE_OPTS=
   ```

3. Remember to save the file after making your changes.

4. Make sure all PC cards are properly inserted, and restart Linux.

5. While rebooting, listen for a series of beeps, which indicate whether your PC cards are recognized and configured by the `cardmgr` daemon. See Table 9.1 for the codes.

SEE ALSO

➤ *To find out how to reboot Linux, see page 13.*

➤ *For more information on editing text files see page 64.*

Table 9.1 *cardmgr* Daemon Beep Codes

Number/Type of Beep	Indication
One beep	PC card ejected
Two high beeps	PC card identified and configured during booting
High beep, lower beep	PC card identified, not configured during booting
Low beep	PC card not identified
Two high beeps	PC card inserted
Two high beeps	PC card service uninstalled during reboot or shut down

Some cards, such as flash memory cards, drive cards, or CD-ROM adapters, must be mounted by the file system. In order to do this, you have to edit `/etc/fstab` or manually mount the card as a new drive on the system.

SEE ALSO

➤ *To learn how to use the* `/etc/fstab` *database or file system table, see page 124.*

➤ *For further information about mounting drives file systems, see page 124.*

Using the *cardmgr* Command

The cardmgr daemon is used to monitor your computer's PC card sockets for inserted or removed cards and will load or unload the device needed for your PC card. The proper driver is found in the cardmgr's database of PC cards, in the file config under the /etc/pcmcia directory. The database entry for your card tells the cardmgr daemon which code module to load or unload. (Code modules are usually found under the /lib/modules/*kernel-version* directory.)

Listing Your PC Card and Drivers

When starting up, or when PC cards are inserted or ejected, the cardmgr daemon creates and updates a system table called stab under the /var/run directory. To see a list of the current PC cards and drivers in use, look in this stab system table like so:

```
# cat /var/run/stab
socket 0: empty
socket 1: Serial or Modem Card
1       serial  serial_cs       0       ttyS1   4       65
```

This particular stab file shows that two PC card sockets are available (socket 0 and 1) and that socket 1 contains a serial or modem card that uses the serial_cs code module to provide serial service for the /dev/ttyS1 device. If another card is inserted, the cardmgr daemon does the following:

1. It notes the insertion.

2. It looks up the card in the /etc/pcmcia/config database.

3. It attempts to load the appropriate module.

4. It beeps twice if the card is recognized and configured.

The /var/run/stab file is then updated with this new information, and might look like the following:

```
# cat /var/run/stab
socket 0: ATA/IDE Fixed Disk Card
0       fixed   fixed_cs        0       hdc     22      0
socket 1: Serial or Modem Card
1       serial  serial_cs       0       ttyS1   4       65
```

This shows that a fixed disk card in socket 0 was detected, recognized, and configured as a hard drive, using the /dev/hdc volume, while the serial or modem card, using the /dev/ttyS1 serial port, still resides in socket 1.

Disabling *cardmgr* Command Event Notification

After you've determined that your PC cards are being properly recognized, you can silence any cardmgr beep notification by editing the pcmcia start up script or config file. Use the -q (quiet) command-line option, where the cardmgr command is used in the pcmcia script. After this change, you won't hear any beeps when the cardmgr command is used to recognize and configure your PC card(s) while booting Linux. (I leave mine enabled so that I know there's a problem if I don't hear them.)

Disabling PC card notification

1. Make sure you're logged in as the root operator.

2. Open the file /etc/init.d/pcmcia with your favorite text editor. This file's path will vary according to your distribution, so check your distribution's documentation to learn the location of your system's init scripts.)

   ```
   # vi -w /etc/rc.d/init.d/pcmcia
   ```

3. Look for the portion of the script containing the cardmgr command. It will look something like this:

   ```
   /sbin/cardmgr $CARDMGR_OPTS
   ```

4. Add the -q (quiet) option to the cardmgr command line:

   ```
   /sbin/cardmgr -q $CARDMGR_OPTS
   ```

5. Save the changes and exit.

6. Restart Linux.

SEE ALSO

➤ *For more information on where your distribution keeps its startup scripts, see your distribution's documentation.*

➤ *For more information on editing text files, see page 64.*

Using the *cardctl* Command

Use the cardctl (card control) command to control your PC card slots. You can also use this command to gather information about your PC cards or to load a PC card *scheme*. A scheme allows you to set the role of your laptop, such as a node on the network instead of dial-up machine. This will, of course, affect the types of cards that are installed in your computer. The default scheme, located under the /var/run directory, is named pcmcia-scheme. Details about using PC card schemes are found in the PCMCIA-HOWTO, in your documentation directory.

Obtaining the Status of PC Cards

To check on the status of your PC card(s), use cardctl's status option like so:

```
# cardctl status
socket 0:
  Function 0:
  card present, ready, battery low
socket 1:
  Function 0:
  card present
```

The cardctl command reports on the number of sockets and the status of any cards currently inserted and in use in each socket.

Listing Your PC Card Configuration

To see your PC card's configuration, use the cardctl command with the config option, as follows:

```
# cardctl config
socket 0:
  Vcc = 5.0, Vpp1 = 0.0, Vpp2 = 0.0
  Card type is memory and I/O
  IRQ 3 is exclusive, level mode, enabled
  Function 0:
    Config register base = 0x0200
      Option = 0x41, status = 0000, pin = 0000, copy = 0000
    I/O window 1: 0x0100 to 0x010f, auto sized
socket 1:
  Vcc = 5.0, Vpp1 = 0.0, Vpp2 = 0.0
  Card type is memory and I/O
  IRQ 9 is exclusive, level mode, enabled
  Speaker output is enabled
  Function 0:
    Config register base = 0x0300
      Option = 0x61, status = 0x08
    I/O window 1: 0x02f8 to 0x02ff, 8 bit
```

This information can be handy if you need to see power settings, interrupts, or other information about inserted, configured, or active cards. For specific details about configuring PC cards, see the section titled "Overview of the PCMCIA

Configuration Scripts" in David Hinds's PCMCIA-HOWTO, found in your documentation directory. For the latest PC card support information, check out the following site:

http://pcmcia.sourceforge.org

Inserting a PC Card

Although the cardmgr daemon automatically recognizes and configures a supported PC card after physical insertion, you can also use cardctl's insert command to restore the card's socket after you perform a software eject. This saves you the trouble of physically removing and then reinserting the PC card to get the cardmgr daemon to configure and reinstall the card.

To perform a software PC card insert for socket 0, use the insert command, like so:

```
# cardctl insert 0
```

This command line performs a software insert of a card in the PC card socket 0.

Ejecting a PC Card

Although the cardmgr daemon will automatically unload the required software modules needed to configure and use a PC card after the card is physically ejected, you can also use the cardctl command to perform a software eject of the card and then cut power to the PC card socket. This is a handy way for laptop users to save battery power without resorting to physical removal of the PC card.

To eject a PC card using socket 0, use cardctl's eject command, like this:

```
# cardctl eject 0
```

This command will software eject and power off socket 0 of your PC card interface.

Do not disable sockets while in use!

Do not use the eject or suspend cardctl command option while a PC card device is in use. You can scramble the structure of a memory disk or cause your computer to hang (although you can kill the offending processes). Use the cardctl command judiciously, and make sure no other applications are using your device before you eject or power off a PC card's socket.

Suspending and Restoring PC Card Power

Another method of saving battery power for laptop users with PC cards is to suspend and restore power to a card. The `cardctl` command allows you to shut down and disable a socket with the `suspend` command, like this:

```
# cardctl suspend 0
```

This shuts down and powers off socket 0. To restore this socket for use after you've executed the `suspend` command, use the `resume` `cardctl` command-line option, as follows:

```
# cardctl resume 0
```

chapter

10

Adding a Pointing Device

Adding a mouse

Installing a joystick

Adding a Mouse

Mouse support for Linux is fairly extensive. A wide variety of devices is supported. Although you can use a keyboard to control your mouse pointer when using the X Window System, a mouse or other hardware device to control the pointer is indispensable. You'll use your mouse to pull down menus, click buttons in dialog boxes, and copy and paste text between programs.

When you install Linux, you will be probably be guided through a brief program that configures your mouse. The installation program actually checks to see whether you have any pointer devices plugged in and tries to detect their types for you. If it does not find anything, you will be given a list of mouse devices to select from. Generally, the generic 3-Button Mouse option will work. A symbolic link is then created, called /dev/mouse, that points to the correct pointing device. To see the device that /dev/mouse points to for your system, use the ls, or list directory, command like this:

```
# ls -l /dev/mouse
lrwxrwxrwx   1 root     root          5 Mar  9 07:54 /dev/mouse -> psaux
```

This shows that /dev/mouse points to the psaux, or PS/2 mouse device. However, you can install other pointing devices, or configure your mouse in many ways. Sometimes it takes awhile for new types of devices to be supported. Be careful about obtaining the latest pointer gizmo without first checking to see that Linux supports it.

Using and Configuring *gpm*

gpm is a small utility that allows you to use your mouse within command-line consoles (that is, outside the graphical X Window System). It is typically installed with a normal Linux installation and is initialized at boot time. In its default configuration, it allows you to select text on the console by highlighting it with the left mouse button. Highlighting text within Linux automatically copies that text to the clipboard. To paste that text, just move your cursor to the desired location and click the middle mouse button. With gpm you can use this convenient feature even when using different virtual terminals. If you only have a two-button mouse, you can configure gpm to paste either with your right button or by pressing both buttons at once.

Table 10.1 lists some command line options for gpm.

Table 10.1 Basic *gpm* Options

Action	Commands
Set the type of mouse	-t *type*
Change button sequence (1,2,3 to 3,2,1)	-B *sequence*
Determine the button number that corresponds to "tapping" with glidepoint devices	-g *number*
Sets time interval between multiple clicks	-i *interval*
Increases or decreases responsiveness	-r *number*
Force to 2-button mode	-2
Force to 3-button mode	-3

gpm is not really designed to be run at the command line. It is usually turned on when you boot your system. It reads from a configuration file whose name, format, and location varies from distribution to distribution. Check your distribution's documentation to find out where it is stored on your system.

SEE ALSO

➤ *To learn more about the X Window System, see page 167.*

➤ *For more information about virtual terminals, see page 172.*

➤ *To learn more about copying and pasting text in X11, see page 206.*

Configuring a Synaptics Touchpad

If you use a laptop for Linux and have a Synaptics touchpad, use the tpconfig command to configure your touchpad. The tpconfig program, by C. Scott Ananian, can be found by browsing to the following Web address:

```
http://www.pdos.lcs.mit.edu/~cananian/Projects/Synaptics/
```

Use the tpconfig program to configure your touchpad button mode, taps, tap mode (such as no taps for left mouse-button presses), or pressure sensitivity. You will have to exit X and kill gpm before running tpconfig to avoid conflicts.

Installing and configuring the *tpconfig* command

1. Download the tpconfig archive. Log on as the root operator and uncompress the archive using the tar command:

```
# tar xvzf synaptics-latest.tar.gz
```

2. Change directory to the software's directory:

```
# cd syn*
```

3. Run the included configure shell script:

```
# configure
```

4. Use the `make` command followed by the word `install` to compile, build, and install the `tpconfig` command in the `/usr/local/bin` directory:

```
# make install
```

5. To configure your touchpad, you must not be running X11 or the `gpm` mouse daemon (which supports cut and paste for console displays). To stop the `gpm` daemon, search for the process number of the `gpm` daemon by using the `ps` and `fgrep` programs in a pipe:

```
# ps aux | fgrep gpm
root      220  0.0  0.1   732    40 ?  S   11:21   0:00 gpm -t PS/2
```

Then use the `kill` command with the `gpm` process number (returned from the earlier example), like this:

```
# kill -9 220
```

6. To get information about your touchpad, use the `-i`, or info, option:

```
# tpconfig -i
Synaptics Touchpad, firmware rev. 3.5 [Standard OEM]
Sensor: Standard-size module
Geometry: Standard module
Rightside-up/Landscape New-style abs-mode packets.
Corner taps disabled. Tap mode: Tap and non-locking drag
Edge motion only during drag.     Z-threshold 3 of 7
Relative mode                        Low  sample rate.
2 button mode          Corner tap is right button click
```

7. The `tpconfig` command has 11 different command-line options, but it is easy to use. For example, to turn off the tap mode, use the `-t` option, followed by the number 0:

```
# tpconfig -t0
```

SEE ALSO

➤ *To learn more about file compression and archiving, see page 505.*

➤ *For more information about using the* make *command or other programming utilities, see page 342.*

Installing a Joystick

A *joystick* is a handy pointing device, especially when playing arcade-style games or using flight simulators, such as the *fly8* simulator (shown in Figure 10.1).

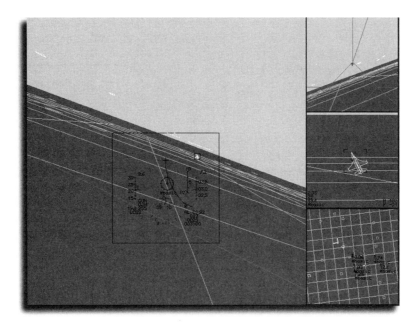

FIGURE 10.1
Using a joystick in the X Window System under Linux makes using the fly8 flight simulator and other games easier.

To use a joystick with Linux, your computer must support the joystick hardware, usually through a joystick port on the back of the main box. You also need to have software support available as a loadable kernel module. You can check to see if your particular model of joystick is supported by going to either of the following URLs:

http://www.atrey.karlin.mff.cuni.cz/~vojtech/joystick/
http://www.linuxgames.com/joystick/

Kernel 2.2 and above comes with support and drivers for most joysticks. Because these are installed by default when you install Linux, you should not need to do anything to make your joystick work other than plug it in. Just make sure that you can find your joystick on the list of supported devices in one of the URLs listed earlier.

SEE ALSO

➤ *For more information about loadable kernel modules, see page 535.*

Configuring a Joystick

Two programs, js and jscal, are included with the joystick driver. Use the js program followed by a number corresponding to your joystick device (in this case 0 because it's the first installed joystick; the second joystick would be 1) to test your joystick:

```
$ js 0
```

The program runs continuously, reporting on button presses and the location of your cursor while you move the joystick. Press Ctrl+c to quit the program.

Use the jscal command to adjust your joystick by specifying the joystick number on the command line, like this:

```
$ jscal 0
```

The jscal program asks you to move your joystick to the lower-right corner, and then press a joystick button. Press Ctrl+c to quit the program.

chapter

11

Configuring a Modem and Fax Service

Selecting a modem for Linux •

Creating the /dev/modem device •

Enabling dial-in service •

Configuring fax service •

Selecting a Modem for Linux

Many different types of modems work with Linux. In order to use a modem, you must first determine which serial port is connected to your modem. Modems can be installed in serial ports on the back of a desktop computer or internal PC serial board, or as a PC card. Built-in modems often come with laptops and are indicated by the RJ-11 jack on the back of the laptop. Serial port devices for Linux are found in the /dev directory, with filenames containing tty. (Some older Linux systems can also have cua devices and newer systems might still show cua devices but be mapped to ttyS devices.) Table 11.1 lists the eight most common serial devices, along with the corresponding "traditional" DOS and Windows port names and addresses.

Table 11.1 Linux Serial Devices and Their Equivalent DOS Port Addresses

Linux Device	Port Name, Address, and Interrupt
/dev/ttyS0	COM1, 0x3F8 IRQ 4
/dev/ttyS1	COM2, 0x2F8 IRQ 3
/dev/ttyS2	COM3, 0x3E8 IRQ 4
/dev/ttyS3	COM4, 0x2E8 IRQ 3

Will my modem work with Linux?

Although nearly any modem works with Linux, there are at least two types to avoid: WinModems and Mwave. Both of these modems require special drivers for Windows that are unavailable for Linux. Although you can use the Mwave board to support sound by booting Linux from DOS, you should avoid any type of modem or serial board that requires special drivers (at least until manufacturers recognize that Linux is a part of mainstream computing). "Plug-and-Pray" devices might also work, but in general, you should stick with "normal" modems to avoid trouble.

Using the *dmesg* Command to Check Serial Port Status

Use the dmesg command to determine whether your serial ports are enabled. The dmesg command displays the dmesg startup log, found under the /var/log directory. Look for lines in the dmesg output that list any recognized serial drivers and ports, such as the following:

```
Serial driver version 4.13 with no serial options enabled
tty00 at 0x03f8 (irq = 4) is a 16550A
tty03 at 0x02e8 (irq = 3) is a 16550A
```

This output shows that Linux found two serial ports at COM1 and COM4. If a serial driver or port is not listed, make sure that serial-line support is enabled for your Linux kernel, or that the proper serial devices exist under the /dev directory. Read the MAKEDEV manual page for details on how to create serial devices.

SEE ALSO

➤ *For more details about enabling serial support, see Chapter 31, "Managing the Kernel."*

PC card serial ports and modems

PC card owners must first enable PCMCIA services to get Linux to recognize and configure a PC card. Fortunately, most serial and modem PC cards work under Linux with few problems. For details about how to install PCMCIA services, refer to Chapter 9, "Enabling a PC Card Device," and read the PCMCIA-HOWTO, often found under the /usr/share/doc directory.

Testing Your Modem with the *echo* Command

You can test your modem by using the echo command to send a command string through a serial port.

Testing your modem

1. Log in as the root operator.
2. Make sure your modem is switched on, or if you have an external modem, that it is plugged in.
3. Check any serial cable connections for your external modem.
4. Make sure your phone lines are properly connected to the modem or modem card.
5. Choose the proper tty serial device corresponding to your modem port. If necessary, find the DOS COM port used, and then choose the device listed in Table 11.1.
6. Type the following at the console or terminal window, replacing <u>N</u> with the serial port you want to test:
   ```
   echo ATDT/n > /dev/ttySN
   ```
7. Wait at least 10 seconds; you should then hear a dial tone.

SEE ALSO

➤ *To learn more about the* echo *command, see page 39.*

Your modem's *AT* commands

Not all modems possess the same **AT** command set, and minor variations exist between modems from different manufacturers. The best reference to use is your modem manual, which should specify your modem's **AT** command set in detail.

Creating the */dev/modem* Device

You don't have to always remember which serial port is connected to your modem. An easy way to determine what port your modem is attached to is to create a device called /dev/modem. You can create one from the command line using the ln command.

Creating */dev/modem* with the *ln* Command

You can also create the /dev/modem device from the command line by using the ln (link) command. To create /dev/modem if your modem is connected to ttyS0, log in as the root operator and enter the following:

```
# ln -s /dev/ttyS0 /dev/modem
```

This command line creates a symbolic link, /dev/modem, which points to the ttyS0 serial port. Check this link with the ls (list directory) command, like so:

```
# ls -l /dev/modem
lrwxrwxrwx   1 root     root          9 Feb 19 07:56 /dev/modem -> /dev/ttyS0
```

Getting Serial Port Information with the *setserial* Command

The setserial command reports on the status, type, and configuration of the four default serial ports. This command can also be used to configure how the kernel recognizes additional serial ports or to alter how the kernel acts with an existing port.

To get information about a specified port, use the -a (all available information) option followed by the port's device name, like so:

```
# setserial -a /dev/modem
/dev/modem, Line 1, UART: 16550A, Port: 0x02f8, IRQ: 2
        Baud_base: 115200, close_delay: 50, divisor: 0
        closing_wait: 3000, closing_wait2: infinte
        Flags: spd_normal skip_test
```

This information shows the device, line, hardware chip, port, and interrupt used by the specified port. The highest speed supported by the serial port, along with other operational features such as the delay used before closing a connection, is also listed.

Enabling Dial-In Service

Linux supports dial-in service. This means that you can call in from another computer and log in over the phone. If you have two modems and phone lines for your computer, you can log in and then either dial out on the spare phone line or use Internet services if the spare line maintains an active Internet connection.

Setting up Linux for dial-in service requires the following:

- An incoming phone line
- A serial port and attached modem

It also requires that you do the following:

- Configure the modem.
- Edit the system initialization table.
- Restart Linux.

Serial port technical details

For technical information regarding Linux and serial ports, see the Serial-HOWTO and Serial-Programming-HOWTO, often under the `/usr/doc` directory.

Configuring Linux for Dial-in Service

Configuring Linux for dialing in is easy. You can perform one of the first steps, configuring the modem, while running the Linux `minicom` communications program.

Creating dial-in service

1. Attach your modem to a recognized serial port. Make sure the modem is connected properly and turned on.

2. Start a communications program such as `minicom`. Use the AT command &V to display your modem's profile, like this:

```
AT&V
ACTIVE PROFILE:
B1 E1 L1 M1 N1 Q0 T V1 W0 X4 Y0 &C1 &D2
&G0 &J0 &K3 &Q5 &R1 &S0 &T5 &X0 &Y0 ~Z0
S00:000 S01:000 S02:043 S03:013 S04:010
S05:008 S06:004 S07:045 S08:002 S09:006
S10:014 S11:095 S12:050 S18:000 S25:005
S26:001 S36:007 S37:000 S38:020 S44:020
S46:138 S48:007 S51:012 S52:012 S53:010
S54:010 S95:000
```

3. If your modem is set to the following, you're all set:

```
E1 Q0 V1 S0=0 &C1 &S0
```

   If not, set your modem by using the following AT command string:

```
ATE1Q0V1S0=0&C1&S0&W
```

   This command string configures your modem with the proper settings and then saves the configuration by using the &W command. Make sure your modem echoes an OK string.

4. Ensure that you're logged in as the root operator.

5. Using your favorite text editor, create a file called conf.uugetty.ttys*N* in the /etc directory, in which *N* matches the device number of your modem's serial port (if your modem is connected to /dev/ttyS0, create the file conf.uugetty.ttyS0). Type the following:

```
ALTLOCK=ttyS0
ALTLINE=ttyS0
# line to initialize
INITLINE=ttyS0
# timeout in seconds before disconnect
TIMEOUT=60
# initialize modem
INIT="" AT\r OK\r\n
WAITFOR=RING
# modem connect
CONNECT="" ATA\r CONNECT\s\A
# delay in seconds before sending contents of /etc/issue
DELAY=1
```

   Make sure values for ALTLOCK, ALTLINE, and INITLINE match your modem's serial port.

   Set the TIMEOUT value to the amount of time in seconds you want your modem to wait for a carriage return from the caller before disconnecting.

   Set the DELAY value to the amount of time in seconds you want before the file /etc/issue, or welcome text, is echoed to the caller.

6. Save the file and exit your text editor.

7. Open your system's initialization table, inittab, under the /etc directory. Look for these lines:

```
# Run gettys in standard runlevels
1:12345:respawn:/sbin/mingetty tty1
2:2345:respawn:/sbin/mingetty tty2
3:2345:respawn:/sbin/mingetty tty3
4:2345:respawn:/sbin/mingetty tty4
5:2345:respawn:/sbin/mingetty tty5
6:2345:respawn:/sbin/mingetty tty6
```

. Specifically, locate this line:

```
3:2345:respawn:/sbin/mingetty tty3
```

Change it to the following:

```
3:2345:respawn:/sbin/uugetty -d /etc/conf.uugetty.ttyS0
\ttyS0 38400 vt100
```

This change to `inittab` makes Linux run the `uugetty` command when you boot your system. These lines specify commands to run and at which run levels to run them. This particular change says that in run levels 2, 3, 4, and 5, run the `uugetty` command. When the command exits, the `respawn` directive tells Linux to run another one. The `uugetty` command uses the configuration file you created, watches for an incoming call on the specified serial port, and then answers when a modem is detected. If you'd like to support faster dial-in speeds, enter `57600` instead of `38400`.

8. Save the file, exit the text editor, and restart your system.

There are alternatives to *uugetty*

`uugetty` is not the only program that can answer your modem. Your system might have **ngetty**, **mgetty**, or others in addition to, or instead of, **uugetty**. Check your distribution's documentation for more details.

SEE ALSO

➤ *To learn more about using the* /etc/inittab *file for the X Window System and the* xdm *chooser client, see page 171.*

After you restart Linux, the `uugetty` command constantly checks the `/dev/ttyS0` serial port for incoming calls. When you call in, wait for the modem to connect, and then press Enter. Linux then echoes back a login prompt.

Use caution when editing system files

To set up your system to accept incoming calls, you must edit the system's initialization table, `/etc/inittab`. If you edit this file incorrectly, you might hang your system. Keep a boot disk handy, and copy the `/etc/inittab` file before making changes. For details about creating an emergency boot disk, see the section titled "Performing Hard Drive Recovery" in Chapter 29, "Managing the File System."

Configuring Linux for Dial-in PPP Service

The point-to-point protocol allows two computers (or networks) to be connected as peers. This is the most common method for connecting systems that talk to the Internet or use other TCP/IP services over a standard phone line. Before PPP can be enabled in the kernel, PPP support must be compiled into the kernel or must be available as a loadable module and the PPP software needs to be installed. After connecting two computers by dial-in as mentioned earlier, the PPP (pppd) daemon is run, usually automatically. The pppd program, however, has a fair number of options that should be set for it to run properly. This is typically done by setting values in a file called /etc/ppp/options. You should already have a template for this file at /etc/ppp/options.tpl. Copy this template to options, and then open it with your favorite text editor.

```
# cp /etc/ppp/options.tpl /etc/ppp/options
# emacs /etc/ppp/options
```

The template has explanations for each option and further information can be found in the pppd man page or the PPP-HOWTO. Some of the most important options are listed in Table 11.2.

Table 11.2 PPPD Options

Option	Meaning
-detach	Prevent pppd from forking into the background. Useful for debugging.
modem	Use the modem control lines. (Yes, there are some configurations to use pppd without a modem; however, those are beyond the scope of this book.)
lock	Use a locking mechanism to guarantee exclusive access to the modem.
crtscts	Set your modem to handle flow control.
defaultroute	Make changes to your system routing table setting the modem as the default.

If the machine you are connecting to requires you to use the password authentication protocol (PAP) or challenge handshake authentication protocol (CHAP), you need an additional file called /etc/ppp/pap-secrets or /etc/ppp/chap-secrets, respectively. This file contains your username, the name of the machine you're connecting to (often a * to allow any machine), and your password.

```
michael    *    mypassword
```

If your computer is the one dialing, you might want to use the scripts provided in /etc/ppp/ppp-on and /etc/ppp/ppp-off to automate the dialing process. These scripts need to be edited to set a few options correctly, such as the phone number to be dialed. If, on the other hand, your computer is the one answering the phone, you might want to edit the startup scripts for the user account that is being dialed into so that pppd automatically runs on login.

 If you have KDE installed, you can use the kppp utility to configure and run your PPP scripts.

1. Start kppp either by selecting it from your desktop menu or by typing kppp at a command line.

2. You will see a dialog box that lets you choose between the dialup connections you've configured. If you haven't configured any yet, click Setup.

3. Click New to bring up a dialog box where you can enter the phone number and other relevant information.

4. Click OK to close the dialog box.

5. You should now have a new entry in the Account Setup window of the setup box. You can make other setup changes by selecting the appropriate tab along the top of the setup box.

6. Click OK when you are finished with your setup. You can now select a connection from the main kppp dialog box.

SEE ALSO

➤ *To learn more editing text files, see page 64.*

➤ *To learn more about setting up user accounts, see page 362.*

➤ *For information about connecting to the Internet, see page 250.*

Configuring Fax Service

If you have a fax modem, you should be able to send and receive faxes using Linux. Fax transmission and reception requires a fax modem and graphics translation of files to be sent and received. You should have your modem's technical documentation on hand, along with the efax software package. This software package includes the modem and graphics programs to translate files to be sent.

Table 11.3 The *efax* Software Package

File	Purpose
/usr/bin/fax	Comprehensive shell script to create, send, receive, view, and print faxes
/usr/bin/efax	Driver program to send and receive faxes
/usr/bin/efix	File conversion program
/usr/man/man1/fax.1	Fax script manual page
/usr/man/man1/efax.1	efax manual page
/usr/man/man2/efix.1	efix manual page
/usr/doc/efax-0.8a	Directory containing a README file

Make sure to read the fax, efax, and efix manual pages, along with the README documentation, before you start configuring your Linux system for fax service.

Fax service packages

You can use a number of other fax software packages to set up fax service for your Linux system, such as mgetty+sendfax, or the Hylafax network fax package. For more information about these software packages, check your favorite Linux Internet Web site. The following is one good place to look:

http://www.freshmeat.net/

Configuring the *fax* Shell Script

Setting up for sending and receiving faxes involves editing the /usr/bin/fax shell script. You'll need to check some of the configuration lines, and you must edit other lines to customize your fax headers and specify your modem. The script contains easy-to-follow instructions, but the basic changes are outlined here.

Editing the *fax* shell script

1. After you've made sure you're logged in as the root operator, open the /usr/bin/fax shell script with your favorite text editor.

2. The /usr/bin/fax shell script lists the pathnames for the FAX, EFAX, and EFIX commands. Make sure the script has the correct pathnames for the efax programs,like this:

```
FAX=/usr/bin/fax
EFAX=/usr/bin/efax
EFIX=/usr/bin/efix
```

3. Edit the entry specifying your modem's serial port:
```
DEV=ttyS0
```

Use the word `modem` if you've created the symbolic link /dev/modem. If your system is configured for dial-in use, enter the actual name of the device, such as ttyS0.

4. Specify the fax `CLASS` type your modem supports. Comment out the undesired `CLASS` by using the pound sign (#), and uncomment the desired `CLASS` by removing the pound sign:
```
# CLASS=1
CLASS=2
# CLASS=2.0
```

Make sure only one `CLASS` is selected, or uncommented.

5. Specify your phone number:
```
FROM=16505551212
```

6. Enter your name:
```
NAME=Michael Turner
```

7. Specify the default fax page size, again using the pound sign to comment out the undesired sizes, and by removing the pound sign in front of the proper size:
```
PAGE=letter
# PAGE=legal
# PAGE=a4
```

Ensure that only one size is specified.

8. Save the file and exityour text editor.

Testing Your Fax Configuration

Test your fax configuration and fax modem by using the fax script's `test` command-line option, like so:
```
# fax test
```

The `fax` script prints three pages of information to your display. A better way to see the test results is to redirect the output of the test to a file, like this:
```
# fax test > test.txt
```

Look for error messages in the output file. Common errors include specifying the wrong serial port for your fax modem and having more than one fax `CLASS` or default `PAGE` size specified.

Sending a Fax Using the *fax* Shell Script

Fax a text document using the `fax` script's `send` and `-1` command-line options, followed by a fax number and filename, like so:

```
# fax send -1 afaxphonenumber test.txt
```

This command line sends a low-resolution fax to the specified fax number using the specified file. High-resolution faxes are sent by default if you don't use the `-1` command-line option.

Setting Up to Wait for Incoming Faxes

You can use the `fax` script to have your computer automatically wait for incoming faxes. Use the `fax` script's `wait` command-line option:

```
# fax wait &
```

The `fax` command uses your fax modem to answer incoming fax calls and then saves incoming faxes under the `/var/spool/fax` directory.

Checking the Status of Incoming or Outgoing Faxes

To make sure the `fax` script is waiting for faxes, use the `fax` command's `status` command-line option:

```
# fax status
```

To see if you've received any faxes, use the `fax` script's `queue` command:

```
# fax queue
```

This command line causes the `fax` script to list the contents of the `/var/spool/fax` directory.

Viewing Received Faxes

After checking the fax queue, use the `fax` script's `view` option along with a received fax's filename to read a fax:

```
# fax view 1204164646*
```

The `fax` command automatically runs the X11 `xv` graphic program to view or print your incoming faxes.

Printing a Received Fax

Although the X11 xv client can be used to print faxes while viewing, you can also use the `fax` script's `print` command-line option as an alternative way to print a fax. Give the fax's filename as an argument to this command:

```
# fax print 1204164646*
```

SEE ALSO

➤ *For more information about setting up your printer for Linux, see page 88.*

Deleting a Received Fax

To delete a fax, use the `fax` script's `rm` command-line option, and give the fax's filename, like so:

```
# fax rm 120417243*
```

SEE ALSO

➤ *For more information about deleting files, see page 49.*

Be careful when deleting faxes

Always specify a fax filename, as returned by the `fax` script's `queue` option, when deleting a fax using the `rm` command-line option. This command can be dangerous and can unnecessarily delete critical files, especially if used with the wildcard character (*). Use specific filenames when deleting faxes.

part

III

THE X WINDOW SYSTEM

Running and Configuring X   169   **12**

Using a Window Manager   189   **13**

Performing Common X Operations   197   **14**

Using Graphics and Multimedia
Tools   215   **15**

chapter

12

Running and Configuring X

Configuring XFree86 with XF86Setup •

Configuring XFree86 with
XConfigurator •

Starting X11 •

Stopping X •

System and X session control with
display managers •

Customizing the .xinitrc startup script •

Customizing your workspace •

Using X11 resources •

The default graphic interface for Linux is the X Window System, usually the port of X11 from the XFree86 Project, Inc. This collection of software includes nearly 3,500 files, almost 200 programs (or clients), more than 500 fonts, and more than 500 graphics in nearly 50MB of software.

There are other sources for distributions of the X Window System for Linux. A commercial distribution, which can cost from $50 to several hundred dollars, can be especially helpful if you can't get X running on your computer, if you want special-ized technical support, or if the distribution includes commercial programs—such as a word processor or database manager. For information about other sources of X for Linux, check out the following sites:

```
http://www.calderasystems.com/
http://www.xig.com/
http://www.redhat.com/
http://www.metrolink.com/
```

Configuring XFree86 with XF86Setup

XF86Setup has become a common tool for configuring X and is now included in most distributions. From the command line, type

```
# XF86Setup
```

Configuring XFree86 with XConfigurator

Red Hat Linux includes its own tool for configuring X called Xconfigurator. If you are installing Red Hat Linux, the install procedure automatically runs XConfigurator. You can also re-configure X at any time by typing the following from the command line:

```
# Xconfigurator
```

Configuring Your Graphics Card

After Xconfigurator has been started, you are prompted to select your graphics card. If your card is on the list, select it and click OK to move to the next step.

If you cannot find your card on the list, try looking for your graphics chipset instead. Many times the Xconfigurator list will not include every brand of card that uses a particular chipset. Your video card's manual should contain information regarding the chipset that it uses. Common chipsets that can be found in Xconfigurator include the Riva 128 and TNT and Cirrus Logic chips.

If neither your card nor your card's chipset are on the list, select "Generic VGA ***". The generic VGA driver should work on any graphics card, but may not use your card to the best of its capabilities.

For more information about supported cards in XFree86 visit

```
http://www.xfree86.org/
```

Starting X11

There are two basic methods for starting the X windowing system. You can choose to have Linux start up directly into X, presenting you with a graphical login screen. In doing this, you gain the advantage of experiencing Linux entirely in a graphical system. For details, see the "System and X Session Control with Display Managers" section later in this chapter.

You can also choose to log in to Linux in text mode, and then manually start X. If your Linux machine is going to be used primarily as a server, you may want to choose this option. This gives you the flexibility to run Linux without the overhead of a graphical system if necessary.

Using the *startx* Command

After installing Linux and the X Window System, you can use the `startx` shell script from the command prompt to start an X session, like so:

```
# startx
```

> **Note**
> Under OpenLinux, this starts twm.

The `startx` script is used to feed options to the `xinit` (X initializer) command, which is discussed later in this chapter in the "Customizing the `.xinitrc` Startup Script" section.

If you've configured X to use different color depths (such as 8, 16, 24, or 32 bits per pixel), use the `-bpp` option followed by the color depth you want to use for your X session:

```
# startx -- -bpp 16
```

This command line starts X and tells the X server to use 16 bits per pixel color.

Using Virtual Consoles with X

Linux was built to handle multiple simultaneous users and includes the capability to switch between several "virtual consoles." Each virtual console presents the user with a separate login screen, enabling him to work in isolation from any other users.

For the casual user, virtual consoles can be used to provide several virtual desktops or work areas, each available with simple keypresses.

Switching between X11 and the console

1. Start an X11 session. To move to the first virtual console, press Ctrl+Alt+F1.

2. If you started X from the first virtual console (the default console) with the `startx` command, you won't be able to use this console because it will be displaying output and debug information for the X session. Press Alt+F2 to go to the second virtual console.

3. You should see a logon prompt. Log on to get to another shell prompt. To return to your X session, press Alt+F7. By default, most distributions support six virtual consoles, available through the F1–F6 function keys.

> **Note**
> Alt+F8 on systems using kdm returns to the X session.

Starting Multiple X Sessions

Virtual consoles begin in text mode, but they can be used to launch additional X sessions. Because an original X Session is already using the default display, ":0", it is necessary to specify the display for any additional sessions.

To start an X session on display number ":1" using the startx script:

```
# startx -- :1
```

Additional sessions can be started by specifying a unique display number for each session. By default, you will be able to reach additional X sessions (if they exist) by pressing Alt+F8 through Alt+F12.

Note that X sessions are memory intensive since separate graphics engines must load for each session. Most users will not have a need for more than one instance of X.

Stopping X

Window managers usually provide a graceful way to exit from your X session. Many times this takes the form of "logout" or "exit session" menu choices.

Always shut down properly!

Anytime you want to stop your X11 session or shut down Linux, use the proper keystrokes or commands. Never, *never* simply turn off your computer. This can wreak havoc with the file structure of your Linux partition!

You can also immediately exit from your X session by pressing Ctrl+Alt+backspace. Exiting through your window manager is preferable, however, because it gives the window manager the opportunity to save user preferences and exit any running programs gracefully.

System and X Session Control with Display Managers

Using the startx script is only one way to start an X session. Linux has the capability to boot directly into an X session, displaying the login prompt in a graphical fashion. The login prompt can be presented by the traditional xdm (X Display Manager) client, the more recent gdm (Gnome Display Manager), or kdm (K Display Manager) clients.

Logging In with xdm

The xdm (X Display Manager) client is used to display a logon screen before running your window manager. It eliminates the need to use the startx script because the X session is started before logging in. To use xdm (as shown in Figure 12.1), you must configure Linux to boot directly to X11.

Be careful editing /etc/inittab!

Make a backup copy of your system's /etc/inittab file before making any changes. Incorrect settings in this file can render your system inoperable by not supporting the boot process correctly (but can be easily fixed by using an emergency boot disk).

It is important that you ensure that X is configured correctly by first starting an X session with the startx command. After you have successfully installed and tested X, it is safe to setup Linux to boot directly to X.

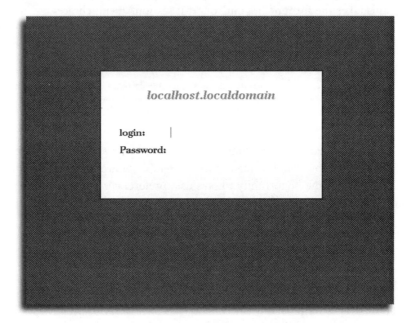

FIGURE 12.1
The xdm client displays a logon console to start an X session.

Configuring Linux to use *xdm*

1. To configure Linux to boot directly to X11 through the xdm client, first log on as the root operator.

2. Use your favorite text editor (such as pico), and open the file inittab under the /etc directory by entering the following:

```
# pico /etc/inittab
```

3. Move your cursor to the default initialization entry, which looks like this:

   `id:3:initdefault`

4. Change the number 3 to the number 5:

   `id:5:initdefault`

5. Save and close the file.

6. Restart Linux, using the `shutdown -r` (reboot) command:

   `# shutdown -r now`

7. After Linux restarts, you are presented with the default `xdm` logon screen, shown in Figure 12.2.

Tip

Also, both Red Hat and OpenLinux (at least) default to starting in run level 5 in most cases. In this case, editing `/etc/inittab` or using `linux 3` at the LILO prompt can be a lifesaver if something goes wrong with your X configuration.

FIGURE 12.2
The Red Hat Linux xdm logon display uses the `xbanner` command for a custom look.

If you just want to try xdm between Linux reboots, first make sure you're not running X11, and then log on as the root operator. Use xdm and the -nodaemon option, like this:

```
# xdm -nodaemon
```

Your display clears, and the xdm screen appears (refer to Figure 12.2).

Customizing the *xdm* Banner Screens

Some Linux distributions include a custom xdm configuration, and use the xbanner command to spiff up the display with a title, graphic, and background color. The xbanner command, used by xdm's setup function, is defined in the Xsetup_0 file (found under the /usr/X11R6/lib/xdm directory) with an entry such as the following:

```
/usr/X11R6/bin/xbanner
```

To change the title, or to insert your own graphic into the xdm logon screen, edit the file Xbanner, found under the /usr/X11R6/lib/X11/app-defaults directory. Xbanner is an X11 resource file (discussed later in this chapter in the "Using X11 Resources" section), and contains settings that you can change to personalize your xdm logon screen.

Creating a custom logon screen

1. Log on as the root operator. Using a text editor such as pico, open the Xbanner resource file under the /usr/X11R6/lib/X11/app-defaults directory by entering the following:

```
# pico -w /usr/X11R6/lib/X11/app-defaults/XBanner
```

2. Scroll through the document until you reach the Xbanner.Label section, which looks like the following:

```
! The text that will appear! This gets parsed for environment variables
! as in the shell. So $HOSTNAME and ${HOSTNAME} will work!
XBanner.Label:          Red Hat Linux
```

3. Typing over the default .Label entry, enter your own title:

```
XBanner.Label           Laptop Linux
```

4. Scroll through the file until you reach the effects section. Select an effect from the list of effects, shown here:

```
! Type of effect to render the text with. Allowed keywords:
! None               : Draw the text in the Foreground color.
! Shadow             : Add shadow under the text using the ShadowColor.
! Outline            : Add an outline to the text.
! Shadowed-Outline   : Outline with a shadow.
```

```
! 3D-Shadow        : Outline in a 3D fashion.
! Thick            : Shows text with thick letters.
! StandOut         : 3D thing standing out of the screen.
! StandIn          : Opposite of StandOut...
! PopArt           : Alternating HiColor/ShadowColor.
! Coin             : Somewhat like a coin.
! Fade             : Shadow/Thickness along a color gradient.
! Backlight        : Text with a color gradient.
! FatText          : Text fat and with a shadow.
! StandOut2        : Different way to do it.
! StandIn2         : Same here...
! FunnyOutline     : The wider areas of text filled with HiColor.
! FgGrad           : Color gradient on text and shadow.
! FgPlasma         : Foreground oftext is PlasmaCloud.
! Shake            : Nervous? Tense? Tired?
```

5. Set the desired effect (in this case, PopArt) by typing the following:

```
XBanner.Effect:        PopArt
```

6. To change the default penguin graphic, scroll down to the image section, which looks like the following:

```
! *** PASTE PIXMAP OPTIONS ***


! XBanner can put an image on the screen. Currently only .XPM!
! If your filename starts with '@', then it is a file _containing a list
! of pixmaps of the format:
! <pathname> <x> <y>
! And the PixmapX/PixmapY have no effect.
XBanner.DoPixmap:      True
XBanner.PixFile:       /usr/X11R6/include/X11/pixmaps/rhpenguin.xpm
XBanner.PixmapX:       30
XBanner.PixmapY:       400
```

7. Enter the location of your new graphic (which must be in XPM format) by changing the `PixFile` entry, like so:

```
XBanner.PixFile    /usr/X11R6/include/X11/pixmaps/escherknot.xpm
```

Note that the `Xbanner`, `.PixmapX`, and `.PixmapY` settings are used to place the graphic on the display at specified x and y coordinates (0,0 being the upper-left corner of your display).

8. Save the changes and exit your text editor. If you're running X, quit your session. To see your changes, start `xdm` by entering the following:

```
# xdm -nodaemon
```

The new `xdm` logon screen appears as shown in Figure 12.3.

FIGURE 12.3
Customize the xdm logon screen by using the xbanner command.

The xbanner program has nearly 80 command-line options, but curiously, no manual page. To read all the xbanner documentation, use the Lynx web browser to reach the following:

```
# lynx /usr/doc/xbanner-1.31/index.html
```

Customizing the *.xinitrc* Startup Script

The .xinitrc, or X initialization script, is a file used by the xinit command (started by the startx command) to configure your X session, or to start other window managers and clients. The default initialization script is found under the /etc/X11/xinit directory. If you customize this file as the root operator, any changes are systemwide and affect all users. To make individual changes, copy xinitrc to your home directory with .xinitrc as the file's name by entering the following:

```
# cp /etc/X11/xinit/xinitrc $HOME/.xinitrc
```

SEE ALSO

➤ *To learn how to use* .xinitrc *to start different window managers for X, see page 193.*

Customizing Your Workspace

The XFree86 X Window System distribution comes with a variety of clients that you can use as screen savers, to set background colors and patterns, or to configure your cursor and mouse. You can also load pictures and even animated screen savers into your root desktop display. Insert particularly pleasing screen savers or desktop color settings into your `.xinitrc` file so you can use them during your X sessions.

Setting a Screen Saver

Screen savers for X11 are not only fun to watch, but can also be used to password-protect your computer while you're using X. Linux distributions may include several screen-saving clients, such as `xset`, `xscreensaver`, and `xlock`.

xset

The `xset` client manages the screen-saving facilities of your X server, and can be used to set, turn on, test, and turn off screen savers.

Screen saving with the *xset* client

1. Start the `xset` client with the s command-line option, followed by a timeout interval (in seconds):

   `# xset s 30`

   This command sets the time that passes before a screensaver kicks in.

2. To turn on screen saving, use `xset` with the s option, followed by `on`, like this:

   `# xset s on`

3. To test screen saving right away instead of waiting for your timeout, follow the s option with `activate`, like so:

   `# xset s activate`

4. All you get is a blank screen. Not much fun, huh? To use a graphic and background pattern, use the s option with `noblank`, like this:

   `# xset s noblank`

5. Repeat step 3. You should see a light gray screen with a black X logo.

6. To turn off screen saving, follow the s option with `off`:

   `# xset s off`

xscreensaver

For a more animated display, use the xscreensaver and _xscreensaver-command clients. The xscreensaver client has 16 command-line options, but is easy to use.

Screensaving with *xscreensaver*

1. Start the xscreensaver client as a background process with the -timeout option, followed by a number (in minutes), like so:

```
# xscreensaver -timeout 5 &
```

2. After five minutes of no keyboard or mouse activity, xscreensaver runs a screen saver. Use the xscreensaver-command client to control xscreensaver. For example, to immediately test xscreensaver, use the -activate option, like this:

```
# xscreensaver-command -activate
```

Your screen slowly fades, and a screen saver starts.

3. To lock your screen saver and require a password to return to your X session, use the -lock option, like so:

```
# xscreensaver-command -lock
```

4. To turn off xscreensaver, use xscreensaver-command followed by the exit option, like so:

```
# xscreensaver-command -exit
```

5. To run a demonstration of xscreensaver, use the -demo option, like so:

```
# xscreensaver-command -demo
```

Your screen fades, and a dialog box appears, from which you can select a screen saver. An easier way to see an individual screen saver is to enter the screen saver's name from a command line, because each screen saver is a standalone client. For example, to see the shade sphere screen saver (©1988 by Sun Microsystems) program, use a command line like the following:

```
# sphere
```

The screen saver runs in an X11 window, as shown in Figure 12.4.

6. Another option is to run the animated screen saver in your root desktop, like an animated wallpaper. To work with X11 clients in the foreground while your background display is filled with movement and color, use the name of a screen saver, followed by the -root option, like this:

```
# forest -root &
```

FIGURE 12.4
Sun Microsystems' sphere drawing program can be used with the xscreensaver command.

For a list of screen savers for the xscreensaver client, see the xscreensaver manual page or the file Xscreensaver in the /usr/X11R6/lib/X11/app-defaults directory.

xlock

The xlock client is a sophisticated terminal-locking program with nearly 50 command-line options and more than 50 built-in screen savers. Use this client to password-protect your X session while you're away from your desk.

You can use xlock as a simple screen saver without password protection by using the -nolock option. For example, to see a random selection of xlock's screen savers every 15 seconds, use the -duration option, followed by a number (in seconds), the -nolock and -mode options, and the word random, like so:

```
# xlock -duration 15 -nolock -mode random
```

Like xscreensaver, xlock offers animation in your root display. Use the -inroot command-line option, like this:

```
# xlock -inline -mode random &
```

Setting the Background Desktop Color

Use xsetroot to change the color of your root display. For example, to use the color LavenderBlush3, use the xsetroot command's -solid option followed by the color's name (from the file rgb.txt under the /usr/X11R6/lib/X11 directory), like so:

```
# xsetroot -solid LavenderBlush3
```

Setting the Background Desktop Pattern

Use the xsetroot client along with the -bitmap option and the name of an X11 bitmap to set a pattern for your root display. You'll find nearly 90 bitmap graphics in the /usr/include/X11/bitmaps directory. To set a blue basket-weave pattern for your desktop, use the -bitmap option followed by the path to a graphic, and the -bg (background) option, followed by a color's name, like this:

```
# xsetroot -bitmap /usr/include/X11/bitmaps/wide_weave -bg blue
```

Using a Desktop Wallpaper

Using a wallpaper, or graphic image, in the root display of your desktop can enhance how your screen looks during your X sessions. The clients xloadimage and xv support many different graphics formats, and can be used to load pictures onto your desktop.

xloadimage

Use the xloadimage client to display a picture on your desktop. This program supports a number of graphics file formats, which are listed in Table 12.1.

Table 12.1   xloadimage-supported file formats

File Type	Description
cmuraster	CMU WM raster
faces	Faces project
fbm	FBM image
gem	GEM bit image
gif	GIF image
jpeg	JFIF-style JPEG image

File Type	Description
macpaint	MacPaint image
mcidas	McIDAS area file
niff	Native image file format (NIFF)
pbm	Portable bitmap (PBM, PGM, PPM)
pcx	PC paintbrush image
rle	Utah RLE image
sunraster	Sun rasterfile
vff	Sun visualization file format
vicar	VICAR image
xbm	X bitmap
xpm	X pixmap
xwd	X window dump

For example, to load a GIF graphic as a wallpaper graphic, use xloadimage with the -onroot option, followed by the graphic's name, like this:

```
# xloadimage -onroot /usr/lib/tk8.0/demos/images/earth.gif
```

This command line displays the earth in a tiled format in the background display. Use xloadimage with the -fullscreen option along with the -onroot option to fit the graphic to the size of your display, like this:

```
# xloadimage -onroot -fullscreen/usr/lib/tk8.0/demos/images/earth.gif
```

Note that you might have to experiment with different graphics to get the best effect.

XV

The xv client (usually used as an image viewer, editor, or conversion program) displays an image in the root window. Use the -root option followed by name of the graphic, like so:

```
# xv -root /usr/lib/tk8.0/demos/images/earth.gif
```

Setting the Mouse Pointer

Use the xsetroot command to change the mouse pointer for X. If you use Red Hat's AnotherLevel window manager for X, use the Set Root Cursor menu, found under the Root Cursor section of the Preferences menu.

Changing cursors with *xsetroot*

1. To use the xsetroot client to change your cursor, first use the less pager to read the cursorfont.h file under the /usr/X11R6/include/X11 directory, like this:

   ```
   # less /usr/X11R6/include/X11/cursorfont.h
   ```

2. You'll see a list of nearly 80 cursor definitions that will resemble the following:

   ```
   ...
   #define XC_box_spiral 20
   #define XC_center_ptr 22
   #define XC_circle 24
   #define XC_clock 26
   #define XC_coffee_mug 28
   #define XC_cross 30
   #define XC_cross_reverse 32
   #define XC_crosshair 34
   #define XC_diamond_cross 36
   #define XC_dot 38

   ...
   ```

3. To set your cursor to coffee_mug, use the xsetroot client along with the -cursor_name option and the name of the cursor, like so:

   ```
   # xsetroot -cursor_name coffee_mug
   ```

4. To reset your cursor to the normal X11 cursor, use xsetroot with X_cursor name, like so:

   ```
   # xsetroot -cursor_name X_cursor
   ```

5. To see a character grid of the available cursors, use the xfd (X11 font display) client with the -fn command-line option followed by the name of the cursor font, like so:

   ```
   # xfd -fn cursor
   ```

   A window containing a small graphic of each cursor appears, as shown in Figure 12.5.

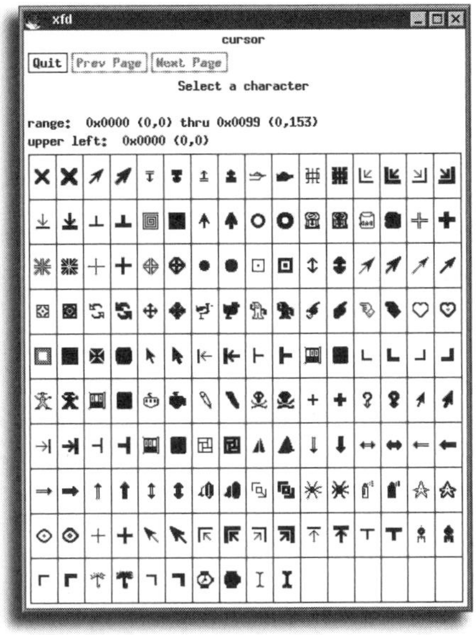

FIGURE 12.5
The xfd client can display pictures of available X11 cursors in the cursor's font.

Configuring the Mouse

Use the xmodmap and xset clients to configure how your mouse works with X11. The xmodmap client can change the order of your mouse buttons, while the xset client can set your mouse acceleration.

Setting your mouse with *xmodmap* and *xset*

1. Use xmodmap with the -e (expression) option followed by the pointer specification to switch your mouse buttons. For example, to reverse the order of the buttons, use xmodmap like so:

```
# xmodmap -e "pointer 3 2 1"
```

2. Use the xset client with the m (mouse) option followed by two numbers to set the acceleration of your pointer. For example, to slow down your mouse, use xset like so:

```
# xset m "1 5"
```

Too slow? Try the following:

```
# xset m "40 20"
```

Too fast? Try the following:

```
# xset m "4 8"
```

3. To reset your mouse, use `xset` with the `m` option followed by the word `default`, like this:

```
# xset m "default"
```

SEE ALSO

➤ *For more information about using a mouse with Linux, see page 148.*

Configuring Terminal Windows

Terminal emulator clients such as `xterm`, `rxvt`, `kvt`, or Gnome Terminal display an open window with a shell command line. Terminal windows are resizable, and can be moved, minimized (iconified), or maximized. A minimized terminal window can appear on the desktop or, if you are using Gnome or KDE, may appear on a taskbar at one side of the screen.

Chapter 14, "Performing Common X Operations," discusses many of the X Toolkit command-line options that you can use to configure terminal windows. However, some terminal emulators, such as `nxterm`, can be configured via a combination of the keyboard and your mouse.

Your default X configuration should include at least one root menu item for a terminal. In many window managers, you will find the root menu by middle- or right-clicking your mouse on the desktop. In Gnome or KDE, the menu may appear on one side of the screen. By default, several terminals are usually available.

Configuring xterm Terminals

`xterm` is probably the most common terminal client on Linux installations. It is almost always included with a distribution's default configuration options and can be found in the default root menu.

Starting xterm for the first time is usually a matter of selecting the xterm menu choice from your window manager. This will start xterm with its default options. To start another xterm session from any terminal, start it from the command line.

```
# xterm
```

xterm is one of the most common and stable terminals available, but it lacks some of the function of some of the newer terminals, especially in terms of ease-of-use and configurability. For a more configurable terminal, try kvt or gnome terminal.

Using X11 Resources

Many X Window System clients use a configuration, or resource, file. This is a text file that contains line-item settings, or resource strings, used to determine how the client looks or runs. Many of these settings can be specified by using the `-xrm` X11 Toolkit option followed by a resource string, but most programs use only a resource file.

To change resource settings for an X11 client, first read the program's manual page. Alternatively, look for a resource file in the `app-defaults` directory under `/usr/X11R6/lib/X11` by entering the following:

```
# ls -A /usr/X11R6/lib/X11/app-defaults
```

Beforelight	RXvt	XGammon	XRn	Xgopher
Bitmap	Seyon	XGetfile	Xscreensaver	Xgopher color
Bitmap-color	Seyon-color	XLoad	XSm	Xloadimage
Chooser	Viewres	XLock	XSysinfo	Xmag
Clock-color	X3270	XLogo	XSysinfo-color	Xman
Editres	XBanner	XLogo-color	XTerm	Xmessage
Editres-color	XCalc	XMailbox	XTerm-color	Xmh
Fig	XCalc-color	XMdb	Xditview	Xvidtune
Fig-color	XClipboard	XMixer	xosview	
GV	XClock	XPaint	Xedit	
GXditview	XConsole	XPat	Xfd	
KTerm	XDbx	XPlaycd	Xfm	
Nxterm	XFontSel	Playmidi	Xgc	

Each resource file (usually with the name of the corresponding client, but with a leading capital letter) contains resource strings that not only determine how a program is displayed, but also the contents and handling of menus, buttons, and other parts of a program.

Read the X manual page to learn how to define resource strings. As an example, the resource settings for the `xcalc` calculator client are defined in the `Xcalc` resource file.

Changing resource settings

1. Log on as the root operator. Using your text edit (`pico`, for example), open the resource file `Xcalc` for the `xcalc` calculator by entering the following:
    ```
    # pico -w /usr/X11R6/lib/X11/app-defaults/XCalc
    ```

2. Scroll through the resource file. You see definitions for the title, cursor, icon name, and other settings, such as the font used for the calculator keys. To change the calculator to use words instead of numbers for the calculator keys,

look for the `*ti.buttonxxLabel` resource definitions, which resemble the following:

```
*ti.button22.Label:          7
```

3. Change the numeral 7 to the word seven:

```
*ti.button22.Label:          seven
```

4. Change the labels for the other keypad numerals, save the file, and exit. To see your changes, run the xcalc client by entering the following:

```
# xcalc &
```

Your new calculator should look like the one on the right in Figure 12.6.

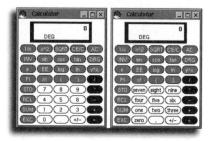

FIGURE 12.6
Change resource settings for X11 clients, such as xcalc, to alter the client's appearance.

Always make a backup copy of the original file before committing changes to a resource file. Also, make sure that any changes to a program's default window size work with your display. (In other words, don't create a default 1024×786 window for a program if you use only an 800×600 display.)

# chapter 13

Using a Window Manager

Window managers and desktop
environments

Selecting an X11 window manager

Starting a window manager

Window Managers and Desktop Environments

The recent evolution of Linux desktops has caused some confusion between "desktop environments" and "window managers." Most modern distributions include several window managers as well as one or more desktop environments. The two major desktop environments for Linux are GNOME and KDE (the K Desktop Environment).

The *desktop environment* provides features that work on top of window managers, including application drag-and-drop support, file managers, menuing systems, and a suite of standard applications. Your *window manager* is the program that controls the look and feel of your window "decorations," window icons, and desktop management.

It is possible to choose your window manager and desktop environment independent of each other. (Desktop environments are relatively new and are not actually required at all.) KDE, however, comes with its own window manager, kwm.

Selecting an X11 Window Manager

One great feature of X11 is that it provides the freedom to choose how to manage the windows or programs on your screen. Through a window manager, users can select the look and feel of their desktop and customize much of its behavior.

There are several different window managers for Linux and the X Window System. Though you have dozens of good choices, this chapter looks only at KDE/kwm, GNOME/Enlightenment, and Window Maker.

Window managers vary in ease of use, convenience, size, and style. Although you can use only one window manager at a time on a single display, you might have several installed on your system. Window managers demonstrate the graphic flexibility of the X Window System and show that there is no such thing as a standard graphical user interface for X.

SEE ALSO

➤ *For more information about using the X Window System, see page 167.*

The K Desktop Environment and *kwm*

 The *K Desktop Environment*, or *KDE*, is one of the newest and most popular desktop environments for Linux and X11. KDE is a complete graphical environment for X11 (see Figure 13.1) and provides many features, including the following:

- An integrated suite of more than 100 programs and games

- Configuration of window scrollbars, fonts, color, and size using graphical dialog boxes

- Mounting of file systems, such as CD-ROMs, using the mouse pointer

- *Network Transparent Access*, or *NTA*, in which clicking a graphic file in an FTP listing results in an automatic download and display of the graphic

- Support for background (desktop) wallpaper graphics in JPEG format

- Support for session management (applications and window positions are remembered between sessions)

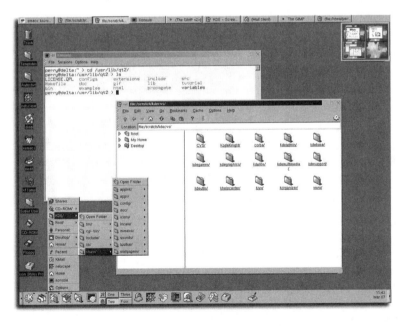

FIGURE 13.1
KDE comes with nearly 100 programs and is one of the newest and most popular desktop environments for Linux.

KDE is included in most modern distributions. If it was not included in your distribution, visit KDE's homepage at http://www.kde.org to get instructions for obtaining the package for your distribution. KDE even makes prebuilt packages for the major distributions available on its FTP site.

Enlightenment

The Enlightenment window manager (often referred to as *E*, and shown in Figure 13.2) began as a project to make a window manager that was extremely configurable and graphically appealing. It is now one of the most popular window managers for Linux.

You can use either GNOME or KDE with Enlightenment as well, adding even more customizability to your desktop. On most distributions, however, Enlightenment defaults to a stand-alone window manager or starts GNOME.

Enlightenment remains one of the fastest developing window managers for X, and I highly recommend it for showing off the power and configurability of Linux.

Learn more about Enlightenment by visiting the official Web site, `http://www.enlightenment.org`.

FIGURE 13.2
Enlightenment is one of the most configurable and graphically appealing window managers for X.

Window Maker

Window Maker (shown in Figure 13.3) is another popular Linux window manager. It boasts easy-to-use configuration tools and very fast operation.

Window Maker is famous for its use of *docked applets*, small applications that run in Window Maker icons. These small applets range from system monitoring tools to tiny video games. You can find demonstrations of many of these applets at `http://www.windowmaker.org/projects.html`.

FIGURE 13.3
Window Maker runs docked applets in icons.

Starting a Window Manager

Most window managers are started by line entries in a file called `.xinitrc` in your home directory. The systemwide default `.xinitrc` file is found under the `/etc/X11/xinit` or `/usr/X11R6/lib/X11/xinit` directory. When you first start X (as detailed in the section "Starting X11" in Chapter 12, "Running and Configuring X11"), the `xinit` program (started by the `startx` command) first looks for the initializer file `.xinitrc` in your home directory. If it is not found, `xinit` then looks for `.xinitrc` in the `/usr/X11R6/lib/X11/xinit` directory.

You do not have to use the default `.xinitrc` system file, but if you want to experiment, use the `cp` command to copy and create your own `.xinitrc` file, like this:

```
# cp /usr/X11R6/lib/X11/xinit/xinitrc $HOME/.xinitrc
```

SEE ALSO

➤ *To learn more about using* `.xinitrc`, *see page 178.*

Starting KDE

 Use your text editor to create or edit your `.xinitrc` file in your home directory. Comment out any previous window managers, and insert the `startkde` command in your `.xinitrc` file.

```
startkde
```

Save your file, and then use the `startx` command to start X11 and run KDE.

```
# startx
```

Starting Enlightenment/GNOME

 Use your text editor to create or edit your `.xinitrc` file in your home directory. Comment out or remove any previous window managers and insert the following command to start Enlightenment:

```
exec /usr/local/enlightenment/bin/enlightenment
```

To make sure that this is the correct path to Enlightenment on your machine, use the `which` command:

```
# which enlightenment
```

Save your file, and use the `startx` command to start X and run Enlightenment.

```
# startx
```

If GNOME is installed on your system and you want to start it as well, add the following line instead of the command to start your window manager.

```
exec gnome-session
```

GNOME will begin its session and load its default window manager (usually Enlightenment).

Starting Window Maker

To start Window Maker for an X session, you must tell the `startx` script to launch Window Maker. Window Maker comes with a script to perform all the necessary configuration and modify your `.xinitrc` file. To run this script and configure X to start Window Maker, type the following:

```
# wmaker.inst
```

After running this script, exit from any running X sessions and restart X.

```
# startx
```

To start Window Maker from a line in your own `.xinitrc` file, use your text editor to create a `.xinitrc` file in your home directory, and then add the following line. If the `.xinitrc` file already exists, edit the existing file, remove the line that starts your old window manager (usually beginning with an `exec` statement), and insert this line:

```
# exec /usr/X11R6/bin/wmaker'
```

Be sure to use the path to Window Maker on your local machine. You can find out where (and if) Window Maker is installed by using the `which` command:

```
# which wmaker
```

# chapter 14

Performing Common X Operations

Using X11 Toolkit command-line options •

Moving, resizing, and managing windows •

Viewing X11 fonts •

Using the xfd client to view font character maps •

Copying and pasting text •

Capturing windows and the desktop •

Using X11 Toolkit Command-Line Options

Nearly all X Window System clients, or programs, accept a set of similar command-line options, known as X11 Toolkit options. These options provide a range of choices for the window size, placement, colors, title, or fonts used when a client starts. Most of the standard X11 Toolkit options are discussed in the x manual page.

SEE ALSO

➤ *To learn more about the X Window System, see page 171.*

Using Geometry Settings to Set Window Size

Use the -geometry option followed by width, height, and xoffset or yoffset values to start your program with a specific window size, in a specified area of your display, or in a virtual desktop.

Placing *rxvt* terminal windows by using *-geometry*

1. Use the -geometry setting with the rxvt terminal emulator to place the initial window in the upper-right corner of your display. Assuming you have a desktop that's 800×600 pixels, start rxvt with an 80-character wide by 24-line window by typing the following at the command line:

   ```
   # rxvt -geometry 80x24+216+0 &
   ```

   The value 216 is the xoffset value and forces the rxvt window to start 216 pixels from the left side of the screen. A yoffset value of 0 forces the rxvt window to the top of screen.

2. Use the -geometry setting again, but this time, start rxvt in the lower-right corner of your screen by entering the following at the command line:

   ```
   # rxvt -geometry 80x24+216+232 &
   ```

3. Use geometry offset settings greater than your desktop size to start the rxvt client offscreen in an adjacent virtual desktop. If your screen size is 800×600 pixels, use an xoffset value slightly greater than 800 to place the terminal window in the desktop to the right, like this:

   ```
   # rxvt -geometry 80x25+801+0
   ```

   This command line starts rxvt in the upper-left corner of the desktop that is located to the right of your screen.

4. To start rxvt in a desktop below your current screen, use a yoffset slightly greater than your screen's height, like so:

   ```
   # rxvt -geometry 80x25+0+601
   ```

This command line starts `rxvt` in the upper-left corner of the desktop below your current screen.

5. Substituting the plus sign with a minus sign tells X to reference the bottom or right side of the screen. For instance, to place a window in the bottom-right corner:

```
# rxvt \geometry 80x25-0-0
```

Using geometry to place a window

You can also use `-geometry -0+0` to place a client window in the upper-right corner of your display. This saves you the effort of manually moving the window or performing subtraction of a client's window size from your desktop's size.

Automatically placing windows in the lower-right corner

`-geometry -0-0` does the same thing, and places any client's window in the lower-right corner of your desktop!

Use geometry settings to start clients in each of your desktops. For example, one desktop could be dedicated to Web browsing or email, another could be dedicated to a sports graphics program, and a third could be occupied by your word processor or text editor.

Setting Foreground and Background Colors

Use the `-bg` and `-fg` X11 Toolkit options to set the background and foreground colors of an X11 client's window. The list of colors supported by the XFree86 256-color servers are in the file rgb.txt under the /usr/X11R6/lib/X11 directory, or you can use the showrgb client to display the list of colors by typing the following at the command line:

```
# showrgb
```

To start the `rxvt` terminal emulator with a BlanchedAlmond background and MidnightBlue text for the foreground, for example, use the `-bg` and `-fg` options:

```
# rxvt -bg BlanchedAlmond -fg MidnightBlue &
```

If you must use the XF86_VGA16 server ffor your X11 sessions, only 16 colors are available. Use the xcmap client to display the available colors, like this:

```
# xcmap &
```

The available colors will be displayed in a grid, as shown in Figure 14.1. Users of black-and-white–display servers, such as the monochrome server XF86_Mono, might want to experiment with the -rv and +rv reverse video modes to invert the display of terminal windows or text editors.

FIGURE 14.1
The xcmap client displays a grid of available colors for your X11 desktop.

SEE ALSO
➤ *To learn more about using the XFree86 series of X11 servers, see page 171.*

Moving, Resizing, and Managing Windows

The types and features of windows used by X11 clients depend on the X11 window manager used during your X Window System sessions.

The anatomy of an X11 window is shown in Figure 14.2.

Specifying an X11 Window Title

The topmost portion of an X11 window is called the *title bar*, and usually contains the name of the X11 client. You can change the name that appears on the title bar by using the X11 Toolkit -title option. For example, to start the rxvt X11 terminal emulator with a custom title bar, enter a command line such as the following:

```
# rxvt -title "Welcome to Linux! Have a nice day! :-)"
```

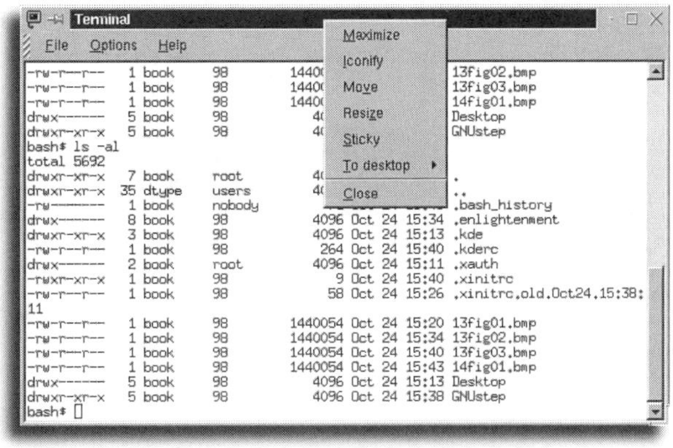

FIGURE 14.2
A typical KDE X11 window, showing common window features, such as a title bar, scrollbars, and window control buttons.

SEE ALSO

➤ *For more information about configuring X11 terminal emulators, such as* rxvt *or* xterm, *see page* 179.

Minimizing, Maximizing, or Closing Windows

Depending on your window manager, common window functions might be slightly different than described later. Every window manager has slightly different ways to control window behavior, but they generally follow established standards. For simplicity, the following description describes behavior in KDE.

In the title bar of each window are three buttons: Minimize, Maximize, and Close. If you click the Minimize button, the window will shrink, appearing only as a button in the taskbar or as an icon (shown in Figure 14.3). If you click the Maximize button, the window will enlarge to fill your display, or will be restored to a previous size (note that in some window managers you can also double-click the window's title bar to maximize or restore a window's size). Although you should usually use an X11 client's documented method to quit, you can close the client or window by clicking the Close button.

There are several ways to resize a window. To resize a window horizontally using your mouse, move your cursor to right or left edge of the window and click and drag the window until it reaches the desired width. To resize a window vertically using your mouse, move your cursor to the top or bottom of the window, and click and drag the window until it reaches the desired height. To resize vertically and horizontally at the same time, move your mouse cursor to one of the window's four corners, and click and drag the window until it reaches the desired size.

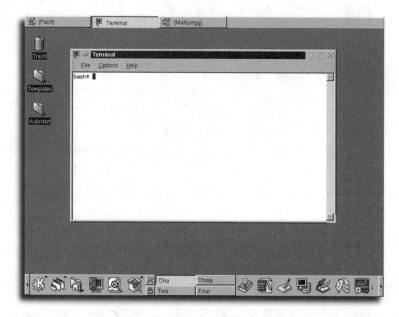

FIGURE 14.3
The KDE desktop provides a Start menu and desktop control functions. The taskbar (top) provides placement for minimized X11 windows.

Viewing X11 Fonts

Use the xlsfonts program to list the fonts recognized by the X Window System. Use wildcards or patterns to match font names to find specific fonts. For example, to list all bold fonts from the Adobe Utopia family, use xlsfonts with the -fn (font) option and a wildcard, like so:

```
# xlsfonts -fn *utopia*bold*
-adobe-utopia-bold-i-normal-0-0-0-0-p-0-iso8859-1
-adobe-utopia-bold-r-normal-0-0-0-0-p-0-iso8859-1
```

Use the xlsfonts program to find font names for the -fn X11 Toolkit option, or with the xfontsel or xfd clients discussed in this section.

xlsfonts outputs the raw X font names, which can be confusing at first. The naming convention, although cryptic, is designed to allow selection of the proper font, including all its variations. The font name includes a descriptive name, weight (bold, normal), style (italic, roman, and so on), spacing, size, and character set information.

SEE ALSO

➤ *To learn how X uses fonts, see page 171.*

Viewing X11 Fonts with the *xfontsel* Client

The xfontsel client provides an easy way to see samples of each font available during your X11 session. By default, xfontsel attempts to read the names of every available font, but when used with the -pattern option, displays fonts matching a wildcard pattern. For example, to force xfontsel to use all Adobe fonts, use the -pattern option followed by a wildcard pattern:

```
# xfontsel -pattern *adobe*
```

The xfontsel client presents a window, as shown in Figure 14.4, along with a sample of the first font found. To display different fonts, click any of the fmly, wght, or slant names, and then select an option from the ensuing shortcut menu.

FIGURE 14.4
The xfontsel client displays a character-set sample of a selected font.

Using the *xfd* Client to View Font Character Maps

Use the X11 xfd (X font display) client to see all the characters in a font. The font must be made available to your X11 server through the Files section of your system's XF86Config file (described in Chapter 12, "Running and Configuring X," in the section "Starting X11"). If you're not sure about what font to display, use the xfontsel client or look under the /usr/X11R6/ lib/X11/fonts directory. For example, to display all the available miscellaneous fonts, use the ls command, as follows:

```
# ls /usr/X11R6/lib/X11/fonts/misc
10x20.pcf.gz        8x16rk.pcf.gz        deccurs.pcf.gz
12x24.pcf.gz        9x15.pcf.gz          decsess.pcf.gz
12x24rk.pcf.gz      9x15B.pcf.gz         fonts.alias
3270-12.pcf.gz      clB6x10.pcf.gz       fonts.dir
3270-12b.pcf.gz     clB6x12.pcf.gz       gb16fs.pcf.gz
3270-20.pcf.gz      clB8x10.pcf.gz       gb16st.pcf.gz
3270-20b.pcf.gz     clB8x12.pcf.gz       gb24st.pcf.gz
3270.pcf.gz       clB8x13.pcf.gz       hanglg16.pcf.gz
3270b.pcf.gz      clB8x14.pcf.gz       hanglm16.pcf.gz
3270d.pcf.gz      clB8x16.pcf.gz       hanglm24.pcf.gz
3270gt12.pcf.gz     clB8x8.pcf.gz        heb6x13.pcf.gz
3270gt12b.pcf.gz    clB9x15.pcf.gz       heb8x13.pcf.gz
3270gt16.pcf.gz     clI6x12.pcf.gz       hex20.pcf
3270gt16b.pcf.gz    clI8x8.pcf.gz        jiskan16.pcf.gz
3270gt24.pcf.gz     clR4x6.pcf.gz        jiskan24.pcf.gz
3270gt24b.pcf.gz    clR5x10.pcf.gz       k14.pcf.gz
3270gt32.pcf.gz     clR5x6.pcf.gz        nil2.pcf.gz
3270gt32b.pcf.gz    clR5x8.pcf.gz        olcursor.pcf.gz
3270gt8.pcf.gz    clR6x10.pcf.gz       olgl10.pcf.gz
3270h.pcf.gz      clR6x12.pcf.gz       olgl12.pcf.gz
5x7.pcf.gz        clR6x13.pcf.gz      olgl14.pcf.gz
5x8.pcf.gz        clR6x6.pcf.gz       olgl19.pcf.gz
6x10.pcf.gz       clR6x8.pcf.gz       vga.pcf
6x12.pcf.gz       clR7x10.pcf.gz
6x13.pcf.gz       clR7x12.pcf.gz
6x13B.pcf.gz      clR7x14.pcf.gz
6x9.pcf.gz       clR7x8.pcf.gz
7x13.pcf.gz       clR8x10.pcf.gz
7x13B.pcf.gz      clR8x12.pcf.gz
7x14.pcf.gz       clR8x13.pcf.gz
7x14B.pcf.gz      clR8x14.pcf.gz
7x14rk.pcf.gz     clR8x16.pcf.gz
8x13.pcf.gz      clR8x8.pcf.gz
8x13B.pcf.gz     clR9x15.pcf.gz
8x16.pcf.gz      cursor.pcf.gz
```

Note that each font is compressed (with the .gz extension). This is a feature of X Window System release X11R6.3, which can use compressed fonts to save disk space. If you're using an earlier release of X11 (such XFree86 3.1.2), the fonts are not compressed.

SEE ALSO

➤ *To learn more about compressed files, see page 504.*

Displaying X11 font characters

1. Use the xfd client from the command line of a terminal window, followed by the -fn (font) option and the name of the desired font. The xfd client also supports many standard X11 Toolkit options, so you can use geometry, foreground, or background settings to customize how the characters are displayed. For example, to display the characters contained in a tiny font, use the xfd client like this:

```
# xfd -geometry 500x400 -fn 5x7
```

The xfd client displays a window like the one shown in Figure 14.5.

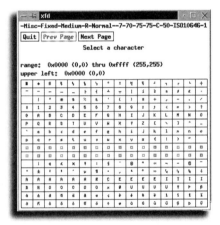

FIGURE 14.5
The xfd client displays characters defined in a specified X11 font.

2. To see the available X11 cursors, use the xfd client along with geometry settings for size and color and the -center option to center each character in the display:

```
# xfd -geometry 500x400 -bg blue -fg white -center -fn cursor
```

This displays a 500×400–pixel window, with each X11 cursor in white on a blue background.

SEE ALSO

➤ *For more information about using compression programs, see page 504.*

Copying and Pasting Text

Copying and pasting text between terminal windows is a common X11 operation and involves using your mouse to select, drag, and then paste selected portions of text. Your keyboard can also play a part in these operations, especially for selecting large areas of text.

Copying and pasting text is handy for quickly copying complex command lines for later use in shell scripts, for duplicating text blocks or for moving chunks of text from a program's output in a terminal window into a text editor window.

Copying and pasting words, lines, and blocks

1. To copy a word from text in a terminal window, double-click the word. Move to another window and press the middle mouse button (or both left and right mouse buttons simultaneously if you use a two-button mouse) to paste the word.

2. To copy a line of text, triple-click the line, and then paste using the same technique as described in step 1. Note that if you copy a command line from a terminal window, you might also get a carriage return in your pasted text.

3. To copy a large chunk of text, you must first highlight it. Move your cursor to the beginning of the text area, and then drag to the end of the area with the left mouse buttons held down. Alternatively, you can click at the beginning of the text and then, holding down the Shift key, click at the end of the text.

To paste the highlighted selection, press the middle mouse button (or simultaneously press the left and right mouse buttons if you use a two-button mouse). Alternatively, hold down the Shift key, and then press the Insert key.

SEE ALSO

➤ *To learn how to configure your mouse for X11, see page 185.*

Using the *xcutsel* Client to Copy Text

Use the xcutsel client to copy text from one window to another. This client offers a convenient way of copying text from one application to another through the use of buttons in dialog boxes, and can serve as a temporary holding place for copied text. It is similar in function to the basic mouse click method described earlier, but allows you to view the buffer to ensure accuracy.

Copying text with *xcutsel*

1. Start the xcutsel client from the command line of a terminal window by typing the following:

```
# xcutsel &
```

2. The `xcutsel` client window, shown in Figure 14.6, appears. Two buttons (`copy PRIMARY to 0` and `copy 0 to PRIMARY`) are used to copy text.

FIGURE 14.6
The `xcutsel` client supports the copying and pasting of text between X11 clients.

3. Highlight a word, line, or block of text in a terminal window.

4. Click the `copy PRIMARY to 0` button.

5. Click the `copy 0 to PRIMARY` button.

6. Move your mouse cursor to the terminal or client window where you want to paste the text.

7. Paste the text by clicking the middle mouse button or by pressing Shift+Insert.

Copying Text with the *xclipboard* Client

Use the `xclipboard` client to copy and paste text. This client works just like the `xcutsel` client, but in addition to copying large sections of text and serving as a temporary holding place, it displays the copied text before your paste operation, supports multiple buffers of copied text, and can save buffers or copied text into text files.

Copying, saving, and pasting text with *xclipboard*

1. Start the `xclipboard` client from the command line of terminal window by typing the following:
   ```
   # xclipboard &
   ```

2. A small window appears (see Figure 14.7). Note the Quit, Delete, New, Save, Next, and Prev buttons.

3. Highlight the desired word, line, or block of text in a terminal or client window.

4. Move your mouse cursor to the `xclipboard` window.

5. Paste the highlighted text into the `xclipboard` window. Unlike with normal cut-and-paste operations, you must use your middle mouse button (or a simultaneous left- and right-button press if using a two-button mouse) to paste.

6. To save the text to a file, click the Save button. A small dialog box with the default name (`clipboard`) will appear.

FIGURE 14.7
The xclipboard client offers multiple buffers for copied text and enables you to save copied text to disk.

7. If you don't want to use the default name, enter a new filename. Click the Accept button.

8. To save multiple buffers, click the New button. The Prev button should become active, and a 2 should appear next to it.

9. Repeat step 3 to highlight text, and then paste the text into the xclipboard window. You now have two buffers of copied text.

10. To paste the first buffer, click the Prev button. Your previously copied text appears.

11. Highlight the text displayed in the xclipboard window.

12. Move your mouse to the desired terminal or client window, and use your middle mouse button (or press Shift+Insert) to paste the text.

Capturing Windows and the Desktop

Use the xwd, xmag, or xv client, found under the /usr/X11R6/bin directory, to capture a window picture, a portion of the X11 display, or the entire desktop. This is a handy way to capture, copy, or print graphics from your X11 sessions. Some of the techniques and X11 clients described in this section might come in handy if you use any of the graphics programs described in Chapter 15, "Using Graphics and Multimedia Tools."

Using *xwd* to Capture Windows

Use the xwd (X11 window dump) program to take snapshots of your desktop or of a desired terminal or client window.

Saving window dumps with *xwd*

1. Start the xwd client from the command line of a terminal window, using the standard output redirection operator (>) to create a file with an .xwd extension:

   ```
   # xwd >dump1.xwd
   ```

2. By default, xwd sends its output, a special text graphics format, to the standard output. Alternatively, you can use the -out option followed by a filename to save the graphic, like so:

   ```
   # xwd -out dump1.xwd
   ```

3. When you start xwd, your cursor turns into cross hairs (+). To capture a window, click the window or its border. The window graphic is saved to the specified filename. Even if a selected window is overlapped by another window, the contents of the selected window are captured.

4. To capture the entire screen, click the root desktop or display.

SEE ALSO

➤ *To learn more about using shell redirection operators, see page 24.*

Using *xwud* to Display Window Dumps

Use the xwud (X11 window undump) client to view your captured graphic.

Viewing window dumps

1. Start the xwud client from the command line of a terminal window, using the -in option followed by the name of your window dump, like so:

   ```
   # xwud -in dump1.xwd
   ```

2. Alternatively, you can use the shell's standard input redirection operator (<) to read in your captured graphic:

   ```
   # xwud <dump1.xwd
   ```

3. By default, the xwud client quits when you click the displayed window. If you want to disable this feature, use the -noclick option. If you want to distort the graphic or rescale the window, use the -scale option, which allows you to resize the graphic's window.

Using the *xloadimage* Client to View Captures

Use the `xloadimage` client, found under the `/usr/X11R6/bin` directory, to view graphics captured by the `xwd` command. To view a captured window dump, use `xloadimage` followed by the name of the dumped graphic, like so:

```
# xloadimage dump1.xwd
```

The `xloadimage` client displays a series of screen dumps one at a time after each press of N when you use the `-goto` option, like so:

```
# xloadimage dump1.xwd dump2.xwd dump3.xwd -goto dump1.xwd
```

This command line causes `xloadimage` to repeat the sequence of graphics on your display until you press Q to quit. See the `xloadimage` manual page for more information about this program, such as graphics file format conversion.

SEE ALSO

➤ To learn more about converting graphics formats, see page 229.

Capturing and Viewing Screens with the *xv* Client

Use the `xv` client to capture or display X11 windows or desktops. This command has a bewildering array of more than 100 command-line options, but you can read the `xv` documentation by using the `gv` client (which is in PostScript format) like this:

```
# gv /usr/doc/xv-3.10a/xvdocs.ps
```

SEE ALSO

➤ For more information about the `gv` PostScript previewer, see page 234.

Capturing X11 windows by using the *xv* client

1. Start the `xv` client from the command line of terminal window like so:
   ```
   # xv &
   ```

2. The `xv` title screen appears. Right-click the title screen to display the main `xv` dialog box.

3. To capture a window, click the Grab button.

4. The `xv` Grab dialog box, shown in Figure 14.8, appears. Click the dialog box's Grab button, and then click the desired window.

5. The `xv` client beeps once, and then again after it displays the captured graphic in a window (see Figure 14.9).

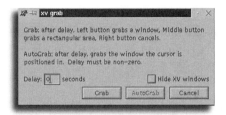

FIGURE 14.8
The xv Grab dialog box is used to capture all or portions of your X11 desktop.

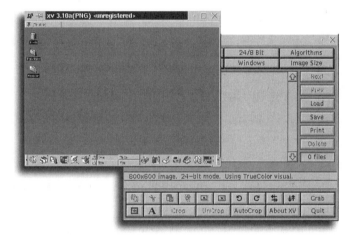

FIGURE 14.9
After a screen capture, the xv displays the graphic in a separate window.

6. To capture a portion of a window, hold down your middle mouse button (or both mouse buttons if you're using a two-button mouse), and drag to create a rectangle. To capture a window using a time delay, move your mouse to the Delay field, enter the number of seconds for the delay, click the AutoGrab button, and then move your mouse to the desired window (or select the rectangular area to grab). Use the Hide XV Windows button to make the xv client disappear when performing the graphics capture.

7. After capturing your graphic, click xv's Save button. A Save dialog box appears. Select the desired graphics output format by clicking the Format button. To save the graphic as a grayscale or black-and-white image, click the Colors button.

Although the xv command-line options (detailed starting on page 74 of xv's 128-page manual) might at first be confusing, the xv client is simple to use when displaying window dumps. Use the xv command followed by the name of your dumped graphic like this:

```
# xv dump1.xwd
```

Use the handy -expand command-line option followed by a positive or negative number to display captured images as larger or smaller. For example, to display a small window graphic at three times its original size, use the -expand option:

```
# xv -expand 3 dump1.xwd
```

To display a full-screen image capture at one-half its original size, use -expand -2 like so:

```
# xv -expand -2 dump1.xwd
```

Using the *xmag* Client to Capture Magnified Images

You can use the xmag client to capture or magnify portions of your display, such as window buttons or icons.

Capturing images with the *xmag* client

1. Start the xmag client from the command line of a terminal window like this:
   ```
   # xmag &
   ```

2. To specify a level of magnification to use when capturing magnified images, use the -mag option followed by a positive number (xmag will not capture reduced images). For example, to capture a graphic at three times its original size, use the -mag option like this:
   ```
   # xmag -mag 3 &
   ```

3. After you start the xmag program, your cursor changes to a character that resembles a rotated L. To capture the default 64×64-pixel area, click a desired portion of the window. The main xmag window, shown in Figure 14.10, appears.

4. To capture an area larger or smaller than the default, hold down your middle mouse button and drag to select a larger rectangular area before releasing the button. You can also use the -source option followed by an X11 Toolkit geometry setting to specify a custom area. For example, to capture a 200×200-pixel area, use the -source option:
   ```
   # xmag -source 200x200 &
   ```

FIGURE 14.10
The xmag client captures magnified portions of your X11 desktop.

> **Handling areas larger than your desktop**
>
> Be careful! By using this option with the default magnification level 5, the resulting xmag window will cover the entire desktop of an 800×600 display, and you won't be able to use the program (press the Q key or Ctrl+C to quit). The best approach is to use the -mag and -source options to find the optimum results for your screen display—for example, -mag 2 at 200×200 works well with an 800×600 display.

5. The xmag window (refer to Figure 14.10) has five buttons: Close, Replace, New, Cut, and Paste. Click the Close button to quit the xmag client. Click the Replace button to select a new area to be displayed in the original xmag window. Click the New button to select a new area to be displayed in a new xmag window.

6. To copy the currently captured area, click the Select button.

7. To paste the graphic, move your mouse cursor to an open window of an X11 graphics program, such as xpaint or GIMP (discussed in Chapter 15), and paste the image.

8. The xmag Paste button can be used to paste a selected image from one xmag window to another. To scale an xmag image, hold down the Shift key, move your mouse to a corner of an xmag window, and drag (with your left mouse button held down) to make the xmag window smaller or larger.

chapter

15

Using Graphics and Multimedia Tools

Selecting a graphics program •

Translating or converting graphics •

Previewing graphics and
PostScript documents •

Playing music CDs •

Watching and listening to
Internet TV and radio •

Playing animations and movies
with the *xanim* client •

Selecting a Graphics Program

Linux is distributed with many different programs, and many distributions include a wealth of graphics programs for creating, editing, and converting graphics images. These programs range from simple to complex. Some programs work only on the command line for translating graphics file formats, whereas others rival commercial-quality graphics software applications.

Using the GIMP Client

One of the best and newest graphics tools for Linux is GIMP, the GNU Image Manipulation Program. This X11 client, shown in Figure 15.1, is a full-featured image-editing program with many menus, tools, and filters.

FIGURE 15.1
The GIMP image editor has features that rival commercial image-manipulation programs.

The GIMP features include

- Floating menus (which you access by right-clicking an image window)
- Graphics layers (so that effects can be superimposed)
- More than 100 plug-in filters and tools
- More than 20 editing tools
- Multiple image windows (for cutting and pasting graphics, or for multiple views of a file)
- Multiple undo levels
- Scripting language to automate image processing or to create new filters
- Six floating tool, brush, colors, and pattern windows
- Support for the importing and exporting of 24 graphics formats

GIMP requires nearly 23MB of hard drive space for its software libraries, support files, and related directories, which are installed under the /usr/share/gimp/*x.xx* directory (where *x.xx* is the current version). A library of GIMP plug-ins is installed in the /usr/lib/gimp/*x.xx*/plug-ins directory. *Plug-ins* are compiled modules, or programs, run by GIMP from different menus.

X Toolkit options and GIMP

Although you must run the X Window System to use GIMP, it does not support any X11 Toolkit options such as geometry settings.

Starting GIMP

1. First, start an X11 session. Then start GIMP from the command line of a terminal window, with the name of a graphic file:

```
# gimp rhpenguin.gif &
```

2. When you use GIMP for the first time, the program will present a dialog box such as the one shown in Figure 15.2. This dialog box contains various details, such as version number, required resources, and installation procedures. To proceed, click the Install button.

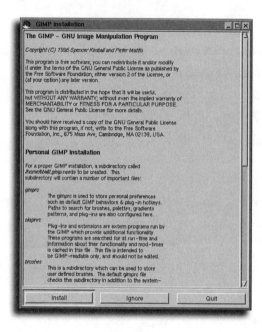

FIGURE 15.2
The first time you use the GIMP editor, it will ask whether you want to configure itself in your home directory.

3. A dialog box such as the one shown in Figure 15.3 will appear after GIMP creates its `.gimp` directory in your home directory.

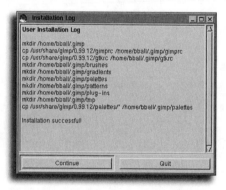

FIGURE 15.3
After installing its resources in your home directory, GIMP summarizes what it has done.

4. Click the Continue button. GIMP will load and present the graphics image you specified in step 1, as shown in Figure 15.4.

FIGURE 15.4
GIMP loads your images into a floating window, with a separate operations menu.

5. To open the Brush Selection dialog box, shown in Figure 15.5, press Shift+Ctrl+B. This dialog box boasts 115 brush patterns, 15 drawing modes, and sliding controls to change the size or opacity of the brush.

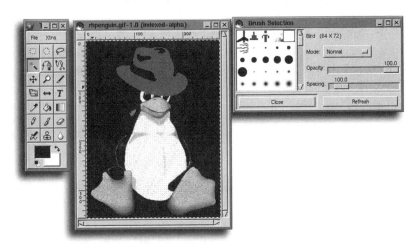

FIGURE 15.5
GIMP's brushes window offers 115 different brush patterns to use when creating or editing images.

6. Click a brush to select it. Click the Mode pop-up menu to select a drawing mode, and drag the slider controls to change the opacity or spacing of the brush pattern.

7. To view GIMP's Pattern Selection dialog box, shown in Figure 15.6, press Shift+Ctrl+P. This dialog box boasts 168 patterns that you can select for painting or filling image areas.

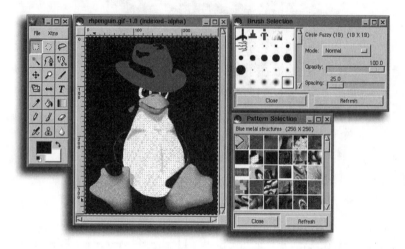

FIGURE 15.6
The GIMP Pattern Selection dialog box offers 168 patterns that you can use when editing images.

8. Click a pattern to select it, or use the scrollbar to view more patterns.

9. There are several ways to quit GIMP: Click the File menu and select Quit; press Ctrl+Q; or right-click the graphic's window and select Quit from the shortcut menu.

Use your keyboard or mouse with GIMP

GIMP's floating toolbar (refer to Figure 15.4) provides access to a number of drawing, painting, and selection tools. You can also use a number of keyboard commands, as listed in Table 15.1.

SEE ALSO
➤ *For more information about X11 Toolkit options, such as geometry settings, see page 198.*

Table 15.1 Common GIMP Keyboard Commands

Command	Description
Ctrl+K	Clear selection
Ctrl+W	Close file

Command	Description
Ctrl+C	Copy selection
Ctrl+N	Create new file
Ctrl+X	Cut selection
Ctrl+.	Fill selection
Ctrl+B	Lower layer
Ctrl+M	Merge layer
Ctrl+O	Open file
Ctrl+V	Paste Clipboard
Ctrl+Q	Quit GIMP
Ctrl+F	Raise layer
Ctrl+R	Redo last action
Ctrl+S	Save file
A	Select Airbrush tool
Ctrl+A	Select all
Shift+B	Select Bucketfill tool
Shift+E	Select Eraser tool
F	Select Free-selection tool
Z	Select Fuzzy selection tool (magic wand)
P	Select Paintbrush tool
Shift+P	Select Pencil tool
R	Select Rectangular selection tool
Shift+Ctrl+H	Sharpen selection
Shift+Ctrl+B	Show Brushes dialog box
Ctrl+G	Show Gradient editor
Ctrl+L	Show Layer Channel editor
Ctrl+P	Show Palette dialog box
Shift+Ctrl+P	Show Patterns dialog box in active window
Shift+Ctrl+T	Show Tool Options dialog box from main menu
Shift+Ctrl+T	Show guides

continues…

Table 15.1 Continued

Command	Description
Shift+Ctrl+R	Show rulers
Ctrl+Z	Undo last action
=	Zoom in
-	Zoom out

After starting GIMP, you might want to configure some of its default settings. To configure GIMP, edit the file `gimprc` in the `.gimp` directory under your home directory.

Configuring GIMP

1. The `.gimp` directory contains tool resources and settings, along with your GIMP preferences. Use the `ls` command to see the installed GIMP files:

```
# ls -l .gimp
total 15
drwxrwxr-x 2 bball bball 1024 Apr 6 13:21 brushes
-rw-r--r-- 1 bball bball 7277 Apr 6 13:21 gimprc
drwxrwxr-x 2 bball bball 1024 Apr 6 13:21 gradients
-rw-r--r-- 1 bball bball  379 Apr 6 13:21 gtkrc
drwxrwxr-x 2 bball bball 1024 Apr 6 13:21 palettes
drwxrwxr-x 2 bball bball 1024 Apr 6 13:21 patterns
drwxrwxr-x 2 bball bball 1024 Apr 6 13:21 plug-ins
drwxrwxr-x 2 bball bball 1024 Apr 6 13:21 tmp
```

Another way to set GIMP's undo levels

You can also change the number of undo levels while GIMP is running through its Preferences menu.

2. The `gimprc` file <contains settings for defaults, such as brushes, patterns, palettes, measurements, number of undo levels, and temporary directories. For example, one way to change the number of GIMP's undo levels is to use your favorite text editor, such as `pico`, and edit the `gimprc` file (disabling line-wrapping):

```
# pico -w $HOME/.gimp/gimprc
```

3. Scroll though the `gimprc` file until you come to the undo default section, which looks like this:

```
# Set the number of operations kept on the undo stack
(undo-levels 5)
```

4. Change the number following `undo-levels` to the number you want. For example, to change the number of actions you can undo to 2, edit the line to look like this:

```
# set the number of operations kept on the undo stack
(undo-levels 2)
```

5. If you don't have a lot of memory, such as 32MB, configure GIMP for `stingy-memory-use`. If you try to edit graphics as large as 640×480 pixels, GIMP will use nearly 16MB of your system memory. Scroll through the `gimprc` file until you come to the memory section, which looks like this:

```
# There is always a tradeoff between memory usage and speed. In most
# cases, the GIMP opts for speed over memory. However, if memory is
# a big issue, set stingy-memory-use
# (stingy-memory-use)
```

6. To use this feature, remove the pound (#) character in front of the memory setting like so:

```
# There is always a tradeoff between memory usage and speed. In most
# cases, the GIMP opts for speed over memory. However, if memory is
# a big issue, set stingy-memory-use
(stingy-memory-use)
```

7. If you try to edit a large graphics file such as a full-page, color TIFF document, you can also run out of disk space. GIMP creates large temporary files during editing sessions, typically three times the memory required to load an image. A little math can show you that editing a 20MB graphic can translate to a lot of used disk space. Scroll to the swap file section, which looks like this:

```
# Set the swap file location. The gimp uses a tile based memory
# allocation scheme. The swap file is used to quickly and easily
# swap files out to disk and back in. Be aware that the swap file
# can easily get very large if the gimp is used with large images.
# Also, things can get horribly slow if the swap file is created on
# a directory that is mounted over NFS. For these reasons, it may
# be desirable to put your swap file in "/tmp".
(swap-path "${gimp_dir}")
```

If your system has a second hard drive or a little-used partition, say at `/d2`, use the `mkdir` command to create a swap file directory for GIMP:

```
# mkdir /d2/tmp
```

To configure GIMP to use this new directory, change the `swap-path` from the default `${gimp_dir}` directory (`tmp` under `.gimp` in your home directory) to the path of your second drive or partition:

```
(swap-path "/d2/tmp")
```

8. Save the `gimprc` file and exit your text editor.

SEE ALSO

➤ *For more information about text editors, see page 64.*

➤ *For details about using `mkdir`, see page 43.*

GIMP's floating tool, pattern, and brush windows are convenient to use when editing an image. Access the complete GIMP menu system by right-clicking over your image; GIMP's menus will cascade.

The best sources of documentation for GIMP can be found online.

`http://www.gimp.org/docs.html`

`http://manual.gimp.org/`

For a series of tutorials to learn how to use GIMP, browse to the following Web site:

`http://abattoir.cc.ndsu.nodak.edu/~nem/gimp/tuts/`

To read a series of Frequently Asked Questions (FAQs), browse to

`http://www.rru.com/~meo/gimp`

For the latest tools, or plug-ins, go to

`http://registry.gimp.org`

SEE ALSO

➤ *For more information about using a Web browser to download files from the Internet, see page 293.*

Using ImageMagick

The ImageMagick software package is a collection of seven graphics-manipulation programs for the X Window System, although several of these programs, such as the `convert` command, can be used from the command line of the console. Table 15.2 describes each ImageMagick component.

Table 15.2 ImageMagick Program Requirements and Descriptions

Name	X11 Required	Description
`animate`	X	Display a series of graphics
`combine`		Combine, or overlay, multiple images
`convert`		Translate, or convert, graphics file formats
`display`	X	Interactive image-editing, manipulation program
`import`	X	Window capture utility

Name	X11 Required	Description
montage		Create tiled images, combine graphics files
mogrify		Convert, overwrite multiple graphics files

Using ImageMagick's *display* client

1. Use the display command within an X11 client to edit or modify graphics. First, start an X11 session. Then, from the command line of a terminal window, use the display command, followed by a graphics filename:

   ```
   # display rhpenguin.gif &
   ```

   The display command will show the ImageMagick splash screen and then load your graphic. Click the image window to view the display command's menu, as shown in Figure 15.7.

FIGURE 15.7
ImageMagick's display command for X11 uses a menu system and separate window for manipulating graphic images.

2. Another feature of the display command is a visual directory view of all specified graphics in a directory. To use a visual directory, click the ImageMagick File menu and select Visual Directory. A File dialog box will appear, as shown in Figure 15.8.

3. To create a visual directory of all files in the current directory, click the Directory button. To display only certain files—such as those with filenames beginning with the letter *m*—type a wildcard pattern in the Filename field:
   m*

FIGURE 15.8
ImageMagick's display command uses file dialog boxes to open, save, or create a visual directory.

4. Press Enter, and the display command will build a visual directory of the selected files (see Figure 15.9).

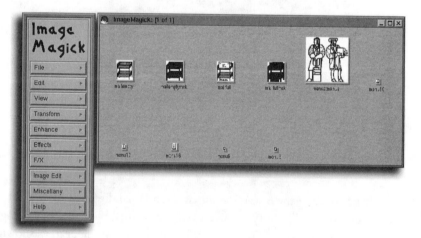

FIGURE 15.9
ImageMagick's visual directory is a convenient way to display and open graphics files.

5. To open a file from the visual directory, right-click the file's thumbnail graphic, and select Load from the shortcut menu. The display command will load the file.

6. Use `display`'s View menu to resize your image. To reverse, flip, or rotate the image, use the Transform menu. To change the brightness, contrast, or other qualities of the image, use the Enhance menu. For special effects, use the F/X menu. For example, to distort the image, click F/X on `display`'s menu and select Swirl. A dialog box such as the one shown in Figure 15.10 will appear.

FIGURE 15.10
Many of ImageMagick's special effects offer controls, such as numeric settings.

7. Enter a number, such as `60`, and click the Swirl button. ImageMagick will distort the image, as shown in Figure 15.11.

FIGURE 15.11
ImageMagick comes with a number of special effects, such as swirl, that you can apply to images.

8. To save your image, click the File menu and select the Save menu item. A Save dialog box will appear, as shown in Figure 15.12. If you click the Save button to save your image, the display program will quit.

FIGURE 15.12
ImageMagick's Save dialog box offers the choice of saving your image in a different graphics format.

9. To save your image in a different graphics format, such as JPEG, click the Format button instead of the Save button to open the Format Selection dialog box (shown in Figure 15.13).

10. Scroll through the list of formats and click JPEG to select it. Click the Select button to return to the Save dialog box. The selected extension of the graphic's type will be appended to your image's name. Click the Save button to save your image and exit the display program.

Much of the "magic" of the ImageMagick software distribution is through the convert command. Use this program from the command line to change your image with more than 70 different effects and to then save your graphic into more than 70 different file formats.

For example, to convert your sample file, originally a GIF (Graphical Interchange Format) to a JPEG (Joint Photographic Expert Group), use the convert command with the original file's name, followed by the new file's name:

```
# convert rhpenguin.gif rhpenguin.jpeg
```

FIGURE 15.13
ImageMagick can save your image in 60 different graphics formats.

The convert command automatically translates the original graphic to a new format based on the new filename's extension. To apply the swirl effect demonstrated previously, use the convert command with its -swirl option followed by the number 60. You can also convert the file at the same time:

```
# convert rhpenguin.gif -swirl 60 rhpenguin.jpeg
```

For more information about ImageMagick, see its manual page and the manual pages for its component programs (refer to Table 15.2). Use your favorite Web browser to load and read ImageMagick's hypertext documentation, found in the /usr/doc/ImageMagick directory.

Translating or Converting Graphics

Using ImageMagick's convenient and capable convert command is only one way to translate graphics. Most Linux distributions include a host of programs in the Portable Bitmap (pbm) and Portable Anymap (pnm) series. Many (but not all) of these programs can be combined with other commands to work as conversion filters in piped commands.

Table 15.3 lists many different graphics file formats, along with pertinent conversion programs you'll find for Linux. Chances are good that if you're faced with the task of converting a graphics file to a readable format, you'll find a program for Linux that will help you!

Table 15.3 Linux Graphics Formats and Conversion Programs

Extension	Format Type	Conversion Program
.10x	Gemini 10X	pbmto10x
.3d	Red/Blue 3D pixmap	ppm3d
.asc	ASCII text	pbmtoascii
.atk	Andrew Tookit raster	atktopbm pbmtoatk
.avs	AVS X image	convert
.bie	Bi-level image expert	convert
.bg	BBN BitGraph graphic	pbmtobg
.bmp	Windows, OS/2 bitmap	bmptoppm convert ppmtobmp
.bmp24	Windows 24-bit bitmap	convert
.brush	Xerox doodle brush	brushtopbm
.cgm	Computer graphics metafile	convert
.cmu	CMU window manager bitmap	cmuwmtopbm pbmtocmuwm
.dcx	ZSoft Paintbrush	convert
.ddif	DDIF image	pnmtoddif
.dib	Windows bitmap image	convert
.dxb	AutoCAD database file	ppmtoacad sldtoppm
.dvi	TeX printer file	dvips dvilj4 dvilj4l dvilj2p dvilj
.eps2	Encapsulated PostScript Level II	convert
.epsi	PostScript preview bitmap	pbmtoepsi convert
.epsf	Encapsulated PostScript	convert
.epson	Epson printer graphic	pbmtoepson
.fax	Group 3 fax	convert
.fig	TransFig image	convert
.fits	FITS file	fitstopnm pnmtofits convert

Extension	Format Type	Conversion Program
.fpx	FlashPix file	convert
.g3	Group 3 fax file	g3topbm pbmtog3
.gif	Graphics Interchange	giftopnm gif2tiff ppmtogif convert
.gif87	Graphic Interchange	convert
.go	Compressed GraphOn	pbmtogo
.gould	Gould scanner file	gouldtoppm
.icn	Sun icon	icontopbm pbmtoicon
.ilbm	IFF ILBM file	ilbmtoppm ppmtoilbm
.img	GEM image file	gemtopbm pbmtogem imgtoppm
.icr	NCSA ICR raster	ppmtoicr
.jbig	Joint Bi-level image	convert
.jpeg	JPEG	cjpeg djpeg jpegtran convert
.lj	HP LaserJet data	pbmtolj
.ln03	DEC LN03+ Sixel output	pbmtoln03
.mgr	MGR bitmap	mgrtopbm pbmtomgr
.miff	MNG multiple-image network	convert
.mitsu	Mitsubishi S340-10 file	ppmtomitsu
.mpeg	Motion Picture Group file	convert
.mtv	MTV ray tracer	mtvtoppm convert
.pbm	Portable bitmap	pbm*
.pcd	Photo CD	convert
.pcl	HP PaintJet PCL	ppmtopjxl convert
.pcx	PCX graphic (PC Paintbrush)	pcxtoppm ppmtopcx convert
.pgm	Portable graymap	pbmtopgm pgmtoppm ppmtopgm convert
.pi1	Atari Degas file	pi1toppm ppmtopi1
.pi3	Atari Degas file	pbmtopi3 pi3topbm
.pict	Macintosh PICT file	picttoppm ppmtopict convert
.pj	HP PaintJet file	pjtoppm ppmtopj
.pk	PK format font	pbmtopk pktopbm

continues...

Table 15.3   Continued

Extension	Format Type	Conversion Program
.plasma	Plasma fractal	convert
.plot	UNIX plot file	pbmtoplot
.png	Portable network graphic	pngtopnm pnmtopng convert
.pnm	Portable anymap	pnm* convert
.pnt	MacPaint file	macptopbm pbmtomacp
.ppm	Portable pixmap	ppm* convert
.ps	PostScript (lines)	pbmtolps pnmtops convert
.ptx	Printronix printer graphic	pbmtoptx
.qrt	QRT ray tracer	qrttoppm
.rad	Radiance image	convert
.ras	Sun rasterfile	pnmtorast rasttopnm
.rla	Alias/Wavefront image	convert (read only)
.rle	Utah run-length encoded	convert (read only)
.sgi	Silicon Graphics image	pnmtosgi sgitopnm convert
.sir	Solitaire graphic	pnmtosir sirtopnm
.sixel	DEC sixel format	ppmtosixel
.spc	Atari Spectrum file	spctoppm
.sun	Sun rasterfile	convert
.spu	Atari Spectrum file	sputoppm
.tga	TrueVision Targa file	ppmtotga tgatoppm convert
.tiff	Tagged file format	pnmtotiff tifftopnm ppmtotiff tiff2ps convert
.tiff24	Tagged file format (24-bit)	convert
.txt	Text file bitmap	pbmtext convert (read only)
.uil	Motif UIL icon	ppmtouil convert
.upc	Universal Product Code	pbmupc
.uyvy	16-bit YUV format	convert
.vicar		convert
.viff	Khoros Visualization image	convert

Extension	Format Type	Conversion Program
.x10bm	X10 bitmap	pbmtox10bm
.xbm	X11 bitmap	pbmtoxbm xbmtopbm convert
.xim	Xim file	ximtoppm
.xpm	X11 pixmap	ppmtoxpm xpmtoppm convert
.xv	xv thumbnail	xvminitoppm
.xvpic	xv thumbnail file	xvpictoppm
.xwd	X11 window dump	pnmtoxwd xwdtopnm convert
.ybm	Bennet Yee face file	pbmtoybm ybmtopbm
.yuv	Abekas YUV file	ppmtoyuv yuvtoppm convert
.zeiss	Zeiss confocal file	zeisstopnm
.zinc	Zinc bitmap	pbmtozinc

Using the *pbm, ppm,* and *pnm* Utilities

The Portable bitmap, pixmap, and anymap series of commands can be combined to translate and even change graphics. These commands are meant to be used from the command line of the console or an X11 terminal window but do not require you to run X. This makes them ideal for inclusion in shell scripts for large scale batch image maniuplation.

However, if you are running X11, you can take an instant screen shot of your X11 desktop from the command line of a terminal window using several of these programs. Use the xwd (X window dump) command with its -root option in a shell pipe with the xwdtopnm (X window dump to Portable anymap) command. This will capture your entire display and translate the output of the xwd client, which is the X Window dump format, to the Portable anymap format.

The output of the xwdtopnm command can then be piped through other commands, such as pnmflip, to flip the image upside down using its -tb (top-to-bottom) option. Finally, the graphic can be converted to a third format, such as TIFF, using the pnmtotiff command, which translates Portable anymap graphics to Tagged File Format. Construct the pipe like this:

```
# xwd -root | xwdtopnm | pnmflip -tb | pnmtotiff >xwd.tiff
```

SEE ALSO
➤ *For more information about using pipes with the shell, see page 24.*

Previewing Graphics and PostScript Documents

Linux distributions include a number of programs for the X Window System that you can use to preview or print a variety of graphics, such as PostScript or Portable Document Format, also known as pdf.

Using the *gv* PostScript Previewer

The gv command is a PostScript previewer for the X Window System. Use gv to read PostScript documents or to print PostScript graphics. This command is an improved version of the earlier ghostview client for X.

Using the *gv* client

1. The gv command, like many X11 clients, obeys X11 Toolkit options, such as geometry settings. To read the PostScript documentation for the xv X11 graphics client, use gv with the -geometry option, followed by a window size and the name of the document, like so:

   ```
   # gv -geometry 750x550 /usr/doc/xv-3.10a/xvdocs.ps
   ```

   The gv client will load the file. After a slight pause, the first page of the document will appear as shown in Figure 15.14, in a window 750 pixels wide by 550 pixels high.

2. To scroll the document window, click the rectangular button below the Save Marked button. The displayed page will shift inside gv's main window.

3. To move to the next page, click the Next button, which is the one with two greater-than symbols (>>). The next page of the document will be displayed.

4. To jump several pages, scroll through the list of page numbers below the Next button and click the desired page number. The gv command will then display that page. Note that the Previous button—marked with two less-than symbols (<<)—will become active as soon as you jump past the first page of a PostScript document.

5. To view your document in a different size, use gv's Scales button at the top of its main window. This button is a number, 1.000 by default. Click the button, and a menu of percentages will appear. Select a number less than 1.000 to reduce the PostScript window's size. Select a number greater than 1.000 to enlarge the displayed page. For example, selecting a value of 8.000 will enlarge the view 800 percent, as shown in Figure 15.15.

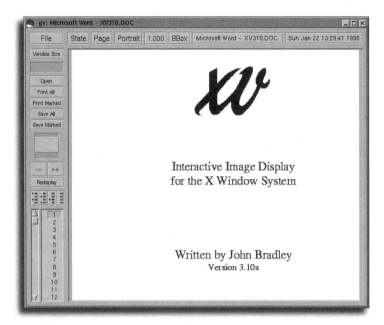

FIGURE 15.14
Use the gv program to read PostScript documents during your X Window session.

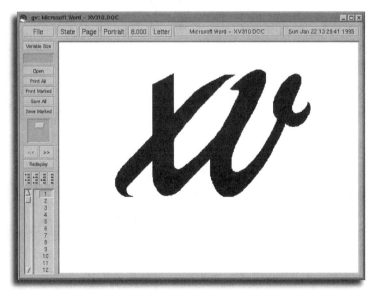

FIGURE 15.15
The gv X11 client can be used to view PostScript graphics or documents in different sizes.

Note that the Scroll button has automatically reduced in size. This is because the gv window is much smaller relative to the viewing size of the displayed graphic.

6. To print a graphic or pages of a PostScript document, pages must first be marked. Four marking buttons are located beneath the Redisplay button (which is used to redisplay draft documents). Clicking the first button marks all odd-numbered pages. Clicking the second button marks all even-numbered pages (this is a handy feature for printing double-sided documents—simply mark and print all odd pages and then reinsert the printed pages in your printer and mark and print all even pages). Clicking the third button marks the currently displayed page, whereas clicking the last button unmarks all marked pages.

7. After marking the desired pages, click the File button and select Print Document (alternatively, you can press the P key). The Print dialog box, shown in Figure 15.16, will appear.

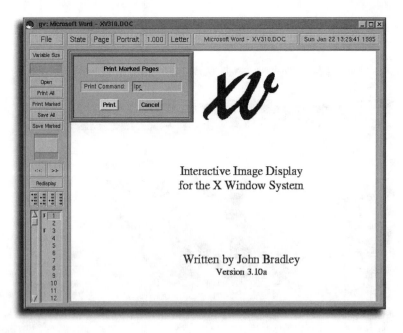

FIGURE 15.16
To print from the gv client, specify a print command in its print dialog box.

8. To use the default printer, click the Print button. To use a different printer, use the `lpr` command's `-P` option followed by a printer's name (as found in the `/etc/printcap` database):

```
lpr -Pmycolorprinter
```

9. To exit the `gv` client, select Quit from the File menu, or press the Q key.

SEE ALSO

➤ *For more details about printing documents or graphics, see page 87.*

➤ *For more information about using geometry settings with X11 clients, see page 198.*

For more details about using `gv`, see its manual page or browse its hypertext documentation under the `/usr/doc/gv` directory. For example, to use the Lynx Web browser, use a command such as this:

```
# lynx /usr/doc/gv-3.5.8/gv.html
```

Using Adobe Acrobat

The Adobe Acrobat Reader, from Adobe Systems, Inc., is an X11 client that you can use to read Portable Document Format (PDF) files. To obtain the latest copy for Linux, browse to this address:

```
http://www.adobe.com/prodindex/acrobat/readstep.html
```

If you'd rather retrieve the file using the `ftp` command, try the following:

```
ftp.adobe.com/pub/adobe/acrobatreader/unix/3.x/acroread_linux_301.tar.gz
```

After downloading the compressed Acrobat archive, use the `tar` command with the `xvzf` option to decompress and unarchive the file:

```
# tar xvzf acroread_linux-ar-40.tar.gz
```

Follow the instructions in the file INSTGUID.TXT to install Acrobat. After you install the `Acrobat4` directory under `/usr/local`, `/usr/local` will contain more than 12MB of the Acrobat software. The Acrobat application is named `acroread` and is found under the `/usr/local/Acrobat4/bin` directory. To create a symbolic link to a known directory, log in as the root operator and use the `ln` command:

```
# /usr/local/Acrobat4/bin/acroread /usr/local/bin/acroread
```

To read a PDF file, use the `acroread` command from the command line of a terminal window, followed by the name of a file (in this case its user manual), like so:

```
# /usr/local/Acrobat4/bin/acroread /usr/local/Acrobat4/Reader/Acrobat.pdf
```

The Acrobat reader will start and display its main window with the first page of the document, as shown in Figure 15.17. Acrobat can also be configured as a helper application for use by the Netscape Web browser.

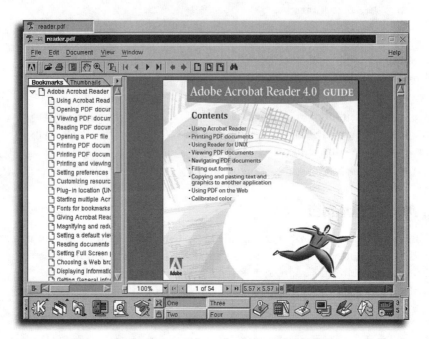

FIGURE 15.17
The Adobe Acrobat reader for Linux displays Portable Document Format (PDF) files in an X11 window.

Installing Acrobat as a Netscape helper application

1. Start the Netscape browser from the command line of a terminal window:
   ```
   # netscape &
   ```

2. Select the Preferences menu item from Netscape's Edit menu.

3. Click the triangle next to the Navigator Category item in the Preferences dialog box.

4. Two new items, Languages and Applications, will appear below the Netscape item. Click Applications to open the Applications preferences dialog box, shown in Figure 15.18.

5. Click the New button, found beneath the Applications list in the dialog box. A blank dialog box will appear, as shown in Figure 15.19.

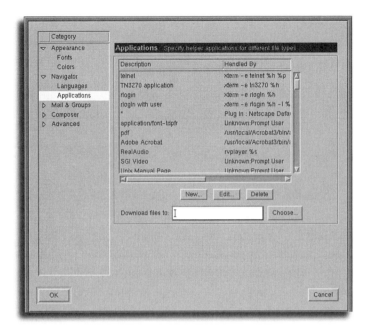

FIGURE 15.18
Netscape's Applications preferences dialog box is used to configure Netscape to start external applications when encountering foreign documents.

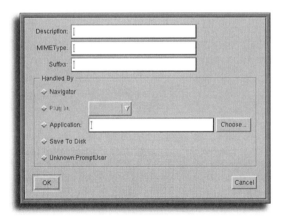

FIGURE 15.19
Configure external applications for Netscape, such as Adobe Acrobat, by entering a description, type, suffix, and pathname to the program.

6. In the Description field, enter the following:
```
Adobe Acrobat
```

In the MIMEType field, enter the following:
```
application/pdf
```

In the Suffixs field, enter the following:
```
pdf
```

7. Click the Application field and type the pathname to the Acrobat reader:
```
/usr/local/Acrobat3/bin/acroread
```

8. Click the check box to the left of the Application field and then click the OK button.

9. Click the Applications preferences dialog box's OK button to save your preferences. Netscape will now use Acrobat if it encounters PDF files when browsing the Internet; Netscape can even be used to open a PDF file, like so:
```
# netscape myfile.pdf
```

For more information about Adobe Acrobat, select the Reader Online Guide from Acrobat's Help menu.

Playing Music CDs

To play music CDs while working with Linux, your system's kernel must be configured to use your sound card. Sound support must either be installed in your kernel or available as a loadable module.

Singing the sound card configuration blues?

Having a hard time configuring your system for sound? If you don't want to waste the time and effort by recompiling your Linux kernel, or if Red Hat's `sndconfig` program does not work for you, take heart. A much easier way to configure Linux for sound is to use the Open Sound System from 4Front Technologies. The OSS software package is easy to install and use, and could solve your sound-configuration problems. The software uses self-configuring, loadable kernel modules, and contains support for many types of sound cards not found in Linux distributions. For more information, browse to `http://www.4front-tech.com`

If your sound card works with Linux and you have a CD-ROM drive, you should be able to play music CDs. Most Linux distributions come with music CD programs for the console and X11. To play a CD from the command line of the console or a terminal window, use the `cdp` command.

SEE ALSO

➤ *To learn how to configure Linux to use your sound card, see page 532.*

Playing music using *cdp*

1. Log in as the root operator. Make sure that there is a device named cdrom under the /dev directory by using the ls command:
   ```
   # ls -l /dev/cdrom
   lrwxrwxrwx 1 root root 3 Mar 9 07:55 /dev/cdrom -> hdc
   ```

2. If the /dev/cdrom device is not found, use the ln command to create a symbolic link from your CD-ROM's device to /dev/cdrom:
   ```
   # ln -s /dev/XXX /dev/cdrom
   ```

   where XXX is the name of your CD-ROM drive, such as hdb, hdc, and so on.

3. Make sure that the /dev/cdrom device is publicly readable by using the chmod command:
   ```
   # chmod 666 /dev/cdrom
   ```

4. Insert a music CD into your CD-ROM drive.

5. Start the cdp command from the command line:
   ```
   # cdp
   ```

6. Before pressing the Enter key, activate the Num Lock feature by pressing the Num Lock key on your keyboard. The cdp command will start and display a list of the tracks on your CD, as shown in Figure 15.20.

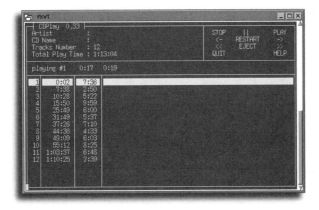

FIGURE 15.20
The cdp music CD player displays a list of your CD's tracks when playing music.

SEE ALSO

➤ *To learn more about creating and using symbolic links, see page 46.*

7. Use the keypad controls, listed in Table 15.4, to control the `cdp` player (you can also use the regular numbers on your keyboard).

Table 15.4 Keypad Controls for the *cpd* Command

Control	Keypad Key
Back 15 seconds	1
Eject CD from drive	2
Exit, but continue music	0 or Q
Forward 15 seconds	3
Help	.
Next track	6
Play	9
Previous track	4
Replay CD	5
Stop	7
Toggle pause/resume	8

The `cdp` command's companion program, a symbolic link called `cdplay`, can be used to play music without an interactive screen. For example, to start playing a music CD at track number four, use `cdplay` followed by the `play` option and a track number:

```
# cdplay play 4
```

Use the `xplaycd` client to play music CDs during your X11 session. Start `xplaycd` from the command line of a terminal window:

```
# xplaycd &
```

The `xplaycd` client will display a small window with CD controls, horizontal stereo volume bars, and a list of buttons representing the tracks on the CD, as shown in Figure 15.21.

You can also rearrange the order of tracks to be played from the music CD. Click a track number to select it, and drag the number to the front or back of the list of track numbers. To play the same track several times, select a track number with your middle mouse button (hold down the left and right mouse buttons if using a two-button mouse), and drag the track along the CD track sequence. When you release your mouse button(s), the track number will be duplicated.

FIGURE 15.21
The X11 xplaycd client features CD controls and music track resequencing.

The xplaycd also supports a music CD database to create play lists of tracks for your favorite CDs. Read the xplaycd manual page for more details about creating its CD database.

Watching and Listening to Internet TV and Radio

One of the most exciting aspects of getting connected to the Internet is that you can listen or watch live radio and TV broadcasts. The program of choice for this is RealNetwork's RealPlayer 5.0 for Linux, shown in Figure 15.22. To get a copy of rvplayer for your system, browse to:

http://www.real.com

FIGURE 15.22
RealNetwork's Internet video client, rvplayer, plays live radio or TV broadcasts during your Internet and X11 sessions.

To configure the Netscape Web browser to use the `rvplayer` client, see the section titled "Using the Netscape Browser" in Chapter 19, "Using Web Browsers."

Using RealPlayer

The `rvplayer` X11 client is usually used as a Netscape Communicator plug-in or external program that adds features to the browser. After you properly configure Netscape, the `rvplayer` will automatically play audio or video when you click an audio or video link on a Web page.

You can also use `rvplayer` to play video clips downloaded from remote computers. These video clips must be in RealVideo format and usually have `.rm` as a filename extension. For example, to play a clip of one of the infamous dancing baby animations, start an X11 session and use the `rvplayer` client from the command line of a terminal window, like so:

```
# rvplayer bluesuede.baby &
```

The `rvplayer` program loads the video clip and starts playing, as shown in Figure 15.23.

FIGURE 15.23
Not only will RealNetwork's rvplayer load and play video clips without an Internet connection, it can also make a baby dance!

> **SEE ALSO**
> ➤ *For more information about starting the X Window System, see page 171.*
> ➤ *For details about configuring Netscape Communicator to use* rvplayer, *see page 300.*

After downloading and installing `rvplayer`, look under the `/usr/doc/rvplayer` directory for information about how to use the RealVideo Player.

> **Picture this: more colors!**
>
> The `rvplayer` client requires an 8-bit, or 256-color, display. When you use X, other applications can use many of the available colors needed to provide good-looking video. If your computer's graphics chip and X11 configuration support X sessions with more than 256 colors, `rvplayer`'s video display will look much better. Start your X session at a greater color depth by using the `startx` command's `-bpp` (bits-per-pixel) option, followed by a color depth. For example, to start an X11 session using 16 bpp, use `startx` from the console command line like so:
>
> `# startx -- -bpp 16`
>
> For details about how to use your X11 server and computer graphics card, see the various **READMEs** under the `/usr/X11R6/lib/X11/doc` directory, the `startx` manual page, or the documentation for your distribution of X11. For XFree86 users, different color depths are supported in your X11 configuration file, `XF86Config` (found under the `/etc` directory).

Playing Animations and Movies with the *xanim* Client

Another X11 client you can use to play sound or video clips is the `xanim` program. The `xanim` client will play a variety of audio and video clips in different formats. Some of the formats supported by this program are listed in Table 15.5.

Table 15.5 Audio and Video Clips Supported by *xanim*

Type	Description
AU	Audio track of animation
AVI	Windows animations (not all types supported)
DL	Animation
FLC	Animation
FLI	Animation
GIF	Single, multiple images
IFF	Animation
JFIF	Single images
MOV	QuickTime animations (not all supported)
MPEG	Animation (not all supported)
MovieSetter	Amiga animation

continues...

Table 15.5 Continued	
Type	Description
PFX	Amiga PageFlipper Plus
RLE	Utah Raster Toolkit animations, images
WAV	Audio track of animation

By default, xanim does not play audio tracks of specified video clips. To configure xanim to use sound and display video, use its +Ae (audio-enable) command-line option and the name of the video clip, like so:

```
# xanim +Ae blownaway.avi &
```

This will run xanim, as shown in Figure 15.24, with a floating controls window and a video window. The xanim controls allow you to stop, start, set the volume, or play the video clip frame by frame. For more information, see the xanim manual page.

FIGURE 15.24
Oh no! Another dancing baby, courtesy of the xanim X11 video player client.

part

IV

CONNECTING TO YOUR
INTERNET SERVICE PROVIDER

Connecting to Your Internet
Service Provider   249   **16**

Using Electronic Mail   265   **17**

Using FTP   283   **18**

Using Web Browsers   295   **19**

Using telnet, Internet Relay Chat,
and AOL's Instant Messenger   309   **20**

# chapter 16

Connecting to Your Internet Service Provider

Configuring a PPP connection •

Configuring PPP for your ISP •

Configuring your PPP connection scripts •

Configuring PPP with kppp •

Starting a PPP connection •

Checking your PPP connection •

Configuring a PPP Connection

Connecting to the Internet using Linux is easy. The method by which you connect to your Internet service provider (ISP) via a modem is called the Point-to-Point Protocol, or PPP. If you follow the steps outlined in this chapter, you'll be able to quickly connect to and disconnect from the Internet through your ISP. After you are connected, you can send and retrieve email, download files, read Usenet news, or use a Web browser to surf World Wide Web sites.

SEE ALSO

➤ *To learn more about email, see Chapter 17, "Using Electronic Mail."*

➤ *To learn more about Web browsers, see Chapter 19, "Using Web Browsers."*

In this chapter, you find the basic steps for checking your hardware, configuring your software, and connecting to your ISP. You'll also learn about commands that you can use to check your connection. You'll need the basic hardware required for modem connections, several standard Linux programs, and some technical information from your ISP in order to begin. These hardware and software items include the following:

- A working serial port and attached modem. Internal modems include their own serial port.

- A Linux kernel supporting the PPP and TCP/IP protocols. Most Linux distributions should provide this.

- The PPP software package, which includes the pppd daemon, the chat dialer program, associated scripts, and the pppstats command. This might be an installation option for your Linux distribution, labeled as Dialup Workstation or PPP.

- The minicom communications program (optional)

- An active account with an ISP supporting PPP. Nearly all ISPs use PPP.

Setting up PPP and then connecting to your ISP involves several steps, including the following:

1. Check your serial port and modem.
2. Check your kernel for PPP and TCP/IP support.
3. Edit and customize the PPP connection scripts.
4. Edit or create required system configuration files.
5. Dial out and establish a PPP connection.

6. Check the connection.

7. Disconnect and shut down the PPP connection.

Checking Your Serial Port and Modem

To check your serial port and modem, you need a phone line, modem, and modem cable (if you have an external modem). If you know your modem works under Linux, you can skip to the next section, "Checking Your Linux Kernel and File System for PPP Support."

Checking the modem connection

1. Make sure your phone line is attached to your modem and that your modem is connected to your computer. If your modem is internal, make sure that the phone line is connected to your computer's internal modem.

2. Pipe the output of the `dmesg` command through the `less` pager to determine whether your serial port is enabled and working:

```
# dmesg | less
```

3. Look for lines detailing serial driver information similar to these:

```
Serial driver version 4.27 with no serial options enabled
tty00 at 0x03f8 (irq = 4) is a 16550A
tty03 at 0x02e8 (irq = 3) is a 16550A
```

4. If you don't find serial support, refer to Chapter 11, "Configuring a Modem and Fax Service," for details about configuring your modem. If you have defined a symbolic link called `/dev/modem` that points to your modem's serial port, test the modem and phone-line connection by using the `echo` command like this:

```
# echo "ATDT\n" >/dev/modem
```

You should hear a dial tone after a few seconds. If not, reread Chapter 11 to find out how to create the `/dev/modem` symbolic link.

SEE ALSO

➤ *To learn more about pipes, see page 26.*

➤ *For more details about installing and configuring a modem, see page 154.*

Checking Your Linux Kernel and File System for PPP Support

Your Linux kernel must support PPP in order to connect to your ISP. Support can be compiled into your kernel or loaded as a code module. The PPP module, `ppp.o`, is found under the `/lib/module/2.x.xx/net` directory (where `2.x.xx` is your kernel's version).

Checking for PPP support

1. Use the output of the `dmesg` command, piped through the `less` pager, to determine whether PPP support is enabled for your kernel:

```
# dmesg | less
```

2. Look for lines detailing TCP/IP and PPP support similar to these:

```
Swansea University Computer Society TCP/IP for NET3.034
IP Protocols: IGMP, ICMP, UDP, TCP
PPP: version 2.2.0 (dynamic channel allocation)
PPP Dynamic channel allocation code copyright 1995 Caldera, Inc.
PPP line discipline registered.
```

3. If you do not see this support enabled, you must enable the TCP/IP and PPP networking support. This means that you must either ensure that the required modules or network services are enabled or rebuild the kernel with built-in support. See Chapter 26, "Managing Network Connections," and the section titled "Recompiling the Kernel" in Chapter 31, "Managing the Kernel," for details.

SEE ALSO

➤ *To learn more about the* `less` *pager, see page 41.*

➤ *To learn more about kernel modules, see page 535.*

➤ *For more details about installing networking support, see page 406.*

You also must ensure that the required PPP connection software and directories are installed on your system.

Checking for PPP software

1. Ensure that the `pppd` daemon, the `chat` dialing command, and the PPP connection scripts are installed by using the `ls` (list directory) command:

```
# ls /usr/sbin/pppd
/usr/sbin/pppd
# ls /usr/sbin/chat
/usr/sbin/chat
# ls /etc/ppp
chap-secrets     options      ppp-on-dialer
connect-errors   pap-secrets  ppp-on
ip-up     ppp-off
```

2. If you don't find these programs and scripts on your system or on your CD-ROM, you must find and download the PPP software.

3. After downloading, if you are using a distribution that uses the Red Hat package manager, install PPP using `rpm` (substitute for the version of PPP you are installing):

```
# rpm -i ppp-2.2.0f-5.i386.rpm
```

4. If the PPP scripts `ppp-on`, `ppp-on-dialer`, and `ppp-off` are not found in the
`/etc/ppp` directory after installation, copy them from the `/usr/doc/`
`ppp-2.2.0f-5/scripts` directory by issuing the following command (substitute for
the version of PPP you installed):

```
# cp /usr/doc/ppp-2.2.0f-5/script/* /etc/ppp
```

SEE ALSO

➤ *To learn more about Linux software package management, see page 482.*

➤ *To learn more about shell scripts, see Chapter 21. "Basic Shell Programming."*

Configuring PPP for Your ISP

You must have a PPP account with an Internet service provider to connect to the
Internet. At a minimum, you'll need the following information about your account:

- The username and password.

- The phone number for your ISP's modem.

- The Internet Protocol (IP) addresses of your ISP's domain name servers, and the
  ISP's domain name. The addresses will look something like `205.198.114.1` or
  `205.198.114.20`, and the domain name might be the name of the ISP with `.com`,
  `.org`, or `.edu` appended.

After you have this information, the next step is to create or edit the resolver configuration file, `/etc/resolv.conf`. This file contains the DNS addresses used by email,
newsreaders, or Web browsers to look up valid Internet addresses. The DNS
addresses are the Internet addresses of your ISP's computer running the domain
name system, which translates a text address, such as `staffnet.com`, to its numerical
address (in this case, `207.226.80.14`).

Creating */etc/resolv.conf*

1. Make sure you're logged on as the root operator. Using your favorite text editor,
   create or edit the file `/etc/resolv.conf`:

```
# touch /etc/resolv.conf
# pico /etc/resolv.conf
```

2. Add the search path for DNS searches by entering the resolver keyword search,
   followed by your ISP's domain name:

```
search myisp.com
```

3. Add the IP addresses of the DNS server or servers, preceding each address with the `nameserver` keyword:

```
nameserver 205.198.114.1
nameserver 205.198.114.20
```

4. Save and close the file.

SEE ALSO

➤ *For details about domain name service, see page 413.*

Configuring Your PPP Connection Scripts

In order to dial out and connect with your ISP, you must configure the PPP connection script `ppp-on`, found under the `/etc/ppp` directory. This script contains all the necessary information needed to connect to your ISP. When started, `ppp-on` uses the `/etc/ppp/ppp-on-dialer` script to make the call. Use your account information from your ISP, and enter the correct username, phone number, password, and addresses to make the `ppp-on` script work correctly.

Editing the *ppp-on* Connection Script

Standard Linux installations include a command-line script called `ppp-on` that allows dialup connections to most ISPs. The script makes a connection by controlling your modem, dialing into the ISP, and connecting via the standard PPP protocol. When it's connected, your computer can access the Internet through the connection at the ISP. Before using the script, however, you must edit it to reflect your configuration.

Customizing the *ppp-on* script

1. Make sure you're logged in as the root operator.

2. Using your favorite text editor, open the `ppp-on` file in the `/etc/ppp` directory.

3. Enter the phone number for your ISP's modem in the TELEPHONE field:

```
TELEPHONE=555-1212 # The telephone number for the connection
```

4. Enter your username in the ACCOUNT field (where `myusername` is the username assigned by your ISP):

```
ACCOUNT=myusername   # The account name for logon
```

5. Enter your password in the PASSWORD field (where `mypassword` is your password):

```
PASSWORD=mypassword  # your assigned password
```

6. If your ISP has assigned you an IP address, enter it in the LOCAL field. If your IP address is assigned dynamically when you log in, enter the address as follows:

```
LOCAL_IP=0.0.0.0   # Local IP address
```

7. If you've created a symbolic link for your modem's serial port, use /dev/modem followed by the highest speed supported by your modem in the pppd command line (if you do not have a dynamically assigned IP number, see the sidenote "Dynamic addresses and the pppd daemon"):

```
exec /usr/sbin/pppd lock modem crtscts /dev/modem 57600\
     asyncmap 20A0000 escape FF $LOCAL_IP:$REMOTE_IP \
        noipdefault netmask $NETMASK defaultroute           connect \
           $DIALER_SCRIPT &
```

8. Make both the ppp-on and ppp-on-dialer scripts executable by using the chmod program and its +x command-line option:

```
# chmod +x /etc/ppp/ppp-on*
```

SEE ALSO

➤ *For more information about changing file permissions, see page 378.*

Configuring PPP with *kppp*

KDE comes with a graphical PPP client program called kppp that allows for easy setup and management of your dialup accounts. To start kppp from KDE, select Internet/kppp from the graphical menu, or from the command line:

```
#kppp
```

You will be presented with the main kppp screen (see Figure 16.1).

FIGURE 16.1
kppp is the KDE graphical PPP client that simplifies dialup connections.

Setting up a new dialup account

1. Select the Setup button.

2. Create a new PPP dialup account by clicking New. You will be presented with a new account screen as shown in Figure 16.2.

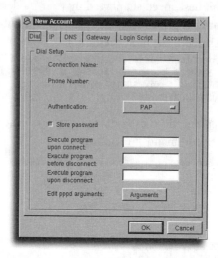

FIGURE 16.2
kppp allows you to configure many dialup accounts.

3. Select the Dial tab.

4. Descriptively name your connection under Connection Name.

5. Fill out the phone number field for your local ISP dialup number. Don't forget to include any additional phone or dial codes you might need for your local phone service.

6. For most dialup connections, the Authentication field should be set to PAP. This is the same authentication scheme that Windows clients use.

7. Select the IP tab. If your ISP has assigned you a static IP address, fill it in here. Otherwise, select Dynamic IP Address.

8. Select the DNS tab.

9. Fill out DNS IP Address with the appropriate information provided by your ISP. Click Add for each IP address entered.

10. Click OK to save this configuration.

The default kppp setup options should work for most users. If you experience problems, you might need to adjust the device settings from the kppp setup screen.

Dynamic addresses and the pppd daemon

If you have a permanently assigned IP address (also called a *static IP address*), remove the `noip_default` option from the `pppd` command line in the `ppp-on` script (see step 7 of "Customizing the `ppp-on` script") and change the `$REMOTE_IP` string to the IP address provided by your ISP. If your ISP uses dynamic addressing, you don't have to make this change; your IP address will be different every time you log in.

Starting a PPP Connection

There are many ways to start a phone-line PPP connection. In this section, you learn how to start your Internet session using the `minicom` communications program, the `ppp-on` script, or `kppp`.

Starting a PPP Connection Using the *minicom* Program

The `minicom` communications program, found under the `/usr/bin` directory, can establish a PPP connection with your ISP. Although using this approach is not as convenient as using the `ppp-on` script, it is a good method to verify that your username, password, and PPP connection work with your ISP.

This approach works because you can quit `minicom` without hanging up and resetting your modem (not always a good idea, especially if making long-distance connections).

Connecting to the Internet with the *minicom* command

1. Log in as the root operator; make sure your modem is plugged in and turned on.

2. Run the `minicom` program from the command line, like this:
   ```
   # minicom
   ```

3. Use the modem `ATDT` command followed by your ISP's modem number, and then press Enter to dial out:
   ```
   ATDT555-1212
   ```

4. Wait for the connection. Your ISP's computer should present a login prompt. Enter your username and your password.

5. Press Ctrl+Q to exit `minicom` without hanging up and resetting your modem.

6. Start your PPP connection from the command line, using the `pppd` daemon on the command line, and type the following:
   ```
   # pppd -d detach /dev/modem &
   ```

7. Test your connection by using the `ifconfig` command (see the later section "Checking Your PPP Connection").

Starting a PPP Connection with the *ppp-on* Script

After you've verified that your PPP connection works, you can use the `ppp-on` script to start your Internet sessions. Using this script is a lot easier than using the `minicom` program.

Starting Internet sessions by using the *ppp-on* script

1. Make sure you're logged in as the root operator.

2. Either copy the `ppp-on` script to a recognized program directory, such as `/usr/local/bin`, or create a symbolic link in a recognized directory, like this:

```
# ln -s /etc/ppp/ppp-on /usr/local/bin/ppp-on
```

3. To let all users of your system start PPP connections, use the `chmod` command to change the execute permissions of the `ppp-on` script:

```
# chmod 4711 /etc/ppp/ppp-on
```

4. Start a PPP connection using the script:

```
# ppp-on
```

5. After a few seconds, you should hear your modem dial out and then connect with your ISP's modem. After several seconds, test or close the connection.

Starting a PPP Connection with *kppp*

kppp provides one of the easiest ways to initiate a PPP connection in Linux. To connect to your ISP, start kppp as you did for the initial setup, or if you have not closed kppp, return to the main kppp dialog box (refer to Figure 16.1).

The connection you just configured should be shown in the Connect To field. Fill out your ISP-supplied login ID and password in the appropriate fields and select Connect to initiate the connection.

Closing Your PPP Connection

If you initiated your connection with the ppp-on script, use the `ppp-off` script, found under the `/etc/ppp` directory, to stop your PPP connection:

```
# /etc/ppp/ppp-off
```

Unlike the `ppp-on` script, the `ppp-off` script must be run by the root operator. This is not a problem unless your system's users must dial long distance to make a connection; most ISPs configure their systems to hang up after a set period of inactivity.

If you used a graphical tool to connect, use the same tool to disconnect from your ISP. `kppp` will display a Disconnect option. `netcfg` requires that you deactivate the PPP interface.

Checking Your PPP Connection

Most Linux distributions come with a number of commands that you can use to check your PPP connection. Many of these commands are network utilities. You can also look at system logs to diagnose or troubleshoot a bothersome connection.

Checking PPP Connections with the *ifconfig* Command

Although usually used by network administrators to configure network interfaces, the `ifconfig` command, found under the `/sbin` directory, can be used to gather a report on the status of your PPP connection. The `ifconfig` command lists information about active network interfaces. The first PPP connection started on your system is represented by the `ppp0` device. To see the status of your PPP connection, start a PPP session and use the `ifconfig` command with the `ppp0` device command-line option:

```
# ifconfig ppp0
ppp0      Link encap:Point-to-Point Protocol
          inet addr:207.226.80.155  P-t-P:207.226.80.214
Mask:255.255.255.0
          UP POINTOPOINT RUNNING  MTU:1500  Metric:1
          RX packets:109 errors:0 dropped:0 overruns:0
          TX packets:117 errors:0 dropped:0 overruns:0
```

Along with IP address of your computer and the connected computer, using the `ifconfig` command shows the number of characters received (RX) and transmitted (TX) over your PPP interface. See the `ifconfig` manual pages for more details.

SEE ALSO

➤ *For more details about configuring network services, see page 406.*

Getting PPP Statistics with the *pppstats* Command

Use the pppstats command, found under the /usr/sbin/ directory, to print short reports about the statistics (such as incoming and outgoing data) of a specified PPP device connection (such as ppp0, as returned by the ifconfig command). To use the pppstats command, specify the unit number of the PPP interface on the command line, like this:

```
# pppstats 0
      in    pack   comp uncomp    err  |    out   pack   comp   uncomp  ip
  285567    281    143     91      0  |   9472    282    126      111  45
```

The pppstats command displays a line of information every five seconds while your connection is active. This information includes the number of 512-byte packets received and sent, along with some technical packet-compression information. The pppstats program is most useful to at least verify your PPP connection. Change the update rate by setting the -i (interval) command-line option to the desired number of seconds between report updates. See the pppstats manual page for more information.

Getting PPP Statistics with *kpppload*

KDE includes an application to monitor the status of your PPP connection called kpppload (see Figure 16.3). It displays information about the amount of network traffic through your connection. kpppload will also indicate if there is not an active PPP link, providing an easy way to check link integrity.

FIGURE 16.3
kpppload can be used to diagnose connection problems. There is a problem with the connection on this machine, as kpppload reports that it cannot find the ppp link.

Testing PPP Connection Speed with the *ping* Command

Use the ping command to verify an Internet hostname or address and to test response times of your host servers. This command sends small test packets of data to the specified computer, and then measures the time it takes for the computer to send back the information. Use the ping command, followed by a host computer's name or address, as follows:

```
# ping www.mcp.com
PING www.mcp.com (198.70.146.70): 56 data bytes
64 bytes from 207.226.80.14: icmp_seq=0 ttl=254 time=4296.3 ms
64 bytes from 207.226.80.14: icmp_seq=1 ttl=254 time=3900.0 ms
64 bytes from 207.226.80.14: icmp_seq=2 ttl=254 time=2940.0 ms


--- staffnet.com ping statistics ---
6 packets transmitted, 3 packets received, 50% packet loss
round-trip min/avg/max = 2940.0/3712.1/4296.3 ms
```

The ping command will continuously send and receive information until you tell it
to quit by pressing Ctrl+C.

Getting PPP Interface Information with the *route* Command

Use the route command, found under the /sbin directory, to get additional information about your active PPP interface. Although the route command is usually used as
a network-administration tool to set up or delete networking routes for interfaces,
route's report, especially the Flags column, can be useful in showing your PPP interface status. Use the route command as shown in Figure 16.4.

```
# route
Kernel IP routing table
Destination     Gateway           Genmaks          Flags Metric Ref    Use Iface
pm0.staffnet.co *                 255.255.255.255  UH    0      0      0   pppo
127.0.0.0       *                 255.0.0.0        U     0      0      2   lo
default         pm0.staffnet.co   0.0.0.0          UG    0      0      2   ppp0
```

FIGURE 16.4
The route report shows detailed technical information about your network connection. It can be useful when debugging connections.

In this report, the U flag shows that the interface is up (running). See the route command's manual page for more information.

Troubleshooting PPP Connections with Your System Log

Use your Linux system's logs to troubleshoot problems in establishing a PPP connection. Some of these problems include the following:

- PPP kernel services not available
- pppd kernel not loading
- Modem not dialing out
- Abrupt disconnects from your ISP

- Problems logging in to your ISP
- Unrecognized Internet addresses or hostnames

To see what's going on in detail when you start a PPP connection, read the file called messages found under the /var/log directory. Make sure you're logged in as the root operator, and then pipe the contents of the messages file through the less pager:

```
# less /var/log/messages
```

The output, shown in Listing 16.1, shows the details of starting a PPP connection, including PPP code module loading, dialing out with the chat command (started by the ppp-on script), connecting, logging in, and assigning a dynamic IP address for your computer after login.

Listing 16.1 PPP Connection Details in */var/log/messages*

```
Feb 24 09:26:15 localhost kernel:
PPP: version 2.2.0 (dynamic channel allocation)
Feb 24 09:26:15 localhost kernel:
PPP Dynamic channel allocation code copyright 1995 Caldera, Inc.
Feb 24 09:26:15 localhost kernel: PPP line discipline registered.
Feb 24 09:26:15 localhost kernel: registered device ppp0
Feb 24 09:26:15 localhost pppd[5147]: pppd 2.2.0 started by bball, uid 500
Feb 24 09:26:16 localhost chat[5148]: timeout set to 3 seconds
Feb 24 09:26:16 localhost chat[5148]: abort on (\nBUSY\r)
Feb 24 09:26:16 localhost chat[5148]: abort on (\nNO ANSWER\r)
Feb 24 09:26:16 localhost chat[5148]: abort on (\nRINGING\r\n\r\nRINGING\r)
Feb 24 09:26:16 localhost chat[5148]: send (rAT^M)
Feb 24 09:26:16 localhost chat[5148]: expect (OK)
Feb 24 09:26:16 localhost chat[5148]: rAT^M^M
Feb 24 09:26:16 localhost chat[5148]: OK -- got it
Feb 24 09:26:16 localhost chat[5148]: send (ATH0^M)
Feb 24 09:26:16 localhost chat[5148]: timeout set to 30 seconds
Feb 24 09:26:16 localhost chat[5148]: expect (OK)
Feb 24 09:26:16 localhost chat[5148]: ^M
Feb 24 09:26:16 localhost chat[5148]: ATH0^M^M
Feb 24 09:26:16 localhost chat[5148]: OK -- got it
Feb 24 09:26:16 localhost chat[5148]: send (ATDT102881540555-1212^M)
Feb 24 09:26:17 localhost chat[5148]: expect (CONNECT)
Feb 24 09:26:17 localhost chat[5148]: ^M
Feb 24 09:26:37 localhost chat[5148]: ATDT102881540555-1212^M^M
Feb 24 09:26:37 localhost chat[5148]: CONNECT -- got it
```

```
Feb 24 09:26:37 localhost chat[5148]: send (^M)
Feb 24 09:26:37 localhost chat[5148]: expect (ogin:)
Feb 24 09:26:37 localhost chat[5148]:  57600^M
Feb 24 09:26:45 localhost chat[5148]: ^M
Feb 24 09:26:45 localhost chat[5148]: ^M
Feb 24 09:26:45 localhost chat[5148]: Staffnet PM0 login: -- got it
Feb 24 09:26:45 localhost chat[5148]: send (bball^M)
Feb 24 09:26:46 localhost chat[5148]: expect (assword:)
Feb 24 09:26:46 localhost chat[5148]: bball^M
Feb 24 09:26:46 localhost chat[5148]: Password: -- got it
Feb 24 09:26:46 localhost chat[5148]: send (mypasswd^M)
Feb 24 09:26:46 localhost pppd[5147]: Serial connection established.
Feb 24 09:26:47 localhost pppd[5147]: Using interface ppp0
Feb 24 09:26:47 localhost pppd[5147]: Connect: ppp0 <--> /dev/modem
Feb 24 09:26:49 localhost pppd[5147]: local  IP address 207.226.80.155
Feb 24 09:26:49 localhost pppd[5147]: remote IP address 207.226.80.214
```

Examine your log for modem or login errors. Common problems include use of the incorrect phone number, username, or password.

Troubleshooting PPP connections

Still having trouble making a connection? Read Robert Hart's PPP-HOWTO, along with Al Longyear's PPP-FAQ (he's the author of the **ppp-on** and **ppp-on-dialer** scripts). These documents, found under the **/usr/doc** directory, contain loads of valuable tips about setting up and troubleshooting PPP connections and discuss other issues, such as security.

chapter
17

Using Electronic Mail

Retrieving electronic mail •

Selecting a mail program •

Managing electronic mail •

Retrieving Electronic Mail

Configuring Linux for sending and retrieving electronic mail can be a complex task but, fortunately, most Linux distributions automatically configure and set up the main email software and directory components during installation. In simple terms, the two types of programs involved in email are as follows:

- *Transport agents.* Programs, such as the sendmail daemon, which send mail files from one computer to another.
- *User agents.* Programs, also called *mail readers*, such as mail, pine, or Netscape Messenger, used to compose and manage messages.

The sendmail daemon is started when you boot Linux. Its job is to send, not retrieve, email. To retrieve mail over a Point-to-Point Protocol (PPP) *interface*, or connection, you must use a retrieval program.

The basic approach to handling mail over a PPP connection is to log on, connect with your Internet service provider's computer, retrieve your waiting mail, and then either disconnect or stay connected to browse the Web, read news, or download files.

***sendmail:* a black art?**

Thanks to the efforts of the individuals who prepared your Linux distribution, you won't have to suffer the heartache of configuring the sendmail electronic mail transport agent, a task that can make even the most experienced system administrators tremble. This also means that you should never edit the sendmail configuration file (sendmail.cf, found under the /etc directory) unless you absolutely know what you're doing. For details about Linux mail handling and for other sources of information, see the Mail-HOWTO under the /usr/doc/HOWTO directory.

Using *fetchmail*

To get your email, you'll need the IP address or name of your ISP's mail server (such as mail.mcp.com), the mail-retrieval protocol used by your ISP, and a retrieval program such as fetchmail. Most ISPs use the IMAP or POP3 protocols, which are supported by the fetchmail command, found under the /usr/bin directory.

There are a number of ways to configure the fetchmail program to retrieve mail. Retrieving mail from a remote computer usually involves passwords. Following is the simplest and most secure way to get your mail.

Retrieving mail with *fetchmail*

1. Dial out and establish your PPP connection.

2. Use the `fetchmail` program, along with your ISP's mail protocol and domain name, like this:

```
# fetchmail -u username -p pop3 mail.mcp.com
```

3. After you press the Enter key, the `fetchmail` program prompts for a password:

```
Enter password for username@mail.mcp.com:
```

   Enter the password used to establish your PPP connection, not the system password for your computer. The `fetchmail` command does not echo back your password, so be sure to enter it correctly.

4. `fetchmail` retrieves any waiting mail messages from your ISP. Incoming mail is stored in a file with your username under the `/var/spool/mail` directory. This is the default directory for your user mail on your Linux system. Mail reader programs will pull mail from this directory.

The `fetchmail` program works only one way: It retrieves your mail, and, by default, tells your ISP's mail server to delete the retrieved mail messages. Table 17.1 lists some of the common `fetchmail` command-line options that you can use to manage waiting or retrieved mail. Also included are the corresponding keywords for use in the `.fetchmailrc` file. These options are case sensitive. See the `fetchmail` manual page for more options.

Table 17.1 Common *fetchmail* POP3 Retrieval Options

Option	Specifies
-B n	Do not retrieve more than n messages. (keyword: fetchlimit)
-F	Delete previously retrieved messages before retrieving new messages on the remote mail server. (keyword: flush)
-K	Delete retrieved messages on the remote mail server. (keyword: no keep)
-a	Retrieve all messages from remote mail server, including old messages. (keyword: fetchall)
-c	Check only for mail (no retrieval).
-d n	Daemon mode: Check for mail and retrieve every n seconds.
-e	Delete waiting messages. (keyword: expunge)
-k	Keep retrieved messages on the remote mail server; do not delete them. (keyword: keep)

continues...

Table 17.1 Continued

Option	Specifies
-l n	Do not retrieve messages larger than n characters. (keyword: limit)
-t secs	Abort retrieval if you receive no response in secs from the mail server. (keyword: timeout)
-u name	Retrieve mail for the user with the username name. (keyword: user)
-v	Operate verbosely; print all status messages.

The fetchmail program also recognizes a resource, or configuration file, called
.fetchmailrc, if present in your home directory. Using keywords documented in the
fetchmail manual pages, you can configure fetchmail to automatically retrieve your
mail without requiring you to type numerous options on the command line.

Configuring .fetchmailrc

1. Use your favorite text editor to create a file called .fetchmailrc in your home
   directory.

2. Enter the poll keyword, followed by your ISP's domain name, like this:
   ```
   poll mail.mcp.com
   ```

3. On the same line, enter the protocol keyword, followed by the mail protocol
   supported by your ISP's mail server:
   ```
   poll mail.mcp.com protocol pop3
   ```

4. Again, on the same line, add the user keyword followed by your username, like
   this:
   ```
   poll mail.mcp.com protocol pop3 user username
   ```

5. If you don't want to enter your mail service password each time you use fetchmail, use the password keyword followed by your mail server's password:
   ```
   poll mail.mcp.com protocol pop3 user username password mon6key
   ```

6. Save and close the file.

7. Use the chmod command to change the file permissions of the .fetchmailrc file
   to user read-write, or -rw------ (as returned by the command ls -l), like this:
   ```
   # chmod 600 .fetchmailrc
   ```

8. To retrieve your mail, start your PPP connection and then use the fetchmail
   command:
   ```
   # fetchmail
   ```

SEE ALSO

➤ *To learn more about the* chmod *command to change file ownership and permissions, see page 379.*

You can also use command-line options in conjunction with your .fetchmailrc settings. For example, to retrieve your mail but not erase retrieved messages, and to retrieve only short messages, use the -k (keep) option along with the -l (limit) option, like so:

```
# fetchmail -k -l 32000
```

This command line won't erase retrieved messages from your ISP's mail server and won't download files larger than 32,000 characters.

Selecting a Mail Program

After you've retrieved your messages, a user agent, or mail program, is used to list, read, delete, forward, or create new messages to send. Selecting a mail program is primarily a matter of taste; some are easy to use, whereas others might offer more complex functions such as address books or file attachments. In this section, you are introduced to several simple and popular mail programs that work with Linux.

Using *mail*

The simplest mail program is called mail and is usually found under the /bin directory. This program does not have a full-screen editor and does not require the X Window System. The mail command, similar to the mailx program distributed with other versions of UNIX, supports the basic features needed to compose, send, list, and read messages.

Be careful when mailing from the command line

Use redirection with care. It's not a good idea to mail someone the contents of your system's spelling dictionary!

Creating and sending mail by using *mail*

1. At the command line, enter the word mail followed by the destination email address, like this:

```
# mail dstreib@mcp.com
```

2. The mail command will respond with the prompt Subject. Enter a short subject line:

```
Subject: Y2K Programming Project
```

3. Press Enter and type the text of your message:

```
I have a great consulting opportunity for you! The
firm we spoke to on Wednesday is interested in hiring
your programming staff. Please give me a call to confirm
availability.
```

4. After you finish typing your text, enter a period (.) on a line by itself to send the message:

```
.
EOT
```

5. The `mail` program responds by printing the letters `EOT` (end of text) and sending the message.

Use the `mail` command to retrieve your mail from the `/var/spool/mail` directory. To read your mail, use the `mail` command on the command line, as follows:

```
# mail
Mail version 8.1 6/6/93.  Type ? for help.
"/var/spool/mail/dstreib": 1 message 1 new
>N  1 dstreib@localhost.loca  Sun Sep 19 15:34  17/610    "Y2K Programming
➥Project"
&
```

When you use the `mail` command, it prints a short version message and then lists your messages. The ampersand (&) is a command-line prompt. Use a single-letter command (see Table 17.2) to read, delete, save, or reply to the current mail message, which is denoted by a greater-than character (>). By default, saved messages are stored in a file called `mbox` in your home directory. Table 17.2 lists the most common `mail` program commands; for a complete list of `mail` commands, see the `mail` manual page.

Table 17.2 Common *mail* Program Commands

Key	Specifies
+	Move to the next message and list it
-	Move to the previous message and list it
?	Print a helpful list of mail commands
R	Reply to sender
d	Delete the current message
h	Reprint the list of messages (after listing a message)
n	Go to the next message and list it

Key	Specifies
q	Quit, and save messages in the default mailbox, mbox
r	Reply to the sender and all recipients
t	Type, or list, the current message
x	Quit, and don't save messages in mbox

SEE ALSO

➤ *To learn more about using pipes and redirection in the shell, see page 24.*

The mail command also supports command-line redirection operators and pipes of your shell. This is an easy way to quickly send program output or large files as messages. To use a pipe, use the mail command along with the -s (subject) command-line option followed by an email address. For example, to quickly mail a copy of the current month's calendar, pipe the output of the cal command through mail, as follows:

```
# cal | mail -s "This Month's Calendar" dstreib@mcp.com
```

To quickly send a large file, redirect the contents of a file using the standard input, like this:

```
# mail -s "This is a big file""dstreib@mcp.com </usr/dict/words
```

Using *pine*

The pine mail program, developed by the University of Washington, is a software package consisting of a mail program and an easy-to-use text editor called pico (pico is discussed in Chapter 4, "Using Text Editors," in the section titled "Using Screen Editors"). The pine and pico commands do not require the X Window System and work especially well if you have set up Linux to support dial-in logons. These easy-to-use programs are favorites among Linux users because of their compact size and numerous features, such as spell checking and built-in help.

SEE ALSO

➤ *To learn more about the* pico *editor, see page 72.*

Using the *pine* mail program

1. Start the pine program from a command line:

   ```
   # pine
   ```

   The program automatically creates a directory called mail in your home directory, along with a configuration file called .pinerc.

2. Configure pine by entering your username, your ISP's domain name, and your ISP mail server's name (listed as smtp-server in Figure 17.1). Do this by typing an s, and then type a c to get to the configuration screen.

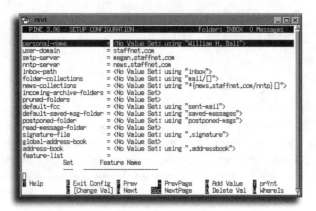

FIGURE 17.1
The pine mailer configuration screen specifies your username and mail server name.

3. After you enter your username, the domain of your ISP, and the name of your ISP's mail server, type an e. The pine program asks whether you want to save the changes in the .pinerc file. Press Y to save the changes.

4. Press C to compose a message; pine enters compose mode, shown in Figure 17.2.

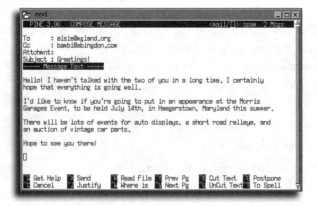

FIGURE 17.2
The pine compose mode is used to create a mail message.

5. Type the name of the addressee in the To field, and press Enter. If you want to copy the message to someone else, enter another addressee in the Cc field. After you've entered all the addressees, press Enter. To send a file as an attachment with the message, enter a valid pathname for a file and press Enter:

`/home/dstreib/quebook/chapter11.sdw`

6. Enter a subject line in the Subject field, and press Enter. Now compose your message. Lines automatically wrap when you reach the far right margin.

7. After you finish, send the message by pressing Ctrl+X. To cancel the message, press Ctrl+C. To postpone sending the message, press Ctrl+O. Table 17.3 summarizes the `pine` commands that are supported for creating or editing a message.

Table 17.3 *pine* Keyboard Motion, Action, and Editing Commands

Command	Specifies
Ctrl+@	Go to the next word
Ctrl+A	Go to the beginning of the line
Ctrl+B	Go back one character
Ctrl+C	Cancel the message
Ctrl+D	Delete one character
Ctrl+E	Go to the end of the line
Ctrl+F	Go forward one character
Ctrl+G	Show the help screen
Ctrl+H	Backspace one character
Ctrl+J	Justify the paragraph
Ctrl+K	Delete the current line
Ctrl+N	Go down one line
Ctrl+O	Postpone sending and save the message
Ctrl+P	Go up one line
Ctrl+R	Insert a file
Ctrl+T	Spell check the message
Ctrl+V	Page down
Ctrl+W	Search for a word
Ctrl+X	Send the message
Ctrl+Y	Page up

Like the `mail` command, `pine` extracts your messages from the `/var/spool/mail` directory. Incoming messages are displayed in a list, as shown in Figure 17.3; you can select messages by scrolling up and down with the cursor keys. From the main list of messages, you can delete, undelete, save, read, and export messages to your home directory. To read a message, move your cursor to the desired message and press Enter.

FIGURE 17.3
The `pine` mail program displays messages in a scrolling list.

Using Netscape Messenger to Create, Send, and Read Mail

Netscape Communicator, perhaps best known as a Web browser, also supports electronic mail through the Netscape Messenger component. Netscape Messenger must be configured before you can use it to send or retrieve email. You must be running the X Window System in order to use Netscape.

SEE ALSO

➤ *To learn more about using Netscape, see page 300.*
➤ *To learn more about PPP connections, see page 250.*

Bug fix: Can't get help with Netscape?

Netscape Communicator 4.04 has comprehensive built-in help for each included component, including Netscape Messenger. However, Netscape's installation script, `ns-install`, does not create required directories or links for Netscape's built-in help files. If you click Netscape's Help button, you'll get an error message dialog box indicating that required files and directories are not available. You can fix this problem by creating a symbolic link (symbolic links are discussed in Chapter 3, "Navigating the Linux File System," in the section titled "Creating Symbolic Links") with the following:

```
# ln -s /opt/netscape /usr/local/lib/netscape
```

After you create this symbolically linked directory, Netscape 4.04 will know where to find its help files.

Configuring Netscape Messenger

1. Start Netscape Messenger from the command line of a terminal window by typing the following:

```
# netscape -mail &
```

2. This launches Netscape; the Netscape component bar will appear (see Figure 17.4), along with the main window for Netscape Messenger (as shown in Figure 17.5).

FIGURE 17.4
The Netscape component bar.

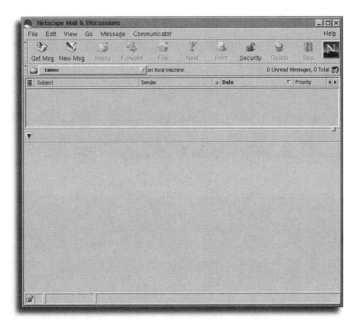

FIGURE 17.5
The Netscape Messenger application supports email for X11 Linux users.

3. Pull down the Edit menu and select Preferences. This displays the Messenger Preferences dialog box (shown in Figure 17.6).

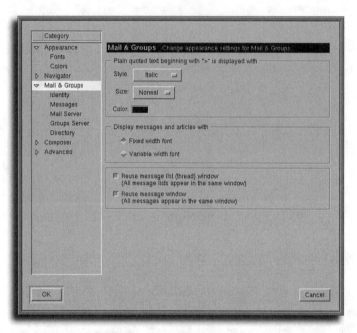

FIGURE 17.6
Configure Netscape Messenger through its Preferences dialog box.

4. Move the cursor to the Identity item in the Category list and click it to display the Identity dialog box. Type your name in the Your Name field and type your email address in the Email Address field, as shown in Figure 17.7.

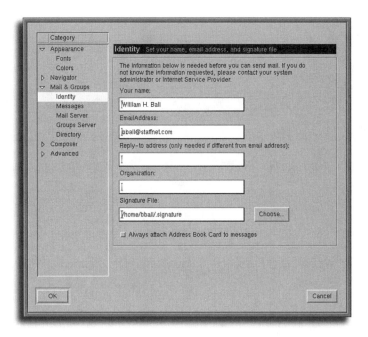

FIGURE 17.7
The Netscape Messenger Identity Preference dialog box contains email identification information, such as your name and email address.

5. Move the cursor to the Mail Server item in the Category list, and click it to display the Mail Server dialog box, shown in Figure 17.8. Enter your username (assigned to you by your ISP) in the Mail Server User Name field. Enter the name of your outgoing mail server in the Outgoing Mail (SMTP) Server field. Enter the name of your incoming mail server (the name of your ISP's mail server) in the Incoming Mail Server field.

6. If your ISP's mail server uses the POP3 mail protocol, make sure the diamond next to POP3 is selected, and then press Enter. Netscape automatically creates a directory called nsmail in your home directory. This directory contains the following files:

```
Drafts        Sent          Unsent Messages
Inbox         Trash
```

These files represent email you create, edit, send, or postpone while using Netscape Messenger.

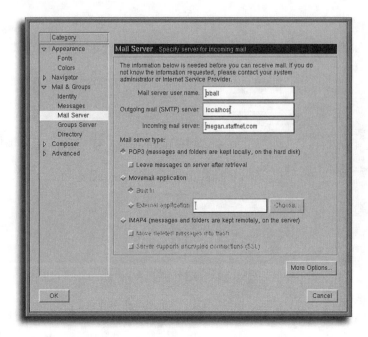

FIGURE 17.8
The Netscape Messenger Mail Server dialog box contains information about your username as well as incoming and outgoing mail services and protocols.

Retrieving and creating mail

1. Launch Netscape Messenger. Start your PPP connection with your ISP.

2. Click the Get Msg button (refer to Figure 17.5). Netscape Messenger prompts you for your ISP mail server's password. Enter the password and press Enter.

3. Netscape Messenger downloads waiting mail messages from your ISP's mail server, and then displays the list of messages in the Messenger window (see Figure 17.9). To view a message, click it in the message list.

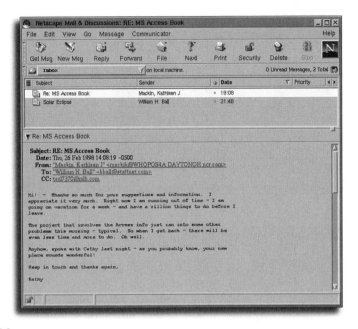

FIGURE 17.9
Read received messages by clicking them in the message list of Netscape Messenger's main window.

4. After you read the message, you can reply to, forward, or file it by selecting the appropriate button in Netscape Messenger's toolbar (refer to Figure 17.9).

5. To create a message, click the New Msg button. Netscape Messenger displays its Message Composition window, shown in Figure 17.10.

6. Move your mouse cursor to the To line and type an email address.

7. Move the cursor to the Subject line, and enter a subject. Press Enter and start typing your message.

8. When finished, click the Send Now button on the Message Composition window toolbar (refer to Figure 17.10) to send the message right away. To save the message as a draft, click the Save button on the toolbar.

FIGURE 17.10
Create new messages in Netscape Messenger's Message Composition window.

Managing Electronic Mail

Junk email, also known as *spam*, can be annoying. Email addresses are often "harvested" from the Internet by companies for inexpensive advertising. If you have an email address, chances are that at some time it will end up on someone's spam list. Spam is not usually dangerous, but can quickly fill your email inbox and result in your spending extra time trying to sort out bulk mail from your private messages.

Sick of spam?

I mean spurious email, not the delightful food product trademarked by Hormel, Inc. Nonetheless, if you want to learn more about what you can do to protect yourself against these despicable bulk emailers, browse to the following sites to learn how to protect yourself, write more complex `procmail` recipes, and complain to the proper authorities in case of suspected fraud:

http://spam.abuse.net/spam/

http://www.cauce.org/

http://www.elsop.com/wrc/

http://www.chooseyourmail.com/spamindex.cfm

What can you do about spam? I list some general rules to follow, but not all might be effective:

- Unless you know and trust the company or vendor, never enter your email address in a request form on a Web site.

- If you regularly post or reply to Usenet newsgroup messages, configure your mail program to send your real username accompanied by an embedded string that can be easily removed. This clues in the truly concerned, but foils email villains who use extraction software to harvest email addresses from newsgroup postings to build bulk emailing lists. Try an email address like the following:
  dstreib@FIGHT-ALL-spam-mcp.com

- If you receive particularly obnoxious email, complain in writing to pertinent local, state, or federal authorities, and include a printed copy of the message.

- At the end of the body text of any posted Usenet message, include valid email addresses of your state attorney general or of pertinent federal postal or commerce fraud-reporting authorities. This will help ensure that these addresses, if harvested, are included in future spam mailings.

- Complain to your ISP about unwanted email from bulk emailers.

- Don't bother complaining to spammers: These worms are scofflaws of dubious lineage. Don't fall for any encouraged procedures, such as the TO BE REMOVED, REPLY TO: bait; verifying your email address in this way will certainly ensure more spam!

- Use mail filters to delete or organize all incoming email from unwanted sources.

Configuring *procmail* to Filter Mail

procmail, a mail-processing program, is a first-line-of-defense weapon in the war against spam. This command, found under the /usr/bin directory, filters incoming mail so that you can automatically delete or organize messages by sender, subject, recipient, or text. Mail handling is accomplished by using procmail's command syntax to write short filters, or *recipes*.

Writing *procmail* recipes

1. Using your favorite text editor, create a text file called .procmailrc in your home directory. Specify the name of your mail directory (mail, if you use pine), the location of the .procmail directory, and the name of your procmail filter file, like this:
   ```
   MAILDIR=$HOME/mail
   PMDIR=$HOME/.procmail
   INCLUDERC=$HOME/rc.mailfilter
   ```

2. Save this file, and then create a text file called .forward in your home directory, with the following line (replace *username* with your username):

```
"|IFS=' ' && exec /usr/bin/procmail -f- || exit 75 #username"
```

3. Save the .forward file and then use the chmod command to change the permissions of the .forward file and your home directory, as follows:

```
# chmod 644 .forward
# chmod a+x /home/bball
```

4. Use the mkdir command to create a directory called .procmail:

```
# mkdir .procmail
```

5. Switch to the .procmail directory by entering the following:

```
# cd .procmail
```

6. Create a text file called rc.mailfilter, and enter three procmail recipes, like this:

```
:0:
*^From:.*aol.com
AOL
:0:
*^From:.*hotmail.com
/dev/null
:0:
*^Subject:.*CASH
/dev/null
:0:
```

7. Save the file rc.mailfilter.

8. Connect to your ISP and retrieve your mail. From now on, procmail will filter all incoming mail (the .forward file specifies that all your incoming mail be forwarded through the procmail program). The first recipe saves mail messages from anyone at aol.com into a mail folder called AOL. The next recipe sends all messages from the domain hotmail.com to a place where they rightfully belong: the ol' bit bucket, /dev/null. This means that as you receive a message with the string hotmail.com in the From field, procmail won't even save it on your hard drive. The last recipe sends all messages with the word CASH on the Subject line to the same boneyard.

9. As you receive additional spam, enter new recipes to filter unwanted mail.

To add more features to your procmail recipes, read the procmailrc manual page. For a great selection of procmail recipe examples, see the procmailex manual page.

chapter

18

Using FTP

Using the `ftp` command •

Using the `ncftp` command •

Using Netscape to download files •

Using the *ftp* Command

Use the `ftp` (file transfer) command to download files directly to your computer from another computer on the Internet. `ftp` supports the standard File Transfer Protocol (FTP) and was originally designed to transfer files to and from other networked computers on the Internet.

`ftp`, found under the `/usr/bin` directory, has five command-line options and dozens of built-in commands. Use this program from the command line of the console or a terminal window, followed by a name of a remote computer, like this:

```
# ftp ftp.mcp.com
Connected to ftp.mcp.com.
220 iq-mcp FTP server (Version wu-2.4(4) Sun Dec 21 13:01:32 EST 1997) ready.
Name (ftp.mcp.com:ds):
```

You can also use an Internet (IP) address to connect to a remote computer, like this:

```
# ftp 206.246.150.88
Connected to 206.246.150.88.
220 iq-mcp FTP server (Version wu-2.4(4) Sun Dec 21 13:01:32 EST 1997) ready.
Name (206.246.150.88:ds):
```

Both command lines connect you to the same remote computer. You don't even have to specify a hostname on the command line when using `ftp`; you can run the program interactively—repeatedly connecting to and disconnecting from different computers—by using `ftp`'s `open` and `close` commands:

```
# ftp
ftp> open ftp.mcp.com
Connected to ftp.mcp.com.
220 iq-mcp FTP server (Version wu-2.4(4) Sun Dec 21 13:01:32 EST 1997) ready.
Name (ftp.mcp.com:ds): anonymous
331 Guest login ok, send your complete e-mail address as password.
Password:
230 Guest login ok, access restrictions apply.
Remote system type is UNIX.
Using binary mode to transfer files.
ftp> close
221 Goodbye.
```

After using the `close` command, you can then open a new connection to another computer by using the `open` command, followed by the name of an FTP server:

```
ftp> open ftp.tenon.com
Connected to toady.tenon.com.
220-_220-Welcome to ftp.tenon.com, Tenon Intersystem's FTP server.
220-             - Thanks, Tenon Tech Support
220-                      support@tenon.com
220 toady FTP server (Version wu-2.4(2) Wed May 10 19:20:08 GMT-0800 1995)
ready.
Name (ftp.tenon.com:ds): anonymous
331 Guest login ok, send your complete e-mail address as password.
Password:
230 Guest login ok, access restrictions apply.
Remote system type is UNIX.
Using binary mode to transfer files.
ftp> bye
221 Goodbye.
```

In this example, I first connected to the FTP server at Macmillan USA (`ftp.mcp.com`) by using the `open` command. After logging in, I disconnected from Macmillan's server by using the `close` command, connected to Tenon's FTP server, and then closed the connection by using the `bye` command. Most of the commands you'll use with `ftp` are listed in Table 18.1.

Table 18.1   Common *ftp* Commands

Command Name	Action
!	Run a shell command on the local system.
ascii	Specify text file downloads.
binary	Specify binary file downloads.
bye	Close the open connection and exit `ftp`.
cd nnn	Change to directory `nnn`.
close	Close the open connection.
exit	Close any open connection and quit.
get file	Download `file` from the current directory of the remote computer.
help	List help topics for `ftp`'s commands.
help str	List help for specific topic `str`.

continues...

Table 18.1 Continued

Command Name	Action
ls	List files or directories in the current directory of the remote computer.
mget nnn	Download multiple files according to pattern nnn.
mput nnn	Send (upload) multiple files to remote computer according to pattern nnn.
open	Open a connection to a remote computer.
prompt	Turn off prompting during multiple file transfers. Turn prompting on if prompting has been turned off.
pwd	Print the current working directory on the remote computer.
put	Send (upload) a file from your computer to the remote computer.

Using *ftp* to Download Files

After ftp connects to a remote computer, the remote computer usually presents a login prompt. If you do not have an account on the remote computer system (such as a username or password), type anonymous at the Name prompt and press Enter. At the Password prompt, type your email address. Your email address will not be echoed back to your screen. Entering your email address, although usually unnecessary to make the connection, is considered polite practice because the service to which you are connecting is usually free.

SEE ALSO

➤ *To learn more about changing directories using the cd command, see page 36.*

➤ *To learn more about using electronic mail, see Chapter 17.*

➤ *To learn more about the Internet network services and Linux, see Chapter 26.*

Linux and *ftp*

When you install Red Hat Linux, a user named ftp is created, along with a directory called ftp under the /home directory. (You can check this by looking at the contents of your system's /etc/passwd file.) To enable FTP access for your system, log in as the root operator, start X11, and use Red Hat's tksysv Control Panel tool to start inet services. To test your system to see whether FTP access is available, use the ftp command followed by the name of your computer, like this:

```
# ftp localhost
```

If you get a login prompt, FTP has been enabled. For more information about Internet network services for Linux, see the services manual page.

Logging in, navigating, and downloading files

1. Start your Internet connection—a PPP connection, for example. At the command line of the console or a terminal window, use the `ftp` command followed by the name of a remote computer, like so:

```
# ftp metalab.unc.edu
Connected to metalab.unc.edu.
Connected to metalab.unc.edu.
220-
220-                   Welcome to UNC's MetaLab FTP archives!
220-            at the site formerly known as sunsite.unc.edu
220-
220-You can access this archive via http with the same URL.
220-
220-example:    ftp://metalab.unc.edu/pub/Linux/ becomes
220-            http://metalab.unc.edu/pub/Linux/
220-
220-For more information about services offered by MetaLab,
220-go to http://metalab.unc.edu
220-
220- We're using wu-ftpd.  You can get tarred directories if you issue
220-the following command:
220-
220-    get dirname.tar
220-
220- You can also get gzipped or compressed tarred directories by
220-following the .tar with .gz or .Z, respectively.
220-
220-Have suggestions or questions?  Please mail ftpkeeper@metalab.unc.edu.
220-
220 helios.oit.unc.edu FTP server (Version wu-2.5.0(1) Tue Aug 31 15:21:58
➥EDT 1999) ready.
Name (metalab.unc.edu:ds):
```

2. Type anonymous at the `Name` prompt:

```
Name (metalab.unc.edu:ds): anonymous
331 Guest login ok, send your complete e-mail address as password.
Password:
```

3. Enter your email address at the `Password` prompt—for example, `ds@valinux.com`:

```
Password:
230 Guest login ok, access restrictions apply.
Remote system type is UNIX.
Using binary mode to transfer files.
ftp>
```

   Remember: You won't see any text entered at the `Password` prompt!

4. To see the contents of the current directory, use `ftp`'s `ls` (list directory) command:

```
ftp> ls
200 PORT command successful.
150 Opening ASCII mode data connection for /bin/ls.
total 28797
```

287

```
dr-xr-xr-x    9 root     other         512 Feb 16 16:22 .
dr-xr-xr-x    9 root     other         512 Feb 16 16:22 ..
-r--r--r--    1 root     other    29428182 Mar 31 07:26 IAFA-LISTINGS
lrwxrwxrwx    1 root     other           7 Jul 16  1997 README -> WELCOME
-r--r--r--    1 root     other         608 Jan 13  1997 WELCOME
dr-xr-xr-x    2 root     other         512 Jul 16  1997 bin
dr-xr-xr-x    2 root     other         512 Jul 16  1997 dev
dr-xr-xr-x    2 root     other         512 Jul 18  1997 etc
drwxrwxrwx    6 root     other       18944 Mar 30 01:48 incoming
dr-xr-xr-x   17 root     root          512 Mar 19 22:13 pub
dr-xr-xr-x    3 root     other         512 Jul 16  1997 unc
dr-xr-xr-x    5 root     other         512 Jul 16  1997 usr
226 Transfer complete.
        ftp>
```

5. To navigate to a different directory, use `ftp`'s `cd` (change directory) command followed by the name of a directory:

```
ftp> cd pub
250 CWD command successful.
ftp>
```

6. To navigate to a specific subdirectory, use a more complete path specification with the `cd` command:

```
ftp> cd pub/Linux/games/arcade
250 CWD command successful.
ftp>
```

7. To list specific files, use `ftp`'s `ls` command along with a wildcard pattern:

```
ftp> ls xcen*
200 PORT command successful.
150 Opening ASCII mode data connection for /bin/ls.
-rw-rw-r--    1 67       1002         6884 Aug 01  1996 xcentipede-0.01.ELF.gz
-rw-rw-r--    1 67       1002         1595 Aug 01  1996 xcentipede-0.01.README
-rw-rw-r--    1 67       1002         1104 Aug 01  1996 xcentipede-0.01.lsm
-rw-rw-r--    1 67       1002        10016 Aug 01  1996 xcentipede-0.01.src.tgz
226 Transfer complete.
ftp>
```

8. To prepare to download a binary file, such as a compressed Linux `gzip` archive, use `ftp`'s `binary` command:

```
ftp> binary
200 Type set to I.
ftp>
```

9. To download a single file, use `ftp`'s `get` command followed by the filename:

```
ftp> get xcentipede-0.01.ELF.gz
local: xcentipede-0.01.ELF.gz remote: xcentipede-0.01.ELF.gz
200 PORT command successful.
150 Opening BINARY mode data connection for xcentipede-0.01.ELF.gz (6884
➥bytes).
```

```
226 Transfer complete.
6884 bytes received in 2.37 secs (2.8 Kbytes/sec)
ftp>
```

10. If you can't remember the current directory of the remote computer, use ftp's pwd (print working directory) command:

```
ftp> pwd
257 "/pub/Linux/games/arcade" is current directory.
ftp>
```

11. To prepare to download text files, use ftp's ascii command. Because Windows and UNIX/Linux machines use different characters to separate lines, if you are transferring text files across these platforms, it is always best to use the ascii command before making the transfer:

```
ftp> ascii
200 Type set to A.
ftp>
```

12. To download multiple files, use ftp's mget command followed by a filename pattern:

```
ftp> mget xb*.lsm
mget xbattle.patch.lsm? y
200 PORT command successful.
150 Opening ASCII mode data connection for xbattle.patch.lsm (286 bytes).
226 Transfer complete.
295 bytes received in 0.0602 secs (4.8 Kbytes/sec)
mget xbill-2.0.lsm? y
200 PORT command successful.
150 Opening ASCII mode data connection for xbill-2.0.lsm (606 bytes).
226 Transfer complete.
623 bytes received in 0.131 secs (4.6 Kbytes/sec)
mget xblast-2.2.1.lsm? y
200 PORT command successful.
150 Opening ASCII mode data connection for xblast-2.2.1.lsm (858 bytes).
226 Transfer complete.
879 bytes received in 0.161 secs (5.3 Kbytes/sec)
mget xboing-2.3.lsm? y
200 PORT command successful.
150 Opening ASCII mode data connection for xboing-2.3.lsm (465 bytes).
226 Transfer complete.
479 bytes received in 0.111 secs (4.2 Kbytes/sec)
ftp>
```

Before retrieving each file, ftp prompts and asks for a Y or an N. Press Y to download the file; press N to skip the file and go to the next file.

13. To download multiple files without a prompt, use ftp's prompt command to toggle interactive downloads:

```
ftp> prompt
Interactive mode off.
ftp> mget xb*.lsm
```

```
local: xbattle.patch.lsm remote: xbattle.patch.lsm
200 PORT command successful.
150 Opening ASCII mode data connection for xbattle.patch.lsm (286 bytes).
226 Transfer complete.
295 bytes received in 0.0602 secs (4.8 Kbytes/sec)
local: xbill-2.0.lsm remote: xbill-2.0.lsm
200 PORT command successful.
150 Opening ASCII mode data connection for xbill-2.0.lsm (606 bytes).
226 Transfer complete.
623 bytes received in 0.121 secs (5 Kbytes/sec)
local: xblast-2.2.1.lsm remote: xblast-2.2.1.lsm
200 PORT command successful.
425 Can't create data socket (152.2.254.81,20): Address already in use.
local: xboing-2.3.lsm remote: xboing-2.3.lsm
200 PORT command successful.
150 Opening ASCII mode data connection for xboing-2.3.lsm (465 bytes).
226 Transfer complete.
479 bytes received in 0.0906 secs (5.2 Kbytes/sec)
ftp>
```

Return to *ftp* with the *exit* command

Using `ftp`'s shell prompt can be handy but confusing, especially if you type the exclamation-point character and press the Enter key without a trailing command. You'll find yourself at your shell prompt and might think you've disconnected and quit the program. Type the word `exit` to return to the `ftp` program.

---

14. To use a shell command from inside `ftp`, use the exclamation-point character (!), also known as the "bang" character, followed a command line:

```
ftp> ! ls -l xb*.lsm
-rw-rw-r--   1 ds      ds        286 Mar 31 12:41 xbattle.patch.lsm
-rw-rw-r--   1 ds      ds        606 Mar 31 12:41 xbill-2.0.lsm
-rw-rw-r--   1 ds      ds        858 Mar 31 12:39 xblast-2.2.1.lsm
-rw-rw-r--   1 ds      ds        465 Mar 31 12:43 xboing-2.3.lsm
ftp>
```

15. To close the connection without quitting `ftp`, use the `close` command:

```
ftp> close
221 Goodbye.
ftp>
```

16. To quit and exit `ftp`, use the `quit` or `exit` command:

```
ftp> quit
```

SEE ALSO

➤ *To learn more about using a shell with Linux, see Chapter 2.*

Using *ftp* Help Commands

ftp has built-in help that you can use as a quick reminder about its different commands. This help system can be used before or during a remote connection; simply type help to print a list of all built-in commands:

```
# ftp
ftp> help
Commands may be abbreviated.  Commands are:

!     debug    mdir      sendport    site
$     dir      mget     put     size
account    disconnect     mkdir     pwd      status
append     exit     mls     quit     struct
ascii     form     mode     quote     system
bell     get     modtime     recv     sunique
binary     glob     mput     reget     tenex
bye     hash     newe     rstatus     tick
case     help     nmap     rhelp     trace
cd     idle     nlist     rename     type
cdup     image     ntrans     reset     user
chmod     lcd     open     restart     umask
close     ls     prompt     rmdir     verbose
cr     macdef     passive     runique     ?
delete     mdelete     proxy     send
ftp> help prompt
prompt force interactive prompting on multiple commands
ftp> help exit
exit terminate ftp session and exit
ftp>
```

Typing help and then the name of a command will print a short description of the command.

Use ftp's built-in help to supplement its manual page. More extensive documentation can be found under the /usr/doc/wu-ftpd directory.

Using the *ncftp* Command

The ncftp command is similar to the ftp command, but has additional features, including the following:

- Three visual (screen) modes
- 15 command-line options
- A command line separate from a main scrolling window
- A status line showing download progress with elapsed and remaining time to completion
- An editor for bookmarks (abbreviated hostnames of remote computers)

The ncftp command also features a built-in help facility that is similar to ftp's. You can read more about ncftp by browsing to this address:

```
http://www.probe.net/~mgleason
```

Downloading with the *ncftp* Command

The ncftp command features several command-line options that can save you time and typing.

Downloading files with the *ncftp* command

1. Use the ncftp command followed by the -a (anonymous) option to quickly log in to a remote computer, like so:
```
# ncftp -a ftp.ncftp.com
```

2. Your screen clears, and ncftp automatically logs you in to the remote computer, sending information to your display that is similar to the following:
```
Trying to connect to ftp.ncftp.com...
You are user #2 of 50 simultaneous users allowed.

Welcome to ftp.ncftp.com
Logged in anonymously.
```

3. If you know the complete path to a desired file on a remote computer, use ncftp's -a option followed by the name of the FTP server, a colon, and the complete path or directory specification to the desired file:
```
# ncftp -a metalab.unc.edu:/pub/Linux/NEW
```

This command line retrieves a list of the newest software for Linux at the sunsite.unc.edu FTP server (with the very latest files at the bottom of the list).

4. To save even more time, use ncftp's -c command to pipe the retrieved file through the tail and less commands, like so:

```
# ncftp -ac sunsite.unc.edu:/pub/Linux/NEW | tail | less
```

After a pause, following ncftp's automatic login and retrieval, you should see something like the following:

```
system/network/serial/ppp/gppp-1.0.tar.gz (183724 bytes)
   ppp setup program with a similar user interface to Windows' Internet
➥Wizard (Mar 30, 1998 16:38:13 EST)

kernel/patches/cdrom/linux-2.0.30-cm205ms-0.10.tgz (41435 bytes)
   new cdrom device driver Philips/LMS cm205ms/cm206 (Mar 30, 1998
➥20:59:44 EST)

system/mail/mua/mr0721beta.tar.gz (71392 bytes)
   mr is a colorful mailreader (Mar 31, 1998 2:29:3 EST)
```

5. While logged in to a remote machine, you can download complete directories (with all subdirectories) using the -r option to the get command. Be careful with this though! Make sure you know what you're downloading so that you don't end up with lots of files you don't need.

```
>get -r entiredirectory
```

SEE ALSO

➤ *To learn more about using the* less *pager command, see page 41.*

Using Netscape to Download Files

Netscape Communicator not only interactively browses the Web, but can be directed to retrieve files from remote computers through the command line of a terminal window.

Netscape Navigator, a component of the Netscape Communicator distribution for Linux, recognizes a uniform resource locator (URL) specification of the FTP protocol (ftp://). This is handy for quickly downloading known files from familiar places on the Internet.

SEE ALSO

➤ *For more information about Netscape Communicator for Linux, see page 300.*

➤ *To learn more about the X Window System, see Chapter 12.*

To navigate an FTP site using Netscape, simply type the URL into the Location bar, as shown in Figure 18.1. You can then browse the site graphically.

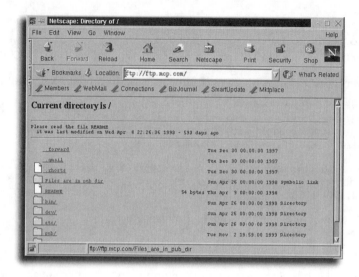

FIGURE 18.1
Using Netscape Navigator to surf an FTP site.

To download most files in Netscape, all you need to do is click them. This will not work for all files, however, and sometimes Netscape will display the file rather than download it. You can force Netscape to download and save a file, rather than display it on the screen, by holding down the Shift key and clicking the file.

# chapter 19

Using Web Browsers

Using the Lynx browser •

Using Netscape Communicator •

Using the Lynx Browser

The Lynx Web browser, hosted at the University of Kansas, is a text-only browser. This program does not load Web page graphics, play sounds, or use any of the plug-in features of today's modern Web browsers. However, Lynx is fast and efficient and does not take up much disk space (around 500KB versus up to 46MB for Netscape).

You don't need to use X11 to browse the Web; use Lynx from the command line:

```
# Lynx http://www.mcp.com
```

The Lynx browser connects to Macmillan USA's Web page and shows it on your display or in a terminal window, as shown in Figure 19.1.

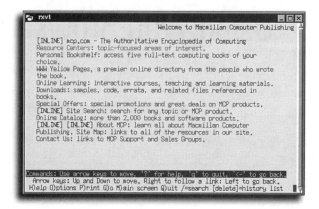

FIGURE 19.1
The Lynx program is a text-only Web browser.

If you're using the X Window System, you can also use Lynx to browse the Web in the window of an X11 terminal client. Use Lynx to quickly browse Web pages without the delay caused by advertisements, large graphics, or animations that can get in the way of getting information.

The Lynx browser has 66 different command-line options but is easy to use. The most common keystroke commands used to navigate Web pages are listed in Table 19.1.

Table 19.1   Common Lynx Keyboard Commands

Action	Keystroke
Add page to bookmark file	a
Download highlighted file	Enter key or d key
Edit current URL before jump	G
Get help	? key or h key
Jump to an URL	g
Jump to topic	Enter key or Cursor right
Mail current page	p, followed by cursor down, Enter key
Next topic	Cursor down
Previous page	Cursor left
Previous topic	Cursor up
Save link to bookmark file	a
Save page to a file	p, followed by Enter key
Scroll backward one page	PageUp key
Scroll backward one-half page	(
Scroll forward one page	spacebar key
Scroll forward one-half page	)
Search page	/

SEE ALSO

➤ *To learn more about PPP connections, see Chapter 16, "Connecting to Your Internet Service Provider."*

➤ *To learn more about the X Window System and X11 terminals, see Chapter 12, "Running and Configuring X."*

Using Lynx command lines

1. Start your PPP connection. To browse to a specific page on the Internet, enter the Web address (also known as a Uniform Resource Locator, or URL):

   ```
   # Lynx http://www.mcp.com
   ```

2. To go to a File Transfer Protocol (FTP) server, use an FTP URL address:

   ```
   # Lynx ftp://sunsite.unc.edu/pub/Linux
   ```

   This command line logs you in to the specified ftp server, and display a list of available files, as shown in Figure 19.2.

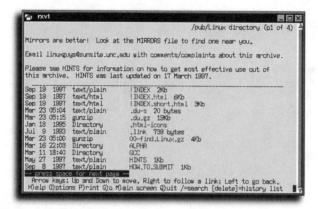

FIGURE 19.2
The Lynx browser lists and retrieves files from FTP servers.

Save time and effort downloading files

If you frequently use the `ftp` command to retrieve files from remote computers, try using the Lynx browser instead. Many FTP sites now include index files in `.html` format that makes listings much easier to read. To download a file, hold down the Shift key and click the filename.

---

3. To use the Lynx browser to retrieve text files without browsing, enter a known URL and then use the `-dump` option, followed by the shell's standard output redirection operator, like this:

```
# Lynx http://www.yahoo.com/headlines/news/summary.html -dump >news.raw
```

This command line will dump the text of the requested page into a text file on your disk (note that the URL might be outdated by the time you read this).

Configuring the Lynx Browser

To configure the `Lynx` command, log in as the root operator and edit the file `Lynx.cfg` under the `/etc` directory. Make a backup copy first if you want (but you'll find an original copy under the `/usr/doc/Lynx` directory). The `/etc/Lynx.cfg` file contains systemwide settings for the Lynx browser's features.

Configuring the Lynx browser

1. Using your favorite text editor, such as pico, open the `Lynx.cfg` file and turn off line wrapping:

```
# pico -w /etc/Lynx.cfg
```

2. To change the default Web address used when starting Lynx from the command line without an URL, change the default address used with the STARTFILE variable, from

   STARTFILE:http://Lynx.browser.org/

   to a different address (Red Hat Linux users will find STARTFILE defined as /usr/doc/HTML/index.html):

   STARTFILE:http://www.yahoo.com/

3. To configure Lynx to use its help files installed on your disk in the /usr/doc/Lynx/Lynx_help directory, change the HELPFILE variable, from its default Web address:

   HELPFILE:http://www.crl.com/~subir/Lynx/Lynx_help/Lynx__help_main.html

   to the location of the Lynx_help_main.html file:

   HELPFILE:localhost/usr/doc/Lynx-2.7.1/Lynx_help/Lynx_help_main.html

   After making this change, Lynx reads in the help files installed on your system following a question mark (?) keypress, as shown in Figure 19.3, instead of browsing to its home page for help information. (Check your /usr/doc directory to make sure that you enter the correct path for the Lynx help file.)

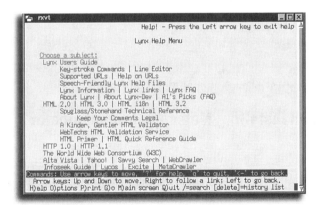

FIGURE 19.3
The Lynx program can display online help from files on your hard drive, or through links to Web pages on the Internet.

SEE ALSO
➤ *For more information about text editors, see page 67.*

4. To configure Lynx to work as a Usenet newsreader, find the NNTPSERVER line and enter the name of your Internet service provider's (ISP) news server:

```
NNTPSERVER:your.ISPnewserver.com
```

5. To read articles in newsgroups specified in your .newsrc file in your home directory, use the news URL prefix, followed by your news server name:

```
# Lynx news://your.ISPnewserver.com
```

6. To download files while using Lynx, navigate to the filename on the display Web page and press the d key. Lynx then downloads the file and prompts you for a local filename. Type the path and filename under which you want to save the file and press Enter.

Using Netscape Communicator

This section details how to install, configure, and use some basic features of Netscape Communicator. This program is much more than a Web browser and includes a suite of three tools: Navigator for Web browsing; Messenger for electronic mail and Usenet news; and Composer for creating and editing Web pages.

For the latest information about Netscape Communicator for Linux, browse to Netscape's home page at

```
http://home.netscape.com
```

SEE ALSO

➤ *For more information about electronic mail, see Chapter 17, "Using Electronic Mail."*

Downloading and Installing Netscape Communicator

The Netscape Communicator Web browser is one of the most popular browsers for all computer systems, including Linux. Thanks to Netscape, Linux users will continue to enjoy this browser for a long time (see the earlier sidenote, "Freely licensed Netscape Communicator source"). Netscape is now a standard Web browser for Linux.

Most Linux distributions come with Netscape Communicator. You can check for an installation by trying to run Communicator from the command line.

```
# netscape &
```

Freely licensed Netscape Communicator source

Along with Netscape's decision to make Netscape Communicator 4.0 free for all users, the company shocked and delighted many Linux software developers by announcing plans "to make the source code for the next generation of its highly popular Netscape Communicator client software available for free licensing on the Internet."

What does this mean for you? Expect to see rapid development of the Netscape Communicator suite of Internet tools, with many enhancements. Expect to see this program become a standard part of nearly all Linux distributions in the future. (It's currently included with all new Red Hat Linux CD-ROM distributions.) For Netscape, one of the first large commercial software companies to endorse and credit the power of the Free Software Foundation's GNU Public License, this means that the company will benefit from seeing rapid enhancements, improvements, and variations to its browser tools.

Kudos to Netscape for taking this bold step. You can be sure that the worldwide community of Linux software developers will repay this generosity tenfold with some "insanely great" improvements to your favorite browser in the near future. For more information about Netscape's source licensing of Communicator and related programs, see

`http://developer.netscape.com/`

If Communicator is not installed on your machine, navigate to the Netscape home page (using the Lynx browser), `http://home.netscape.com`, to download the proper version of Netscape Communicator for your version of Linux.

Be prepared for a long download if you're getting Communicator over a PPP connection. The latest version (4.7 as of this writing) is more than 16MB in compressed form and will require even more disk space when installed. Also consider that the installed default `.netscape` directory in your home directory can grow to several megabytes after using Netscape for awhile due to disk caching.

It is not very likely that you will have any problems, but I have had Netscape upgrades damage my bookmarks and mail files in the past. Just to be safe, you might want to back up these items, which are all contained in the .netscape directory. The easiest way to do this is with the `tar` command (discussed in Chapter 30, "System Maintenance").

```
# tar cvf ~/netscape-backup.tar ~/.netscape
```

Installing and configuring Communicator

   1. Log in as the root operator. Start your PPP connection, navigate to Netscape's home page, `http://home.netscape.com`, and download Netscape Communicator for Linux.

2. Use the `mkdir` command to create a temporary directory and copy the file into it. Then change directory into the temporary directory and use the `tar` command to decompress and extract the Netscape package:
```
# tar xvzf *
```

3. Remove any existing RPM installations of Communicator. If you are using a distribution that manages installations with RPM, you will want to remove any existing installations so that the RPM package manager doesn't get confused by the upgrade. Depending on your installation you might need to substitute the words `netscape-common`, `netscape-navigator`, or `netscape-communicator` for `netscape` in the following command line. It doesn't hurt to try all these commands just to make sure any existing installation is removed.
```
#rpm -e netscape
```

4. Begin installing Netscape Communicator by using its installation script:
```
# ./ns-install
```

5. The installation script asks some simple questions and then extracts required files, creates any necessary directories, and installs the browser. By default, Communicator and its files are installed into the `/opt/netscape` directory.

6. Check out the `README` file in the `netscape` directory for information on release notes, features, or known problems.

7. To start Netscape from the command line of a terminal window, specify its full path:
```
# /opt/netscape/netscape
```

8. A much better way to configure Netscape is to create a symbolic link, called `netscape`, in the `/usr/local/bin` directory:
```
# ln -s /opt/netscape/netscape /usr/local/bin/netscape
```

9. Netscape's installation script does not create a required symbolic link to use the client's built-in help. If you try to use Netscape help, you'll get an error message. You can configure Netscape in two different ways. One way is to create the required link with the `ln` command:
```
# ln -s /opt/netscape /usr/local/lib/netscape
```

The other way is to create an environment variable, NS_NETHELP_PATH, which points to the `/opt/netscape/nethelp` directory, and add the `/opt/netscape` directory to your shell's PATH environment variable. Open the bash shell's Startup file, `/etc/profile`, and enter the following:
```
NS_NETHELP_PATH=/opt/netscape/nethelp
PATH=$PATH:/opt/netscape
export NS_NETHELP_PATH PATH
```

Save the file. To use this variable right away, use the `bash` shell's `source` command:

```
# source /etc/profile
```

SEE ALSO

➤ *For more information about symbolic links and using the* `ln` *command, see page 46.*

➤ *To learn more about shell environment variables, see page 100.*

Working with Netscape Communicator

Netscape Communicator has nearly 30 different command-line options. Like most well-behaved X11 clients, this program also supports several X11 Toolkit options, such as geometry settings. For example, if you want a smaller initial window, specify a smaller starting window using geometry settings.

Starting Netscape from the command line

1. Use Navigator's `--help` option to see a list of supported command-line options:

   ```
   # netscape --help
   ```

   If the list is too large for your terminal window, redirect the standard error output to a file:

   ```
   # netscape --help 2>netscape.options
   ```

   The file `netscape.options` contains the output from the `--help` option.

2. To start Netscape with a specific window size, use the X11 Toolkit `-geometry` setting, followed by a window size in horizontal and vertical pixels:

   ```
   # netscape -geometry 600x400 &
   ```

SEE ALSO

➤ *For more information about X11 Toolkit options, see page 198.*

➤ *To learn more about input or output redirection, see page 24.*

3. The Navigator window appears, as shown in Figure 19.4.

Setting Navigator preferences

1. To set preferences for Navigator, move your mouse cursor to the Navigator Edit menu and select the Preferences menu item. The Preferences dialog box appears, as shown in Figure 19.5.

2. To configure Communicator to launch a specific component, select one of the components under the Appearance setting. To configure the appearance of Communicator's component bar, select a Show Toolbar As setting.

3. Click the Fonts or Colors settings to customize the font size of menus and the background or foreground colors used by Communicator.

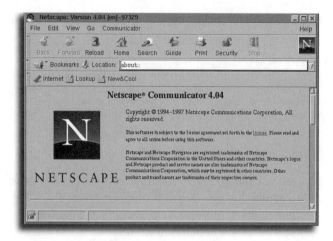

FIGURE 19.4
The Navigator window size can be specified with X11 -geometry settings.

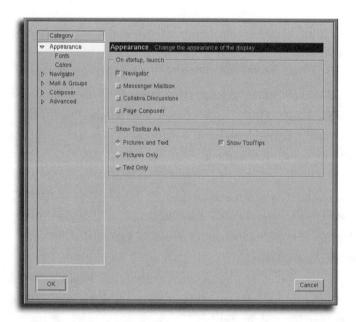

FIGURE 19.5
Numerous Communicator preferences are set through the Navigator Preferences dialog box.

4. Much of Netscape's behavior can be modified in the Navigator preference section. Move your mouse cursor to the Navigator item under the Category menu (as shown in Figure 19.6). Click the Navigator item. The Navigator settings appear, as shown in Figure 19.6.

FIGURE 19.6
The Navigator settings determine how Navigator works on starting, what the default home page is, and how long Navigator retains its cache list of visited Web pages.

SEE ALSO

➤ *To learn more about configuring your mouse for the X Window System, see page 184.*

5. Select your preference for how Communicator should start, the default home page, and the cache or history settings. Then move your mouse cursor to the Navigator menu item under the Category list. Click your left mouse button on the small triangle next to the word *Navigator*. The preferences dialog box will then list the Languages and Applications menu items. Click the Applications menu item, and the Navigator preferences dialog box will change as shown in Figure 19.7.

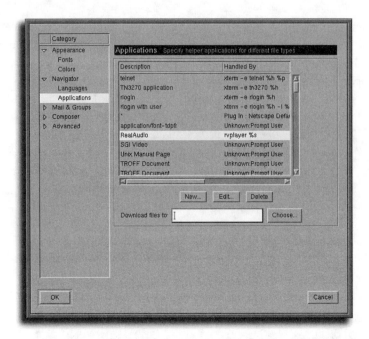

FIGURE 19.7
The Navigator Applications setting is used to add support for external programs or plug-ins, such as RealPlayer.

Netscape Communicator supports *plug-ins*, or additional programs that can add features to the browser. One of these is the RealPlayer plug-in named rvplayer, which you can use to listen to audio or video broadcasts through the Internet (audio or video will be played automatically when you click audio or video links on a Web page).

Installing Internet video support for Netscape

1. To add support for the RealPlayer plug-in, continue from the previous step-by-step and scroll through the list of applications. Select the RealAudio application and then click the Edit button with your left mouse button. A dialog box appears, as shown in Figure 19.8.

SEE ALSO

➤ *To learn about more multimedia tools for Linux, see Chapter 15, "Using Graphics and Multimedia Tools."*

2. Add the filename extension .rm to the list, edit the Handled by Application field to read realplay %s, and then click the OK button. Click the OK button again to exit and save your Navigator Preferences.

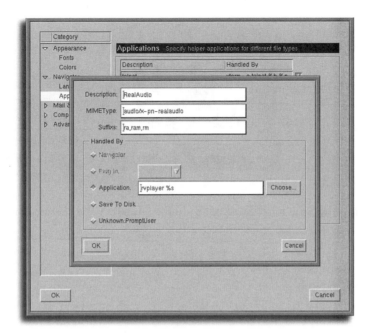

FIGURE 19.8
Use the Navigator Application Edit dialog box to add specific support for RealPlayer.

3. To test the rvplayer plug-in, first make sure that it is installed on your system (look under the /usr/local/RealPlayerG2 directory for the realplay program), and then use Navigator to read in the rvplayer sample video from your hard drive:

```
# netscape file:/usr/local/RealPlayerG2/audiosig.rm
```

After Navigator displays its initial window, the RealPlayer starts and play a short music and video clip, as shown in Figure 19.9.

To get the latest RealPlayer application for Linux, browse to

```
http://www.real.com/products/player/linux.html
```

For more information about using Communicator helper applications, browse to

```
http://home.netscape.com
```

FIGURE 19.9
The RealPlayer plug-in plays audio and video clips during your Internet sessions when you use Netscape Navigator.

chapter

20

Using telnet and Internet Relay Chat

Using the `telnet` command   ●

Chatting with Internet Relay Chat   ●

Using the *telnet* Command

The telnet command is used to log on to remote computers on the Internet. Use telnet to log on, usually with a user name and password, and run programs, view files, or download data. The telnet command is used on the command line, followed by a hostname, or remote computer system's name to start a telnet session.

For example, to connect to the U.S. Environmental Protection Agency (which runs open information services on several remote computer systems), use the telnet command, like this:

```
# telnet ttnbbs.rtpnc.epa.gov
```

This command connects you to the EPA's remote computer, and you receive a logon prompt (as shown in Figure 20.1).

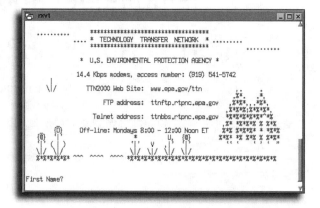

FIGURE 20.1
Log on to remote federal government or other computer systems by using the telnet command.

> **SEE ALSO**
> ➤ *For more information on using Netscape Communicator, see page 300.*

Connecting to Other Computers

You usually need an active username and password on the remote computer in order to log on to the remote system using the telnet program. This means that you generally need an account on the remote computer system to get in. Few system administrators allow anonymous telnet access, although you can find a list of computer systems with open telnet access (such as those that run bulletin-board systems, or BBSs) by using a search engine through a favorite Web search site (such as http://www.yahoo.com).

Netscape does it all—telnet too!

The Netscape Navigator component of Netscape's Communicator can also be used to `telnet` to remote computers, because it recognizes a uniform resource locator (URL) specification of the `telnet` protocol, such as `telnet://ttnbbs.rtpnc.epa.gov`. If you enter a `telnet` address in Netscape's Location field or click on a `telnet` link on a Web page, a separate program (the X11 terminal client, `xterm`) is launched by Netscape to start your `telnet` session.

The `telnet` command, like the `ftp` command, can also be used in an interactive mode, so you can open and close sessions to different remote computers without exiting the program. The `telnet` command also has built-in help (accessed by the keyword help without an active session). Table 20.1 lists many of `telnet`'s built-in commands.

Table 20.1 Common telnet commands (accessed by Ctrl+] during an active session)

Command	Action
!	Run a shell from `telnet`.
?	Show help.
close	Close the current connection.
display	Display control characters.
environ	List or change environment variables.
logout	Log off remote system and close the connection.
open	Connect to a remote computer.
quit	Exit the `telnet` program.
send	Send special characters to remote computer.
set	Set various operating parameters status. Print connection status.
toggle	Toggle various operating parameters.
unset	Unset various operating parameters.
z	Suspend `telnet`.

Starting a *telnet* session

1. Start your Internet session (such as through a Point-to-Point Protocol, or PPP, account with your Internet service provider).

2. From the command line of the console or an X11 terminal window, use the `telnet` command, followed by the name or Internet Protocol, or IP, address, like this:

   ```
   # telnet fbminet.ca
   ```

3. The `telnet` program prints the IP address of the remote computer, like this:

   ```
   Trying 199.214.6.227...
   ```

4. The `telnet` program then (hopefully) connects, informs you of the escape character you can use to run `telnet` commands (Ctrl+]), and presents the logon screen for the remote computer:

   ```
   Connected to fbminet.ca.
   Escape character is '^]'.
   MAXIMUS/2 v2.02MAXIMUS/2 v2.02
   ±±±±±±±±Ü ±±±±±±±±Ü  ±±±±±±±±±Ü  ±±±±Ü
   ±±ÛBBB±±Û  ±±ÛBBB±±Û  ±±ÛB±±ÛB±±Û    ±±ÛB
   ±±Û    BB  ±±Û  ±±Û   ±±Û ±±Û ±±Û    ±±Û  ±±±±±Ü±±Ü ±±±±±±Ü Â±±±±±±±±Ü
   ±±±±±Ü    ±±±±±±±ÛB  ±±Û ±±Û ±±Û    ±±Û  ±±Û±±Û±±Û ±±ÛBBBB  ÂBB±±ÛBBB
   ±±ÛBBB    ±±ÛBBB±±Û  ±±Û ±±Û ±±Û    ±±Û  ±±Û±±Û±±Û ±±±±Ü       Â±±Û
   ±±Û       ±±Û  ±±Û   ±±Û BB ±±Û    ±±Û  ±±Û±±Û±±Û ±±ÛBB       Â±±Û
   ±±±±Û     ±±±±±±±±±Û ±±±±Û   ±±±±Û ±±±±Û ±±Û±±±±±Û ±±±±±±Ü    Â±±Û
   BBBB      BBBBBBBB  BBBB      BBBB  BBBB  BB BBBBB  BBBBB     ÂBB
                Farm Business Management Information Network
                A project of the Canadian Farm Business
                Management Council

            National Internet Telnet Site -- Telnet://FBMInet.ca
                 FBMInet Node 2001:1/101   Telnet Line 4

   If your Telnet client does not support ANSI emulation,
   Zmodem file transfers, and IBM boxdraw characters, we
   suggest you try NetTerm.You can download a shareware
   version of NetTerm from this BBS or directly from the
   FBMInet web site at http://FBMInet.ca
   ```

5. Log on to the remote computer. (Note that some remote computers use logon prompts much different than your Linux system's!)

   ```
   William Ball [Y,n]?
   Password: ******


   Hi there, and welcome back to FBMInet-CFBMC Telnet Site
   Telnet://FBMInet.ca!


   We're glad that you called back, and we hope that you'll
   call again in the future.  Enjoy your stay!
   ```

6. When you finish with the `telnet` session (by using the `logout`, `exit`, or `close` `telnet` commands, or through the remote computer's commands—refer to Table 20.1), the `telnet` program quits and prints a message like this:

```
Connection closed by foreign host.
```

Use *ping* to test your session

If you have trouble connecting to the remote computer with the `telnet` command, make sure you're using the correct name of the computer or Internet Protocol (IP) address. To see if the name is correct, use the `ping` command, followed by the computer's name:

```
# ping staffnet.com
PING staffnet.com (207.226.80.14): 56 data bytes
64 bytes from 207.226.80.14: icmp_seq=0 ttl=249 time=315.7 ms
64 bytes from 207.226.80.14: icmp_seq=1 ttl=249 time=179.8 ms
64 bytes from 207.226.80.14: icmp_seq=2 ttl=249 time=167.2 ms


--- staffnet.com ping statistics ---
3 packets transmitted, 3 packets received, 0% packet loss
round-trip min/avg/max = 167.2/220.9/315.7 ms
```

The `ping` command continues until you press Ctrl+C. You can also use the computer's IP address with the `ping` command like this:

```
# ping 207.226.80.14
PING 207.226.80.14 (207.226.80.14): 56 data bytes
64 bytes from 207.226.80.14: icmp_seq=0 ttl=249 time=161.6 ms
64 bytes from 207.226.80.14: icmp_seq=1 ttl=249 time=150.1 ms
64 bytes from 207.226.80.14: icmp_seq=2 ttl=249 time=150.5 ms


--- 207.226.80.14 ping statistics ---
3 packets transmitted, 3 packets received, 0% packet loss
round-trip min/avg/max = 150.1/154.0/161.6 ms
```

Downloading Files During *telnet* Sessions

Downloading programs from a remote computer during a `telnet` session can present a problem. The `telnet` command is not an FTP connection, so you must use programs on each end of the `telnet` connection to transfer files. To download a program from the remote computer, the remote computer should have a program, such as `sz` or send ZMODEM. To download files from the remote computer, use the rz, or receive ZMODEM, communications program. The sz and rz commands are included in Red Hat Linux and most other Linux distributions.

Downloading a file with the *sz* and *rz* commands

1. To retrieve a file called program.tgz from a remote computer, start your telnet session, and then use the sz command from the command line of the remote computer. Start the file transfer by using sz like so:

   ```
   # sz -w 2048 filename.tgz
   ```

   This command sends the file filename.tgz using the _ZMODEM communications protocol.

2. Immediately after starting the sz command on the remote computer, press Ctrl+] to escape to the telnet prompt, which looks like the following:

   ```
   telnet>
   ```

3. Type the telnet shell command (the exclamation point) followed by the rz command and a press of the Enter key to start receiving the file:

   ```
   telnet> ! rz
   ```

   The file starts transferring from the remote computer to your computer. See the sz and rz manual pages for more information.

   SEE ALSO
   ➤ *To learn more about the shell, see page 24.*

Chatting with Internet Relay Chat

Use the irc, or Internet Relay Chat, command, to converse with other people on the Internet. When you run irc, use its built-in commands to connect to chat servers, to see who is chatting, and to set other options. The irc command's built-in help documents more than 110 commands and topics. To use irc, you should have an active Internet connection.

Starting an *irc* Session

Starting a chat session with *irc*

1. Start your Internet connection. To start an irc session, use irc on the command line of the console or an X11 terminal window like this:

   ```
   # irc
   ```

The irc program connects to a default chat server, or other computer supporting irc, as shown in Figure 20.2.

```
rxvt                                                          _ □ X
*** Connecting to port 6667 of server irc-2.mit.edu
*** Welcome to the Internet Relay Network bball
*** If you have not already done so, please read the new user information with
    /HELP NEWUSER
*** Your host is irc-2.mit.edu[rastro], running version 2.8.21+CSr29
*** This server was created Mon May 26 1997 at 12: 19:34 EDT
*** umodes available oiwsfcukbdl, channel modes available biklmnopstv
*** There are 55 users and 30 invisible on 1 servers
*** 43 channels have been formed
*** This server has 85 clients and 0 servers connected
*** Highest connection count:  110 (110 clients)




[1] bball [Mail: 1]
>
```

FIGURE 20.2
The irc command displays a scrolling screen with a command line at the bottom of the screen.

2. If you're using irc for the first time, use the /HELP command, followed by the keyword newuser, as shown:

   > /HELP newuser

   A screen or two of helpful information is printed to your display. You can also browse through the irc command's help facility and read introductory information by using the /HELP command followed by one of these keywords, or topics: basics, commands, etiquette, expressions, intro, ircII, menus, news, newuser, and rules.

3. To see a list of active chat groups on the server, use the /LIST command on the irc command line, like this:

   > /LIST

   After a slight pause, the screen scrolls a list of current discussion groups, as shown in Figure 20.3.

FIGURE 20.3

The irc /LIST command displays a list of current discussion groups.

4. To see details about the members of a particular group, use the /WHO command, followed by the name of the group, like this:

```
> /WHO #giggles
```

The irc command lists the names of any current members.

5. To become a member of a discussion group, use the /JOIN command, followed by the name of the group, like this:

```
> /JOIN #giggles
```

Your screen starts scrolling messages as member of the group talk (as shown in Figure 20.4). From now on, all text you type followed by the Enter key is broadcast to all members of the group. See the ircII manual page (found under the /usr/doc/irc/doc directory) for more information about using irc.

6. To quit the irc program, use irc's /QUIT command and press Enter. The irc program exits and severs your connection.

SEE ALSO

➤ *For more information about starting PPP connections, see page 257.*

FIGURE 20.4
Group discussions continuously scroll up the screen after you've joined an `irc` chat session.

part

V

SYSTEM ADMINISTRATION

Basic Shell Programming	321	**21**
Using Basic Programming Tools	339	**22**
Using Boot Managers	351	**23**
Managing Users and Groups	361	**24**
Managing Scheduling Services	389	**25**
Managing Network Connections	405	**26**
Managing Daemons	431	**27**
Managing the File System	453	**28**
Managing Applications	481	**29**
System Maintenance	503	**30**
Managing the Kernel	527	**31**

# chapter 21

Basic Shell Programming

What shell scripts are used for •

Writing shell programs •

Using shell variables •

Using shell constructs •

Writing shell functions •

The part of any system that interprets keyboard or mouse commands is called the *shell*. Under MS-DOS, for example, the shell is called COMMAND.COM; under Windows 95/98, the graphical shell is called EXPLORER.EXE. Under most UNIX systems, users have their choice of shells in both the graphical and text-mode environments.

The most popular Linux shell is bash. This stands for *Bourne Again Shell*, and is named after one of the original UNIX shell designers. bash has a lighter relative, ash, which lacks some features such as command-line histories, but requires substantially less memory and is therefore found in some Linux distributions and on emergency recovery disks. Clones of the standard UNIX shells, sh (the Bourne shell), csh (the c shell), and ksh (the Korn shell) are also available.

Another point to remember is that a shell under Linux (as well as under other UNIX systems, and interestingly enough, under DOS and OS/2) is just another program. You can start another shell from the shell you're in, just like you can start the program ls to get a directory listing. This is significant because many shell scripts are not interpreted by the same type of shell in which you type the command; instead, a different shell is started to process the command. The different shells have different syntaxes. If a program is written using sh but you are running bash, it makes sense that sh would be started when your shell script is started.

What Shell Scripts Are Used For

Shell scripts are actually one of the most common types of programs on all UNIX systems. They are relatively easy to write and maintain, and they can tie together other programs (for example, other shell scripts) to get a lot of work done with one simple command.

Every time you log in to your Linux system, the system executes a shell script before you even see the first $ prompt. Almost all aspects of system startup, including network initialization, are controlled by shell scripts. For a regular Linux system user, shell scripts can make work easier and more productive. For the Linux system administrator, a basic understanding of shell scripts makes all the difference between a well-run and trouble-free Linux system and one that can get really ugly, really fast.

Writing Shell Programs

Shell programs are similar to batch files in the DOS world. Unlike DOS batch files, however, shell programs have much more advanced functionality; they are akin to conventional programming languages. Entire books have been written about most available shells; this chapter covers only bash because it is the most popular, and because it is used by default on Red Hat, Caldera, and most popular Linux distributions.

Good Programming Practice

Good shell programs are easy to read and understand. This is vital if someone else must modify your work, or if you come back to it months later to fix or extend something. Badly written code is very difficult to work with and understand. Don't kid yourself about being able to remember what you've written (let alone understand what someone else has written) if the code is not formatted and commented properly. I hate preaching, but remind yourself when looking at the examples that the indentations and so on are there to help you understand the code. Give others who have to work with your code the same courtesy.

A simple shell script consists of regular shell commands, like the ones that would be typed interactively at the shell command line. Shells can also define commands that are only used in scripts. Because it's handy to document what you're doing in a shell script for when you need to modify or fix it, comment lines can be included in a script by preceding the line with a # character. bash then treats the rest of the line as a comment.

Indentation is an important tool to help make your code readable when things get complicated. Blank lines can be used as well. Too many blank lines, indents, and comments, however, can make the code look just as jumbled as if it all had been crammed on one line.

A Sample Program

The last thing the world needs is another "Hello, World!" program. Instead, I want to show you something useful. For example, suppose you want a nicely formatted printout of what is in the current directory. The code shown in Listing 21.1 provides a means to do just that (the numbers at the beginning of each line are for your use; they do not actually appear in the code).

Listing 21.1   *printdir* Sends an Appropriately Paginated List of Files and Directories to the Printer

```
01 #!/bin/bash
02 #Sample Program for Practical Linux
03 # Jan Walter jwalter@rogers.wave.ca
04 # Practical, Chapter 21
05 # Copyright 2000 Macmillan Computer Publishing and Jan Walter
06 # All rights reserved.
07 # This code comes without warranty of any kind. If it breaks you get
08 # to keep both pieces.
09 ls -l > /tmp/lstemp
10 pr /tmp/lstemp | lpr
11 rm /tmp/lstmp
12 #end of script
```

This script works best when you're logged in as a regular user rather than system administrator; it assumes that you have a printer installed and correctly configured. Simply put, it executes the commands in the file in sequence. The more interesting aspects of this listing are as follows:

- Line 1 tells the system which shell the system should start to execute the script. This is vital because different shell programs sport different built-in commands.

- Line 9 executes the program ls -l and redirects output to a file in the system temporary directory.

- Line 10 feeds the contents to pr (which breaks the file into pages and, depending on the arguments, numbers the pages, adds a nice header, and so on) and feeds the output of pr to lpr, the system print spooler. The important point here is the redirection of the output of commands, not the commands themselves.

- Line 11 removes the temporary file created in line 3. (Just a reminder: Make sure your programs are polite to other users on the system and clean up after themselves.)

Now try the script out:

1. Start an editor, such as joe, like this:
   joe printdir

2. After the editor starts, enter the script text in Listing 21.1.

3. If you are using joe, press Crtl+K, and then press X to save the file and quit.

4. You still need to tell Linux that this file is indeed something it can execute. To do this, use the chmod command:

```
chmod a+x printdir
```

5. Try out your creation by issuing the following command:

```
./printdir
```

Your printer should spit out a long listing of the contents of your directory.

I admit that all of this can be done easily at the command line with the following command:

```
ls -l | pr | lpr
```

All this really does is create a long directory listing, along with file permissions, sizes, and so on, and uses a pipe to redirect the output of the program. In this case, the output gets sent to pr, which formats the text into nice 60-line pages, with page numbers, time and date, and the output of pr gets passed on to lpr.

> **Note**
>
> You can look up these commands in the system manual by using the command man.

> **Tired of typing ./to start your scripts?**
>
> You can put your frequently used scripts into a directory called **bin** in your home directory. This directory's contents are always in your application path (the directories the system searches when looking for a program whose name was not preceded by a directory name), which allows you to use the script without using the path just as with a regular system program. Be aware that you run a security risk by doing this. If, for example, a malicious hard drive–eating program called **ls** makes its way into your **./bin** directory, you could end up running it whenever you try to list your directory.

Nonetheless, the point is that you can now do all this with the simpler command ./printdir. The idea also carries on to the bigger scripts that actually do something significant, such as add a new user to the system. Every expression you use in a shell script can also be used interactively.

In Listing 21.2, I've tweaked the script in Listing 21.1 to provide what programmers call instrumentation. *Instrumentation* is the process of indicating to the user of the program what is actually happening. This prevents users from prematurely terminating the program (possibly while the program is in the middle of doing something critical) because the system appears to be sitting there and doing nothing.

Listing 21.2 *printdir2* Sends the Nicely Paginated List of Files in the Current Directory to the Printer and Provides Feedback to the User While Doing So

```
01 #!/bin/bash
02 # printdir2
03 # Jan Walter jwalter@rogers.wave.ca
04 # Practical Linux, Chapter 22
05 # Copyright 2000 Macmillan Computer Publishing and Jan Walter
06 # All rights reserved.
07 # This code comes without warranty of any kind. If it breaks you get
08 # to keep both pieces.
09 echo -n "Getting Directory listing ..."
10 ls -l > /tmp/lstmp
11 echo " done."
12 echo -n "Formatting and printing Directory listing ..."
13 pr /tmp/lstmp | lpr
14 echo " done."
15 echo -n "Cleaning up ..."
16 rm /tmp/lstmp
17 echo " done."
18 # end of script
```

The output of the program looks something like this:

```
[jwalter@jansmachine samples_22]$ ./printdir2
Getting Directory listing ... done.
Formatting and printing Directory listing ... done.
Cleaning up ... done.
[jwalter@jansmachine samples_22]$
```

If the directory listing is large or the system that's being used is heavily loaded, the first step might take some time; it's nice to see what's happening as a program proceeds through the work it's doing. This is, of course, much more useful when many more steps are involved.

The command echo is just another program (type man echo to view echo's man page), and the -n parameter simply tells echo to not output a newline character after printing something on the display. In this case, I use echo -n to keep progress information on a single line, which, in my opinion, looks nicer.

Using Shell Variables

Variables are temporary placeholders for information, either numbers or sequences of characters (called *strings*). The system (that is, the shell) has a number of useful predefined variables, such as the user name, home directory, and system name. Using the env command generates a listing of all *persistent* environment variables (meaning that they don't stop existing when the current command or script ends, instead they exist for your Linux login environment as a whole) defined in your shell. Listing 21.3 is the output generated by the env command on my machine. This will vary somewhat from machine to machine, of course.

Listing 21.3 Sample Output Listing of the *env* Command

```
[jwalter@jansmachine samples_22]$ env
USERNAME=
ENV=/home/jwalter/.bashrc
BROWSER=xterm -font 9x15 -e lynx
HISTSIZE=1000
HOSTNAME=jansmachine.censvcs.net
LOGNAME=jwalter
HISTFILESIZE=1000
MAIL=/var/spool/mail/jwalter
TERM=xterm
HOSTTYPE=i386
PATH=/usr/local/bin:/bin:/usr/bin:/usr/X11R6/bin:/opt/kde/bin:/usr/bin/mh:
/home/jwalter/bin
KDEDIR=/opt/kde
HOME=/home/jwalter
SHELL=/bin/bash
USER=jwalter
MANPATH=/usr/man:/usr/X11R6/man:/usr/local/man
DISPLAY=:0.0
OSTYPE=Linux
MM_CHARSET=ISO-8859-1
SHLVL=5
=/usr/bin/env
[jwalter@jansmachine samples_22]$
```

The majority of the environment variables are used for library and application pathnames, and things like the OS type and platform.

327

> **Modifying variables in your login shell**
>
> It's not a good idea to mess with the predefined shell variables in your system unless you know exactly the effect you're trying to achieve. If **PATH** or some other vital variable is filled with invalid data, you will have difficulty executing normal commands—even `exit`, which you need to log out. If you modify your login script (the `.bash_profile` script in your home directory), you might not even be able to log in.
>
> Be sure to keep this in mind when you modify root's login scripts! I find it best to keep another root login on another terminal to ensure that I have a usable shell if the new login script does not work.

Using Variables in Scripts

Unlike most conventional programming languages, variables in bash shell scripts are *optionally* typed (that is, classified as to whether they contain integers, characters, or floating point numbers). Some numerical operations are faster when bash is informed that a variable contains only a number. Variables are not required to be declared before they are used, but it does make the code more readable.

After a variable is *referenced* (that is, used by having something assigned to it), you can use the value of the variable in expressions by prefixing the variable name with a $ character.

To make a persistent environment variable, use the `export` command. This command is useful for modifying shell variables that already exist (like the ones you see when the `env` command is executed) because changes made to the values of the variables already declared will otherwise be lost after the script finishes.

A Sample Script

The script in Listing 21.4 uses shell variables, decision-making constructs, and some more advanced shell techniques to clear all files owned by the current user from the /tmp directory. This is a common operation done by system administrators because some programs don't clean up after themselves properly, and some users like to use the /tmp directories for other things. As an option, if the user is root, the script accepts a user name argument and clears that user's files instead.

Listing 21.4 Use *cleantmp* to Clean Up Files in the */tmp* Directory Left by the Current User (or If the User of the Script Is Root, the Name Specified on the Command Line)

```
01 #!/bin/bash
02 # cleantmp
03 # bash script that cleans up the files left in /tmp by a user
```

```
04 # usage: cleantmp <user>
05 # the user argument is only valid if the script is run as root
06 # Jan Walter jwalter@rogers.wave.ca
07 # Practical Linux, Chapter 22
08 # Copyright 2000 Macmillan Computer Publishing and Jan Walter
09 # All rights reserved.
10 # This code comes without warranty of any kind. If it breaks you get
11 # to keep both pieces.
12
13 #check to see if root executed this
14 if [ $LOGNAME = 'root' ]; then
15 if [ $1 ]; then
16         DELNAME=$1
17    else
18        DELNAME=$LOGNAME
19    fi
20 else
21    if [ $1 ]; then
22        echo "Only root is allowed to specify another user id."
23        exit 1
24    else
25        DELNAME=$LOGNAME
26    fi
27 fi
28 echo "User's files to remove: " $DELNAME
29 echo "Proceeding with this script can cause problems if other applications"
30 echo "still require access to those files."
31 echo -n "Proceed with clearing the files? [y/N]"
32 read
33
34 if [ $REPLY ]; then
35        if [ $REPLY = 'y' -o $REPLY = 'Y'  ]; then
36            echo "You pressed yes."
37        else
38            echo "You pressed no."
39        exit 0
40        fi
41 else
42    echo "You did not press anything."
```

continues...

Listing 21.4 Continued

```
43      exit 0
44 fi
45
46 # all this leads up to one big finale ...
47 echo -n "Deleting files in /tmp directory tree belonging to "$DEL_NAME" ... "
48 rm -f $( find /tmp -user $DELNAME )
49 echo "done."
50
51 # end of script
```

Following is a review of the use of variables and the more complex parts of the script:

- Line 14 introduces the `if` condition and the test expression (more about these later), and references your first variable. This variable is also listed in the output of the program `env` and, as you might have guessed by the output there, contains the name under which the user is currently logged in. The `if` executes all statements immediately following the `then` if the expression that immediately follows it is true (or equal to 1). In this case, it compares the variable `LOGNAME` to the string `root` to determine whether the user who typed the command is root.

Command-line arguments in *bash*

Command-line arguments are defined by `bash` as anything following the first word of a command. These arguments are separated from the command by a space. For example, with `ls -l`, `ls` is the command and `-l` is an argument.

- Line 15 uses the `if` condition and the test expression to determine whether the program has a command-line argument. Command-line arguments are referenced by their position on the command line, `$1` being the first, `$2` being the second, and so on. If you want to use all command-line arguments in a list, for example to document what's happening, you can use `$@` to use them all as one string. A single variable in a test expression is evaluated by `bash` to determine whether the variable actually contains anything.

- Line 16 assigns a value to the variable DELNAME. Note that there are no spaces between the equal sign (=) and the value being assigned to the variable. If you must have spaces in the value you're assigning, make sure to enclose the value in single quotes, with no space between the quote and the equal sign.

- Lines 14–27 essentially check the user ID and command-line arguments according to the following logic:

```
If the user is root
    then
    if there is a command line argument
        accept another name as a command line argument and set
        DELNAME to that argument
    else
        set DELNAME to root
    end if
else
    if there is a command line argument
        then tell the user they are not allowed to do this and exit
    else
        set DELNAME to the user's name
    end if
end if
```

The only other thing to note here is that, unlike with some other programming languages, if statements in bash are ended with fi instead of with endif or end (refer to line 27 of Listing 21.4).

A word about warnings

It's especially important to notify users when a script is about to delete any data that might belong to them, and to give them the opportunity to abort the operation!

- Lines 28–30 basically provide documentation and a warning to users that what they are about to do can have potentially undesirable effects. It's important to tell users this; otherwise, you, the system administrator, are likely to get a lot of complaints or service calls about weird things happening on the system.

- Line 31 uses the echo -n command that was introduced earlier to provide a prompt for confirmation from the user, and to ensure that the cursor stays on the same line as the question to underscore to the user that the program requires a response.

- Line 32 introduces the `read` command. This command reads a line of input from the user, and then puts each word into the variable names that follow, one per variable, placing any remaining words (if applicable) into the last variable. If no variable is given, as in this case, the `read` command places everything that was read into the `REPLY` variable, which is the default.

- Lines 34–44 check whether there is something in the `REPLY` variable (if there is nothing, this indicates that the user simply hit the Enter key), and if there is, check for a lowercase or a capital Y. The only way the program can proceed is if the `REPLY` variable contains y or Y; all other conditions cause the script to terminate (note that the `echo` statements provide documentation to users to make sure they understand why the program did not continue).

- Line 48 does all the work of the program—it calls `rm -f` for all files found with the name contained in `DELNAME`'s user ID. This is all wrapped up in another `echo` statement to give the user some idea of the completion status. Note that the `find` command contained in the `$( ... )` expression is executed first, and the output of the program used as input for the `rm -f` statement.

You must wonder whether all this is really necessary to execute what essentially boils down to one command. I would argue that the extra checks, and moreover the ease of use of the script, will make it more likely for someone with limited Linux experience to complete the task successfully. Creating a friendlier environment for the user is paramount in the continued acceptance of Linux.

Most shell programs are not full-blown applications, but helpers in everyday tasks. It's relatively easy to make them somewhat interactive, and so they are very useful if you want to prompt users as to whether they are certain they want to do something.

Using Shell Constructs

`bash` provides the following constructs:

- Conditional constructs—These are statements that cause code to be executed depending on a decision.

- Looping constructs—These are statements that repeat the themselves a given number of times.

As stated before, this chapter is not intended to teach you how to program, only to introduce you to the most commonly used parts of shell programming so that if you're confronted with a shell script, you'll be able to figure out what's happening.

Conditional Constructs: The *if* Statement

The `if` statement executes lines of code depending on whether the expression following the keyword `if` evaluates to a true result. The code following the `else` keyword (if any) is executed if the expression evaluates to false. The syntax of the `if` statement is shown in Listing 21.5.

Listing 21.5 *if* Expression Syntax

```
if <expression>
then
    <code executed if expression true>
else
    <code executed if expression false>
fi
```

The `else` statement and subsequent code is unnecessary if nothing needs to be done when the expression evaluates to a false result.

How *bash* interprets *true* and *false*

Conventional programming languages (specifically C and C++) interpret true and false as numerical values, where 0 is false, and any other result is true. In **bash**, however, true and false values are reversed: **bash** interprets 0 as true and 1 as false. This is because `if` expressions were designed to test the return codes of actual programs and commands, and a 0 typically indicated success, not failure, of the program.

All **bash** constructs and expressions automatically handle this for you; you need only worry about whether the expression is true or false without worrying about the actual numerical values. But remember to take this into account when dealing with programs that don't follow the conventions for return values.

Also keep this in mind if you are providing result codes when ending your shell scripts with the `exit` command. The statement `exit 0` indicates a successful completion of a shell script, while `exit 1` is failure. Using `exit` enables you to easily use other shell scripts within your script and determine if they've worked successfully.

Testing Expressions with *test*

`test` provides the other half of the functionality of `if`. Test expressions perform mathematical, Boolean, and other tests and return true or false depending on the outcome.

Test expressions can appear in two forms:

- With the keyword `test`, like so:
  ```
  test $LOGNAME = 'root'
  ```

- With square brackets, like so:

```
[ $LOGNAME = 'root' ]
```

Both forms of test expressions work in the same way.

Integer Expressions

Test expressions are remarkable compared to other programming languages' comparison expressions because they do not use operators such as >, <, >=, and so on for greater-than and less-than comparisons. Instead, integer expressions, which are discussed in Table 21.1, are used.

Table 21.1 Integer Test Expressions

Expression	True If
x -eq y	x equals y
x -ne y	x is not equal to y
x -ge y	x is greater than or equal to y
x -gt y	x is greater than y
x -le y	x is less than or equal to y
x -lt y	x is less than y

String Expressions

String expressions, on the other hand, can test to determine whether strings are identical, not identical, zero or non-zero lengths, or null values (that is, empty or not initialized). Note that bash discriminates between zero-length strings and empty ones. Table 21.2 illustrates how string expressions operate.

Table 21.2 String Test Expressions

Expression	True If
-z string	string has a length of zero
string	string is not null, (that is, it is uninitialized)
-n string	string has a nonzero length
string1 = string2	string1 is identical to string2
string1 != string2	string1 is not identical to string2

File-Testing Expressions

File-testing expressions test for information about files, and are typically used by scripts to determine whether the file should be backed up, copied, or deleted. There are numerous file-testing expressions, so I will list only some of the more common ones in Table 21.3. See the bash(1) manual page, or more specifically, the test(1) manual page for more of these expressions.

Table 21.3 File Test Expressions

Expression	True If
-e file	file exists
-r file	file is readable
-w file	file is writable
-d file	file is a directory
-x file	file exists and is executable
file1 -nt file2	file1 is newer than file2
file1 -ot file2	file1 is older than file2

Negation and Boolean Operators

Test expressions support the basic AND, OR, and NOT Boolean operators. Table 21.4 illustrates how these expressions operate.

Table 21.4 Boolean Test Expressions

Expression	Effect
!expression	Reverses the evaluation of expression (that is, it changes the evaluation to true if expression is false, and vice versa)
expression1 -a expression2	True if both expressions are true (expression1 AND expression2)
expression1 -o expression2	True if either expression is true (expression1 OR expression2)

Repeating Commands with *while*

`while` is used to repeat commands until a given condition evaluates to false. It's used when it cannot be predicted or calculated how many iterations the loop will go through. Listing 21.6 shows the `while` syntax.

Listing 21.6 *while* Syntax

```
while expression
do
     <code executed while the expression is true>
done
```

Repeating Commands with *for*

`for` works differently in `bash` than it does in any other programming language: It is used to traverse lists, and to process each item of the list in sequence. This is useful because so much work deals with handling lists. Command-line arguments are lists of separate strings, as are multiple words that can be returned from `readline`. To `bash`, "words" are defined as tokens that are separated by a white space; therefore, `The-big-cat` is considered a single word.

Writing Shell Functions

Shell functions are one of the more advanced features of the `bash` shell programming language. In most programming languages, programmers accumulate snippets of code that are useful in more than one program. To make the reuse of code easier between programs, these snippets of code are grouped into functions. They are essentially subprograms that your shell programs can call. BASIC calls these *subroutines*; Pascal and Modula-2 call them *procedures*; and C, C++, and `bash` call them *functions*.

Functions usually take an argument or more to pass to them the data they are supposed to work on. The idea is that the code in a function should be packaged in such a way as to make it useful in more than one circumstance. To allow more than one shell program to use the same function library, and to prevent multiple copies of these functions from littering the `bin` directories of hapless shell programmers, `bash` introduces the concept of including files in your script.

> **Note**
>
> I tend to put my `bash` functions in a directory called `include` in my home directory's `bin` directory, because `include` directories are conventionally used for containing header files that programs written in C and C++ use. I do plenty of programming in all of these languages, and so the less I have to change my way of working, the better.
>
> I also group my functions into separate categories, and keep them in different files according to category —such as `fileman` (short for file management), which I use for the finding and handling files. I admit that my procedure libraries are pretty sparse—I spend too much time moving from system to system to really accumulate a comprehensive function library.

Consider for a moment the advantages of doing this. There would be one file (or different files containing groups of functions useful for different things) that contains functions that any other script can use. When a problem is discovered in one of those functions and fixed, all scripts using this function automatically use the updated—and hopefully less problematic—code. This reduces the time spent maintaining scripts, and frees the shell programmer to do other things.

Using functions in a single script can make programming easier and less likely to contain errors. Using functions in multiple scripts has the same advantage, but also requires some forethought. Different files containing functions scattered all over the place tend to make reusing code difficult. However, if you are distributing a useful script you've written, sometimes it is more convenient to include all the functions in a single file. You can always be sure that someone using your software has the most recent version of all of your functions without having to download separate support libraries.

A Simple Shell Function

From `bash`'s point of view, a shell function is essentially a script within a script. Functions can do anything that scripts can do, with the added benefit that properly designed functions can be reused in other scripts.

To declare a function, use the (appropriately named) `function` keyword. Functions, just like scripts, take arguments, and these are treated the same way in the code. All code contained within a function is enclosed in curly braces (`{ }`). As an example, the following function would print the words `function called` on the screen and list the arguments given.

```
function test_function()
{
```

```
        echo "This function was called with the following _arguments:"
        echo   $@
}
```

Note that $@ means "all arguments" in bash.

The function would be called in the script like this:

```
... (preceding code)
test_function argument1 argument2 and so on
... (code afterwards)
```

The output on the screen (excluding anything else the script might put up, of course) would look like this

```
This function was called with the following arguments:
argument1 argument2 and so on
```

All in all, functions don't behave much differently from separate scripts, but because they are in the same file, the additional overhead of starting yet another instance of bash to process the script is not incurred.

Using a Library

By definition, a library contains only functions and environment variable definitions. To load a library of functions (you need to do this before using the function in the library), you must execute the file containing the library. Because the file does not contain any code that bash will immediately execute, bash will load only the functions from the file. After this, you can use all the functions just as though they were in the local file.

Libraries follow the same conventions as regular scripts and executable files in most respects—including the PATH environment variable. For example, this technique provides one single point of maintenance for the init scripts on your system for functions dealing with process control. To include a file of functions (this example is from the init scripts in your /etc/rc.d/init.d directory), type the following at the command line:

. /etc/rc.d/init.d/functions

The . indicates that the file following the space should be loaded and executed. Because library files contain nothing but functions, they are simply loaded and then available for use. bash also has another keyword that does the same thing: source. The . is easier, and most people use this to get bash to load a file full of functions.

chapter
22

Using Basic Programming Tools

Recompiling code ●

Compiling programs with gcc ●

Linking programs with the ld linker ●

Building programs with the
make command ●

Specifying different makefiles ●

Getting started quickly with
new programs ●

Building X11 makefiles with the
xmkmf script ●

Recompiling Code

One of the greatest strengths of Linux is that it can run almost any UNIX program. But many UNIX machines don't use the Intel (or Digital Alpha) processors. What's more, when UNIX was designed, binary emulation of different machine architectures was prohibitive in terms of hardware requirements and was unworkable in business environments in which UNIX was deployed. Nonetheless, UNIX systems are, for the most part, *source-code compatible*, so a program's source code (typically in C) can be recompiled on a different platform and will usually work. Of course, this is not guaranteed, so sometimes minor changes are required.

Even DOS and Windows programmers have reason to thank UNIX systems: The standard C libraries are part of the ANSI C standard. This means that code complying with the standard will also compile and run on any platform that complies with this standard. The standard enables most programs to *port* (to compile on a new platform) with minimal changes...or none at all.

This chapter covers compiling programs that are available in their source-code form. The Linux project has been busy, and just about every available free program—certainly every program from the GNU project—has been both ported and confirmed to work with Linux.

Compiling Programs with *gcc*

The C and C++ compiler included with Linux is gcc. This compiler supports all the latest features that would be expected from a commercial compiler, including a very good code optimizer (better than some compilers costing a significant amount of money), support for ANSI C and C++, C++ templates and template classes, and the C++ Standard Template Library. The gcc compiler is part of a complete development system, including a debugger (gdb), a profiler (gprof), various code-processing tools (such as make), and the runtime library itself.

The gcc program provides a front end to several compilers and allows you to compile C, C++, and other languages from a single command. The program manages this "magic" by expecting certain file extensions on the source code files.

The gcc compiler is the equivalent of cc on other UNIX systems. In fact, Linux sets a symbolic link so that all programs (such as make, when compiling programs actually written for other UNIX systems) that are told to call cc will call gcc instead. make calls gcc to compile all source files written in the C and C++ languages.

The gcc compiler can call ld and link your program for you, and it also can produce intermediate files. To compile a program with a single C file, use the following command:

```
gcc -o program name sourcefile
```

Using this command, gcc produces an executable file with the name *program name* from the source file given. The source files for gcc usually end in .c. If you don't specify an output file, gcc assumes the file a.out.

By default, gcc does not use its built-in code optimizer. To use the optimizer, you can use the -O switch to make the compiler do everything it can to increase the performance of the program. -O can be followed by a number up to 6 to denote the level of optimization the compiler will apply to the code. Note that when you enable optimizations, you should make sure the compiler is not producing debugging information as well. Unless you have a lot of experience with the GNU tools and debugging code, trying to debug optimized code can be frustrating. To instruct the program to produce output that the code profiler can read and from which it can generate reports, add the -pg switch to the compiler's command line.

Often, the programs will be modular, which means that they are comprised of several C modules that must be linked together. The gcc compiler can handle more than one source file at a time, but more than a few will begin to result in a lot of typing, and it's not worth the trouble for use on a regular basis. To automate this process, you use makefiles and usually process C files one at a time; then you link together the object files with ld at the end. The gcc compiler provides a command-line option specifically for this: -c. For example, you use the following command to generate a file called greeting.o from the C file greeting.c:

```
gcc -c greeting.c
```

The gcc compiler automatically uses the same filename in this case to generate a file with the .o extension.

If you need to debug the program

This command does not include the additional information for the debugger. To use the debugger on the program, give gcc the -ggdb switch, in addition to any others.

Linking Programs with the *ld* Linker

The ld linker links object files (the intermediate files that gcc generates) to system library files to produce executable files. Because most programs that Linux runs are usually based on shared code, incompatibilities sometimes occur when moving programs between different releases or distributions of Linux.

The ld linker knows about the standard libraries on your system and attempts to link these with the object files of the program. For example, if you have an object file called greeting.o that you have compiled with gcc, you would use the following command to produce an executable file with the same name:

```
ld -o greeting greeting.o
```

The ld linker would take the standard library files and dynamically link everything it could to reduce the memory your program takes. If you wanted to make sure this code runs on all systems, or that versioning of the dynamic libraries did not affect the program, you would use the following command to link the program:

```
ld -Bstatic -o greeting greeting.o
```

This file would naturally be quite a bit larger than the dynamically linked version.

Linux uses dynamic linking, too

Shared code uses dynamic linking to reduce the amount of memory a program takes. For example, many programs use the same code to put text on the screen; shared code enables many programs to use this code at the same time while keeping only one copy in memory. This is the same idea used for .dll files on Windows and OS/2 systems. However, differences in the versions of the shared code libraries can cause programs to malfunction. When you compile your programs, you can optionally tell the linker to include the versions of the libraries it has statically instead of using shared libraries. Although this prevents version conflicts, it wastes memory on the system.

Building Programs with the *make* Command

The make utility provides a mechanism for automating the compilation and linking of programs. If the program's source code comes with a makefile—and if the documentation says the program supports Linux—making the program work on your system should be quite easy.

The syntax of the make command is as follows:

```
make options make target
```

Because make works based on *targets*, it is often used to automate not only the building of programs but also other tasks such as program installation and object file maintenance. make runs based on *dependencies*, which means that a certain condition must be met before the system can carry out another action. This process is usually implemented to force make to build the program before building the install target, which makes sense—you cannot install a program before you compile it.

make also has built-in defaults that are, for a UNIX program, relatively sane. I would suppose this to be the case because UNIX is one of the most common utilities used by programmers, and programmers certainly are in a position to modify programs to do exactly what is required. make calls these sane defaults the *default rules*, which state, for instance, that a file ending with .c should be compiled with the system's C compiler, and that files ending in .cc, .cpp, and .c++ should be compiled with the C++ compiler, and so on. Most of these work pretty much as a programmer would expect.

Different makefiles for different platforms

Some programs' source distributions come with different makefiles for different platforms. This is often the case with older programs, which had to support platforms in which the **make** program was not as functional as the one included with Linux or most other UNIX systems. This is also often the case for programs that support DOS as well as Linux.

These programs usually have makefiles with the platform name as the extension, such as `Makefile.linux`, `Makefile.borland` (indicating this would be a makefile for Borland's C/C++ compilers on the DOS, OS/2, and Win32 platforms), `Makefile.msc` (makefile for Microsoft compilers on DOS and Win32 platforms), `Makefile.sco` or `Makefile.sunos` (for SCO UNIX and Sun SunOS systems, respectively).

A Sample Program

Let's start developing for Linux using C by writing, compiling and running the most famous of all programs, Hello World. The code is shown in Listing 22.1 (the numbers at the beginning of each line are for your use; they do not actually appear in the code).

Listing 22.1 *hello-world.c*

```
1   #include <stdio.h>
2   #include <stdlib.h>
3   int main(void)
4   {
5       printf("Hello World\n");
6       0;
}
```

Type this program using your favorite text editor and save it as `hello-world.c`. After you save the file, compile and link the program using the command

```
gcc -o hello-world hello-world.c
```

To view the output of the program from the command line type

```
$ ./hello-world
```

For instance, the command to compile the C program `myprogram.c`

```
gcc -o my program my program.c
```

can get pretty tedious, even if you consider the functionality that a shell such as `bash` provides with regard to command-line histories to repeat commands easily. Instead, typing `make myprogram` would be a lot easier. `make` looks for any compilable file of that name and then compiles and links it for you. The programmer does not have to think about the language in which his program is written because `make`—having been configured correctly by the system administrator—knows about most, if not all, compilers installed on the system. If you're the system administrator, don't worry too much about configuring `make` because the installation script in most cases does this.

The only drawback to using `make` in this way is that it provides little facility for programs composed of multiple files, which unfortunately covers the majority of programs. The other disadvantage is that `make`'s default settings offer little control over the optimizations the compiler uses to compile your program, which can have some impact on overall program performance.

`make` does support optimizations, as well as the building of multiple source file programs; this, in fact is the capability for which `make` was intended. All the programmer has to do is write his or her own makefile.

make Options

Typing the `make` command is often all that is needed to prepare a program to run on your system. When you type `make` at the command line, `make` looks for a file called `GNUmakefile`, `makefile`, or `Makefile` in the current directory to decipher what actions to perform. `make` performs the first action it finds in the file. By convention, this builds the program but does not install it for everyone to use on the system. The reason for this is simple: If you're logged in as root and type `make`, the last thing you want is for your directories to be littered with new programs that might not be working yet.

A Sample Program: the *make* Command

Taking the Hello World program a step further lets build a simple Makefile for it. The code is shown in Listing 22.2.

Listing 22.2 Simple Makefile for *hello-world.c*

```
hello-world: helloworld.c
     gcc -o hello-world hello-world.c
```

This simple makefile allows you to build `hello-world.c` but does not install the program for everyone to use. To test this out type the code listed in Listing 22.2 and save it as `Makefile`.

Now from the command line type `make` and the `hello-world` program will be compiled for you. To run this program type `./hello-world`.

To build and install the program, use the `make install` command. This tells `make` to build the program and, if everything is successful, to install its executable and configuration files in the appropriate directories, with the correct permissions, ready for users on your system to use.

The typical program installation

Typically, you would run `make` first and then try the program to make sure it works and is configured correctly. You would then use `make install` to first ensure that the program files generated by `make` are up to date and then to copy them to their intended locations in the system.

Be sure to read the documentation to make sure that programs are configured with the defaults you want. Otherwise, the programs you install might not work as expected—and could even damage data.

A Sample Program

Taking the Hello World program another step further lets build a Makefile that installs the compiled hello-world program onto your system so that everyone can use it. The code is shown in Listing 22.3. (The numbers at the beginning of each line are for your use; they do not actually appear in the code.)

Listing 22.3 Makefile with *install* functions for *hello-world.c*

```
1    CC=gcc
2    INSTDIR=/usr/bin
3
4    all: hello-world
5
6    hello-world: hello-world.c
7        $(CC) -o hello-world hello-world.c
8
9    install: all
10       cp hello-world $(INSTDIR);\
11       chmod a+x $(INSTDIR)/hello-world;\
12       chmod og-w $(INSTDIR)/hello-world;\
13       echo "Hello-World was installed in $(INSTDIR)";\
```

This makefile allows you to build `hello-world.c` and provides an install routine for the compiled file `hello-world`. To test this out type the code listed in Listing 22.3 and save it as `Makefile`.

From the command line type `make` and the `hello-world` program will be compiled for you. Now type `make install` from the command line and `hello-world` will be installed in `/usr/bin/`; the permissions on `hello-world` will also be changed so that every user on your system can run this program. To run this program type `hello-world` (after copying to `/usr/bin`) to see the output.

configure

Large programs with numerous configuration options often come with a `configure` target. This option usually walks you through a script to establish the program's configuration and to configure other files before you run `make` and `make install`. I appreciate the programs that come with a `configure` script because this tends to take care of the really minor version differences between systems if they are at issue with the program with which I am working. If the documentation says the program supports the `configure` option, you can run it by typing `make configure` or `make config`, depending on the program. If you're lucky, many programs now come with `autoconf` support, allowing you to type `./configure` in the source directory to configure the makefile for your system.

Constants

The `make` command also enables you to define constants for the program. In beta distributions (or in distributions in which not much time was spent on the makefile), you might have to define a constant to ensure that compilation and linking completes successfully. Usually, this takes the form of `make -D_LINUX` to define the constant `LINUX` to the preprocessor of the code.

clean

Finally, most makefiles provide the option to clean up after themselves. Large programs often leave a substantial number of intermediate files lying about in their source directories, which can consume a significant amount of space. To make sure that these are cleaned up, or to clean up after a failed build of the program, try using the command `make clean`. This should also be run after the configuration of the program is changed, such as after `make config` has been run.

Getting Started Quickly with New Programs

This section is intended to help you get started quickly with programs that were downloaded as source code. The text assumes that the source distribution of the program already supports Linux.

Checking for documentation

1. The first thing you'll want to do is extract the program's source directory tree. Some programmers use a fairly intricate directory structure to manage their programs and distribute everything, but this depends on the program complexity as well as the number of programmers who worked on the project.

2. Look for files with names such as `readme.1st`, `readme.install`, `README`, or `readme`. As the names imply, these contain additional information that might not have made it into the program's primary documentation in time. They usually document peculiarities in the configuration, installation, and running of the program.

3. The next place to check for additional hints or documentation is a subdirectory in the source tree that is usually called `doc` or `Documentation` (remember that directory names are case sensitive).

4. The root of the distribution directory should contain a file called `Makefile`. This is the file that `make` reads by default, and it contains all the rules and targets `make` follows when making the program. You should peruse the file for comments (as with shell scripts, the comments begin with #) indicating that certain things should be commented, filled in, or commented out.

At this point, you're ready to try making the program for the first time.

Making the program

1. Unless the documentation states otherwise, type `make`. The source code begins to compile, link, and sometimes run text processors (such as `TeX` to make printable manuals) or other commands to make `man` or `info` pages. If the program stops with an error message, you might have overlooked some configuration option in the `makefile`, the `make` target, or another file. Reread the documentation on making the program and what you need to configure. You might have to edit header files, or run `make config` or a configuration script. Make sure that you run the cleanup script (usually called `make clean`) after rerunning `make config`.

2. Assuming that the `make` process completed successfully, you should now have some programs in the source tree that you can try out. Some `make` scripts generate or copy the final programs to the root directory of the source tree, but this might vary—the `readme` and other files tell you where the software will be installed.

3. Try the program. Verify that the program works to your satisfaction and that everything behaves as expected.

4. When you finish testing the program—or when selected users on your system confirm that the program works as expected—you are ready to install the program for everyone's use. You can use the `make install` command or run an installation script mentioned in the program documentation. This is the only step for which you're required to log in as root because only root can put new programs in the `/bin`, `/usr/bin`, and `/usr/local/bin` directories, where programs are normally installed.

Security precautions

When you first compile and test new programs, make sure you're logged in as a regular user to ensure that the program does not affect your system integrity. Although there is a great deal of trust in the Linux community, you'll want to make sure that you don't trip up your system by missing something important in the program's configuration.

The point I want to emphasize is that you must read the documentation to make sure you get all this right. It's not as difficult as it sounds when you have done it a few times.

Specifying Different Makefiles

You have the option of copying or renaming the makefile you want to use, but often it's just as fast to specify the makefile by giving the command make -f *makefile*.

Building X11 Makefiles with the *xmkmf* Script

The X11 system is much more complicated than the conventional Linux text mode. Many more configurations and quirks must be accounted for, as must differences between XFree86 and commercial X11 distributions. Most X11 source distributions come with a file called the Imakefile, which contains detailed information about how the program should be configured for various platforms running various X11 systems. This is not a file you want to feed directly to make because the contents and format are quite different.

Instead of feeding this file to make, the file is fed to a program that generates a makefile specifically for your system and other information for make (called *dependencies*). The script xmkmf does all this for you and ensures that the program generating the makefile (called imake) is called with all the appropriate options for your system. Optionally, the script can call make a few times to finish the configuration and make the dependencies.

Compiling an X11 program

1. To generate the correct configuration to compile an X11 program, go into the source's root directory (where the Imakefile is located), and enter the following command:

    xmkmf

2. Optionally, if you want xmkmf to also call make makefiles to process the makefiles for the subdirectories (if any) and to call make include and make dep (which generate additional information that the complete make process needs to complete), you would use the following:

    xmkmf -a

    Whether you use xmkmf or xmkmf -a depends on the documentation you received with your X11 program.

3. When xmkmf is finished, you can run make to build the program.

23

Using Boot Managers

How Linux Boots: LILO/LOADLIN •

Configuring LILO •

Using LOADLIN •

How Linux Boots: LILO/LOADLIN

Loading Linux is not as simple as booting traditional operating systems such as Windows. The kernel requires a preloader that can pass it options necessary to its operation. For example, you can have multiple different kernels on your system; how do you tell Linux which one to boot from? In most cases you use a piece of software called LILO or LOADLIN. Some distributions, such as OpenLinux, use SYSLINUX.

These programs provide a vital service to Linux: They load the kernel (the part of the operating system that does all the work) into memory and then *boot* it. You will need one of these programs to get Linux going.

Configuring LILO

LILO (short for *Linux loader*) is the standard Linux loader. This program is the most flexible of the Linux boot loaders. LILO can be configured to reside in either the master boot record of your hard disk or the boot sector of a partition of a hard disk. You will have made this decision when installing Linux; depending on your system, one or the other will work best for you.

If your mind stalled when reading the previous paragraph, you're not alone. The most modern PC today boots very much like a PC did in 1982. However, the hardware has changed so much that the boot process requires the operating system and the loader for the operating system to be aware of the various workarounds that have been implemented on PCs to support, such as larger hard disks and changes in technology, such as bootable CD-ROMs and bootable tapes.

The boot procedure for every PC is relatively straightforward when viewed from a distance. It works like this:

1. When the PC is turned on, the processor begins executing the code in the BIOS. This code sizes the installed memory, tests the processor and hardware, and initializes the hardware to a known state.

2. The BIOS then looks for the boot drive (usually either a floppy disk or a hard disk); if it's a hard disk, BIOS reads the master boot record and executes it. This master boot record (usually installed by DOS, a.k.a. Windows 95) looks for the first active partition and then attempts to load the boot located on this partition.

3. The partition's boot sector contains instructions on how to load the boot loader. Size limitations are in effect here, so the boot loader must be very small. DOS

itself is small enough to fit there, so for a DOS system, the boot process is finished. Other systems will have a program here that loads the operating system kernel and boots it, such as LILO loading the Linux kernel, decompressing it, and then booting it. The memory the boot loader uses is then usually reclaimed by the operating system that has been booted.

LILO's options are set and configured while Linux is running, which means that if LILO won't boot Linux, you must use your emergency boot disks to access the system's hard disk and then configure LILO. You might need to experiment to determine whether LILO works best for you in the hard disk's MBR or in the boot sector of your boot partition.

LILO reads its configuration from a file in your systems /etc directory called lilo.conf. This file tells LILO the operating systems for which to configure and where to install itself. At its most basic is the lilo.conf file, which tells LILO to boot only one operating system, as shown in Listing 23.1.

Listing 23.1 A Typical *lilo.conf* File

```
1    boot=/dev/sda hda4
2    map=/boot/map
3    install=/boot/boot.b
4    prompt
5    timeout=50
6    image=/boot/vmlinuz-2.2.12 0.32
7            label=linux
8            root=/dev/sda1 hda4
9              read-only
```

Line 1 tells LILO to place itself in the boot sector of the partition /dev/sda hda4. Lines 4 and 5 instruct LILO to wait for five seconds for user input at the LILO: prompt, and to boot the kernel image vmlinuz-2.2.12 0.32 located in the /boot directory of the /dev/sda1 hda4 partition. LILO puts up a prompt and waits for five seconds for input before booting the first image in the lilo.conf file. Note the time-out value for five seconds is 50—LILO measures time in .10 second increments.

It's also possible to have a choice of several different Linux kernels to boot; this is handy if you're trying out the latest one but want to have the option of booting the old one just in case. It's worth the effort to set this up because it can save you—and those who depend on your system—a lot of frustration if a new kernel has problems.

> **Using other boot loaders in conjunction with LILO**
>
> If you're using System Commander or IBM's Boot Manager (this ships with OS/2, as well as the latest versions of PartitionMagic by PowerQuest) to boot multiple operating systems, you can also use it to boot Linux. Simply configure LILO to install itself into the boot record of the Linux partition, and then configure your boot loader to boot that partition like a DOS one.

Changing the Default Boot

The first entry in the `lilo.conf` file is the default boot configuration, which LILO starts when the timeout value has been reached. Changing the boot order is a simple matter of cutting and pasting, using your preferred text editor, and rerunning LILO to install the new boot sector. If it is not convenient to make these changes to the `lilo.conf` file, add the directive `default = label` (where `label` is the text on the label of the image you want LILO to boot by default).

LILO uses labels to allow the booting of multiple operating systems or different Linux kernels. Typing the word `dos` at the `LILO:` prompt instructs LILO to boot DOS on your system.

Passing Kernel Parameters

The Linux kernel can take command-line arguments, much like a regular program. LILO supports this and can pass parameters from either the `LILO` prompt or the configuration file. Generally, the command line for the kernel is used to tell the kernel to expect more than one network card or device address. These options can be manually entered at boot time to permit experimentation or one-time modifications to the way the system or kernel loads. Alternatively, the options can be entered into the `lilo.conf` file. When changing `/etc/lilo.conf` options, you must always rerun `/sbin/lilo` to save the changes to your boot sector.

To pass a parameter from the `LILO` prompt, you first must give the name of the image to which you want to pass the parameter, and then you must give the parameters. For example, if you have a system with more than one network card, you must tell the kernel to keep looking for a second network card, or it will stop looking after finding and initializing the first one. The following command tells the stock kernel to do this:

```
LILO: linux ether=0,0,eth0 ether=0,0,eth1
```

The two `ether` parameters tell the kernel that there should be two auto-detectable Ethernet cards in the system. The order in which they are found depends on the network card drivers involved. If you need to have specific cards assigned to certain Ethernet device names rather than the Linux defaults, you must determine the card parameters by using this method. Note the interrupt number and the I/O address that the Linux kernel reports (these also are in the kernel log file [/var/log/messages] after the system comes up), and then set those parameters in your lilo.conf file.

This lilo.conf file lists three boot images:

- /vmlinuz
- /vmlinuz.old
- A DOS partition

Note how the kernel parameters are attached via the append command, as shown in Listing 23.2.

Listing 23.2 A *lilo.conf* File Is Set Up to Boot Either of Two Linux Kernels, as Well as a DOS Partition

```
boot=/dev/sda hda2
map=/boot/map
install=/boot/boot.b
prompt
timeout=50
image=/boot/vmlinuz-2.2.12
        label=linux
        append="ether=0,0,eth0 ether=0,0,eth1"
        root=/dev/sda1 hda2
        read-only
image=/boot/vmlinuz-2.2.7-1.15 .old
        label=old d
        root=/dev/sda1 hda2
        read-only
other=/dev/sdb hda1
        label=dos
        table=/dev/sdb hda
```

Booting to a Specific Run Level

You can override the run level to which Linux boots by passing a command-line argument to the kernel at the LILO prompt. For example, to boot Linux into single-user mode, enter the following command at the LILO prompt (you can also substitute 1 in place of the word single):

```
lilo: linux single
```

Single-user mode is a maintenance mode for UNIX systems and does not start any daemons, networking, or login programs. This basically ensures that the system boots successfully (as long as the hard disk, kernel files, and so on, are okay). To boot another run level (for example, to test whether it's configured correctly), make the run level number the last item on the kernel command line at the LILO prompt.

You can make such a change to the append command in the lilo.conf file, but I don't suggest that you do so. Instead, modify your initrc file, as described in Chapter 26, "Managing Network Connections."

There are some things you don't really want to do at the LILO command prompt. For example, don't set the system to run level 0 or 6 (which are shutdown and reboot, respectively) because the system will happily boot up—only to shut down immediately afterward.

Using LOADLIN

LOADLIN is designed to boot Linux from a DOS prompt, which means that it is possible to boot Linux from DOS without actually rebooting the machine. This has inherent advantages, because it requires no modifications to the hard-disk structure to work, other than the creation of the Linux data and swap partitions.

One other advantage exists, which relates to unsupported hardware. Sound cards, in particular, often have SoundBlaster emulation modes, and these modes can be reached only by using DOS programs. Because LOADLIN does not reboot the machine, the sound card stays in a mode compatible with SoundBlaster and allows the regular Linux sound driver to work with it. I don't recommend doing this, but it *is* an option if nothing else works. For me, LOADLIN is just plain convenient.

Booting from DOS to Linux

Setting up LOADLIN is somewhat simpler than using LILO because LOADLIN is run as a regular DOS program and takes all the information it needs to boot Linux from its command line. For example, the following command causes LOADLIN to load the Linux kernel image vmlinuz and point it at partition /dev/hda4, initially read-only:

```
loadlin vmlinuz /dev/hda4 ro
```

Setting Up LOADLIN

LOADLIN is archived at the main Linux software distribution point, `http://metalab.unc.edu/`. If you purchased Linux as a CD set, it will be worth your while to look through those disks first because the Linux Archive is usually quite busy. The distribution of LOADLIN as of this writing is version 1.6, and the file is called `lodlin16.tgz`. The latest version can be found in the `/pub/Linux/system/boot/dualboot/` directory at Sunsite (accessible via FTP or HTTP) or on the equivalent directory on your CD distribution. When you have the file, you can extract it to its own directory by issuing the following command:

```
tar xzf lodlin16.tgz
```

LOADLIN comes with a sample batch file that you can use to boot Linux. This file must be modified for your particular setup.

The *.tgz* extension

Some extraction programs for DOS enable you to extract the contents of this file. A good place to look for utilities is in the wc archive at `ftp://ftp.cdrom.com/pub`.

Text files, DOS, and Linux

When editing text files, remember that the DOS text-file convention includes a line feed as well as a carriage return in the file, whereas Linux and other UNIX systems use only the line-feed character. This is why text files often appear stair-stepped when sent directly to the printer from Linux. Although Linux usually understands DOS text files with the carriage-return characters in them, DOS does not extend Linux the same courtesy. Thus, when editing text files intended to be read on a DOS (or Windows, Windows NT, or OS/2) system, add the carriage-return character manually by pressing Ctrl+M, or by using conversion utilities such as **fromdos** and **todos** afterward. These utilities can be downloaded in the easy-to-use **rpm** format from `ftp://ftp.redhat.com/pub/contrib/`.

Setting up LOADLIN and the batch file

1. You'll need to know the partition on which Linux is installed. To do so, type the following:

```
$ mount
```

This is the result:

```
/dev/hda4 on / type ext2 (rw)
/proc on /proc type proc (rw)
/dev/hdb7 on /mnt/f type vfat (rw)
/dev/sda4 on /mnt/zip type vfat (rw,nosuid,nodev)
```

This shows you the partitions Linux has mounted and the location of those partitions. The root partition (that is, the one mounted at the / mount point) is the partition from which Linux boots. In this case, /dev/hda4 is the root partition. You also might have noted this information when you installed your system, in which case you can skip this step.

2. You'll need to know any kernel parameters that your system requires (for example, whether you have two network adapters in your machine). The best way to check the parameters for your kernel is to check the append command in the lilo.conf file from your current installation. Most systems do not require parameters for anything vital, except for the multiple network card switch.

3. You'll need to know the name of the kernel file itself, which is often /boot/vmlinuz. Unfortunately, this varies between distributions.

Why is the kernel called *vmlinuz*?

The z at the end is there because the kernel image is compressed to reduce the amount of disk space it takes by using a method similar to gzip; the image is uncompressed when booted. If you really want to, you can change the kernel file's name; just make sure that you point LILO to the right file!

---

4. Determine whether your machine requires the initial ramdisk (initrd) to boot. The initial ramdisk is loaded by the boot loader and contains the device drivers that Linux needs to access the actual device(s) from which Linux boots. Most SCSI adapters, for example, allow simple DOS access without a device driver, but 32-bit operating systems cannot use this method. The boot loader (as with LILO and LOADLIN) uses the DOS method to load the ramdisk and the kernel, and the kernel then loads the device driver modules from the ramdisk to continue booting the system.

If you have an SCSI adapter, you will generally have to use initrd.

5. Get the ramdisk file, /boot/initrd-2.0.31.img. Make sure that the version number of the file is the same as the version of the kernel you're using!

Setting up a LOADLIN boot disk

1. Using DOS or Windows 95, format a bootable floppy disk. From the DOS or Windows 95 command prompt, type the following:

```
format a: /u /s
```

The /u parameter prevents DOS 6.x from saving unformat information to the disk, and it also speeds up the operation. The unformat information that DOS puts on the disk, in theory, would enable you to recover data from the disk if it were formatted accidentally. However, it's impossible to unformat a disk after a significant amount of data has been written to it.

2. Copy the files `loadlin.exe` (the program itself), `vmlinuz` (the Linux kernel), and `initrd-2.0.31.img` (the initial ramdisk, if you need one) to the floppy disk. You will want to rename `initrd-2.0.31.img` to `initrd.img` to get a short filename that DOS supports.

3. Using your favorite text editor, create a DOS batch file on the floppy disk. If you want to boot Linux automatically, name the file `autoexec.bat`. Otherwise, call it `linux.bat`. This file will call LOADLIN with the correct list of arguments. You could do it manually every time, but using a batch file is probably more convenient. You might want to add DOS sound drivers, a boot-up menu, or other objects to the floppy's `autoexec.bat` and `config.sys` files (either now or later). However, don't add the driver `EMM386.EXE` because this driver can cause you lots of grief when booting Linux with LOADLIN.

   The command line that tells LOADLIN to boot your system without an initial ramdisk is as follows:

   ```
   loadlin vmlinuz root=/dev/hda2 ro
   ```

   If you had to use an initial ramdisk, you'd use the following:

   ```
   loadlin vmlinuz initrd=initrd.img root=/dev/hda2 ro
   ```

   This example assumes that your system boots from the partition `/dev/hda2`. Be sure to specify the correct partition for your installation. The `ro` at the end tells the Linux kernel to initially mount the root file system as read-only. This enables you to check the file system if necessary.

4. Try it out. Remember that if you did not put the `loadlin` command in the `autoexec.bat` on the disk, you must issue the command `linux` to run the `linux.bat` batch file.

Passing Kernel Parameters with LOADLIN

LOADLIN interprets everything after the first argument (which it expects to be the kernel name) as a kernel argument. Therefore, to boot Linux to run level 5 with LOADLIN, use the following command:

```
loadlin vmlinuz root=/dev/hda2 ro 5
```

The previous command assumes that your Linux root partition is `/dev/hda2`. If you are booting from a floppy disk and LOADLIN sees some of the LOADLIN header and copyright information or some information about your current operating system (such as DOS), LOADLIN begins to load the ramdisk and kernel image, displaying dots as it proceeds. The system then boots the kernel. If you're running LOADLIN from a hard disk, this all happens too quickly to see—unless you have an older machine, of course.

# chapter 24

Managing Users and Groups

Users, groups, and their relation to
the system

Using the usercfg Tool

Adding, editing, and deleting users
using the command line

Adding, editing, and deleting groups

Changing user and group ownership

Changing file ownership and
permissions

Advanced concepts: password
authentication module

Users, Groups, and Their Relation to the System

Unlike many other operating systems currently available on the market, Linux supports the concept of multiple *users* and *groups*. A *user* is someone who has a unique identifier on the system, both a name and a number. This information allows the system to control how access is granted to the system and what the person might do after he or she has been allowed in. Users' activities are tracked by the system using their unique user identification number.

The difference between *login* and *username*

You will often find that people use the terms *login* and *username* interchangeably. Within most contexts, they mean the same thing.

A *group* is a collection of users. Every group also has a unique identification number as well as a unique name by which it can be referenced. Systems administrators often control access by groups. (For example, users in the group undergrad may not log in to the server insocoxygen.)

Every user and group has some peripheral information attached to it. The information is listed in Table 24.1.

Table 24.1 What Makes Up a User

Field	Description
Login	The user's unique name in the system.
Password	The password by which the user may access the system (encrypted).
UID	Short for *user identification*. This number pairs up with the login name. Every login/UID combination must be unique.
GID	Short for *group identification*. This number pairs up with the group the user belongs to by default. All users must belong to at least one group. (See Table 24.2 for more information.)
Comment	A free-form entry used to describe the user. Usually this is the user's full name. This entry does not have to be unique.
Home Directory Path	The directory where the user's files are stored. Each user's personal configuration files are kept here. When the user logs in, his or her default directory will be here as well.

Field	Description
shell	The program that is run automatically when the user logs in. This is usually a shell program such as /bin/bash, which gives the user a UNIX prompt (much the same way the command.com program gives users access to DOS under Windows).

Table 24.2 What Makes Up a Group

Field	Comment
Name	The group's name. Every group name must be unique.
Password	If a group has a password to control access to it, this must be set. In most instances, you do not need to worry about setting this.
GID	Short for *group identification*. This associates a number to the group name. All group name/group number combinations must be unique.
User list	A comma-delimited list of users who are part of this group—for example, the list sshah, hornbach, jnguyen indicates that the three users, sshah, hornbach, and jnguyen are in this particular group.

These two tables are stored in the files /etc/passwd and /etc/group, respectively. The programs that manage users in one way or another essentially edit these files for you. If you are feeling adventurous, take a look at the password file in its raw format with the command:

```
[root@insocoxygen /root]# more /etc/passwd
```

Table 24.1 explains each field, but don't worry if it doesn't make too much sense. All you *need* to know is that they are there.

The following sections use this information to establish, edit, and remove users using the tools built into Red Hat Linux.

Using the *usercfg* Tool

The usercfg tool is an all-in-one package for manipulating user and group information. Because of its graphical interface, it is easy to use.

To start the program, simply run usercfg like so:

Starting the User Configurator

1. Log in as the root user.

2. Start the X Window System with the startx command.

3. Open up an xterm and run the command usercfg.

The opening window should look something like Figure 24.1.

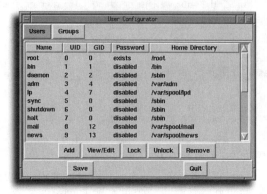

FIGURE 24.1
The User Configurator window as it appears when first started.

At the top of the window you see two buttons, one for Users and one for Groups. On startup, the Users button is always highlighted. Below those two buttons is the list of the current users in the system. The first column is the login name; then the user identification (UID); the group identification (GID); whether the user's password exists, is disabled, or empty; and finally, the location of the user's home directory.

If you click the Groups button at the top of the window, you can see what the group configuration currently looks like. A stock configuration should look something like Figure 24.2.

Don't change the User Identification (UID)

As mentioned earlier, you cannot change a user's login name in the View/Edit dialog box. You have the option, however, to change the User ID (UID). *Don't.* Changing a user's ID number will cause a great deal of confusion because Linux associates file ownership to UIDs, not login names. Thus, changing a person's UID will cause him to lose ownership of all his files.

If for whatever reason you need to do this, be sure you read the section later in this chapter on how to use the chown command to reassign ownership to files.

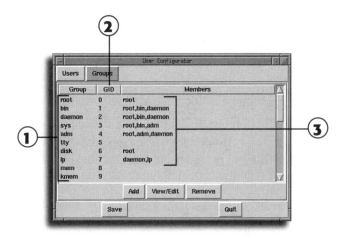

FIGURE 24.2
In the first column below the User and Group buttons is the name of the groups, the second column is their group identification (GID), and the last column contains a list of group members.

① Name of groups   ③ Group members

② Group identification

Adding a User with *usercfg*

Adding a new user

1. Click the top button labeled Users to bring the user list back. The list of buttons on the bottom two rows show which functions are available. Click the Add button to bring up a new Edit User Definition dialog box, as shown in Figure 24.3.

FIGURE 24.3
The Edit User Definition dialog box. Notice the defaults set by the system.

usercfg will automatically fill in the UID and GID for you. In our example, that is UID 514 and GID 514. In addition, usercfg fills in the Full Name field with a default string Red Hat Linux User. Finally, usercfg gives you the default shell setting to /bin/bash.

2. Select a new login name. The login name should not be greater than eight characters. This should consist of only letters and numbers.

3. Click the down arrow button next to the password entry. Select the second option, Change. This will bring up a dialog box like the one shown in Figure 24.4.

FIGURE 24.4
Change the entry.

4. Enter the password you want to assign to the user and press Enter. The dialog box will then prompt you to verify the password by reentering it. (The system wants to be sure that you haven't made a typing mistake.) Enter the password again and press Enter. The first line of the dialog box will show the encrypted version of the string as in Figure 24.5.

FIGURE 24.5
Click the Done button to make that the password entry.

5. usercfg will have already filled in a UID and GID for you. If you want the user to be part of an existing group, provide that group number instead of the suggested one. Of course, you can always add that user to the group by editing the groups file, as you will see shortly.

6. In the Full Name entry, fill in the complete name of the user. If the user wants to go by an alias—for example, Steveoid—enter the alias here.

7. The entries for Office, Office Phone, and Home Phone are optional. They are only used when the user is queried by other people using the finger command.

8. In the Home Directory entry, specify where the user's home directory will be. By default, the home directory will be /home/login where login is the user's login name. For most systems, this is acceptable and can be left alone. If you maintain a different home directory structure, replace this entry with the appropriate directory.

9. In the default shell entry, specify which shell the user will use when he logs in. The default shell is /bin/bash, which is fine for most users. If the user wants a different shell, you can click the down arrow button to see a listing of available shells based on the contents of the /etc/shells file. If you want to give the user a shell not listed, simply erase the entry and enter whatever shell you want to assign them.

10. After you have completed the dialog box, click the Done button. You should see your new entry in the main User Configurator window.

Password information

Accounts should always have passwords. It is bad practice to leave accounts open to login without passwords, especially if your machine attaches to a network in any way. Furthermore, you need to use a good password—one that cannot be guessed using any of the automated password guessing programs available on the Internet.

A good password is at least six characters long, contains a mixture of uppercase letters, lowercase letters, punctuation, and numbers. One good technique is to pick a phrase and use the first letter of each word in the phrase. This makes the password easy to remember but difficult to crack. For example, "Always remember: It's a great big disco world" would be **ArIagbdw**.

View/Edit Users

After a user has been added, you might find it necessary to go back and edit her information. To bring up the Edit User Definition dialog box, follow these steps:

Editing user settings

1. Either double-click the user or click once on the user and click the View/Edit button at the bottom of the window. The Edit User Definition window looks just like the Add User window without the option to change the login name (see Figure 24.6).

2. Each field containing the user's current information will be available for you to edit, except for the login name. You may change any of the other fields as you deem necessary.

FIGURE 24.6
The Edit User Definition dialog box. Note the striking similarity to the Add User dialog box.

   3. When you have finished making changes, click the Done button at the bottom of the active window. This will commit your changes to the system.

Locking a User

There eventually will come a time when a user on your system has become so troublesome that you need to lock him out of the system until you've had a chance to talk with him and set him straight. For example, you've just found out that the user named vector has formed the Internet Terrorist Task Force and is attacking other sites. To lock him out, do the following:

Locking out a user

   1. At the top of the usercfg window, click the Users button. This should bring up the list of users on the system.

   2. Click once on vector's entry.

   3. Click the Lock button at the bottom of the usercfg window. This will bring up the Archive User window, as shown in Figure 24.7.

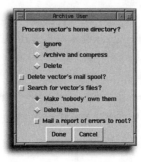

FIGURE 24.7
Open the Archive User window.

4. The first choice is what you want to do with vector's home directory. The three options are to ignore it, archive and compress it, or delete it altogether. Ignoring it will leave his home directory intact. Archiving and compressing will cause his home directory to be combined into one large file and compressed with the tar and gzip commands. (Together, they work similarly to the way WinZip works under Windows.) The last option to is delete his files altogether. In most instances, you will only want to disallow access to your system until you've had a chance to talk to your user about inappropriate behavior; thus, select the first option, Ignore.

5. The second option is whether you want to delete the user's undelivered mail. Unless you have a specific reason to remove it, leave it alone.

6. The last option is whether you want to change the ownership of all the user's files to the user nobody. In most instances, you will not want to do so. Select the option accordingly.

7. Click Done. Another dialog box will appear warning you that locking out a user will cause any changes made so far to be written to disk. Click Really Archive if you want to proceed; otherwise, you can cancel the operation.

After the home directory is dealt with, the password entry is locked by placing an asterisk character in it, thereby preventing the user from logging in.

Unlocking a User

After you've had a chance to talk with vector and you feel that he should have access to the system once again, you will want to unlock his account. To do so, follow these directions:

Unlocking a user

1. Click once on the user's login name in the User Configurator. This will highlight the entry.

2. Click the Unlock button at the bottom of the window. A dialog box will inform you that unlocking a user will cause any changes made so far to be written to disk. If you are sure that you want to unlock the account, click Really Unlock; otherwise, click Cancel.

With the home directory back in place, the password entry will have the asterisk character removed, thereby allowing the user to enter the system.

Removing a User

Occasionally, you will need to remove a user from the system. To remove the user named vector from the system, follow these directions:

Removing a user

1. Click vector's login name in the User Configurator dialog box. This will highlight his entry.

2. Click the Remove button at the bottom of the User Configurator dialog box. This will bring up the Delete User dialog box, as shown in Figure 24.8.

FIGURE 24.8
The Delete User dialog box. Note the similarity to the Lock User dialog box shown in the preceding section.

The menu options in this window are identical to the ones in the Lock User window. Here, however, you will want to take more drastic options if you're looking to completely remove him from the system. In most cases, you do want all traces of him removed.

3. The first option allows you to specify how you want the contents of vector's home directory dealt with. You will probably want to remove it. Click the Delete button.

4. Click the option Delete vector's Mail Spool.

5. Click the option Search for vector's Files to tell the system that you want to find files outside vector's home directory that he owns (for example, files stored in /tmp).

6. Click the radio button to Delete Them under the Search for vector's Files button. This will cause any files owned by vector found outside vector's home directory to be deleted.

7. Just to be on the safe side, click the button to Mail a Report of Errors to Root.

8. The Delete User window should look like Figure 24.9 for the options you have selected.

FIGURE 24.9
The Delete User dialog box after it has been filled out.

9. Click Done to indicate that you are happy with the selections you have made. You will get a warning about this operation not being undoable. Click Really Delete if you are sure; otherwise, click Cancel.

Adding a Group

Adding a group

1. Click the Groups button at the top of the User Configurator window. The window will show the current listing of groups in the system, similar to Figure 24.10.

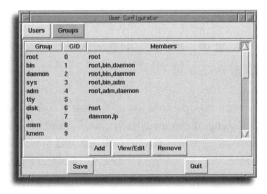

FIGURE 24.10
The User Configurator when listing groups.

2. Click the Add button at the bottom of the window. This will bring up the Edit Group Definition window similar to the one shown in Figure 24.11.

FIGURE 24.11
The Edit Group Definition dialog box.

3. Enter the name you want to call your new group. Like a login name, group names cannot be longer than eight characters and can only consist of letters and numbers.

   Note: The next two steps are identical to the steps used to set the password when adding a user. The figures used to describe this process in the "Adding a User" section (Figures 24.4 and 24.5) apply here as well.

4. Click the down arrow button next to the password entry. Select the second option, Change.

5. Enter the password you want to assign the user and press Enter. The dialog box will then prompt you to verify the password by reentering it. (The system wants to be sure that you haven't made a typing mistake.) Enter the password again and press Enter. The first line of the dialog box will show the encrypted version of the string. Remember! Linux is case sensitive! You *must* enter the password exactly the same way both times, with the exact same mix of capital and lowercase letters!

6. Click the Done button to make that the password entry.

7. The GID entry will already be filled in with the next available GID and can be left alone.

8. The user list is a comma-separated list of the users whom you want to be part of this group. For example, if the users sshah, heidi, and jnguyen are working on a new project, you could create a group for them and have each login listed as a member. When they use the newgrp command to switch into that group, they will not have to give a password to gain access.

9. After you have completed the form, click the Done button. The new group should appear in the User Configurator window.

Editing an Existing Group

Editing groups

1. Click the Groups button at the top of the User Configurator window.

2. Click once on the group's entry to highlight it and then click the View/Edit button at the bottom of the User Configurator window.

3. Make the changes you want to the group's information. It should be noted that changing the value of the GID will cause confusion because files will need their group ownership reset. In general, the only changes you need to make to a group after it is created is to either add or delete users who are members of the group. Remember that the list of users who are members of a group must be comma separated.

4. Click Done to finalize changes.

Removing a Group

Removing a group is even simpler than removing a user.

Removing groups

1. Click the Groups button at the top of the User Configurator window.

2. Click the group you want removed.

3. Click the Remove button at the bottom of the User Configurator window. The group will be removed immediately.

Finishing Up with *usercfg*

Unless otherwise mentioned, the changes you make with the usercfg program will not take effect until you explicitly click the Save button at the bottom of the User Configurator window. After you have saved your changes, you can click Quit to exit the User Configurator.

Adding, Editing, and Deleting Users Using the Command Line

Unfortunately, it isn't always possible to use a graphical tool such as usercfg to manipulate users. In these instances, you can manipulate users with the command-line versions of using the tools called useradd, usermod, and userdel for adding, modifying, and deleting users, respectively.

Adding Users with *useradd*

To add a user with the `useradd` command, log in to the root account and enter the following command:

```
[root@insocoxygen /root]# useradd -d homedir -s /bin/tcsh [ic]
              -c "User's Real Name" newlogin
```

`homedir` is the home directory of the user being created, set by the `-d` option. `User's Real Name` is the real name of the user, added using the comment, `-c`, flag. (Be sure to have the user's name inside the double quotation marks.) The `-s` sets the user's shell to `/bin/tcsh`, and finally, `newlogin` is the login name of the user being added.

Study this example:

```
[root@insocoxygen /root]# useradd -d /home/sshah -s /bin/tcsh [ic]
          -o "Steve Shah" sshah
```

See the man page regarding `useradd` for the complete details on all the options available.

Modifying Users with the *usermod* Command

The `usermod` command allows you to change all the parameters you set for a user when adding him or her to the system. Note that the user cannot be logged in when you are changing his or her login, UID, GID, or home directory because the system will get very confused.

To change a user's configuration information, log in as the root user and enter the following command:

```
[root@insocoxygen]# usermod -c "New Name" -d homedir -m -g groupname -s shell
➥-l newlogin currentlogin
```

where `New Name` is the user's new real name (for example, if a user named Kurt Valaquen wanted to change his name to Kurt Harland), `homedir` is the new home directory for the user, `groupname` is the name of the default user group he will belong to, `shell` is the desired shell of the user, `newlogin` is the new login name the user wants, and finally `currentlogin` is the login name of the user you want to change. The command-line options given in the `useradd` option are specific to Red Hat Linux. Because users are added in different ways in different systems, be sure to check the man page (`man useradd`) for your distribution's utility to find the appropriate options.

For example, if a user wants to set his name to "Kurt Harland" with a home directory of /home/vector, a default group setting to ittf, using the shell /bin/bash and using the login name vector, you would use the following command:

```
[root@insocoxygen /root]# usermod --o "Kurt Harland" --d /home/vector --m --q
➥ittf --s /bin/bash --l vector vector
```

What am I typing?

If the preceding command appears cryptic to you, don't worry. Its design was geared toward functionality over readability. Let's dissect the preceding command to see what it is doing.

The **usermod** portion simply specifies the command we are running. This program will interpret the remainder of the line.

The first thing that will be interpreted is the string --o "Kurt Harland". The --o tells the program that we want to change the comment field of the password entry to "Kurt Harland". Quotation marks are placed around his name so that the program doesn't get confused and think the string "Harland" is the next parameter.

Each of the parameters works in a similar way where strings that start with a hyphen character tell **usermod** that we want to change an aspect of the user's settings and the string that immediately follows is the desired value. The last parameter is the user's login, which is required for this command.

See the man page regarding usermod for a list of all the available command-line options.

Deleting Users with the *userdel* Command

To remove a user from your system, use the userdel command. Note that the user must be logged out of the system before you can remove him. To use userdel, log in as the root user and enter the following command:

```
[root@insocoxygen /root]# userdel -r login
```

where login is the login name of the user you want to remove.

For example, if you want to remove the user vector, you would use userdel as follows:

```
[root@insocoxygen /root]# userdel -r vector
```

If you use the userdel command without the -r, the user will be removed from the system but his or her files will be left behind. Use the -r to remove all traces of the user. See the man page for userdel of a list of all the command-line options.

Adding, Editing, and Deleting Groups

Similar to the user commands, there are commands for controlling groups as well. They are

groupadd	Add groups
groupmod	Modify groups
groupdel	Delete groups

Adding Groups with the *groupadd* Command

The groupadd command allows you to add groups to the system from the command line. To do so, log in as the root user and enter the following command:

```
[root@insocoxygen /root]# groupadd groupname
```

where groupname is the name of the group you want to add to the system.

For example, to add the group www to your system, you would use the command:

```
[root@insocoxygen /root]# groupadd www
```

See the man page regarding groupadd for a full list of all the command-line options available.

Modifying Groups with the *groupmod* Command

To modify the name of a group after it has been created, use the groupmod command. To make the change, log in as the root user and enter the following command:

```
[root@insocoxygen /root]# groupmod -n newgroup currentgroup
```

where newgroup is the new name you want to give the group, and currentgroup is the current name of the group.

For example, to change a group name from admin to sysadmin, you would use the following command:

```
[root@insocoxygen /root]# groupmod -n sysadmin admin
```

See the man page groupmod for a full list of all the command-line options available.

Deleting Groups with the *groupdel* Command

To remove an existing group, use the groupdel command as described here. Log in as the root user and enter the following command:

```
[root@insocoxygen /root]# groupdel groupname
```

where `groupname` is the group you want to delete. There is one catch, however. You cannot delete a group if it is the primary group of any users. You either need to remove the users or change their primary group using the `usermod` command first.

For example, to remove the group `ittf`, you would use the command

```
[root@insocoxygen /root]# groupdel ittf
```

Changing User and Group Ownership

Linux provides two programs to help you manage user and group ownership from the command line. The first, `gpasswd`, allows you to administer a group with relative ease. `chgrp`, the second program, allows users to change the group of particular files.

Managing Groups with *gpasswd*

To add users to an existing group, log in as the root user and enter the following command:

```
[root@insocoxygen /root]# gpasswd -a loginname groupname
```

where `loginname` is the login name of the user you want to add to the group `groupname`.

For example, to add the user `vector` to the group `ittf`, you would use the command

```
[root@insocoxygen /root]# gpasswd -a vector ittf
```

To remove a user from an existing group, log in as the root user and enter the following command:

```
[root@insocoxygen /root]# gpasswd -d loginname groupname
```

where `loginname` is the login that you want to remove from the group `groupname`.

For example, if you wanted to remove the user `yoko` from the group `beatles`, you would use the command

```
[root@insocoxygen /root]# gpasswd -d yoko beatles
```

For a full list of command-line options available for the `gpasswd` command, see the related man page.

Using the *chgrp* Command

To change the group of a file, use the chgrp command. Log in as the root user and enter the following command:

```
[root@insocoxygen /root]# chgrp groupname filename
```

where groupname is the name of the group you want to change the file's group setting to, and filename is the name of the file for which you want the group changed.

For example, if you wanted to change the group for the file index.html to www, you would use chgrp as follows:

```
[root@insocoxygen /root]# chgrp www index.html
```

To change the group of a directory and all its subdirectories and files, you can use the chgrp command with the -R option. For example, to change the group on all the files in the htdocs directory to www, you would use

```
[root@insocoxygen /root]# chgrp -R www htdocs
```

Changing File Ownership and Permissions

Two programs in the command-line arsenal help change file ownership and permissions. chown, or Change Ownership, lets you change a file (or group of files) to another owner. chmod lets you change the access permissions to individual files.

Using the *chown* Command

To change the owner of a file, you use the chown command. Log in as the root user and enter the following command:

```
[root@insocoxygen /root]# chown ownername filename
```

where ownername is the login name of the user you want to change the file's owner setting to, and filename is the name of the file for which you want the owner changed.

For example, if you wanted to change the owner for the file index.html to sshah, you would use chown as follows:

```
[root@insocoxygen /root]# chown sshah index.html
```

To change the owner of a directory and all its subdirectories and files, you can use the chown command with the -R option. For example, to change the owner on all the files in the htdocs directory to sshah, you would use

```
[root@insocoxygen /root]# chown -R sshah htdocs
```

Using the *chmod* Command

Before we can explain the usage of the `chmod` command, you need to first understand file permissions.

> **How does this compare to Windows NT?**
>
> Linux is similar to Windows NT in regard to the concept of users. Each user has a designated set of permissions, which allows them to run certain programs, save files in a certain place, and read files owned by other users provided that other users have set their file permissions accordingly.

In Linux, every file and directory has three sets of access permissions: those applied to the owner of the file, those applied to the group the file has, and those of all users in the system. You can see these permissions when you do an `ls -lg`. For example

```
drwxr-xr-x   2 sshah    sysadmin     1024 Feb 14 15:49 wedding_plans
-rw-------   1 sshah    sysadmin     2465 Feb  5 19:22 index.html
```

The first column of the listing is the permissions of the file. The first character represents the type of file (`d` means directory, `l` means symbolic link, and so on), and the next nine characters are the permissions. The first three characters represent the permissions held by the file's owner, the second three are for the group the file is in, and the last three represent the world permissions.

The following letters are used to represent permissions:

Letter	Meaning
r	Read
w	Write
x	Execute

Each permission has a corresponding value. The read attribute is equal to 4, the write attribute is equal to 2, and the execute attribute is equal to 1. When you combine attributes, you add their values. See the following examples.

The most common groups of three and their meanings are

Permission	Values	Meaning
---	0	No permissions
r--	4	Read only
rw-	6	Read and write

continues...

...continued

rwx	7	Read, write, and execute
r-x	5	Read and execute
--x	1	Execute only

Although other combinations do exist (for example, -wx), they are nonsensical, and the likelihood you'll ever run across them is almost nil.

When you combine these values, you get three numbers that make up the file's permission. Common permission combinations include the following:

Permission	Value	Meaning
-rw-------	600	The owner has read and write permissions. This is what you want set on most of your files.
-rw-r--r--	644	The owner has read and write permissions. The group and world has read-only permissions. Be sure you want to let other people read this file.
-rw-rw-rw-	666	Everybody has read and write permissions on a file. This is bad. You don't want other people to be able to change your files.
-rwx------	700	The owner has read, write, and execute permissions. This is what you want for programs that you want to run.
-rwxr-xr-x	755	The owner has read, write, and execute permissions. The rest of the world has read and execute permissions.
-rwxrwxrwx	777	Everyone has read, write, and execute privileges. Like the 666 setting, this is bad. Allowing others to edit your files is a cookbook formula for disaster.
-rwx--x--x	711	The owner has read, write, and execute privileges. The rest of the world has execute only permissions. This is useful for programs that you want to let others run, but not copy.
drwx------	700	This is a directory created with the mkdir command. Only the owner can read and write into this directory. Note that all the directories must have the executable bit set.
drwxr-xr-x	755	This directory can be changed only by the owner, but everyone else can view its contents.

Permission	Value	Meaning
drwx--x--x	711	A handy trick to use when you need to keep a directory world-readable, but you don't want people to be able to see a directory listing via the `ls` command. Only if the person knows the filename she wants to retrieve will she be allowed to read it.

Now that you're fluent with permissions, learning `chmod` is easy. To change the permissions on a file, log in as the root user and enter the following command:

```
[root@insocoxygen /root]# chmod permissions file
```

where `permissions` is a numeric value (three digits), discussed earlier, and `file` is the name of the file for which you want this to affect.

For example, to set the `index.html` file to be changeable by the owner, but only readable by the file's group and the world, the command would be

```
[root@insocoxygen /root]# chmod 644 index.html
```

To recursively change the permissions on all the files in a specific directory, use the `-R` option in `chmod`. For example, to make all the files in `/usr/bin` set to the permissions 755, you would use

```
[root@insocoxygen /root]# chmod -R 755 /usr/bin
```

What are SetUID programs?

SetUID is a special permission applied to programs. Remember how everything in Linux has an owner? This concept of ownership applies to programs in execution (processes) as well. Each process is owned by the person who invoked it. For example, if you log in as yourself, start the program `xtetris`, and then list the running processes using the `ps` command, you'll see that you are the owner of the `xtetris` process. But if you do a directory listing on the `xtetris` program using `ls -l`, you'll see that the file itself is owned by the root user.

Under normal circumstances, this is good. You want to make programs available to your users to run without giving away the privilege to change them. However, you occasionally run across a need for the program to run not as the user who invokes it but as the user the file is owned by. The `ping` command is a common instance of this. For `ping` to work, it must be run as the root user. To allow normal users of the system to use `ping`, you can make it SetUID.

To make a file SetUID, prefix the permissions with the number 4. For example

```
[root@insocoxygen /root]# chmod 4755 /bin/ping
```

> **SetGID**
>
> SetGID works similarly to SetUID. Programs that are SetGID are executed with the permissions of the group that owns the program rather than the group of the user. You can set a file to be SetGID by prefixing the permissions with the number 2. For example
>
> `[root@insocoxygen /root]# chmod 2755 /usr/local/backups/backup_level_0`
>
> When listing a file with the `ls -l` command, you can visually see whether a file is SetUID or SetGID. SetUID files have an **s** where the first **x** should be, and SetGID files have an **s** where the second **x** should be.

Advanced Concepts: Password Authentication Module

The Password Authentication Module (PAM) is for those who want to modify the security model that comes with Red Hat. By default, the model is reasonably strict about who can enter the system and in most instances, does not need to be adjusted. Like the password and group configuration files, though, understanding this subsystem will better prepare you for troubleshooting problems.

Improving System Security Using PAM

In an effort to separate authentication techniques from applications, the Linux development community took hints from the Solaris operating system and created its own implementation of PAM, Pluggable Authentication Modules. By separating the method of authentication from applications, it is possible for system administrators to implement their own authentication techniques and have application software automatically use them.

This section explains the key components of the PAM system, its installation, configuration file, and some modules that come with Red Hat Linux.

Installing PAM

If you chose a standard installation procedure with Red Hat Linux, you probably have PAM already installed. If you don't have it installed, don't worry, it's very straightforward.

Begin by acquiring the RPM package for PAM. This should be on the distribution you installed with. If not, you can always download it from Red Hat's Web site at `http://www.redhat.com`. Our distribution for this section is version 0.57 with configuration file version 0.51. We would use the following commands to install the RPMs:

```
[root@insocoxygen /root]# rpm -i pam-0.57-2.i386.rpm
[root@insocoxygen /root]# rpm -i pamconfig-0.51-2.i386.rpm
```

If you already had the packages installed, rpm should have told you. If they are older versions, be sure to specify the -U instead of -i option with rpm so that it will upgrade older files correctly.

The PAM Configuration Files

As of version 0.56, PAM prefers to use the directory-based approach for managing its configuration files. These files are located in the /etc/pam.d directory, and each filename represents a particular service. For example, ftpd and login are considered services.

Each file consists of lines in the following format:

```
module_type    control_flag    module_path    arguments
```

where module type represents one of four types of modules, auth, account, session, or password. Comments must begin with the hash (#) character.

auth	Instructs the application program to prompt the user for a password and then grants not only user privileges but group privileges too.
account	Performs no authentication but determines access based on other factors, such as time of day or location of the user. For example, the root login can be given only console access this way.
session	Specifies what, if any, actions need to be performed before or after a user is logged in—for example, logging the connection.
password	Specifies the module that allows users to change their password (if appropriate).
control_flag	Allows you to specify how you want to deal with the success or failure of a particular authentication module.
required	The module must succeed in authenticating the individual. If it fails, the returned summary value must be failure.
requisite	Similar to required; however, if this module fails authentication, modules listed after this one in the configuration file are not called, and a failure is immediately returned to the application. This allows you to require that certain conditions hold true before even accepting a login attempt. (For example, the user must be on the local area network and cannot come in from over the Internet.)

continues...

...continued

`sufficient`	If the module returns a success and there are no more `required` or `sufficient` `control_flags` in the configuration file, PAM returns a success to the calling application.
`optional`	This flag allows PAM to continue checking other modules even if this one has failed. You will want to use this when the user is allowed to log in even if a particular module has failed.

The `module_path` specifies the actual directory path of the module that performs the authentication task. For a full list of modules that came with PAM, check out the file `/usr/doc/pam-0.59/html/pam-6.html` using your favorite Web browser. Text versions of the document are also available in the `/usr/doc/pam-0.59` directory.

`arguments` are the parameters passed to the authentication module. Although the parameters are specific to each module, some generic options can be applied to all modules. They are

`debug`	Send debugging information to the system logs. (Usually located at `/var/log`—check `/etc/syslog.conf` for details.)
`no_warn`	Do not give warning messages to the calling application.
`use_first_pass`	Do not prompt the user for a password a second time. Instead, use the password entered the first time to determine the user's eligibility to enter the system.
`try_first_pass`	Similar to `use_first_pass` where the user is not prompted for a password the second time; however, if the existing password causes a failure to be returned from the module, the user is then asked to enter a second password.
`use_mapped_pass`	Passes the password from a previous module into the current one much like `use_first_pass`; however, the password is then used to generate an encryption or decryption key.

One special feature of PAM is its "stackable" nature. That is, every line in the configuration file is evaluated during the authentication process (with the exceptions shown later). Each line specifies a module that performs some authentication task and returns either a success or failure flag. A summary of the results is returned to the application program calling PAM.

Let's examine a sample PAM configuration file, `/etc/pam.d/login`.

```
#%PAM-1.0
auth        required      /lib/security/pam_securetty.so
auth        required      /lib/security/pam_pwdb.so shadow nullok
auth        required      /lib/security/pam_nologin.so
account     required      /lib/security/pam_pwdb.so
password    required      /lib/security/pam_cracklib.so
password    required      /lib/security/pam_pwdb.so shadow nullok use_authtok
session     required      /lib/security/pam_pwdb.so
```

You can see that the first line begins with a hash symbol and is therefore a comment. You can ignore it.

Now go through the rest of the file line by line:

```
auth        required      /lib/security/pam_securetty.so
```

specifies that the `module_type` is `auth`, which means it will want a password. The `control_flag` is set to `required`, so this module must return a success or the login will fail. The module itself is the `pam_securetty.so` module, which verifies that logins on the root account can only happen on the terminals mentioned in the `/etc/securetty` file.

```
auth        required      /lib/security/pam_pwdb.so shadow nullok
```

Similar to the previous line, this line wants to use a password for authentication, and if the password fails, the authentication process will return a failure flag to the calling application. The `pam_pwdb.so` module behavior is based on the `module_type`. In this case, the `auth` type allows `pam_pwdb.so` to do basic password checking against the `/etc/passwd` file. The shadow parameter tells it to check the `/etc/shadow` file if it is there, and the `nullok` parameter tells the module to allow users to change their password from an empty one to something. (Normally, it treats empty passwords as an account locking mechanism.)

```
auth        required      /lib/security/pam_nologin.so
```

The `pam_nologin.so` module checks for the `/etc/nologin` file. If it is present, only root is allowed to log in, and others are turned away with an error message. If the file does not exist, it always returns a success.

```
account     required      /lib/security/pam_pwdb.so
```

Because the `module_type` is account, the `pam_pwdb.so` module will silently check that the user is even allowed to log in (for example, has his password expired?). If all the parameters check out okay, it will return a success.

```
password    required      /lib/security/pam_cracklib.so
```

385

The `password module_type` account means that we will be using the `pam_cracklib.so` module during a password change. The `pam_cracklib.so` module performs a variety of checks to see whether a password is too easy to crack by potential intruders.

```
password    required    /lib/security/pam_pwdb.so shadow nullok use_authtok
```

This is another example of the versatility of the `pam_pwdb.so` module. With the `module_type` set to password, it will perform the actual updating of the `/etc/passwd` file. The shadow parameters tell it to check for the existence of the `/etc/shadow` file and update that file if it does exist. `nullok` allows users to change their passwords from empty entries to real passwords. The last option, `use_authtok`, forces `pam_pwdb.so` to use the password retrieved from a previous `module_type` entry of password.

```
session     required    /lib/security/pam_pwdb.so
```

This is the fourth and final usage of the `pam_pwdb.so` module. This time it sends login successes and failures to the system logs because the `module_type` is set to session.

The *other* File

What happens when you need to authenticate someone for a service, but you don't have a PAM configuration file for him? Simple. Use the `/etc/pam.d/other` configuration file—a sort of catch-all type of setup.

In this situation, if a user tries to authenticate himself using a PAM-aware application (for example, the FTP server) but the configuration file for it is not there (in the case of the FTP server, the `/etc/pam.d/ftp` file got accidentally removed), PAM will default to using the configuration file `/etc/pam.d/other`.

By default, the other configuration file is set to a paranoid setting so that all authentication attempts are logged and then promptly denied. It is recommended that you keep it that way.

Oh No! I Can't Log In!

In the immortal words of Douglas Adams, "Don't panic." Like many other configuration errors that can occur under Linux, this one can be fixed by either booting into single user mode or booting off a floppy. (See Chapter 23, "Using Boot Managers," for details on booting into single user mode.)

After you are back into the system in single user mode, simply edit the
`/etc/pam.d/login` file so that it contains only the following lines:

```
auth        required    /lib/security/pam_unix_auth.so
account     required    /lib/security/pam_unix_acct.so
password    required    /lib/security/pam_unix_passwd.so
session     required    /lib/security/pam_unix_session.so
```

This simplified login configuration will stick to the original UNIX authentication
method, which should hopefully work well enough to get you back into the system
in multiuser mode.

After you are back in multiuser mode, be sure to go back and fix the login configuration file to reflect what you really wanted to do instead of what it did—lock you out!

Debugging/Auditing

While you are debugging the PAM configuration files, be sure to keep an eye on the
system log files. (Usually in `/var/log`.) Most of the error logging will occur there.

When you have things working the way you like, be sure to check those files for
auditing information from PAM. It reports not only authentication successes but
failures as well. Multiple failures for a particular person or for a range of people in a
short time could indicate trouble.

chapter

25

Managing Scheduling Services

Configuring `inittab` and `rc` files •

Configuring `crontab` scheduling
service •

Configuring the `at` command service •

Scheduling resources is a management process. Whether you are scheduling a workforce, a tournament, or a class load, you are required to look at each piece from the perspective of the whole. For example, it is good to take English and math in high school, but it is not good to schedule them both at 9:00 in the morning. Part of scheduling, then, is making sure that there are enough resources for all the work. There is only one you, and you can be in only one class at a time.

Scheduling a computer's resources is also a management process. Certain processes, by their very nature, use more of the computer's resources than other processes. Some require dedicated time or dedicated access, whereas other processes work regardless. As the system administrator, it is your job to manage all the processes so that maximum efficiency is achieved, and so that the users can get their work done with as little interruption as possible. Fortunately, there are tools that allow you to manage your resources, and even start and stop processes when you are not around. Scheduling services are broken down into three areas:

- Processes that run all the time (or once, but always at startup)
- Processes that run repeatedly, at a specific time or on a specific day
- Processes that run only occasionally

For processes that run all the time, you have two tools: `inittab` and the `rc` files. For processes that run repeatedly, at a specific time or on a specific date, you have the `crontab` tool. For processes that need to be run only occasionally, you have the `at` tool.

Configuring *inittab* and *rc* Files

Before discussing the ins and outs of `inittab` and `rc` files, a brief discussion is needed on `init`, the parent process of `inittab`. When `init` is kicked off, it reads the file `/etc/inittab`, which tells `init` what to do. Usually, it tells `init` to allow user logons (`gettys`), and controls autonomous processes and other "at boot time" processes.

The `init` process can run at one of 15 levels. The run level is changed by having a privileged user (root) run `/sbin/telinit`, which sends appropriate signals to `init`, telling it which run level to change to.

After it has spawned all its processes, `init` waits for one of its child processes to die, for a power fail signal, or for a signal from `/sbin/telinit` to change the system's run level. When one of these changes occurs, the `/etc/inittab` file is reexamined. Root can also force the file to be reloaded with the command `init q`. `init` does not read files until one of these events occurs.

The *inittab* File

The `inittab` file, which tells `init` what to do, is a list of colon-delimited entries that use the following format:

```
id:runlevels:action:process
```

Table 25.1 examines and describes each of these entries.

Table 25.1   The Makeup of Each Line in the *inittab* File

Entry	Description
`id`	Identifies a unique sequence of 1–4 characters, which identifies an entry.
`runlevel`	Describes at which run level this action should occur.
`action`	Dictates which action is to be taken.
`process`	Specifies the process to be executed. If the process field starts with a +, `init` does not do `utmp` and `wtmp` accounting for that process.

`action` and `process` are easily confused. The action is what `init` does, not what the process does. There are 14 possible actions, as illustrated in Table 25.2.

Table 25.2   Possible Actions *init* Can Take

Action	Description
`respawn`	`init` restarts the process whenever the process terminates.
`wait`	`init` starts this process and waits for it to complete before continuing to the next process.
`once`	`init` starts this process and moves on. If/when this process terminates, it is not restarted.
`boot`	This process runs during system boot. The `runlevel` field is ignored.
`bootwait`	`init` starts this process at system boot, and waits for it to complete before continuing. The `runlevel` field is ignored.

continues…

Table 25.2	Continued
off	This does not run.
ondemand	This process is run whenever the specified ondemand run level is called. No actual run level change occurs. ondemand run levels are a, b, and c.
initdefault	This entry specifies the run level that should be entered after system boot. If none exists, init asks for a run level on the console. The process field is ignored. The default value is 3.
sysinit	This process is executed during system boot, and before any boot or bootwait entries. The runlevel field is ignored.
powerwait	This process is executed when init receives the SIGPWR signal, indicating that there is something wrong with power. init waits for the process to finish before continuing.
powerfail	This process is executed when init receives the SIGPWR signal, indicating that there is something wrong with power. init does not wait for the process to finish before continuing.
powerokwait	init executes this command when it receives the SIGPWR signal, provided that there is a file called /etc/powerstatus containing the word OK. This indicates that the power has come back on again.
ctrlaltdel	init executes this process when it receives the SIGINT signal. This means that someone on the system console has pressed the Ctrl+Alt+Del key combination. Typically, this is either a shutdown command or a boot to single-user mode.
kbrequest	This is one of the newer actions. When init receives a signal from the keyboard handler that a special key combination was pressed on the console keyboard, this command is executed. See documentation found in the kbd-x.xx package for more information.

Listing 25.1 shows an example inittab file from a machine running Red Hat Linux 6.1.

Listing 25.1	A Sample *inittab* File from a System Running Red Hat Linux 6.1

```
# inittab        This file describes how the INIT process should set up
# the system in a certain run-level.

# Author:       Miquel van Smoorenburg, <miquels@drinkel.nl.mugnet.org>
# Modified for RHS Linux by Marc Ewing and Donnie Barnes


# Default runlevel. The runlevels used by RHS are:
# 0 - halt (Do NOT set initdefault to this)
```

```
# 1 - Single user mode
# 2 - Multiuser, without NFS (The same as 3, if you do not have networking)
# 3 - Full multiuser mode
# 4 - unused
# 5 - X11
# 6 - reboot (Do NOT set initdefault to this)

id:3:initdefault:

# System initialization.
si::sysinit:/etc/rc.d/rc.sysinit

l0:0:wait:/etc/rc.d/rc 0
l1:1:wait:/etc/rc.d/rc 1
l2:2:wait:/etc/rc.d/rc 2
l3:3:wait:/etc/rc.d/rc 3
l4:4:wait:/etc/rc.d/rc 4
l5:5:wait:/etc/rc.d/rc 5
l6:6:wait:/etc/rc.d/rc 6

# Things to run in every runlevel.
ud::once:/sbin/update

# Trap CTRL-ALT-DELETE
ca::ctrlaltdel:/sbin/shutdown -t3 -r now

# When our UPS tells us power has failed, assume we have a few minutes
# of power left.  Schedule a shutdown for 2 minutes from now.
# This does, of course, assume you have powerd installed and your
# UPS connected and working correctly.
pf::powerfail:/sbin/shutdown -f -h +2 "Power Failure; System Shutting Down"

# If power was restored before the shutdown kicked in, cancel it.
pr:12345:powerokwait:/sbin/shutdown -c "Power Restored; Shutdown Cancelled"


# Run gettys in standard runlevels
1:2345:respawn:/sbin/mingetty tty1
2:2345:respawn:/sbin/mingetty tty2
```

continues...

Listing 25.1 Continued

```
3:2345:respawn:/sbin/mingetty tty3
4:2345:respawn:/sbin/mingetty tty4
5:2345:respawn:/sbin/mingetty tty5
6:2345:respawn:/sbin/mingetty tty6

# Run xdm in runlevel 5
# xdm is now a separate service
x:5:respawn:/etc/X11/prefdm -nodaemon
```

A number of the lines should now be familiar. It is good to point out that the id of each of these entries corresponds with the entry itself (for example, pf = power fail). This is a good habit to get into. Also, from the lilo line, you can specify a level by entering the following (in which # is the runtime level you want to use):

```
linux #
```

The *rc* Files

This section focuses particular attention on the lines in the inittab file that call the rc files (refer to Listing 25.1):

```
l0:0:wait:/etc/rc.d/rc.0
l1:1:wait:/etc/rc.d/rc.1
l2:2:wait:/etc/rc.d/rc.2
l3:3:wait:/etc/rc.d/rc.3
l4:4:wait:/etc/rc.d/rc.4
l5:5:wait:/etc/rc.d/rc.5
l6:6:wait:/etc/rc.d/rc.6
```

What is actually being called is the /etc/rc.d/rc file. This file is receiving an argument for the run level. At the end of this file, the following commands are called:

```
# Now run the START scripts.
for i in /etc/rc.d/rc$run level.d/S*; do
# Check if the script is there.
[ ! -f $i ] && continue
# Check if the subsystem is already up.
subsys=${i#/etc/rc.d/rc$run level.d/S??}
[ -f /var/lock/subsys/$subsys ] && \
[ -f /var/lock/subsys/${subsys}.init ] && continue
# Bring the subsystem up.
```

```
$i start
done
```

This loop is checking for a directory associated with that particular run level. If the directory exists, each process in that directory is initiated. After all other `rc` files are run, `/etc/rc.d/rc.local` is initiated. This is the best place to put your changes to the system. Note that this file overwrites the `/etc/issue` file at every bootup. So if you want to make changes to the banner that is displayed at logon, make your changes in the `rc.local` file rather than in the `/etc/issue` file.

With `inittab` and `rc` files, you have an excellent set of tools for starting processes at boot time, capturing keystroke events (such as Ctrl+Alt+Delete), and reacting in a appropriate manner.

Configuring *crontab* Scheduling Service

Certain processes must be run at a specific time, over and over again. An example of this might be a backup process that is kicked off each night, or a log analyzer that must be run every minute. These processes are run at specific times or on specific days; the rest of the time, they are not running.

`cron` starts from either `rc` or `rc.local`, forks, and puts itself in the background. There is no need to background this command. `cron` searches `/var/spool/cron` for entries that match users in the `/etc/passwd` file; found entries are loaded into memory. `cron` also searches `/etc/crontab` for system entries.

`cron` "wakes up" once a minute and does several things:

- It checks the entries that it knows about and runs any commands that are scheduled to run.
- It determines whether the `modtime` on the `cron` directory has changed.
- If the `modtime` on the `cron` directory has changed, `cron` checks each of the files and reloads any that have changed.

Do I need to restart *cron* after a change?
Since `cron` checks for changes every minute, it is unnecessary to restart `cron` when the `cron` files are changed.

Enabling *crontab* Service

It is the crontab file's job to schedule these services. The cron daemon reads the crontab file. The main system crontab file is stored in /etc/crontab and must be edited manually. Each user can also have her own version of this file that runs commands as that user. To set an individual user's crontab file, the appropriately named crontab command is invoked. Flags associated with the crontab application specify whether to open crontab for listing, editing, or removal.

The syntax for the crontab program is as follows:

```
crontab [-u user] file
crontab [-u user] -l -e -r
```

These parameters indicate the following:

- The -u option tells the system the name of the user whose crontab file is about to be used. If the -u option is omitted, the system assumes that you are editing your crontab. The switch user (su) command can confuse crontab, so if you are su'ing to someone else, be sure to use the -u option.

- The -l option tells crontab to list the file to standard output (in other words, to list the file).

- The -e option tells crontab to edit the file. cron uses the editor defined by EDITOR or by VISUAL. If neither is defined, it defaults to vi. When the file is exited, it is immediately placed in the correct location and the time stamp is updated.

- The -r option removes the specified crontab file. If no file is specified, it removes that user's crontab file.

crontab Entries

Two types of entries are allowed in the crontab file:

- Environment settings
- Command settings

These entries are discussed in the following sections.

Environment Settings

Environment settings use the following form:

```
name = value
```

cron already knows about several environment settings. For example, SHELL is set to /bin/sh. Other environment variables, such as LOGNAME and HOME, are associated with the owner of the file. SHELL and HOME can be overridden in the script; LOGNAME cannot. If MAILTO is defined (that is, MAILTO actually appears in a line in the crontab file and is not set to ""), it mails any messages to the specified user. The following shows MAILTO set to a specific user:

```
# mail any output to 'paulc', no matter whose crontab this is MAILTO=paulc
```

Any errors that occur while processing a crontab entry are sent in email to the MAILTO user. By default, messages are sent to the owner of a crontab file if not explicitly set with MAILTO.

Command Settings

Command settings use a standard format: Each line starts with five time/date fields. If this is the system crontab, the next field is the username associated with the entry. Following this entry is the command to be executed. The command is executed only when the current date and time meet all five of the time/date field criteria.

Here you see the available time/date fields and the ranges of values for each field. A time/date field can contain an asterisk instead of a number or a name; an asterisk indicates that any valid value should be matched.

Field	Allowable Values
minute	0–59
hour	0–23
day	0–31
month	0–12 (alternatively, three-letter, not case sensitive abbreviations of names can be used)
day of the week	0–7 (with 0 and 7 being Sunday; alternatively, three-letter, not case sensitive abbreviations of names can be used)

Using ranges to specify starting times

Ranges can be specified through the use of a hyphen. A value of 1-5 indicates that this field is valid for numbers 1 through 5. If you use a name instead of a number, you cannot specify a range.

Using step values to specify starting times

Step values can be used in conjunction with ranges. To specify a step value, follow the range with a forward slash (/) and a number. The number specified is the step value. For example, the following specifies that every third value (in this case, 2, 5, 8, and 11) should be matched:

`0-12/3`

Step values can also be used with asterisks. The value `*/3` in the hour field would match every third hour (0, 3, 6, 9, 12, 15, 18, and 21).

Using lists to specify starting times

Lists are also acceptable; each item in a list is separated by a comma. It is common to use lists in conjunction with ranges, like so:

`1-15,31-45`

This example matches all numbers from 1 through 15 and from 31 through 45. If you use a name instead of a number, you cannot specify a list.

Listing 25.2 shows the default `/etc/crontab` that comes with Red Hat Linux version 6.1.

Listing 25.2   An Example of a *crontab* File

```
[jray@pointy jray]$ more /etc/crontab
SHELL=/bin/bash
PATH=/sbin:/bin:/usr/sbin:/usr/bin
MAILTO=root
HOME=/

# run-parts
01 * * * * root run-parts /etc/cron.hourly
02 4 * * * root run-parts /etc/cron.daily
22 4 * * 0 root run-parts /etc/cron.weekly
42 4 1 * * root run-parts /etc/cron.monthly
```

Be aware that this is the system level `crontab` and it includes the username that the command should operate under. This field is *not* included in the `crontab` files of individual users; otherwise, the file structure is the same.

Notice that this crontab actually calls four different crontabs:

- One associated with hourly events
- One associated with daily events
- One associated with weekly events
- One associated with monthly events

If you are using a system that switches between Linux and another operating system, such as Windows 95, you might want to kick off some of these cron jobs yourself (if, for example, their scheduled time lapsed while you were in another operating system). Remember: The system does not go back and "pick up" cron jobs; it executes them only if the current date/time matches the entry.

Allowing and Preventing Access to the *crontab* Service

Two files enable root to allow or deny crontab service to users:

- /etc/cron.allow. This file does not exist by default; you must create it. Any entries you place in this file override entries placed in /etc/cron.deny. If the /etc/cron.allow file exists, only those users specified in that file can use the crontab service.

Specifying a day

The day that a command runs is specified by two fields; day of the week and day. The command runs if either of these is true. For example, the following entry specifies that the command be executed at 5:00 p.m. on the 1st and 15th of the month, and on every Friday:

```
0 17 1,15 *, 5
```

- /etc/cron.deny. This file exists by default. In it, you enter the usernames of users who are not allowed to use the crontab service.

It is important that only root be allowed to edit or add these files to the system.

If a user attempts to use cron (crontab -e), but his or her username has been placed in the /etc/cron.deny file, the following error occurs:

```
You (account name) are not allowed to use this program (crontab).
See crontab(1) for more information.
```

It is generally unwise to enable crontab abilities for all users. crontab files are a good way for users to eat up system resources without knowing it. Creating an /etc/cron.allow file for users who have a legitimate use for cron jobs is, by far, a better approach than creating an /etc/cron.deny file for those who shouldn't.

Configuring the *at* Command Service

crontab is great for processes that must be run on a regular schedule, but is a poor tool for something you want to run only once. The at tool enables you to specify a command to run at a certain time; the time can be the current time or it can be a specified time in the future.

To go along with the at command is the batch command, which executes commands when system load levels permit—that is, when the load average (measured by /proc/loadavg) drops below 1.5 or some other value specified at the invocation of atrun.

Enabling *at* Command Service

The at command service (as well as the batch command service) reads commands from standard input or a specified file that is to be executed at a later time via /bin/sh. The syntax for the at command is as follows:

```
at [-V] [-q queue] [-f file] [-mldbv] TIME
at -c job [job...]
atq [-V] [-q queue] [-v]
atrm [-V] job [job...]
batch [-V] [-q queue] [-f file] [-mv] [TIME]
```

Table 25.3 briefly describes what each command does.

Table 25.3 The *at* Commands

Command	Description
at	Executes commands at a specified time
atq	Lists the user's pending jobs (unless the user is the superuser, in which case it lists everyone's pending jobs)
atrm	Removes at jobs
batch	Executes commands when system load levels permit

Options for the at command include the following:

- -b. An alias for batch.

- -c. Shows jobs listed on the command line to standard output (the monitor).

- -d. An alias for atrm.

- -f. Reads the job from a file rather than standard input.

- -l. An alias for at.

- -m. Mails the user when the job is complete. This sends mail to the user specified (even if there is no output).

- -q. Uses a specified queue. A queue designation consists of a single letter, with c being the default for at, and E for batch. Valid designations are a..z and A..Z. Queues with letters closer to z (A is closer to z than z is) run with increased performance. If a job is submitted to a queue with an uppercase designation, the job is treated as a batch job. If atq is given a specific value, it shows jobs pending for only the specified queue.

- -v. Shows jobs that are complete, but not yet deleted.

- -V. Prints the version number to standard output.

Common Problems with the *at* Command

Several people have had problems with at jobs, some to the point where they would prefer to make the job a cron job, and then go back after the fact and remove the cron job.

Most of the problems with at jobs are in defining them. A straight at job is simple enough if you are calling a single word for a command, but it can easily get confusing. For example, I tried to run the following simple at job:

```
at now + 2 minutes touch ~/touch_file
```

When I pressed Enter, I got an error with the time:

```
parse error.  Last token seen: touch
Garbled Time.
```

Using the echo command, you can turn this at job around, and thus avoid the problems with "garbled time." Following is the same command, except I have turned it around with an echo command:

```
echo touch ~/touch_file | at now + 2 minutes
```

Sure enough, this one worked without a problem, and two minutes later my file in my home directory (`touch_file`) had its access date set to the current time.

The same problem occurs when you try to configure a `shutdown` command to run at a specific time:

```
echo shutdown -fr now | at now + 4 hours
```

This shuts down the system exactly four hours after this at job is initiated.

You can also run at interactively. This is one way to avoid the command-line problems entirely. Run the at utility with the time that you want your job to run, and then enter the commands you want to run, each on a separate line. Press Ctrl+D to finish up. For example, the `touch file` command can be activated like this:

```
[root@contempt jray]# at now +2 minutes
at> touch ~/touch_file
at> <EOT>
warning: commands will be executed using /bin/sh
job 2 at 1999-10-29 19:52
```

at jobs can accept the standard `hh:mm` time, but if the specified time has already passed, the system assumes that you mean that time tomorrow. You can use some common words with at jobs to specify time, including NOON, MIDNIGHT, TEATIME (4:00 p.m.), TODAY, TOMORROW, and NOW. The use of am and pm is also allowed. Days in the future can also be specified, and months can be designated with their three-letter abbreviations. For example, if you wanted to execute something at 4 a.m. two days from now, the command would look like this:

```
at 4am + 2 days
```

To run a job at noon on my birthday (November 25th), you would use the following:

```
at noon Nov 25
```

Finally, to shut down the system at 1 a.m. tomorrow, you would use the following:

```
echo shutdown -fr now | at 1am tomorrow
```

Determining who can use the *at* command

Root can always use the `at` command. All others depend on the `at.allow` and the `at.deny` files.

Problems with Specifying Time with *at*

One of the more common problems with at is specifying times. The command takes a wide variety of time and date syntaxes, listed here.

Specifying the Date

Month Day Year (November 12 1999)	You can explicitly spell out the date.
MMDDYY, MM/DD/YY, DD.MM.YY	You can also specify the date using traditional date shorthand.
today/tomorrow	at also takes relative dates rather than specific values.

Specifying the Time

now, midnight, noon, or teatime (4pm) HH[:MM]<AM/PM>	Self explanatory, but unfortunately "lunchtime" isn't one of the options.
	You can dictate times by giving the hour with an optional minute and an AM or PM designation.

Specifying a Time Relative to a Given Time

+ hours/minutes/days/weeks	Given a time, you can tell at to add a certain number of hours, minutes, days, or weeks to that time before executing.

Allowing and Preventing Access to the *at* Command Service

By default, an empty /etc/at.deny file exists. Because it is empty, every user is allowed to use the at command. If there are usernames (as defined in the /etc/passwd file) in this file, then those users are *not* allowed to use the at command.

By default, /etc/at.allow does not exist. If it does exist, only users whose usernames are entered in this file can use the at command. This means that /etc/at.allow has precedence over /etc/at.deny. If both exist, only the /etc/at.allow file is checked, and only those entries are allowed to use the at command. If neither file exists, then only root can run at commands.

If a user attempts to run the at command, but his or her username appears in the /etc/at.deny file (or an /etc/at.allow file exists and his or her username is not one of the entries), the following error occurs:

```
You do not have permission to use at.
```

# chapter 26

Managing Network Connections

Configuring network connections manually

Configuring network connections with `linuxconf`

Adding a PLIP interface

Adding an Ethernet interface

Enabling the file system service

Enabling dial-in service

Configuring Network Connections Manually

Linux distributions offer their own proprietary tools for configuring network interfaces and often store configuration information in different places. This section of the chapter walks you through configuring a network card so that it can talk on your network. When it's configured, you'll need to repeat these commands each time your system boots. The easiest way to do this is to add them to the end of one of your system initialization files, such as `/etc/rc.d/rc.local`. The drawback to this approach is that by manually configuring the network, you can cause problems later if you decide to use the system's configuration tools. Chances are, they won't store the configuration in the same place and might end up adding redundant information to the files you've already set up. With this configuration trouble in mind, a universal configuration utility was created: `linuxconf`. `linuxconf` enables the administrator to configure network settings, Apache, Sendmail, and many other parts of your system settings. Setting up your network using `linuxconf` is discussed later in the chapter.

In order to fully set your system up, you'll need the following information for your network:

- IP address
- Subnet mask
- Default gateway
- Domain name servers

Don't ever guess these values; doing so could cause problems for your network and network administrator.

Configuring the Loopback Interface

The computer uses the loopback interface to make connections to itself. Information requests made by computers using the Internet Protocol go through interfaces. If a computer wants to get information from itself, the fastest way to obtain this information is to have a software interface. This interface should have been configured by your computer during the installation procedure; nonetheless, the instructions for setting it up are included here.

The easiest way to set up this interface is to use the `ifconfig` and `route` commands, like so:

```
# ifconfig lo 127.0.0.1
# route add -host 127.0.0.1 lo
```

Make sure the loopback interface has the right IP address

The loopback interface is always assigned the IP address `127.0.0.1`. This standardization means you can be sure that connections made to the IP address `127.0.0.1` are always made to the local computer, not some other computer.

The `ifconfig` command tells the computer to enable the interface `lo` (short for *loopback*) with an IP address of `127.0.0.1`. The `route` command tells the computer to add a route to the host `127.0.0.1` through the interface `lo`. When these commands have been executed, you can test whether the loopback address is working by typing the following:

```
# ping -c 1 localhost
```

This results in the following output:

```
[root@pointy jray]# ping -c 1 localhost
PING localhost (127.0.0.1) from 127.0.0.1 : 56(84) bytes of data.
64 bytes from 127.0.0.1: icmp_seq=0 ttl=255 time=0.2 ms

--- localhost ping statistics ---
1 packets transmitted, 1 packets received, 0% packet loss
round-trip min/avg/max = 0.2/0.2/0.2 ms
```

When the loopback interface has been configured, it must be named.

Naming the interface

1. Open the `/etc/hosts` file in your favorite editor.

2. Include a line that looks like this:

   ```
   127.0.0.1       localhost       localhost.localdomain
   ```

3. Exit and save the file you are editing.

This process can be used to give names to other IP addresses as well, but very few IP addresses need to be named on systems using name servers.

Configuring an Ethernet Card

Now that you have the loopback interface up and running, the process of configuring an Ethernet card should seem very familiar. Assuming you already have a card `eth0` recognized by your system, it's easy to configure the necessary properties to be up and running on a TCP/IP network.

Once again you employ the ifconfig command to bring up your network card. This is a relatively painless process—just use the syntax ifconfig *device ipaddress* netmask *network mask* broadcast *broadcast address*.

For example, in order to configure a network card (eth0) with the address 192.168.0.1, a subnet mask of 255.255.0.0, and a broadcast address 192.168.255.255, you would use the following syntax:

```
[root@pointy network-scripts]# ifconfig eth0 192.168.0.1 netmask 255.255.0.0
➥broadcast 192.168.255.255
```

You can verify that your network interface is up and running at any time by using the ifconfig command by itself.

```
[jray@pointy jray]$ ifconfig
eth0      Link encap:Ethernet  HWaddr 00:A0:C9:B3:5B:A2
          inet addr:192.168.0.1  Bcast:192.168.255.255  Mask:255.255.0.0
          UP BROADCAST RUNNING MULTICAST  MTU:1500  Metric:1
          RX packets:214 errors:0 dropped:0 overruns:0 frame:0
          TX packets:195 errors:0 dropped:0 overruns:0 carrier:0
          collisions:0

lo        Link encap:Local Loopback
          inet addr:127.0.0.1  Mask:255.0.0.0
          UP LOOPBACK RUNNING  MTU:3924  Metric:1
          RX packets:0 errors:0 dropped:0 overruns:0 frame:0
          TX packets:0 errors:0 dropped:0 overruns:0 carrier:0
          collisions:0
```

As you can see, eth0 is indeed configured as intended. Pretty simple, huh? You should, at this point, make a note of the command you used; you'll need to add it to a file executed at startup, such as rc.local, when you're sure that everything is working like you want.

Setting a Default Route

Now, turn your attention to the default gateway for your network. This is the device that is used to connect your network to the rest of the world or to other networks within your organization. If you don't configure your default route, you'll only be able to talk to computers on your local subnet. If you're only operating a LAN, you probably don't need to configure the gateway.

The syntax for add your default gateway is `route add default gw gateway address`. To add a default gateway of `192.168.0.2`, you would type the following:

```
route add default gw 192.168.0.2
```

At this point, your machine should be able to talk to other computers on the network by using their IP addresses; you haven't configured DNS information yet, so hostnames are still out of the picture. To test your connectivity, try pinging a host outside of your network, such as one of your nameservers. For example

```
[root@pointy jray]# ping 140.254.85.225
PING 140.254.85.225 (140.254.85.225) from 24.93.100.123 : 56(84) bytes of data.
64 bytes from 140.254.85.225: icmp_seq=0 ttl=251 time=26.1 ms
64 bytes from 140.254.85.225: icmp_seq=1 ttl=251 time=125.7 ms
64 bytes from 140.254.85.225: icmp_seq=2 ttl=251 time=63.1 ms
64 bytes from 140.254.85.225: icmp_seq=3 ttl=251 time=73.9 ms
64 bytes from 140.254.85.225: icmp_seq=4 ttl=251 time=30.9 ms

--- 140.254.85.225 ping statistics ---
5 packets transmitted, 5 packets received, 0% packet loss
round-trip min/avg/max = 26.1/63.9/125.7 ms
```

If `ping` fails to receive a response from the remote machine, go back and check your default route. If that looks good, check your IP address and subnet mask. Any variation from the numbers assigned to your network could result in a wide variety of strange problems.

Configuring Hostname and DNS Information

Now that your computer can talk on the network, you need to give it the means by which it can identify other computers (and itself) by name. This is primarily accomplished by listing known hosts in the `/etc/hosts` file and adding name servers to `/etc/resolv.conf` (no, that isn't a typo).

As you saw earlier, `/etc/hosts` is a simple textfile that contains a list of IP address and hostname pairs. In the sample configuration you've seen so far, the network interface was configured with the address `192.168.0.1`. If you (for some strange reason) wanted to call your machine `pointy` (for short) and `pointy.poisontooth.com`, you could edit the `/etc/hosts` file to include this information:

```
127.0.0.1       localhost           localhost.localdomain
192.168.0.1     pointy              pointy.poisontooth.com
```

The `localhost` settings should be there from your earlier configuration of the loop-back interface.

You can also add IP addresses and hostnames of other machines that you might want to contact. It might seem a bit strange to hard-code hostname/IP pairs into your `/etc/hosts` file when you can just use a domain name server to return lookup results. Keeping commonly used hosts in your hosts file, however, can be a lifesaver when network problems arise.

There is a great deal of responsibility placed on name servers. Almost all network connections are made by hostname rather than IP address. Because of this reliance, a network can be rendered useless when a name server fails. If you keep your commonly used hosts and their IP addresses listed in `/etc/hosts`, in the event of a name server failure, you'll still be able to contact your remote system.

When you've configured your host/IP mappings, you'll probably want to configure a nameserver. To do this, you'll need to edit the `/etc/resolv.conf` file. You can include up to three different nameservers; at least two are recommended.

Here is a sample `/etc/resolv.conf` file (these numbers *will not* work for you):

```
search brevardmpo.com poisontooth.com
nameserver 192.30.29.7
nameserver 192.30.29.8
nameserver 168.146.1.7
```

The first line specifies a *search path* for name lookups. The search path includes the domains that are appended to a hostname lookup if the hostname is not fully qualified. For example, if I try to connect to the host `maddy` instead of `maddy.poisontooth.com`, the system will first look for `maddy.brevardmpo.com` and then `maddy.poisontooth.com`. This line is optional, but it can save you quite a bit of typing if you commonly connect to hosts outside of your local network.

The remaining three lines of the file specify three different nameservers. Each line must contain `nameserver` followed by the IP address of the server. You can list more than three servers, but only the first three will be used.

To test your system to see if name resolution is working, use `nslookup` *hostname* to test your DNS configuration.

```
[root@pointy /etc]# nslookup www.cnn.com
Server:  name.farwestcom.net
Address:  192.30.29.7

Non-authoritative answer:
```

```
Name:     cnn.com
Addresses: 207.25.71.26, 207.25.71.27, 207.25.71.28, 207.25.71.29
          207.25.71.30, 207.25.71.82, 207.25.71.199, 207.25.71.5, 207.25.71.6
          207.25.71.7, 207.25.71.8, 207.25.71.9, 207.25.71.12, 207.25.71.20
          207.25.71.22, 207.25.71.23, 207.25.71.24, 207.25.71.25
Aliases:  www.cnn.com
```

Here, the test lookup was performed on www.cnn.com, and the multiple IP addresses of the CNN servers were returned.

When you've verified that your configuration is complete, you're finished! You've successfully configured your network by hand. You should go ahead and add the commands used to produce a working configuration to one of your startup files; this will bring your network up each time your computer boots.

Using DHCP to Configure Your Network Settings

If you're using a network that supports DHCP, chances are you don't need to do nearly as much work to configure your network settings. Depending on your Linux distribution, you might have a slightly different procedure to follow. Most distributions use dhcpcd; although Red Hat Linux has shifted to pump, it still includes dhcpcd.

To activate an Ethernet interface (eth0) with dhcpcd, type the following:

```
[root@pointy /etc]# dhcpcd eth0
```

If everything worked as it should, ifconfig, as before, displays your network settings as if you had configured them manually. dhcpcd automatically configures your routing as well as DNS information. In some cases, you might want to keep dhcpcd from replacing your /etc/resolv.conf file because of custom configuration you might have done. To prevent the file from being erased, invoke dhcpcd with the -R option.

dhcpcd automatically keeps your DHCP connection up and running and renews DHCP leases as appropriate. When you've started the process, it forks into the background and ensures that your network access is not interrupted.

Configuring Network Connections with *linuxconf*

Managing network connections with Linux is straightforward, thanks to the user-friendly configuration tool linuxconf. This tool provides for the enabling and configuring of network connections in a graphical interface. If you do not have linuxconf on your system, I recommend that you install it as soon as possible.

Currently, `linuxconf` supports Red Hat, Debian, SuSE, Caldera, and Slackware distributions. This is the most universal configuration tool available. If you operate computers running different Linux distributions, providing a common interface to system configuration greatly eases administration. `linuxconf` is a large project under very active development. With its open module model, developers are encouraged to use it as a front-end to *any* Linux software configuration task.

`linuxconf` enables you to configure many different aspects of your system, including the X Window System, the command line, and even a Web browser. The `linuxconf` homepage is located at `http://www.solucorp.qc.ca/linuxconf/`.

Using the Network Configuration Tool

To launch `linuxconf`, type the following at root's prompt:

```
# linuxconf
```

Within a few seconds, the `linuxconf` screen should appear. Navigate through the hierarchical settings on the right to reach the network configuration options: Networking, Clients, Basic Host Information. Figure 26.1 shows `linuxconf` up and running.

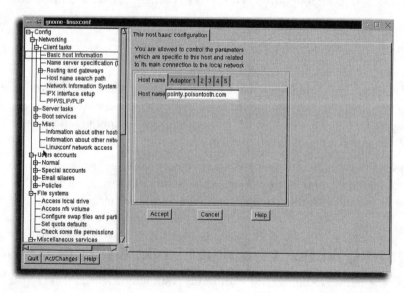

FIGURE 26.1
This screen shows the basic network configuration screen of `linuxconf`.

Setting the Hostname and the Domain Name

When linuxconf is running, setting a machine's hostname is simple. Just click in the Host Name text field and type the name you want to give the machine. To save the hostname, click the Accept button. If you want to set multiple options, there is no need to click Accept after each one. Just move from screen to screen and make your changes.

Set the hostname and domain name correctly

For most people, hostnames and domain names are provided by their Internet service provider or their school or business. In such cases, it is important that the name entered in the Hostname and the Domain field is the same as the name provided by the ISP or other entity.

Setting the Name Servers

To add a name server, click the Name Server Specification item in the configuration option listing on the right, and then be sure that the Resolver Configuration tab is selected in the pane on the left. You can now specify up to three name servers and several different search paths. This information can be obtained from your ISP or network administrator.

Adding a PPP Interface

The Point-to-Point Protocol (PPP) is a method of creating and running IP over a serial link made using modems and phone lines. With PPP, a client connects to a PPP server. When connected, the client can access resources on the PPP server's network as though it were connected directly to the network. PPP is one of the most common ways for personal computers to connect to the Internet.

Configuring PPP on a Linux machine

1. Navigate to the PPP/SLIP/PLIP linuxconf options.
2. Choose PPP from the device list, and click Accept to create a new interface. Figure 26.2 shows the configuration screen for your newly created PPP interface.
3. Type the phone number, username, and password for the PPP connection that you'll be making. Be sure to also choose the appropriate serial port for your computer. If you want to customize the settings for your modem, click the Customize button. Figure 26.3 shows PPP interface customization options.

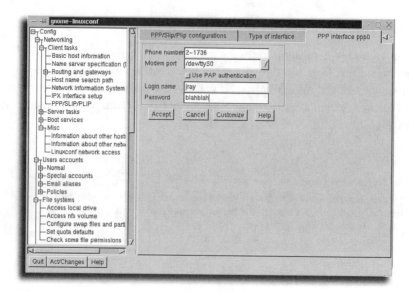

FIGURE 26.2
linuxconf can control all your PPP options.

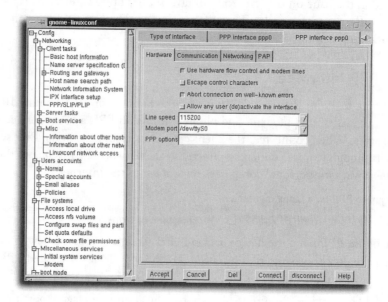

FIGURE 26.3
You can customize all aspects of your PPP connection.

4. Here you can change the speed of your modem port as well as handshaking options for the port. Each tab at the top of the screen enables you to configure other aspects of the PPP connection.

5. Click the Communication tab to view and update all the commands that will be sent to your modem. It's usually best not to change anything here unless you're familiar with the modem's command set.

6. The Networking tab offers few options that you'll want to change. One potential exception to note is the Activate Interface at Boot Time option. With this option selected, when the computer boots, the PPP interface will become active and dial into the network. A summary of these options follows:

- *Activate Interface at Boot Time.* This means that when your computer boots up, it will dial your modem and establish a PPP link. This is useful if your service provider grants you unlimited connection time.

- *Set Default Route.* This means that all packets requested by your machine for addresses other than the local host will be sent to the PPP interface. This is useful when PPP is the main network connection for your machine.

- *Restart Link When Connection Fails.* This useful option prevents you from having to restart PPP every time the connection fails.

- *MRU/MTU.* The maximum transmission unit is the maximum size in bytes of a packet that can be sent and received by your machine. The allowable range is 296–1,500 bytes. The value you enter depends on the quality of your phone line. Noisy lines require smaller numbers, and clean lines can use larger numbers.

- *Local IP Address and Remote IP Address.* These options are useful only for machines with static IP addresses. If you have a static IP address, these values will be provided to you by your company or service provider.

7. The PAP options are useful if you use PAP authentication on your PPP connection (this is *very* common); fill in your username and password to log in to the system.

8. When you're finished configuring, click Accept. Your PPP interface will now be listed in the main PPP/SLIP/PLIP configuration screen.

9. You can add additional interfaces by repeating these steps.

> **Run *linuxconf* as root**
>
> It is important to root run `linuxconf`; otherwise, the modifications made to the network will not be applied.

Adding a SLIP Interface

Adding a new SLIP interface follows exactly the same procedure as the PPP interface configuration:

1. Click the PPP/SLIP/PLIP option from the main selection list, and then choose Add.

2. Instead of choosing PPP, choose SLIP and click Accept. Type the phone number, username, and password for the SLIP connection that you'll be making. Be sure to also choose the appropriate serial port for your computer. If you want to customize the settings for your modem, click the Customize button. Figure 26.4 shows SLIP interface customization options.

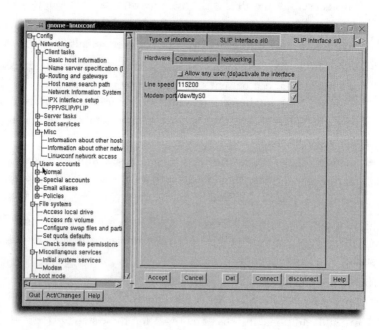

FIGURE 26.4
`linuxconf` also offers easy SLIP configuration options.

3. Here you can change the speed of your modem port as well as handshaking options for the port. Each tab at the top of the screen enables you to configure other aspects of the PPP connection.

4. Click the Communication tab to view and update all the commands that will be sent to your modem. It's usually best not to change anything here unless you're familiar with the modem's command set.

5. The Networking tab offers few options that you'll want to change. One potential exception to note is the Activate Interface at Boot Time option. With this option selected, when the computer boots, the SLIP interface will become active and dial into the network. A summary of the available options follows:

   - *Activate Interface at Boot Time.* This means that when your computer boots up, it will dial your modem and establish a PPP link. This is useful if your service provider grants you unlimited connection time.

   - *Set Default Route.* This means that all packets requested by your machine for addresses other than the local host will be sent to the SLIP interface. This is useful when SLIP is the main network connection for your machine.

   - *MTU.* The maximum transmission unit is the maximum size in bytes of a packet that can be sent and received by your machine. The allowable range is 296–1,500 bytes. The value you enter depends on the quality of your phone line. Noisy lines require smaller numbers, and clean lines can use larger numbers.

   - *Local IP Address and Remote IP Address.* These options are useful only for machines with static IP addresses. If you have a static IP address, these values will be provided to you by your company or service provider.

When you're finished configuring your options, choose Quit from the main linuxconf window. When the system prompts you to make sure you want to save changes, tell it Yes.

After your PPP or SLIP interface is configured, you'll want to test it to make sure it works the way you want.

Testing the PPP/SLIP interface

1. Open a terminal session and type ifup *interface name*. If you've just configured PPP, the interface is probably ppp0 or, for SLIP, sl0.

2. After the connection is established, ping a well-known host (for example, try pinging 192.31.7.130, which is www.cisco.com):

```
kanchi 1555$ ping -c 3 192.31.7.130
PING 192.31.7.130 (192.31.7.130): 56 data bytes
64 bytes from 192.31.7.130: icmp_seq=0 ttl=248 time=38.5 ms
64 bytes from 192.31.7.130: icmp_seq=1 ttl=249 time=32.5 ms
64 bytes from 192.31.7.130: icmp_seq=2 ttl=249 time=30.7 ms

--- 192.31.7.130 ping statistics ---
3 packets transmitted, 3 packets received, 0% packet loss
round-trip min/avg/max = 30.7/33.9/38.5 ms
```

If your output is similar to this, your connection is working correctly.

To easily activate and deactivate a PPP interface, just use the ifup and ifdown commands followed by the name of the interface you want to control. Non-root users might not be able to use ifup and ifdown, depending on the system configuration.

Activating and deactivating an interface

The ifconfig command will show you the interfaces that are currently active on your machine. If there is an interface that you'd like to bring online, you can use the ifup *interface name* command to activate the interface. Likewise, the ifdown *interface name* command will deactivate an interface.

Be sure to be logged in locally when changing states of interfaces. If you telnet in and start reconfiguring your network, you might find that you've disabled the interface you're connected to!

Adding a PLIP Interface

The Parallel Line Internet Protocol (PLIP) is similar to SLIP because it provides a point-to-point connection between two machines. The difference between the two is that PLIP uses the parallel ports on the computer to provide higher speeds (megabytes per *second* versus megabytes per minute).

Configuring a PLIP interface

1. Launch linuxconf and choose PPP/SLIP/PLIP from the Networking, Client Tasks section.

2. Click the PLIP checkbox and Accept.

3. Click the Networking tab to bring up the PLIP configuration options, which are shown in Figure 26.5.

4. Click the Local IP field and type the local machine's IP address.

5. Click the Remote IP field and type the remote machine's IP address.

6. Click the Netmask field and enter the network mask for the local machine's IP address.

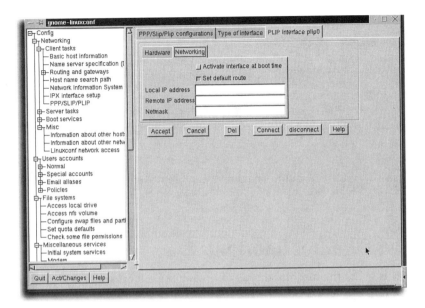

FIGURE 26.5
Configure a new PLIP interface using `linuxconf`.

7. If you want the PLIP interface to be active when your machine boots, select the Activate Interface at Boot Time option.

8. A new entry, `plip0`, will be added to the system. Click Accept and Quit to exit from `linuxconf`.

9. Use the command `ifup plip0` to bring the interface online.

10. Test the PLIP interface by pinging the remote machine. For example, if the remote machine's IP address is 10.8.11.5, ping would produce the following output:

```
kanchi 1572$ ping -c 3 10.8.11.5
PING 10.8.11.5 (10.8.11.5): 56 data bytes
64 bytes from 10.8.11.5: icmp_seq=0 ttl=255 time=1.7 ms
64 bytes from 10.8.11.5: icmp_seq=1 ttl=255 time=1.7 ms
64 bytes from 10.8.11.5: icmp_seq=2 ttl=255 time=1.7 ms

--- 10.8.11.5 ping statistics ---
3 packets transmitted, 3 packets received, 0% packet_loss
round-trip min/avg/max = 1.7/1.7/1.7 ms
```

If your output looks similar, your PLIP interface is working properly.

TCP/IP connections over serial lines

The three common protocols for running TCP/IP on serial or parallel lines are the Point-to-Point Protocol (PPP), the Serial Line Internet Protocol (SLIP), and the Parallel Line Internet Protocol (PLIP).

Of these, SLIP is the oldest and has problems dealing with noisy low-speed telephone lines. SLIP predates the standardization process for protocols, so it is not considered one of the Internet standard protocols.

The Internet standard replacement for SLIP is PPP. This protocol provides similar functionality to SLIP, but in a reliable manner over all types of phone lines. Currently, PPP is the most widely used protocol for running TCP/IP over phone lines.

PLIP is a variant of SLIP, which enables TCP/IP to be run over the parallel port of a computer. PLIP is faster than PPP or SLIP but is not widely used for connecting computers over phone lines.

Adding an Ethernet Interface

Ethernet is by far the most used type of hardware for local area networks because it is cheap, fast, and reliable.

Configuring an Ethernet interface

1. Launch `linuxconf`.

2. Navigate to the Networking, Basic Host Information section of `linuxconf` (refer to Figure 26.1).

3. Click the number of the adapter you want to configure—most likely 1.

4. The Adapter Configuration screen will appear, as shown in Figure 26.6.

5. If your network uses Bootp or DHCP to assign network information, click the appropriate radio button and skip ahead to step 9.

6. Click the IP field and type the IP address of the interface. If Ethernet is your machine's primary interface, type the machine's IP address.

7. Click the Netmask field and enter the network mask for the IP address entered in step 5.

8. Fill the in the Primary Name + Domain field with a fully qualified hostname for your computer. Add any additional names to the Aliases field.

9. Click the Enabled option.

10. Fill in the appropriate Ethernet device name—usually `eth0` for adapter 1, `eth1` for adapter 2, and so on.

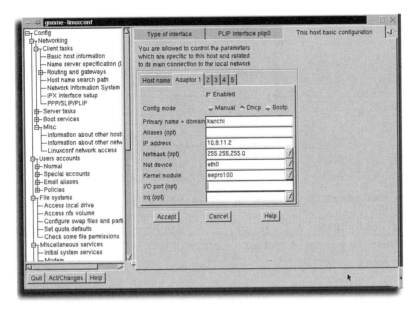

FIGURE 26.6
Configure a new Ethernet interface using `linuxconf`.

11. In the Kernel Module field, select the name of the driver module for your
    Ethernet card from the drop-down menu. Do the same with the IRQ and I/O
    address if necessary.

12. Click Accept and then Quit to save your configuration.

Setting Up a Router

The previous steps configure your Ethernet interface, but for your machine to be
able to talk to other machines, the routing must be set up. The following example
covers setting up a machine to be a *router*. Client setups for Linux, Windows, and
Mac OS are covered in separate subsections.

For the purposes of the following examples, assume that the local network is the one
shown in Figure 26.7 and that the `eth0` interface for `kanchi` has been configured with
the parameters shown in Figure 26.6.

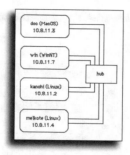

FIGURE 26.7
This is a sample network, used to illustrate connecting hosts to a Linux machine.

The network illustrated in Figure 26.7 boasts four hosts, which will be used to demonstrate the process of configuring different types of machines to talk to a Linux machine acting as a router:

- doc. This is a Macintosh running system 8.1 with open transport. Its local IP address is 10.8.11.3.

- win. This is an x86 machine running Windows NT Workstation 4.0. Its local IP address is 10.8.11.7.

- kanchi. This main Linux machine is the router for all the other machines in the network. Its IP address is 10.8.11.2.

- melkote. This is a client Linux machine. Its local IP address is 10.8.11.4.

To configure kanchi to route packets for all machines, several routes must be added to the routing table, which helps the kernel keep track of where packets should be sent. The routing table is used to track three main types of routes:

- Host routes
- Network routes
- Default routes

Setting up routes

1. The first type of route you must set up is a host route to yourself. To do this, use the route command (while acting as root), as follows:

```
# route add -host 10.8.11.2 netmask 255.255.255.255 dev lo
```

This creates a route to the host 10.8.11.2 through the interface lo (loopback).

2. Add a route to all hosts with IP addresses starting with 10.:

```
# route add -net 10.0.0.0 netmask 255.0.0.0 dev eth0
```

The route that is created enables the computer to use the Ethernet interface
eth0 to communicate with all hosts that have an IP address of the form 10.*x.x.x*,
where x is a number between 1 and 254. Some examples of valid IP address
starting with 10. are 10.0.0.1 and 10.8.11.2.

3. For all packets going to hosts without 10.*x.x.x* addresses, you must add the
default route. In the case of this machine, the default route runs through itself,
so you add it as follows:

```
# route add default gw 10.8.11.2 dev eth0
```

Now that the main Linux machine, kanchi, is configured, you can configure the
other machines.

Connecting Two Linux Systems

Connecting two Linux machines is easy. This is usually referred to as configuring
one Linux machine to be the client of another. In this case, melkote is configured to
be a client of kanchi.

Configuring *melkote*

1. Make sure that melkote's lo and eth0 interfaces have been configured properly.

2. Add a route to the kanchi (10.8.11.2). This route will be used by the local
machine for sending and receiving packets from kanchi. Entering the following
at the command line adds a route to kanchi via the eth0 interface:

```
# route add -host 10.8.11.2 netmask 255.255.255.255 dev eth0
```

3. For the local machine (melkote) to communicate with the other computers on
the network, you must add the default route. The default route is used to communicate with hosts that do not have explicit entries in the routing table. To add
the default route for melkote via kanchi, enter the following:

```
route add default gw 10.8.11.2 dev eth0
```

This adds a default route for all packets to be sent to the router at 10.8.11.2 on
your eth0 interface. A program such as Telnet or PING will confirm that the
routing is working properly.

Connecting a Mac OS Machine to a Linux System

Connecting the machine doc, which runs Mac OS as a kanchi, is straightforward
under Open Transport.

Configuring *doc*

1. Click the Apple menu and select Control Panels.

2. In the Control Panels window, select the TCP/IP icon. The TCP/IP screen shown in Figure 26.8 appears.

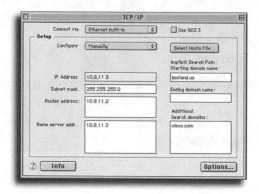

FIGURE 26.8
Configure TCP/IP on a computer running Mac OS using the TCP/IP control panel.

3. Click the Connect Via drop-down list and select the Ethernet built-in option.

4. Click the Configure drop-down list and select the Manually option.

5. In the IP Address field, enter doc's IP address (in this example, the IP address is 10.8.11.3).

6. In the Subnet mask field, enter the network mask for the IP address entered in step 6.

7. In the Router Address field, enter kanchi's address (10.8.11.2).

8. Close the window to initialize the network by clicking the Close box in the upper-left side of the window.

Connecting a Windows Machine to a Linux System

Configuring a Windows machine is similar to configuring a Macintosh. This example demonstrates how to configure Windows NT; configuring Windows 95 (and, presumably, Windows 98) works in exactly the same way.

Configuring *win*

1. Click the Start menu, click Settings, and then choose Control Panel to open the Control Panel window.

2. Click the Network icon to open the Network window.

3. Click the Identification tab.

4. Click the Computer Name field and type the name of the computer. (I've typed win in this example.)

5. Click the Protocols tab.

6. If TCP/IP Protocol is displayed in the list of network protocols, double-click it. If not, click the Add button and select TCP/IP Protocol. Return to the Protocols tab, and then double-click the newly added TCP/IP Protocol entry.

7. In the ensuing Microsoft TCP/IP Properties dialog box, click the Specify an IP address option.

8. Click the IP Address field and type the computer's IP address. (In this case, I entered 10.8.11.7.)

9. Click the Subnet Mask field and type the computer's subnet mask. (In this case, I entered 255.255.255.0.)

10. Click the Default Gateway field and type the computer's gateway, which is the machine through which all packets are routed. (I entered 10.8.11.2 because win's gateway is kanchi.)

11. Click OK in the Microsoft TCP/IP Properties window, and then click OK in the Network window.

12. Click Yes in the window that asks whether you want to reboot the machine for the new network configuration.

After the machine reboots, the network will be properly configured. I used the dos shell and the PING program to test this.

Enabling the Network File System Service

The Network File System (NFS) provides for the mounting of directories across a network. Directories on a remote machine mounted via NFS on the local machine actually become part of the local machines file system.

Configuring the NFS service involves two parts:

- *Configuring the NFS server.* This is the machine from which a directory is mounted. In my sample network, the NFS server is kanchi.

- *Configuring the NFS client.* This is the machine mounting the directory. In my sample network, the NFS client is melkote.

This example demonstrates how to mount the kanchi's /home directory on melkote so that users have the same /home directory on both machines.

Configuring an NFS server

1. As root, open the file /etc/exports in your editor. If the file existed prior to opening it in the editor, its contents will be displayed in your editor's window. If the file did not exist when you opened it, your editor will create the file and display a blank screen.

2. A shorthand for allowing everyone to mount a directory is to simply give the permissions and not list any host names. Take a look at a sample:

```
# exports file for kanchi
/mnt/cdrom      (ro)
/mnt/zip        (rw)
/store/pub      (rw)
```

This is the /etc/exports file on kanchi; the three entries in it correspond to directories that can be mounted by NFS clients. In this case, all three directories are mountable by everyone. The permissions are clearly seen in this file:

- (ro). This indicates read-only permissions.
- (rw). This indicates read and write permissions.

3. Make the /home directory available for NFS mounting on melkote by entering the following line:

```
/home           melkote(rw)
```

This indicates that melkote can mount /home with read and write permissions.

The syntax of /etc/exports

The syntax of the /etc/exports file is simple. The directories available for NFS mounting are specified one per line. On each line, the first entry is the directory that you want to mount. The next two entries are a pair. The first entry in this pair is the name of a machine that should be capable of mounting this directory; the second entry in this pair is the permissions with which this machine can mount the directory. As many host and permission pairs can exist as you want.

Now that you have configured the NFS server kanchi, you can configure the NFS client melkote. To the client, mounting an NFS directory is the same as mounting any other type of device, such as a hard drive or CD-ROM.

Configuring an NFS client

1. For `melkote` to mount `/home` properly, you must add an entry to its `/etc/fstab` file. In this case, the entry is as follows:
   ```
   kanchi:/home      /home    NFS
   ```

2. After you have added this entry, you can mount `kanchi`'s `/home` directory as root by typing the following:
   ```
   mount kanchi:/home
   ```

3. Now anyone who logs in to `melkote` will get the same `/home` directory as on `kanchi`.

Enabling Dial-In Service

Enabling dial-in service on a Linux system requires two programs:

- The PPP daemon (PPPD), which is used to detect incoming connections and to shut down active PPP links when a connection terminates.
- The `getty` program, which handles modem communications intelligently. This chapter gives an overview of the format of the file, `/etc/gettydefs`, used to handle login process for a dial-in user.

These programs are available on every Red Hat Linux installation.

The process in which a user establishes a PPP link is as follows:

1. The phone number of the modem connected to the Linux system (the PPP server) is dialed from a remote host (the PPP client).

   The user logs in to the server with a valid username and password.

2. At the shell prompt, the user issues the following command to start PPP on the server:
   ```
   exec /usr/sbin/pppd detach
   ```

3. The user starts PPP on the client.

Setting Up the PPP Options Files

Two files must be present to grant PPP access to a Linux system. The first file, `/etc/ppp/options`, contains the common PPP options required for modem connections. These options are listed one per line in the file as shown here:
```
asyncmap 0
```

```
netmask 255.255.255.0
proxyarp
lock
crtscts
modem
```

The line for `netmask` should be modified to be the netmask for your Linux system's IP address.

The second file that must be created is the `/etc/ppp/options.tty01` file. This file contains a list of IP addresses or hostnames and the PPP interfaces with which they are associated. For example, if the `/etc/ppp/options.tty01` file contained the following line, when a PPP client connects to the ppp0 interface, it is automatically given the name `srv-ss2` along with the IP address of `srv-ss2`:

```
srv-ss2:ppp0
```

Configuring Getty Devices

When a user dials into a Linux system, three actions must be performed before the user can log in:

1. Open tty lines and set their modes.

2. Print the login prompt.

3. Initiate the login process for the user.

These actions are handled by the `getty` program, which keeps a list of tty lines and their modes and sets the mode of dial-in connection to the appropriate entry in the list. Each individual entry in the list is referred to as a `getty` device. After the line has been set up, `getty` prints the login prompt and initiates the login process.

The process of configuring `getty` devices is done by adding entries to the `/etc/gettydefs` file. The default version of this file is fine for most installations, but occasionally, entries for newer or faster modem types must be added.

---

gettydefs file format

The `/etc/gettydefs` file has the same convention as most UNIX configuration files, in that lines starting with the # character or completely blank lines are ignored. All other lines are treated as configuration entries.

Usually a configuration entry consists of two lines. The first line is a description of the entry, and the second is the entry itself. Strictly speaking, only the configuration lines are required, but it is a good idea to include a description for each entry.

Entries are made up of five values separated by the # character.

A sample entry in the /etc/gettydefs files looks like this:

```
# 19200 fixed-baud modem entry
F19200# B19200 CS8 # B19200 SANE -ISTRIP HUPCL #@S login: #F19200
```

The first and the last value in each entry describe the speed of the modem. These must always be the same. In this case, we see that the speed is 19200, which corresponds to a 19.2Kbps modem.

The second and third values are called the init flags and the final flags. These are given in this format:

```
B[speed] [options]
```

Because the speed for this entry is 19200, the init flags are set as B19200 CS8 and the final flags are set as B19200 SANE -ISTRIP HUPCL. Usually the only option specified for init flags is CS8. The options that can be specified for the final flags are covered in great detail in the getty man page, but the most common options used are the ones listed in this entry.

The fourth entry is the prompt to be issued for the user to log in. This can be set to any value, but the standard is either login: or username:.

chapter
27

Managing Daemons

Editing and creating run levels ●

Editing `inittab` ●

Using `chkconfig` ●

Editing startup and shutdown scripts ●

Customizing the login greeting ●

Enabling and customizing the MOTD ●

Using the `tksysv` tool ●

Using the `ntsysv` tool ●

Enabling FTP access ●

Enabling a Web server ●

Linux, and all other UNIX variants, starts a number of services at system startup. It is these services—called *daemons*—that the users, and you, the administrator, interact with. To increase flexibility, all these systems give you the option of starting the system in different modes, called *run levels*, each of which configures the system to operate in a certain way. Understanding how the entire process works is fundamental to successfully managing a Linux system.

Many beginning administrators have trouble understanding *parent processes*. All processes on the system have a parent process, which starts the actual program. For example, every time you type ls at the command line, your shell starts the program ls—in this case, the shell is the parent process. *Login* is the parent process of the shell you get when you log in. The parent of all processes is called init; this process controls what happens when the system starts, and controls how the system runs.

Because Linux is a multiuser system, it must have several modes of operation. For example, the halt and reboot modes of operation make the system do things not typically associated with a valid state for an operating system. UNIX and Linux call the state of the operating system a run level. As shown in Table 27.1, six run levels are implemented for a stock Red Hat Linux system:

Table 27.1 Linux System Run Levels

Run Level	Name	Purpose
0	Halt	When the system is at this run level, nothing is running, and the disk volumes are not mounted. The only things you can do at this level are to turn off the system or press Ctrl+Alt+Delete.
1	Single User Mode	This is the system's maintenance mode. This mode guarantees that only the person at the console of the system is able to use the system. This mode is used for checking disks or for serious system-maintenance work that cannot be done when users are on the system or when processes are accessing the disk. You can think of this as similar to Safe Mode for Windows or booting with the Shift key down on the Macintosh.

Run Level	Name	Purpose
2	Multi-User Mode Without Networking	This allows multiple logins via the console sessions or via serial ports, but does not configure the network or anything that relates to it, such as the Web and Samba servers. Typically, this run level is not used, but some sysadmins use it to make changes to network configurationswithout having to kick all the users off the system. On some other systems, this run level only disables nfs, the network file system.
3	Multi-User Mode	This is the normal operating mode for which Linux is configured. All services required for the full capability of the system are started.
4	Multi-User Mode, Spare	This mode is a spare multiuser mode. On Red Hat systems, it does pretty much the same things that level 3 does. Because it's a spare, you can test new configurations with this run level before rolling out a configuration to run level 3.
5	XDM Mode	This mode keeps XDM, the X11 login manager, running. On KDE-based systems, XDM is replaced with a work-alike program called KDM. Likewise, GNOME systems use GDM. Its most notable change is that you now get a graphical login prompt, and the user's X11 configuration starts up immediately after login. This is great for systems that are used as workstations rather than network servers, because workstations are not normally running (many) other services that might need the extra memory this takes. Take my advice: For high-load servers, you don't want to start at this run level.
6	Reboot	This run level's ultimate goal is to reboot your Linux computer. No services should be running when the computer finally reboots.

The point to remember for both run levels 0 and 6 is this: It's not the run level itself that is significant, it's *getting there* that matters. In the process of switching run levels, init starts and stops the services to make the system conform to the specification of that run level. This is a complicated way of saying that if a process is called for at the run level where the system is (or is going to), init makes sure that it's running. The opposite also applies—if a service is not called for at the run level the system is going to, init stops it.

Editing and Creating Run Levels

init reads its configuration from the file /etc/inittab, which contains a number of pieces of information for init. It outlines what processes init should keep running (and restart if necessary) at each run level. Your login prompts (called getty processes) are started and restarted by init. init reads the names of scripts to run when the system changes run level. This is probably the most confusing point about init and how the system starts: The scripts can (and usually do) also start processes. These are very different from the processes directly controlled by init, because they are not absolutely vital to the operation of the system (*vital* being defined here as being necessary to prevent the system from being completely inaccessible, as in not being able to log in at the console). The script that init calls, as well as exactly how it operates, is very much distribution dependent.

Red Hat Linux's set of init scripts (so named because they are called by init, not because they are the initialization scripts) are kept in the /etc/rc.d and /etc/rc.d/init.d directories. The scripts in /etc/rc.d are there primarily for backward compatibility with other Linux distributions. The most noteworthy file is called rc.local, which is a shell script in which modifications specific to the particular Linux system would go on other systems. The standard installation's rc.local script sets the /etc/issue file only to the version of Red Hat Linux that's being used. Other Linux distributions also follow this same model, but might have their directory structures configured slightly differently.

The two UNIX camps

The UNIX world is divided into two differing camps: Berkeley and Sys V. Because Linux straddles the ground between the two, each distribution has a lot of leeway as to how to implement the run-level mechanism.

The more interesting directory is called the init.d directory. This directory holds a number of scripts that control the non-vital system services. If none of the services in this directory start, your system won't do much, but hopefully init will have managed to start a login prompt.

These directories are pretty vital to your system. In fact, I recommend that the entire /etc/ directory tree appear in every backup you do. Thank me later for reminding you.

Editing *inittab*

Adding a process to the inittab file is pretty easy. Like many of the system files in Linux, this file is delimited by the colon (:) character.

Remember the 3 *B*s of system administration: back up, back up, and back up again

Make sure you have a backup copy of the inittab file before you start editing it.

Each line has the following format:

```
[ID]:[Runlevels to be running at]:[Action]:[program name and arguments]
```

Table 27.2 describes each field in the preceding code.

Table 27.2   Inittab File Layout

Field Name	Description
ID	This is a short description of the line or event. For example, pressing Ctrl+Alt+Delete causes init to look for the ctrl-alt-del event in the inittab file. There are events for power failure as well, and along with the proper service process (also called daemon) this mechanism can provide for UPS monitoring (look up powerd in the man pages if you want to see how to do this). Services that are attached to terminal devices (virtual terminals or serial ports) use the name of the port after the letters tty as their ID (for example, ttyS1 becomes S1), because the tty prefix is implied.
Runlevels	This section contains the numbers for the run level on which the command should be executed (for example, 345).
Action	This tells init what action to take. A whole list of actions is documented in the inittab(5) man page, but the most commonly used actions are wait, respawn, and boot.
Program name and arguments	The last part of the inittab line contains the name of the program and the command-line arguments.

Using *chkconfig*

chkconfig is an automated init script-management tool. It acts as a sanity checker to make sure that the system will stop a service when leaving a run level.

chkconfig requires some additional comment lines in the actual init script to tell it in which run levels the service should be started, and when, relatively, the service should be started during the initialization of the run level. (init scripts are processed in a specific order to ensure that services dependent on others are started after the services they depend on.) These lines, taken from the httpd init script, are as follows:

```
# chkconfig: 345 85 15
# description: Apache is a World Wide Web server.  It is used to serve
# HTML files and CGI.
```

The first line, which is a marker for chkconfig, tells it that the given script should be run for run levels 3, 4, and 5, with a start order of 85, and a stop order of 15. This means that http is one of the last services to start when entering one of these run levels, and one of the first ones to get stopped when leaving one of them.

What's a sanity checker?

Tools that solve—or that help solve—particularly irritating problems for programmers and systems administrators have become known as *sanity checkers*. In particular, setting up init scripts has caused systems administrators significant amounts of grief since the early days of the UNIX operating system. Many systems administrators have burned up days (and nights!) looking for a problem with their system configuration or trying to configure things. Frustration over extended periods of time, lack of sleep, too much coffee, and probably heartburn from pizza, have been known to make even the most level-headed systems administrators behave irrationally.

Listing Services by Using *chkconfig*

To get a list of which services are started at which run level, use the command chkconfig --list. Optionally, you can add a name as an additional argument, and chkconfig will list only the information for that service. Following is the output of chkconfig --list httpd on my system:

```
[jwalter@jansmachine jwalter]$ /sbin/chkconfig --list httpd
httpd 0:off 1:off 2:off 3:on 4:on 5:on 6:off
```

In this case, chkconfig reports that the httpd service is to be started for run levels 3, 4, and 5.

Removing a Service by Using *chkconfig*

To remove a service from a certain run level, use the following command:

```
chkconfig --level <runlevel> <servicename> off
```

runlevel is the run level number you want to modify, and servicename is the name of the service. The commands on and off enable and disable the service, respectively. For example, to turn off httpd for run level 3, you would issue the following command:

```
chkconfig --level 3 httpd off
```

This command removes the service only for a specific run level, which is the most common operation. You can list multiple run levels (for example, you could type 345 on the command line to change the settings for multiple run levels). If you need to remove a service altogether, you would use the following command:

```
chkconfig --del httpd
```

This command has the effect of removing httpd from all rcX.d directories. It does not remove the service's script from the /etc/rc.d/init.d directory; it just removes the symbolic links to the file from the directories that the init scripts search.

Adding a Service by Using *chkconfig*

To add a service to a specific run level, use the following command:

```
chkconfig --level <runlevel> <servicename> on
```

To add httpd back to run level 3, use the following command:

```
chkconfig --level 3 httpd on
```

To add a new service to all run levels according to the recommendations given to chkconfig, use the following command:

```
chkconfig --add <servicename>
```

chkconfig sets all the links for the service in the correct directories in one swoop.

Resetting Service Information

Playing with services is educational, as long as you have a backup of your /etc/rc.d directory tree and a way to get back into the system to restore it. However, this type of drastic action is usually not necessary. Instead, you can restore the service's startup priority and other information to the recommended settings by issuing the following command

```
chkconfig <servicename> reset
```

This command returns everything to a (hopefully) sane default.

Editing Startup and Shutdown Scripts

The startup and shutdown scripts reside in the /etc/rc.d directory subtree. These are generally bash scripts that start daemons. Each run level has its own subdirectory of /etc/rc.d, which contains the run level number (as in /etc/rc.d/rc0.d for run level 0, /etc/rc.d/rc3.d for run level 3, and so on). These subdirectories contain *symbolic links* to actual scripts in /etc/rc.d/init.d. This ensures that all run levels read from the same set of scripts. There is something else to account for, however: Certain processes and daemons must start before other processes. For example, it makes little sense for the system to start the Web server (httpd) before having started the networking on the system because the Web server needs a network interface on which to initialize.

So this is how it happens: Depending on whether the script is designed to start a service or to ensure that a service is stopped, the first letter of the script name is either S (for start) or K (for kill). Then comes a (by convention) two-digit number, and then the name of the script in the init.d directory. When the system changes to a different run level, the K scripts are run first, in numerical order, and then the S scripts, again in numerical order.

The chkconfig utility checks the recommended numbers for the script you're using, for both start and kill scripts (the example in the previous section using httpd's init script lists 85 as the startup number and 15 as the kill number). You should, for the most part, use these numbers unless you have a good reason to do otherwise.

The init scripts do make things easy for you, however—the difficult scripting has been done for you and packaged into functions that your script can call to do most of the dirty work.

A Sample *init* Script

The init script in Listing 27.1 is for httpd, the Apache Web server that comes packaged with most distributions of Linux. I use this as an example because the majority of additional services out there work very similarly to this.

Listing 27.1   Listing of */etc/rc.d/init.d/httpd*, the *init* Script for the Web Server

```
01: #!/bin/sh
02: #
03: # Startup script for the Apache Web Server
04: #
05: # chkconfig: 345 85 15
06: # description: Apache is a World Wide Web server.  It is used to serve \
07: # HTML files and CGI.
08: #
09: #
10:
11:
12: # Source function library.
13: . /etc/rc.d/init.d/functions
14:
15: # See how we were called.
16: case "$1" in
17:   start)
18:     echo -n "Starting httpd: "
19:     daemon httpd
20:     echo
21:     touch /var/lock/subsys/httpd
22:     ;;
23:   stop)
24:     echo -n "Shutting down http: "
25:     kill `cat /var/run/httpd.pid`
26:     echo httpd
27:     rm -f /var/lock/subsys/httpd
28:     rm -f /var/run/httpd.pid
29:     ;;
30:   status)
31:     status httpd
32:     ;;
33:   restart)
34:     $0 stop
35:     $0 start
36:     ;;
37:   *)
38:     echo "Usage: httpd.init {start|stop|restart|status}"
```

continues...

Listing 27.1 Continued

```
39:
40:     exit 1
41: esac
42:
43: exit 0
```

The easiest way to set up another program as a daemon in your system is to copy an existing script to a new file, and edit the file to suit your needs. The only lines in the script shown in Listing 27.1 that are specific to httpd are lines 3–7, 18–21, 24–28, 31, and 33. These lines either provide feedback while the script is executing, or actually start the program.

Lines 25 and 28 are specific to Apache because Apache stores its process ID numbers in a file in the /var/run/httpd.pid file to make stopping the process easier. If the daemon you want to add cannot be configured to do this, the script called functions that is included at the beginning contains a function to automatically find the PID(s) of the daemon in question and to kill the process. For example, if your program were called mydaemon, lines 24–28 would look like the following:

```
24:     echo -n "Shutting down mydaemon : "
25:     killproc mydaemon
26:     echo mydaemon
27:     rm -f /var/log/subsys/mydaemon
28:     ;;
```

Note that the line to remove the PID file in /var/run is not there (of course, you could leave it in if mydaemon were to support it).

init Script Checklist

Using this short checklist should ensure that all necessary features are present to make working with the script you created easy and painless for both you and other systems administrators.

- The script supports start and stop command-line arguments.
- The script has appropriate lines for chkconfig to manage the script. If you're in doubt of the order the program should be started, start it with a high number and stop it with a low number. If your process depends on another to be running first, be sure your process has a higher number than the other process.

- Make sure that the script handles creating the lock files in /var/lock/subsys and the PID files in /var/run; the status command-line argument and the killproc function for the script use these. A status check is nice to have for a daemon process.

- Make sure that the script provides appropriate feedback to make clear to the user what is happening. Be especially sure of this if the daemon that's starting needs to start connections that need some time to initialize. Otherwise, observers might get the impression that the system has hung, and take some drastic actions that might not be warranted.

Where should I start?

Most system services are not absolutely vital. If you need init to baby-sit the process to make sure it's always running, it would be worthwhile for the daemon to be started from the inittab file. Thankfully, the majority of daemon programs do not require this sort of attention, and for ease of maintenance are best started from a script in /etc/rc.d/init.d and managed through the available tools discussed in this chapter.

However, if the daemon is started from the inittab file and init needs to *respawn* (the term used for restarting a daemon process) the program too often, it disables the program for a while. You'll see a message like the following in the kernel message file (/var/log/messages):

```
init: process respawning too fast. disabled for 5  minutes
```

Customizing the Login Greeting

The getty programs that manage logins over terminals and network connections prints a message to the screen before asking for the login ID. The default message is as follows:

```
Red Hat Linux release 6.1 (Cartman)
Kernel 2.2.12-20 on an i586
```

Many organizations dealing with computer security recommend that there be no information about the operating system, or about the company whose machine is in the login message. All operating systems have potential security holes that system crackers can exploit if they know which version of the system they are working with. Making this information more difficult to obtain goes a long way toward thwarting an attack. On a more upbeat note, it's nice to be able to modify this to put either amusing or informative messages at the login prompt.

Red Hat Linux generates its `issue` file at every system boot by default, and this should be the first thing that gets turned off if you want to customize the login greeting. The code that does this is in the file `/etc/rc.d/rc.local`. The lines look like this on my system (I included the comments as well):

```
# This will overwrite /etc/issue at every boot.  So, make any changes you
# want to make to /etc/issue here or you will lose them when you reboot.
echo "" > /etc/issue
echo "$R" >> /etc/issue
echo "Kernel $(uname -r) on $a $SMP$(uname -m)" >> /etc/issue

cp -f /etc/issue /etc/issue.net
echo >> /etc/issue
```

Putting the # character before each of the offending lines will comment them out and render them harmless to your system's `issue` file. Then, feel free to edit the `/etc/issue` file with any message that pleases you and, hopefully, your users. In some cases, you might need to edit `/etc/.issue` depending on your Linux installation.

Customizing the Login Greeting for Network Connections

Linux copies the `/etc/issue` file to the greeting file for network connections (aptly named `/etc/issue.net`), so I refer you to the previous section for information on where to disable this. After this is complete, feel free to edit the `/etc/issue.net` file to say the same thing, or anything else.

It is common—and recommended—for corporate Linux systems to have different messages for network and local connections. Most crackers use networks, not local terminals, so on network connections it is especially important not to give out any information that these individuals might be able to use against you. Be careful about what you use as a network greeting message because some installations go a bit over-board warning the potential intruder about the site's security. Depending on the intruder, this "warning" might seem more like a challenge. The more "uninteresting" your system seems, the better. Be sure to check your company's official policy on this before setting it up—in some cases you *must* provide warnings.

Disclaimers and other legal notifications

It is possible that some states, countries, or provinces require systems administrators to make sure that people logging in to the system understand that their actions or transmissions might be monitored. It can be argued that this possibility is implied in the use of any computer or data network (including public phone systems), but some people might not feel the same way about this. In this case, the best place to put a message like this is in the `/etc/issue` and `/etc/issue.net` files. If you really want to be safe, mention this in the `motd` (Message of the Day) file as well.

Enabling and Customizing the MOTD

MOTD stands for Message of the Day, and has long been something that administrators use to convey important information, such as scheduled shutdowns or maintenance to users. The MOTD should be provided for users after they log in but before they come to the shell prompt.

The file the message of the day is kept in is `/etc/motd`. The contents of this file are displayed every time a user logs in. It's that simple. When you first install the system, the file is empty.

Changing the Message of the Day

1. Start your favorite editor to edit `/etc/motd`. In this case, I use `vi`, so the command `vi /etc/motd` will do the trick.

2. Press the I key on your keyboard to begin inserting text.

3. Type your message.

4. Press the Esc key to stop inserting text.

5. Type the command `:wq` to save the file and quit `vi`.

Using the *tksysv* Tool

`tksysv` is the X11 manager for system services. This program allows you to start and stop services and reorganize them for various run levels.

To start `tksysv`, start X11, open an `xTerm`, and type `tksysv &`. Make sure that you're logged in as or su'd to root.

Adding a Service with *tksysv*

The left pane in Figure 27.1 lists which services are currently available for use in the system. The right pane lists the services that are started and stopped for each run level.

Don't count on a confirmation request

tksysv does not request confirmation when removing a service from a run level, so pause a moment and ask yourself whether you really want to remove the service before clicking that Remove button.

Make it a habit to ask yourself each time you prepare to perform a serious action as root whether that action is really what you want to do. Most system commands, as you will likely have discovered by now, don't require confirmation.

```
Run a chkconfig
```

When editing multiple run levels, ntsysv marks a service as being started if it is started on any run level that is currently being edited. You should confirm that any changes made did not have any undesirable effects by running chkconfig after running ntsysv this way.

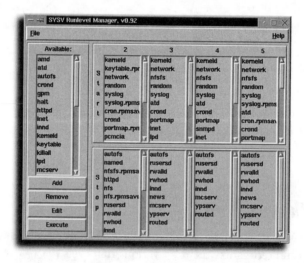

FIGURE 27.1
Don't worry about the frills on the windows—these vary depending on the X11 window manager that's installed.

To add a service to a run level, select the service and click the Add button (see Figure 27.2).

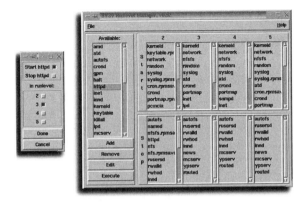

FIGURE 27.2
Choose which run level to add a service to.

Choose whether to start or stop the service, specify the run level you want to modify, and then click Done (see Figure 27.3).

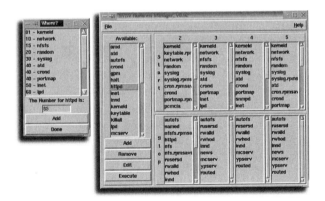

FIGURE 27.3
Choose the starting order for the service.

tksysv then asks for the starting number (order) for the service. If the service has a chkconfig entry, tksysv reads it and fills in the order number for you—stick with the recommendations unless you have a very good reason not to. Click Add. To cancel, click Done.

Removing a service with *tksysv*

1. With tksysv running, click the service on the run level side that you want to remove.

2. Click Remove.

Starting and stopping a service

1. Choose from the left pane the service you want to start or stop (see Figure 27.4).

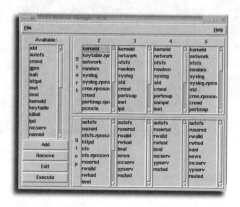

FIGURE 27.4
The service start/stop dialog box.

2. Click Execute.

3. Click Start or Stop to start or stop the service, respectively.

Using *ksysv*

The KDE environment also comes with a Sys V run level editor that is as simple as drag-and-drop. If you have KDE installed on your system, you can start ksysv from a terminal or run the application by clicking the main KDE pop-up menu and choosing Sys V Init Editor from the System menu. Figure 27.5 shows the KDE run level editor.

Adding a service

1. To add a service using ksysv, first locate the service you want to add from the left side of the window. All the available init.d files are listed here.

2. Using the mouse, drag the service to the run level where you want it to be.

3. Release the mouse and you're finished! Choose Save Configuration from the file menu to make the changes permanent.

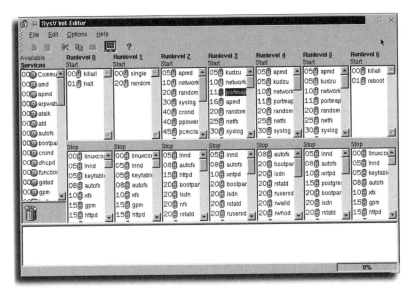

FIGURE 27.5
KDE features its own run level editor.

Deleting a service

1. Deleting a service is just as easy as adding one. First, locate the service you want to remove in the run level that you want to remove it from.

2. Drag the service to the trashcan on the left side of the window.

3. Choose Save Configuration from the file menu to make the changes permanent.

The ksysv utility provides a simple and user-friendly interface to the run level directories. If you have KDE on your system, I wholeheartedly recommend using it.

Starting and Stopping Network Services

When starting and stopping network services, make sure that you stop all network-related services first. For the most part, these services continue to run if not stopped, generating errors and filling up log files. Furthermore, stopping the services properly ensures that all network connections have had the time to close down properly.

Using the *ntsysv* Tool

ntsysv is the text-mode service manager for Red Hat Linux. It is quite a bit simpler to use than tksysv, mainly because it deals with things one run level at a time.

To start ntsysv, type the command ntsysv --level <runlevel>, in which <runlevel> is the run level you want to edit. To edit multiple run levels with ntsysv, list them all (for example, 234).

Adding or removing a service to a run level by using *ntsysv*

1. Log in as root.

2. Issue the command ntsysv --level <runlevel> in which <runlevel> is the number of the run level you want to edit.

3. Use the up and down arrow keys to move to the service that you want to modify.

4. Press the Spacebar to turn the service on or off for the run level.

5. Repeat steps 3 and 4 to turn any additional services on or off, as you need.

6. Press the Tab key to highlight the OK button.

7. Press Enter while OK is selected to save your work.

Stopping the service before removing it

When you remove or disable a service, you have no guarantee that the system will stop the service gracefully the next time the system changes run levels. To make sure a service is stopped properly, do it manually before removing the service from the run levels.

You can use tksysv, ksysv, or ntsysv to manually stop a service—these are graphical front ends to manage the services on the system for X11 and text mode, respectively.

You can also simply call the script that manages the service by employing the stop command-line argument. For example, you would use the following command to stop httpd before disabling it:

```
/etc/rc.d/init.d/httpd stop
```

Incidentally, you can use this method to start services outside of their normal run level or before adding them by using the start command line argument instead, or restart them with restart. This is useful for determining whether the services are running properly.

Enabling FTP Access

The FTP network service is controlled by the Internet service daemon, inetd. To ensure that inetd knows how to respond to FTP connection requests, you must edit /etc/inetd.conf to ensure that the FTP service is enabled.

There are two types of FTP access—one type for regular users of your system (who have user accounts), and the other for *anonymous* user access. Anonymous user access allows anyone to download files from a set of defined directories on your system by logging in as user *anonymous* and by convention, leaving his email address as a password.

Determining whether FTP is enabled on your system

1. Make sure you have the FTP server installed on your system. Issue the command `rpm -q wu-ftpd`. If the system responds with the message `package wu-ftpd is not installed` then you must install the package before continuing. If you do not have `ftpd` on your system and are not running Red Hat Linux, you can download WU-FTPD from `http://www.wu-ftpd.org/`.

2. Ensure that the FTP service line in `/etc/inetd.conf` exists and is not commented out. Issue the command `less /etc/inetd.conf` and then make `less` perform a forward search for the word ftp by using the command `/ftp`. `less` should stop at a line like the following:

   ```
   ftp     stream tcp    nowait root    /usr/sbin/tcpd  in.ftpd -l -a
   ```

   If this line starts with a # you need to remove this before continuing.

3. If you had to edit the `inetd.conf` file, you must notify `inetd` of the change to the file. Issuing `/etc/rc.d/init.d/inet restart` should do this for you.

Your system is now configured to accept incoming FTP connections.

To enable anonymous FTP access, first follow the preceding steps. The `wu-ftpd` server included with Red Hat and other Linux distributions provides anonymous FTP server capabilities immediately on installation, but the additional directories are not installed with the server. You will need the package `anonftp` for this. Anonymous FTP access can be very dangerous and should not be enabled unless it is absolutely necessary.

If you are a Red Hat user, you can check whether you have `anonftp` installed by typing `rpm -q anonftp` at the command line, and install the file if necessary. If you are using a different distribution of Linux, CERT (Computer Emergency Response Team) offers a guide on setting up a secure anonymous server at `ftp://ftp.cert.org/pub/tech_tips/anonymous_ftp_config`.

The anonymous FTP server directories are in `/home/ftp`. Anything in the `/home/ftp/pub` directory can be downloaded by anonymous users.

Providing support for anonymous uploads

1. Log in as root.

2. Change directories to /home/ftp.

3. Create a directory called incoming.

4. Change the write permissions to all everyone write access to the chmod a+w /home/ftp/incoming directory.

Testing your FTP server before letting other users onto it

1. FTP to your server with the command ftp localhost.

2. Log in as user anonymous. Enter a password when prompted. If the password was not a valid email address, the server should issue a warning but still let you in.

3. Change to the incoming directory.

4. Set your FTP client's binary mode by typing the command bin at the ftp> prompt.

5. Attempt to upload a file to the server using the command <filename> where filename is the name of the file you want to upload.

6. Try to download a file from your FTP server to make sure that everything works as expected.

Enabling a Web Server

The stock Web server that Linux ships with is Apache. This is the most popular Web server used on the Internet by a large margin, and is fast and relatively efficient. It's not unreasonable to use Linux as a high-volume Web server with Apache, and a great many sites on the Internet run this combination.

To set up Apache on your system, ensure that you have the correct package installed:

1. Confirm that Apache is installed on your system by issuing the command rpm -q apache at the command line. If the system reports that the package is not installed, you must install it before proceeding. Installations not using RPMs can download and install the Web server from the main Apache site at http://www.apache.org/.

2. Although Apache can be run under the auspices of inetd, this is not common. Web clients are an impatient bunch, and the added time it takes for inetd to start Apache to handle a request for each connection adds too much wait time

for all but the least-loaded Web servers. Apache is usually started as a regular daemon, and is left to manage itself after that. Use `chkconfig` to see if the service `httpd` (the generic name for Web services) is started: `chkconfig --list httpd`. If the service is listed as `on` for the run level where your system is (probably 3), Apache starts for this run level.

3. If `httpd` is not configured to start for your run level, typing `chkconfig httpd reset` should set up Apache to run in the run levels in which it should be running.

4. If you're sure that Apache was not started when the system last entered your current run level, you can start it manually by giving the command `/etc/rc.d/init.d/httpd start`. Watch for error messages.

5. Test your Web server by starting a Web client on your machine, such as `lynx` for text mode, or Netscape for X11, and going to address `http://localhost`. You should get the page entitled "It Worked!"

The files that your Web server reads by default are in `/home/httpd/html`.

Configuring the Apache Web Server

Apache's configuration files are kept in `/etc/httpd/conf`.

`httpd.conf` contains the main server configuration. You might need to change the `ServerName` directive for the server if, when started, the server responds with the message `Unable to resolve host name` or `Unable to determine local host name`. If your computer has multiple DNS entries, you might also want to change this to the hostname that you want displayed in the user's browser when she visits your site. This file typically contains other server-specific settings used to fine-tune the server, such as the minimum and maximum number of servers processes to run at the same time, and the number of requests each server should process before terminating. Each server process services one request at once, so it's important to keep these numbers appropriate to the load on the server.

`srm.conf` contains information for Apache on how to handle different file types, and which directory to treat as the root directory for the server.

`access.conf` contains all the access control options for all the directories on the server. With `access.conf` it is possible, for example, to exclude certain addresses from accessing the server, or certain directories on the server.

These files are very well commented and each setting is documented in detail. If you point your Web browser at `localhost` (or if you are on another machine, the Linux machine's host name) and follow the links to Apache Documentation, you see the most current documentation that shipped with the version of the server that is installed.

If you'd like to consolidate your Apache configuration directory, you can actually combine the individual files into a single file (httpd.conf); the latest versions of Apache support reading any configuration options from any file. Different versions of Linux will name and divide these files differently.

# chapter 28

Managing the File System

Mounting and unmounting file systems •

Setting up new file systems •

Creating new file systems •

Repairing file systems •

Disaster recovery •

Mounting and Unmounting File Systems

The file systems on your hard disk drives are mounted for you automatically when the system boots. The removable devices (for example, floppy disks and CD-ROM drives) are not.

All the people using a Linux machine see the same view of the file system (although many of them are unable to access all parts of it). This means that mounting a file system is an action reserved for the superuser. The superuser can indicate that some file systems can be mounted and unmounted by ordinary users (the user option in the file /etc/fstab is used for this).

The superuser sets up the /etc/fstab file to specify what file systems are used on each device, using either the linuxconf command or a text editor directly on the /etc/fstab file.

SEE ALSO

➤ *To learn more about being a superuser and using the* su *command with Linux, see page 8.*

Using the *usermount* Command

Red Hat Linux comes with a command called usermount that provides a GUI for mounting and unmounting file systems. The usermount command must be run during an X11 session. When you start usermount, it shows you what file systems you can *mount* (or format). The usermount program is shown in Figure 28.1.

FIGURE 28.1
The usermount program.

SEE ALSO

➤ *To learn more about the X Window System, see page 171.*

The buttons for /mnt/cdrom (the CD-ROM drive) and /mnt/floppy (the floppy disk drive) are labeled Mount and Format. If you click the Mount button with a disk in the drive, the disk is mounted and the button changes to Unmount, as shown in Figure 28.2.

FIGURE 28.2
The disk is mounted and the button changes to Unmount.

If you try to mount the floppy disk (/dev/fd0) without having a disk in the drive, you receive an error message in a dialog box similar to the one shown in Figure 28.3.

FIGURE 28.3
Mounting without the disk in the drive results in this dialog box.

Formatting a floppy disk with *usermount*

1. To format a floppy disk with the usermount command, your system must be set up so that you are allowed (have permission) to write to the floppy disk drive.

2. Insert a blank disk in your disk drive, and start the usermount command from the command line of a terminal window like this:

```
# usermount
```

3. The Format button is active for the floppy drive. Ensure that there is no data that you want to keep in the drive before clicking this button.

4. Click the Format button. A dialog box appears, asking if you are sure. There is also a checkbox on the dialog box that asks if you want to do a low-level format (as shown in Figure 28.4).

FIGURE 28.4
Specify whether you want to do a low-level format.

If you don't elect to do the low-level format because the disk has already been formatted, Linux builds a new, clean file system on the disk, which takes a second or so. A low-level format, on the other hand, takes quite a while.

Although you can reformat your hard disk partitions by using Linux's `fdisk` and `mkfs` programs, they are omitted from the `usermount` program in the interests of safety.

Formatting a Floppy Using the *kfloppy* Command

If you are not using Red Hat Linux, you might still have a graphical formatting utility available for your use. The KDE graphical user interface is now included with several Linux distributions and has the handy `KFloppy` utility. If you're running KDE you can access `KFloppy` by clicking the main KDE pop-up menu, and choosing Utilities, and then KFloppy. Figure 28.5 shows the `KFloppy` interface.

The available KDE floppy formatter options are

- *Floppy Drive.* The drive and floppy type that you intend to format. For most machines, drive A and 3.5 are the appropriate values.
- *Density.* HD, or high density, is the standard 1.44MB floppy format. If you are using an old 720KB disk, you should change to the DD, double density, option.
- *File System.* You can choose to create a DOS or ext2 file system on the disk. If you intend to use the disk on an MS-DOS or Windows based machine, choose Dos.

FIGURE 28.5
KFloppy presents a friendly formatting interface for KDE Linux users.

- *Format Type.* Two types of formatting are available: Quick Erase, which just re-creates the file system, and Full Format, which does exactly what its name suggests.

- *Create Label.* Last, you can specify a label to be given the disk on completion of the format.

After you've set the options you like, simply click the Format button and you're in business. The progress bar at the bottom of the window indicates how far along the disk is in the formatting process.

SEE ALSO

➤ *For more information about using or setting permissions, see page 378.*

Using the *mount* Command

To mount a block device into the file system, use the mount command. You must specify what device contains the file system, what type it is, and where in the directory hierarchy to mount it.

A mount command looks like this:

```
mount [-t type] [-o options] device mount-point
```

device must be a block device; or, if it contains a colon, it can be the name of another machine from which to mount a file system. mount-point should be an existing directory; the file system appears at this position (anything previously in that directory is hidden). The file system type and options are optional, and the variety and meaning of options depend on the type of file system being mounted. If the file system you want to mount is specified in the /etc/fstab file, you need to specify only the mount point or the device name; the other details will be read from /etc/fstab by mount.

Mounting a floppy with the *mount* command

1. Use the mount command, followed by the device name, the -t (file system type) option, the name of a file system, and the mount point in your system's directory structure. For example, to mount a floppy disk, first log in as the root operator, and then use the mkdir command to create a mount point like this:

   ```
   # mkdir /mnt/floppy
   ```

2. Use the mount command, specifying your floppy drive's device name, and the type of file system (the available file system types are listed in /usr/src/linux/fs/filesystems.c), like this:

   ```
   # mount /dev/fd1 -t vfat /mnt/floppy
   mount: block device /dev/fd1 is write-protected, mounting read-only
   ```

3. The disk's contents become available at the specified mount point (directory). Use the ls (list directory) command to verify that the disk is mounted, like this:

   ```
   # ls /mnt/floppy
   grub-0.4.tar.gz
   ```

4. After you have finished reading, copying, or deleting files on the disk, use the umount command, followed by the mount point or pathname, to unmount the file system, like this:

   ```
   # umount /mnt/floppy
   ```

Make sure that you are not currently in the directory structure contained on the mounted device before you attempt to umount. If you are in the mounted device, you get a device busy error when attempting to umount.

SEE ALSO

➤ *To learn more about drivers, code modules, and the magic of the Linux kernel, see page 535.*

Is it magic or the Linux *kerneld* daemon?

Mounting a vfat floppy disk causes the Linux kernel to automatically load the vfat driver into the kernel while it is needed. These (and other) drivers are loaded by the system daemon kerneld; when the drivers are no longer being used, such as after a file system is unmounted, the drivers are unloaded to recover the memory.

Mounting and Unmounting File Systems **CHAPTER 28**

Any one of several things can cause the mount command to fail. It is possible to specify an incorrect device name (that is, to specify a device file that does not exist, one for which a driver is not available in the kernel, or one for which the hardware is not present). Other error conditions include unreadable devices (for example, empty floppy drives or bad media) and insufficient permissions (mount commands other than those sanctioned by the administrator by listing them with the option user in /etc/fstab are forbidden to ordinary users). Trying to mount a device at a mount point that does not already exist also will not work.

Still more error conditions are possible but unlikely (for example, exceeding the compiled-in limit to the number of mounted file systems) or self-explanatory (for example, most usage errors for the mount command itself).

Don't forget the mount point

In order to mount a file system, the point at which it is to be mounted (that is, the mount point) must be a directory. This directory doesn't have to be empty, but after the file system is mounted any files "underneath" it will be inaccessible. Be careful when mounting disks or other media!

Linux provides a *singly rooted* file system, in contrast to those operating systems that give each file system a separate drive letter. Although this might seem less flexible, it is actually *more* flexible, because the size of each block device (that is, the hard disk, or whatever) is hidden from programs, and things can be moved around.

For example, if you have some software that expects to be installed in /opt/umsp, you can install it in /big-disk/stuff/umsp and make /opt/umsp a symbolic link. There is also no need to edit a myriad of configuration files that are now using the wrong drive letter after you install a new disk drive, for example.

There are many options governing how a mounted file system behaves; for example, it can be mounted read-only. There are options for file systems such as msdos, and others, such as the nfs file system, which has so many options that it has a separate manual page (man nfs).

Table 28.1 contains options useful for mount, given in alphabetical order. Unless otherwise indicated, these options are valid for all file system types, although asking for asynchronous writes to a CD-ROM is no use! Options applicable only to nfs file systems are not listed here; refer to the nfs manual page for those.

459

Table 28.1 *mount* Options

Option	Description
async	Write requests for the file system normally should wait until the data has reached the hardware; with this option, the program continues immediately instead. This does mean that the system is slightly more prone to data loss in the event of a system crash, but, on the other hand, crashes are very rare with Linux. This option speeds up nfs file systems by a startling extent. The opposite of this option is sync.
auto	Indicates to mount that it should mount the device when given the -a flag. This flag is used by the startup scripts to make sure that all the required file systems are mounted at boot time. The opposite of this option is noauto.
defaults	Turns on the options rw, suid, dev, exec, auto, nouser, and async.
dev	Allows device nodes on the system to be used. Access to devices is completely determined by access rights to the on-disk device node. Hence, if you mount an ext2 file system on a floppy and you have previously placed a writeable /dev/kmem device file on the disk, you've just gained read/write access to kernel memory. System administrators generally prevent this from happening by mounting removable file systems with the nodev mount option.
exec	Indicates to the kernel that it should allow the execution of programs on the file system. This option is more frequently seen as noexec, which indicates to the kernel that execution of programs on this file system shouldn't be allowed. This is generally used as a security precaution or for nfs file systems mounted from another machine that contain executable files of a format unsuitable for this machine (for example, intended for a different CPU).
noauto	Opposite of auto; see auto table entry.
nodev	Opposite of dev; see dev table entry.
noexec	Opposite of exec; see exec table entry.
nosuid	Opposite of suid; see suid table entry.
nouser	Opposite of user; see user table entry.
remount	Allows the mount command to change the flags for an already-mounted file system without interrupting its use. You can't unmount a file system that is currently in use, and this option is basically a workaround. The system startup scripts, for example, use the command mount -n -o remount,ro / to change the root file system from read-only (it starts off this way) to read/write (its normal state). The -n option indicates to mount that it shouldn't update /etc/fstab because it can't do this while the root file system is still read-only.
ro	Mounts the file system read-only. This is the opposite of the option rw.
rw	Mounts the file system read/write. This is the opposite of the option ro.

Option	Description
suid	Allows the set user ID and set group ID file mode bits to take effect. The opposite of this option is nosuid. The nosuid option is more usual; it is used for the same sorts of reasons that nodev is used.
sync	All write operations cause the calling program to wait until the data has been committed to the hardware. This mode of operation is slower but a little more reliable than its opposite, asynchronous I/O, which is indicated by the option async (see preceding).
user	Allows ordinary users to mount the file system. When there is a user option in /etc/fstab, ordinary users indicate which file system they want to mount or unmount by giving the device name or mount point; all the other relevant information is taken from the /etc/fstab file. For security reasons, user implies the noexec, nosuid, and nodev options.

Options are processed by the mount command in the order in which they appear on the command line (or in /etc/fstab). Thus, it is possible to allow users to mount a file system and then run set user ID executables by using the options user, suid, in that order. Using them in reverse order (suid, user) doesn't work because the user option turns the suid option off again. An SUID program runs with the permissions of the user who owns the executable. If a program is made SUID root, any operation it performs will be done with root privileges. Actions such as erasing the hard drive could immediately become accessible to other users.

SEE ALSO

➤ *For more information about using the* mount *command, see page 124.*

There are many other options available, but these are all specific to particular file systems. All the valid options for mount are detailed in its manual page. An example is the umask flag for the vfat and fat file systems, which allows you to make all the files on your MS-DOS or Windows partitions readable (or even writeable if you prefer) for all the users on your Linux system.

Setting Up New File Systems

When the kernel boots, it attempts to mount a root file system from the device specified by the kernel loader, LILO. The root file system is initially mounted read-only. During the boot process, the file systems listed in the file system table /etc/fstab are mounted. This file specifies which devices are to be mounted, what kinds of file systems they contain, at what point in the file system the mount takes place, and any options governing *how* they are to be mounted. The format of this file is described in fstab.

> **Importance of the** /etc/fstab **table**
>
> Always make a backup copy of the file system table, /etc/fstab, before making changes to your system, such as adding additional hard drives, or editing the table. If you make a mistake in the file, your system might not boot properly or at all. With a backup copy you can easily restore your system's settings.

Starting *linuxconf*

linuxconf resides in the /bin directory. You start it by typing linuxconf.

You can also access linuxconf through its Web interface by pointing a browser running locally to port 98—that is, http://localhost:98/.

Adding a New Local File System by Using *linuxconf*

If you want to add a file system to the fstab file, you can use linuxconf, which is included in Red Hat and other popular Linux systems. If you do not have linuxconf, you can download it from http://www.solucorp.qc.ca/linuxconf/.to thto t See Chapter 7, "Working with Hard Drives," for instructions on formatting and making file systems. If the partition already exists, either because it belongs to another operating system or because you just finished following the instructions in Chapter 7, please continue.

> **File system mount points**
>
> If you mount a file system on a >directory, this hides anything that was previously there. When you unmount the file system, it is again visible.

Adding an existing partition to the file system

1. Invoke linuxconf by typing linuxconf at a command line. You'll need to be root in order to perform these operations.

2. Choose Access Local Drive from the File Systems menu hierarchy.

3. Select Add.

4. In the field Partition type the name of the partition or device that you've prepared, such as /dev/hdb1 or /dev/sdb1.

5. In the Type field, enter the file system type that you prepared on this device. For most Linux native devices, this would be ext2.

6. The Mount Point field is the local directory on your drive where you'd like the device to be mounted. This directory must exist before you attempt to mount it.

7. You can also configure several options for the drive, including mounting the device read-only and making it user-mountable.

8. After choosing the options you'd like to apply to this mount point, choose Accept to save your changes. If you'd like to immediately mount the device, choose Mount instead.

Adding a New Network File System by Using *linuxconf*

If you want to mount a network file system, you must first ensure that you can communicate over the network to the server machine. For more information about this, please see Chapter 26, "Managing Network Connections." You also need to ensure that the remote machine permits you to mount its shared file systems. You might need to consult with the administrator of that machine to confirm this.

Ensuring that you can communicate with the server

1. Start the `linuxconf` command. Select Access nfs Volume from the File Systems section.

2. Choose Add from the NFS mount point selection list.

3. Provide the name of the server in the Server field.

4. Enter the directory of the remote file system into the Volume field and the mount point directory into the Mount Point field.

5. Select any options you require from General Options section. The defaults are usually appropriate; for `nfs`, however, there is a separate NFS options section, some of which might be useful to change. Select Accept when you are finished.

6. Choose Quit to exit from `linuxconf`.

SEE ALSO
➤ For instructions on adding Zip drives, see page 132.
➤ For more information on networked file systems, see page 425.

File System Options

When you create a new entry for a file system using `linuxconf`, as described in the preceding sections, you are given the opportunity to change the options pertaining to it. Many options are possible, but only some of them are commonly used.

The options fall fairly neatly into those suitable for removable devices and those suitable for nonremovable ones.

Options Useful for Removable Devices

Removable devices such as floppy disks must be mounted and unmounted in order to be used (unless you use the mtools package for floppy disks). The Users Can Mount Filesystem option (which appears as user in /etc/fstab) is required for this to happen. Conversely, for nonremovable devices such as hard disk partitions, allowing just anybody to unmount the /usr file system would pretty much be a disaster. The various Ignore options for linuxconf are listed in Table 28.2.

Table 28.2 Removable Device Mounting Options

Long Name	Short Name
No setuid programs allowed	nosuid
No special device file support	nodev
No program allowed to execute	noexec

The first two options, nosuid and nodev, are security features, which prevent any old person from bringing along a specially prepared UNIX file system and using it to compromise your machine. If you have entries in your file system table for removable ext2 file systems, set these two options for them.

If you'd like to set the removable device options outside linuxconf, you can manually edit the fstab file. Before editing the fstab file, be sure to back it up. When you're ready to make your changes, follow these instructions:

1. Log in as the root operator. Using your favorite text editor, such as pico, open the /etc/fstab file:

   ```
   # pico -w /etc/fstab
   ```

2. If you have a removable device, such as a Zip drive, you can make your system a bit more secure by inserting the nosuid and nodev mount options. Look for your device's entry in the fstab file:

   ```
   /dev/sda4   /mnt/zip    vfat    user,noauto,dev,exec,suid    0 0
   ```

3. Make sure the devices are not mounted. Then change the dev and suid options to nodev and nosuid, like this:

   ```
   /dev/sda4   /mnt/zip    vfat    user,noauto,nodev,exec,nosuid    0 0
   ```

4. Save the fstab and quit your word processor.

The third ignore option is also sometimes used on network servers. Some file systems are designed to be mounted only by client machines and aren't of much use to the server itself. They might, for example, contain executables for a bunch of client machines running some incompatible version of UNIX. If this is the case, you should set the noexec option so that nobody can try to run the incompatible kinds of programs.

Options Useful for Fixed Devices

Most fixed devices need to be mounted at boot time, so that option should normally be set for nonremovable devices. On the other hand, this option should not normally be set for removable devices because there often is no disk in the drive at boot time.

The writeable (rw) flag is usually set, but one might unset it for CD-ROM drives that aren't writeable anyway, or for file systems containing important archive data.

The updateatime option is relatively new to Linux and isn't used by most people. Normally one of the three timestamps on a file is a record of the time that it was last accessed. If a file system is heavily read from and rarely written to, the endless updating of access-time timestamps can lead to an unproductive waste of performance.

Access timestamps and Linux

Although the access timestamp is an integral part of all UNIX file systems, including Linux's ext file system, disabling usually doesn't break anything. The most significant thing that this breaks is the reporting of new mail; if the modification time for your mailbox is newer than its access time, you must have received new mail since you last read mail. Conversely, if the access time is newer, you have no unread mail. This fact is used by the finger program. Some specialized systems benefit from the noatime option, particularly Usenet News servers with a lot of clients. For most other machines, this option is usually left alone.

The user option is occasionally used for file systems belonging to other operating systems; it allows ordinary users to mount Microsoft Windows file systems (for example) and access the files on them without falling afoul of the fact that Windows (except Windows NT in some cases) does not keep track of who owns files.

Mount Options for NFS File Systems

When you set up an NFS file system, there are also NFS options that allow you to customize the way the file system is mounted and used.

Most of the nfs options are concerned with what should happen if the server machine is unreachable (because, for example, either it or the network has failed). This perhaps seems unlikely but, believe me, you'll care on the day it happens.

The default options just make the system keep trying indefinitely until the file system can be mounted. Many file systems are essential but some are not. For nonessential file systems, you should check the Background Mount checkbox. This allows your Linux system to continue to boot if the remote file system is not available. If a program has to use a file on the failing server, it waits until the file system has been mounted (the upper limit on how long this takes until it gives up is also configurable).

The read and write sizes are configurable. Again, the defaults are conservative and should be satisfactory. The default read and write size is 1,024 bytes (this conveniently fits inside a 1,500-byte Ethernet packet), but often the system performs much better if this size is increased to 4,096 or even 8,192 bytes (that is, 4KB or 8KB). Sometimes doing this actually makes things worse rather than better, however; it depends on the server and the quality of the network cards, as well as the amount of network traffic.

linuxconf

As you've seen, `linuxconf` is a quick and easy way to configure the file systems on your Linux computer. Besides offering text and Web-browser interfaces, `linuxconf` also has an X Window GUI, as shown in Figure 28.6.

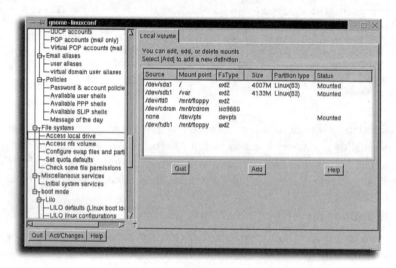

FIGURE 28.6
`linuxconf` includes a graphical X Window interface.

Unlike previous tools, linuxconf is consistent between all three of the different access methods. No longer do you need to master a text-based tool as well as a graphical tool. With linuxconf installed on your system, you can manage almost all aspects of your Linux computer from anywhere in the world with a familiar and easy-to-use interface.

Editing */etc/fstab* Manually

The file system table /etc/fstab is just a text file; it is designed to have a specific format that is readable by humans and not just computers. /etc/fstab is separated into columns by tabs or spaces and you can edit it with your favorite text editor. You must take care, however, if you modify it by hand, because removing or corrupting an entry can make the system unable to mount that file system next time it boots. My /etc/fstab looks like this:

```
#
# /etc/fstab
#
# You should be using fstool (control-panel) to edit this!
#
#<device> <mountpoint> <filesystemtype> <options>    <dump> <fsckorder>


/dev/hda1     /            ext2    defaults  1           1
/dev/hdb5     /home        ext2    defaults,rw  1        2
/dev/hda3     /usr         ext2    defaults    1      2
/dev/hdb1     /usr/src     ext2    defaults    1      3


/dev/hdc      /mnt/cdrom   iso9660   user,noauto,ro   0       0
/dev/sbpcd0   /mnt/pcd     iso9660   user,noauto,ro   0       0
/dev/fd1      /mnt/floppy  vfat    user,noauto    0        0


/proc         /proc         proc    defaults
/dev/hda2     none          swap    sw
```

The first four entries are the ext2 file systems comprising my Linux system. When Linux is booted, the root file system is mounted first; all other local (that is, non-network) file systems are mounted next.

Order is important in */etc/fstab*

File systems appear in /etc/fstab in the order in which they are mounted; /usr must appear before /usr/src, for example, because the mount point for one file system exists on the other. Be sure to use the proper order if you have partitioned your hard drive in order to separate parts of the Linux file system.

The following three file systems are all removable file systems: two CD-ROM drives and a floppy disk drive. These have the noauto option set so that they are not automatically mounted at boot time. These removable devices have the user option set so that I can mount and unmount them without having to use su all the time. The CD-ROMs have the file system type iso9660, which is the standard file system for CD-ROMs, and the floppy drive has the file system type vfat, because I often use it for interchanging data with MS-DOS and Windows systems.

/proc is a special file system provided by the kernel as a way of providing information about the system to user programs. The information in the /proc file system is used to provide information to utilities such as ps, top, xload, free, netstat, and so on. Some of the "files" in /proc are really enormous (for example, /proc/kcore) but don't worry—all the information in the /proc file system is generated on-the-fly by the Linux kernel as you read it; no disk space is wasted. You can tell that they are not real files because, for example, root can't give them away with chown.

The final "file system" isn't, in fact, a file system at all; it is an entry that indicates a disk partition used as swap space. Swap partitions are used to implement virtual memory. Files can also be used for swap space. The names of the swap files go in the first column where the device name usually goes.

The two numeric columns on the right relate to the operation of the dump and fsck commands, respectively. The dump command compares the number in column five (the *dump interval*) with the number of days since that file system was last backed up so that it can inform the system administrator that the file system needs to be backed up. Other backup software—for example, Amanda—can also use this field for the same purpose. (Amanda can be found at the URL http://www.cs.umd.edu/projects/amanda/amanda.html.) File systems without a dump interval field are assumed to have a dump interval of zero, denoting "never dump." For more information, see the manual page for dump.

The sixth column is the fsck pass, which indicates the file systems that can be checked in parallel at boot time. The root file system is always checked first, but after that, separate drives can be checked simultaneously, Linux being a multitasking operating system. There is no point, however, in checking two file systems on the same hard drive at the same time, because this results in lots of extra disk head movement and wasted time. All the file systems that have the same pass number are checked in parallel, from 1 upward. File systems with a 0 or missing pass number (such as the floppy and CD-ROM drives) are not checked at all.

Creating New File Systems

When you install Linux, the installation process makes some new file systems and sets the system up to use them. Many operating systems don't distinguish between the preparation of the device's surface to receive data (formatting) and the building of new file systems. Linux does distinguish between the two, principally because only floppy disks need formatting in any case, and also because Linux offers as many as half a dozen different file systems that can be created (on any block device).

SEE ALSO

➤ *For a list of a number of different file systems for Linux, see Table 7.1 on page 114.*

Linux provides a generic command, mkfs, that enables you to make a file system on a block device. In fact, because UNIX manages almost all resources with the same set of operations, mkfs can be used to generate a file system inside an ordinary file!

Because of the tremendous variety of file systems available, almost all the work of building the new file system is delegated to a separate program for each; however, the generic mkfs program provides a single interface for invoking them all. It's common to pass options to the top-level mkfs (for example, -v to make it show what commands it executes or -c to make it check the device for bad blocks). The generic mkfs program also enables you to pass options to the file system-specific mkfs. There are many of these file system-dependent options, but most of them have sensible defaults, and you normally would not want to change them.

The only options you might want to pass to mke2fs, which builds ext2 file systems, are -m and -i. The -m option specifies how much of the file system is reserved for root's use (for example, for working space when the system disk would otherwise have filled completely). The -i option is more rarely exercised and is used for setting the balance between inodes and disk blocks; it is related to the expected average file size. As stated previously, the defaults are reasonable for most purposes, so these options are used only in special circumstances.

Formatting and creating a Linux floppy *fstab* entry

1. Log in as the root operator and insert a blank disk into your floppy drive.

2. Use the `mkfs` command, followed by the `-t` option, the name of a file system, and the floppy device name on the command line to format a floppy:

```
# mkfs -t ext2 /dev/fd1
mke2fs 1.10, 24-Apr-97 for EXT2 FS 0.5b, 95/08/09
Linux ext2 filesystem format
Filesystem label=
360 inodes, 1440 blocks
72 blocks (5.00) reserved for the super user
First data block=1
Block size=1024 (log=0)
Fragment size=1024 (log=0)
1 block group
8192 blocks per group, 8192 fragments per group
360 inodes per group

Writing inode tables: done
Writing superblocks and filesystem accounting information: done
```

3. After the `mkfs` command creates the file system on your disk, you can include the disk in your file system's table by changing an existing line referring to a `vfat` file system on `/dev/fd1`, or by creating a new line.

Using your favorite text editor, open the `/etc/fstab` file (make a backup!). Type an entry for your floppy like this:

```
/dev/fd1      /mnt/floppy    ext2    user,sync,errors=continue 0 0
```

4. You can then use the `mount` command to mount your new Linux disk, like this:

```
# mount -t ext2 /dev/fd1 /mnt/floppy
```

5. Use the `ls` command, along with the `-la` (long-format and all) options, to verify the contents of the new disk:

```
# ls -la /mnt/floppy
total 14
drwxr-xr-x   3 root      root       1024 Aug  1 19:49 .
drwxr-xr-x   7 root      root       1024 Jul  3 21:47 ..
drwxr-xr-x   2 root      root      12288 Aug  1 19:49 lost+found
```

6. Finally, you can unmount the disk with the `umount` command, followed by the mount point of the disk:

```
# umount /mnt/floppy
```

The structure and creation of an `ext2` file system on a floppy shows that there is no volume label, and there are 4,096 bytes (4KB) per inode ($360 \times 4 = 1,440$). The block size is 1KB and 5% of the disk is reserved for root. These are the defaults (which are explained in the `mke2fs` manual page).

The first three columns in the floppy disk's `/etc/fstab` entry are the Device, Mount Point, and File system type. The Options column is more complex than previous ones. The `user` option indicates that users are allowed to mount this file system. The `sync` option indicates that programs writing to this file system wait while each write finishes, and only then continue.

This might seem obvious, but it is not the normal state of affairs. The kernel normally manages file system writes in such a way as to provide high performance (data still gets written to the device, of course, but it doesn't necessarily happen immediately). This is perfect for fixed devices such as hard disks, but for low-capacity removable devices such as floppy disks, it's less beneficial. Normally, you write a few files to a floppy, and then unmount it and take it away. The unmount operation must wait until all data has been written to the device before it can finish (and the disk can then be removed).

Having to wait like this is annoying, and there is always the risk that someone might copy a file to the floppy, wait for the disk light to go out, and remove it. With asynchronous writes, some buffered data might not have yet been written to disk. Hence, synchronous writes are safer for removable media.

The `ext2` file system has a configurable strategy for errors. If an `ext2` file system encounters an error (for example, a bad disk block), there are three possible responses to the error:

- *Remount the device read-only.* For file systems that contain mostly nonessential data (for example, `/tmp`, `/var/tmp`, or news spools), remounting the file system read-only so that it can be fixed with `fsck` is often the best choice.

- *Panic.* Continuing in the face of potentially corrupted system configuration files is unwise, so a kernel *panic* (that is, a controlled crash—or emergency landing, if you prefer) can sometimes be appropriate.

- *Ignore it.* Causing a system shutdown if a floppy disk has a bad sector is a little excessive, so the `continue` option tells the kernel to "carry on regardless" in this situation. If this actually does happen, the best thing to do is to use the `-c` option of `e2fsck`, for example, with `fsck -t ext2 -c /dev/fd1`. This runs `e2fsck`, giving it the `-c` option, which invokes the `badblocks` command to test the device for bad disk blocks. After this is done, `e2fsck` does its best to recover from the situation.

How to Organize Your File System Tree

It is often useful to have major parts of the Linux file system on separate partitions; this can make upgrades and reinstalls easier, and it can also facilitate backup and network administration.

Good Candidates for Separate File Systems

The best candidate for being on a separate file system is the /home tree. A separate /home file system means that your own data will survive unscathed even if you have to reinstall everything from scratch. If you have more than one machine, it is often useful to mount /home over the network so that your files can be shared between all the machines.

Other file systems are made separate for different reasons—for example, so that they can be mounted over the network, or so that they can have different mount options.

Because the /usr file system is large, it is often on a separate file system, sometimes mounted from another machine. A separate /usr also allows you to have a much smaller root (/) partition. Having a small root partition is beneficial because this tends to reduce the chances of it becoming corrupted when the power fails as well as slowing down due to fragmentation. Having a separate /var partition can help for the same reason.

Some of the machines that I administer are security-critical. On these machines I make /var/log a separate, huge file system. There are two reasons for this. First, it means that filling up /var will not mean that the system cannot continue to log activity. Second, making /var/log large means that an attacker (or "cracker") can't fill up the partition in order to prevent the logging of future activities.

Bad Candidates for Separate File Systems

There are some directories that absolutely must be part of the root file system. These are listed in Table 28.3.

Table 28.3 Essential Linux Directories of the *root* File System

Directory Name	Description
/bin	The mount command lives in /bin and if it is not available on the root file system, there is no way to mount any other file system.
/sbin	Contains programs essential to booting, such as /sbin/init, the very first program to be started (the kernel starts it in order to get the system going).

Directory Name	Description
/etc	Contains many configuration files that must be present at boot time, such as /etc/inittab and /etc/fstab.
/dev	Contains device files for all the other file systems in /dev. The mount command needs these in order to work.
/lib	Contains libraries to which many programs needed at boot time are dynamically linked.
/root	It's a good idea to have root's home directory available even when some file systems cannot be mounted; useful backup files can be kept there.

Almost any other directories can be on separate file systems. Insightful users will note that the /boot directory is not in this list. That is because the files in /boot are not needed at boot time; they are needed only when you run the program /sbin/lilo. As long as the BIOS can read these files by sector-by-sector BIOS calls, the kernel can be loaded by the boot loader. After the kernel is loaded and the root file system is mounted, these files have done their job. Having a separate /boot file system allows you to ensure that it resides near the start of a large <hard disk. This can be vital for some older PC-compatible machines.

Repairing File Systems

Some disk data is kept in memory temporarily before being written to disk, for performance reasons (see the previous discussion of the sync mount option). If the kernel does not have an opportunity to actually write this data, the file system can become corrupted. This can happen in several ways:

- The storage device (for example, a floppy disk) can be manually removed before the kernel has finished with it.
- The system might suffer a power loss during a storm or power surge.
- The user might mistakenly turn off the power or accidentally press the reset button.

As part of the boot process, Linux runs the fsck program, whose job it is to check and repair file systems. Most of the time, the boot follows a controlled shutdown (see the manual page for shutdown), and in this case, the file systems will have been unmounted before the reboot. In this case, fsck says that they are "clean." It knows this because before unmounting them, the kernel writes a special signature on the file system to indicate that the data is intact. When the file system is mounted again for writing, this signature is removed.

If, on the other hand, one of the disasters listed earlier takes place, the file systems will not be marked "clean," and when fsck is invoked, as usual, it will notice this and begin a full check of the file system. This also occurs if you specify the -f flag to fsck. To prevent errors creeping up on it, fsck enforces a periodic check; a full check is done at an interval specified on the file system itself (usually every 20 boots or every six months, whichever comes sooner), even if it was unmounted cleanly.

The boot process checks the root file system and then mounts it read-write. (It's mounted read-only by the kernel; fsck asks for confirmation before operating on a read-write file system; and you should *never* allow fsck to operate on such a system because you risk serious data corruption.) First, the root file system is checked with the following command:

```
fsck -V -a /
```

Then all the other file systems are checked by executing this command:

```
fsck -R -A -V -a
```

These options specify that all the file systems should be checked (-A) except the root file system, which doesn't need checking a second time (-R), and that operations produce informational messages about what it is doing as it goes (-V), but that the process should not be interactive (-a). This last option is included because, for example, there might not be anyone present to answer any questions from fsck.

In the case of serious file system corruption, the approach breaks down because there are some things that fsck will not do to a file system without your say-so. In this case, it returns an error value to its caller (the startup script), and the startup script spawns a shell to allow the administrator to run fsck interactively. When this has happened, this message appears:

```
*** An error occurred during the filesystem check.
*** Dropping you to a shell; the system will reboot
*** when you leave the shell.
Give root password for maintenance
(or type Control-D for normal startup):
```

This is a very troubling event, particularly because it might well appear if you have other problems with the system—for example, a lockup (leading you to press the Reset button) or a spontaneous reboot. None of the online manuals are guaranteed to be available at this stage, because they might be stored on the file system whose check failed. This prompt is issued if the root file system check failed, or the file system check failed for any of the other disk file systems.

When the automatic `fsck` fails, you need to log in by specifying the root password and running the `fsck` program manually. When you have typed in the root password, you are presented with the following prompt:

```
(Repair filesystem) #
```

You might worry about what command to enter here, or indeed what to do at all. At least one of the file systems needs to be checked, but which one? The preceding messages from `fsck` should indicate which, but it isn't necessary to go hunting for them. There is a set of options you can give to `fsck` that tells it to check *everything* manually, and this is a good fallback:

```
# fsck -A -V ; echo == $? ==
```

This is the same command as the previous one, but the `-R` option is missing, in case the root file system needs to be checked, and the `-a` option is missing, so `fsck` is in its "interactive" mode. This might enable a check to succeed just because it can now ask you questions. The purpose of the `echo == $? ==` command is to unambiguously interpret the outcome of the `fsck` operation. If the value printed between the equal signs is less than 4, all is well.

If this value is `4` or more, on the other hand, more recovery measures are needed. The meanings of the various values returned are as follows:

0	No errors
1	File system errors corrected
2	System should be rebooted
4	File system errors left uncorrected
8	Operational error
16	Usage or syntax error
128	Shared library error

If this does not work, this might be because of a *corrupted superblock*—`fsck` starts its disk check and if the superblock is corrupted, it can't start. By good design, the `ext2` file system has many backup superblocks scattered regularly throughout the file system. Suppose the command announces that it has failed to clean some particular file system—for example, `/dev/fubar`. You can start `fsck` again, using a backup superblock by using the following command:

```
# fsck -t ext2 -b 8193 /dev/fubar
```

`8193` is the block number for the first backup superblock. This backup superblock is at the start of block group 1 (the first is numbered 0). There are more backup superblocks at the start of block group 2 (`16385`), and block group 3 (`24577`); they are spaced at intervals of 8192 blocks. If you made a file system with settings other than the defaults, these might change. mke2fs lists the superblocks that it creates as it goes, so that is a good time to pay attention if you're not using the default settings. There are other things you can attempt if fsck is still not succeeding, but further failures are very rare and usually indicate hardware problems so severe that they prevent the proper operation of fsck. Examples include broken wires in the IDE connector cable and similar nasty problems. If this command still fails, you might seek expert help or try to fix the disk in a different machine.

These extreme measures are very unlikely; a manual fsck, in the unusual circumstance where it is actually required, almost always fixes things. After the manual fsck has worked, the root shell that the startup scripts provide has done its purpose. Type exit to exit it. At this point, in order to make sure that everything goes according to plan, the boot process is started again from the beginning. This second time around, the file systems should all be error-free, and the system should boot normally.

Disaster Recovery

Easy disaster recovery, in computing as in life, requires forward planning. This means making regular backups of your computer, and checking that those backups work properly.

The actual backup process is covered in Chapter 30, "System Maintenance," but here we discuss the other aspects of disaster recovery.

What's Vital and What Isn't?

There was a time when PC floppy disks were 360KB and hard disks were 10MB. A complete system backup might fit onto 30 floppy disks. A few years later, floppies were 1.44MB and hard disks were 100MB—that's over 60 floppies. Today, floppy disks are still the same size but disks are 4GB. Even if you could buy 3,000 floppy disks, system backups would be ridiculously impractical.

There are many solutions to this problem. Floppy disks are no longer viable for backups of a whole system. Tapes and recordable CDs are perfectly good in their place.

A useful backup strategy takes into account several things:

- What is the maximum acceptable downtime?
- How much data must be backed up?

- How quickly does the data change?
- What backup devices are available?

If all the data you need to back up will fit on your backup device, the simplest solution works best—back everything up, every time.

If a complete backup every time is impractical, you have to find a balance between the risk to your data and the cost of making backups. As an example, my own system has almost 4GB of file systems. Much of this is occupied by the operating system and could easily be restored from the installation CD-ROM. Of the rest, the majority consists of packages either from CDs or downloaded from the Internet (WINE, POV, Gnome, LCLint, and so on). These come to over half a gigabyte. All these things can either be reinstalled from the CDs or downloaded again.

SEE ALSO

➤ *For more information about doing system backups for Linux, see page 504.*

Altogether, the files on which I work actively come to under 100MB, including the intermediate compiler output files, which don't really need to be backed up. I keep these files separate from the things that I don't work on. So, for me it is practical to back up my vital data to a series of floppy disks. This is not ideal, but it's reasonable. This strategy is only possible because the file system is organized so as to keep the various kinds of data separate; I don't mix my own files (which I have to keep safe) with downloaded packages or documents (which I can delete).

When to Back Up

When you have a catastrophe, you will lose everything modified since it was last backed up. So, there are two factors that determine how often you back your data up: what the capacity of your backup device is and how much suffering you can bear.

Nontraditional backup devices

If you don't have a traditional kind of backup device, this does not mean that you cannot back up your important data. See your backup device's documentation for more information, and remember that backing up is absolutely crucial.

What to Do with the Backups

After you've backed up your data, the three most important things to do are as follows:

- *Write-protect the media.* There's nothing worse than trying to restore from backup in a panic and accidentally deleting the backup.

- *Label your backup.* If you can't identify the most recent backup when you need it, it's no use. Keep your backups in a safe place.

- *Test your backup.* Make sure you can restore from it.

This last point is particularly important. Many people have a backup routine that they follow day in and day out but find out only too late that their backups are useless. A cautionary tale that sticks in my memory is that of a vendor of backup software whose code had a bug; it would make multivolume backups, but the second and following volumes were useless and could not be read back. Unfortunately, they used their own software to back up their systems and amazingly had never done a trial restore with their tapes.

Reviewing Your Backup Strategy

Don't forget to periodically reconsider your backup strategy. Circumstances change; your data might grow, or it might suddenly be more important that you be able to recover from backup suddenly. For example, while writing this chapter I added up the size of my working data and realized it was larger than I thought. Part of my next paycheck will go for a larger backup device; probably a SCSI tape drive or (if I can afford it) a CD-ROM recorder.

Coping with Disaster

When the worst happens, it's important to be extra careful about what you do. If you've just typed `rm -rf /tmp *` instead of `rm -rf /tmp/*`, by all means immediately interrupt this. After you realize that data has been lost, take a moment to calm down and review your options. Determine the answers to these questions:

1. What data has been lost?
2. Where is my most recent backup?
3. Where is my system installation media (boot disk and installation CD-ROM)?

Restoring System Files

If you've just lost a few system files, you might be able to fix everything by reinstalling a few packages from the CD-ROM. People with even quite badly destroyed systems have recovered simply by booting from the installation floppy and selecting Upgrade. The Red Hat upgrade process can replace only missing files. If the destruction is more extensive, you might need to consider reinstalling from scratch.

> **System won't boot? Don't panic!**
>
> Don't panic if your Red Hat Linux system won't start. The problem could be with your LILO configuration or errors in your file system table. One fail-safe approach to try is to restart your computer with your Red Hat Linux boot disk or CD-ROM. At the boot prompt, enter the word `rescue`. Red Hat Linux will try to find and mount existing Linux volumes or partitions, and you can either try to fix the problem or salvage your data.

Strictly speaking, it is quite possible to recover from losing almost everything just by booting the installation floppy in `rescue` mode and knowing how to haul yourself up by your bootstraps. However, if you're not an expert, you might find a reinstallation easier. If you do this, however, the installation process will destroy any data on partitions that the operating system installs onto. That is, if you only have one file system, `/`, a reinstall will delete the contents of your home directory, too. If you have your `/home` file system on a separate drive, the reinstall will not delete it (unless you tell it to format that partition by accident).

If a reinstall would destroy your own data and you have no useful backup, you're in a tight spot. The best approach is to avoid the reinstall, perhaps by recruiting the help of an expert. Lastly, if you do reinstall your system, consider putting your own important data on a separate file system (`/home`, for example).

Restoring User Files

After the system files are taken care of, you can restore your own data from a backup. The actual details of this are explained in Chapter 30.

chapter

29

Managing Applications

Package Management with *rpm*

Converting between different
package methods

Package Management with *rpm*

One of the most powerful and innovative utilities available in Red Hat Linux is rpm, the Red Hat package manager. It can be used to install, uninstall, upgrade, query, verify, and build software packages. The RPM system provides all the functions of the installer/uninstaller model of Windows, but actually works! The RPM system is so popular that it has been adopted by other Linux distributions as the primary means of packaging software. Unfortunately, there isn't a true standard for packaging, and there are other means of distributing software for your computer. Debian Linux has its own system packages that are similar in function to the Red Hat package system. At the end of this chapter, I'll look at a way to convert between these different packaging methods to provide compatibility across different Linux distributions. A software package built with rpm is an archive of files and some associated information, such as a name, a version, and a description. A few of the advantages of rpm packages over the traditional tar.gz method of software distribution are as follows:

- *Upgrading.* A new version of the software can be installed without losing customization files.

- *Uninstalling.* A software package that installs files in several locations can be cleanly removed.

- *Verification.* After its installation, a package can be verified to be in working order.

- *Querying.* Information about what package a file belongs to can be easily obtained.

In addition to these features, rpm is available for many flavors of Linux and UNIX, making it one of the emerging utilities for distributing software packages.

SEE ALSO

➤ *For more information about other software backup or archiving utilities for Linux, see Chapter 30, "System Maintenance.*

The *rpm* Command's Major Modes and Common Options

Following are the major modes in which rpm can be run:

- Install (rpm -i)
- Uninstall (rpm -e)
- Query (rpm -q)
- Verify (rpm -V)

The options to invoke the major modes are given in parentheses. These major modes are covered in detail in subsequent sections.

All these major modes understand the following options:

- -vv. Prints out all debugging information; this mode is useful for seeing what exactly RPM is doing.

- --quiet. Prints out very little information—only error messages.

In addition to these, there are a few other minor modes that are useful:

- --version. The version mode is invoked as the following:

  ```
  # rpm --version
  ```

  This mode prints out a line containing version information, similar to the following:

  ```
  RPM version 3.0.3
  ```

- help. The help mode prints out an extensive help message:

  ```
  # rpm --help
  ```

- If a message is long, it is handy to have a large xterm to pipe the output to more. To get a shorter help message, just type the following:

  ```
  # rpm
  ```

  --showrc. This prints out a usage message. The showrc mode prints out a list of variables that can be set in the files /etc/rpmrc and $HOME/.rpmrc:

  ```
  # rpm --showrc
  ```

  The default values are adequate for most installations.

- --rebuilddb. The --rebuilddb option is used to rebuild the database that rpm uses to keep track of which packages are installed on a system. Although this option is rarely needed, it is invoked as follows:

  ```
  # rpm --rebuilddb
  ```

Installing Packages

One of the major uses of rpm is to install software packages. The general syntax of an rpm install command is as follows:

```
rpm -i [options] [packages]
```

options can be a common option given earlier or an install option covered in the following list; packages is the name of one or more rpm package files. The RPM system is so advanced that it can take an FTP or HTTP URL as the package name. Some of the install options are listed in Table 29.1.

Table 29.1   *rpm* Install Options

Option	Description
-v	Prints out what rpm is doing
-h or --hash	Prints out 50 hash marks (or pound signs; #) as the package is installed
--percent	Prints out percentages as files are extracted from the package
--test	Goes through a package install, but does not install anything; mainly used to catch conflicts
--excludedocs	Prevents the installation of files marked as documentation, such as man pages
--includedocs	Forces files marked as documentation to be installed; this is the default
--nodeps	No dependency checks are performed before installing a package
--replacefiles	Allows for installed files to be replaced with files from the package being installed
--replacepkgs	Allows for installed packages to be replaced with the packages being installed
--oldpackage	Allows for a newer version of an installed package to be replaced with an older version
--Force	Forces a package to be installed

When giving options to rpm, regardless of the mode, all the single-letter options, known as *short options*, can be lumped together in one block:

```
# rpm -i -v -h kernel-2.2.12-20.i386.rpm
```

This command is equivalent to the following:

```
# rpm -ivh kernel-2.2.12-20.i386.rpm
```

All options starting with --, called *long options*, must be given separately, however.

Now take a look at a few examples of installing rpm packages. The first example installs defrag (a file system defragmenter) from the following package:

```
defrag-0.73-5.i386.rpm
```

Installing the *vim rpm* package

1. rpm software packages generally follow a standard naming convention:

   ```
   name-version-release.arch.rpm
   ```

name is the package's name, version is the package's version, release is the package's release level, arch is the hardware architecture the package is for, and rpm is the default extension. This naming scheme is quite handy because some of the essential information about a particular package can be determined from just looking at its name.

2. For this example, defrag package, defrag version 0.73, release 5 is installed for a computer with the i386 architecture.

3. Use cd to change to the appropriate directory containing the RPM or find a URL where you can download the package and then install defrag by using the rpm command's i, v, and h options, followed by the name and URL of defrag's rpm file, like so:

```
# rpm -ivh ftp://contrib.redhat.com/contrib/libc6/i386/
defrag-0.73-5.i386.rpm
```

As the package is installed, the output will look like the following:

```
defrag                       ###############
```

When the install is finished, 50 hash marks are displayed.

In this example, I used the pound sign (#) to indicate the root prompt because only root can properly install packages for an entire system. If you try to install this package as a user other than root, an error similar to the following will be generated:

```
failed to open //var/lib/rpm/packages.rpm
error: cannot open //var/lib/rpm/packages.rpm
```

Occasionally, the files that one package installs conflict with the files of a previously installed package. If you had defrag version 0.65 installed, the following message would have been generated:

```
/sbin/e2defrag conflicts with file from defrag-0.65-5
error: defrag-0.73-5.i386.rpm cannot be installed
```

If you wanted to install these files anyway, the --replacefiles option can be added to the command.

Another type of conflict that is sometimes encountered is a *dependency conflict*. This happens when a package that is being installed requires certain other packages to function correctly. For example, perhaps you try to install the following package:

```
# rpm -ivh quicktest-1.5.2-1.i386.rpm
```

You can get the following dependency errors:

```
failed dependencies:
kernel >= 2.2.12 is needed by quicktest-1.5.2-1
quicktest = 1.5.1 is needed by xquicktest-1.0.1-1
```

This indicates two things. You must upgrade your kernel to 2.2.12, and if you install a newer version of quicktest, you must also install a newer version of xquicktest. Although it is usually not a good idea to ignore dependency problems, using the --nodeps option causes rpm to ignore these errors and install the package.

Upgrading Packages

rpm's *upgrade mode* provides an easy way to upgrade existing software packages to newer versions. Upgrade mode is similar to install mode:

```
rpm -U [options] [packages]
```

options can be any of the install options or any of the general options.

Here is an example of how to upgrade packages. Suppose that on your system you are currently running emacs version 19.31, but you want to upgrade to the newer emacs version 20.4. To upgrade, use the following command:

```
# rpm -Uvh emacs-20.4-4.i386.rpm
```

The upgrade mode is really a combination of two operations: uninstall and install. First, rpm uninstalls any older versions of the requested package and then installs the newer version. If an older version of the package does not exist, rpm simply installs the requested package.

An additional advantage of upgrade over a manual install and uninstall is that upgrade automatically saves configuration files. For these reasons, some people prefer to use upgrade rather than install for all package installations.

Uninstalling Packages

The uninstall mode of rpm provides for a clean method of removing files belonging to a software package from many locations.

SEE ALSO
➤ *To learn about other ways to delete files, see page 49.*

Many packages install files in /etc, /usr, and /lib, so removing a package can be confusing, but with rpm an entire package can be removed as follows:

```
rpm -e [options] [package]
```

options is one of the options listed later in this section, and package is the name of the package to be removed. For example, if you want to remove the package for dosemu, the command is as follows:

```
# rpm -e quicktest-1.5.2-1
```

The name specified here for the package is just the name of the package, not the name of the file that was used to install the package. Perhaps you ask for the following:

```
# rpm -e quicktest-1.5.2-1.i386.rpm
```

The following error would have been generated:

```
package quicktest-1.5.2-1.i386.rpm is not installed
```

Another common error encountered while trying to uninstall packages is a _dependency error_. This occurs when a package that is being uninstalled has files required by another package. For example, when you try to remove the quicktest package from your system, you get the following error:

```
removing these packages would break dependencies:
quicktest = 1.5.2 is needed by xquicktest-1.0.5-1
```

This means that the package xquicktest does not function properly if the package quicktest is removed. If you still want to remove this package, rpm could be presented with the --nodeps option to make it ignore dependency errors.

The other useful option is the --test option, which causes rpm to go through the motions of removing a package without actually removing anything. Usually there is no output from an uninstall, so the -vv option is presented along with the --test option to see what would happen during an uninstall:

```
# rpm -e -vv --test kernelcfg-0.5-5
```

This example produces the following output on the system:

```
D: opening database mode 0x0 in //var/lib/rpm/
D: getting list of mounted filesystems
D: will remove files test = 1
D:    file: /usr/share/icons/kernelcfg.xpm action: remove
D:    file: /usr/lib/rhs/kernelcfg/kernelcfg.pyc action: remove
D:    file: /usr/lib/rhs/kernelcfg/kernelcfg.py action: remove
D:    file: /usr/lib/rhs/kernelcfg action: remove
D:    file: /usr/lib/rhs/control-panel/kernelcfg.xpm action: remove
D:    file: /usr/lib/rhs/control-panel/kernelcfg.init action: remove
D:    file: /usr/bin/kernelcfg action: remove
D:    file: /etc/X11/wmconfig/kernelcfg action: remove
D: removing database entry
```

As you can see, the files that would have been removed are clearly indicated in the output.

Querying Packages

The querying mode in `rpm` allows for determining the various attributes of packages. The basic syntax for querying packages is as follows:

```
rpm -q [options] [packages]
```

`options` is one or more of the query options listed later in this section. The most basic query is one similar to the following:

```
# rpm -q kernel
```

On my system, this prints out the following line for the kernel package:

```
kernel-2.2.12-20
```

In a manner similar to uninstall, `rpm`'s query mode uses the name of the package, not the name of the file that the package came in for queries.

Now for a few more sample queries. If you want to retrieve a list of all the files owned by the kernel package, you can use the `-l` option:

```
# rpm -ql kernel
```

This outputs the following list of files on my system:

```
/boot/System.map-2.2.12-20
/boot/module-info-2.2.12-20
/boot/vmlinux-2.2.12-20
/boot/vmlinuz-2.2.12-20
/lib/modules
/lib/modules/2.2.12-20
/lib/modules/2.2.12-20/.rhkmvtag
/lib/modules/2.2.12-20/block
/lib/modules/2.2.12-20/block/DAC960.o
/lib/modules/2.2.12-20/block/cpqarray.o
/lib/modules/2.2.12-20/block/ide-floppy.o
/lib/modules/2.2.12-20/block/ide-tape.o
/lib/modules/2.2.12-20/block/linear.o
/lib/modules/2.2.12-20/block/loop.o
/lib/modules/2.2.12-20/block/nbd.o
/lib/modules/2.2.12-20/block/raid0.o
/lib/modules/2.2.12-20/block/raid1.o
/lib/modules/2.2.12-20/block/raid5.o
/lib/modules/2.2.12-20/block/xd.o
...
(and several more)
```

In addition to getting a list of the files, you can determine their state by using the -s option:

```
# rpm -qs kernel
```

This option gives the following information about the state of files in my kernel package:

```
normal          /boot/System.map-2.2.12-20
normal          /boot/module-info-2.2.12-20
normal          /boot/vmlinux-2.2.12-20
normal          /boot/vmlinuz-2.2.12-20
normal          /lib/modules
normal          /lib/modules/2.2.12-20
normal          /lib/modules/2.2.12-20/.rhkmvtag
normal          /lib/modules/2.2.12-20/block
normal          /lib/modules/2.2.12-20/block/DAC960.o
normal          /lib/modules/2.2.12-20/block/cpqarray.o
normal          /lib/modules/2.2.12-20/block/ide-floppy.o
normal          /lib/modules/2.2.12-20/block/ide-tape.o
normal          /lib/modules/2.2.12-20/block/linear.o
normal          /lib/modules/2.2.12-20/block/loop.o
normal          /lib/modules/2.2.12-20/block/nbd.o
normal          /lib/modules/2.2.12-20/block/raid0.o
normal          /lib/modules/2.2.12-20/block/raid1.o
normal          /lib/modules/2.2.12-20/block/raid5.o
normal          /lib/modules/2.2.12-20/block/xd.o
```

If any of these files report a state of missing, there are probably problems with the package.

In addition to the state of the files in a package, the documentation files and the configuration files can be listed. To list the documentation that comes with the emacs package, use the following:

```
# rpm -qd emacs
```

This produces the following list:

```
/usr/doc/emacs-20.4/BUGS
/usr/doc/emacs-20.4/FAQ
/usr/doc/emacs-20.4/NEWS
/usr/doc/emacs-20.4/README
/usr/info/ccmode-1.gz
/usr/info/ccmode-2.gz
```

```
/usr/info/ccmode-3.gz
/usr/info/ccmode.gz
/usr/info/cl-1.gz
/usr/info/cl-2.gz
/usr/info/cl-3.gz
/usr/info/cl-4.gz
```

To get the configuration files for a package, use the following query:

```
# rpm -qc apache
```

This results in the following list:

```
/etc/httpd/conf/access.conf
/etc/httpd/conf/httpd.conf
/etc/httpd/conf/magic
/etc/httpd/conf/srm.conf
/etc/logrotate.d/apache
/etc/rc.d/init.d/httpd
/etc/rc.d/rc0.d/K15httpd
/etc/rc.d/rc1.d/K15httpd
/etc/rc.d/rc2.d/K15httpd
/etc/rc.d/rc3.d/S85httpd
/etc/rc.d/rc5.d/S85httpd
/etc/rc.d/rc6.d/K15httpd
/home/httpd/html/index.html
```

In addition to these queries, complete information about a package can be determined by using the `info` option:

```
# rpm -qi kernel
```

This example gives the following information about the installed kernel package:

```
Name        : kernel                    Relocations: (not relocateable)
Version     : 2.2.12                          Vendor: Red Hat Software
Release     : 20                          Build Date: Mon Sep 27 10:31:59 1999
Install date: Wed Oct  6 14:24:00 1999   Build Host: porky.devel.redhat.com
Group       : System Environment/Kernel  Source RPM: kernel-2.2.12-20.src.rpm
Size        : 11210657                       License: GPL
Packager    : Red Hat Software <http://developer.redhat.com/bugzilla>
Summary     : The Linux kernel (the core of the Linux operating system).
Description :
The kernel package contains the Linux kernel (vmlinuz), the core of your
Red Hat Linux operating system.  The kernel handles the basic functions
of the operating system:  memory allocation, process allocation, device
input and output, etc.
```

A summary of the query options appears in Table 29.2.

Table 29.2	Summary of rpm's query options
Option	Description
-a	Lists all installed packages
-c	Lists all files in a package that are marked as configuration
-d	Lists all files in a package that are marked as documentation
-f *file*	Lists the package that owns the specified file
-i	Lists the complete information for a package
-l	Lists all the files in a package
-p *package*	Query an uninstalled RPM file
-s	Lists the state of files in a package

If any of these options, except for -i, is given along with a -v option, the files are listed in ls -l format:

```
# rpm -qlv kernel
```

This example outputs the following:

```
-rw-r--r--   root   root    191244 Sep 27 10:30 /boot/System.map-2.2.12-20
-rw-r--r--   root   root     11773 Sep 27 10:30 /boot/module-info-2.2.12-20
-rwxr-xr-x   root   root   1544561 Sep 27 10:30 /boot/vmlinux-2.2.12-20
-rw-r--r--   root   root    622966 Sep 27 10:30 /boot/vmlinuz-2.2.12-20
drwxr-xr-x   root   root      1024 Sep 27 10:30 /lib/modules
drwxr-xr-x   root   root      1024 Sep 27 10:31 /lib/modules/2.2.12-20
-rw-r--r--   root   root       149 Sep 27 10:30 /lib/modules/2.2.12-20/.rhkmvtag
...and so on...
```

If you want to learn about a package before it is installed, you can use the rpm -p query format. This will query a package file (either located on your local drive, or on a remote server) and present you with the same query information as if the package were installed.

Verifying Packages

Verifying packages is an easy way to determine whether there are any problems with an installation. In verification mode, rpm compares information about an installed package against information about the original package, which is stored in the package database at install time.

The basic syntax for verifying a package is as follows:

```
rpm -V [package]
```

If a package is verified correctly, rpm does not output anything. If rpm detects a difference between the installed package and the database record, it outputs an eight-character string in which tests that fail are represented by a single character, and tests that pass are represented by a period (.). The characters for failed tests are listed in Table 29.3.

Table 29.3 Characters for Failed Verification Tests

Letter	Failed Test
5	MD5 Sum
S	File Size
L	Symlink
T	Mtime
D	Device
U	User
G	Group
M	Mode (permissions and file type)

For example, on my system, verifying the bash package using # rpm -V bash fails:

```
.M..L...   /bin/bash
....L...   /bin/sh
```

This indicates that the size of my bash is different from the information stored in the database. This is okay on my system because I have recompiled bash.

In addition, it is possible to use the query option -f to verify a package containing a particular file, which is helpful when diagnosing problems with programs:

```
# rpm -Vf /bin/ksh
```

If ksh were behaving peculiarly, the preceding line would verify the package that ksh came in. If any of the tests fail, at the very least you will be closer to understanding the source of the problems.

Using KDE's *kPackage* System to Manage RPMs

 One of the nicest components of the KDE environment is the kpackage RPM management system. kpackage supports RPMs as well as the Debian packages that were mentioned earlier. By enabling you to use either packaging system, kpackage is valuable no matter what Linux distribution you're using. To start kpackage, you can select kpackage from the Utilities menu of the main KDE pop-up menu. You can also start the application by typing kpackage at a command-line.

After kpackage has loaded, a window similar to Figure 29.1 appears.

FIGURE 29.1
The primary kpackage window displays a hierarchy of installed software packages.

SEE ALSO
➤ *For more information about the X Window System, see Chapter 12.*
➤ *To learn more about how to begin a superuser, and using the* su *command with Linux, see page 11.*

The folders displayed in the right pane of this window correspond to different groups or classes of packages. In each group, there can be subgroups as well, which are represented as folders within folders. Any files displayed in the folders represent the currently installed packages of a particular group. These are the main groups into which packages can be installed:

- Amusements
- Applications
- Daemons
- Development
- Documentation
- Networking
- Libraries
- Networking
- System environment
- User interface
- Utilities

You can expand the categories down to the individual packages that are installed on the system. Selecting a package displays information about it on the right side of the screen. If you'd like to list all the files that are a part of the package, just click the File List tab. Figure 29.2 shows a selected networking package.

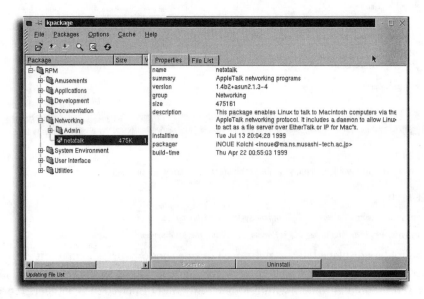

FIGURE 29.2
You can get information about an individual package by selecting it in the package listing.

If you'd like to remove the selected package, you can do so by clicking the uninstall button. You will then be prompted for whether or not to use uninstall scripts, check dependencies, or just run in test mode, as shown in Figure 29.3. To finish the uninstall, just click Uninstall.

FIGURE 29.3
Uninstalling a selected package is a simple point-and-click away.

If you'd like to install a new piece of software, that's just as easy.

1. From the File menu, choose Open or Open URL.

2. If you are opening a URL, input the Web or FTP address of the site with the package you want to install. Otherwise, choose the file from the standard file listing, and click OK.

3. Within a few seconds, a screen similar to Figure 29.4 will be shown.

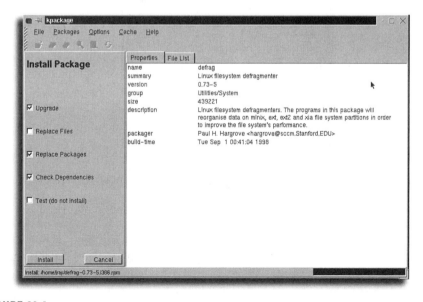

FIGURE 29.4
Software installation can be performed from local or remote files.

4. Choose the install options that are appropriate for your package: Upgrade, Check Dependencies, and so on.

5. Click Install to install the package or Cancel to exit the process.

The kpackage manager should provide all the functions that you need in a package manager, whether using RPMs or Debian packages.

Installing and Using the *xrpm* Client

Another graphical X11 package management utility similar to kpackage is xrpm. Its interface is slightly different, but it provides RPM support for those who aren't using KDE.

xrpm is freely available from http://www.gmsys.com/xrpm.html. It is distributed in both rpm and tar.gz formats. As of this writing, the newest version is 2.2.

After installed, xrpm can be invoked from the command line of an X11 terminal window by typing the following:

```
# xrpm
```

This brings up the xrpm main window, shown in Figure 29.5.

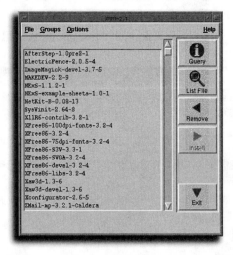

FIGURE 29.5
Main window of xrpm.

The main window of xrpm contains a list of all installed packages at the left and the following buttons at the right:

- *Query.* Queries a package and outputs the results into a window (see Figure 29.6).

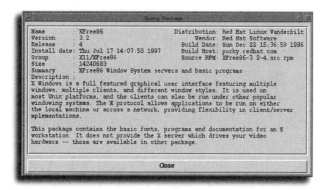

FIGURE 29.6
Results of a package query in xrpm.

- *List Files.* Lists the files in a given package in a separate window.
- *Remove.* Removes an installed package.
- *Install.* Installs a selected package.
- *Exit.* Exits xrpm.

When xrpm first starts up, all the buttons except Install are active. Take a look at the functionality of each of these buttons.

In xrpm, to execute a query on a package, simply click a package name in the list and then click the Query button. The resulting query is slightly different than kpackage: The files included in the package are not listed. An example of a package query is given in Figure 29.6.

To list the files in a package, click a package name in the list and then click the List Files button. This action produces a list of files in the selected package. The listing is slightly different than kpackage, because it does not include extra information about the files.

To remove a package, simply click a package and then click the Remove button. This action brings up the Remove RPM window shown in Figure 29.7. To remove the package you selected, click the Remove button in this window. Any errors encountered during removal are reported in separate windows. To cancel the removal, click the Close button. The Options button gives access to some of the more advanced options, which are not usually required.

FIGURE 29.7
Remove RPM window in xrpm.

xrpm also provides the ability to list packages by their groups. For example, to list all the packages installed in the Applications group, select the Applications menu item from the Groups menu. A new list appears, listing each package's subgroup, as shown in Figure 29.8.

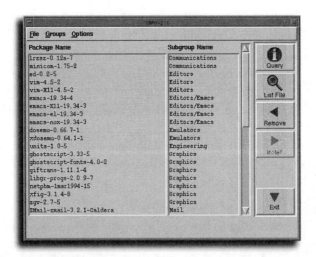

FIGURE 29.8
Application group listing in xrpm.

To restore the full list of all installed packages, select List Installed from the File menu.

To install a new package using xrpm, simply select a location containing RPM files. This location can be on either the local machine or an FTP site. To install packages from the local machine, select Open Directory from the File menu. This brings up a dialog box, shown in Figure 29.9, from which a directory containing RPMs can be selected.

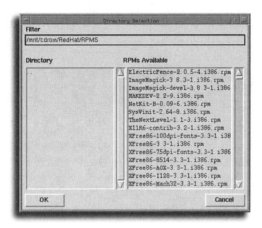

FIGURE 29.9
Selecting a directory containing RPMs in xrpm.

After a directory has been selected, the list in the main xrpm window changes to a list of all the available RPMs for installation in that directory. At this point, the Install button becomes active and the Remove button becomes inactive. Figure 29.10 shows all the available RPMs on the Red Hat Power Tools CD-ROM.

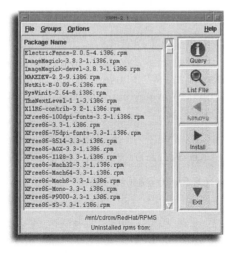

FIGURE 29.10
Available RPMs for installation.

System Administration

Managing Applications

To install a package, click the package and then click the Install button, which brings up the Install RPM window (shown in Figure 29.11). To install the selected package, click the Install button. This installs the package and reports any errors in a separate window. To cancel the installation, click the Close button. As in the Remove RPMs window, the Options button gives access to several advanced options, which are not usually needed.

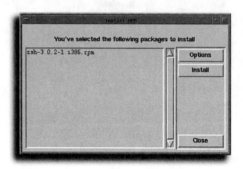

FIGURE 29.11
Install RPM window in xrpm.

Converting Between Different Package Methods

Although this chapter focused on the RPM system, there are other packaging methods that you might run into or might need to use on your system. Luckily, a utility called Alien enables you to convert between different packages. Alien can convert between rpm, dpkg, Stampede slp, and Slackware tgz file formats.

You can download the latest version of Alien from its homepage at http://kitenet.net/programs/alien/. The installation instructions vary from Linux distribution to distribution, so I urge you to check out the Web site for full installation directions for your computer.

After Alien is installed, you can perform the following conversions, as documented here: ftp://ykbsb2.yk.psu.edu/pub/alien/alien-extra.info.

To convert a tgz (or tar.gz) file to a deb or rpm

```
alien --to-deb filename.tgz (or alien -d filename.tgz)
alien --to-rpm filename.tgz (or alien -r filename.tgz)
```

500

To convert a `deb` file to a `tgz` or `rpm`

```
alien --to-tgz filename.deb (or alien -t filename.deb)
alien --to-rpm filename.deb (or alien -r filename.deb)
```

To convert a `rpm` to a `tgz` or `deb`

```
alien --to-tgz filename.rpm (or alien -t filename.rpm)
alien --to-deb filename.rpm (or alien -d filename.rpm)
```

To convert a `slp` to `tgz` or `rpm`

```
alien --to-tgz filename.slp (or alien -t filename.slp)
alien --to-rpm filename.slp (or alien -r filename.slp)
```

To convert a `rpm` or `tgz` to a `slp`

```
alien --to-slp filename.rpm
alien --to-slp filename.tgz
```

Although Alien should be used for applications that install critical system components, it provides more than enough functions to get most packages up and running
on your system.

chapter
30

System Maintenance

Performing system backups •

Performing file system maintenance •

Maximizing disk space •

Performing System Backups

Making backups is the only way to ensure that you can replace files that become accidentally deleted. To get the most bang for your backup buck (if you can't back up everything), identify the most important files on your own system. If you use your Linux machine exclusively as a Web server, your backup requirements are probably a little different than those of someone who tests software. Try to archive the most critical parts of your system on a regular basis. There is little need to back up applications that you loaded from another storage device (CD-ROM, floppy, and so on) unless you have made major modifications to them. If you are supporting a machine with multiple users, you should definitely set up a backup schedule for the /home directory tree.

Compressing and Decompressing Files and Directories

Often you will need to compress files when backing them up. Compression can also reduce the size of files you are emailing or transferring to someone on diskettes. Linux provides several ways to compress files and directories: The gzip (gnu zip) command is generally considered the best of the bunch for most purposes. gzip's alter ego, gunzip, decompresses files compressed by gzip. gzip's basic syntax is as follows:

```
#gzip filename
```

gunzip's syntax is similar:

```
#gunzip filename
```

Using *gzip* and *gunzip* to compress and decompress files

1. First, choose a file to compress:
   ```
   #ls --l frankie.txt
   --rw--r----r-   1 tb   users        1425 Mar 31 09:22 frankie.txt
   ```

2. Compress the file using the gzip command:
   ```
   #gzip frankie.txt
   ```

3. Use ls to check the file again (don't list a filename on the command line). You can see that gzip replaces the file whose filename you provide (frankie.txt in our example) with a compressed version whose name ends in the suffix .gz. The permissions, ownership, and date stamp of the original uncompressed file are retained in the compressed version.
   ```
   #ls --l
   total 1
   --rw--r----r-   1 tb   users        705 Mar 31 09:22 frankie.txt.gz
   ```

4. Use `gunzip` to uncompress the compressed file we just made:

```
#gunzip frankie.txt.gz

#ls -l
total 1
--rw--r----r-    1 tb users        1425 Apr  1 09:22 frankie.txt
```

`gunzip` restores the original filename (removing the `.gz` suffix) and file attributes, removing the compressed file.

`gunzip` can expand files created with other Linux compression utilities, such as the `compress` command. Table 30.1 contains useful command-line options for the `gzip` and `gunzip` commands. You can also use the `info` or `man` command to look at online documentation for `gzip`:

#info gzip

Table 30.1 Commonly Used Command-Line Options for *gzip* and *gunzip*

Option	Mnemonic	Description
h	help	Lists command-line options for `gzip` and `gunzip`
v	verbose	When used with `gzip`, produces a verbose information listing, including the name of the compressed file and the degree of compression (as a percentage of the original file size)
l	list	Lists the original filename(s) of file(s) contained in a compressed file
t	test	Tests to determine the result of a `gzip` or `gunzip` command. Indicates expected results without actually executing the specified command
r	recursive	Recursively descends a directory tree, compressing or uncompressing files that match the filename(s) given on the command line
c	concatenate	Accepts input from the standard input, or places output onto the standard output (allows the use of pipes when generating filenames to be compressed or uncompressed)

SEE ALSO
➤ *To find out how to use* `ls` *to list files and directories, see page 38.*

Compressed Archiving with the *tar* Command

`gzip` does not allow you to easily compress entire directories or directory trees; to compress directories you must also use the `tar` (tape archive) command. `tar` can accept entire file systems as its input, placing all their directories and files into one file, called a tar *file*:

```
#tar -cf tarfile.tar file(s)
```

This command creates (-c) an archive file (f tarfile.tar) containing all the listed files. The file(s) argument can be a directory in a directory tree; tar archives everything beneath that directory (inclusive), maintaining all the directory relationships, including links, permissions, ownership information, and date stamps. To tell tar exactly what type of archiving job to perform, specify one function as the first argument on the command line (see Table 30.2 for a list of tar's major function identifiers).

Table 30.2 *tar's* Major Function Identifiers

Function Identifier	Mnemonic	Action
c	create	Instructs tar to make a new archive, putting the listed files and directories in the tar file you designate.
x	extract	Instructs tar to recreate a set of original files (and directories) using the specified tar archive file.
t	list	Generates a list of the listed files that are stored in the tar file (if no files are listed on the command line, lists all files in tar).
u	update	Updates an existing tar file with the files listed if they are not currently contained in the tar file, or have more recent modification times (m times) than the file(s) already contained in the tar file.
z	gzip	Passes the archive through gzip. Used to automatically compress or uncompress archives without a separate call to gzip or gunzip.
r	append	Adds listed files to the end of an existing tar archive file.

tar command-line options do not require leading dashes

Unlike most Linux commands, the initial arguments on the command line of a tar command do not require leading dashes to set them apart. This is partly because the first argument after the tar command must be one of the major tar functions (c, x, t, u, and so on), so the shell doesn't need an additional cue to determine how to parse the command line.

In addition to using functions to designate the major action it will perform, `tar` accepts dozens of additional options. Listed here are some of the ones most often used:

`I.f filename`	Designates `tar` filename
`2k`	Keeps old files (doesn't overwrite with files being extracted)
`3v`	Verbose (provides information while running)
`4z`	Archives/extracts by using `gzip` compression/decompression
`5M`	Multivolume (indicates an archive that can use several floppy disks or tapes)
`V`	Volume name (stored in `tar` file for reference)

Using *tar* to Archive Directories

tar can archive an entire directory if you use a directory name on the command line:

```
#pwd
/public/sharedfiles/me


#ls -l
total 27
--rwxrwxr--x   1 me       users        22843 Apr  1 20:40 README.txt
--rwxrwxr--x   1 me       me            1519 Mar 15 21:29 iousage
drwxrwxr--x    2 me       users         1024 Jun  8  1996 fileshare
lrwxrwxr--x    2 me       users            8 Dec 12 20:39 thtfil -> thisfile


#tar cf share.tar /public/sharedfiles/me
tar: removing leading / from absolute pathnames in the archive


#ls -l
total 28
--rwxrwxr--x   1 me       users        22843 Apr  1 20:40 README.txt
--rwxrwxr--x   1 me       me            1519 Mar 15 21:29 iousage
drwxrwxr--x    2 me       users         1024 Jun  8  1996 fileshare
--rwxrwxr--x   1 me       users        46058 Apr  1 20:40 share.tar
lrwxrwxr--x    2 me       users            8 Dec 12 20:39 thtfil -> thisfile
```

tar uses relative pathnames; it creates an archive of the `me` directory in the preceding code without referring to the root pathname (the first slash). (That's what the `tar:` ... system message means.) You can place archived directories in other directories without worrying about the archive's original pathnames and parent directories.

You can think of tar as a way to graft a directory branch to another directory tree; you can use one tar file to move an entire set of directories and subdirectories from place to place on your system, or from system to system (many ftp files are tar files).

Moving and Extracting *tar* Files

After you create a tar file, anyone with read and write permissions for the directory containing the file (such as the user notme) needs to add the me directory that was archived earlier to his or her home directory:

```
#pwd
/home/notme

#ls -l
total 53
--rw--rw--r-   1 notme    users      8432 Apr  1 20:40 zipcode.c
--rw--rw--r-   1 notme    users     21519 Mar 14 21:29 stadd.o
drwxrwxr--x   2 notme    users      1024 Dec  4 20:39 docfiles
drwxr-xr-    1 notme    users      1024 Jan 11  1996 perlscripts
drw--r---r-   2 notme    users      1024 Mar 14 21:29 progfiles

#cp /public/sharedfiles/me/share.tar .

#tar xvf share.tar
public/sharedfiles/me/README.txt
public/sharedfiles/me/iousage
...

#ls -l
total 80
--rw--rw--r----   1 notme    users      8432 Apr  1 20:40 zipcode.c
--rw--rw--r----   1 notme    users     21519 Mar 14 21:29 stadd.o
drwxrwxr--x   2 notme    users      1024 Dec  4 20:39 docfiles
drwxr-xr----   1 notme    users      1024 Jan 11  1996 perlscripts
drw--r---r----   2 notme    users      1024 Mar 14 21:29 progfiles
drwxrwxrwx   2 notme    users      1024 Apr  1  1996 public

#ls -l public
drwxrwxr-x   2 notme    users      1024 Aug 17 08:42 me
```

Because the user notme ran the tar extraction command, the extracted directory public (and its subdirectories) are now owned by notme rather than me. The v (verbose) option in the last example provides a listing of relative pathnames for each file `tar` processes (abbreviated for space). Increasing the number of v options listed increases the amount of information `tar` provides (vv lists date stamps and sizes as well as pathnames, such as the `ls -l` command).

Compressing Archive Files with *tar*

`tar` can also serve double duty as an archive compression/expansion utility. When used with the z option, `tar` gzips (or gunzips) the `tar` archive file it creates (or extracts) by using `gzip` compression. To compress our `sharedfiles` tree, use the following:

```
#tar czf meshare.tar.gz me
```

`tar` compresses and archives in one step. If you use the `filename.tar.gz` naming convention for gzipped `tar` files, it helps you keep track of when to use the z option to extract a `tar` file.

SEE ALSO

➤ *For more information about file attributes, see pages 50 and 378.*

➤ *For more information about command-line syntax, see page 20.*

Using *find* to Locate Files for *tar* Backups

Often you must back up certain kinds of files based on their type, owner, creation date, or other file attributes. The `find` command helps you look for those files by using a large number of options.

```
#find pathname(s) to search search rule expression
```

For instance, you can use `find` to look for HTML files like so:

```
#find . -name '*.html' -print
```

Used this way, `find` locates all files in the current directory and any of its subdirectories with filenames ending in .html, and then prints a list of those filenames. (Actually, you would not have to list the . before html to indicate the current directory; `find` automatically searches the current directory if no pathname(s) are listed.)

`find` works like an inspection line in a factory. It passes each filename it finds in the specified path(s) to the first rule in the search rule expression. Each rule in the search processes the file in some way, and then either passes the file to the next rule or excludes the file from the search.

Using *find* to Help with System Maintenance

You can use `find` to search using a number of different rules. When using `find` for system maintenance purposes, often you will need to locate files based on one of three criteria: file ownership, file size, or other file attributes (such as file access time, file type, or file permissions). `find` is equipped to handle most jobs simply. For instance, you can print a list of all files of type `d` (the directories) in `/usr`:

```
#find /usr -type d -print
```

```
#find $HOME -size +5k -print
```

In the preceding example, `find` prints a list of files with sizes larger than 5KB in your home directory. (In `find` test expressions, `+number` represents all values greater than the number, `-number` represents all values less than the number, and a number with no plus or minus attached stands for the value of the number itself.)

Using the `atime` and `fprint` options, you can print a list of man page files that have not been accessed within the last five days in the log file `unhit_man_files.log`.

```
#find /usr/man -atime +5 -fprint unhit_man_files.log
```

`find` can use a version of the `ls` command as an option. The following command prints a list of files on the current device (`-xdev`) belonging to the user `tb` in the `ls -dils` format to the file `all_tb_files.lst`.

```
#find / -xdev -user tb -ls > all_tb_files.lst
```

This last example illustrates a way to use `find` with `tar`. If the user `tb` were taking a sabbatical, you could round up all the files owned by that user and back them up by using the `tar` command.

```
#cd /

#find / -user tb -print
/usr/local/proj1/stadd.o
/usr/local/proj1/stadd.c
/home/tb/docfiles/mk2efs_notes
/home/tb/scripts/perlscripts/hform1
...

#find / -xdev -user tb -fprint all_tb_files.lst

#tar -cvz -T all_tb_files.lst -f all_tb_files.tar.gz
```

The -T option instructs tar to look for the list of files to archive inside a file, instead of on the command line. (When using the -T option with tar, you must separate command-line options with leading dashes.) If you were to delete all the tb files, and needed to reinstall them when tb returned, you would have to extract the all_tb_files.tar.gz archive from the same spot you created it (to ensure that the tar extraction replaced the files in the original spots recorded by the find command).

There are more options available for the find command than for almost any other Linux utility. See Table 30.3 for useful search rules to use with find.

Table 30.3 *find* Command Search Expressions

Expression	Type	Function
-atime/-mtime/-ctime	test	Tests whether file(s) were created before (+n), after (-n), or on (n), where n is an integer representing n number of days before today. (For example, -ctime -5 would find all files changed within the last five days.)
-depth	option	Processes the files in each directory before checking the permissions of the directory itself.
-exec command {} \;	action	Executes *command* for each file passed to it. Braces ({}) used in the command will be replaced with the current file being examined. A semicolon (;) terminates the command string, whereas the backslash (\) is used to escape the ; so it isn't misinterpreted by the shell.
-group groupname	test	Tests whether files are owned by group *groupname*.
-name filename	test	Tests whether filenames passed to it match *filename*.
-nouser	test	Tests for files with no user associated; useful for finding orphaned files that could be archived or deleted.
-ok command {} \;	action	Like exec, except prompts user before executing *command* on each file passed to it.
-path pathname	test	Tests whether the path of the file(s) passed to it matches *pathname*.
-prune	action	Skips directories passed to it (often used with -path, where -path identifies the directory to skip and passes the name to prune).
-regex expression	test	Tests whether the filename(s) passed to it match a regular expression.

continues...

Expression	Type	Function
-size nk	test	Tests whether files passed to it are n KB in size (can use +n or -n for greater or less than n).
-type d	test	Tests whether files are of type d (directories).
-user *username*	test	Tests whether files are owned by user *username*.
-xdev	option	Instructs find to search on the current device only (for example, only on the hard drive).

Locating Files Based on Their Access Times

You've seen how find can locate files based on their access times (for example, the most recent time the file was accessed, or used) in Chapter 3, "Navigating the Linux File System."

```
#find /dev -atime +30 -print
```

This command prints to the screen the device files that haven't been accessed for the past 30 days. You can build a list of files to archive based on their most recent access times. However, it's sometimes necessary to change files' access times to make sure the find command locates them during a search.

To update a file's access times, use the touch command:

```
#touch $HOME/*
```

Using the touch command like this changes the access times of all files in your home directory to the current system time.

You can then use the tar command to select files based on access times when archiving.

```
#ls -l $HOME
total 2
--rwxrwxr--x   1 me       users        22843 Apr  1  9:40 README.txt
--rwxrwxr--x   1 me       me            1519 Apr  1  9:40 iousage
```

```
#tar -cvz -N DATE -f home.tar.gz $HOME
```

The N option tells tar to archive only those files with access times more recent than DATE, where the date is given in the format of the date command.

For more information about the find and tar commands, consult their respective man pages.

SEE ALSO

➤ *For more information about regular expressions, see page 31.*

➤ *For more information about file attributes (date stamps, permissions, and ownership) see page 50 and page 378.*

Using *taper* for Backups

Several versions of Linux include a backup utility developed by Yusuf Nagree called `taper`.

If you do not have the `taper` package installed, you can download the latest version for free from `http://www.omen.net.au/~yusuf/`.

You can run the `taper` utility entirely from the command line, but it is made to use a menuing system. The main piece of information you must supply is the type of backup device you use.

```
#taper -T device type indicator
```

Table 30.4 lists the device types you can use with `taper`, and the device type indicator for each.

Table 30.4 Device Type Options to Use When Starting *taper*

Device Indicator	Mnemonic	Description
z	zftape	Newest floppy drive tape driver, recommended for use if you have the `zftape` device driver
f	ftape	Older floppy drive tape driver, use if the `ftape` version you use is earlier than version 3.0
r	removable	Use when backing up to floppies and other removable devices (such as Zip drives)
s	scsi	Use with SCSI tape drives

`taper` works best with tape drives connected to a floppy disk drive controller. To find out if you have a version of `ftape` more recent than 3.0, you can look in your `/dev` directory. To download a recent version of the new `zftape` driver, point your browser to `ftp://sunsite.unc.edu/pub/Linux/kernel/tapes/zftape-1.06.tar.gz`. Or check out `http://www.math1.rwth-aachen.de/~heine/ftape/` for the latest versions of `ftape` and `zftape`. For more information about the differences between these drivers, see the `taper` documentation in `/usr/doc/taper-6.9a`. You can view it with a pager command such as `less`.

After you have determined which driver to run with taper, you can use the menu system to set up an interactive backup. Figure 30.1 shows the main taper menu.

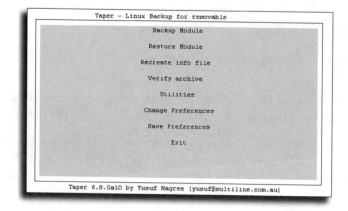

FIGURE 30.1
From the main taper menu, you can archive and restore files as well as change your taper preferences.

Selecting the backup module brings up a three-part selection menu (see Figure 30.2).

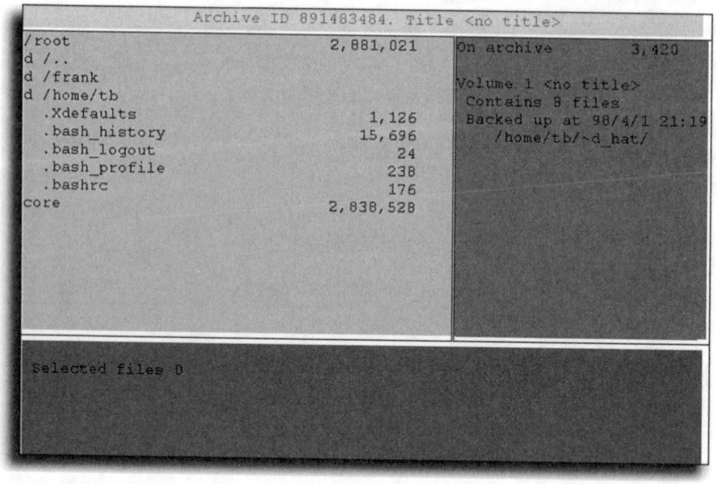

FIGURE 30.2
The taper backup menu lets you examine existing taper archives and select files for a new archive.

To maneuver within the taper menus and screens, you can use arrow, Tab, and other keys (see Figure 30.3).

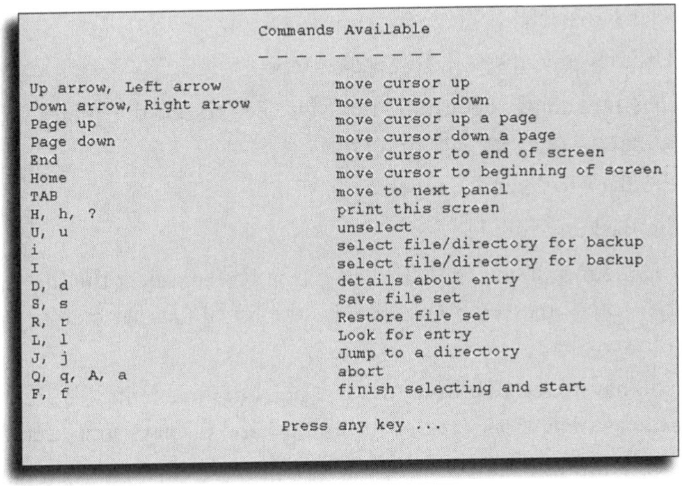

```
                              Commands Available
                              - - - - - - - -

Up arrow, Left arrow              move cursor up
Down arrow, Right arrow           move cursor down
Page up                           move cursor up a page
Page down                         move cursor down a page
End                               move cursor to end of screen
Home                              move cursor to beginning of screen
TAB                               move to next panel
H, h, ?                           print this screen
U, u                              unselect
i                                 select file/directory for backup
I                                 select file/directory for backup
D, d                              details about entry
S, s                              Save file set
R, r                              Restore file set
L, l                              Look for entry
J, j                              Jump to a directory
Q, q, A, a                        abort
F, f                              finish selecting and start

                         Press any key ...
```

FIGURE 30.3
You can use various keys to maneuver in a `taper` menu.

Across the top of the backup module screen is the archive ID number and the title of the archive (you will be asked to enter a title for your backup when you enter this menu). The upper-left portion of the screen lists the files contained in the current directory. You can move to subdirectories by selecting their names using the arrow keys and then pressing Enter (move into the parent directory by selecting the .. item). The upper-right portion of the screen lists current archives created with `taper` on the device you selected when starting `taper`. The bottom portion of the screen lists files that you have selected for the current backup. Select files by using the `i` command. If you select a directory, all the files within that directory are selected; you can unselect files by using the `u` command.

Now that you have some familiarity with the `taper` menu interface, you can use it to make backups. Start with a new, preformatted tape on a floppy tape drive (the process is similar for other storage devices and floppies).

Backing up with *taper*

1. Determine the backup device you want to use and ensure that you have the appropriate device driver (`taper` was developed using a Colorado tape drive, so it works well with those).

2. Start `taper` by using the appropriate command-line instruction (`taper -T z`, `taper -T f`, `taper -T r`, and so on—refer to the previous device selection instructions). After you have started `taper`, you can save this device driver information by using the Preferences menu so you do not have to enter it again.

3. After `taper` has started, enter the Utilities menu.

4. In the Utilities menu, select Test Make Tape.

5. Test Make Tape might determine that you need to run the `mktape` utility; assuming this is a new tape, it's safe to do this now.

6. Select the Back to Main Menu option.

7. Enter the Backup Module.

8. Using the menu system at the top-left of the screen, select the files and the directories to be archived. `taper` displays the list of files selected in the bottom half of the screen.

9. When you have selected all the files you need to include in this archive, press F to start the archive. `taper` creates the archive and displays some details about it.

10. You might want to make a note of the title of the archive to use to label the tape. `taper` records this information in an archive index file for use whenever the archive is used. You can now begin selecting files for another archive, or exit the Backup Module and exit `taper`.

Be careful

Use the Test Make Tape option only on *new* tapes because it will erase data and write some data onto the tape.

If you do not have a preformatted tape, you can use a third-party application in Windows or MS-DOS (for floppies, you can use the Linux utility `fdformat`—see the man page on `fdformat` for details). Some aspects of `taper` differ from `tar`. `taper` uses a proprietary compression utility by default; you can change the compression utility to `gzip` in Preferences menu. Also, `taper` makes incremental backups by default (it only overwrites a file if the archived version is older than the selected file). Likewise, `taper` automatically restores the most recent version of a file if several versions exist in different `taper` archives. Most of these behaviors can be changed using the Preferences menu.

For more information about `taper`, including available drivers (Iomega, for example), refer to the taper documentation (`/usr/doc/taper-6.9a/`).

SEE ALSO

➤ *For more information about the Red Hat package manager (`rpm`) and `kpackage`, see Chapter 29.*

➤ *For more information about setting up peripheral storage devices for use with Linux, see Chapters 7–9.*

Backing Up with Floppy Disks

`taper` allows you to use several kinds of peripherals to back up files. Standard Linux utilities also work with a number of different devices, including SCSI drives and other external hard drives. Often, though, backups use a tape drive or floppies. Floppy disks are convenient for small backups, or at times when you need to store a few files or directories for physical transport to another location.

To use floppy disks as storage devices, you must know the device name your floppy disk drive uses. Usually, this is `/dev/fd0`, but you might need to do some snooping to verify this—one way to snoop is to try the procedures for formatting or mounting floppies (described later in this section) on different device files (`/dev/fd0`, `/dev/fd1`, and so on). Then you must mount a floppy disk (you must have more than one disk handy, so format extras if you need to). You can do a low-level format (similar to the one performed by the MS-DOS command `format`) using the `fdformat` utility to preformat a floppy:

```
#fdformat /dev/fd0H1440
```

> **Use *fdformat* with care**
>
> Using `fdformat` erases all data on the floppy disk. Try mounting and reading from it (using the `mount` and `ls` commands) to make sure it is empty before formatting if you're not sure.

After the floppy disk has been formatted with `fdformat`, you must configure it for the `ext2` file system. The `mkfs` command sets up the parameters for the Linux Second Extended file system:

```
#mkfs -t ext2 /dev/fd0 1440
```

The `1440` indicates that the floppy disk contains 1,440 kilobytes of storage, or 1.44MB.

Finally, we can mount the floppy disk by using the default mount point `/mnt/floppy`.

```
#mount -t ext2 /dev/fd0 /mnt/floppy
```

Be sure to use one mount point per mounted device. Now that you have a mounted floppy disk at your disposal, you can start to back up information onto it:

```
#tar -cvfz /dev/fd0 files
```

The preceding command creates an archive on the device `/dev/fd0`. Note that in this command, you use the name of a device and not the `tarfile.tar` filename structure.

tar recognizes that /dev/fd0 is a device, but allows you to treat the device like an archive file. Usually, when backing up onto floppy disks, you will use the M option with tar to signify that this is a backup with multiple volumes.

```
#tar -cvzMf /dev/fd0 files
```

tar prompts you when you need to change floppy disks. Make sure you mark the disk order number on each floppy used, or you will have problems when you try to restore the archive.

SEE ALSO

➤ *For more information about formatting and mounting devices, see Chapter 9.*

➤ *For more information about the* tar *command, see page 505.*

Backing Up with Removable Drives

If you plan to use removable tape drives connected to your floppy disk controller for backups, you must determine the device file associated with your tape drive. Usually, tape drives are divided into two types: rewindable (represented by the device files /dev/rft0, /dev/rft1, /dev/rft2, and so on) and non-rewindable (represented by the device files /dev/nrft0, /dev/nrft1, /dev/nrft2, and so on). *Rewindable* tape devices rewind the tape automatically after tar finishes writing an archive to the tape, so they are best used when you use a tape for only one archive file. *Non-rewindable* tape devices do not automatically rewind after tar finishes, so you can place several archive files, one after the other, on one tape. If you are using SCSI hardware, the device names use st rather than ft.

Consider the following commands:

```
#tar -cvzf /dev/rft0 /usr/doc
```

When used with a rewindable tape drive, this tar command creates a compressed archive of all the files in /usr/doc installed on your main system. After the command has finished running, the tape rewinds automatically. Running tar again on the same tape overwrites this archive (so label your tapes well). Conversely, with a non-rewindable tape drive, you can put several successive archives on one tape.

```
#tar -cvzf /dev/nrft0 /usr/src
```

This command creates an archive of all the standard source code on the main system. Assuming there is enough space left on the tape, after this command runs you can run another tar command to create a second archive on the tape.

```
#tar -cvzf /dev/nrft0 /usr/lib
```

This command is not the same as using `tar` with the `-A` function to append files to an existing archive. This command creates a second archive, distinct from the first, on the device `/dev/nrft0`. To restore the second archive, you must use the `mt` command to skip over the first archive file on the tape:

```
#mt /dev/nrft0 fsf 1
```

If you use another kind of drive for backups, you can substitute the device file it uses for the previous floppy tape device files. So, if you use a SCSI tape device, for instance, you'd indicate it with the nomenclature `/dev/st0`, as follows:

```
#tar -cvzf /dev/st0 /home
```

Likewise, if you use an Iomega Zip drive on a SCSI port, you would use the `/dev/sda1` drive (`sda1` usually refers to the first SCSI device that is removable, but not a tape):

```
#tar -cvzf /dev/sda1 /home
```

The device you use depends on the device that the kernel supports . To check available devices, you can run `mount` with no arguments:

```
#mount
/dev/hda5 on / type ext2 (rw)
/dev/hda7 on /usr type ext2 (rw)
/dev/fd0 on /mnt/floppy type msdos (rw)
/dev/sda1 on /mnt/zip type ext2 (rw)
```

SEE ALSO

➤ *For more information about formatting and mounting devices, see Chapter 7.*

➤ *For more information about using tape drives and Iomega Zip drives with Linux, see Chapter 8.*

➤ *For more information about the* `tar` *command, see page 505.*

Automating Incremental Backups

You can use the `find` and `tar` commands to automatically back up files that have changed since the last time the entire system was backed up. Backing up the entire system, called a *full backup*, usually involves backing up everything that was created or changed after the initial installation. There is little need to include in a full backup most packages that can be reloaded from the main Linux distribution CD, because these packages exist on separate devices. However, if you have added some utilities via ftp from the Internet, or have lost the original disks that packages came on, you should make sure you have at least one good backup copy.

If you have enough room on tapes, a full backup can be simple:

```
#tar -cvzMf /dev/rft0 /
```

Or, you could be more selective:

```
#tar -cvzMf /dev/rft0 /etc /var /sbin /usr/local /home
```

This command archives many of the files unique to most systems.

Again, if you cannot back up everything, make sure you are backing up everything important.

After you have a full backup, you can begin to take advantage of the tar and find command options to make backups of files that have changed since the last full backup (incremental backups).

To track the date of the last backup, sometimes it makes sense to store it in a file:

```
#ls -l lastarchive.tar | cut -f6-8 > lastarchive.date
```

If you are backing up with tar, the -N option backs up only files with more recent access times than the date provided:

```
#tar -cz -g archlog.txt -N DATE -V 'latest backup' /home
```

The -g option creates a log file archlog.txt, which contains the archive time and a list of the directories archived. -V electronically labels the archive latest backup. The -N option specifies that tar is only to back up files newer than DATE, where the date is entered in the same format as the date command's. So, if you know the date of the last archive, you could use this date to generate an incremental backup. (Actually, this command is a bit redundant. The -g archlog option looks for an existing file named archlog and, using the date recorded from the last backup in this file, instructs tar to archive only files newer than that date. So this command assumes you have not yet created a -g archlog file.)

If you need to archive files that could be anywhere on the system, the find command comes in handy:

```
#find / -atime -1 -print > /home/backuplists/todaysfiles
#tar -cvz -f /dev/rft0 -T /home/backuplists/todaysfiles
```

These commands place an archive of files accessed within the last 24 hours on the tape mounted at /dev/rft0. (Make sure to change the tape each day if you need to store more than one day's backup.)

---

find uses three general kinds of search rules

Find recognizes three basic kinds of rules: tests, actions, and options. *Tests*, such as `name`, run tests on each file they process, and forward only those files that pass the test to the next rule in the search. *Actions*, such as `print`, perform some action on all the files that reach them; they also can pass the file to the next rule in the search. `find` *options* determine how the command runs generally; they don't process individual filenames.

You can use the `crontab` feature to avoid having to run this backup manually:

```
* 3 * * * find / -atime -1 -print > \
 /home/backuplists/todaysfiles; mt -f /dev/rft0 rewind; \
 tar -cvz -f /dev/rft0 -T /home/backuplists/todaysfiles
```

You can also use shell scripts to automate backups. A simple example would be to take the `cron` bash commands in the preceding example and type them into a shell script called `todaysbu`. You could then just add the following to `crontab`:

```
* 3 * * * /home/backupscripts/todaysbu
```

SEE ALSO

➤ *For more information about using dates and* `crontab` *with Linux, see page 395.*
➤ *For more information about using shell scripts to automate tasks, see Chapter 22.*

Performing File System Maintenance

It's good to be in the habit of snooping around your system a little for unnecessary files. Besides keeping space free, it familiarizes you with the layout of your directories, and the way users (including you) are using the system.

Deleting Unnecessary Files

In addition to using `find` to locate files to back up, you can use it to search for files that are no longer needed. After you have found those files, you can delete them from the command line, or use an automated process (`crontab` entry or shell script) to remove them. (Warning: Make sure you back up any files you might *ever* need again before removing them.)

For instance, you can search for files belonging to users who no longer have access to the system, archive them to a tape, and delete the originals (make sure your backup is good):

```
#find / -user tb -print > tbfiles
#tar -cvz -f tbfile.tar.gz -T tbfiles
#find / -user tb -print0 | xargs -r0 rm
```

The last command line makes use of the xargs utility. xargs processes each argument piped to it and runs a command on that argument. The find print0 option separates filenames with a NULL (0) character instead of a newline, in case some files or directories have a newline in their names (unlikely, but better safe than sorry). The -r0 options tell xargs to expect input separated by NULL characters (0), and make sure the command doesn't run if the input is a blank line (r). To remove directories, use the following command:

```
#find / -user tb -print0 | xargs -r0 rmdir
```

For more information about xargs, see its man page.

SEE ALSO

➤ *For more information about shell scripts, see Chapter 22.*
➤ *For more information about using* crontab, *see page 395.*
➤ *For more information about the* rm *and* rmdir *commands, see page 49.*
➤ *For more information about the* tar *command, see page 505.*

Undeleting Files

The only way to undelete files with Linux is to use a backup system such as tar or taper. There is no Recycle Bin or Trash icon where deleted files are kept indefinitely. To examine archives for a lost file, use the tar command

```
#tar -tvz -f monthlybackup.tar.gz lostfile(s)
```

tar lists any files in the monthly backup matching lostfile(s). To restore lost files, create a lost file directory and extract the designated files there (rather than trying to place them back in their original habitat immediately). Sometimes directory permissions or pathnames might have changed, and occasionally someone will have created a new file in the same place, with the same name, as the one you are restoring. Use the following commands:

```
#cd /home/me/restored_lostfiles
#tar -xvz -f monthlybackup.tar.gz lostfile(s)
```

Then you can move the files back to the original places after you have verified that no conflicts or problems with file attributes exist.

SEE ALSO

➤ *For more information about the* tar *command, see page 505.*

Maximizing Disk Space

Generally, it's best not to allow free space on your hard drive to fall below 25–30 percent of your hard drive's total capacity. The following sections examine ways to keep an eye on disk space, and (more importantly) ways to reclaim parts of a shrinking hard disk pie.

Performing System Cleanups

While the kernel and other Linux processes run, they generate a number of house-keeping files. Often, Linux automatically disposes of these files but sometimes you must take matters into your own hands. For instance, if you are creating your own logs, use a redirect command such as >> (append); the files used by that redirect will continue to grow until removed.

Linux provides two commands to check on disk usage, df and du, described in the following two command examples:

```
[jray@pointy jray]$ df -h
Filesystem          Size  Used Avail Use% Mounted on
/dev/sda1           1.8G  1.2G  512M  71% /
/dev/sdb            3.9G  2.9G  805M  79% /mnt/storage
```

df (disk free space) reports on the total number of blocks used and free on all mounted partitions. The -h option produces a nice human-readable format. It's good for getting an overall snapshot of the space available on the entire system. Its compatriot, du, allows you to examine individual files and directories for space usage, a little like ls with the -l option:

```
[root@pointy sbin]# du -h
50k     ./CommuniGate/WebAdmin/Accounts
34k     ./CommuniGate/WebAdmin/Monitors
47k     ./CommuniGate/WebAdmin/Settings
200k    ./CommuniGate/WebAdmin
1.0M    ./CommuniGate/WebGuide
```

```
39k     ./CommuniGate/Migration
47k     ./CommuniGate/WebUser/Account
7.0k    ./CommuniGate/WebUser/Lists
98k     ./CommuniGate/WebUser
3.0M    ./CommuniGate
3.8M    .
```

Once again, the -h option produces a nicely formatted result. You can also use -s to provide a usage summary for an individual directory.

You can use these commands in shell scripts to automate monitoring of system space usage.

You can also use the find command with the size (-s) option to generate lists of large files that bear examining:

```
#find -size +1000k -print > /home/me/filemaint/bigfilelist
```

This command prints a list of files larger than 1MB (1,000KB) in the designated log file. You can also run this command using the crontab feature to receive email listing those files:

```
* 8 * * Mon find -size +1000k -print
```

This command checks for large files every Monday at 8:00 a.m. (a good way to enjoy light entertainment on Monday mornings is to see some of the gargantuan files created over the last week).

Aside from looking for files created by users, there are several places that you can check for files that need to be cleaned up. The best place to start is in the /etc/syslog.conf file. This file maintains a listing of all the logs used by the syslogd daemon, a system logger started when you boot Linux:

```
#cat /etc/syslog.conf
# Log all kernel messages to the console.
# Logging much else clutters up the screen.
kern.*                                  /dev/console
# Log anything (except mail) of level info or higher.
# Don't log private authentication messages!
*.info;mail.none;authpriv.none          /var/log/messages
# The authpriv file has restricted access.
authpriv.*                              /var/log/secure
# Log all the mail messages in one place.
mail.*                                  /var/log/maillog
```

```
# Everybody gets emergency messages, plus log them on another # machine.
*.emerg                                                     *
# Save mail and news errors of level err and higher in a
# special file.
uucp,news.crit                                    /var/log/spooler
```

In this file, the lines starting with # signs are comments; the other lines instruct the syslog daemon how to handle log messages. The Linux system logs a variety of messages to help with everything from lost mail to system crashes. Almost every message contains a time, machine name, and the name of the program that generated it. The syslog daemon also categorizes messages by order of importance, ranging from simple system debugging and info messages to high-priority critical and emergency (emerg) messages.

In addition to being routed by severity, messages are earmarked based on the facility (cron, mail, and so on) associated with them. So, as you can see, mail log messages are handled differently than kernel (kern) messages. Some of these logs can be good places to look if you're having problems with a particular feature of Linux (such as mail).

You can see how, if the system were left up for some time with no other housecleaning done, some of the files might get large. Almost all these syslogd logs are stored in /var/log, so this is a good place to check for files experiencing runaway growth:

```
#find /var/log -size +250k -print
```

It's also worth becoming a little familiar with the Linux File System Standard to help identify other likely places to clean. Two candidates are the tmp directories: /tmp and /var/tmp. These directories are used as dumping grounds by various applications and utilities, and if the system isn't rebooted periodically, they too can become larger than you'd like:

```
#ls /var/tmp
taper00291oaa
taper00291paa
taper00420caa
taper00420daa
taper01047caa
taper01047daa
```

The /var/tmp file contains a set of taper-related files. If you're not sure whether taper still needs these (it probably doesn't), move them to another directory and run a taper backup and/or restore. Assuming taper runs satisfactorily, it should be safe to remove these files.

> **The Filesystem Hierarchy Standard describes the general layout of most Linux systems**
>
> For more information about the standard configuration of most Linux file systems, you can review the Filesystem Hierarchy Standard (often abbreviated FHS) at `http://www.pathname.com/fhs/`.

SEE ALSO

➤ *For more information about the* `crontab` *utility, see page 395.*

➤ *For more information about Linux kernel management, see Chapter 31.*

➤ *For more information about using the Linux* `mail` *utility, see page 269.*

➤ *For information about Linux system daemons, see Chapter 27.*

Compressing Unused Documents and Directories

By knowing where the bodies are buried on your system, you can often find a way to restore underused space. For instance, perhaps you are engaged in a project to code a sequel to Doom: Doom B. Unfortunately, things didn't work out with the licensing, and you're ready to put Doom B on the back burner. The following command would help you move along:

```
#tar -cvz -f /dev/rft0 /projects/DoomB /home/lib/DoomB /usr/local/
➥DoomB_graphics
```

This last directory, `/usr/local/DoomB_graphics`, contains graphics, which usually don't compress well. However, they are often not used by many users, and can sometimes be archived until needed.

chapter

31

Managing the Kernel

Adding a module to the kernel
configuration •

Editing the Linux kernel
configuration files •

Managing modules •

Managing processes •

Recompiling the kernel •

The *kernel* is the core component of every operating system. The performance of the kernel determines the most fundamental properties of the operating system, as it is an application's gateway to the computer hardware. Modern kernels provide *pre-emptive multitasking* capability, which allows multiple programs to operate seemingly at the same time. This is physically impossible with only one system processor, but the kernel schedules the processes in such a way that they seem to be running concurrently.

Although the Linux kernel is a complicated piece of software, it is one of the most simple 32-bit kernel designs in common use. Linux has always been on the leading edge of feature support, as well as performance—a truly rare combination. The simplicity of the kernel also increases the system's reliability, which is another of Linux's hallmarks.

The Linux kernel requires very little maintenance after it is set up to run correctly. The process of getting it that way, however, is what many newcomers to Linux have complained about.

Modern Linux distributions are almost completely configurable at run-time, with few reboots required. This means that networking, sound cards, file systems, and even device support can be dynamically reconfigured, added, and removed from the system as necessary to facilitate almost any configuration.

Adding a Module to the Kernel Configuration

Only SCSI host and ethernet device modules need to be added to the kernel configuration. Most of these devices benefit from command-line arguments, and using `kernelcfg` is a good way to keep things consistent and reduce the amount of searching the driver has to do to find your particular hardware.

Booting from a SCSI device

If your system is booting from a SCSI device, the Linux kernel must load the SCSI device driver module before `kerneld` is even running. This is achieved by using an initial ramdisk, from which the driver is loaded. By convention, this SCSI adapter is still configured for `kerneld`, but in reality it has no effect because the driver is vital to system operation.

1. Log on as root and start X Window.

2. From the Control Panel, select Kernel Daemon Configuration. You might have to start the Control Panel application yourself before doing this. Open an X Terminal window and enter `control-panel &` to open the Control Panel, shown in Figure 31.1.

FIGURE 31.1
Clicking the topmost icon in the Control Panel starts the `kernel` Daemon Configuration applet.

3. Click the topmost icon in the Control Panel to open the Kernel Configurator applet, shown in Figure 31.2. Click the Add button.

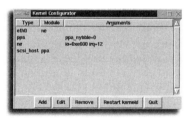

FIGURE 31.2
This is how the Kernel Configurator applet looks on the author's system.

4. From the dialog box shown in Figure 31.3, choose the module type that you want to add (click the Module Types button to get a list of them). The most common additions are ethernet devices (`eth`) and SCSI host adapters (`scsi_hostadapter`). Occasionally, a proprietary-interface CD-ROM must be configured (`cdrom`). The remainder of the additions deal with Token-Ring networks, parallel-port networking, and other more advanced configuration topics.

FIGURE 31.3
Click the module type you want to add to your system's configuration.

For this example, configure `kerneld` to automatically load and unload the device driver for our parallel port Zip drive. Choose `scsi_hostadapter`, and then click OK.

5. The Kernel Configurator now requires the exact module name. In this example, it is `ppa`. Click the Which Module? button in the Define Module dialog box (shown in Figure 31.4) to find the module you want. Click OK to proceed.

FIGURE 31.4
In this case, the ppa module was selected.

6. Now comes the module-specific part. Most modules accept a number of arguments, such as device addresses and interrupt numbers. These depend on the device, and most device drivers are able to autodetect the device parameters. Autodetection of device parameters is not fool-proof, however, and can cause your machine to hang, crash, or do other undesirable things. Fortunately, the Kernel Configurator seems to know about the parameters a particular module can take. Click Done when you're satisfied that everything is set up correctly.

Figure 31.5 shows the options available for the `ppa` parallel port Zip drive.

FIGURE 31.5
Entering the module options for the ppa module.

7. To get `kerneld` to recognize the changes to the configuration, click the Restart `kerneld` button.

Editing the Linux Kernel Configuration Files

`kerneld`, `kmod`, and other programs can do a lot more for you when they are configured by hand. Granted, this is not as nice as a graphical configuration program, but Linux's roots (in fact, UNIX's roots) are in text mode, and these systems for the most part have been run by hackers (the good ones, that is) who do not care too much for glitzy configuration tools when `vi` will do.

Finding information on module parameters

Module documentation has always been something of a weak point in Linux. The most up-to-date information is always included in the kernel, but some repositories on the Internet are also starting to keep this information. (A good place to start looking is the Linux Documentation Project, at `http://www.linuxdoc.org/`.) The problem with the information included with the kernel source itself is that it is scattered in all the directories in various Readme files, and for some modules the only way to find out what the parameters are called is to read the source code for the module.

That being said, later revisions of the 2.2 Linux kernel sport both text-based menus and point-and-click X compile-time configuration tools in addition to the obtuse step-by-step configuration method. Recompiles are now rarely required for systems running production kernels. Only kernel updates themselves require compilation of the kernel for your system. If you're really allergic to compiling and installing kernels, a number of packages can be found that can install a later kernel for you.

The main file for kernel module configuration is `/etc/conf.modules`. `kerneld` and the supporting programs know about most modules that ship with the stock Linux kernel, and attempt to take care of these automatically. The only ones that `kerneld` needs help with are network, SCSI, and CD-ROM devices. The reason for this is pretty simple—autodetection of hardware is not something that should have to happen on a running system if it can be avoided, because the PC platform is just far too complex for things to be 100% reliable in this regard.

Other modules take other parameters

Other modules, such as networking, ask for IRQ and I/O address information.

`kerneld` comes preconfigured for the majority of modules that now come with Linux. To find out about which modules `kerneld` is currently aware of, run the following command:

```
/sbin/modprobe -c | grep -v '^path' | less
```

This command gives you a listing of what the `/etc/conf.modules` file would look like if `kerneld` knew nothing about the modules on your system. Fortunately this is not the case, but it is handy to be able to see how `kerneld` actually sees the world. `kerneld` keeps some configuration information elsewhere on your system to allow it to know about the modules it listed for you, and to provide the basic functionality to keep your system running. The `modprobe` command is a tool that can be used to manually manage modules, and is documented in detail later in this chapter. As far as the preceding command goes, the call to `grep` just filters out all the extraneous information such as the actual paths of the module files, which are irrelevant to the current discussion.

Configuring Your Sound Card

As mentioned before, the 2.x Linux kernel is almost entirely modular. Chances are that there is a module already compiled for your sound card, and that all you need to do is add the appropriate line to your module's configuration file to point the system to the right file. Although it's possible to load and unload sound modules on-the-fly, I don't recommended it because some sound card drivers need to allocate contiguous areas of memory for buffering. A contiguous piece of memory space is one in which the storage space to be used is not fragmented. At boot-up, this is easy, but it becomes increasingly difficult the longer the system has been running.

Determining the device driver module for your sound card

Determining what device driver module supports your sound card can take quite a bit of time because there is a lot of documentation to wade through for some of the weirder configurations. The Creative Labs' ubiquitous SoundBlaster series is well supported, and can even be made to work without recompiling the kernel. Even the cheaper Opti and Crystal audio chipsets can be made to work with some effort, but these are the cards in which it's best to combine all the drivers you need into one module.

With the advent of Plug and Play PC hardware (most affectionately known by most PC support techs as *Plug and Pray*), things can get complicated with configuring sound cards at times, and the only advice I can give is *be patient*. Eventually it will work if the hardware is directly supported. Asking questions on Usenet newsgroups can be especially enlightening if you're absolutely stuck. In some cases, it's best to recompile the kernel and collect the sound drivers you need into one module rather than a whole mess of them. I am trying to spare you the hours of fighting with the sound system and detail a way to get only the drivers you need and the base sound functionality into one module instead of three or four. I detail this later in the section "Using `make config`."

Configuring your sound card

1. Determine what device driver module supports your sound board. The best place to start looking for information is in the HOWTOs of the Linux Documentation Project. The most up-to-date copies are kept at `http://www.linuxdoc.org/`, but relatively current copies of these documents are usually included with CD-ROM distributions.

2. Determine the device addresses for your audio card. If you have a manually jumpered card, just check the jumpers for the I/O port and IRQ. If not, the easiest way to do this on a dual-boot Windows 95/Linux machine is to look up the audio card in the device manager to get the interrupt and I/O addresses. Barring that, it is possible to configure Plug and Play devices as discussed in the next section.

3. Using your favorite text editor, edit the `/etc/conf.modules` file. Make sure you have a backup of this file somewhere so you can restore it in case things go wrong. My `/etc/conf.modules` looks like this:

```
alias eth0 ne
options ne io=0xe000 irq=12
alias scsi_hostadapter ppa
options ppa ppa_nybble=0
alias sound sb
```

Using *sndconfig* to configure SoundBlaster cards

If you have a SoundBlaster, SoundBlaster Pro, SoundBlaster 16, 16 Pnp, AWE 32, or AWE 64 sound card, you can use `/usr/sbin/sndconfig` on Red Hat systems to configure Plug and Play and the sound modules for you. Although these are the only cards `sndconfig` officially supports, you can use `sndconfig` to gain insight into how sound configuration works by looking over the output files (that is, the changes to `/etc/conf.modules` and `/etc/isapnp.conf` files). If all this works for you and your SoundBlaster card, you can stop reading this section right now…

The key element here is the line `alias sound sb`, which tells the system that the sound hardware uses the `sb` (SoundBlaster) module. In this case, the `init` scripts included with Linux look for the sound alias in the `/etc/conf.modules` file and, if they find it, load the sound modules. In this case, the defaults work fine.

The modules attempt to find the sound card, and in the case of common hardware, everything will work just fine.

4. If you (or the sound card's configuration program) have set the configuration to non-default settings, you might need to specify these when adding your sound card. Generally, the I/O address, IRQ(s), and DMA channels must be specified. The following example tells the SoundBlaster driver to look for the card at the factory default values:

```
alias sound sb
options sound ioaddr=220 irq=5 dma=1,5
```

This tells the driver to look for the SoundBlaster card at I/O address 220, interrupt 5, and using DMA channels 1 and 5. For 8-bit SoundBlaster and SoundBlaster Pros, only one 8-bit DMA channel is required.

Plug and Play Devices

ISA Plug and Play hardware is becoming more and more common. Although it is a common myth that only Windows 95 supports Plug and Play devices, PCI devices are inherently Plug and Play, and are managed (for the most part) by your PC BIOS with little operating system intervention. ISA Plug and Play is another matter altogether because the ISA bus predates the Plug and Play standard by more than a few years. Most people mean *ISA Plug and Play* when they utter the words *Plug and Play*.

Linux can be made to work with ISA Plug and Play devices. The first tool that can be used to make Plug and Play devices work with Linux is your system's BIOS. Most PC BIOSes have a setting to indicate whether a Plug and Play operating system is installed. Changing the setting to No often causes the BIOS to activate all ISA Plug and Play devices before booting the system. This means that, for the most part, these devices act as regular jumpered devices.

Some BIOSes, however, either do not have this capability or don't support the correct Plug and Play specification. There are two specifications: the Intel one, and the Microsoft one. Each is somewhat compatible with the other, but more so in theory than in practice. If this is the case for you, all is not lost.

The definitive ISA Plug-n-Play toolset is located at `http://www.roestock.demon.co.uk/isapnptools/`. If you have ISA PnP devices, be sure to check out the Web site for extensive information on configuring your system.

Managing Modules

Most modules on your system are managed by `kerneld`, but there are times during which manual intervention is required. One limitation is having multiple SCSI adapters of different types in the system. The main SCSI adapter is in the `conf.modules`' `scsi_hostadapter` alias, but because `kerneld` allows only one SCSI setting in the `conf.modules` file, you have a problem. The answer is not overly complicated—the additional SCSI adapter must be managed manually. This is not as big a deal as it seems because the SCSI driver can be loaded with one command and then left in memory. In most cases, this is a parallel port SCSI device anyway, such as a Zip drive.

Other circumstances can occur where it is more convenient to manage modules manually. Sound driver modules should be tested by manually loading and unloading them, rather than immediately configuring them into the `/etc/modules.conf` file.

Installing Modules

To load a module manually from the command line, log on as root and issue the following command:

```
/sbin/modprobe <module-name>
```

In this case, `<module-name>` is the name of the module you want to install (for instance, use `ppa` to install the Zip driver module). `modprobe` reads its configuration from `/etc/conf.modules` as well, and it accepts aliases as well as real module names on the command line.

Listing Loaded Modules

Listing loaded modules is fairly easy; you simply issue the following command:

```
/sbin/lsmod
```

If you're logged on as root

If you have logged on as root rather than having **su**'d from a user account, you can leave out the **/sbin** at the beginning of the command.

Output of the program on my system looks like this:

```
[root@jansmachine jwalter]# /sbin/lsmod
Module    Pages    Used by
ppa    1    1 (autoclean)
sd_mod    4    1 (autoclean)
scsi_mod    7        [ppa sd_mod] 2 (autoclean)
vfat    3    1 (autoclean)
fat    6        [vfat]1 (autoclean)
ne    2    1 (autoclean)
8390    2        ?    0 (autoclean)
sound    19    0
```

The entries followed by (autoclean) are modules managed by kerneld. Note that the sound module is not followed by this designation, even though it is listed in the /etc/conf.modules file. This is because the module is actually loaded from an init script when the system boots.

Creating Module Dependencies

In many cases, loadable modules depend on one another to work—for example, the SCSI CD-ROM driver requires that a SCSI adapter driver be loaded before the CD-ROM driver is loaded, so it can actually access the CD device. This is a critical function of the system, and the system must keep detailed information on which module requires another module to be loaded first. There is another advantage to having interdependent modules in a system—common functionality can be built into one module, and provide this functionality to other, more specific modules. Both the SCSI and sound module systems work this way, as do some file system driver modules. For instance, the Windows 95 long-filename system, vfat, is essentially a modified version of the standard DOS file system. Thus it makes sense for the vfat module to use the functionality found in the msdos file system module for most of it functions. The benefit here is that the new module can take advantage of extremely well-tested, dependable code, and if a standard (non-vfat) msdos file system is mounted, there is no code being loaded twice.

The system automatically creates the module dependencies at boot-time. Under certain circumstances, it is convenient, or even necessary, to update the dependency information. It is usually done when installing modules that are not part of the standard kernel distribution, such as the latest versions of ftape, the module that provides access to QIC tape drives. You also want to run module dependencies if you have changed your modules.conf to include additional directories where modules are kept. This prevents surprises if there are errors or problems with the modules in the directories that have been added and the system is rebooted, because you'll see any error messages while the system is still in a state at which these problems can be fixed.

To have the system generate new module dependencies, log on as root and issue the following command:

```
/sbin/depmod -a
```

The system searches the standard module directory trees and generates dependencies for every module it finds.

If you want to keep certain modules in directories outside the standard module directory tree /lib/modules/<kernel-version>, where <kernel-version> is the current version of the Linux kernel), you must add the following to the top of your modules.conf file and restart kerneld:

```
keep
path=<path name>
```

Again, <path name> points to the directory where the additional modules are kept. The keep directive tells the module utilities to *append* the directory name to the module paths. If this directory is not there, the module path will be *replaced*, which most likely is not what you want.

Enabling Modules at Boot Time

The module management utilities can be configured to load entire directories of modules at boot time. This is not the same as using initrd to get the kernel to pre-load modules. initrd loads modules into a device that can be mounted and used before the kernel starts. The method discussed here allows modules to be loaded from the standard file at boot.

> **In case you forget...**
> The kernel must be able to read the hard disk to load modules at boot time, which means that this is *not* the place to put entries for the SCSI adapter drivers that your system boots from because by the time the kernel has booted, the drivers must already be loaded and initialized for Linux to read the hard disk. These SCSI drivers that allow your system to boot are loaded from the *initial ramdisk*.

This process is a viable alternative to listing individual modules to be loaded at boot time in init scripts, or to letting kerneld automatically load and unload them.

Loading a module at boot time by using *modules.conf*

1. Create a directory in which these modules should be kept. Use something like `/lib/modules/<kernel version>/boot` to keep the modules with the kernel version they were compiled for, and also within the directory tree where the rest of the world expects to see modules.

2. Copy the modules you need to load at boot time to the directory.

3. Make sure the first line of `/etc/conf.modules` is the directive `keep`. You don't want your module utilities thinking that this is the *only* thing you want them to do.

4. Add the line `path[boot]=/lib/modules/'uname -r'/boot` as the next line of `/etc/conf.modules`. If you want to make sure that you have typed this correctly before saving your changes, execute the command `echo /lib/modules/'uname -r'/boot` on another virtual terminal or `xterm`. The output should have your current kernel version in place of the `'uname -r'`.

5. Restart `kerneld`. There are lots of ways to do this, but the command `/etc/rc.d/init.d/kerneld restart` works adequately.

Managing Processes

As introduced in Chapter 27, "Managing Daemons," the Linux process model places significant importance on the ideas of process ownership and parent processes. Managing all the programs that run on a Linux system is a task that requires constant attention from the system administrator. The "mother of all processes" is called `init`, which is part of the kernel, and this process *spawns* all other processes, usually via the `inittab` file entries and the `init` scripts that define the system run levels.

Because Linux is a multiuser operating system, its processes also have other information attached to them. The user ID and the group ID, as well as a priority setting, are part of the process. You see, the process has all the rights of the user that started the process on the system. This is an important concept: The process is what prevents a user's programs from overwriting another user's home directory or reading his email. The process also makes it dangerous to run programs, especially unattended *daemon* programs, on the system as root because the program can read from and write to any file and all networks.

Rights, as specified by user and group IDs, are *inherited* by all processes spawned by any other process. For example, when a user logs on, the shell that is started to process the user commands, usually `bash`, has the same user ID as the user who has logged on, and so any process that the shell starts (such as `ls`, `pine`, and so on) has the same settings as well. When a process's parent process finishes before the child process does, the child process is *orphaned*. In this case, `init` takes over as the parent process. If the user is no longer on the system and the process has not been flagged to continue running after the user logs off, using the command `nohup` (meaning "no hang-up," or "ignore hangup signals that are sent to the process"), the process will be terminated because it is orphaned.

Because every process must have a parent, and many programs use multiple processes to accomplish their tasks, child programs are frequently created in order to help their parents complete a task. It is the parent's responsibility to make sure that the child processes are terminated appropriately when finished with their task (they aren't the friendliest of parents) by accepting the child's exit code. If a child process is not disposed of properly, it becomes what is considered a *zombie* process. Zombie processes can fill up your process table and be a bit of a nuisance, necessitating a reboot in some cases. The children will be killed by `init` if the parent no longer exists.

Using the */proc* Directory Information

The `/proc` directory tree is a special virtual directory structure that is a window on the running Linux kernel. This structure contains files and directories with all sorts of information that the kernel collects, and is useful for troubleshooting the system or learning about how it works. Utilities can use the information in `/proc` to provide statistics to the user.

Some files in `/proc` are security sensitive—in particular, the file `/proc/kcore` is essentially a file pointing to all the system's memory, and as such can contain passwords or other information that others should not see. As a result, this file and any other files that contain sensitive information have the appropriate permissions set on them to prevent this sort of abuse. Table 31.1 covers a few files of interest in the `/proc` directory.

Table 31.1 A Few Files of Interest in the */proc* Directory

File	Description
cpuinfo	Contains information about the processor(s) in the system, including the capabilities and bugs that the Linux kernel has detected. For example, many Intel processors contain the F0 0F bug that can cause the system to completely freeze when certain machine instructions are executed. Current Linux kernels can detect this and take appropriate measures to minimize the impact of these problems with the system processor. Other processor problems include the Pentium floating point math bug, but the kernel also accounts for differences in how floating point coprocessors and halt instructions are handled.
version	Contains the kernel version number, the system name, and the time and date that the kernel was compiled.
pci	Contains information about the devices on the system's PCI bus, as well as the detected capabilities of the hardware that's on the bus.
interrupts	Contains a count of all interrupts the system has processed, and the device that they are attached to.

The majority of these files are used by Linux developers and administrators to debug their systems.

Viewing the System Load Average

The load on a system in the UNIX world is measured by using a number called the *load average*. This number is based on the number of processes waiting to run at a given time. The higher the load average, the less CPU time each process is getting.

The best command for viewing the system load average is uptime. The output of this command also reveals how long the system has been up, along with the load average over the last 1, 5, and 15 minutes and number of users logged on. If you'd rather gather all this information yourself, it's in /proc/loadavg—the first three numbers are the load average.

Viewing Processes with the *top* Command

top is a dynamic process-viewing utility. It essentially combines the output of several other utilities in a compact and relatively easy-to-read format. top provides the means to sort processes by the percentage of processor time they use, the memory they use, or the total amount of time they have run on the system.

To start top, simply type `top` from a command prompt. A screen comes up showing you the memory allocated, the system-uptime and load averages, and a list of processes sorted by the amount of CPU time they are using.

top's commands are pretty simple, and are summarized in Table 31.2.

CPU time versus how long a process has been running

CPU time for a process is a reasonable estimate of how long a process has run on the processor. This is different from how long the program has been running, from a human perspective, because there are a lot of other programs running at the same time. Time used gives an estimate on how far along the process would be if it had been the only thing running on the system.

Case sensitivity with *top*

top's commands are case sensitive!

Table 31.2 Command Summary for the *top* Utility

Command	Usage
h	Help. This brings up a detailed help screen.
M	Sorts processes by memory used in descending order. Use this to find the program that is using the most memory on your system.
S	Changes top's statistics to include the amount of time all its children have used in the CPU time display.
T	Sorts by the amount of processor time the process has used in descending order, either cumulative or since the last refresh of the top screen.
P	Sorts the display by the percentage CPU time a process has had, in descending order, since the last time the top display refreshed itself.
r	Re-nices a process. The nice value of a process is the priority the process has in the system, ranging from 19 to –20. The lower the nice value, the higher the process's priority in the system. Only processes owned by root can have negative nice values. You must be the owner of the process or logged on as root to change its nice value.
k	Kills a process. This sends the appropriate signal to a process to indicate that it should finish processing and exit. top enables you to send different signals to a process—it prompts you for the one to send. Normally, the TERM signal (15) works fine to terminate a process. Processes that are hung, or those that ignore the TERM signal, however, might need some stronger persuasion to terminate, such as the KILL signal (9). This signal makes Linux unconditionally terminate the process.

Viewing Processes with the *ps* Command

ps is the UNIX standard utility used to manage processes on a system. This utility provides pretty much the same functionality as top, but is command-line driven rather than providing an interactive interface.

The ps command alone produces a list of all processes owned by the current user, along with the process ID, the terminal the process is running on, the process status, the CPU time used, and the command line and name of the process itself.

At its most basic, the output of ps looks like this:

```
[jwalter@irksome jwalter]$ ps
  PID TTY STAT   TIME COMMAND
 1296  p1 S     0:00 -bash
 1310  p1 R     0:00 ps
[jwalter@irksome jwalter]$
```

I own only two processes in this session: bash (my shell) and ps (the program that produced this data). The STAT column tells me what the processes are currently up to—whether the program is running (R), sleeping (S), stopped (T), or zombie (Z).

ps Command-Line Parameters

The ps utility accepts command-line parameters without requiring a hyphen, like so:

```
ps <options>
```

ps command-line options are discussed in Table 31.3.

Table 31.3 *ps* command-line options

Option	Effect
a	Lists all processes, even those not owned by the user running ps.
x	Lists processes that don't have a controlling terminal (daemon programs and so on).
u	Prints user ID and memory usage information. This looks remarkably like the process list for top.
j	Prints job information. This lists the process user and group IDs in numerical format, along with the parent process IDs.
f	Prints process information in a tree format showing parent processes and their relations.
l	Display a long listing. This is extremely useful if the output is cut off at the end of lines.
t	Prints only process attached to the terminal name that immediately follows. The preceding tty is assumed, so ps tS1 would list all processes with ttyS1 as the owning terminal.

Of course, there are plenty of other options listed in the man pages for ps. The ones in Table 31.3 are simply the ones that systems administrators use the most often.

Using the *kill* and *killall* Commands and Process IDs

The kill utility is used to send signals to processes. One of the uses, as the name of the utility suggests, is for terminating or removing unwanted processes from the system. kill can also send other signals to processes. For instance, the HUP signal by convention causes most daemon programs to re-read their initialization files.

Another noteworthy point is that most shells, such as bash, contain their own built-in kill utilities. On some shells, this can be quite different than the kill that's described here, and you'd do well to check your shell's documentation to see how that behaves. In this section, you learn about bash's kill behavior.

> **Confusing signal names**
>
> Signal names such as **HUP** and **KILL** are often referred to as **SIGHUP** and **SIGKILL**. Either way of writing them is usually valid, but some utilities might accept only one or the other.

The bash shell is capable of getting a process ID for you, provided the process is running in the background of that session. For other processes, you must use the ps utility to get the process ID. You can kill only processes that your user ID owns—unless, of course, you are logged on as root.

This syntax of the kill command is as follows:

```
kill -<signal> <process id>
```

To print a list of signals and their numbers, execute the following command:

```
kill -l
```

The default signal that kill sends is TERM signal.

Killing a process

1. Obtain the process ID by running ps. If the list is too long, and if you know the process name, try piping the output to the grep utility to find the word for you.

2. With the process ID handy, type the command kill <PID>, where <PID> is the process ID number. The command prompt returns. If bash complains about there being no such process, you have the wrong number, or the process has already terminated.

3. After the next command is executed, bash should produce a message such as the following:

```
[1]+  Terminated              find / -name what
```

If it does not produce such a message, the process is not responding to TERM signals. In this example, the program find was terminated.

4. If bash does not issue that message, and another look using ps shows that the process is still merrily gobbling up your CPU time, you'll need to do something more drastic. First make sure that the program is not doing some sort of shutdown processing that needs to be completed, and then issue the following command to kill the process:

```
kill -9 <PID>
```

Getting impatient when sending signals to programs

Some programs need to do some work before shutting down, such as saving open files. Be sure to give the program enough time to do this, or data loss can occur.

This is a signal that a program cannot ignore, so the process is terminated even if it does not want to be. After the next command (or just after pressing Enter if you have nothing else to do), bash should print the following message to tell you that the program has been killed:

```
[1]+  Killed                  find / -name what
```

If you're running a recent version of Linux, there's a good chance that you have a variant of the kill command on your system called killall. The killall command lets you kill processes by their name, rather than the process ID. This is extremely convenient if you don't want to search for a particular process. You use killall exactly the same as kill, except you substitute a process's name in place of the process ID. For example, if you want to kill the httpd processes on your system with the TERM signal (9), all you'd need to do is

```
killall -9 httpd
```

Of course, you'd have to be root in order to do this. Not every user can kill any process on the system.

Recompiling the Kernel

Every once in a while, it is worthwhile to see whether a new kernel for Linux has been released. Usually new kernels provide fixes for problems that people have experienced, or provide performance improvements (usually both). The new kernels can also contain more device drivers. This section discusses how to obtain, compile, and install a new kernel on your Linux system.

The official repository for Linux kernels is the FTP site `ftp://ftp.kernel.org/pub/linux/kernel/`. The Linux installation program might have placed the source code to your current kernel in the `/usr/src/linux` directory on your hard disk. This might be a symbolic link to the actual source directory.

The disclaimer

The process of compiling and installing kernels is not for the technically faint-of-heart: Mistakes here could leave your system in an unbootable state, or worse, could damage your hardware or disk contents. You have been warned.

Installing the New Kernel Source

After you have downloaded the kernel source, you must decompress it and extract the directories within. You must be logged on as root, as well, or at least have full permissions to the `/usr/src` directory. This assumes that you have downloaded the kernel source to the `/root` directory. Be sure to substitute the directory that the kernel was downloaded to for your system. You must also have about 10–15MB of free space to extract and compile a new kernel.

1. Delete the symbolic link pointing to the current Linux kernel source directory. The idea is to avoid overwriting the current source directory because it might contain modifications you have made. It's also a setup that you should be able to restore if something goes wrong. The command is as follows:

   `rm linux`

   If `rm` tells you you're deleting a directory, there is something wrong. Check the directory you're in, and make sure that `linux` is a symbolic link to the current source directory.

2. Create the new directory to hold the kernel source. The reason this is being done is that the source distribution wants to extract itself to a directory called `linux`, but this is not the way it is intended to be used. Create a directory with

an appropriate name, usually `linux-`, followed by the kernel version (for example, `linux-2.2.12`).

3. Create the new symbolic link to the new directory by entering the following:
```
ln -s <your directory name> linux
```

4. Extract the file to the new directory by entering the following:
```
tar xzvf <kernel file name>
```

Your new kernel source is now correctly installed and you can configure the kernel. Depending on the speed of your system, this can take some time.

Before Configuring the Kernel

Make sure that you note the following information about your system before configuring a kernel that you intend to use:

- Your processor type.
- Whether your machine is PCI.
- The type of IDE controller in your system (if there is one).
- The type of SCSI controller in your system, if you have one: Manufacturer, model number, chipset number, and revision are important here.
- The type of interface your CD-ROM uses.
- The type of network card that's in your system. Having the make and model number of the chipset on the network card is also quite handy.
- The make, model, and chip number of your sound card. You should also note the interrupt request line (IRQ, for short), the I/O addresses the card uses, and the DMA line(s) the card uses.

PC hardware is a complex thing. Not only is there a myriad of possible combinations of hardware for your computer, but also many manufacturers and their products, although not officially supported by Linux, use chipsets and other components that work just fine. Sometimes it's a matter of trial and error to figure out what works, but often, the answer can be determined easily by getting the chip numbers from the cards, and looking into the appropriate directory containing similar drivers.

In fact, the writers of the drivers for Linux often go as far as to include one or more documentation files with the drivers to explain some of the "gotchas" for a particular piece of hardware. Just look in the `drivers` subdirectory of the `linux` directory. The documentation files in the `drivers/sound` and `drivers/net` are particularly detailed.

Also, I recommend that, if you have never built a Linux kernel before, you review all the sections, in particular the make config and the make xconfig sections. They both deal with the same kernel, but the material (and configuration programs) are organized slightly differently. These differences might shed some light on items that might not be apparent from reading just one section.

Using *make config*

This section describes the classic way to configure the Linux kernel, and is entirely text based.

If the descriptions in this section differ from what you see on your system

The kernel configuration examples here use a kernel that is slightly modified from the Red Hat 6.0 distribution. Some additional support for devices has been added to the newer kernels, and the additional information about these devices is included in this section.

To configure your kernel by using make config, change to the /usr/src/linux directory and, as root or someone with write permissions there, type the following command:

```
make config
```

You are greeted by the following friendly message:

```
[root@jansmachine linux]# make config
rm -f include/asm
( cd include ; ln -sf asm-i386 asm)
/bin/sh scripts/Configure arch/i386/config.in
#
# Using defaults found in .config
#
*
* Code maturity level options
*
Prompt for development and/or incomplete code/drivers _
➡(CONFIG_EXPERIMENTAL)[Y/n/?]
```

The questions usually list choices of valid answers, with the default answer in capital letters. If you cannot decide, type a question mark and press Enter. Usually there is some text to help you, but sometimes the answers are quite cryptic.

In the case of the preceding code, you'll normally want to answer Y, especially if you have a PCI-based PC.

The configuration script continues here:

```
*
* Processor type and features
*
Processor family (386, 486/Cx486, 586/K5/5x86/6x86, Pentium/K6/TSC,
PPro/6x86MX)
 [386]
  defined CONFIG_M386
Math emulation (CONFIG_MATH_EMULATION) [Y/n/?]
MTRR (Memory Type Range Register) support (CONFIG_MTRR) [Y/n/?]
Symmetric multi-processing support (CONFIG_SMP) [N/y/?]
*
* Loadable module support
*
Enable loadable module support (CONFIG_MODULES) [Y/n/?]
Set version information on all symbols for modules (CONFIG_MODVERSIONS) [Y/n/?]
Kernel module loader (CONFIG_KMOD) [Y/n/?]
```

For normal configurations, accept the default on all the above. If you want to turn off kernel daemon support, here is where it's done. As far as processor types are concerned, choose the one you have. It doesn't hurt to use a kernel built for a 386 on a Pentium system, but a kernel compiled for a Pentium won't run on a 386. If you have a NexGen processor, compile for 386 and make sure that Math Emulation is turned on. If you have any other non-Intel processor, answer 486 here. Some processors identify themselves as Pentium processors, but some differences still exist. Besides, these processors tend to have more advanced features, such as out-of-order instruction execution, and do not need any of the more advanced optimizations to function at peak efficiency. The configuration script continues here:

```
*
* General setup
*
Networking support (CONFIG_NET) [Y/n/?]
PCI support (CONFIG_PCI) [Y/n/?]
PCI access mode (BIOS, Direct, Any) [Any]
  defined CONFIG_PCI_GOANY
    PCI quirks (CONFIG_PCI_QUIRKS) [Y/n/?]
    PCI bridge optimization (experimental) (CONFIG_PCI_OPTIMIZE) [N/y/?]
    Backward-compatible /proc/pci (CONFIG_PCI_OLD_PROC) [Y/n/?]
```

If you turn off kernel daemon support

Turning off kernel daemon support can cause your system to lose network connectivity because there will be nothing to load the drivers when the network cards are configured in the `init` scripts on system boot. If you turn off this support, either compile the drivers for your network card into the kernel rather than as modules, or modify your `init` scripts to manually load the modules for your network card before the `network` script is called.

These questions should be pretty clear. The next section of script configures the binary formats the kernel supports, as well as other compatibility options:

```
MCA support (CONFIG_MCA) [N/y/?]
SGI Visual Workstation support (CONFIG_VISWS) [N/y/?]
System V IPC (CONFIG_SYSVIPC) [Y/n/?]
BSD Process Accounting (CONFIG_BSD_PROCESS_ACCT) [Y/n/?]
Sysctl support (CONFIG_SYSCTL) [Y/n/?]
Kernel support for a.out binaries (CONFIG_BINFMT_AOUT) [M/n/y/?]
Kernel support for ELF binaries (CONFIG_BINFMT_ELF) [Y/m/n/?]
Kernel support for MISC binaries (CONFIG_BINFMT_MISC) [M/n/y/?]
Kernel support for JAVA binaries (obsolete) (CONFIG_BINFMT_JAVA) [M/n/y/?]
```

These options allow you to set the types of binaries supported by the kernel. Respond Y to the ELF binaries options, because this is the most common and current type of Linux binary. The others can be compiled as modules.

The next section deals with floppy and IDE devices:

```
*
* Floppy, IDE, and other block devices
*
Normal floppy disk support (CONFIG_BLK_DEV_FD)[Y/m/n/?]
Enhanced IDE/MFM/RLL disk/cdrom/tape/floppy support (CONFIG_BLK_DEV_IDE)[Y/n/?]
```

Both questions should be answered with Y, unless you don't want to use either of these devices.

The next section of script assumes you have answered Y to IDE device support:

```
*
* Please see Documentation/ide.txt for help/info on IDE drives
*
  Use old disk-only driver on primary interface (CONFIG_BLK_DEV_HD_IDE) [N/y/?]

  Include IDE/ATA-2 DISK support (CONFIG_BLK_DEV_IDEDISK) [Y/m/n/?]
  Include IDE/ATAPI CDROM support (CONFIG_BLK_DEV_IDECD) [Y/m/n/?]
```

```
Include IDE/ATAPI TAPE support (CONFIG_BLK_DEV_IDETAPE) [M/n/y/?]
Include IDE/ATAPI FLOPPY support (CONFIG_BLK_DEV_IDEFLOPPY) [M/n/y/?]
SCSI emulation support (CONFIG_BLK_DEV_IDESCSI) [M/n/y/?]
CMD640 chipset bugfix/support (CONFIG_BLK_DEV_CMD640) [Y/n/?]
  CMD640 enhanced support (CONFIG_BLK_DEV_CMD640_ENHANCED) [N/y/?]
RZ1000 chipset bugfix/support (CONFIG_BLK_DEV_RZ1000) [Y/n/?]
Generic PCI IDE chipset support (CONFIG_BLK_DEV_IDEPCI) [Y/n/?]
  Generic PCI bus-master DMA support (CONFIG_BLK_DEV_IDEDMA) [Y/n/?]
  Boot off-board chipsets first support (CONFIG_BLK_DEV_OFFBOARD) [N/y/?]
  Use DMA by default when available (CONFIG_IDEDMA_AUTO) [N/y/?]
  OPTi 82C621 chipset enhanced support (EXPERIMENTAL)
(CONFIG_BLK_DEV_OPTI621) [N/y/?]
  Tekram TRM290 chipset support (EXPERIMENTAL)
(CONFIG_BLK_DEV_TRM290) [N/y/?]
  NS87415 chipset support (EXPERIMENTAL) (CONFIG_BLK_DEV_NS87415) [N/y/?]
  VIA82C586 chipset support (EXPERIMENTAL) (CONFIG_BLK_DEV_VIA82C586) [N/y/?]

  CMD646 chipset support (EXPERIMENTAL) (CONFIG_BLK_DEV_CMD646) [N/y/?]
  Other IDE chipset support (CONFIG_IDE_CHIPSETS) [N/y/?]
```

As stated here, more information on IDE peculiarities can be gleaned from the Documentation subdirectory of the linux source directory. To summarize, this section of script allows you to enable the new IDE/ATAPI device capabilities. Some IDE CD changers use a protocol similar to the SCSI Logical Units to control the several devices attached, and SCSI emulation support allows the use of regular SCSI tools to exploit this feature. With each new release of the kernel, more and more devices are supported. If you're using a more recent version of the kernel than was used in the creating this chapter (2.2.12), there's a good chance that the kernel configuration screens will be slightly different from what has been covered here.

The following section is presented next:

```
*
* Additional Block Devices
*
Loopback device support (CONFIG_BLK_DEV_LOOP) [M/n/y/?]
Network block device support (CONFIG_BLK_DEV_NBD) [M/n/y/?]
Multiple devices driver support (CONFIG_BLK_DEV_MD) [Y/n/?]
Autodetect RAID partitions (CONFIG_AUTODETECT_RAID) [Y/n/?]
  Linear (append) mode (CONFIG_MD_LINEAR) [M/n/y/?]
  RAID-0 (striping) mode (CONFIG_MD_STRIPED) [M/n/y/?]
  RAID-1 (mirroring) mode (CONFIG_MD_MIRRORING) [M/n/y/?]
  RAID-4/RAID-5 mode (CONFIG_MD_RAID5) [M/n/y/?]
```

```
    Translucent mode (CONFIG_MD_TRANSLUCENT) [N/y/m/?]
    Logical Volume Manager support (CONFIG_MD_LVM) [N/y/m/?]
RAM disk support (CONFIG_BLK_DEV_RAM) [Y/m/n/?]
    Initial RAM disk (initrd) support (CONFIG_BLK_DEV_INITRD) [Y/n/?]
XT hard disk support (CONFIG_BLK_DEV_XD) [M/n/y/?]
Mylex DAC960/DAC1100 PCI RAID Controller support (CONFIG_BLK_DEV_DAC960)
[M/n/y/?]
Compaq SMART2 support (CONFIG_BLK_CPQ_DA) [M/n/y/?]
    Support for PCI SMART2 adapters (CONFIG_BLK_CPQ_DA_PCI) [Y/n/?]
    Support for EISA SMART2 adapters (CONFIG_BLK_CPQ_DA_EISA) [Y/n/?]
Parallel port IDE device support (CONFIG_PARIDE) [M/n/?]
```

These devices are a bit more interesting than those in the run-of-the-mill IDE controller section. The loopback device allows the use of files as "virtual file systems" inside files. This is often used for creating disk images for writing CD-ROMs. There are some other uses for this as well—for example, this device is used by the script that makes a SCSI system's initial ramdisk. In the preceding case, the makefile recommends this to be a module. It does no harm to leave it this way, and could come in useful.

The multiple devices driver allows several partitions to be accessed as one. Additional tools and configurations are required to implement this. Ramdisk support is important for systems that boot from SCSI disks with modular kernels—answer Y to the initial ramdisk support option that is displayed if you have a SCSI system. The Linux kernel now supports RAID (Redundant Array of Inexpensive Disks), as seen in this section. RAID can improve performance of your I/O subsystem and provide fault tolerance at the same time.

Your initial ramdisk and the loopback adapter

If your system requires an initial ramdisk (in other words, your system boots off a SCSI adapter), you need the loopback device to generate that ramdisk in the first place.

On to configuring your kernel's networking:

```
*
* Networking options
*
Packet socket (CONFIG_PACKET) [Y/m/n/?]
Kernel/User netlink socket (CONFIG_NETLINK) [Y/n/?]
Routing messages (CONFIG_RTNETLINK) [Y/n/?]
```

```
Netlink device emulation (CONFIG_NETLINK_DEV) [Y/m/n/?]
Network firewalls (CONFIG_FIREWALL) [Y/n/?]
Socket Filtering (CONFIG_FILTER) [Y/n/?]
Unix domain sockets (CONFIG_UNIX) [Y/m/n/?]
TCP/IP networking (CONFIG_INET) [Y/n/?]
IP: multicasting (CONFIG_IP_MULTICAST) [Y/n/?]
IP: advanced router (CONFIG_IP_ADVANCED_ROUTER) [N/y/?]
IP: kernel level autoconfiguration (CONFIG_IP_PNP) [N/y/?]
IP: firewalling (CONFIG_IP_FIREWALL) [Y/n/?]
IP: firewall packet netlink device (CONFIG_IP_FIREWALL_NETLINK) [Y/n/?]
IP: transparent proxy support (CONFIG_IP_TRANSPARENT_PROXY) [Y/n/?]
IP: masquerading (CONFIG_IP_MASQUERADE) [Y/n/?]
*
* Protocol-specific masquerading support will be built as modules.
*
IP: ICMP masquerading (CONFIG_IP_MASQUERADE_ICMP) [Y/n/?]
*
* Protocol-specific masquerading support will be built as modules.
*
IP: masquerading special modules support (CONFIG_IP_MASQUERADE_MOD) [Y/n/?]
IP: ipautofw masq support (EXPERIMENTAL) (CONFIG_IP_MASQUERADE_IPAUTOFW)
[M/n/y/?]
IP: ipportfw masq support (EXPERIMENTAL) (CONFIG_IP_MASQUERADE_IPPORTFW)
[M/n/y/?]
IP: ip fwmark masq-forwarding support (EXPERIMENTAL) (CONFIG_IP_MASQUERADE_MFW)
[M/n/y/?]
IP: optimize as router not host (CONFIG_IP_ROUTER) [N/y/?]
IP: tunneling (CONFIG_NET_IPIP) [M/n/y/?]
IP: GRE tunnels over IP (CONFIG_NET_IPGRE) [M/n/y/?]
IP: broadcast GRE over IP (CONFIG_NET_IPGRE_BROADCAST) [Y/n/?]
IP: multicast routing (CONFIG_IP_MROUTE) [N/y/?]
IP: aliasing support (CONFIG_IP_ALIAS) [Y/n/?]
IP: ARP daemon support (EXPERIMENTAL) (CONFIG_ARPD) [N/y/?]
IP: TCP syncookie support (not enabled per default) (CONFIG_SYN_COOKIES)
[Y/n/?]

*
* (it is safe to leave these untouched)
*
IP: Reverse ARP (CONFIG_INET_RARP) [M/n/y/?]
```

```
IP: Allow large windows (not recommended if <16Mb of memory) (CONFIG_SKB_LARGE)
[Y/n/?]
The IPv6 protocol (EXPERIMENTAL) (CONFIG_IPV6) [N/y/m/?]
```

This section of script details the kernel's networking options for the base networking tool in Linux: TCP/IP. I strongly recommend that you compile network support here even if you do not have a network card because the default selections should always work in your favor unless your system has already been reconfigured previously. Your system has a loopback network configured to support local programs whose operation assumes there to be a network. There are many programs (X Window, for instance) on your system that prefer to use network sockets.

The majority of cases do not need either network firewalling or aliasing. (For a more detailed description of how these options work see the Firewall-HOWTO on your CD and available online at `http://www.linuxdoc.org` and on many mirror sites.)

Multicasting is relatively new for the rest of the Internet, and many ISPs' equipment does not support it. Say N here while the rest of the world gets multicasting sorted out.

Syn and Rst cookies are designed to reduce the effectiveness of certain attacks on your system. There has been significant attention paid to "syn flooding" attacks on systems connected to the Internet in recent months, and this change in Linux networking is designed to reduce the effectiveness of the attack significantly. Select Y.

IP accounting allows you to keep track of network traffic going over your system. It's really useful only if Linux is being used as a network router—a topic, unfortunately, beyond the scope of this book. Select N.

Optimizing as router not host makes some changes to the networking in Linux. I recommended you leave it off unless you're setting up a router.

IP tunneling is used similarly to Virtual Private Networks under Windows, and although the two are incompatible, it should be noted that this feature can be used to join two LANs over the Internet by using Linux. Most users can say N here.

IP aliasing is the other half of the network aliasing option, and as mentioned earlier, most people won't need it.

The next section of the script allows you to enable support for other networking protocols and other kernel functions:

*

*

*

```
The IPX protocol (CONFIG_IPX) [M/n/y/?]
IPX: Full internal IPX network (CONFIG_IPX_INTERN) [N/y/?]
IPX: SPX networking (EXPERIMENTAL) (CONFIG_SPX) [N/m/?]
Appletalk DDP (CONFIG_ATALK) [M/n/y/?]
CCITT X.25 Packet Layer (EXPERIMENTAL) (CONFIG_X25) [N/y/m/?]
LAPB Data Link Driver (EXPERIMENTAL) (CONFIG_LAPB) [N/y/m/?]
Bridging (EXPERIMENTAL) (CONFIG_BRIDGE) [N/y/?]
802.2 LLC (EXPERIMENTAL) (CONFIG_LLC) [N/y/?]
Acorn Econet/AUN protocols (EXPERIMENTAL) (CONFIG_ECONET) [N/y/m/?]
WAN router (CONFIG_WAN_ROUTER) [M/n/y/?]
Fast switching (read help!) (CONFIG_NET_FASTROUTE) [N/y/?]
Forwarding between high speed interfaces (CONFIG_NET_HW_FLOWCONTROL) [N/y/?]
CPU is too slow to handle full bandwidth (CONFIG_CPU_IS_SLOW) [N/y/?]
```

These options are only for the technologically savvy. IPX can be used with some programs to provide services to Novell clients. The others are best left off.

The next section of script allows you to configure generic SCSI support for your kernel:

```
*
* SCSI support
*
SCSI support (CONFIG_SCSI) [Y/m/n/?]
*
* SCSI support type (disk, tape, CD-ROM)
*
SCSI disk support (CONFIG_BLK_DEV_SD) [Y/m/n/?]
SCSI tape support (CONFIG_CHR_DEV_ST) [Y/m/n/?]
SCSI CD-ROM support (CONFIG_BLK_DEV_SR) [Y/m/n/?]
   Enable vendor-specific extensions (for SCSI CDROM) (CONFIG_BLK_DEV_SR_VENDOR)
[Y/n/?]
SCSI generic support (CONFIG_CHR_DEV_SG) [M/n/y/?]
*
* Some SCSI devices (e.g. CD jukebox) support multiple LUNs
*
Probe all LUNs on each SCSI device (CONFIG_SCSI_MULTI_LUN) [Y/n/?]
Verbose SCSI error reporting (kernel size +=12K) (CONFIG_SCSI_CONSTANTS)
[Y/n/?]
```

These options cover the common functionality for SCSI drivers and devices under Linux. The choices here depend on the hardware you have, although I recommend that verbose SCSI reporting be left off for performance and kernel size reasons.

If you have answered Y to SCSI support, you are now prompted to specify the actual SCSI card or chip your system has:

```
*
* SCSI low-level drivers
*
7000FASST SCSI support (CONFIG_SCSI_7000FASST) [M/n/y/?]
ACARD SCSI support (CONFIG_SCSI_ACARD) [M/n/y/?]
Adaptec AHA152X/2825 support (CONFIG_SCSI_AHA152X) [M/n/y/?]
Adaptec AHA1542 support (CONFIG_SCSI_AHA1542) [M/n/y/?]
Adaptec AHA1740 support (CONFIG_SCSI_AHA1740) [M/n/y/?]
Adaptec AIC7xxx support (CONFIG_SCSI_AIC7XXX) [M/n/y/?]
   Enable Tagged Command Queueing (TCQ) by default (CONFIG_AIC7XXX_TCQ_ON_BY_
DEFAULT) [N/y/?]
   Maximum number of TCQ commands per device (CONFIG_AIC7XXX_CMDS_PER_DEVICE)
[8]
   Collect statistics to report in /proc (CONFIG_AIC7XXX_PROC_STATS) [Y/n/?]
   Delay in seconds after SCSI bus reset (CONFIG_AIC7XXX_RESET_DELAY) [5]
AdvanSys SCSI support (CONFIG_SCSI_ADVANSYS) [M/n/y/?]
Always IN2000 SCSI support (CONFIG_SCSI_IN2000) [M/n/y/?]
AM53/79C974 PCI SCSI support (CONFIG_SCSI_AM53C974) [M/n/y/?]
AMI MegaRAID support (CONFIG_SCSI_MEGARAID) [M/n/y/?]
BusLogic SCSI support (CONFIG_SCSI_BUSLOGIC) [M/n/y/?]
  Omit FlashPoint support (CONFIG_SCSI_OMIT_FLASHPOINT) [N/y/?]
DTC3180/3280 SCSI support (CONFIG_SCSI_DTC3280) [M/n/y/?]
EATA ISA/EISA/PCI (DPT and generic EATA/DMA-compliant boards) support (CONFIG_
SCSI_EATA) [M/n/y/?]
  enable tagged command queueing (CONFIG_SCSI_EATA_TAGGED_QUEUE) [Y/n/?]
  enable elevator sorting (CONFIG_SCSI_EATA_LINKED_COMMANDS) [N/y/?]
  maximum number of queued commands (CONFIG_SCSI_EATA_MAX_TAGS) [16]
EATA-DMA [Obsolete] (DPT, NEC, AT&T, SNI, AST, Olivetti, Alphatronix) support
(CONFIG_SCSI_EATA_DMA) [M/n/y/?]
EATA-PIO (old DPT PM2001, PM2012A) support (CONFIG_SCSI_EATA_PIO) [M/n/y/?]
Future Domain 16xx SCSI/AHA-2920A support (CONFIG_SCSI_FUTURE_DOMAIN) [M/n/y/?]
GDT SCSI Disk Array Controller support (CONFIG_SCSI_GDTH) [M/n/y/?]
Generic NCR5380/53c400 SCSI support (CONFIG_SCSI_GENERIC_NCR5380) [M/n/y/?]
   Enable NCR53c400 extensions (CONFIG_SCSI_GENERIC_NCR53C400) [N/y/?]
NCR5380/53c400 mapping method (use Port for T130B) (Port, Memory) [Port]
  defined CONFIG_SCSI_G_NCR5380_PORT
Initio 9100U(W) support (CONFIG_SCSI_INITIO) [M/n/y/?]
Initio INI-A100U2W support (CONFIG_SCSI_INIA100) [M/n/y/?]
```

```
IOMEGA parallel port (ppa - older drives) (CONFIG_SCSI_PPA) [M/n/?]
IOMEGA parallel port (imm - newer drives) (CONFIG_SCSI_IMM) [M/n/?]
  ppa/imm option - Use slow (but safe) EPP-16 (CONFIG_SCSI_IZIP_EPP16) [N/y/?]
  ppa/imm option - Assume slow parport control register (CONFIG_SCSI_IZIP_SLOW_
CTR) [N/y/?]
NCR53c406a SCSI support (CONFIG_SCSI_NCR53C406A) [M/n/y/?]
symbios 53c416 SCSI support (CONFIG_SCSI_SYM53C416) [M/n/y/?]
NCR53c7,8xx SCSI support (CONFIG_SCSI_NCR53C7xx) [M/n/y/?]
    always negotiate synchronous transfers (CONFIG_SCSI_NCR53C7xx_sync) [N/y/?]
    allow FAST-SCSI [10MHz] (CONFIG_SCSI_NCR53C7xx_FAST) [Y/n/?]
    allow DISCONNECT (CONFIG_SCSI_NCR53C7xx_DISCONNECT) [Y/n/?]
NCR53C8XX SCSI support (CONFIG_SCSI_NCR53C8XX) [M/n/y/?]
  default tagged command queue depth (CONFIG_SCSI_NCR53C8XX_DEFAULT_TAGS) [8]
  maximum number of queued commands (CONFIG_SCSI_NCR53C8XX_MAX_TAGS) [32]
  synchronous transfers frequency in MHz (CONFIG_SCSI_NCR53C8XX_SYNC) [20]
  enable profiling (CONFIG_SCSI_NCR53C8XX_PROFILE) [Y/n/?]
  use normal IO (CONFIG_SCSI_NCR53C8XX_IOMAPPED) [N/y/?]
  assume boards are SYMBIOS compatible (CONFIG_SCSI_NCR53C8XX_SYMBIOS_COMPAT)
[N/y/?]
PAS16 SCSI support (CONFIG_SCSI_PAS16) [M/n/y/?]
PCI2000 support (CONFIG_SCSI_PCI2000) [N/y/m/?]
PCI2220i support (CONFIG_SCSI_PCI2220I) [N/y/m/?]
PSI240i support (CONFIG_SCSI_PSI240I) [M/n/y/?]
Qlogic FAS SCSI support (CONFIG_SCSI_QLOGIC_FAS) [M/n/y/?]
Qlogic ISP SCSI support (CONFIG_SCSI_QLOGIC_ISP) [M/n/y/?]
Qlogic ISP FC SCSI support (CONFIG_SCSI_QLOGIC_FC) [M/n/y/?]
Seagate ST-02 and Future Domain TMC-8xx SCSI support (CONFIG_SCSI_SEAGATE)
[M/n/y/?]
Tekram DC390(T) and Am53/79C974 SCSI support (CONFIG_SCSI_DC390T) [M/n/y/?]
  _omit_ support for non-DC390 adapters (CONFIG_SCSI_DC390T_NOGENSUPP) [N/y/?]
Trantor T128/T128F/T228 SCSI support (CONFIG_SCSI_T128) [M/n/y/?]
UltraStor 14F/34F support (CONFIG_SCSI_U14_34F) [M/n/y/?]
  enable elevator sorting (CONFIG_SCSI_U14_34F_LINKED_COMMANDS) [N/y/?]
  maximum number of queued commands (CONFIG_SCSI_U14_34F_MAX_TAGS) [8]
UltraStor SCSI support (CONFIG_SCSI_ULTRASTOR) [M/n/y/?]
SCSI debugging host adapter (CONFIG_SCSI_DEBUG) [M/n/y/?]
```

These options are for specific SCSI devices in your system. Particularly, if you want to support more than one or two SCSI devices, setting them as modules is a good idea. If your boot drive is a SCSI disk, and you decide to use modules, ensure that the Initial ramdisk support is enabled and that you remember to make the initial ramdisk with the SCSI driver(s) for your system. The reason for this ramdisk is that it contains the modules necessary for SCSI support. The ramdisk is read by the boot loader before the Linux kernel is started.

If you do not want to use a SCSI module for your boot device, however, make sure that you delete the `initrd<kernel _version>.img` file in the `/boot` directory, or that you have turned off `initrd` support in the kernel. Otherwise, the kernel's now built-in device driver will initialize the device, and then the device driver included in the initial ramdisk will try to do the same, and fail. This would not be so bad, except that the failed device driver load in this case will trigger a kernel panic. If you neglect to delete the `initrd<kernel version>.img` file, you can give to the boot the kernel image from the LILO command line with the `noinitrd` option.

The online help here is most helpful for drivers that give you additional configuration options. In general, Tagged Command Queuing is an option you should enable for the best performance, but check the other options there to ensure that there is not something else in the driver that can affect this.

The kernel configuration now takes us to the choices for network devices:

```
*
* Network device support
*
Network device support (CONFIG_NETDEVICES) [Y/n/?]
ARCnet support (CONFIG_ARCNET) [N/y/m/?]
Dummy net driver support (CONFIG_DUMMY) [M/n/y/?]
EQL (serial line load balancing) support (CONFIG_EQUALIZER) [M/n/y/?]
Ethertap network tap (CONFIG_ETHERTAP) [M/n/y/?]
```

This set of options is for base network device support. For anything but specialized configurations, answer Y to network device support. Making these modules is your choice.

The next question really means: "Do you have a network card?"

```
Ethernet (10 or 100Mbit)(CONFIG_NET_ETHERNET)[Y/n/?]
```

Answer Y here for a walk-though of the choices of different network adapters, including SLIP and PPP options. The list is pretty lengthy, so take your time. Most network adapters require no parameters or anything, so as long as you know what you have, you should be fine.

```
*
* ISDN subsystem
*
ISDN support (CONFIG_ISDN)[N/y/m/?]
```

ISDN support for Linux is pretty new, and not that many adapters are supported. For up-to-date information about using ISDN with Linux, have a look in the Documentation/isdn subdirectory, where you'll find information on configuration issues and software required.

The next section of script deals with non-SCSI and non-IDE CD-ROM drives:

```
*
* CD-ROM drivers (not for SCSI or IDE/ATAPI drives)
*
Support non-SCSI/IDE/ATAPI CDROM drives (CONFIG_CD_NO__IDESCSI)[N/y/?]
```

Answering Y here causes the configuration program to go through a list of non-SCSI and non-IDE CD-ROM drives; most users should be able to type N here. There are some issues with some proprietary CD controllers and some network cards in which the system might hang if the kernel has to probe for the CD controller's I/O address. Read the documentation for the CD drivers and specify an I/O address at the kernel command line if this happens.

Things will now get interesting again—the next section of script allows you to configure file system support for your Linux kernel:

```
*
* Filesystems
*
Quota support (CONFIG_QUOTA) [Y/n/?]
Kernel automounter support (CONFIG_AUTOFS_FS) [M/n/y/?]
ADFS filesystem support (read only) (EXPERIMENTAL) (CONFIG_ADFS_FS) [N/y/m/?]
Amiga FFS filesystem support (CONFIG_AFFS_FS) [N/y/m/?]
Apple Macintosh filesystem support (experimental) (CONFIG_HFS_FS) [M/n/y/?]
DOS FAT fs support (CONFIG_FAT_FS) [M/n/y/?]
  MSDOS fs support (CONFIG_MSDOS_FS) [M/n/?]
  UMSDOS: Unix-like filesystem on top of standard MSDOS filesystem (CONFIG_
UMSDOS_FS) [M/n/?]
  VFAT (Windows-95) fs support (CONFIG_VFAT_FS) [M/n/?]
ISO 9660 CDROM filesystem support (CONFIG_ISO9660_FS) [Y/m/n/?]
Microsoft Joliet CDROM extensions (CONFIG_JOLIET) [Y/n/?]
Minix fs support (CONFIG_MINIX_FS) [M/n/y/?]
NTFS filesystem support (read only) (CONFIG_NTFS_FS) [N/y/m/?]
OS/2 HPFS filesystem support (read only) (CONFIG_HPFS_FS) [M/n/y/?]
/proc filesystem support (CONFIG_PROC_FS) [Y/n/?]
/dev/pts filesystem for Unix98 PTYs (CONFIG_DEVPTS_FS) [Y/n/?]
QNX filesystem support (EXPERIMENTAL) (CONFIG_QNX4FS_FS) [N/y/m/?]
ROM filesystem support (CONFIG_ROMFS_FS) [M/n/y/?]
```

```
Second extended fs support (CONFIG_EXT2_FS) [Y/m/n/?]
System V and Coherent filesystem support (CONFIG_SYSV_FS) [M/n/y/?]
UFS filesystem support (CONFIG_UFS_FS) [M/n/y/?]
   UFS filesystem write support (experimental) (CONFIG_UFS_FS_WRITE) [N/y/?]
```

A great number of file systems are supported by Linux. Other file system drivers are available for download as well. Quota support provides a means of limiting the disk space that a certain user can use.

Personally, I never set ext2fs to be a module—it's just too much of a hassle. Trust me here. Every other file system you want can be set to be a module. I tend to not bother with Minix or the old ext file systems; instead, I simply compile the MS-DOS fat and vfat file systems, hpfs, and iso9660 as modules. kerneld is usually smart enough to pick the right file system and load the driver for you when you try to mount one.

Automounting enables the system to automatically mount NFS (network file system) drives when they are needed. Unless you're on a network with lots of UNIX and Linux machines, the time spent making this work is probably better spent doing other things.

On to configuring character-based devices, such as modems, and so on:

```
*
* Character devices
*
Virtual terminal (CONFIG_VT) [Y/n/?]
Support for console on virtual terminal (CONFIG_VT_CONSOLE) [Y/n/?]
Standard/generic (dumb) serial support (CONFIG_SERIAL) [Y/m/n/?]
   Support for console on serial port (CONFIG_SERIAL_CONSOLE) [Y/n/?]
Extended dumb serial driver options (CONFIG_SERIAL_EXTENDED) [Y/n/?]
   Support more than 4 serial ports (CONFIG_SERIAL_MANY_PORTS) [Y/n/?]
   Support for sharing serial interrupts (CONFIG_SERIAL_SHARE_IRQ) [Y/n/?]
   Autodetect IRQ on standard ports (unsafe) (CONFIG_SERIAL_DETECT_IRQ) [N/y/?]
   Support special multiport boards (CONFIG_SERIAL_MULTIPORT) [Y/n/?]
   Support the Bell Technologies HUB6 card (CONFIG_HUB6) [N/y/?]
Non-standard serial port support (CONFIG_SERIAL_NONSTANDARD) [Y/n/?]
Comtrol Rocketport support (CONFIG_ROCKETPORT) [M/n/y/?]
Digiboard Intelligent Async Support (CONFIG_DIGIEPCA) [M/n/y/?]
Cyclades async mux support (CONFIG_CYCLADES) [M/n/y/?]
Stallion multiport serial support (CONFIG_STALDRV) [Y/n/?]
   Stallion EasyIO or EC8/32 support (CONFIG_STALLION) [M/n/y/?]
   Stallion EC8/64, ONboard, Brumby support (CONFIG_ISTALLION) [M/n/y/?]
SDL RISCom/8 card support (CONFIG_RISCOM8) [M/n/y/?]
```

```
Specialix IO8+ card support (CONFIG_SPECIALIX) [M/n/y/?]
Specialix DTR/RTS pin is RTS (CONFIG_SPECIALIX_RTSCTS) [Y/n/?]
Hayes ESP serial port support (CONFIG_ESPSERIAL) [M/n/y/?]
Multi-Tech multiport card support (CONFIG_ISI) [M/n/?]
Microgate SyncLink card support (CONFIG_SYNCLINK) [M/n/?]
HDLC line discipline support (CONFIG_N_HDLC) [M/n/?]
Unix98 PTY support (CONFIG_UNIX98_PTYS) [Y/n/?]
Maximum number of Unix98 PTYs in use (0-2048) (CONFIG_UNIX98_PTY_COUNT) [256]
Parallel printer support (CONFIG_PRINTER) [M/n/?]
  Support IEEE1284 status readback (CONFIG_PRINTER_READBACK) [N/y/?]
Mouse Support (not serial mice) (CONFIG_MOUSE) [Y/n/?]
*
* Mice
*
ATIXL busmouse support (CONFIG_ATIXL_BUSMOUSE) [M/n/y/?]
Logitech busmouse support (CONFIG_BUSMOUSE) [M/n/y/?]
Microsoft busmouse support (CONFIG_MS_BUSMOUSE) [M/n/y/?]
PS/2 mouse (aka "auxiliary device") support (CONFIG_PSMOUSE) [Y/n/?]
C&T 82C710 mouse port support (as on TI Travelmate) (CONFIG_82C710_MOUSE)
[M/n/y/?]
PC110 digitizer pad support (CONFIG_PC110_PAD) [M/n/y/?]
QIC-02 tape support (CONFIG_QIC02_TAPE) [N/y/m/?]
Watchdog Timer Support (CONFIG_WATCHDOG) [Y/n/?]
```

The preceding script is the character device configuration section, as you can probably tell by its title. Things such as mice and serial and parallel ports fall into this category.

The next section of script is the sound card configuration section:

```
*
* Sound
*
Sound card support (CONFIG_SOUND) [M/n/y/?]
Ensoniq AudioPCI (ES1370) (CONFIG_SOUND_ES1370) [M/n/?]
Creative Ensoniq AudioPCI 97 (ES1371) (CONFIG_SOUND_ES1371) [M/n/?]
S3 SonicVibes (CONFIG_SOUND_SONICVIBES) [M/n/?]
Support for Turtle Beach MultiSound Classic, Tahiti, Monterey (CONFIG_SOUND_
MSNDCLAS) [M/n/?]
  Full pathname of MSNDINIT.BIN firmware file (CONFIG_MSNDCLAS_INIT_FILE)
[/etc/sound/msndinit.bin]
  Full pathname of MSNDPERM.BIN firmware file (CONFIG_MSNDCLAS_PERM_FILE)
[/etc/sound/msndperm.bin]
```

Support for Turtle Beach MultiSound Pinnacle, Fiji (CONFIG_SOUND_MSNDPIN)
[M/n/?]
  Full pathname of PNDSPINI.BIN firmware file (CONFIG_MSNDPIN_INIT_FILE)
[/etc/sound/pndspini.bin]
  Full pathname of PNDSPERM.BIN firmware file (CONFIG_MSNDPIN_PERM_FILE)
[/etc/sound/pndsperm.bin]
OSS sound modules (CONFIG_SOUND_OSS) [M/n/?]
ProAudioSpectrum 16 support (CONFIG_SOUND_PAS) [M/n/?]
100% Sound Blaster compatibles (SB16/32/64, ESS, Jazz16) support
(CONFIG_SOUND_SB) [M/n/?]
Generic OPL2/OPL3 FM synthesizer support (CONFIG_SOUND_ADLIB) [M/n/?]
Gravis Ultrasound support (CONFIG_SOUND_GUS) [M/n/?]
16 bit sampling option of GUS (_NOT_ GUS MAX) (CONFIG_GUS16) [Y/n/?]
GUS MAX support (CONFIG_GUSMAX) [Y/n/?]
MPU-401 support (NOT for SB16) (CONFIG_SOUND_MPU401) [M/n/?]
PSS (AD1848, ADSP-2115, ESC614) support (CONFIG_SOUND_PSS) [M/n/?]
  Enable PSS mixer (Beethoven ADSP-16 and other compatibile) (CONFIG_PSS_MIXER)
[N/y/?]
Microsoft Sound System support (CONFIG_SOUND_MSS) [M/n/?]
Ensoniq SoundScape support (CONFIG_SOUND_SSCAPE) [M/n/?]
MediaTrix AudioTrix Pro support (CONFIG_SOUND_TRIX) [M/n/?]
Support for OPTi MAD16 and/or Mozart based cards (CONFIG_SOUND_MAD16) [M/n/?]
Support MIDI in older MAD16 based cards (requires SB) (CONFIG_MAD16_OLDCARD)
[Y/n/?]
Full support for Turtle Beach WaveFront (Tropez Plus, Tropez, Maui)
synth/soundcards (CONFIG_SOUND_WAVEFRONT) [M/n/?]
Support for Crystal CS4232 based (PnP) cards (CONFIG_SOUND_CS4232) [M/n/?]
Support for Yamaha OPL3-SA2, SA3, and SAx based PnP cards (CONFIG_SOUND_
OPL3SA2) [M/n/?]
Limited support for Turtle Beach Wave Front (Maui, Tropez) synthesizers
(CONFIG_SOUND_MAUI) [M/n/?]
Support for Aztech Sound Galaxy (non-PnP) cards (CONFIG_SOUND_SGALAXY) [M/n/?]
Support for AD1816(A) based cards (EXPERIMENTAL) (CONFIG_SOUND_AD1816) [M/n/?]
Yamaha OPL3-SA1 audio controller (CONFIG_SOUND_OPL3SA1) [M/n/?]
SoftOSS software wave table engine (CONFIG_SOUND_SOFTOSS) [M/n/?]
FM synthesizer (YM3812/OPL-3) support (CONFIG_SOUND_YM3812) [M/n/?]
Loopback MIDI device support (CONFIG_SOUND_VMIDI) [M/n/?]
6850 UART support (CONFIG_SOUND_UART6850) [M/n/?]

The Linux Sound System again. If you've decided that you want to re-build your
kernel to support your sound card, you're in the right place. Most people with
Creative Labs sound cards are well served by installing the sb module in

`/etc/conf.modules`, but the rest of us, especially those with later version Plug and Play cards, will likely need to recompile our kernels for more reliable and easier sound support.

If you configure sound as a module, the sound card device drivers will also, by default, want to be made as modules. With some playing you can coax most of them to allow a Y answer instead. This results in the sound drivers being compiled into one module, rather than a whole set of modules, and should also allow you to hard-code some sane default I/O address, IRQ, and DMA settings into the drivers.

I have found that this is the least painful way to get a stubborn sound card working with Linux. After you have configured the card parameters, and if you have a Plug and Play card, I recommend that you use the `isapnp` tools to configure the card to the I/O addresses and other parameters.

The configuration program asks whether you want to see additional low-level drivers. These are pretty non-standard devices, which are documented in the `drivers/sound` directory.

The last section of script has options for kernel developers:

```
*
* Kernel hacking
*
Magic SysRq key (CONFIG_MAGIC_SYSRQ) [Y/n/?]


*** End of Linux kernel configuration.
*** Check the top-level Makefile for additional configuration.
*** Next, you must run 'make dep'.
```

The preceding message signals the end of the kernel configuration. Depending on your Linux distribution, you might see other configuration options in addition to the ones that are covered here. With the release of the Linux 2.2.x kernels, there is support for infrared devices, joysticks, dongles, and other devices that previously were unavailable to the operating system. After you've finished configuring your selections, you should move on to the later section "Building and Installing the Kernel."

Using *make xconfig*

Using `make xconfig` is the preferred way of configuring the kernel. In a pinch, you can use the venerable `make config`, or `make menuconfig`, which is not documented here due to space considerations, but the X configuration program for the Linux kernel is the easiest to use by far.

Starting X Window configuration of the kernel

1. Log on as—or su to—root.

2. Start X Window.

3. Open an xterm session.

4. Change to the Linux kernel source directory, /usr/src/linux.

5. Enter the command make xconfig. You are greeted by the screen shown in Figure 31.6.

FIGURE 31.6
Configuring the Linux kernel by using make xconfig.

Configuring the kernel

The details are the same
Most of the kernel configuration options are discussed in the previous section, and only the finer points are covered here.

1. Start the configuration by clicking the Code Maturity Options button. This should always be your starting point when configuring a new kernel.

2. It is generally safe to answer Y to Prompt for Development and/or Incomplete Code/Drivers, shown in Figure 31.7. For the most part, these changes to the kernel can enhance performance, and truly experimental code will be made obvious to you.

FIGURE 31.7
Selecting the Code Maturity Options.

3. Next, return to the main menu and click the Loadable Module Support button. This configuration screen is shown in Figure 31.8. Answering Y to all three questions here is recommended for Linux, unless you really have a lot of experience with this, or are experimenting to get that experience. Click Next to continue.

Getting help

Note the Help buttons next to the options. By now, most options are well documented in the online help for the kernel. Feel free to use this facility as you see fit. I use it often, even if only to see whether things have changed between versions.

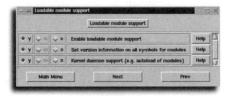

FIGURE 31.8
Configuring the loadable module options.

4. The General Setup screen, shown in Figure 31.9, gets more interesting. Here you can choose to include kernel PCI support, network support, and so on. Fresh kernel sources (ones that have not yet been configured on your system) have pretty safe defaults built in. The same caveats as in the make config section apply to everything here. Return to the main menu.

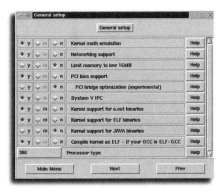

FIGURE 31.9
Configuring the general settings for the kernel.

5. The Block Devices screen, shown in Figure 31.10, configures your floppy disks, IDE drives, and non-SCSI block devices. You will probably have noticed by now that the questions are almost, if not exactly, identical to the questions that make config poses, but appear in a graphical format. Help, of course, is much more accessible. Note that the scrollbars on the right of the screen allow you to see the rest of the configuration options. In this section you get to set up your IDE devices and drivers for them. Click Next to continue.

FIGURE 31.10
The scrollbars on the right of the block device configuration screen allow you to see the rest of the configuration options.

6. Networking options are configured in the next screen, shown in Figure 31.11. These are covered in depth in the make config section earlier in the chapter. Note that if you answer Yes to certain options, other sections become ungrayed. This makes it easy to determine which options must be enabled to allow you do what you want.

FIGURE 31.11
Configuring the network devices.

7. Now, let's move to SCSI configuration. Make sure you're back at the menu and then click the SCSI Support button to load the SCSI configuration screen (see Figure 31.12). Here you can choose to support various generic SCSI devices and how to modularize the SCSI subsystem. Note how this kernel configuration is set up. The commonly used parts are compiled into the kernel (make sure you do this with SCSI Disk Support if you don't want to fight with mkinitrd), and the less commonly used parts are compiled as modules.

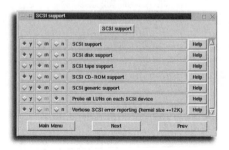

FIGURE 31.12
The Basic SCSI configuration screen is shown. Note how the modules are selected.

8. Click Next to bring up the SCSI Low-level Drivers section (see Figure 31.13). The advantage of the graphical configuration program here is that you can see which questions are coming for I/O Addresses and so forth before you get there. You can also go back and fix things easily if necessary. It's worth noting that some of the tagged command queuing options and SCB paging options have a profound impact on the performance of the system, so be sure to read the driver documentation for your card.

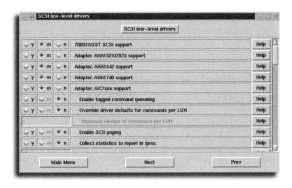

FIGURE 31.13
The SCSI Low-level Drivers selection dialog box is shown.

Again, note that the stock system has your SCSI disk driver as a module if your system boots from it, and make sure that you disable the initial ramdisk if you decide to compile the driver directly into the kernel.

9. The Network Device Support screen, which allows you to configure the network cards as well as SLIP and PPP connectivity for your machine, appears next (see Figure 31.14). Again, making PPP and SLIP modules is reasonable here, because `kerneld` knows about them and automatically loads them.

10. ISDN is also available (see Figure 31.15). Choose the device connected to your computer. If you cannot find your particular device, start looking in the help screens, as well, for documentation in the `/usr/src/linux` subdirectories for any to see if your ISDN modem is compatible with something.

FIGURE 31.14
The Network Device Support screen probably lists the most devices, and can take some time to work though. Take your time.

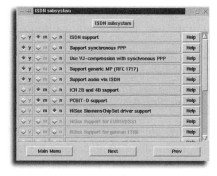

FIGURE 31.15
ISDN configuration options. Note that when experimenting with any device you're not sure of, it's best to use the driver as a module so you don't have to reboot every time you try different settings.

11. To configure a non-IDE and non-SCSI CD-ROM, click the "Old CD-ROM drivers" section from the main menu (see Figure 31.16). There are fewer and fewer of these devices around, but your system might still have one. It's particularly likely if your system has a double-spin drive, because most of these proprietary interfaces date back to that era.

12. In the Filesystems screen (see Figure 31.17), pick your file systems and move on. I recommend making any file system you want modular, except for ext2fs, because your system will need to use that to mount its initial ramdisk and the root partition.

FIGURE 31.16
The CD-ROM configuration screen. Be prepared to give IRQ and I/O Addresses for some CD-ROMs.

Modularizing drivers can be handy

It's probably worthwhile to modularize your drivers if you're experimenting. That way, device addresses and so on can be changed by unloading the module and reloading it with different parameters. You can then possibly recompile a module and use it without rebooting the system in most cases.

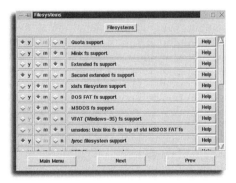

FIGURE 31.17
On the Filesystems configuration screen, make sure that you don't disable the `ext2` file system, or make it a module.

13. Character Devices is where support for parallel ports, serial ports, and non-serial mice is configured (see Figure 31.18). If you plan to use a parallel port Zip drive, you'll want to make your parallel port driver as well as your Zip driver modular; the Zip driver does not yet support sharing the parallel port.

FIGURE 31.18
The Character Devices screen.

14. The sound card for your Linux system is configured from the Sound section (see Figure 31.19). Everything noted in the make config section applies here, but also note that it is possible to hard-set non-standard device addresses for your sound modules using make xconfig. It's worth noting that few of the configuration fields in this section check for "sane" values, so it's up to you to make sure that you enter correct ones. Make the sound driver static (by answering Yes) and then change the option Sound Card Support back to being a module. This has the effect of producing only one module to contain sound support, which is something I have had a lot less trouble with.

15. If there are other sections that you'd like to configure, now is the time. If not, click the Save and Exit button, and you're now ready to build your kernel.

Building and Installing the Kernel

No matter which configuration tool you used to configure your kernel, now you must compile all the source files and produce the kernel itself. After building the kernel and the modules for it, you need to create an initial ramdisk if your system is booting from a SCSI disk, and then re-run LILO, if you're using LILO to boot the system. If you're using LOADLIN, you must copy the kernel and the ramdisk file to a location from which LOADLIN can load the kernel.

FIGURE 31.19
The Sound configuration screen.

Compiling the kernel and modules

1. Make sure you're in the Linux kernel directory. (You're probably already there.)

2. Issue the `make dep` command. This command causes the `make` system to generate dependency files to facilitate the correct building of the kernel.

3. Issue the `make clean` command. `make dep` leaves a lot of files lying around that can prevent the `make` program from compiling some files, and this can cause problems.

4. Issue the `make zImage` command. Note that this command is case sensitive. `make zImage` builds the kernel file. If the build process stops with an error message, run `make clean`, `make dep`, and then `make zImage` again. Any remaining error is likely to be an error in the configuration from the `make config` or equivalent script. Rerun that script, and perhaps take out some of the experimental stuff. If, during the configuration process, a monolithic kernel was configured, you might need to use `make bzImage` to compress the kernel image correctly.

5. If all went well, run the `make modules` command to compile the module files.

6. If the version of the kernel you're compiling is different from the kernel you're currently running, run the `make _modules_install` command. (Note the underscore in this command.) `make modules_install` copies the modules into the correct tree in the `/lib/modules` directory tree. If you want to make backups of the modules you currently have, you can make a quick backup by issuing the following command:

```
tar czvf /root/modules-`uname -r`.tar.gz /lib/modules/`uname -r`
```

This command assumes that you're going to install modules of the same kernel version that you're currently running.

You're now ready to make your initial ramdisk. You must perform this step only if you are booting from a non-IDE block device (such as a SCSI hard disk or RAID array), are using modules for your SCSI block device driver, and have switched kernel versions.

Creating an initial ramdisk with *mkinitrd*

Initial ramdisks and static (non-modular) device drivers

The default installation of Red Hat Linux does use modular device drivers for SCSI hard disks, and if you have compiled drivers specific to your SCSI hardware into your kernel you must make sure that you have either disabled initial ramdisk support in the kernel as well or edited your `/etc/lilo.conf` file to remove the initial ramdisk entry; otherwise, your system attempts to load the drivers for your SCSI card twice. Because your system will not find a SCSI device the second time the driver is initialized, the boot system will stop—this is not what you want!

1. Ensure that the `/etc/conf.modules` file on your system is set up correctly. (Chances are it is, especially if your SCSI system booted from your hard disk successfully.)

2. Make a backup of your current ramdisk. The file is located in the `/boot` directory, usually called either `initrd` or `initrd-<kernel-version>`, where `<kernel-version>` is the version number of the kernel it is compiled for. Because it's probably a good idea to set up your system so that you can still boot the old kernel, rename the file to `initrd.old`.

3. Determine whether your system needs to preload the generic SCSI system support modules. Execute the command `/sbin/lsmod` to obtain a listing of the modules that your system currently has loaded. The generic SCSI modules are called `sd_mod` and `scsi_mod`. If these appear in the output listing, chances are your system needs them.

4. Issue the following command:

   ```
   /sbin/mkinitrd <—needs-scsi-modules> /boot/initrd <kernel-version>
   ```

   The option `—needs-scsi-modules` should be used if you have configured your kernel so that the generic SCSI disk support is modular. `<kernel-version>` is the version of the kernel for which you need to make the ramdisk.

   If you have problems with this command, make sure that your system has support for a loopback block device, either as a module (recommended—`kerneld` will automatically load the module), or as a static device. It would also be worthwhile to check for updates for `mkinitrd` at the Red Hat Web site.

Installing the Kernel

This assumes that you have configured and compiled your kernel, installed your modules, and configured `initrd`. You should also have configured LILO (refer to Chapter 23, "Using Boot Managers") to perhaps include the old boot image and ramdisk so that you can boot those if things go wrong with your new kernel.

The following steps will save you the most typing if you are in the `/boot` directory because you can leave the `/boot` directory path out of every command.

1. Copy the kernel image, `/usr/src/linux/arch/i386/boot/vmlinuz`, to the `/boot` directory as file `vmlinuz-<kernel-version>`. Of course, replace `<kernel-version>` with the version number of your kernel. If you have customized LILO to look for a different filename as the kernel image, make sure you use that instead.

2. Delete the symbolic link `/boot/vmlinuz`. Create a new symbolic link using the command `ln -s /boot/ vmlinuz-<kernel-version> /boot/vmlinuz`.

3. Add, if you'd like, a new kernel boot option to the `/etc/lilo.conf` configuration file. The `lilo.conf` man page is the best place to look for details on this process. If you do modify `lilo.conf`, you'll need to move on to step 4, otherwise you're ready to go!

4. Type the command `lilo`. You should see output something like this:
   ```
   [root@jansmachine /root]# lilo_Added linux *_Added old
   ```

   The `*` character after the `linux` image is the image that LILO will boot by default. If you want to boot another image (for instance, the image `old` that was listed earlier in the chapter), just type the image at the `lilo:` prompt that the system presents you with before it boots.

   You might also want to test to see if LILO will install your configuration successfully. To do this, type `lilo -t` instead of `lilo`. This does everything but actually modify your disk to install LILO.

Enabling Advanced Power Management

Advanced Power Management provides a means to reduce the power a PC consumes, and controls features such as software power off as well. APM was around a long time before the standard was implemented, with significant 16-bit underpinnings, which makes support difficult in 32-bit operating systems. To make matters worse, desktop machines' "Green" BIOSes often don't comply fully with the established APM standard. Use of APM on Linux is at your own risk. My opinion is that it's interesting to try APM even with a desktop machine—just make sure that you have a backup kernel that does not have APM enabled in case things go awry.

The APM driver for Linux was designed specifically for notebook PCs to use the CPU's power-saving features. The driver does not provide support for hard disk spin-down (this is provided separately by the utility hdparm(8)), or VESA-compliant monitor power-saving, which can be enabled by editing a kernel source file. Notebooks, more so than desktop PCs, vary widely in their configuration and adherence to PC standards. This means that your mileage on this information will vary, probably not only from machine to machine, but also depending on the BIOS revision of a given line of machines from the same manufacturer.

Enabling APM is a simple case of checking the Enable Advanced Power Management option under the General Settings section of make xconfig. After you enable APM, there are a few additional choices to make:

- Ignore User Suspend turns off the code that responds to the user suspend APM signal. This must be turned off if the machine hangs or the Linux kernel panics/OOPs (you know you're there when your screen is full of hexadecimal numbers). The documentation specifically mentions the NEC Versa M series notebooks as qualifying for this special setting.

- Enable PM at Boot Time makes the Linux kernel turn on APM as soon as the machine boots. Most machines do this automatically, but it's worth experimenting with if power-saving does not seem to work. NEC Ultralite Versa 33/C and Toshiba 410CDT machines seem to experience problems when this is enabled, and this option is off by default.

- Make CPU Idle calls when Idle makes the Linux kernel call the APM CPU idle routines when not busy. This setting results in significant power savings on machines where this works; it allows the APM BIOS to do things such as slow the CPU clock after the machine has been idle or at a low load for some time.

- Enable Console Blanking Using APM allows the LCD backlight on your notebook PC's LCD screen to be turned off when the stock Linux screen-blanker blanks the screen. This option has known problems with the gpm utility, and if you're using this feature you should disable gpm using the command chkconfig ---del gpm.

- Power Off on Shutdown causes your machine to turn off when the system's halt command is issued, typically by the shutdown script. This feature is possibly of interest to owners of later desktop machines that support soft power-off, if their system has a compliant BIOS.

The main point to keep in mind here is that with the wide variety of implementations of APM in PC systems today, some or all of the features might not work with your particular PC. If you're comfortable with reading C and assembler source code, the `drivers/char/apm_bios.c` file makes for interesting reading (this is subjective, of course) and contains plenty of notes about how varying machines implement APM.

part

VI

APPENDIXES

Resources 579 A

Using Linux HOWTO Documents 585 B

Top 50 Linux Commands
and Utilities 597 C

Glossary 621 D

Resources

- Usenet resources

- World Wide Web resources

Usenet Resources

Following is a list of current Linux Usenet newsgroups. Note that the list does not include international newsgroups in other languages, such as French, German, or Italian.

- `comp.os.linux.advocacy` Rants, raves, taunts, and flame wars between Linux's Defenders of the Faith and the minions of the Dark Side.

- `comp.os.linux.alpha` Discussions of Linux on the Digital Equipment Corporation's Alpha CPU.

- `comp.os.linux.announce` Commercial, user group, and software release announcements.

- `comp.os.linux.answers` The definitive source of new or updated Linux HOWTOs, FAQs, and other Linux documents.

- `comp.os.linux.development.apps` Discussions concerning porting software programs, and using compilers or other languages for Linux.

- `comp.os.linux.development.system` Linux kernel and other programming information, such as modules or device drivers.

- `comp.os.linux.hardware` Questions, answers, and debates concerning using different hardware with Linux.

- `comp.os.linux.m68k` News and development information about Linux on Motorola 68x000-series CPUs.

- `comp.os.linux.misc` Miscellaneous questions, answers, and debates about hardware and software for Linux.

- `comp.os.linux.networking` Discussions about topics such as communications and networking administration and configuration.

- `comp.os.linux.powerpc` News and development information about Linux on the PowerPC series of CPUs.

- `comp.os.linux.setup` Questions and answers about how to install, set up, configure, and maintain Linux.

- `comp.os.linux.security` Linux security issues and discussion.

- `comp.os.linux.x` Discussions about installing, configuring, and using the X Window System and X11 clients with Linux.

- `alt.os.linux` A general discussion of the Linux operating system.

- `alt.os.linux.caldera` Information about the Caldera OpenLinux distribution.

- `alt.os.linux.slackware` Discussion about the Slackware Linux distribution

There are many other Linux newsgroups that might be available on your news server. For a complete list, check out `http://www.linux.org/help/usenetlinux.html`.

World Wide Web Resources

There are too many Linux Web sites to list a them all. Nonetheless, you'll find most of the answers you need through the Linux Documentation Project (LDP), available through the following site:

`http://www.linuxdoc.org/`

For a list of other computers (or mirrors) with the LDP contents, browse to the following address:

`http://www.linuxdoc.org/mirrors.html`

Have you recently installed Linux and now want to see what applications are available? LinuxApps.com is an excellent source for finding new and old applications alike:

`http://www.linuxapps.com/`

Want to see an estimate on the number of people who use Linux around the world? Navigate to this site, and register as a Linux user! The latest estimates are 12,000,000 users worldwide:

`http://counter.li.org`

Looking for a certain Linux logo? This site has a link to three pages of logos for Linux:

`http://pobox.com/~newt/`

Have extra copies of old Linux distributions on CD-ROM you'd like to donate? Navigate to this site for more information:

`http://visar.csustan.edu:8000/giveaway.html`

This site features Caldera's OpenLinux distribution, which includes the StarOffice suite of applications, DR-DOS, the ADABAS-D relational database, along with various Netscape clients and servers:

`http://www.caldera.com/`

Walnut Creek's Web site is a great starting place to get other free UNIX distributions, such as BSD or Slackware Linux:

`http://www.cdrom.com/`

The following site is the definitive Web site for Linux laptop users. This site features many different links and documentation to solve problems and provide solutions to making Linux and X11 work correctly:

`http://www.cs.utexas.edu/users/kharker/linux-laptop`

The definitive site for downloading the Debian Linux distribution is as follows:

`http://www.debian.org/`

Want to know whether your favorite Linux Web site has been updated or new software uploaded? Use this site to watch for daily changes:

`http://webwatcher.org/`

A long-time distributor of Linux, Infomagic offers many different sets of software collections available by FTP or on CD-ROM:

`http://www.infomagic.com`

This site not only offers the oldest and newest kernels, it also offers more than 20GB of software for Linux:

`http://www.kernel.org/`

With more than 4,000,000 visitors during 1997, this site is one of the most popular Linux Web sites, and is generally considered the Linux home page:

`http://www.linux.org/`

Another great home page for Linux is the similarly named Linux.com. A great source for up-to-date press on Linux, this site is definitely worth a look:

`http://www.linux.com/`

This is the place to start looking for Linux books by Sams, Que, and New Riders:

`http://www.mcp.com/`

Ken Lee's X and Motif Web site has more than 700 links to different X Window System Web pages (Ken is the maintainer of the Motif FAQ):

`http://www.rahul.net/kenton/index.shtml`

Red Hat Software, Inc.'s Web site offers links to Linux information, news, and support for Red Hat's Linux distribution, and versions of commercial Linux software, such as Applixware, Motif, and CDE:

`http://www.redhat.com/`

This site is the home of the Linux Journal, a four-color, 70+-page monthly magazine all about Linux:

```
http://www.linuxjournal.com/
```

The great folks of the XFree86 Project, Inc., provide free distributions of the X Window System not only for Linux, but for other operating systems on other computers:

```
http://www.xfree86.org/
```

appendix
B

Using Linux HOWTO Documents

Guide to current Linux HOWTOs

Guide to current Linux mini-HOWTOs

A massive collection of Linux HOWTO documents is usually included with each Linux distribution. Many Linux distributions, including Red Hat Linux 6.1, come with nearly 200 documents, requiring more than 6MB in compressed form! HOWTO documents are comprehensive, detailed guides for solving problems or for obtaining a quick education on specialized aspects of using Linux. If your system does not have these documents, you can download them from the Linux Documentation Project Web site at `http://www.linuxdoc.org/`, the official source for Linux documentation. Be aware that Linux documentation is maintained by individuals, not by a company. As a result, some of the documentation might be out of date. If your HOWTO documentation isn't matching up with the commands on your system, be sure to read the command's man pages for up-to-date info.

To read one of the regular HOWTO documents (compressed text, not `.html`, `.sgml`, `.dvi`, or `.ps`), use the `zless` command, followed by the path and name of the document, like this:

```
# zless /usr/doc/HOWTO/Serial-HOWTO.gz
```

Table B.1 provides a quick summary of each compressed HOWTO.

Table B.1 Red Hat 6.1 HOWTO Documents (Under the */usr/doc/HOWTO* Directory)

HOWTO	Description
3Dfx-HOWTO	Using the 3Dfx graphics accelerator chip with Linux
Access-HOWTO	How to use adaptive technology with Linux to help users with disabilities
Alpha-HOWTO	Discusses Linux for the Alpha series of CPUs
Assembly-HOWTO	How to program in i386 assembly language
AX25-HOWTO	How to install and configure support for AX.25 packet radio protocol
Bash-Prompt-HOWTO	Information on tweaking the command-line to your liking
Benchmarking-HOWTO	Discusses issues with benchmarking Linux systems
Beowulf-HOWTO	Documents the Beowulf Linux clustering system
Bootdisk-HOWTO	How to create Linux boot, utility, or maintenance disks
BootPrompt-HOWTO	Covers boot time arguments at the LILO prompts
Busmouse-HOWTO	How to install and use a bus mouse on Linux
CD-Writing-HOWTO	How to write CDs under Linux

HOWTO	Description
CDROM-HOWTO	How to install, configure, and use CD-ROMs for Linux
Chinese-HOWTO	How to use Chinese software with Linux
Commercial-HOWTO	Lists of commercial software for Linux
Config-HOWTO	How to fine-tune Linux installations
Consultants-HOWTO	Lists of companies providing commercial support for Linux
Cyrillic-HOWTO	How to use Russian language fonts with Linux
Danish-HOWTO	How to use the Danish language with Linux
Database-HOWTO	How to set up and use PostgresSQL with Linux
Disk-HOWTO	How to use multiple disks and partitions with Linux
Diskless-HOWTO	How to set up a diskless Linux workstation
Distribution-HOWTO	Help on how to choose a Linux distribution
DNS-HOWTO	How to administer a small Domain Name Server
DOS-Win-to-Linux-HOWTO	A DOS/Windows user's guide to Linux
DOS-to-Linux-HOWTO	A DOS users guide to Linux
DOSEMU-HOWTO	How to use the `dosemu` DOS emulator with Linux
ELF-HOWTO	How to use the ELF binary format
Emacspeak-HOWTO	How vision-impaired users can use Linux with a speech synthesizer
Esperanto-HOWTO	How to use the Esperanto language with Linux
Ethernet-HOWTO	How to set up and use different ethernet devices with Linux
Finnish-HOWTO	How to use the Finnish language with Linux
Firewall-HOWTO	Discusses the basics of firewalls with Linux
Framebuffer-HOWTO	How to use frame buffers and multiple displays with Linux
French-HOWTO	How to use the French language with Linux
Ftape-HOWTO	Discusses how to use the `ftape` driver
GCC-HOWTO	Setting up and using the GNU C compiler and development libraries for Linux
German-HOWTO	How to use the German language with Linux

continues...

Table B.1 Continued

HOWTO	Description
Glibc2-HOWTO	Installing and using the GNU C library, version 2 (libc 6)
HAM-HOWTO	Assistance for Linux amateur radio operators
Hardware-HOWTO	What types of hardware and drivers exist for Linux
Hebrew-HOWTO	How to use Hebrew characters with Linux
Installation-HOWTO	How to get and install Linux software
Intranet-Server-HOWTO	How to set up an intranet with Linux
IPCHAINS-HOWTO	Install and configure the IP firewalling chains software
IPX-HOWTO	Using the IPX protocol with Linux
IR-HOWTO	Information about by the Linux/IR project
ISP-Hookup-HOWTO	How to connect to the Internet through your Internet service provider (ISP)
Italian-HOWTO	How to use the Italian language with Linux
Java-CGI-HOWTO	How to set up your Linux server to use Java
Kernel-HOWTO	Configuring, compiling, upgrading, and troubleshooting your i386 Linux kernel
KickStart-HOWTO	Information on using Red Hat's KickStart program to rapidly set up multiple workstations
Keyboard-and-Console-HOWTO	Using the Linux keyboard and console
Laptop-HOWTO	How to use Linux on a laptop
LinuxDoc-Emacs-Ispell-HOWTO	Information to assist writers of HOWTO documents
Mail-Administrator-HOWTO	Mail servers and clients
Mail-User-HOWTO	An introduction to email
MGR-HOWTO	How to configure and use the MGR window system
MILO-HOWTO	How to use the milo loader for Linux Alpha systems
MIPS-HOWTO	Using Linux on MIPS processor systems
MP3-HOWTO	How to play and record sound files on Linux
Modem-HOWTO	Installing and using modems in Linux
Multicast-HOWTO	Information about TCP/IP multicasting
Multi-Disk-HOWTO	How to use multiple disks under Linux

HOWTO	Description
NET-3-4-HOWTO	How to install and configure Linux networking software
Networking-Overview-HOWTO	An overview of the capabilities of the Linux network operating system
News-HOWTO	All you need to know about Usenet news and Linux
NFS-HOWTO	How to set up NFS clients and servers under Linux
NIS-HOWTO	Details about the Network Information System and Linux
Oracle-HOWTO	How to use Oracle under Linux
Optical-Disk-HOWTO	Installing, configuring, and using optical disk drives under Linux
PCI-HOWTO	The latest details about Linux and PCI motherboards
PCMCIA-HOWTO	The definitive guide to using PC cards with Linux
PalmOS-HOWTO	All about using the 3Com Palm Pilot and Linux
Parallel-Processing-HOWTO	Parallel Processing information
Plug-and-Play-HOWTO	How to use Plug-n-Play devices on your Linux computer
Polish-HOWTO	Using the Polish language with Linux
PostgreSQL-HOWTO	Information on using the PostgreSQL database server
PPP-HOWTO	How to connect to the Internet with PPP under Linux
Printing-HOWTO	All you need to know about printing under Linux
Printing-Usage-HOWTO	How to use line printer spooling under Linux
Quake-HOWTO	How to install the Quake series of games on your Linux computer
RPM-HOWTO	The definitive guide to the rpm command
Root-RAID-HOWTO	Information on setting up root mounted RAID systems
Reading-List-HOWTO	Suggested books for Linux users
SCSI-HOWTO	Configuring and using SCSI devices with Linux
SCSI-Programming-HOWTO	How to program generic SCSI interface under Linux
SMB-HOWTO	How to use the Session Message Block (SMB) protocol with Linux
SRM-HOWTO	How to boot Alpha Linux systems using SRM
Security-HOWTO	Overview of general security issues

continues…

Table B.1 Continued

HOWTO	Description
Serbian-HOWTO	Information on using Serbian features of Linux
Serial-HOWTO	How to set up serial devices under Linux
Serial-Programming-HOWTO	How to program Linux serial ports
Shadow-Password-HOWTO	How to install and configure Shadow passwords under Linux
Slovenian-HOWTO	How to use the Slovenian language with Linux
Software-Building-HOWTO	Building software packages on your Linux machine
Sound-HOWTO	How to configure Linux to use sound
Sound-Playing-HOWTO	How to play different sound file formats under Linux
Spanish-HOWTO	How to use the Spanish language with Linux
TclTk-HOWTO	Information on the Tcl and Tk scripting languages
TeTeX-HOWTO	How to install and use TeTeX and LaTeX TeX packages with Linux
Text-Terminal-HOWTO	Using text terminals
Thai-HOWTO	How to set up Linux to use Thai language
Tips-HOWTO	Miscellaneous tips and hints to make using Linux easier
UMSDOS-HOWTO	How to use the UMSDOS file system and Linux
UPS-HOWTO	Details about how to use an uninterruptible power supply (UPS) and Linux
UUCP-HOWTO	All you need to know about UUCP and Linux
User-Group-HOWTO	How to set up and maintain a Linux User Group (LUG)
Unix-Internet-Fundamentals-HOWTO	A high-level background of UNIX operating systems and the Internet
VAR-HOWTO	Lists of value-added resellers of Linux software
Virtual-Services-HOWTO	Information on virtual hosting techniques
VME-HOWTO	Using Linux on VME bus systems
VMS-to-Linux-HOWTO	A gentle introduction to Linux for VMS users
VPN-Masquerade-HOWTO	Information on masquerading VPN traffic
WWW-HOWTO	How to set up Web servers and clients

HOWTO	Description
WWW-mSQL-HOWTO	How to use mSQL with a Web server
XFree86-HOWTO	How to use the XFree86 distribution of X11
XFree86-Video-Timings- HOWTO	How to create mode lines for your graphics card and monitor to use with XFree86's X11
XWindow-User-HOWTO	Information on using the X Window System

The mini-HOWTO documents, found under the /usr/doc/HOWTO/mini directory, provide detailed information in a short format, and usually cover specialized subjects. Unlike the regular HOWTOs, the mini-HOWTO is not distributed in compressed form with Red Hat Linux 6.1. Use the less pager, followed by the path and name of the file to read a mini-HOWTO, like this:

```
# less /usr/doc/HOWTO/mini/Advocacy
```

Need to read everything at once?

You can quickly find information in the HOWTO series without listing the /usr/doc/HOWTO directory. First, log on as the root operator, and then use the gunzip command, along with its -r (recursive) option to decompress the entire directory tree under the /usr/doc/HOWTO directory, like this:

```
# gunzip -r /usr/doc/HOWTO/*
```

Next, combine the find, xargs, head, and less commands to find and list the first 20 lines from the top of each file, like this:

```
# find /user/doc/HOWTO/* | xargs head -v -n 20 | less
```

You can now peruse the contents of your HOWTO documents!

Table B.2 contains a guide to current mini-HOWTOs from the Red Hat 6.1 Linux distribution.

Table B.2 Red Hat 5.0 Mini-HOWTO Documents (Under the */usr/doc/HOWTO/ mini* Directory)

HOWTO	Description
3-Button-Mouse	Using three-button serial mice with Linux
ADSL	Asymmetric Digital Subscriber Loop information
ADSM-Backup	Using IBM's ADSM backup system with Linux

continues...

Table B.2 Continued

HOWTO	Description
AI-Alife	Linux and artificial intelligence software
Alsa-sound	Installing Alsa sound drivers in Linux
Advocacy	How to advocate the use of Linux
Apache+SSL+PHP+fp	Information on setting up a secure Apache server with FrontPage extensions
Automount	Information on the `autofs` auto-mounter utility
Backup-With-MSDOS	How to back up Linux using DOS
Battery-Powered	How Linux laptop users can conserve power
Boca	Using the Boca 2016 serial card with Linux
BogoMips	The definitive tome on the infamous Linux BogoMips
Bridge	Creating and using ethernet bridges with Linux
Bridge+Firewall	Creating and using firewalls with ethernet bridges
Bzip2	Information on the new `bzip2` compression utility
Cable-Modem	Using cable modems with Linux
Cipe+Masq	How to set up a virtual private network between your LAN and other LANs using cipe through Linux-masquerading firewall machines
Clock	Keeping correct time with Linux
Coffee	A humorous article on using Linux as a coffee maker
Colour-ls	Using color `ls` command listings
Comeau-C++	Using Comeau C++ with Linux
Cyrus-IMAP	Installing the Cyrus IMAP mail server
DHCP	Information on setting up DHCP servers and clients
Diald	How to set up Linux to dial on demand for Internet connections
Ext2fs-Undeletion	Tips on recovering lost data and undeleting files on `ext2` file systems
Fax-Server	How to set up fax printer service for Linux
Firewall-Piercing	How to use PPP over Telnet through a firewall
GIS-GRASS	How to set up a GRASS mapping system for Linux
GTEK-BBS-550	How to set up and use the GTEK BBS-550, 8-port serial card for Linux
Hard-Disk-Upgrade	How to move Linux from one drive to another

HOWTO	Description
Install-From-ZIP	How to install Linux from a parallel port ZIP drive
IO-Port-Programming	How to program I/O ports for Linux
IP-Alias	How to set up and run IP aliasing for Linux
IP-Masquerade	How to enable IP masquerading for Linux
IP-Subnetworking	How to subnetwork an IP network with Linux
ISP-Connectivity	How to best use your Internet connection
Jaz-Drive	How to configure and use the Iomega Jaz drive
Kerneld	How to configure and use the Linux `kerneld` daemon
LBX	How to use low-bandwidth X with Linux
Large-Disk	All you need to know about large hard drives and Linux
Leased-Line	Using leased line modems
LILO	Examples of LILO configurations
Linux+DOS+Win95	How to configure LILO to boot Linux, DOS, or Win95
Linux+DOS+Win95+OS2	How to configure LILO to boot Linux, DOS, Win95, or OS2
Linux+FreeBSD	How to use Linux and FreeBSD on your computer
Linux+NT-Loader	How to use the NT loader to boot Linux
Linux+Win95	Discusses issues concerning installing Linux on Win95 systems
Loadlin+Win95	How to use LOADLIN.EXE to boot Linux from Win95
Locales	How to use locales with Linux
Loopback-Root-FS	How to set up a Linux file system that can be run from a DOS partition without repartitioning
Mac-Terminal	Information on using a Macintosh as a serial terminal
MIDI+SB	How to use a MIDI keyboard with a Sound Blaster card under Linux
Mail-Queue	Configuring `sendmail` to deliver local mail for Linux
Mail2News	How to set up mailing list and local newsgroups with your Linux news server
Man-Page	How to write man pages for Linux software
Multiboot-with-LILO	How to boot between different operating systems on a single computer
Modules	Using kernel modules with Linux
NCD-X-Terminal	How to connect an NCD X terminal to Linux

continues...

Table B.2 Continued

HOWTO	Description
NFS-Root	How to boot Linux via the Network File System (NFS)
NFS-Root-Client	How to create client root directories on a Linux server
Netrom-Node	How to set up an x25 utilities package for amateur radio such as making Netrom Nodes
Netscape+Proxy	How to create an in-house intranet
Netstation	How to connect an IBM Netstation to your Linux box
Offline-Mailing	How to get mail for multiple users using only one email address
PLIP	How to build and use the Parallel Line Interface Protocol (PLIP) with Linux
Pager	How to set up and use a Linux alphanumeric pager gateway
Partition	How to choose Linux partitions
Partition-Rescue	How to rescue deleted Linux partitions
Path	How to set up the PATH variable
Pre-Installation-Checklist	Pre-installation checklist for Linux
Process-Accounting	How to use process accounting with Linux
Proxy-ARP-Subnet	How to use ARP with subnetting under Linux
Public-Web-Browser	How to set up a public Web browser using Netscape and Linux
Qmail+MH	Using qmail with Linux
Quota	Enabling disk quotas under Linux
RCS	Installing and using the Revision Control System (RCS) and Linux
RPM+Slackware	How to use the rpm command and the Slackware Linux distribution
RedHat-CD	How to make CDs equivalent to the Red Hat commercial distribution
Remote-Boot	Booting Linux in a network environment
Remote-X-Apps	How to run remote X clients using Linux
Saving-Space	How to make the smallest possible Linux installation
SLIP-PPP-Emulator	How to connect to the Internet via a SLIP/PPP emulator
Sendmail+UUCP	Using sendmail and UNIX-to-UNIX-Copy
Sendmail-Address-Rewrite	Set up sendmail's configuration file for dial-up access
Secure-POP+SSH	How to secure POP connections

HOWTO	Description
Software-RAID	Using RAID software with Linux
Soundblaster-AWE	Using SoundBlaster AWE cards with Linux
StarOffice	Installing the StarOffice suite for Linux
Term-Firewall	How to access network information through a TCP firewall under Linux
TkRat	How to use the TkRat mail program
Token-Ring	How to configure Linux to use Token-Ring networks
Update	How to stay up-to-date with Linux information
Upgrade	How to upgrade from one Linux distribution to another
VAIO+Linux	Information on installing Linux on Sony VAIO computers
VPN	How to set up a virtual private network (VPN) under Linux
Visual-Bell	How to disable console bells under Linux
Windows-Modem-Sharing	How to share a modem over a TCP/IP network under Linux
WordPerfect	How to run WordPerfect under Linux
X-Big-Cursor	How to configure large cursors under X
XFree86-XInside	How to convert XFree86 XF86Config modelines to XI modelines
Xterm-Title	How to place titles in `xterm` windows
ZIP-Drive	How to configure and use the Iomega Zip drive with Linux
ZIP-Install	How to install the `ppa` Zip disk driver

Top 50 Linux Commands and Utilities

General guidelines ●

The list ●

This appendix is not meant to replace the man pages; it does not go into anything resembling the detail available in the man pages. This appendix is designed to give you a feel for the commands and a brief description as to what they do. In most cases there are more parameters that can be used than are shown here.

Most of the descriptions also have examples with them. If these examples aren't self-evident, an explanation is provided. This is not an exhaustive list—there are many more commands that you could use—but these are the most common, and you will find yourself using them over and over again.

If you have problems executing these commands, be warned that some of them are privileged utilities and can only be run by the root user. Often these commands are stored in the /sbin or /usr/sbin directory and require the complete pathname in order to work.

To keep things simple, the commands are listed in alphabetical order. I would have preferred to put them in order of how often I use them, but that would make locating them quite difficult. However, I do want to summarize by listing what are, at least for me, the ten most common commands—also alphabetically. This list of essential commands could be compared to a list of the top ten words spoken by the cavemen when searching for food and a mate:

1. cat
2. cd
3. cp
4. find
5. grep
6. ls
7. more
8. rm
9. tar
10. vi

General Guidelines

In general, if you want to change something that already exists, the command to do that will begin with ch. If you want to do something for the first time, the command to do that will usually begin with mk. If you want to remove something completely, the command will usually begin with rm. For example, to make a new directory, you use the mkdir command. To remove a directory, you use the rmdir command.

The List

The commands listed in this appendix are some of the most common commands used in Linux. In cases where the command seems ambiguous, an example is provided. With each of these commands, the man pages can provide additional information, as well as more examples.

The . command tells the shell to execute all the commands in the file that are passed an argument to the command. This works in the bash or pdksh. The equivalent in the tcsh is the source command. The following example will execute the commands in the file adobe:

```
. adobe
```

&

The & after any other command tells the computer to run the command in the background. By placing a job in the background, the user can then continue using that shell to process other commands. If the command is run in the foreground, the user cannot continue using that shell until the process finishes.

adduser

The adduser command is used by root, or someone else who has the authority, to create a new user. The adduser command is followed by the account name to be created—for example,

```
adduser dpitts
```

alias

The alias command is used to make aliases or alternative names for commands. Typically, these aliases are abbreviations of the actual command. In the following example, the user (probably a DOS user) is adding an alias of dir for a directory listing:

```
alias dir=ls
```

Typing alias by itself will give you a list of all your current aliases. Such a list might look like this:

```
svr01:/home/dpitts$ alias
alias d='dir'
alias dir='/bin/ls $LS_OPTIONS --format=vertical'
alias ls='/bin/ls $LS_OPTIONS'
alias v='vdir'
alias vdir='/bin/ls $LS_OPTIONS --format=long'
```

599

apropos

The apropos command literally means appropriate or regarding (others). When it is followed by a parameter, it will search the man pages for entries that include the parameter. Basically, this performs a keyword search on all the man pages. This is the equivalent of the man -k *parameter* command.

banner

banner prints a large, text-based banner to standard output. If the message is omitted, it prompts for and reads one line from standard input. For example, enter $ banner hi to create the following banner:

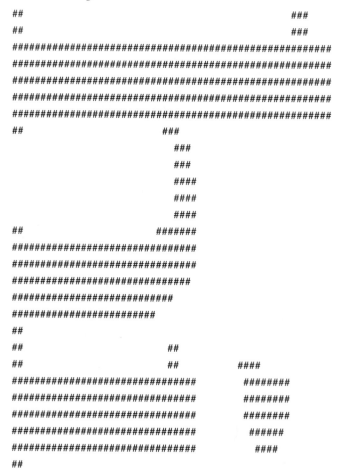

bg

The bg command is used to force a suspended process to run in the background. For example, you might have started a command in the foreground (without using & after the command) and realized that it was going to take a while, but that you still needed your shell. You could take that process that is currently running and hold down the Ctrl key, and, while it is held down, press the Z key. This places the current process on hold. You can either leave it on hold, just as if you called your telephone company, or you could place that process in the background by typing bg. This then frees up your shell to allow you to execute other commands and lets the suspended application continue working.

bind

Used in pdksh, the bind command enables the user to change the behavior of key combinations for the purpose of command-line editing. Many times people bind the up, down, left, and right arrow keys so that they work the way they would in the Bourne Again Shell (bsh). The syntax used for the command is

```
bind key  sequence   command
```

The following examples are the bind commands to create bindings for scrolling up and down the history list and for moving left and right along the command line:

```
bind `^[[`=prefix-2
bind `^XA`=up-history
bind `^XB`=down-history
bind `^XC`=forward-char
bind `^XD`=backward-char
```

cat

cat does not call your favorite feline; instead, it tells the system to "concatenate" the contents of a file to the standard output, usually the screen. If that file happens to be binary, the cat gets a hairball and the output can be a bit ugly. Typically, this is a noisy process as well. What is actually happening is that the cat command is scrolling the characters of the file, and the terminal is doing all it can to interpret and display the data in the file. This interpretation can include the character used to create the bell signal, which is where the noise comes from. As you might have surmised, the cat command requires something to display and would have the following format:

```
cat filename
```

cd

cd stands for change directory. You will find this command extremely useful. There are three typical ways of using this command:

cd ..	Moves one directory up the directory tree.
cd ~	Moves to your home directory from wherever you currently are. This is the same as issuing cd by itself.
cd *directory name*	Changes to a specific directory. This can be a directory relative to your current location or can be based on the root directory by placing a forward slash (/) before the directory name. These examples can be combined. For example, suppose you were in the directory /home/dsp1234 and you wanted to go to tng4321's home account. You could perform the following command, which will move you back up the directory one level and then move you down into the tng4321 directory:

cd ../tng4321

chgrp

The chgrp command is used to change the group associated with the permissions of the file or directory. The owner of the file (and, of course, root) has the authority to change the group associated with the file. The format for the command is simply

chgrp *new group file*

chmod

The chmod command is used to change the permissions associated with the object (typically a file or directory). What you are really doing is changing the file mode. There are two ways of specifying the permissions of the object. You can use the numeric coding system or the letter coding system. If you recall, there are three sets of users associated with every object: the owner of the object, the group for the object, and everybody else. Using the letter coding system, they are referred to as u for user, g for group, o for other, and a for all. There are three basic types of permissions that you can change: r for read, w for write, and x for execute. These three permissions can be changed using the plus (+) and minus (-) signs. For example, to add read and execute to owner and group of the file test1, you would issue the following command:

chmod ug+rx test1

To remove the read and execute permissions from the user and group of the `test1` file, you would change the plus (+) sign to a minus (-) sign:

```
chmod ug-rx test1
```

This is called making relative changes to the mode of the file.

Using the numeric coding system, you always have to give the absolute value of the permissions, regardless of their previous permissions. The numeric system is based on three sets of octal numbers. There is one set for each category of user, group, and other. The values are 4, 2, and 1, where 4 equals read, 2 equals write, and 1 equals execute. These values are added together to give the set of permissions for that category. With the numeric coding you always specify all three categories. Therefore, to make the owner of the file `test1` have read, write, and execute permissions, and no one else to have any permissions, you would use the value 700, like this:

```
chmod 700 test1
```

To make the same file readable and writable by the user, and readable by both the group and others, you would follow the following mathematical logic: For the first set of permissions, the user, the value for readable is 4, and the value for writable is 2. The sum of these two is 6. The next set of permissions, the group, only gets readable, so that is 4. The settings for others, like the group, are 4. Therefore, the command would be `chmod 644 test1`.

The format for the command, using either method, is the same. You issue the `chmod` command followed by the permissions, either absolute or relative, followed by the objects for which you want the mode changed:

```
chmod permissions file
```

chown

This command is used to change the user ID (owner) associated with the permissions of the file or directory. The owner of the file (and, of course, root) has the authority to change the user associated with the file. The format for the command is simply

```
chown new user id file
```

You can also use `chown` as a shortcut to set the group ownership of the file by using this format:

```
chown new user id:new group id file
```

chroot

The chroot command makes the / directory (called the root directory) be something other than / on the file system. For example, when working with an Internet server, you can set the root directory to equal /usr/ftp. Then, when someone logs on using FTP (which goes to the root directory by default), he or she will actually go to the directory /usr/ftp. This protects the rest of your directory structure from being seen or even changed to by this anonymous guest to your machine. If the person were to enter cd /etc, the ftp program would try to put him or her in the root directory and then in the etc directory off of that. Because the root directory is /usr/ftp, the ftp program will actually put the user in the /usr/ftp/etc directory (assuming there is one).

The syntax for the command is

```
chroot original filesystem location new filesystem location
```

cp

The cp command is an abbreviation for copy; therefore, this command enables you to copy objects. For example, to copy the file file1 to file2, issue the following command:

```
cp file1 file2
```

As the example shows, the syntax is very simple:

```
cp original object name new object name
```

dd

The dd command copies and converts file formats. For example, to copy a boot image to a disk (assuming the device name for the disk is /dev/fd0), you would issue the command

```
dd if=filename of-/dev/fd0 obs=18k
```

where filename would be something like BOOT0001.img, of is the object format (what you are copying to), and obs is the output block size.

userdel

The userdel command removes a user account from the system. Use this to delete all the test users that you created with the adduser command—for example,

```
userdel username
```

env

The env command is used to see the exported environment variables. The result of the command is a two-column list where the variable's name is on the left and the value associated with that variable is on the right. The command is issued without any parameters. Hence, typing env might get you a list similar to this one:

```
svr01:/home/dpitts$ env
HOSTNAME=svr01.mk.net
LOGNAME=dpitts
MAIL=/var/spool/mail/dpitts
TERM=vt100
HOSTTYPE=i386
PATH=/usr/local/bin:/usr/bin:/bin:.:/usr/local/java/bin
HOME=/home2/dpitts
SHELL=/bin/bash
LS_OPTIONS=--8bit --color=tty -F -b -T 0
PS1=\h:\w\$
PS2=>
MANPATH=/usr/local/man:/usr/man/preformat:/usr/man:/usr/lib/perl5/man
LESS=-MM
OSTYPE=Linux
SHLVL=1
```

fc

The fc command is used to edit the history file. The parameters passed to it, if there are any, can be used to select a range of commands from the history file. This list is then placed in an editing shell. The editor that it uses is based on the value of the variable FCEDIT. If there is no value for this variable, the command looks at the EDITOR variable. If it is not there, the default is used, which is vi.

fg

Processes can be run in either the background or the foreground. The fg command enables you to take a suspended process and run it in the foreground. This is typically used when you have a process running in the foreground and for some reason, you need to suspend it (thus allowing you to run other commands). The process will continue until you either place it in the background or bring it to the foreground.

file

The `file` command runs each argument through one of three tests: the file system test, the magic number test, or the language test. The first test to succeed causes the file type to be printed. If the file is text (it is an ASCII file), it then attempts to guess which language. The following example identifies the file `nquota` as a text file that contains Perl commands. The file is checked against a list of magic numbers that identify a fixed format of data within the file. Here is an example for checking the file `nquota` to see what kind of file it is:

```
file nquota
nquota: perl commands text
```

find

Did you ever say to yourself, "Self, where did I put that file?" Well now, instead of talking to yourself and having those around you wonder about you, you can ask the computer. You can say, "Computer, where did I put that file?" Okay, it is not that simple, but it is close. All you have to do is ask the computer to find the file.

The `find` command will look in whatever directory you tell it to, as well as all subdirectories under that directory, for the file that you specified. After it has found this list, it will then do with the list as you have asked it to. Typically, you just want to know where it is, so you ask it, nicely, to print out the list. The syntax of the command is the command itself, followed by the directory you want to start searching in, followed by the filename (metacharacters are acceptable), and then what you want done with the list. In the following example, the `find` command searches for files ending with `.pl` in the current directory (and all subdirectories). It then prints the results to standard output.

```
find . -name *.pl -print
./public_html/scripts/gant.pl
./public_html/scripts/edit_gant.pl
./public_html/scripts/httools.pl
./public_html/scripts/chart.no.comments.pl
```

`find` can also be used to look for files of a certain size or date and many other attributes. Be sure to check out the man page for `find`; it can come in handy for lots of searching needs.

ftp

Use the file transfer protocol (FTP) to connect to a remote system. FTP is a basic transfer method that is available for moving data between different computers, regardless of operating system.

grep

The grep (global regular expression parse) command searches the object you specify for the text that you specify. The syntax of the command is grep *text file*. In the following example, I am searching for instances of the text httools in all files in the current directory:

```
grep httools *
edit_gant.cgi:require 'httools.pl';
edit_gant.pl:require 'httools.pl';
gant.cgi:   require 'httools.pl';  # Library containing reuseable code
gant.cgi:       &date;     # Calls the todays date subroutine from httools.pl
gant.cgi:       &date;     #  Calls the todays date subroutine from httools.pl
gant.cgi:   &header;  # from httools.pl
```

Although this is valuable, the grep command can also be used in conjunction with the results of other commands. For example, the following command

```
ps -ef |grep -v root
```

calls for the grep command to take the output of the ps command and take out all instances of the word root (the -v means everything but the text that follows). The same command without the -v (ps -ef |grep root) returns all the instances that contain the word root from the process listing.

groff

groff is the front end to the groff document formatting program. This program, by default, calls the troff program.

gzip

gzip is GNU's version of the zip compression software. The syntax can be as simple as

```
gzip filename
```

but many times also contains some parameters between the command and the file-name to be compressed.

gunzip

gunzip will extract archives compressed with the GNU gzip software. In most cases all you'll need is

gunzip *filename*

This is equivalent to gzip -d (decompress), if you'd prefer.

halt

The halt command tells the kernel to shut down. This is a superuser-only command (you must be root).

hostname

hostname is used to either display the current host or domain name of the system or to set the hostname of the system—for example

svr01:/home/dpitts$ hostname

svr01

kill

kill sends the specified signal to the specified process. If no signal is specified, the TERM signal is sent. The TERM signal will kill processes that do not process the TERM signal. For processes that do process the TERM signal, it might be necessary to use the KILL signal because this signal cannot be caught. The syntax for the kill command is kill *option pid*, and an example is as follows:

svr01:/home/dpitts$kill -9 1438

killall

A simpler method of killing programs is now included in many Linux distributions: killall. You use killall exactly the same as kill, but instead of the process ID, you use the name of the process. This usually eliminates a call to ps.

less

less is a program similar to more, but which allows backward movement in the file as well as forward movement. less also doesn't have to read the entire input file before starting, so with large input files it starts up faster than text editors such as vi.

locate

The locate command is included in most Linux distributions and enables the user to quickly find files based on patterns in the filename. locate works off of an indexed database on your computer, so it is much faster than find. To find a file based on its name, try using locate *filename* like this:

```
[jray@contempt jray]$ locate server
/etc/X11/xdm/Xservers
/etc/CORBA/servers
/etc/CORBA/servers/gnomecc.gnorba
/etc/CORBA/servers/gmc.gnorba
/etc/CORBA/servers/another_clock_applet.gnorba
...
```

login

login is used when signing on to a system. It can also be used to switch from one user to another at any time.

logout

logout is used to sign off a system as the current user. If it is the only user you are logged in as, you are logged off the system.

lpc

lpc is used by the system administrator to control the operation of the line printer system. lpc can be used to disable or enable a printer or a printer's spooling queue, to rearrange the order of jobs in a spooling queue, to find out the status of printers, to find out the status of the spooling queues, and to find out the status of the printer daemons. The command can be used for any of the printers configured in /etc/printcap.

lpd

lpd is the line printer daemon and is normally invoked at boot time from the rc file. It makes a single pass through the /etc/printcap file to find out about the existing printers and prints any files left after a crash. It then uses the system calls listen and accept to receive requests to print files in the queue, transfer files to the spooling area, display the queue, or remove jobs from the queue.

lpq

lpq examines the spooling area used by lpd for printing files on the line printer, and reports the status of the specified jobs or all jobs associated with a user. If the command is invoked without any arguments, the command reports on any jobs currently in the print queue.

lpr

The line printer command uses a spooling daemon to print the named files when facilities become available. If no names appear, the standard input is assumed. The following is an example of the lpr command:

```
lpr /etc/hosts
```

ls

The ls command lists the contents of a directory. The format of the output is manipulated with options. The ls command, with no options, lists all unhidden files (a file that begins with a dot is a hidden file) in alphabetical order, filling as many columns as will fit in the window. Probably the most common set of options used with this command is the -la option. The a means list all (including hidden files) files, and the l means make the output a long listing. Here is an example of this command:

```
svr01:~$ ls -la
total 35
drwxr-xr-x   7 dpitts    users      1024 Jul 21 00:19 ./
drwxr-xr-x 140 root      root       3072 Jul 23 14:38 ../
-rw-r--r--   1 dpitts    users      4541 Jul 23 23:33 .bash_history
-rw-r--r--   1 dpitts    users        18 Sep 16  1996 .forward
-rw-r--r--   2 dpitts    users       136 May 10 01:46 .htaccess
-rw-r--r--   1 dpitts    users       164 Dec 30  1995 .kermrc
-rw-r--r--   1 dpitts    users        34 Jun  6  1993 .less
-rw-r--r--   1 dpitts    users       114 Nov 23  1993 .lessrc
-rw-r--r--   1 dpitts    users        10 Jul 20 22:32 .profile
drwxr-xr-x   2 dpitts    users      1024 Dec 20  1995 .term/
drwx------   2 dpitts    users      1024 Jul 16 02:04 Mail/
drwxr-xr-x   2 dpitts    users      1024 Feb  1  1996 cgi-src/
-rw-r--r--   1 dpitts    users      1643 Jul 21 00:23 hi
-rwxr-xr-x   1 dpitts    users       496 Jan  3  1997 nquota*
drwxr-xr-x   2 dpitts    users      1024 Jan  3  1997 passwd/
drwxrwxrwx   5 dpitts    users      1024 May 14 20:29 public_html/
```

make

The purpose of the make utility is to automatically determine which pieces of a large program need to be recompiled and then to issue the commands necessary to recompile them. You typically use this when downloading source code off the Internet and installing it on your system.

man

The man command is used to format and display the online manual pages. The manual pages are the text that describes, in detail, how to use a specified command. In the following example, I have called the man page that describes the man pages:

```
svr01:~$ man man

man(1)                                              man(1)
NAME
      man - format and display the on-line manual pages
      manpath - determine user's search path for man pages
SYNOPSIS
      man  [-adfhktwW]  [-m system] [-p string] [-C config_file]
      [-M path] [-P pager] [-S section_list] [section] name  .
DESCRIPTION
man  formats  and  displays the on-line manual pages. This
version knows about  the  MANPATH  and  PAGER  environment
variables, so you can have your own set(s) of personal man
pages and choose whatever program you like to display  the
formatted  pages.  If section is specified, man only looks
in that section of the manual.  You may also  specify  the
order to search the sections for entries and which prepro-
cessors to run  on  the  source  files  via  command  line
options  or  environment  variables.  If name contains a /
then it is first tried as a filename, so that you  can  do
```

mesg

The mesg utility is run by a user to control write access others have to the terminal device associated with the standard error output. If write access is allowed, programs such as talk and write have permission to display messages on the terminal. Write access is allowed by default.

mkdir

The mkdir command is used to make a new directory.

mkfs

mkfs is used to build a Linux file system on a device, usually a hard disk partition. The syntax for the command is mkfs *filesystem*, where *filesystem* is either the device name (such as /dev/hda1) or the mount point (for example, /, /usr, /home) for the file system.

mkswap

mkswap sets up a Linux swap area on a device (usually a disk partition).

The device is usually of the following form:

```
/dev/hda[1-8]
/dev/hdb[1-8]
/dev/sda[1-8]
/dev/sdb[1-8]
```

more

more is a filter for paging through text one screen at a time. This command can only page down through the text, as opposed to less, which can page both up and down though the text.

mount

mount attaches the file system specified by specialfile (which is often a device name) to the directory specified as the parameter. Ordinarily, only the superuser can mount files. If the mount command is run without parameters, it lists all the currently mounted file systems. The following is an example of the mount command:

```
svr01:/home/dpitts$ mount
/dev/hda1 on / type ext2 (rw)
/dev/hda2 on /var/spool/mail type ext2 (rw,usrquota)
/dev/hda3 on /logs type ext2 (rw,usrquota)
/dev/hdc1 on /home type ext2 (rw,usrquota)
none on /proc type proc (rw)
```

mv

The mv command is used to move an object from one location to another location. If the last argument names an existing directory, the command moves the rest of the list into that directory. If two files are given, the command moves the first into the second. It is an error to have more than two arguments with this command unless the last argument is a directory. You can use mv to rename files by "moving" the file you want to rename to the filename you want it to be.

netstat

netstat displays the status of network connections on either TCP, UDP, RAW, or UNIX sockets to the system. The -r option is used to obtain information about the routing table. The following is an example of the netstat command:

```
svr01:/home/dpitts$ netstat
Active Internet connections
Proto Recv-Q Send-Q Local Address          Foreign Address         (State)
User
tcp        0  16501 www.mk.net:www         sdlb12119.san_net.:3148 FIN_WAIT1
root
tcp        0  16501 auth02.mk.net:www      sdlb12119.san_net.:3188 FIN_WAIT1
root
tcp        0      1 www.anglernet.com:www  ts88.cctrap.com:1070    SYN_RECV
root
tcp        0      1 www.anglernet.com:www  ts88.cctrap.com:1071    SYN_RECV
root
udp        0      0 localhost:domain       *:*
udp        0      0 svr01.mk.net:domain    *:*
udp        0      0 poto.mk.net:domain     *:*
udp        0      0 stats.mk.net:domain    *:*
udp        0      0 home.mk.net:domain     *:*
udp        0      0 www.cmf.net:domain     *:*
Active UNIX domain sockets
Proto RefCnt Flags    Type        State        Path
unix  2      [ ]      SOCK_STREAM UNCONNECTED  1605182
unix  2      [ ]      SOCK_STREAM UNCONNECTED  1627039
unix  2      [ ]      SOCK_STREAM CONNECTED    1652605
```

passwd

For the normal user (non-superuser), no arguments are used with the passwd command. The command will ask the user for the old password. Following this, the command will ask for the new password twice, to make sure it was typed correctly. The new password must be at least six characters long and must contain at least one character that is either an uppercase or nonalphabetic character. Also, the new password cannot be the same password as the one being replaced, nor can it match the user's ID (account name).

If the command is run by the superuser, it can be followed by either one or two arguments. If the command is followed by a single user's ID, the superuser can change that user's password. The superuser is not bound by any of the restrictions imposed on the user. If there is an argument after the single user's ID, that argument becomes that user's new password.

ps

ps gives a snapshot of the current processes. An example is as follows:

```
svr01:/home/dpitts$ ps -ef

PID TTY STAT  TIME COMMAND
10916  p3 S    0:00 -bash TERM=vt100 HOME=/home2/dpitts PATH=/usr/local/bin:/us
10973  p3 R    0:00 \_ ps -ef LESSOPEN=|lesspipe.sh %s ignoreeof=10 HOSTNAME=s
10974  p3 S    0:00 \_ more LESSOPEN=|lesspipe.sh %s ignoreeof=10 HOSTNAME=svr
```

pwd

pwd prints the current working directory. It tells you what directory you are currently in.

rm

rm is used to delete specified files. With the -r option (Warning: This can be dangerous!), rm will recursively remove files. Therefore if, as root, you type the command rm -r /, you had better have a good backup because all your files are now gone. This is a good command to use in conjunction with the find command to find files owned by a certain user or in a certain group, and delete them. By default, the rm command does not remove directories.

rmdir

`rmdir` removes a given *empty* directory; the word *empty* is the key word. The syntax is simply `rmdir directory name`.

set

The `set` command is used to temporarily change an environment variable. In some shells, the `set -o vi` command will allow you to bring back previous commands that you have in your history file. It is common to place the command in your `.profile` file. Some environment variables require an equals sign, and some, as in the example `set -o vi`, do not.

shutdown

One time during *Star Trek: The Next Generation*, Data commands the computer to "Shut down the holodeck!" Unfortunately, most systems don't have voice controls, but systems can still be shut down. This command happens to be the one to do just that. The `shutdown` command can also be used to issue a "Vulcan Neck Pinch" (Ctrl+Alt+Del) and restart the system. You'll need to give the `shutdown` command a time at which to bring down the system. Typically, if you're issuing shutdown, you'll want to do it now, so that's exactly what you tell the system:

```
[jray@contempt jray]# shutdown now
```

You can add the `-r` option to `shutdown` to reboot, or explicitly use `-h` to halt. By default, shutdown will put the system into runlevel 1.

su

su enables a user to temporarily become another user. If a user ID is not given, the computer thinks you want to be the superuser, or root. In either case, a shell is spawned that makes you the new user, complete with that user ID, group ID, and any supplemental groups of that new user. If you are not root and the user has a password (and the user should!), su prompts for a password. Root can become any user at any time without knowing passwords. Technically, the user just needs to have a user ID of 0 (which makes a user a superuser) to log on as anyone else without a password.

swapoff

No, swapoff is not a move from *Karate Kid*. Instead, it is a command that stops swapping to a file or block device.

swapon

Also not from the movie *Karate Kid*, swapon sets the swap area to the file or block device by path. swapoff stops swapping to the file. This command is normally done during system boot.

tail

tail prints to standard output the last 10 lines of a given file. If no file is given, it reads from standard input. If more than one file is given, it prints a header consisting of the file's name enclosed in a left and right arrow (==> <==) before the output of each file. The default value of 10 lines can be changed by placing a -### in the command. The syntax for the command is

```
tail [-# of lines to see] [filename(s)]
```

talk

The talk command is used to have a "visual" discussion with someone else over a terminal. The basic idea behind this visual discussion is that your input is copied to the other person's terminal, and the other person's input is copied to your terminal. Thus, both people involved in the discussion see the input for both themselves and the other person.

tar

tar is an archiving program designed to store and extract files from an archive file. This tarred file (called a tar file), can be archived to any media including a tape drive and a hard drive. The syntax of a tar command is tar *action optional functions file(s)/directory(ies)*. If the last parameter is a directory, all subdirectories under the directory are also tarred.

telnet

Connect using a terminal to a remote computer. Typically used to connect to another Linux or UNIX computer.

top

Like the ps command, top displays the processes that are running on your system. top, however, offers an updating interactive display that sorts the processes according to their CPU usage, enabling you to see what programs are making your computer *so* slow.

umount

Just as the cavalry unmounts from their horses, file systems unmount from their locations as well. The umount command is used to perform this action. The syntax of the command is

umount *filesystem*

unalias

unalias is the command to undo an alias. In the alias command section, earlier in this appendix, I aliased dir to be the ls command. To unalias this command, you would simply type unalias dir.

unzip

The unzip command will list, test, or extract files from a zipped archive. The default is to extract files from the archive. The basic syntax is unzip *filename*.

wall

wall displays the contents of standard input on all terminals of all currently logged in users. Basically, the command writes to all terminals, hence its name. The contents of files can also be displayed. The superuser, or root, can write to the terminals of those who have chosen to deny messages or are using a program that automatically denies messages.

who

Either the who command calls an owl, which it doesn't, or it prints the login name, terminal type, login time, and remote hostname of each user currently logged on. The following is an example of the who command:

```
svr01:/home/dpitts$ who
root      ttyp0    Jul 27 11:44 (www01.mk.net)
dpitts    ttyp2    Jul 27 19:32 (d12.dialup.seane)
```

```
ehooban  ttyp3    Jul 27 11:47 (205.177.146.78)
dpitts   ttyp4    Jul 27 19:34 (d12.dialup.seane)
```

If two nonoption arguments are passed to the who command, the command prints the entry for the user running it. Typically, this is run with the command who am I, but any two arguments will work; for example, the following gives information on my session:

```
svr01:/home/dpitts$ who who who

svr01!dpitts   ttyp2    Jul 27 19:32 (d12.dialup.seane)
```

The -u option is nice if you want to see how long it has been since that session has been used, such as in the following:

```
svr01:/home/dpitts$ who -u
root     ttyp0    Jul 27 11:44 08:07 (www01.mk.net)
dpitts   ttyp2    Jul 27 19:32   .   (d12.dialup.seane)
ehooban  ttyp3    Jul 27 11:47 00:09 (205.177.146.78)
dpitts   ttyp4    Jul 27 19:34 00:06 (d12.dialup.seane)
```

write

The write command sends a message to the display of another user who is logged in to the system, unless that user has shut off messaging with the mesg command.

xhost

The xhost command provides access control for remote programs outputting their display to your screen. Probably the most common reason that a remote terminal cannot be opened is because the xhost + machine name command has not been run. To turn off the capability for all external programs to connect, the xhost - command is used.

xmkmf

The xmkmf command is used to create the Imakefiles for X sources. It actually runs the imake command with a set of arguments.

xset

The xset command sets some of the options in an X Window session. You can use this option to set your bell (xset b volume frequency duration in milliseconds), your mouse speed (xset m acceleration threshold), and many others.

zip

The `zip` command will list, test, or add files to a zipped archive. The default is to add files to an archive.

Summary

If you read this entire appendix, you will have noticed two things. First, I cannot count. There are about seventy commands here, not fifty as the title of the appendix states. Second, you have way too much time on your hands, and need to go out and program some drivers or something!

I hope this appendix has helped you gain an understanding of some of the commands available for your use, whether you are a user, a system administrator, or just someone who wants to learn more about Linux. I encourage you to use the man pages to find out the many details left out of this appendix. Most of the commands have arguments that can be passed to them, and, although this appendix attempts to point out a few of them, it would have taken an entire book just to go into the detail that has been provided in the man pages.

Glossary

This is a fairly extensive glossary of terms that are related to the UNIX environment and their definitions. All the authors of this book contributed to this section.

Note: The language of the computer field is constantly expanding. If you cannot find a word in this glossary, it is because it is newer than anything the authors knew about or the authors decided is was so obvious that everyone should already know it.

Octothorpe (also called *pound sign* or *hash mark*). Usually denoting a comment.

$HOME   Environment variable that points to your login directory.

$PATH   Pathname environment variable.

$PATH   The shell environment variable that contains a set of directories to be searched for UNIX commands.

$TERM   Terminal-type environment variable.

$USER   Environment variable containing the name of the current user.

.1   Files with this extension contain manual page entries. The actual extension can be any value between 1 and 9 and can have an alphabetic suffix (.3x, .7, and so on).

.ag   Applixware graphics file.

.as   Applixware spreadsheet file.

.aw   Applixware word processing file.

.bmp   Bitmap graphics file.

.bz2   bzip2-compressed file.

.c   C source file.

.C   C++ source file.

.cc   C++ source file.

.conf   Configuration file.

.cxx   C++ source file.

.db   Database file.

.dvi   Device-independent TeX output.

.gif   GIF graphics file.

.gz   File compressed using the GNU gzip utility.

.h   C header file.

.html   HTML document.

.jpg   JPEG graphics file.

.m   Objective C source file.

.o   Compiled object file.

.p   Pascal language source file.

.pbm   Portable bitmap graphics file.

.pdf   Adobe Acrobat file.

.png   Portable network graphics; an alternative to GIFs.

.ps   PostScript file

.s   Assembler file.

.tar   tar file.

.tgz   Gzipped tar file.

.tif   TIFF graphics file.

.txt   Text document.

.z   File compressed using the compress command.

/   Root directory.

/dev   Device directory.

/dev/null **file**   The place to send output that you are not interested in seeing; also the place to get input from when you have none (but the program or command requires something). This is also known as the *bit bucket* (where old bits go to die).

/dev/printer   Socket for local print requests.

/etc/cshrc **file**   The file containing shell environment characteristics common to all users working in the C shell.

/etc/group **file**   This file contains information about groups, the users they contain, and passwords required for access by other users. The password might actually be in another file, the shadow group file, to protect it from attacks.

/etc/inittab **file**   The file that contains a list of processes to be started at boot time. This file defines the standard runlevels.

/etc/motd **file**   Message of the day file; usually contains information the system administrator feels is important for you to know. This file is displayed when the user signs on the system.

/etc/passwd **file**   Contains user information and password. The password might actually be in another file, the shadow password file, to protect it from attacks.

/etc/profile   The file containing shell environment characteristics common to all users of the Bourne and Korn shells.

/usr/local   Locally developed public executables directory.

/var/spool   Various spool directories.

[]   Brackets.

{}   Braces.

ANSI   American National Standards Institute.

API   Application Programming Interface. The specific method prescribed by a computer operating system, application, or third-party tool by which a programmer writing an application can make requests of the operating system. Also known as Application Programmer's Interface.

ar   Archive utility.

arguments   See *parameters*.

ARPA   See *DARPA*.

ASCII   American Standard Code for Information Interchange. Used to represent characters in memory for most computers.

AT&T UNIX   Original version of UNIX developed at AT&T Bell Labs, later known as UNIX Systems Laboratories. Many current versions of UNIX are descendants; even BSD UNIX was derived from early AT&T UNIX.

attribute   The means of describing objects. The attributes for a ball might be rubber, red, 3cm in diameter. The behavior of the ball might be how high it bounces when thrown. Attribute is another name for the data contained within an object (class).

awk   Programming language developed by A.V. Aho, P.J. Weinberger, and Brian W. Kernighan. The language is built on C syntax, includes the regular expression search facilities of grep, and adds in the advanced string and array handling features that are missing from the C language. nawk, gawk, and POSIX awk are versions of this language.

background   Processes usually running at a lower priority and with their input disconnected from the interactive session.

background process   An autonomous process that runs under UNIX without user interaction.

backup   The process of storing the UNIX system, applications, and data files on removable media for future retrieval.

bash   Stands for GNU Bourne Again shell and is based on the Bourne shell, sh, the original command interpreter.

biff   Background mail notification utility.

bison   GNU parser generator (yacc replacement).

block-special   A device file that is used to communicate with a block-oriented I/O device. Disk and tape drives are examples of block devices. The block-special file refers to the entire device. You should not use this file unless you want to ignore the directory structure of the device (that is, if you are coding a device driver).

boot or boot up   The process of starting the operating system (UNIX).

Bourne shell   The original standard user interface to UNIX that supported limited programming capability.

BSD   Berkeley Software Distribution.

BSD UNIX   Version of UNIX developed by Berkeley Software Distribution and written at University of California, Berkeley.

bug   An undocumented and usually unwanted program feature.

bzip2—The latest and greatest compression utility that is slowly gaining ground in the Linux community. Not nearly as prevalent as gzip, but produces smaller files. Use bunzip2 to uncompress a bzip2 file.

C   Programming language developed by Brian W. Kernighan and Dennis M. Ritchie. The C language is highly portable and available on many platforms including mainframes, PCs, and, of course, UNIX systems.

C shell   A user interface for UNIX written by Bill Joy at Berkeley. It features syntax similar to the C programming language.

CAD   Computer-aided design.

cast   Programming construct to force type conversion.

`cat`   Concatenate files command.

CD-ROM   Compact Disc–Read-Only Memory. Computer-readable data stored on the same physical form as a musical CD. Large capacity, inexpensive, slower than a hard disk, and limited to reading. There are versions that are writable (CD-R, CD Recordable) and other formats that can be written to once or many times.

CGI   Common Gateway Interface. A means of transmitting data between Web pages and programs or scripts executing on the server. Those programs can then process the data and send the results back to the user's browser through dynamically creating HTML.

character special   A device file that is used to communicate with character-oriented I/O devices such as terminals, printers, or network communications lines. All I/O access is treated as a series of bytes (characters).

characters, alphabetic   The letters *A* through *Z* and *a* through *z*.

characters, alphanumeric   The letters *A* through *Z* and *a* through *z*, and the numerals *0* through *9*.

characters, control   Any nonprintable characters. The characters are used to control devices, separate records, and eject pages on printers.

characters, numeric   The numerals *0* through *9*.

characters, special   Any of the punctuation characters or printable characters that are not alphanumeric. Include the space, comma, period, and many others.

child process   See *subprocess*.

child shell   See *subshell*.

class   A model of objects that have attributes (data) and behavior (code or functions). It is also viewed as a collection of objects in their abstracted form.

command-line editing   UNIX shells support the ability to recall a previously entered command, modify it, and then execute the new version. The command history can remain between sessions (the commands you did yesterday can be available for you when you log in today). Some shells support a command-line editing mode that uses a subset of the `vi`, `emacs`, or `gmacs` editor commands for command recall and modification.

command-line history   See *command-line editing*.

command-line parameters   Used to specify parameters to pass to the execute program or procedure. Also known as *command-line arguments*.

`compress`   The old standby of compression utilities. The `compress` and `uncompress` commands should be available on any Linux or UNIX installation.

configuration files   Collections of information used to initialize and set up the environment for specific commands and programs. Shell configuration files set up the user's environment.

configuration files, shell   For Bourne shell: `/etc/profile` and `$HOME/.profile`.

For Korn and `pdksh` shells: `/etc/profile`, `$HOME/.profile`, and `ENV= file`.

For C and `tcsh` shells: `/etc/.login`, `/etc/cshrc`, `$HOME/.login`, `$HOME/.cshrc`, and `$HOME/.logout`. Older versions might not support the first two files listed.

For `bash`: `/etc/profile/`, `$HOME/.bash_profile`, `$HOME/.bash_login`, `$HOME/.profile`, `$HOME/.bashrc`, and `~/.bash_logout`.

CPU   Central Processing Unit. The primary "brain" of the computer—the calculation engine and logic controller.

daemon   A system-related background process that often runs with the permissions of root and services requests from other processes.

DARPA   (U.S. Department of) Defense Advanced Research Projects Agency. Funded development of TCP/IP and ARPAnet (predecessor of the Internet).

database server   See *server, database*.

device file   File used to implement access to a physical device. This provides a consistent approach to access of storage media under UNIX; data files and devices (such as tapes and communication facilities) are implemented as files. To the programmer, there is no real difference.

directory   A means of organizing and collecting files together. The directory itself is a file that consists of a list of files contained within it. The root (`/`) directory is the top level and every other directory is contained in it (directly or indirectly). A directory might contain other directories, known as *subdirectories*.

directory navigation   The process of moving through directories is known as navigation. Your current directory is known as the current working directory. Your login directory is known as the default or home directory. Using the `cd` command, you can move up and down through the tree structure of directories.

DNS   Domain Name Server. Used to convert between the name of a machine on the Internet (`name.domain.com`) to the numeric address (`123.45.111.123`) and vice versa.

DOS   Disk Operating System. Operating system that is based on the use of disks for the storage of commands. It is also a generic name for MS-DOS and PC-DOS on the personal computer. MS-DOS is the version Microsoft sells; PC-DOS is the version IBM sells. Both are based on Microsoft code.

`double`   Double-precision floating point.

dpi   Dots per inch.

EBCDIC   Extended Binary Coded Decimal Interchange Code. The code used to represent characters in memory for IBM mainframe computers.

`ed`   A common tool used for line-oriented text editing.

`elm`   Interactive mail program.

`emacs`   A freely available editor now part of the GNU software distribution. Originally written by Richard M. Stallman at MIT in the late 1970s, it is available for many platforms. It is extremely extensible and has its own programming language; the name stands for editing with macros.

email   Messages sent through an electronic medium instead of through the local postal service. There are many proprietary email systems that are designed to handle mail within a LAN environment; most of these are also able to send over the Internet. Most Internet (open) email systems make use of MIME to handle attached data (which can be binary).

encapsulation   The process of combining data (attributes) and functions (behavior in the form of code) into an object. The data and functions are closely coupled within an object. Encapsulation hides a complex interface behind a simpler one. This promotes code reuse and standardized methods of working with the data.

environment variables   See *variables, environmental.*

Ethernet   A networking method where the systems are connected to a single shared bus and all traffic is available to every machine. The data packets contain an identifier of the recipient, and that is the only machine that should process that packet.

expression   A constant, variable, or operands and operators combined. Used to set a value, perform a calculation, or set the pattern for a comparison (regular expressions).

FIFO   First In, First Out. See *pipe, named.*

file Collection of bytes stored on a device (typically a disk or tape). Can be source code, executable binaries or scripts, or data.

file compression The process of applying mathematical formulas to data, typically resulting in a form of the data that occupies less space. A compressed file can be uncompressed, resulting in the original file. When the compress/uncompress process results in exactly the same file as was originally compressed, it is known as lossless. If information about the original file is lost, the compression method is known as lossy. Data and programs need lossless compression; images and sounds can stand lossy compression.

file, indexed A file based on a file structure where data can be retrieved based on specific keys (name, employee number, and so on) or sequentially. The keys are stored in an index. This is not directly supported by the UNIX operating system; usually implemented by the programmer or by using tools from an ISV. A typical form is known as *ISAM*.

file, line sequential See *file, text*.

file, sequential This phrase can mean either a file that can only be accessed sequentially (not randomly), or a file without record separators (typically fixed length, but UNIX does not know what that length is and does not care).

file, text A file with record separators. Can be fixed or variable length; UNIX tools can handle these files because the tools can tell when the record ends (by the separator).

filename The name used to identify a collection of data (a file). Without a pathname, it is assumed to be in the current directory.

filename generation The process of the shell interpreting metacharacters (wildcards) to produce a list of matching files. This is referred to as filename expansion or globbing.

filename, fully qualified The name used to identify a collection of data (a file) and its location. It includes both the path and name of the file; typically, the pathname is fully specified (absolute). See also *pathname* and *pathname, absolute*.

file system A collection of disk storage that is connected (mounted) to the directory structure at some point (sometimes at the root). File systems are stored in a disk partition and are sometimes referred to as being the disk partition.

`finger` User information lookup program.

firewall   A system used to provide a controlled entry point to the internal network from the outside (usually the Internet) and vice versa. This is used to prevent outside or unauthorized systems from accessing systems on your internal network. The capability depends on the individual software package, but the features typically include filter packets and filter datagrams, system (name or IP address) aliasing, and rejecting packets from certain IP addresses. In theory, it provides protection from malicious programs or people on the outside. It can also prevent internal systems from accessing the Internet on the outside. The name comes from the physical barrier between connected buildings or within a single building that is supposed to prevent fire from spreading from one location to another.

flags   See *options*.

`float`   Single-precision floating point.

foreground   Programs running while connected to the interactive session.

`fseek`   Internal function used by UNIX to locate data inside a file or file system. ANSI standard `fseek` accepts a parameter that can hold a value of +2 to -2 billion. This function, used by the operating system, system tools, and applications, is the cause of the 2GB file and file system size limitation on most systems. With 64-bit operating systems, this limit is going away.

FSF   Free Software Foundation.

FTP   File Transfer Protocol. A system-independent means of transferring files between systems connected via TCP/IP. Ensures that the file is transferred correctly, even if there are errors during transmission. Can usually handle character set conversions (ASCII/EBCDIC) and record terminator resolution (linefeed for UNIX, carriage return and linefeed for MS/PC-DOS).

gateway   A combination of hardware, software, and network connections that provides a link between one architecture and another. Typically, a gateway is used to connect a LAN or UNIX server with a mainframe (that uses SNA for networking, resulting in the name SNA gateway). A gateway can also be the connection between the internal and external network (often referred to as a firewall). See also *firewall*.

GID   Group ID number.

globbing   See *filename generation*.

GNOME   GNU Network Object Model Environment. A desktop environment made popular by the Red Hat distribution of Linux. GNOME offers all the functions of modern desktop operating systems in a highly-customizable package. You can download GNOME from `http://www.gnome.org`.

GNU   GNU stands for GNU's Not UNIX, and is the name of free useful software packages commonly found in UNIX environments that are being distributed by the GNU project at MIT, largely through the efforts of Richard Stallman. The circular acronym name ("GNU" containing the acronym GNU as one of the words it stands for) is a joke on Richard Stallman's part. One of the textbooks on operating system design is titled *XINU: XINU Is Not UNIX*, and GNU follows in that path.

GPL   GNU General Public License.

`grep`   A common tool used to search a file for a pattern. `egrep` and `fgrep` are newer versions. `egrep` allows the use of extended (hence the *e* prefix) regular expressions; `fgrep` uses limited expressions for faster (hence the *f* prefix) searches.

GUI   Graphical user interface.

`gzip`   A popular compression tool that produces smaller files than `compress`. `gzip` and `gunzip` are used to manage the compressed files, which usually end in `.gz`.

here document   The << redirection operator, known as *here document*, allows keyboard input (`stdin`) for the program to be included in the script.

HTML   Hypertext Markup Language. Describes World Wide Web pages. It is the document language that is used to define the pages available on the Internet through the use of tags. A browser interprets the HTML to display the desired information.

i-node   Used to describe a file and its storage. The directory contains a cross-reference between the i-node and pathname/filename combination. Also known as *inode*. A file's entry in disk data structure (`ls -i`).

I-Phone   Internet Phone. This is a method of transmitting speech long distances over the Internet in near real-time. Participants avoid paying long distance telephone charges. They still pay for the call to their ISP and the ISP's service charges.

ICCCM   Inter-Client Communications Conventions Manual.

ICMP   Internet Control Message Protocol. Part of TCP/IP that provides a method of communicating status and routing information.

`imake`   C preprocessor interface to `make` utility.

inheritance   A method of object-oriented software reuse in which new classes are developed based on existing ones by using the existing attributes and behavior and adding on to them. If the base object is automobiles (with attributes of engine and four wheels and tires; behavior of acceleration, turning, deceleration), a sports car would modify the attributes: engine might be larger or have more horsepower than the default, the four wheels might include alloy wheels and high-speed–rated tires; the behavior would also be modified: faster acceleration, tighter turning radius, faster deceleration.

inode   See *i-node*.

int   Integer.

Internet   A collection of different networks that provide the ability to move data between them. It is built on the TCP/IP communications protocol. Originally developed by DARPA, it was taken over by NSF, and has now been released from governmental control.

Internet service provider   The company or organization that connects you to the Internet.

IRC   Internet Relay Chat. A server-based application that allows groups of people to communicate simultaneously through text-based conversations. IRC is similar to Citizens Band radio or the chat rooms on some bulletin boards. Chats can be private (between invited people only) or public (where anyone can join in). IRC now also supports sound files as well as text; it can also be useful for file exchange.

ISAM   Indexed Sequential Access Method. On UNIX and other systems, ISAM refers to a method for accessing data in a keyed or sequential way. The UNIX operating system does not directly support ISAM files; they are typically add-on products.

ISO   International Standards Organization.

ISP   See *Internet service provider*.

ISV   Independent Software Vendor. Generic name for software vendors other than your hardware vendor.

K&R   Kernighan and Ritchie.

KDE   Another popular desktop environment, KDE is arguably more stable than GNOME and offers many of the same features. KDE is downloadable from http://www.kde.org/.

kernel   The core of the operating system that handles tasks such as memory allocation, device input and output, process allocation, security, and user access. UNIX tends to have a small kernel when compared to other operating systems.

keys, control   These are keys that cause some function to be performed instead of displaying a character. These functions have names: The end-of-file key tells UNIX that there is no more input; it is usually Ctrl+D.

keys, special   See *keys, control*.

Korn shell   A user interface for UNIX with extensive scripting (programming) support. Written by David G. Korn, the shell features command-line editing and will also accept scripts written for the Bourne shell.

LAN   Local Area Network. A collection of networking hardware, software, desktop computers, servers, and hosts all connected together within a defined local area. A LAN could be an entire college campus.

limits   See *quota*.

link file   File used to implement a symbolic link producing an alias on one file system for a file on another. The file contains only the fully qualified filename of the original (linked-to) file.

link, hard   Directory entry that provides an alias to another file within the same file system. Multiple entries appear in the directory (or other directories) for one physical file without replication of the contents.

link, soft   See *link, symbolic*.

link, symbolic   Directory entry that provides an alias to another file that can be in another file system. Multiple entries appear in the directory for one physical file without replication of the contents. Implemented through link files; see also *link file*.

LISP   List Processing Language.

login   The process with which a user gains access to a UNIX system. This can also refer to the user ID that is typed at the login prompt.

lp   Line printer.

lpc   Line printer control program.

lpd   Line printer daemon.

lpq   Printer spool queue examination program.

`lprm`   Printer spool queue job removal program.

`ls`   List directory(s) command.

man page   Online reference tool under UNIX that contains the documentation for the system—the actual pages from the printed manuals. It is stored in a searchable form for improved ability to locate information.

manual page   See *man page*.

memory, real   The amount of storage that is being used within the system (silicon; it used to be magnetic cores).

memory, virtual   Disk space that is used in place of silicon-based memory. Secondary storage (disk) is used to allow the operating system to enable programs to use more memory than is physically available.

Part of a disk is used as a paging file and portions of programs and their data are moved between it and real memory. To the program, it is in real memory. The hardware and operating system performs translation between the memory address the program thinks it is using and where it is actually stored.

metacharacter   A printing character that has special meaning to the shell or another command. It is converted into something else by the shell or command; the asterisk (*) is converted by the shell to a list of all files in the current directory.

MIME   Multipurpose Internet Mail Extensions. A set of protocols or methods of attaching binary data (executable programs, images, sound files, and so on) or additional text to email messages.

`motd`   Message of the day.

MPTN   Multiprotocol Transport Network IBM networking protocol to connect mainframe to TCP/IP network.

Mrm   Motif resource manager.

mtu   Maximum transmission unit. The largest size frame supported by the network Data Link layer.

`mwm`   Motif window manager.

Netnews   This is a loosely controlled collection of discussion groups. A message (similar to an email) is posted in a specific area, and then people can comment on it, publicly replying to the same place (posting a response) for others to see. A collection of messages along the same theme is referred to as a thread. Some of the groups are moderated, which means that nothing is posted without the approval of the owner. Most are not, and the title of the group is no guarantee that the discussion will be related. The official term for this is Usenet news.

NFS   Network File System. Means of connecting disks that are mounted to a remote system to the local system as if they were physically connected.

NIS   Network Information Service. A service that provides information necessary to all machines on a network, such as NFS support for hosts and clients, password verification, and so on.

NNTP   Netnews Transport Protocol. Used to transmit Netnews or Usenet messages over top of TCP/IP. See *Netnews* for more information on the messages transmitted.

Null Statement   A program step that performs no operation but to hold space and fulfill syntactical requirements of the programming language. Also known as a *NO-OP* for no-operation performed.

object   An object in the truest sense of the word is something that has physical properties, such as an automobile, a rubber ball, and a cloud. These things have attributes and behavior. They can be abstracted into data (attribute) and code (behavior). Instead of just writing functions to work on data, they are encapsulated into a package that is known as an object.

operator   Metacharacter that performs a function on values or variables. The plus sign (+) is an operator that adds two integers.

options   Program- or command-specific indicators that control behavior of that program. Sometimes called *flags*. The -a option to the ls command shows the files that begin with . (such as .profile, .kshrc, and so on). Without it, these files would not be shown, no matter what wildcards were used. These are used on the command line. See also *parameters*.

OSF   Open Software Foundation.

parameters   Data passed to a command or program through the command line. These can be options (see *options*) that control the command or arguments that the command works on. Some have special meaning based on their position on the command line.

parent process   Process that controls another often referred to as the child process or subprocess. See also *process*.

parent process identifier   Shown in the heading of the ps command as PPID. The process identifier of the parent process. See also *parent process*.

parent shell   Shell (typically the login shell) that controls another, often referred to as the child shell or subshell. See also *shell*.

password   The secure code that is used in combination with a user ID to gain access to a UNIX system.

pathname   The means used to represent the location of a file in the directory structure. If you do not specify a pathname, it defaults to the current directory.

pathname, absolute   The means used to represent the location of a file in a directory by specifying the exact location, including all directories in the chain including the root.

pathname, relative   The means used to represent the location of a file in a directory other than the current by navigating up and down through other directories using the current directory as a base.

PDP   Personal Data Processor. Computers manufactured by Digital Equipment Corporation. UNIX was originally written for a PDP-7 and gained popularity on the PDP-11. The entire series were inexpensive minicomputers popular with educational institutions and small businesses.

Perl   Programming language developed by Larry Wall. (Perl stands for "Practical Extraction and Report Language" or "Pathologically Eclectic Rubbish Language"; both are equally valid.) The language provides all the capabilities of awk and sed, plus many of the features of the shells and C.

permissions   When applied to files, they are the attributes that control access to a file. There are three levels of access: Owner (the file creator), Group (people belonging to a related group as determined by the system administrator), and Other (everyone else). The permissions are usually r for read, w for write, and x for execute. The execute permissions flag is also used to control who can search a directory.

PGP   Pretty Good Privacy encryption system.

pine   Interactive mail program.

pipe   A method of sending the output of one program (redirecting) to become the input of another. The pipe character (|) tells the shell to perform the redirection.

pipe file See *pipe, named*.

pipe, named An expanded function of a regular pipe (redirecting the output of one program to become the input of another). Instead of connecting stdout to stdin, the output of one program is sent to the named pipe and another program reads data from the same file. This is implemented through a special file known as a pipe file or FIFO. The operating system ensures the proper sequencing of the data. Little or no data is actually stored in the pipe file; it just acts as a connection between the two.

polymorphism Allows code to be written in a general fashion to handle existing and future related classes. Properly developed, the same behavior can act differently depending on the derived object it acts on. With an automobile, the acceleration behavior might be different for a station wagon and a dragster, which are subclasses of the superclass automobile. The function would still be accelerate(), but the version would vary (this might sound confusing, but the compiler keeps track and figures it all out).

POSIX Portable Operating System Interface, UNIX. POSIX is the name for a family of open system standards based on UNIX. The name has been credited to Richard Stallman. The POSIX shell and Utilities standard developed by IEEE Working Group 1003.2 (POSIX.2) concentrates on the command interpreter interface and utility programs.

PostScript Adobe Systems, Inc. page description language, which is typically used to generate resolution independent text and graphic output.

PPP Point-to-Point Protocol. Internet protocol over serial link (modem).

pppd Point-to-Point-Protocol daemon.

printcap Printer capability database.

process A discrete running program under UNIX. The user's interactive session is a process. A process can invoke (run) and control another program that is then referred to as a subprocess. Ultimately, everything a user does is a subprocess of the operating system.

process identifier Shown in the heading of the ps command as PID. The unique number assigned to every process running in the system.

pwd Print working directory command.

quota General description of a system-imposed limitation on a user or process. It can apply to disk space, memory usage, CPU usage, maximum number of open files, and many other resources.

quoting   The use of single and double quotes to negate the normal command interpretation and concatenate all words and whitespace within the quotes as a single piece of text.

RCS   Revision Control System.

redirection   The process of directing a data flow from the default. Input can be redirected to get data from a file or the output of another program. Normal output can be sent to another program or a file. Errors can be sent to another program or a file.

regular expression   A way of specifying and matching strings for shells (filename wildcarding), `grep` (file searches), `sed`, and `awk`.

reserved word   A set of characters that are recognized by UNIX and related to a specific program, function, or command.

RFC   Request For Comment. Document used for creation of technology standards.

`rlogin`   Remote Login. Gives the same functionality as `telnet`, with the added functionality of not requiring a password from trusted clients, which can also create security concerns (see also *telnet*).

root   The user that owns the operating system and controls the computer. The processes of the operating system run as though a user, root, signed on and started them. Root users are all- powerful and can do anything they want. For this reason, they are often referred to as superusers. Root is also the very top of the directory tree structure.

routing   The process of moving network traffic between two different physical networks; also decides which path to take when there are multiple connections between the two machines. It might also send traffic around transmission interruptions.

RPC   Remote Procedure Call. Provides the ability to call functions or subroutines that run on a remote system from the local one.

RPM   Red Hat Package Manager.

script   A program written for a UNIX utility including shells, `awk`, Perl, `sed`, and others. See also *shell scripts*.

SCSI   Small Computer System Interface.

`sed`   A common tool used for stream text editing, having syntax similar to `ed`.

server, database   A system designated to run database software (typically a relational database such as Oracle, SQL Server, Sybase, or others). Other systems connect to this one to get the data (client applications).

SGID   Set group ID.

shell   The part of UNIX that handles user input and invokes other programs to run commands. Includes a programming language. See also Bourne shell, C shell, Korn shell, `tcsh`, and `bash`.

shell environment   The shell program (Bourne, Korn, C, `tcsh`, or `bash`), invocation options and preset variables that define the characteristics, features, and functions of the UNIX command-line and program execution interface.

shell or command prompt   The single character or set of characters that the UNIX shell displays for which a user can enter a command or set of commands.

shell scripts   A program written using a shell programming language such as those supported by Bourne, Korn, or C shells.

signal   A special flag or interrupt that is used to communicate special events to programs by the operating system and other programs.

SLIP   Serial Line Internet Protocol. Internet over a serial line (modem). The protocol frames and controls the transmission of TCP/IP packets of the line.

SNA   System Network Architecture. IBM networking architecture.

`stderr`   The normal error output for a program that is sent to the screen by default. Can be redirected to a file.

`stdin`   The normal input for a program, taken from the keyboard by default. Can be redirected to get input from a file or the output of another program.

`stdout`   The normal output for a program that is sent to the screen by default. Can be redirected to a file or to the input of another program.

sticky bit   One of the status flags on a file that tells UNIX to load a copy of the file into the page file the first time it is executed. This is done for programs that are commonly used so the bytes are available quickly. When the sticky bit is used on frequently used directories, it is cached in memory.

stream   A sequential collection of data. All files are streams to the UNIX operating system. To it, there is no structure to a file; that is something imposed by applications or special tools (ISAM packages or relational databases).

subdirectory   See *directory*.

subnet   A portion of a network that shares a common IP address component.

subprocess   Process running under the control of another, often referred to as the parent process. See also *process*.

subshell   Shell running under the control of another, often referred to as the parent shell (typically the login shell). See also *shell*.

SUID   Set user ID.

superuser   Usually the root operator.

sysadmin   Burnt-out root operator (system administrator).

system administrator   The person who takes care of the operating system and user administrative issues on UNIX systems. Also called a *system manager*, although that term is much more common in DEC VAX installations.

system manager   See *system administrator*.

tar   Tape archiving utility.

TCP   Transmission Control Protocol.

TCP/IP   Transmission Control Protocol/Internet Protocol. The pair of protocols and also generic name for suite of tools and protocols that forms the basis for the Internet. Originally developed to connect systems to the ARPAnet.

tcsh   Tenex C shell, A user interface, similar to csh, featuring command-line editing.

telnet   Remote login program.

Telnet   Protocol for interactive (character user interface) terminal access to remote systems. The terminal emulator that uses the Telnet protocol is often known as telnet.

termcap   Terminal capability database.

terminal   A hardware device, normally containing a cathode ray tube (screen) and keyboard for human interaction with a computer system.

text processing languages   A way of developing documents in text editors with embedded commands that handle formatting. The file is fed through a processor that executes the embedded commands, producing a formatted document. These include roff, nroff, troff, RUNOFF, TeX, LaTeX, and even the mainframe SCRIPT.

TFTP   Trivial File Transfer Protocol or Trivial File Transfer Program. A system-independent means of transferring files between systems connected via TCP/IP. It is different from FTP in that it does not ensure that the file is transferred correctly, does not authenticate users, and is missing a lot of functionality (such as the `ls` command).

`tin`   Interactive news reader.

`top`   A common tool used to display information about the top processes on the system.

UDP   User Datagram Protocol. Part of TCP/IP used for control messages and data transmission where the delivery acknowledgment is not needed. The application must ensure data transmission in this case.

UID   User ID number.

UIL   Motif User Interface Language.

URL   Uniform Resource Locator. The method of specifying the protocol, format, login (usually omitted), and location of materials on the Internet.

Usenet   See *Netnews*.

UUCP   UNIX-to-UNIX copy program. Used to build an early, informal network for the transmission of files, email, and Netnews.

variables, attributes   The modifiers that set the variable type. A variable can be string or integer, left- or right-justified, read-only or changeable, and other attributes.

variables, environmental   A place to store data and values (strings and integers) in the area controlled by the shell so they are available to the current and subprocesses. They can just be local to the current shell or available to a subshell (exported).

variables, substitution   The process of interpreting an environmental variable to get its value.

WAN   Wide Area Network.

Web   See *World Wide Web*.

whitespace   Blanks, spaces, and tabs that are normally interpreted to delineate commands and filenames unless quoted.

wildcard   Means of specifying filename(s) whereby the operating system determines some of the characters. Multiple files might match and will be available to the tool.

World Wide Web   A collection of servers and services on the Internet that run software and communicate using a common protocol (HTTP). Instead of the users having to remember the location of these resources, links are provided from one Web page to another through the use of URLs.

WWW   See *World Wide Web*.

WYSIWYG   What You See Is What You Get.

X   See *X Window System*.

X Window System   A windowing and graphics system developed by MIT, to be used in client/server environments.

X11   See *X Window System*.

X-windows   The wrong term for the X Window System. See *X Window System*.

yacc   Yet another compiler compiler.

INDEX

SYMBOLS

[ ] (brackets), 624

\ (backslash) character, 22

\! character, 106

\# character, 106

\$ character, 107

\) wildcard, 31

\? wildcard, 31

{ } (braces), 624

! (bang) character, 290

(pound sign), 106, 622
   GIMP memory settings, 223
   inittab files, 391

$abc wildcard, 31

& character, 27

& command, 599

(..) periods (parent directory), 37

* (asterisk) wildcard, 31-32

+ command (mail program), 270

- (hyphen) command
   cd command, 37
   mail program, 270

. command, 599

\[character, 107

\\ character, 107

\] character, 107

^^abc wildcard, 31

| (pipe) operator, 26-27

0123 wildcard, 31

3-button mouse, 591

< (redirection) operator, 24-25, 75

<< (here) operator, 25

<< (redirection) operator, 631

> (redirection) operator, 22-24

>> (append) operator, 24-25

? command (mail program), 270

? wildcard, 31

A

-a option (fetchmail), 267

absolute pathnames, 636

access
   at command, 403-404
   crontab files, 399-400
   FTP
      anonymous, 449
      checking, 449
      enabling, 286, 448-450
      testing, 450
   groups, controlling, 362
   times, 512
   timestamps, 465

account configuration file, 383

accounts (user), 8-10

Acrobat. *See* Adobe Acrobat Reader

acroread command, 237

activating
   Ethernet, 411
   default gateways, 409
   file systems, 462

groups
   groupadd command, 376
   usercfg tool, 371-372
hard drives, 119
modules (kernel), 528-530
partitions to file systems, 462
PLIP interfaces, 418
printers, 89-90
run level services
   chkconfig command, 437
   ksysv utility (KDE), 446
   ntsysv utility (Red Hat Linux), 448
   tksysv utility (X11), 444-445
SLIP interfaces, 416-417
users
   useradd command, 374
   usercfg tool, 365-367

addresses
   DNS, 253
   email, harvesting, 280
   IP, 253, 266
   loopback, 407
   sound card device addresses, 533
   Web (Lynx default), 299

adduser command, 599

Adobe Acrobat Reader
   installing, 237
   Netscape Helper Application, 238-240

ADSL (Asymmetric Digital Subscriber Line), 591

ADSM backup system, 591

Advanced Power Management. *See* APM

advocacy, 592

alias command, 599

aliases, 108

aliasing
Alien utility, 500-501
IP, 593

alphanumeric characters, 626

alphanumeric pager gateways, 594

Alsa sound drivers, 592

Amanda (backup software), 468

amateur radio, 594

American Standard Code for Information Interchange (ASCII), 624

ampersand (&), 27

anonymous FTP access, 449
cautions, 449
enabling, 449-450

ANSI (American National Standards Institute), 624

Apache
inetd daemon, 450
Web server, 592
configuring, 451-452
enabling, 450-451
testing, 451
Web site, 450

API (Application Programming Interface), 624

APM (Advanced Power Management)
drivers, 574
enabling, 573-575
make xconfig command, 574

append command (lilo.config file), 355

appending files, 25

applets
docked, 193
Kernel Configurator, 529
module device parameters, 530
module names, 530

Application Programming Interface (API), 624

applications
Alien utility, 501
calculator, 188
docked applets (Window Maker), 193
graphics
conversion, 230-233
GIMP, 216-217, 220-222
X11, 233
ImageMagick, 226
RealPlayer 5.0, 244
running in background, 27
selecting (email), 269

Applixware office suite, 65

apropos command, 18, 600

ar utility, 624

Archive User window (usercfg tool), 368

archives
compressed, 505, 508-509
directories, 507-508

arguments
command line, 330, 354-355
tar command, 506

ARP, subnetting, 594

artificial intelligence software, 592

ASCII (American Standard Code for Information Interchange), 624

ash shell, 322

asterisk (*) wildcard, 32

Asymmetric Digital Subscriber Line (ADSL), 591

async option (mount command), 460

at command
access, 403-404
enabling, 400-401
options, 401
root, 402
running interactively, 402
scheduling, 400
specifying times, 403
troubleshooting, 401-402

AT command set (modems), 156

AT&T UNIX, 624

atq command, 400

atrm command, 400

attachments (email), 271

attributes, 624, 641

audio
file formats (xanim support), 245-246
music CD-ROMs, 240-243

auth configuration file, 383

auto option (mount command), 460

auto-saves (emacs), 68

autoexpect program, 28-29

autofs automounter utility, 592

automounting
configuring kernels, 559
incremental backups, 519-521

awk, 624

a-z wildcard, 31

B

-b option (fetchmail), 267

background
color (X11 toolkit), 199-200
desktop
pattern, 182
setting color, 182

processes, 625
programs, 27
controlling, 29
kill command, 30-31
ps command, 30
ps command, 31

backslash (\) character, 22

**backups, 477, 504-510,
514-519, 625**
ADSM, 591
Amanda software, 468
bookmarks, 301
cp command, 44
crontab feature, 521
disaster recovery, 476
DOS, 592
file system
restoring, 479
strategy, 477
floppy disks, 517-518
frequency, 477
fstab, 462
full, 519-520
incremental (automating),
519-521
inittab files, 435
mail files, 301
mv command, 45
nontraditional devices, 477
physical storage, 478
recovering lost data, 479
recovery strategy, 478
removable drives, 518-520
rewindable tape devices,
518-519
superblocks, 475
tape drives, 131-132
taper utility, 515
downloading, 513
menus, 514-515
preformatted tapes, 516
*Test Make Tape option,
516*
tar (find command),
509-512

banner command, 600

**banner screens (xdm),
176-177**

bash, 625
.bash_history file, 21
command-line histories, 344
profile, 105

bash shell, 7, 20, 322
arguments, 330
commands (jobs), 30
constructs
conditional, 332-335
looping, 332, 336
environment variables, 100
for statement, 336
prompt characters, 106
true/false values, 333
variables, deleting, 103

bashrc file, 108

bashrc profile, 105

batch command, 400

batch files, 357-358

**beep codes (cardmgr dae-
mon), 140-142**

**Beowulf Linux clustering
system, 586**

**Berkeley Software
Distribution (BSD) UNIX,
92, 434**

bg command, 601

biff utility, 625

bin directory, 325

binary files
downloading, 288
strings, extracting, 61

**binary formats, configuring
kernels, 549**

bind command, 601

BIOS
booting PCs, 352
Plug and Play configura-
tion, 534

bison, 625

bit bucket, 623

block-special files, 625

Boca 2016 serial cards, 592

BogoMIps, 592

bookmarks, backing up, 301

Boolean operators, 335

booting, 353, 625. *See also*
starting
boot disks, creating,
358-359
boot images (lilo.config
file), 355
boot managers, 354
boot messages, 124
boot record, 352
boot time arguments, 586
changing order, 354
from DOS prompt, 356-360
kernel, 352
lilo.config file, 353
LOADLIN, 356-360
modules, loading, 537-538
operating systems (multi-
ple), 354
PCs, 352
rebooting, 13, 474
Red Hat Linux, 479
run levels, 355-356
SCSI device boots, 528,
537, 551, 557, 572
spontaneous reboots, 474
troubleshooting, 353

Bourne Again Shell. *See* bash
shell

Bourne shell. *See* sh shell

braces ({ }), 624

brackets ([ ]), 624

**breaking long command
lines, 22**

bridges, creating, 592

browsers
gmc client, 57
GNOME help browser,
16-17
info utility, 15-16
KDE help browser, 17

kfm client, 55
  creating directories, 56
  directory/file management,
    56-57
  starting, 55
Lynx, 296-299
  command line options,
    296-298
  configuring, 298-300
  downloading files, 300
Netscape Communicator,
  300
  downloading/installing,
    300-302
  downloading files, 293-294

Brush Selection dialog box,
  219

BSD UNIX (Berkeley
  Software Distribution
  UNIX), 92, 625

buffers
  frame, 587
  xclipboard client, 208

bugs, 625

bus mouse, installing, 586

buttons
  Code Maturity Options,
    563
  Loadable Module Support,
    564

bzip2 compression utility,
  592, 625

C

C programming language,
  625
  compiling programs,
    340-341
  make command, 343

C shell. *See* csh shell

C++ programming
  compiling programs,
    340-341
  make command, 343

cabaret file systems. *See* file
  systems

cable modems, 592

CAD (Computer-aided
  design), 625

calculator, 188

Caldera Web site, 581

capacities (Zip disks), 132

capturing
  desktop, 208-213
  magnified images (xmag
    client), 212-213
  viewing captures (xloadim-
    age client), 210
  windows, 208-213
    portions, 211
    X11, 210
    xv client, 210-212
    xwd program, 208-209

carbon copies (email), 273

cardctl command, 142-145

cardmgr daemon, 141
  beep codes, 140
  configuring PC cards,
    139-140
  disabling PC card notifica-
    tion, 142
  listing PC cards, 141
  PC cards support, 138

cards
  Ethernet, configuring, 407
  network, verifying that they
    are running, 408

case sensitivity
  shells, 20
  top command, 541

casts, 625

cat command, 22, 40-41,
  601, 626
  file system contents, 115
  file types, 40
  output redirection, 24
  redirection operators, 24, 40
  viewing fstab, 116

cd command, 36-37, 602

CD-ROMs, 626
  cdplay command, 242
  drives, configuring kernels,
    558, 568
  mounting, 455
  music
    cdp command, 240-242
    playing, 240-243

cdp command, 240-242

cdplay command, 242

CGI (Common Gateway
  Interface), 626

changing
  default boots, 354
  directories, 36
  Linux configuration, 109
  partition types, 121
  passwords, 11
  shells, 33

character maps (fonts),
  203-205

character special file, 626

character-based devices, con-
  figuring kernels, 559-560,
  570

character-mode devices
  (printers), 88

characters
  alphabetic, 626
  alphanumeric, 626
  control, 626
  failed verification tests (pack-
    ages), 492
  metacharacters, 634
  numeric, 626
  prompts (bash shell), 106
  regular, 31
  shell commands, 24-27
  special, 626

chat dialing command, 252

checking
  fax status, 164
  FTP access, 449

PC card status (cardctl command), 143
printers, 89
sound card device addresses, 533

chgrp command, 378, 602

child processes, 539

chkconfig command, 436
adding run level services, 437
comments, 436
deleting run level services, 437
listing run level services, 436
resetting run level service information, 437

chmod command, 379-382, 602-603

chown command, 378, 603

chroot command, 604

chsh command, 33-34

cipe, 592

classes, 626, 632

client root directories, creating, 594

clients
dict, 79
gmc
creating directories, 53-54
directory/file management, 54
starting, 53
symbolic links, 54
kfind, 57-58
kfm, 55
creating directories, 56
directory/file management, 56-57
starting, 55
symbolic links, 57
mail, 588
NFS, configuring, 425, 427
starting in desktop, 199
xman, 15

clocks, 592

closing
connections, ftp command, 290
GIMP, 220
windows (X11), 201

code, polymorphism, 637

Code Maturity Options button, 563

code modules, 6

color
desktop background, 182
directories, 39
foreground (X11 toolkit), 199-200

Comeau C++, 592

command line, 20-22. *See also shells*
arguments, 330
LILO, 354-355
passing with LOADLIN, 359-360
breaking long, 22
chgrp command, 378
chmod command, 379-382
chown command, 378
command completion, 21-22
copying complex, 206
editing, 20-21, 626
emacs options, 68
emailing, 269
environment variables, 102-103
file printing, 93
gpasswd command, 377
groupadd command, 376
groupdel command, 376-377
groupmod command, 376
history, 21
kpackage, 493
LOADLIN, 356
modifying, 586
multiple commands, 22

options
fetchmailrc settings, 269
gunzip command, 505
gzip command, 505
Lynx browser, 296-298
X11 toolkit, 198, 200
parameters, 626
prompt, customizing, 106-108
redirection operators, 271
starting
Netscape Communicator, 303
xrpm client, 496
user account creation, 9
useradd command, 374
userdel command, 375
usermod command, 374-375
using linuxconf utility, 109
wildcards, 31-32

command paths, setting, 104-105

command prompts, 639

command settings (crontab files), 397-399. *See also utilities*

commands, 598-599, 601-619
& command, 599
. command, 599
| (pipe) character, 26-27
adduser, 599
alias, 599
append (lilo.config file), 355
apropos, 18, 600
at
access, 403-404
enabling, 400-401
options, 401
root, 402
running interactively, 402
scheduling, 400
specifying times, 403
troubleshooting, 401-402

commands

AT command set (modems), 156
atq, 400
atrm, 400
banner, 600
bash shell, jobs, 30
batch, 400
bg, 601
bind, 601
cardctl
    checking PC card status, 143
    ejecting PC cards, 144
    inserting PC cards, 144
    listing PC card configuration, 143-144
    PC card schemes, 142
    PC card slots, 142
    suspending/restoring PC card power, 145
cat, 40-41, 601
    file system contents, 115
    redirection operators, 24, 40
cd, 36-37, 602
cdp, playing music CD-ROMs, 240-242
cdplay, 242
chat dialing command, 252
chgrp, 602
chgrp command, 378
chkconfig
    adding run level services, 437
    comments, 436
    deleting run level services, 437
    listing run level services, 436
    resetting run level service information, 437
chmod, 268, 379-382, 602-603
chown, 378, 603
chroot, 604
chsh, 33-34
completion, 21-22

compressed archiving (tar command), 505
compressing files, 504
cp, 44, 604
crontab, 396
dd, 604
decompressing files, 504-505
df, 117
dmesg, serial port status, 154-155
documentation, 325
dump, 468
echo, 39, 155, 331
egrep, 60-62
emacs, 70
env, 102-103, 327, 605
erase (tape drives), 132
exit, 12
export (persistent variables), 328
fax
    checking fax status, 164
    deleting faxes, 165
    incoming faxes, 164
    printing faxes, 165
    sending faxes, 164
    testing fax service configuration, 163
    viewing faxes, 164
fc, 605
fdformat, 517
fg, 605
fgrep, 60-62
file, 41, 606
filters, 80
find, 606
    file searches, 50-51
    restricting searches, 50-51
    search expressions, 511
    tar backups, 509-510
formatting, 81
formatting hard drives, 122-123
fsck, 468
ftp, 607
    ! (bang) character, 290
    closing connections, 290

    common commands, 285-286
    directory navigation, 288
    examples, 284-285
    exit, 290
    file downloads, 286-290
    help, 291
    navigating directories, 288
    opening connections, 287
    quitting, 290
    shell commands, 290
fuser, 104
GNOME panel menu, 23
gpasswd command, 377
grep, 58, 60, 607
groff, 607
groff typesetting, 83-85
groupadd command, 376
groupdel command, 376-377
groupmod command, 376
gunzip, 505, 608
gv, 234
    modifying PostScript window size, 234
    printing documents, 236
    reading documents, 234-236
gzip, 505, 607
halt, 608
hostname, 608
ifconfig (PPP connection), 259, 406
info, 15-16
ispell, 78-79
KDE, 23
keyboard (GIMP), 220-222
kfloppy, 456-457
kill, 30-31, 608
    shell varieties, 543-544
    syntax, 543
killall, 544, 608
kpppload, 260
less, 41, 608
    custom keys, 42
    features, 41
    navigating, 42
ln, 46
    /dev/modem device, 156
    directories, 48

hard links, 47-48
soft links, 47
locate, 51-52, 609
login, 609
logout, 13, 609
lpc, 94, 609
lpd, 609
lpq, 610
lpr, 610
   faxing, 95-96
   line printer, 90
ls, 610
   documentation, 39
   options, 38-39
   sorting, 38
   wildcards, 38
mail program, 270-271
make, 342, 611
   compiling, 344
   configure option, 346
   default rules, 343
   defining constants, 347
   limitations, 344
   options, 344
make clean, 347, 571
make config, 547-562
make dep, 571
make install, 345
make modules, 571
make modules_install command, 571
make xconfig, 562-570
   Code Maturity Options button, 563
   enabling APM, 574
   help, 564
   Loadable Module Support button, 564
make zImage, 571
makefile
   compatibility issues, 343
   mkmf script, 349
   X11, 349
man, 14, 325, 611
manipulating partitions, 123
mesg, 611
mkdir, 43, 223, 612

mkfs (make file system), 469-471, 612
mkinitrd, 572
mkswap, 612
modprobe, 532
more, 41-42, 612
mount, 114, 117, 457-461, 612
   mounting floppy disks, 458
   options, 459-461
mpage, 79-80
mt (magnetic tape), 131-132
multiple, 22
mv, 45-46, 613
ncftp, 292
   downloading files, 292-293
   information Web site, 292
netstat, 613
partitioning hard drives, 120-121
passwd, 11, 614
pico editor, 73
pine program, 273
ping, 260, 313
pppstats, 260
printenv, 100-101
printing, 30
probe, 139
processing, 322
program differences, 27
ps, 30-31, 614
pwd, 36, 614
read, 332
retension, 132
rewind, 132
rm, 614
   deleting directories, 50
   deleting files, 49
   root, 50
rmdir, 49, 615
root, 11-12
route, 406, 422-423
sed editor, 75
set, 615
setserial, 156
sfdisk, 123

shell
   creating, 24-28
   within ftp command, 290
shutdown, 13, 615
sndconfig, 533
startx, 171, 245
strings, 61
su, 11, 615
swapoff, 616
swapon, 616
tail, 616
talk, 616
tar, 508, 616
telnet, 310-314, 616
top, 540-541, 617
touch, 43
tpconfig, 149-150
umount, 617
unalias, 617
unzip, 617
uptime, 540
useradd, 9, 374
userdel, 375, 604
usermod, 374-375
usermount, 454-456
uugetty, 159
vim text editor, 72
wall, 617
whatis, 17
whereis, 52, 104
which, 52
who, 617-618
whoami, 12
write, 618
xbanner, 176
xdm, 173, 176
xhost, 618
xinit, 178
xloadimage (desktop wallpaper), 182-183
xlsfonts, 202-203
xmkmf, 618
xplaycd, 242-243
xset, 618
xsetroot, 182
zgrep, 62
zip, 619

comments
(pound sign), 106
chkconfig, 436
inittab file, 391
shell scripts, 323
users, 362

Common Gateway Interface (CGI), 626

Communicator. *See* Netscape Communicator

compatibility
makefile command, 343
modems, 154
UNIX, 340

compilers
GNU, 587
yaac, 642

compiling
dynamic linking, 342
kernels, 570-572
cautions, 545
make clean command, 571
make dep command, 571
make modules command, 571
make zImage command, 571
recompiling, 545-554
make command, 344
programs
C/C++, 340-341
debugging, 341
ld linker, 341-342
optimizing, 341
troubleshooting, 348
X11, 349
source code, 347-348

compose mode (pine program), 273

compress utility, 627

compressed files, 62

compressed fonts, 204

compressing
archive files (tar command), 505, 508-509
bzip2 compression utility, 592
directories, 504-505
files, 504-505, 629
gzip utility, 631
unused documents/directories, 526

Computer-aided design (CAD), 625

computers, Sony VAIO, 595

concatenate command, 22

conditional constructs, 333-335

configure option (make command), 346

configuring
Apache Web server, 451-452
color depth (rvplayer), 245
configuration files, 383-386, 627
crontab files, 395, 398-400
dial-in PPP service, 160-161
dial-in service, 157-159
dialup accounts (kppp), 256
DNS information, 409-410
doc, 424
Ethernet cards, 407
Ethernet interfaces, 420-421
external applications for Netscape, 239
fax service, 161-164
fax shell script, 162-163
testing configuration, 163
fetchmail, 266-268
firewalls, kernel configuration, 553
gateways, 408
getty devices, 428-429
GIMP, 218, 223
graphics cards, 170

hostnames, 409-410
inittab files, 390-394
Iomega Jaz drives, 593
Iomega ZIP drives, 595
IP accounting, 553
IP Aliasing, 553
IP tunneling, 553
joe editor, 74
joysticks, 152
kanchi to route packets for all machines, 422
kerneld daemon, 593
kernels
adding modules, 528-530
automounting, 559
binary formats, 549
CD-ROMs drives, 558, 568
character-based devices, 559-560, 570
editing files, 531-534
file system support, 558-559, 568
floppy drives, 549-550, 565
IDE devices, 549-550, 565
ISDN support, 558, 567
Kernel Configurator applet, 529-530
kernel developer options, 562
kernel module configuration files, 531-532
loopback devices, 551
make config command, 547-562
make xconfig command, 562-570
multiple devices driver, 551
network connectivity, 549
network devices, 557, 567
networking, 551-554, 566
Plug and Play devices, 534
preparation, 546-547
ramdisk support, 551
SCSI support, 554-555, 557, 566-567
selecting CPU types, 548
sound cards, 532-534, 560-562, 570
LILO, 352-356, 593

Linux, 587
    email options, 266
    Token-Ring networks, 595
LOADLIN, 357-358
loopback interface, 406
Lynx browser, 298-300
melkote, 423
MGR window system, 588
mouse, 148, 185-186
multicasting, 553
Netscape
    Communicator, 302
    help file links, 274
    Messenger, 275, 277
    Navigator, 305
networks
    connections, 407, 411,
        415-417
    netcfg, 412
    security, 553
    settings (DHCP), 411
newsgroups, 580
NFS, 425-426
PC cards
    cardmgr daemon, 139-140
    Linux compatibility, 139
pine program, 272
PLIP interfaces, 419
PostgresSQL, 587
PPP
    connections, 250-251
    ISP, 253
    kppp, 255
    for a Linux machine, 413
    scripts, 254, 257
printers, 90-92
rc files, 394-395
routers, 553
sendmail, 593
sendmail daemon, 266
shadow passwords, 590
SLIP interfaces, 417
sound cards, 240
SoundBlaster cards, 533
Synaptics touchpads, 149
TCP/IP, 424
terminal window, 186

user information (chang-
    ing), 374
win, 424-425
xanim program, 246
xdm use, 174-175
Xfree86, 170
xterm terminals, 186

conflicts (packages), 485

connections
    checking phone lines, 251
    closing (ftp command), 290
    default routes, 415-417
    detecting incoming, 427
    DHCP, 411
    dial-in service, 427
        configuration, 157-159
        PPP service, 160-161
        setup, 157-159
    failure, restarting PPP, 415
    file system support, 251
    Internet
        configuring PPP, 250-251
        minicom, 257
        SLIP/PPP, 594
    kernel daemon support, 549
    Linux systems, 423
    loopback interface, 406-407
    Mac OS to Linux, 423-424
    network
        configuring, 407, 411,
            415-417
        customizing login greet-
            ings, 442
    opening (ftp command),
        287
    PPP
        closing, 258
        customizing, 415
        serial port check, 251
        troubleshooting, 261-263
    TCP/IP, serial lines, 420
    telnet, 310-313
    Windows machine to Linux
        system, 424-425

consoles (virtual), 12

constants, defining, 347

constructs (bash shell)
    conditional, 332-335
    for statement, 336
    looping, 332, 336

control characters, 626

control keys, 633

controllers (PC cards), 139

controlling
    print jobs, 93-96
    programs, 29

**control_flag configuration
file, 383**

**conversion programs (graph-
ics), 217-218, 229**

**convert command
(ImageMagick), 224, 228**

converting
    between package methods,
        500-501
    graphics, 229-233
    XFree86 Xf86Config mode-
        lines to XI modelines, 595

copying
    directories
        cp command, 44
        gmc client, 54
        kfm client, 56-57
    files
        cp command, 44
        gmc client, 54
        kfm client, 56-57
        multiple, 44
    text
        terminal windows, 206
        X11, 206-208
        xclipboard client, 207-208
        xcutsel client, 206-207

core. *See* kernels

Corel Web site, 64

corrupted file systems, 474

corrupted superblocks, 475

cp command, 44, 194, 604

CPU time (processes), 541

cpuinfo file, 540

CPUs, 548, 627

creating
  aliases, 108
  backukps, 504
  boot disks, 358, 586
  client root directories, 594
  custom logon screens, 176
  dictionaries, 78
  email messages
    Netscape Messenger, 279
    pine program, 273
  ethernet bridges, 592
  file systems, 469-471
  filenames, 20
  firewalls, 592
  formatted documents, 80
  host routes, 422
  intranets, 594
  Linux floppy fstab entries,
    470
  man pages, 593
  mount points, 124
  PPP dialup accounts, 256
  printers, 90
  scripts, 29
  shell commands, 28
  swap files, 223
  symbolic links (Netscape
    help files), 274
  visual directories
    (ImageMagick), 226

crontab files, 521
  access, 399-400
  command settings, 397-399
  configuration, 395, 398-399
  cron processes, 395-396
  environment settings, 397
  example, 398
  scheduling, 390
  specifying start times,
    397-398

csh shell, 322

**Ctrl key, editing command
line, 21**

Ctrl+Alt+Del, 13

cursors, 184

custom keys, 42

customizing
  command line prompts,
    106-108
  command-line, 586
  desktop environments, 192
  login greetings, 441-442
    disclaimers, 443
    issue files, 442
    network connections, 442
  logins, 105
  MOTD, 443
  PPP connections, 415
  ppp-on script, 255
  X Windows, 179-185
  xdm banner screens, 176
  xinitrc startup script, 178

D

**-d option (fetchmail),
267-270**

\d character, 107

daemons, 432, 627
  cardmgr, 141
    beep codes, 140
    configuring PC cards,
    139-140
    disabling PC card notifica-
    tion, 142
    listing PC cards, 141
    PC cards support, 138
  inetd
    Apache Web server, 450
    FTP access, 448
  pppd, 160, 257, 637
  restarting, 441
  root cautions, 538
  sendmail, 266
  setting, 440
  starting, 441

DARPA, 627

data
  databases, 639
  encapsulation, 628
  loss, 25
  redirecting, 638
  streams, 639

date
  at command, 403
  command settings (crontab
    files), 397

dd command, 604

Debian Linux distribution
  downloading, 582
  package system, 482

debugging
  debug argument, 384
  gcc compiler, 341

**declaring shell functions,
337-338**

decompressing
  directories, 504-505
  downloaded files, 237
  files, 504-505

**default rules (make com-
mands), 343**

**defaults option (mount com-
mand), 460**

defining
  constants, 347
  default text editor, 74
  environment variables, 102
  variables (ksh shell), 103

Delete User dialog box, 370

deleting
  directories
    gmc client, 54
    rm command, 50
    rmdir command, 49
  environment variables, 103
  faxes, 165
  files
    gmc client, 54
    kfm client, 57
    rm command, 49

system maintenance,
521-522
tmp directory, 328-332
undeleting, 522-523
warnings, 331
groups
groupdel command,
376-377
usercfg tool, 373
password protection (Zip
disks), 135
printers, 89
run level services
chkconfig command, 437
ksysv utility (KDE), 447
ntsysv utility (Red Hat
Linux), 448
stopping services, 448
tksysv utility (X11),
444-445
users
usercfg tool, 370-371
userdel command, 375
variables, 103

dependencies, 342
conflicts, 485
errors, uninstalling packages, 487
modules
benefits, 536
generating, 536
module paths, 537

desktops, 17. See also KDE
backgrounds, 182
capturing, 208-210,
212-213
customizing, 192
environments, 190
GNOME
gmc client, 52-54
help browser, 16-17
Search Tool, 55
wallpaper
xloadimage command,
182-183
xv client, 183

**dev option (mount com-
mand), 460**
/dev directory, 623
/dev/modem device, 156
/dev/null file, 623
/dev/printer socket, 623
devices. See also specific device
types
/dev/modem, 156
block-special files, 625
busy errors, 458
CD-ROM drives, 241
character special file, 626
drivers, 130
files, 627
fixed, 465
floppy disk drive, 517
getty, 428
hard drives, 115-117
identifying, 119
joysticks, 151
mount command, 117, 457
mounting, 124-127
mouse, 148
Plug and Play, 534
BIOS, 534
Plug-and-Play toolset, 534
sound card configuration,
532
printers, 89
removable, 454, 464-465
rewinding tape drives, 130
serial, 154
sound cards, 240
storage, 116-117
support, 6
tape
installing, 130
magnetic, 131
rewinding, 130-132
symbolic links, 131
tension strength, 132
terminals, 640
touchpads, 150
volume, 114-117
Zip drives, 132

df command, 117, 523
DHCP, 411, 592
**dial tone (modem check),
251**
dial-in service
configuration, 157-159
enabling, 427
PPP service, 160-161
setup, 157-159
dialog boxes
Delete User, 370
Edit User Definition,
365-367
linuxconf utility, 109
**dialup accounts, configuring
(kppp), 256**
dict clients, 79
dictionaries
creating, 78
Internet, 79
web2, 77
words, 77
directories, 627
archiving, 507-508
bin, 325
cd command, 36-37
changing, 36
client root, 594
colors, 39
compressing, 504-505
copying
cp command, 44
gmc client, 54
kfm client, 56-57
creating
gmc client, 53-54
kfm client, 56
current directory printout,
323-326
decompressing, 504-505
deleting
gmc client, 54
rm command, 50
rmdir command, 49
echoing contents, 39

/etc/pam.d, 383
ftp, 286
GIMP, 217
hard drives, 115-117
hierarchies, 43
HOWTO documents, 586
links, 48
lists, printing, 89
listing, 37
   echo command, 39
   ls command, 38-39
mkdir command, 43
mount-point, 457
mounting from across a network, 425
moving, 45-46
   gmc client, 54
   kfm client, 57
navigating, 36-37, 627
parent, 37
printing contents
   list of, 89
   program example, 343,
   345
/proc, 539
   cpuinfo file, 540
   interrupts file, 540
   pci file, 540
   security, 539
   version file, 540
programs, locating docu-
mentation, 347
pwd command, 36
renaming, 45-46
   gmc client, 54
   kfm client, 57
root file system, 472
saving shell functions, 337
searching, 50-52
tmp, removing files,
328-332
touch command, 43

disabling
initial ramdisk, 572
PC card notification (cardmgr daemon), 142

disclaimers
customizing login greetings,
443
MOTD, 443

discussion groups
irc, 315
Netnews, 635

**diskless Linux workstations,
587**

disks
floppy
   backups, 517-518
   mounting, 455
minimizing space, 523,
525-526
mounting, 455
multiple, 588
quotas, 594, 637
Zip disks, 132

**display command
(ImageMagick), 225**

displaying
captured images, 212
environment variables
   env command, 102
   printenv command,
   100-101
fonts (X11), 205
fstab, 116
graphics (ImageMagick),
226
HOWTO documents, 586,
591-592
profiles (modems), 157
window dumps (xwud), 209
X11 fonts, 203-204

distributing
GPL, 6
open-source software, 7

**dmesg command, 154-155,
252**

DNS, 627
addresses, 253
information
   configuring, 409-410
   testing, 410

doc, 422-424

**docket applets (Window
Maker), 193**

documentation, 39. *See also*
help
commands, 325
emacs, 71
email, 266
Linux drivers, 546
ls command, 39
modules, 531
PC cards configuration, 139
programs, locating, 347
rvplayer, 244
serial ports, 157

documents
formatted, creating, 80, 83-86
HOWTO
   directories, 586
   mini, 592
   viewing, 586, 591
PostScript
   previewing, 234
   printing, 236
text, printing, 92
text-processing systems, 82

domain names, setting, 413

DOS, 628
backups, 592
partitions, 118
prompt, booting from,
356-360
text-file convention, 357

dosemu, 587

downloading
Alien, 500
Debian Linux, 582
files
   ftp command, 286-290
   Lynx, 300
   ncftp command, 292-293
   Netscape, 293-294
FTP server package, 449
KDE, 632
kernels (FTP site), 545
linuxconf, 462

LOADLIN, 357
Netscape Communicator, 300-303
Plug-and-Play toolset, 534
programs, compiling source code, 347-349
taper backup utility, 513
xrpm client, 496
zftape drivers, 513

dpi, 628

drivers
Alsa sound, 592
APM, 574
joysticks, 152
Linux, documentation, 546
modularizing, 569
SCSI, 528, 537, 551, 557, 572
sound cards, selecting, 532-533

drives. *See also* hard drives
CD-ROM, 241
Iomega Zip, 519
removable, 518-520
tape
backups, 132
floppy controller, 131
installing, 130-131
mt (magnetic tape) command, 131-132
retensioning tapes, 132
rewinding tapes, 132
Zip, 132-134

du command, 523

dump command, 468

dump interval, 468

dvi documents (TeX), 86

dynamic code-module loading, 6

dynamic IP addresses, 257

dynamic linking, 342

E

-e option (fetchmail), 267

EBCDIC (Extended Binary Coded Decimal Interchange Code), 628

echo command, 39, 155, 331

echoing directory contents, 39

ed utility, 628

Edit User Definition dialog box, 365-367

editing. *See also* stream editors; text editors
command line, 20-21, 586, 626
configuration files (kernel), 531-534
ed utility, 628
emacs, 68, 628
fstab, 124-125, 467-468
graphics
convert command (ImageMagick), 229
display command (ImageMagick), 227
GIMP, 216
large, 223
memory use, 223
saving (ImageMagick), 228
groups
groupmod command, 376
usercfg tool, 373
inittab files, 435
run level services (Red Hat Linux), 444
run levels, 434-435
scripts
fax shell scripts, 162
ppp-on, 255
shutdown, 438-441
startup, 438-441
sendmail daemon configuration, 266

spell checking, 78-79
stream text, 638
system files, 159
text files, 357
users
usercfg tool, 367-368
usermod command, 374-375
variables
login shell scripts, 328
PATH, 105

EDITOR environment variable, 101-102

efax software, 95, 161-162

egrep command, 60-62

ejecting
PC cards, 144
Zip disks, 135

Elightenment, starting, 194

elm utility, 628

else statement, 333

emacs, 628
command line options, 68
commands, 70
documentation, 71
installation, 68
jmacs, 74
opening, 23
querying emacs package, 489
text editor, 68-71
tutorial, 69
Web site, 71
Xemacs, 69

email, 588, 628
carbon copies, 273
command line, 269
Cyrus IMAP mail server, 592
documentation, 266
elm utility, 628
fetchmail, 266
configuring, 266
options, 267-268
retrieving, 269

file attachments, 271
filtering, 281-282
forwarding, 279
mail program, 269-271
mail readers, 266
mailing lists, 593
Netscape Messenger
    accessing help, 274
    configuring, 275-277
pine program, 271, 636
    commands, 273
    configuring, 272
    manipulating messages,
    274
POP connections (secure),
    594
protocols, 266
qmail utility, 594
queues, 593
replying to, 279
retrieving
    fetchmail, 267-268
    Netscape Messenger, 278
sendmail daemon, 266
spam, 280-281
TKRat mail program, 595
transport agents, 266
user agents, 266, 269-276

emptying trash, 57

emulators (SLIP/PPP), 594

enabling
Apache Web server,
    450-451
at command, 400-401
cron processes (crontab
    files), 396
dial-in service, 427
FTP access, 286, 448-450
NFS, 428
PPP networking support,
    252
TCP/IP networking sup-
    port, 252

encapsulation, 628

Enlightenment Web site,
192

env command, 102-103, 327,
605

environment settings
(crontab files), 397

environment variables, 622,
641
bash shell, 100
command line, deleting
    from, 103
displaying
    env command, 102
    printenv command,
    100-101
EDITOR, 102
profile files, 100
setting, 100-105
temporary, 103
User Environment
    Variables, 101

environments
desktop, 190
    customizing, 192
    KDE, 191
emacs, 68
GNOME, 631
KDE, 632
shell, 639

erase command (tape drives),
132

errors
dependency, 485-487
errors.log file, 26
messages
    device busy, 458
    mounting floppy disks, 471
output, 26
stderr, 639
terminating processes, 544

escape codes, character
effects, 107

Esperanto, 587

/etc directory, 108

/etc/cshrc file, 623

/etc/exports file, 426

/etc/group file, 623

/etc/inittab file, 174, 623

/etc/motd file, 624

/etc/pam.d directory, 383

/etc/pam.d/login file, 387

/etc/pam.d/other configura-
tion file, 386

/etc/passwd file, 624

/etc/profile file, 624

/etc/resolv.conf file (PPP con-
nection), 253

Ethernet, 628
cards, configuring, 407
creating bridges, 592
interfaces, 420
    activating, 411
    configuring, 421
    routers, 421-423

exclamation point (!)
ftp command, 290
mount command, 460

exit (ftp command), 290

exit commands, 12-13

expect script, 29

exporting
persistent variables, 328
variables, 102

expressions, 628
file-testing, 335
integer, 334
regular, 638
string, 334
test, 333-335

ext2 file system, 471

ext2fs file system, 114

extensions
file, 622-623
MIME, 634

extracting tar files, 506-509

F

-f option (fetchmail), 267

facility (messages), 525

fax service
configuration, 161-162
fax shell script, 162-163
testing, 163
faxes
checking status, 164
deleting, 165
incoming, 164
printing, 165
sending, 164
viewing, 164
software
efax, 161-162
Web sites, 162
faxes

faxing, 95-96, 592

fc command, 605

fdformat command, 517

fdisk command, 120-121

fetchmail, 266-268
chmod command, 268
configuration file, 268
configuring, 266
creating .fetchmailrc file, 268
options, 267
POP3 retrieval options, 267-268
retrieving email, 267-269

fg command, 30, 605

fgrep command, 60-62

fgrep search utility, 102

FIFO, 628

file command, 41, 606

file system table. *See* fstab

file systems, 629
adding, 462
appearance in fstab, 468

backups, 476
frequency, 477
reviewing strategy, 478
storage, 478
strategy, 476
configuring kernel file system support, 558-559, 568
corruption, 474
creating, 469
mkfs command, 470-471
separate, 472
directories not to be made separate file systems, 472
exported from NFS servers, 126
ext2, 471
ext2fs, 114
fixed devices, 465
/home, 472
mkfs command, 469
mount command, 114
mounting, 454-455, 458-461
linuxconf utility, 126
options, 459
usermount command, 454-456
msdos, 114
network, 463
NFS
autmounting, 559
mount options, 465
options, 463
PPP connection support, 251-252
/proc, 468
removable, 468
removable devices, 464-465
repairing, 473-476
repartitioning drives, 119
restoring, 479
root, 472
selecting, 118-119
separate, 472-473
setup, 461, 469
singly rooted, 459
support, 114-115

tree organization, 472-473
unmounting, 454-455, 458-461
/usr, 472
vfat, 114, 134

File Transfer Protocol. *See* FTP

file-testing expressions, 335

filenames, 629
fully qualified, 629
reserved characters, 20
spaces, 20
wildcards, 641

files, 629
/etc/pam.d/login file, 387
access times, updating, 512
appending, redirection, 25
archives, 506, 509
audio formats, xanim support, 245-246
backups
cp command, 44
mv command, 45
bashrc, aliases, 108
binary, string extraction, 61
bit bucket, 623
changing groups, 378
compressing, 504-505, 629
configuration, 627
Apache, 451-452
editing kernel, 531-534
kernel module configuration, 531-532
loading boot-time modules, 538
Password Authentication Module (PAM), 383-386
copying
cp command, 44
gmc client, 54
kfm client, 56-57
multiple, 44
cpuinfo, 540
crontab
access, 399-400
command settings, 397-399

657

files

configuration, 395, 398-399
  enabling cron processes, 396
  environment settings, 397
  example, 398
  restarting cron processes, 395
  scheduling, 390
  specifying start times, 397-398
  starting cron processes, 395
decompressing, 504-505
deleting
  gmc client, 54
  kfm client, 57
  rm command, 49
  system maintenance, 521-522
  undeleting, 522-523
  warnings, 331
device, 89, 627
downloading
  decompressing, 237
  ftp command, 286-290
  ncftp command, 292-293
  Netscape, 293-294
  telnet sessions, 313-314
email attachments, 271
extensions, 622-623
file systems. See file systems
filenames, 629
gettydefs, 428
housekeeping, 523
i-node, 631
indexed, 629
inittab
  backups, 435
  code example, 392-394
  comments, 391
  configuration, 390-394
  editing, 435
  entries, 391, 435
  init actions, 391-392
  scheduling, 390
interrupts, 540
lilo.config, 353-356
link, 633
login, 100

Makefile, 344
missing state, 489
moving, 45-46
  gmc client, 54
  kfm client, 57
naming, 20
overwriting, 25, 45
ownership (chown command), 378
pci, 540
permissions
  chmod command, 379-382
  SetGID, 382
  SetUID, 381
pico editor, 73
PPP options, 427-428
printing (command line), 93
profile, 100
rc
  configuration, 394-395
  scheduling, 390
removing (tmp directory), 328, 330-332
renaming, 45-46
  gmc client, 54
  kfm client, 57
resource, 100, 187-188
searching, 50
  access time, 512
  egrep command, 60-62
  fgrep command, 60-62
  find command, 50-51, 512
  GNOME Search Tool, 55
  grep command, 58-60
  kfind client, 57-58
  locate command, 51-52
  strings command, 61
  tar backups, 509-510
  whereis command, 52
  which command, 52
  zgrep, 62
sed Script File, 76-77
sequential, 629
spooling to printer, 92-93
swap, 223
system
  editing, 159
  log files, 387

tar, 506
  extracting, 506-509
  moving, 506-509
text, 39-42, 629
touch command, 43
users
  home directory path, 362
  restoring, 479
version, 540
video formats, 245-246
X11
  Imakefile, 349
  resource files, 187-188

filtering, 26
  email, 281-282
  text formatting, 80

find command, 606
  file searches, 50-51
  locating files based on access times, 512
  restricting searches, 50-51
  search expressions, 511
  search rules, 521
  system maintenance, 510, 512
  tar backups, 509-510

finding. See searching

finger program, 629

firewalls, 630
  configuring, 553
  creating, 592
  piercing, 592

fixed devices, 465

flags, 635, 639

flipping graphics, 233

floppy controller tape drives, 131

floppy disks
  backups, 517-518
  drives
    configuring kernels, 549-550, 565
    name, 517
  formatting, 517
    kfloppy command, 456-457
    usermount command, 455-456

fstab entry, 470
mounting, 455, 458
unmounting, 471

fmt command, 81

fonts
character maps (xfd client), 203-205
compressed, 202-204
displaying, 203-205

for statement, 336

foreground, 199-200, 630

formatted documents, 80, 83-86

formatting. *See also* mounting
filter commands, 80
floppy disks, 517
kfloppy command, 456-457
usermount command, 455-456
fmt command, 81-82
graphics, 230, 233
groff typesetting system, 82-85
hard drives, 122-123
manual pages, 82-85
pr command, 81
TeX typesetting system, 85-86
text-process systems, 82-86
typesetting programs, 80

forwarding email, 279

frame buffers, 587

Free BSD, 593

free disk space (df) command, 117

free software, 7

Free Software Foundation (FSF), 6, 630

freshmeat.net Web site, 162

fsck command, 468

fsck program, 473, 475-476

fseek function, 630

FSF (Free Software Foundation), 6, 630

fstab (file system table), 116
backup, 462
editing, 124-125
manually, 467-468
entries, 470
order, 468

ftape module (device driver), 130

FTP (File Transfer Protocol), 630
access
anonymous, 449
checking, 449
enabling, 286, 448-450
testing, 450
ftp directory, 286
ftp user, 286
Lynx browser, 298
Netscape, 293
servers
download site, 449
testing, 450
sites, 545

ftp command, 607. *See also*
ncftp command
! (bang) character, 290
closing connections, 290
common commands, 285-286
directory navigation, 288
examples, 284-285
exit, 290
file downloads, 286-290
help, 291
opening connections, 287
quitting, 290
shell commands, 290

full backups, 519-520

fully qualified filenames, 629

function keyword, 337

functions
libraries, loading, 338
shell
declaring, 337-338
organizing, 337
saving, 337
writing, 336-337

fuser command, 104

G

g command (mail program), 271

gateways, 630
alphanumeric pager, 594
setting default, 408

gcc compiler, 340
debugging programs, 341
-ggdb switch, 341
ld linker, 341-342
-O switch, 341
optimizing programs, 341
-pg switch, 341

gdict, downloading, 79

General Public License (GPL), 6, 631

generating
filenames, 629
module dependencies, 536

geometry settings (window sizes), 198-199

getty program, 427
customizing login greetings, 441-442
devices, 429
logging in to Linux, 428

gettydefs file, 428

-ggdb switch (gcc compiler), 341

ghostview client, 234

GIDs (Group ID numbers), 362-364, 630

GIMP (GNU Image Manipulation Program), 216
configuring, 218, 223
editing graphics, 216
memory use, 223
temporary files, 223
FAQs Web site, 224
features, 217
floating toolbar, 220
.gimp directory, 222
gimprc file, 222
keyboard commands, 220-222
loading images, 219
menu system, 224
Pattern Selection dialog box, 220
plug-ins, 217
quitting, 220
starting, 217
swap files, 223
system requirements, 217
tutorial Web site, 224
viewing installed files, 222
Web site, 224
windows, 224
X11 Toolkit options, 217
gimprc file, 222
gmc client
creating directories, 53-54
directory/file management, 54
starting, 53
symbolic links, 54
GNOME (GNOME Desktop Environment), 52, 631
command tools, 23
gmc client
creating directories, 53-54
directory/file management, 54
starting, 53
symbolic links, 54
help browser, 16-17
Search Tool, 55
starting, 194

GNU, 7, 631
GNU Image Manipulation Program. *See* GIMP
gpasswd command, 377
GPL (General Public License), 6, 631
gpm utility, 148
mouse daemon, 150
options, 149
graphical logins, 8
graphical user interfaces (GUIs), 6, 631
graphics
capturing magnified, 212-213
configuring cards, 170
converting, 229-233
conversion programs, 217-218
X11, 233
displaying
captured, 212
visual directory (ImageMagick), 226
editing
distortion, 227
GIMP, 217
large, 223
memory use, 223
saving (ImageMagick), 228
flipping, 233
formats, 230
GIMP, 216-217
gimprc file, 222
keyboard commands, 220-222
loading, 219
quitting, 220
swap files, 223
tutorial Web site, 224
ImageMagick, 224-226
loading (GIMP), 219
patterns, 220
previewing, 234

repeating sequence (xloadimage client), 210
X11, 170
GRASS mapping system, 592
grep command, 58-60, 607
grep utility, 631
groff command, 607
groff typesetting system, 80-85
commands, 83-85
macros, 84
group identifications (GIDs), 362-364, 630
groupadd command, 376
groupdel command, 376-377
groupmod command, 376
groups, 362-363
access, 362
adding
groupadd command, 376
usercfg tool, 371-372
users, 377
changing groups of files, 378
deleting (groupdel command), 376-377
editing
groupmod command, 376
usercfg tool, 373
information, 362
name, 363
ownership
chgrp command, 378
gpasswd command, 377
passwords, 363
removing (usercfg tool), 373
grun command, 23
GUIs (graphical user interfaces), 6, 631
gunzip command, 504-505, 608
gv command, 234
-geometry option, 234
modifying PostScript window size, 234

Postscript graphics, 222
printing documents, 236
reading documents,
234-236
gzip command, 504-505, 607
gzip compression utility, 631

H

\h character, 107
h command
mail program, 270
top command, 541
halt command, 608
Halt run level, 432
halting, 13
hard drives
adding to Linux, 119
df command, 117
directories, 115-117
formatting, 122-123
hidden space, 123
identifying, 119
installing, 119, 124
mounting, 124-125, 127
NFS, 126
partitioning, 114, 120-121
sharing, 114
hard links, 47-48, 633
hardware
joysticks, 151
laptops, 588
mouse, 148
newsgroup, 580
Plug and Play, 534
   BIOS, 534
   Plug-and-Play toolset, 534
   sound card configuration,
   532
Sony VAIO computers, 595
terminals, 640
touchpads, 150
Hello World program, 345

Help, 14
help, 39. See also documentation
accessing (Netscape
   Messenger), 274
apropos command, 18
ftp command, 291
GNOME help browser,
   16-17
info command, 15-16
KDE help browser, 17
Lynx browser, 299
make xconfig command,
   564
manual pages, 14
   whereis command, 52
   which command, 52
   xman client, 15
whatis command, 17
here document, 631
hierarchies (directories), 43
history (command line), 21
HITSIZE environment vari-
able, 101
home directory
.bash_history file, 21
path, 362
HOME environment vari-
able, 101
/home file systems, 472
$HOME variable, 622
hosting (virtual), 590
hostname command, 608
hostnames
configuring, 409-410
setting, 413
testing name resolution, 410
hosts, acting as routers, 422
HOSTTYPE environment
variable, 101
housekeeping files. See system maintenance

HOWTO documents
directories, 586
mini, 592
viewing, 586, 591
HTML (Hypertext Markup
Language), 631
HUP signal name, 543
hyphen (-), cd command, 37

I

i-node, 631
I-Phone, 631
I/O ports, programming, 593
ICCCM (Inter-Client
Communications
Conventions Manual), 631
ICMP (Internet Control
Message Protocol), 631
IDE devices, configuring
kernels, 549-550, 565
identifying hard drives, 119
IDs, processes, 538, 543
if statement, 333-335
file-testing expressions, 335
integer expressions, 334
string expressions, 334
syntax, 333
test expressions, 333
ifconfig command, 406-407
testing PPP connections,
   259
verifying network cards
   (running status), 408
viewing active interfaces,
   418
ImageMagick, 224
convert command, 228
creating visual directories,
   226
display command, 225
editing graphics, 227
further information, 229

program requirements, 224-225
saving files, 228
images. *See* graphics
imake interface, 631
Imakefile (X11), 349
incoming faxes, 164
incremental backups, automating, 519-521
Independent Software Vendors (ISVs), 632
indexed files, 629
Indexed Sequential Access Method (ISAM), 632
inetd daemon
Apache Web server, 450
FTP access, 448
info command, 15-16
Infomagic Web site, 582
inheritance, 632
init process, 432
actions, 391
chkconfig command, 436
adding run level services, 437
comments, 436
deleting run level services, 437
listing run level services, 436
resetting run level service information, 437
init scripts
development checklist, 440-441
example, 438-440
levels, 390
run levels, 434
sanity checkers, 436
spawning processes, 538
initial ramdisks
creating, 572
disabling, 572

loopback devices, 551, 557
SCSI device boots, 528, 537
inittab files
backups, 435
code example, 392-394
comments, 391
configuration, 390-394
editing, 435
entries, 435
init actions, 391-392
scheduling, 390
input
redirection, 25
stdin, 639
inserting PC cards, 144
install command (rpm), 483-484
installing. *See also* loading
Adobe Acrobat Reader, 237
Netscape Helper Application, 238-240
bus mouse, 586
emacs, 68
hard drives, 119, 124
joysticks, 151-152
kernel source, recompiling kernels, 545-546
kernels, 573
enabling APM, 573-575
Linux, 588
from ZIP drives, 593
Win95 systems, 593
make command, 342
make install command, 345
modems, 588
Netscape
Communicator, 300-303, 306-307
help file links, 274
newsgroup, 580
packages
conflicts, 485
rpm, 483-487
xrpm, 498
Password Authentication Module (PAM), 382-383

pcmcia package, 138
ppa Zip disk driver, 595
printers, 89-90
programs, 345, 348
Quake, 589
shadow passwords, 590
tape drives, 130-131
TeX typesetting system, 85
tpconfig command, 149-150
vim (rpm), 484-485
xrpm client, 496-497, 500
Zip drives, 133
instrumentation (shell scripts), 325-326
integer expressions, 334
Inter-Client Communications Conventions Manual (ICCCM), 631
interfaces
Ethernet, 420-425
loopback, 406-407
PLIP, 418-419
PPP, 266, 413-417
SLIP, 416-417
International Standards Organization (ISO), 632
Internet, 632, 642
connections
minicom, 257
PPP, 250-251
SLIP/PPP, 594
dictionaries, 79
I-Phone, 631
IP addresses, 253
Internet Control Message Protocol (ICMP), 631
Internet Relay Chat (IRC), 314-316, 632
interrupts file, 540
intranets, creating, 594
inttab files, 391
Iomega
Jaz drives, 593
Web site, 133
Zip drives, 519, 595

IP accounting, 553
IP addresses, 253, 266
  aliasing, 593
  dynamic, 257
  loopback interface, 407
  masquerading, 593
  naming, 407
IP Aliasing, 553
IP tunneling, 553
IRC (Internet Relay Chat),
  314-316, 632
ISA Plug and Play. *See* Plug
  and Play hardware
ISAM (Indexed Sequential
  Access Method), 632
ISDN support, configuring
  kernels, 558, 567
ISO (International Standards
  Organization), 632
ispell command, 78-79
ISPs, 588
  email protocols, 266
  PPP, configuring, 253
issue file, customizing login
  greetings, 442
ISVs (Independent Software
  Vendors), 632

J

jed editor, 74
jmacs editor, 74
job control (program flow),
  29
jobs command, 30
joe editor, 74
joysticks, 151-152
jpico editor, 74
js joystick driver, 152
jscal joystick driver, 152
jstar editor, 74

K

k command (top command),
  541
K Desktop Environment. *See*
  KDE
K File Manager. *See* kfm
  client
-k option (fetchmail),
  267-268
K&R (Kernighan and
  Ritchie), 632
kanchi, 422-423
KDE (K Desktop
  Environment), 17, 191. *See
  also* desktops
  Command widget, 23
  floppy formatter options,
    456
  help browser, 17
  kfind client, 57-58
  kfm client, 55
    creating directories, 56
    directory/file management,
    56-57
    starting, 55
    symbolic links, 57
  kpackage, 493
    package groups, 493
    removing packages, 495
  kppp utility, 161
  ksysv utility
    adding run level services,
    446
    deleting run level services,
    447
    starting, 446
  starting, 194
  trash, 57
  Web site, 191
  kdict, downloading, 79
Kernel Configurator applet,
  529-530
kernel messages
  logs, 525

Kernel Module filed, 421
kernel package
querying, 489
kerneld daemon
  configuring, 593
kernels, 6-7, 528, 633
  booting, 352, 461
  compiling, 570-572
    cautions, 545
    make clean command, 571
    make dep command, 571
    make modules command,
    571
    make zImage command,
    571
  configuring
    adding modules, 528-530
    automounting, 559
    binary formats, 549
    CD-ROM drives, 558,
    568
    character based-devices,
    559-560, 570
    editing files, 531-534
    file system support,
    558-559, 568
    floppy drives, 549-550,
    565
    IDE devices, 549-550, 565
    ISDN support, 558, 567
    Kernel Configurator
    applet, 529-530
    kernel developer options,
    562
    loopback devices, 551
    make config command, 559
    multiple devices driver, 551
    network connectivity, 549
    network devices, 557, 567
    networking, 551,
    553-554, 566
    Plug and Play devices, 534
    ramdisk support, 551
    SCSI support, 554-555,
    557, 566-567
    selecting CPU types, 548
    sound cards, 532-534,
    560-562, 570

downloading, 545
file system support, 115
FTP site, 545
init process, 538
installing, 573-575
loading, 352
LOADLIN, 359-360
maintenance, 528
modules
  configuration file, 531-532
  documentation, 531
  sound card device drivers,
  532-533
new features, 6-7
PPP support, 251-252
preemptive multitasking,
  528
/proc directory, 539
  cpuinfo file, 540
  interrupts file, 540
  pci file, 540
  security, 539
  version file, 540
recompiling, 545, 570-572
  installing new kernel
  source, 545-546
  kernel configuration prepa-
  ration, 546-547
  make clean command, 571
  make config command,
  547-562
  make dep command, 571
  make modules command,
  571
  make modules_install com-
  mand, 571
  make xconfig command,
  562-570
  make zImage command,
  571
SCSI device boots, 528,
  537, 551, 557, 572
simplicity, 528
vfat, loading, 458
vmlinuz, 358
Kernighan and Ritchie
(K&R), 632

key bindings, 42
keyboards
commands (GIMP),
  220-222
cpd command controls, 242
custom keys, 42
pico editor, 74
MIDI, 593
Tab key, 21
keys (control), 633
keywords
function, 337
poll, 268
kfind client, 57-58
kfloppy command, format-
ting floppy disks, 456-457
kfm client (K File Manager),
55
creating directories, 56
directory/file management,
  56-57
starting, 55
symbolic links, 57
KickStart program (Red
Hat), 588
kill command, 30-31,
543-544, 608
KILL signal name, 543
killall command, 544, 608
kmod system daemon, 130
Korn shell (ksh shell), 103,
322
kpackage, 493
package groups, 493
removing packages, 495
starting, 493
kppp, 161
configuring PPP, 255
setup options, 256
starting, 255
starting PPP connections,
  258
kpppload command, 260

ksh shell (Korn shell), 103,
322
ksysv utility
adding run level services, 446
deleting run level services,
  447
starting, 446

L

languages
text processing, 640
UIL, 641
LANs, 633
laptops, 588
ld command, 341
ld linker, 341-342
LDP (Linux Documentation
Project), 581
leased line modems, 593
less command, 41-42, 608
custom keys, 42
features, 41
navigating, 42
less than (<) operator, 75
libraries
compiling, 341-342
loading, 338
Netscape Communicator, 301
LILO (Linux loader), 352, 593
booting, changing order, 354
command-line arguments,
  354-355
configuring, 352-356
troubleshooting, 353
using boot managers, 354
lilo.config file, 353-356
line printer (lpr) command, 90
line-feed character, 357
line-printer control (lcp) com-
mand, 93-94
line-printer spooling, 92-93
link files, 633

links
directories, 48
hard, 47-48, 633
ln command, 46-48
PPP, 427
soft, 47
symbolic, 46-48, 633
gmc client, 54
kfm client, 57
mouse, 148
shells, 46
subdirectories, 438
tape drive device, 131

Linux
advocacy, 592
Beowulf clustering system, 586
BogoMips, 592
books, 589
changing configuration, 109
Comeau C++, 592
comparing to Windows NT, 379
compatibility, 340
configuring, 587
connecting
Mac OS machine, 423-424
two systems, 423
Windows machine, 424-425
dictionaries, 77
diskless workstations, 587
DOS text files, 357
email, 266
firewalls, 587, 592
graphics formats, 230
GRASS mapping system, 592
HOWTO documents, 586
joystick support, 151
laptop systems, 588
LILO, 352-353
loading, 352
logging in, 428
moving, 592
Netscape Communicator, 301

playing music CDs, 240
PostgresSQL, 587
Red Hat, 454
screen editors, 67
sharing hard drives, 114
shells (list of), 32
sound, 588
text editors, 64
upgrading, 595
Usenet news newsgroups, 580
VME bus systems, 590
web sites, 581-583
word processors, 64-66
WordPerfect, 65, 595

Linux Documentation Project, 533

Linux Documentation Project (LDP), 133, 531, 581, 586

Linux File System Standard, 525

Linux Journal Web site, 583

Linux User Groups (LUGs), 590

linuxconf, 109-110, 412, 462, 467
adding PLIP interfaces, 418
configuring
Ethernet interfaces, 420-421
network connections, 411
creating user accounts, 9-10
dialog boxes, 109
fixed devices, 465
homepage, 412
mounting file systems, 126
options, 463
removable devices, 464-465
running as root, 416
setting hostnames and domain names, 413, 633
SLIP configuration options, 416

LISP (List Processing Language), 633

Lisp language interpreter (emacs), 68

listings
cleantmp shell variables example, 328, 330
crontab file example, 398
directories, 37
echo command, 39
ls command, 38-39
env command output, 327
hello-world.c, 343
Makefile, 345
makefile with install functions, 346
if statement syntax, 333
init script example, 438-440
inittab file code example, 392, 394
lilo.conf file, 353
modules, 535-536
PC cards
cardmgr daemon, 141
configuration, 143-144
persistent variables, 327
printdir shell script example, 323-324
printdir2 shell script example, 325-326
printing queue, 93
run level services, 436
while statement syntax, 336

ln command, 46
/dev/modem device, 156
directories, 48
hard links, 47-48
soft links, 47
symbolic links (tape drives), 131

load average (system load), 540

loadable code module, 89

Loadable Module Support button, 564

loading, 535. *See also* installing
code modules, 6
images (GIMP), 219

kernel, 352
libraries, 338
Linux, 352
modules
  boot time, 537-538
  manually, 535
video clips (rvplayer), 244

LOADLIN, 352
boot disks, creating,
  358-359
booting, 356-360
command-line
  arguments, 359-360
  functionality, 356
configuring, 357-358
distribution, 357
downloading, 357
preparing, 357-358

LOADLIN.EXE, 593

local printers, adding, 90

locales, 593

localhost settings, 410

locate command, 51-52, 609

locking
terminal, 181
users, 368-369

lockups, 474

log messages, 525

logging in, 633
customizing logins, 105,
  441-442
  disclaimers, 443
  issue files, 442
  network connections, 442
logins
  configuration, 386-387
  files, 100
  graphical, 8
  MOTD, customizing, 443
  process, 432
  root, cautions, 9
  screens, virtual consoles,
    172
  scripts, editing shell vari-
    ables, 328

security, 8
username comparison, 362
users, 362, 609
virtual consoles, 12
Remote Login, 638
telnet, 640
X11, 173, 176

**LOGNAME environment
variable, 101**

logout command, 13, 609

logs (error), 26

long options (rpm), 484

loopback devices
configuring kernels, 551
initial ramdisk, 551, 557

loopback interface, 406-407

looping constructs, 332, 336

low-bandwidth X (LBX), 593

lp, 633

lpc, 633

lpc command, 94, 609

lpd command, 609, 633

lpq command, 95, 610, 633

lpr command, 90, 95-96, 610

lprm, 634

ls command, 610, 634
documentation, 39
options, 38-39
sorting, 38
wildcards, 38

**LUGs (Linux User Groups),
590**

Lynx browser, 296-297
command line options,
  296-298
configuring, 298-300
downloading files, 300
ftp, 298
help files, 299
newsreaders, 300
retrieving text files, 298
Usenet, 300
Web address, 299

M

**M command (top command),
541**

**Mac OS, connecting to Linux
system, 423-424**

macros
editing, 68
groff typesetting system,
  82-85

**magnetic tape (mt) command,
131-132**

**magnified images, capturing,
212-213**

mail command, 270

**MAIL environment variable,
101**

mail program, 269-271

mail readers, 266

Mail Server dialog box, 277

mail servers, 588

mailing lists, 593

maintenance (kernel), 528

**make clean command, 347,
571**

make command, 342-347, 611
compiling, 344
configure option, 346
constants, defining, 347
default rules, 343
limitations, 344
options, 344

**make config command,
547-562**

make dep command, 571

**make file system (mkfs) com-
mand, 469-471**

make install command, 345

make modules command, 571

**make modules_install com-
mand, 571**

make xconfig command, 562, 565-570
  Code Maturity Options button, 563
  enabling APM, 574
  help, 564
  Loadable Module Support button, 564

make zImage command, 571

makefile command, 342
  compatibility issues, 343
  X11, 349

man command, 14, 325, 611

man pages. *See* manual pages

managing
  email, spam reduction, 280
  modules, automatic/manual comparison, 535
  multiple programs, 29
  packages (rpm), 482
  processes, 538-539
  rpm, 493-495

manual pages, 593, 634
  formatting, 82-85
  reading, 14
  searching (whereis command), 52
  xman client, 15

masquerading (IP), 593

maximizing windows, 201

maximum transmission unit (MTU), 417, 634

melkote, 422-423

memory
  editing graphics, 223
  real, 634
  reducing usage (ld linker), 342
  requirements (GIMP), 217
  virtual, 634

mesg command, 611

Message of the Day (MOTD), 443

messages
  email, 273
  facility, 525
  log, 525
  severity, 525

Messenger. *See* Netscape, Messenger

metacharacters, 634-635

MIDI keyboards, 593

Midnight Commander. *See* gmc client

MIME (Multipurpose Internet Mail Extensions), 634

mini-HOWTO documents, 592

minicom, 257

minimizing
  disk space, 523-526
  windows (X11), 201

MIPS processor systems, 588

mkdir command, 43, 223, 612

mke2fs command, 122-123

mkfs (make file system) command, 469-471, 612

mkinitrd command, 572

mkmf script, 349

mkswap command, 612

modems
  AT command set, 156
  cable, 592
  checking for PPP connection, 251
  checking phone lines, 251
  /dev/modem device, 156
  getty program, 427
  installing, 588
  leased line, 593
  Linux-compatible, 154
  Mwave, 154

profiles, displaying, 157
  selecting, 154
  serial ports, 154-155
  sharing, 595
  testing, 155
  WinModems, 154

modifying command-line, 586

modprobe command, 532

modular programs, 341

modularizing drivers, 569

modules
  code, dynamic loading, 6
  dependencies
    benefits, 536
    generating, 536
    module paths, 537
  kernel
    adding, 528-530
    configuration file, 531-532
    device parameters, 530
    documentation, 531
  listing, 535-536
  loading
    boot time, 537-538
    manually, 535
  managing, 535
  modprobe command, 532
  sound card device drivers, 532-533

more command, 41-42, 612

motd, 634

MOTD (Message of the Day), 443

motif window manager (mwm), 634
  failures, 459
  mounting floppy disks, 458
  options, 459-461

mounting
  autofs automounter utility, 592
  creating mount points, 124
  device busy errors, 458

devices, 124-127
directories from across networks, 425
file systems, 454-455, 458-461
  linuxconf utility, 126
  network, 463
  options, 459
  usermount command, 454, 456
floppy disks, 455
  error messages, 471
  mount command, 458
  vfat, 458
hard drives, 124-127
mount-points, 457-459
NFS file systems, 465
NFS hard drives, 126
options, 125
removable devices, 454

mouse, 148-152
configuring, 185-186
copying/pasting text, 148
gpm utility, 148-149
pointer, 184
symbolic links, 148

moving
directories, 45-46
  gmc client, 54
  kfm client, 57
files, 45-46
gmc client, 54, 57
tar files, 506, 508-509
windows (X11), 200

mpage command, 79-80

MPTN (Multiprotocol Transport Network) protocol, 634

Mrm, 634

MRU (maximum receive unit), 415

msdos file system, 114

mSQL, 591

mt (magnetic tape) command, 131-132

MTU (maximum transmission unit), 417, 634

Multi-User Mode (run level), 433

Multi-User Mode Spare (run level), 433

Multi-User Mode Without Networking (run level), 433

multicasting, 553, 588

multimedia, 245

multiple commands, 22

multiple devices driver, 551

multiple disks, 588

multiple operating systems, booting, 354

Multipurpose Internet Mail Extensions (MIME), 634

multitasking, preemptive, 528

music (CD-ROMs), 240-243

mv command, 45-46, 154, 613

mwm (motif window manager), 634

N

\n character, 107

n command (mail program), 270

name resolution, 410

name servers, 410, 413

named pipes, 637

names
files, 20
loopback interfaces, 407
signal
  HUP, 543
  KILL, 543
  SIGHUP, 543
  SIGKILL, 543
  TERM, 543
user, 9

navigating
directories, 36-37, 288, 627
GNOME help browser, 16-17
info utility, 15-16
KDE help browser, 17

Navigator Application Edit dialog box, 307

Navigator Edit menu, 303

NCD X terminals, connecting to Linux, 593

ncftp command, 292-293. *See also* ftp command

Netnews, 635

Netnews Transport Protocol (NNTP), 635

Netrom Nodes, 594

Netscape, 594
Communicator
  downloading, 300-303
  installing, 300-303
  licensing information, 301
  Linux, 301
  plug-ins, 306
  preferences, 303
  rvplayer, 306
  starting from command line, 303
  video support, 306-307
  X11, 303
configuring external applications, 239
downloading files, 293-294
helper applications, 238-240
Messenger, 274
  accessing help, 274
  configuring, 275-277
  creating email messages, 279
  Identity Preference dialog box, 277
  Mail Server dialog box, 278

replying to/forwarding email, 279
retrieving email, 278
setting preferences, 276
starting, 275
Navigator
configuring, 305
telnet, 311
nsmail directory, 277
plug-ins (rvplayer), 244
Real/Video Player, 307
setting preferences, 238
starting from command line, 238

netstat command, 613

network configuration tool. *See* linuxconf

Network File System. *See* NFS

Network Information Service (NIS), 635

Network Transparent Access (NTA), 191

networks
configuring
kernel network devices, 557, 567
kernel network options, 551-554, 566
linuxconf, 412
settings (DHCP), 411
connections
configuring, 407, 411, 415-417
customizing login greetings, 442
connectivity, 549
domain name, 413
file systems, mounting, 463
firewalls, 553, 587, 630
hostname, 413
IP accounting, 553
IP Aliasing, 553
IP tunneling, 553
LANs, 633
loopback interface, 406-407

mounting directories, 425
multicasting, 553
PLIP interfaces, 418
protocols, 553
routers, 421, 553
security, 553
setting default gateways, 408
starting/stopping services, 447
subnets, 640
system administrators, 640
testing
connectivity, 409
name resolution, 410
Token-Ring, 595
virtual private, 592

newsgroups
Linux, 580
newsreaders
Lynx browser, 300
tin, 641

NFS (Network File System), 425, 559, 635
automounting, 559
configuring, 425
clients, 426
servers, 426
enabling, 425-426, 428-429
hard drives,
mounting/unmounting, 126
mount options, 465

NIS (Network Information Service), 589, 635

\nnn character, 107

NNTP (Netnews Transport Protocol), 635

noauto option (mount command), 460

nodev option (mount command), 460

noexec option (mount command), 460

non-rewindable tape devices, 518

nosuid option (mount command), 460

nouser option (mount command), 460

no_warn argument, 384

nsmail directory, 277

NT loader, 593

NTA (Network Transparent Access), 191

ntsysv utility, 448

Null Statements, 635

numeric characters, 626

O

-o switch (gcc compiler), 341

objects, 635

Open Software Foundation (OSF), 635

Open Sound System, 240

open source, 7

opening connections, 287

OpenLinux, starting, 175

operating systems, booting multiple, 354

operators, 635
Boolean, 335
redirection
cat command, 40
shells, 24-25

optimizing programs, 341

optional configuration file, 384

options, 635
file systems, 463
PPP, 427-428
rpm, 482-484

Oracle, 589

ordering print jobs, 95

organizing shell functions, 337

orphaned processes, 539

OSF (Open Software Foundation), 635

OSTYPE environment variable, 101

output
error output, 26
redirection, 24-25
xwdtopnm command, 233

overwriting
files, 25, 45
partitions, 120

ownership
files, 378
groups
chgrp command, 378
gpasswd command, 377

P

P command (top command), 541

packages. *See also* software
conflicts, 485
converting between package methods, 500-501
failed verification tests, 492
installing, 483-486, 498
pcmcia, 138
xrpm client
listing by groups, 498
pcmcia, 138
querying, 482
rpm, 488-489
xrpm, 497
removing xrpm, 497
rpm utility, 482-483, 486, 492, 496, 500
options, 491
querying, 488-491
uninstalling, 487
upgrading, 486
verifying, 491-492

pager commands, 41-42

pagers, 594

PAM (Password Authentication Module), 382-384
configuration files, 383-386
installing, 382-383
login configuration, 386-387
system log files, 387

pam_pwdb.so module, 385-386

paper saving, 79-80

Parallel Line Interface Protocol. *See* PLIP interfaces

parallel port printers, 88

parameters, 635
command line, 626
passing from LILO prompt, 354

parent directory, periods (..), 37

parent processes, 432, 539, 636

parent shells, 636

partitioning, 114-117
adding partitions to file systems, 462
boot record, 352
changing type, 121
DOS partitions, 118
hard drives, 121
manipulating partitions (sfdisk command), 123
overwriting partitions, 120
printing partition tables, 121
rescuing deleted partitions, 594
Windows 95 partitions, 118

passwd command, 11, 614

password configuration file, 383

password keywords, 268

passwords, 367, 636
changing, 11, 382-384
configuration files, 383-386
groups, 363
installing, 382-383
login configuration, 386-387
PPP connections, 160
protecting Zip drives, 134-135
screen savers, 180
system log files, 387
telnet, 310, 312-313
users, 362

pasting text, 206-208

PATH environment variable, 101, 104-108, 594

$PATH variable, 622

pathnames, 636

Pattern Selection dialog box, 220

patterns (wildcards), 31

pbm (Portable Bitmap) programs, 229-233

PC Cards, 138
cardctl command
ejecting cards, 144
inserting cards, 144
listing configuration, 143-144
schemes, 142
slots, 142
status checks, 143
suspending/restoring power, 145
cardmgr daemon, 138, 141
beep codes, 140
configuring, 139-140
disabling PC card notification, 142
listing PC cards, 141
controllers, 139
Linux compatibility, 139
Linux-supported cards list Web site, 139
pcmcia package, 138
serial ports, 155

pci file, 540

PCs, booting, 352

pdf files, 234
  Adobe Acrobat Reader,
    237-240
  previewing, 222
  reading, 237

PDPs (Personal Data
  Processors), 636

periods (..) (parent directory), 37

peripherals
  tape drives, 130-131
  Zip drives, 132, 134

Perl, 636

permissions (files), 636
  chown command, 379-382
  SetGID, 382
  SetUID, 381

persistent variables
  env command, 327
  export command, 328

Personal Data Processors
  (PDPs), 636

-pg switch (gcc compiler),
  341

PGP (Pretty Good Privacy),
  636

phone lines, 251

pico editor, 72-73
  commands, 73
  file protection, 73
  jpico, 74
  keyboard commands, 74

PIDs, 637

pine program, 636
  configuration screen, 272
  creating messages, 273
  email, 271
    commands, 273
    configuring, 272
    manipulating messages,
      274

pico text editor, 72
pine email command, 33

ping command, 313
  pinging hosts, 409
  PPP connection speed, 260

pipe (|) operator, 26-27, 75

pipes, 636-637

PLIP (Parallel Line Internet
  Protocol) interfaces,
  418-419, 594
  configuring, 419
  TCP/IP, 420

Plug and Play hardware, 534
  BIOS, 534
  Plug-and-Play toolset, 534
  sound card configuration,
    532

plug-ins
  GIMP, 217
  Netscape
    Communicator, 306
    rvplayer, 244

pnm (Portable Anymap) programs, 229-233

pnmflip command, 233

pnmtotiff command, 233

point-to-point protocol. See
  PPP

pointers (mouse), 184

poll keywords, 268

polymorphism, 637

POP (Post Office Protocol),
  266, 594

Portable Anymap (pnm) programs, 229-233

Portable Bitmap (pbm) programs, 229-233

Portable Document Format.
  See pdf files

Portable Operating System
  Interface (POSIX), 637

porting, 340

porting software, 580

ports
  parallel, 88
  serial, 154
    modems, 154-155
    PC cards, 155
    setserial command, 156
    status, 154-155
    technical details, 157

POSIX (Portable Operating
  System Interface), 637

Post Office Protocol (POP),
  266, 594

PostScript, 637

PostScript previewers,
  234-236

pound sign (#), 106, 391, 622

power
  APM
    drivers, 574
    enabling, 573-575
    make xconfig command,
      574
  PC cards,
    suspending/restoring, 145

PPIDs (parent process identifiers), 636

PPP (point-to-point protocol), 160, 266, 413, 589,
  637
  activating interface at boot
    time, 415, 417
  activating/deactivating, 418
  closing, 258
  configuring
    connections, 250-251
    ISP, 253
    kppp, 255
    for a Linux machine, 413
    scripts, 254, 257
  creating dialup accounts,
    256
  customizing connections,
    415
  dial-in PPP service,
    160-161

/etc/resolv.conf file,
253-254
enabling support, 252
file system support, 252
firewalls, 592
ifconfig command, 259
interface information, 261
kernel support, 251-252
kppp utility, 161
links, 427
minicom program, 257-258
modem check, 251
options, 427-428
ppp-off script, 258
ppp-on script, 255, 258
pppd daemon, 160
replacing SLIP, 420
restarting, 415
scripts, 252
security, 160
software, 252
speed check, 260
starting, 257-258
statistics, 260
TCP/IP, 420
testing, 417-418
testing connections, 259
troubleshooting, 261-263
PPPD (PPP daemon), 160,
257, 427
pppstats command, 260
pr command, 81
preemptive multitasking, 528
preformatted tapes (taper
backup utility), 516
Pretty Good Privacy (PGP),
636
previewing
graphics, 234
PostScript documents,
234-236
printcap, 637
printcap manual page, 90
printenv command, 100-101

printing
debugging information
(rpm), 483
directories
contents, 343-345
current directory printout,
323-326
list, 89
faxes, 165
files from command line, 93
job numbers, 30
lpc commands, 94
paper savings, 79-80
partition tables, 121
PostScript
documents/graphics,
234-236
print jobs, 95
controlling, 93-96
printers, 133
activating, 89
adding, 88, 90
checking, 88-89
configuring, 90-92
controlling, 93-96
creating file entries, 90
detecting, 89
loadable code module, 89
local, 90
parallel port, 88
selecting, 92
serial, 90
spooling files, 92-93
pwd command, 36
queues, 93
redirecting, 93
reordering jobs, 95
staircase, 91
status, 93
stopping, 95
text documents, 92
variable values, 100
priority settings (processes),
538
probe command, 139
/proc directory, 539
cpuinfo file, 540
interrupts file, 540

pci file, 540
security, 539
version file, 540
/proc file system, 468
procedures. See functions
processes, 637
background, 625
child, 539
CPU time, 541
cron, 395
IDs, 538, 543
init, 432
actions, 391
chkconfig command, 4
36-437
init script development checklist, 440-441
init script example, 438-440
levels, 390
run levels, 434
sanity checkers, 436
spawning processes, 538
kill command, 543-544
killall command, 544
login, 432
managing, 538-539
orphaned, 539
parent, 432, 539, 636
priority settings, 538
rights, 539
running time, 541
subprocesses, 640
system load, 540
terminating
cautions, 544
kill command, 543-544
killall command, 544
user IDs, 543
viewing
ps utility, 542-543
top command, 540-541
zombie, 539
processing commands, 322
procmail program, 281-282
profile files, 100
profiles (modems), 157

programming
awk, 624
C (language), 625
I/O ports, 593
Perl, 636
polymorphism, 637
SCSI, 589
serial ports, 590

programs. *See also* scripts
access timestamps, 465
autoexpect, 28-29
background, killing, 30
bringing to foreground, 30
bugs, 625
compiling
C/C++, 340-341
debugging, 341
ld linker, 341-342
optimizing, 341
troubleshooting, 348
X11, 349
configure target, 346
controlling, 29-30
job control, 29
killing, 31
documentation, 347
downloading, 347-349
email, 269
finger, 629
getty, customizing login
greetings, 441-442
graphics conversion,
230-233
installing, 345, 348
kppp, 255
linuxconf, 462, 467
minicom, 257
modular, 341
pbm, 229-233
pine, 636
pnm, 229-233
RealPlayer 5.0, 244
running
background, 27
listing current, 30
searching, 52
security considerations, 348
shells, 322

sndconfig, 240
TKRat, 595
tpconfig, 149
usermount, 454
writing, 343-345

prompts
characters (bash shell), 106
command line, 106-108
DOS, booting Linux, 356
LILO, passing parameters,
354

protocol keywords, 268

protocols
email (PPP), 266
MPTN, 634
networks, configuring ker-
nel support, 553
POP, 266
PPP, 266, 637
TCP/IP, 640
telnet, 640
TFTP, 641
UDP, 641

ps command, 30-31, 614

ps utility, 542-543

**PS1 environment variable,
101**

**PS2 environment variable,
101**

pwd command, 36, 614, 637

Q

qmail, 594

Quake, 589

querying packages
rpm, 488-489
software, 482
xrpm, 497

queues (email), 593

quitting (ftp command), 290

quotas, 594, 637

quoting, 638

R

**R command (mail program),
270-271**

**r command (top command),
541**

RAID, 595

**ramdisk support, configuring
kernels, 551**

**ranges, command settings
(crontab files), 7, 397**

rc files
configuration, 394-395
scheduling, 390

**RCS (Revision Control
System), 594, 638**

read command, 332

**read-write protection (Zip
disks), 135**

reading
manual pages, 14-15
pdf files, 237

real memory, 634

RealAudio applications, 306

**RealPlayer 5.0, 243-246,
306-307**

Reboot run level, 433

rebooting, 13

recompiling kernels, 545. *See
also* compiling
compiling, 570-572
enabling APM, 573-575
installing, 573
installing new kernel
source, 545-546
kernel configuration preparation, 546-547
make config command,
547-562
make xconfig command,
562-570

Red Hat Linux
adding file systems, 462
CD equivalents, 594

KickStart program, 588
ntsysv utility
  adding run level services,
    448
  deleting run level services,
    448
  editing run level services,
    444
  starting, 448
rpm, 482
starting, 175
unable to boot, 479
usermount command, 454
Web site, 382, 582

redirecting
  appending files, 25
  data, 638
  error output, 26
  input, 25
  printing, 93
  redirection operators, 24,
    40, 75, 271
  standard output, 24
  sed editor, 76

referencing variables, 328

**reformatting hard disk parti-
tions, 456**

regular expressions, 31, 638
  egrep command, 60-62
  wildcards, 32

relative pathnames, 636

Remote Login, 638

**remote machines, pinging,
409**

**Remote Procedure Call
(RPC), 638**

**remount option (mount
command), 460**

removable devices
  drives, 518-520
  mounting options, 464-465

removable file systems, 468

removing. *See* deleting

renaming
  directories, 45-46
    gmc client, 54
    kfm client, 57
  files, 45-46
    gmc client, 54
    kfm client, 57

**repairing file systems,
473-476**

**replacing text (sed editor),
75-77**

replying to email, 279

**Request For Comment
(RFC), 638**

**required configuration file,
383**

reserved characters, 20

reserved words, 638

**resetting run level service
information, 437**

resource files, 100, 187-188

respawning daemons, 441

restarting daemons, 441

restoring
  file systems, 479
  PC card power, 145
  user files, 479

**restricting searches (find
command), 50-51**

retension command, 132

**retensioning tapes (tape dri-
ves), 132**

**reviewing system backup
strategy, 478**

**Revision Control System
(RCS), 594, 638**

rewind command, 132

**rewindable tape devices,
518-519**

rewinding devices, 130

**RFC (Request For
Comment), 638**

**rights (processes), inheriting,
539**

rjoe editor, 74

rm command, 614
  deleting
    directories, 50
    files, 49
  root, 50

rmdir command, 49, 615

**rmp utility, querying pack-
ages, 491**

**ro option (mount command),
460**

root, 638
  at command, 402
  cautions, 9, 538
  file systems, 472
  pathnames, 507
  rm command, 50
  running commands, 11-12

route command, 406, 422-423

routers
  configuring, 553
  host routes, 422
  setup, 421-423

routes, 638
  adding to kanchi, 423
  PPP interface information,
    261

RPC, 638

rpm, 482, 589, 638
  advantages over tar.gz meth-
    ods of software distribution,
    482
  install command, 483-484
  long options, 484
  managing, 493-495
  modes, 482-483
  options, 482-484
  querying packages, 488-491
    emacs, 489
    kernel, 490
  short options, 484
  Slackware Linux, 594

uninstalling packages,
486-487
upgrading packages, 486
verifying packages, 491-492
failed tests, 492
ksh, 492
vim installation, 484-485
xrpm client, installing,
496-497, 500

run levels, 432
booting, 355-356
creating, 434-435
editing, 434-435
Halt, 432
init process, 434
ksysv utility (KDE)
adding run level services,
446
deleting run level services,
447
starting, 446
Multi-User Mode, 433
Multi-User Mode Without
Networking, 433
ntsysv utility (Red Hat
Linux)
adding run level services,
448
deleting run level services,
448
editing run level services,
444
starting, 448
Reboot, 433
services
adding, 437
deleting, 437
listing, 436
resetting run level service
information, 437
Single User Mode, 432
starting run level services,
448
stopping run level services,
448

tksysv utility (X11)
adding run level services,
444-445
deleting run level services,
444-445
starting, 443
starting/stopping run level
services, 446
XDM Mode, 433

running time (processes),
541

rvplayer, 243, 306-307
color depth, 245
documentation, 244

rw option (mount com-
mand), 460

rxvt terminal windows, 198

S

\s character, 107

S command (top command),
541

sanity checkers, 436

Save button (usercfg tool),
373

saving
files, graphics
(ImageMagick), 228
shell functions, 337
text (xclipboard client), 207
window dumps
xwd, 209

scheduling
at command, 400
enabling, 400-401
running interactively, 402
specifying times, 403
troubleshooting, 401-402
atq command, 400
atrm command, 400
batch command, 400
crontab files, 390, 398
command settings,
397-399

configuration, 395,
398-399
enabling cron processes, 396
environment settings, 397
example, 398
restarting cron processes,
395
specifying start times,
397-398
starting cron processes, 395
inittab files, 390
backups, 435
code example, 392-394
configuration, 390-394
editing, 435
entries, 391, 435
init actions, 391-392
rc files, 390, 394-395

schemes (PC cards), 142

screen editors, 67-70, 73-74

screen savers
passwords, 180
X11, 179-181
xlock client, 181
xscreensaver client, 180-181
xset screen saver client, 179

screens, capturing
xv client, 210-212
xwd program, 209

scripts, 322. *See also* programs
automating tasks, 28
configure, 346
editing, 438-441
init
development checklist,
440-441
example, 438-440
login, 328
mkmf, 349
PPP
connections, 252
configuring, 254, 257
ppp-off, 258
ppp-on, 258
sed files, 76-77

shells, 322, 639
  bin directory, 325
  comments, 323
  fax shell script, 162-164
  instrumentation, 325-326
  printdir shell script example, 323-325
  printdir2 shell script example, 325-326
  shell variables example, 328, 330-332
  simplicity, 323
  variables, 328
  writing, 323
startup
  editing, 438-441
  xinitrc, 178
startx, 171
tmp directory, removing files, 328-332

SCSI (Small Computer System Interface), 638
  configuring kernel SCSI support, 554-557, 566-567
  programming, 589
  SCSI devices
    boots, 528, 537, 551, 557, 572
    identifying, 119
    removable drives, 518
  tape drives, 130
    installing, 130-131
  Zip drives, 132

search expressions (find command), 511

search paths, 410

search utilities (fgrep), 102

searching
  access time (files), 512
  directories, 50-52
  files, 50
    egrep command, 60-62
    fgrep command, 60-62
    find command, 50-51, 512
    GNOME Search Tool, 55
    grep command, 58, 60
    kfind client, 57-58

    locate command, 51-52
    strings command, 61
    tar backups, 509-510
    zgrep, 62
  finding lost files, 522
  grep utility, 631
  restricting searches (find command), 50-51
  sed editor, 75-77
  whereis command, 52
  which command, 52

security, 589
  at command, 403-404
  crontab files, 399-400
  email
    filters, 281-282
    Web sites, 281
  locking terminal, 181
  logins, 8
  networks, 553
  Password Authentication Module (PAM), 382-387
    configuration files, 383-386
    installing, 382
    login configuration, 386-387
    system log files, 387
  permissions, 636
  POP connections, 594
  PPP connections, 160
  /proc directory files, 539
  programs, compiling, 348
  spam, 280-281
  Zip disks, 135

sed editor, 75-77

sed Script File, 76-77

selecting
  email programs, 269
  file systems, 118-119
  modems, 154
  modules, 532-533
  patterns (GIMP), 220
  printers, 92
  shells, 32-34
  text editors, 64, 67-70, 73-77

sending faxes, 95-96, 164

sendmail daemon, 266

sequential files, 629

Serbian features, 590

serial devices, 154

Serial Line Internet Protocol. *See* SLIP interfaces

serial ports, 154
  checking for PPP connection, 251
  modems, 154-155
  PC cards, 155
  setserial command, 156
  status, 154-155
  technical details, 157

serial printers, 90

servers
  Apache, 592
  database, 639
  DNS, 627
  ensuring communication, 463
  FTP
    download site, 449
    testing, 450
  mail, 588, 592
  NFS, configuring, 425-426
  Web
    configuring Apache, 451-452
    enabling Apache, 450-451
    setting up, 590
    testing Apache, 451
  XF86_VGA16, 200

session configuration file, 383

sessions
  irc, 314-316
  telnet
    starting, 311-313
    testing, 313
  X11, 171

set command, 615

SetGID, 382

setserial command, 156

setting
    command paths, 104-105
    daemons, 440
    default gateways, 408
    default routes, 415
    dial-in service, 157-159
    environment variables, 102
    name server, 413
    preferences (Netscape
        Messenger), 276
    screen savers, 179

setting up
    file systems, 461, 465, 469
    newsgroup, 580
    PPP connections, 250-251
    routers, 421-423

settings, geometry, 198-199

SetUID, 381

severity (messages), 525

sfdisk command, 123

SGID (Set group ID), 639

sh shell, 322

shared code, 342

sharing modems, 595

shell environment, 639

SHELL environment vari-
    able, 101

shells, 7, 322, 639. *See also*
  command line
    ash, 322
    bash, 7, 322
        arguments, 330
        conditional constructs,
         332-335
        for statement, 336
        jobs command, 30
        looping constructs, 332,
         336
        prompt characters, 106
        true/false values, 333
    case sensitivity, 20
    changing, 33-34
    command line, 639
        editing, 20
        history support, 21

commands, 23
    creating, 24, 26-28
    within ftp command, 290
    processing, 322
configuration files, 627
csh, 322
default, 20
functions
    declaring, 337-338
    organizing, 337
    saving, 337
    writing, 336-337
kill commands, 543
Korn, 633
ksh, 103, 322
list of common, 32
multiple (virtual console),
  12
parent, 636
programs, 322, 343-345
scripts, 322, 639
    automating incremental
      backups, 521
    bin directory, 325
    comments, 323
    copying complex command
      lines, 206
    df command, 524
    du command, 524
    fax shell script, 162-164
    instrumentation, 325-326
    printdir shell script exam-
      ple, 323-325
    printdir2 shell script exam-
      ple, 325-326
    shell variables example,
      328-332
    simplicity, 323
    variables, 328
    writing, 323
selecting, 32-34
    sh, 322
    subshells, 640
    switching between, 33
    symbolic links, 46
    tcsh, deleting variables,
      103
    users, 363
    variables, 100

SHLVL environment vari-
    able, 101

short options (rpm), 484

showrc mode (rpm), 483

shutting down, 13
    editing scripts, 438-441
    rebooting, 13
    shutdown command, 13,
      615

SIGHUP signal name, 543

SIGKILL signal name, 543

signal names, 543

signals, 639

Single User Mode (run
    level), 356, 432

singly rooted file systems,
    459

sites. *See* Web sites

sizing windows, 200

Slackware Linux
    newsgroup, 581
    rpm command, 594

SLIP (Serial Line Internet
    Protocol) interfaces, 639
    activating/deactivating, 418
    adding, 416
    configuring, 417
    default routes, 417
    low-speed telephone lines,
      420
    TCP/IP, 420
    testing, 417-418

SLIP/PPP emulators, 594

slots (PC cards), 142

Small Computer System
    Interface. *See* SCSI

SNA (System Network
    Architecture), 639

sndconfig command, 533

sndconfig program, 240

soft links (ln command), 47

software, 482. *See also* packages

Alien utility, 501
Amanda, 468
Applixware office suite, 65
artificial intelligence, 592
bugs, 625
conflicts, 485
efax, 95
fax
efax, 161-162
Web sites, 162
ImageMagick, 224-228
installing rpm, 483-484
joe editor, 74
man pages (Linux), 593
open source, 7
packages
converting between package methods, 500-501
querying, 488-490
porting (newsgroup), 580
PPP, 252
Quake, 589
RAID, 595
StarOffice, 66, 595
uninstalling, 482
upgrading, 482, 486
verification, 482
Web sites, 64
WordPerfect, 64-65

Sony VAIO computers, 595

sorting directory listings, 38

sound, 588, 592

sound cards
configuring, 240
kernels, 532-534, 560-562, 570
Plug and Play, 532
device addresses, 533
drivers, selecting, 532-533
music, 240
SoundBlaster, 533
SoundBlaster AWE cards, 595

source code
compatibility, 340
compiling, 347-349

space (hard drives)
df command, 117
hidden, 123
TeX installations, 85

spaces in filenames, 20

spam
email filters, 281-282
reducing, 280-281
Web sites, 280

spawning processes, 538

special characters, 24-27, 626

speed (PPP connections), 260

spell checking
email messages, 273
ispell command, 78-79

spooling files to printer, 92-93

st module, 130

standard error output, 26

standard output redirection, 24

StarOffice, 66, 595

starting. *See also* booting
clients in desktop, 199
daemons, 441
Enlightenment, 194
GIMP, 217
gmc client, 53
GNOME, 194
KDE, 194
kpackage, 493
kppp, 255
ksysv utility (KDE), 446
linuxconf utility, 109
multiple X11 sessions, 172
Netscape
from command line, 238
Communicator, 303
Messenger, 275

network services, 447
ntsysv utility (Red Hat Linux), 448
parent processes, 432
PPP connections, 257-258
processes (init process), 538
run level services, 446-448
scripts, editing, 438-441
tksysv utility (X11), 443
top command, 541
usercfg tool, 363-364
Window Maker, 195
window managers, 193
X11, 170-171, 174-176
xclipboard client, 207
xcutsel client, 206
xrpm client, 496
xwud client, 209

startkde command, 194

startx command, 171, 245

startx script, 171

statements
else, 333
for, 336
if, 333, 335
file-testing expressions, 335
integer expressions, 334
string expressions, 334
syntax, 333
test expressions, 333
Null, 635
while, 336

status (faxes), 164

stderr, 639

stdin, 639

stdout, 639

step values (command settings), 398

sticky bits, 639

stingy-memory-use setting (GIMP), 223

stopping
network services, 447
programs, 31
run level services, 446-448

storing
storage devices, 116-117
system backups, 478

stream editors, 75

streams, 639

string expressions, 334

strings, 60-62, 327. *See also* variables

strings command, 61

su command, 11, 615

subnets, 640

subnetworking, 593

subprocesses, 640

subroutines. *See* functions

subshells, 640

substitution variables, 641

sufficient configuration file, 384

SUID (Set user ID), 640

suid option (mount command), 461

Sun Microsystems, 66, 126

Sunsite archive Web site, 357

superblocks, corrupted, 475

superusers. *See* root

support (file systems), 115

suspending PC card power, 145

swap files
changing swap-path, 223
creating, 223, 616

swapon command, 616

symbolic links, 46-48, 633
gmc client, 54
kfm client, 57
mouse, 148
shells, 46
subdirectories, 438
tape drive device, 131

Synaptics touchpad configuration, 149

sync option (mount command), 461

syntax
crontab command, 396
/etc/exports file, 426
if statement, 333
kill command, 543
verifying packages, 492
while statement, 336

sysadmin, 640

syslog daemon, 525

system backups
crontab feature, 521
floppy disks, 518
full, 519-520
incremental, 519-520
removable drives, 518-519

system files, editing, 159

system load
load average, 540
uptime command, 540

system log files
Password Authentication Module (PAM), 387
PPP connection check, 261-263

system maintenance, 521, 523
backups, 504-510, 514-516, 519
cleanup, 523-526
file deletion, 521-523
find command, 510, 512
Linux File System Standard, 525
minimizing disk space, 523, 525-526
undeleting files, 522-523

System Network Architecture (SNA), 639

system requirements (GIMP), 217

System V, 434

systems
backups, 476, 517
run levels, 432
creating, 434-435
editing, 434-435
Halt, 432
init process, 434
Multi-User Mode Without Networking, 433
Reboot, 433
Single User Mode, 432
XDM Mode, 433

T

-t option (fetchmail), 268

\t character, 107

t command (mail program), 271

T command (top command), 541

Tab key (command completion), 21

tail command, 616

talk command, 616

tape drives
backups, 132
floppy controller, 131
installing, 130-131
mt (magnetic tape) command, 131-132
retensioning tapes, 132
rewinding tapes, 130-132, 518-519
symbolic links, 131
taper backup utility, 513

taper backup utility, 513, 516
cleaning files, 525
compared to tar backups, 516
device type options, 513
menus, 514-515
preformatted tapes, 516
Test Make Tape option, 516

tar utility, 640

tar backups
  compared to taper backup
    utility, 516
  floppy disks, 518

tar command, 505, 508, 616
  archiving directories,
    507-508
  arguments, 506
  backups, 509-512
  compression archive files,
    509
  finding lost files, 522
  function identifiers, 506
  options, 507
  rewindable tape drives, 518

tar files, 506-509

targets, 342

Tcl scripting language, 590

TCP/IP (Transmission
  Control Protocol/Internet
  Protocol), 640
  configuring, 424
  connections, 420
  enabling support, 252
  multicasting, 588
  PPP, 420

tcsh shell, deleting variables,
  103

tee command, 27

television (RealPlayer 5.0),
  243-246

telnet, 640
  commands, 310-314, 616
  connections, 310-313
  downloading files, 313-314
  Netscape Navigator, 311
  passwords, 310-313
  Remote Login, 638
  sessions
    starting, 311-313
    testing, 313

temporary environment variables, 103

temporary files, 223

tension strength, 132

TERM environment vari-
  able, 101

TERM signal name, 543

$TERM variable, 622

termcap file, 108

terminal windows
  configuring, 186
  copying text, 206
  pasting text, 206

terminals, 640
  definitions, 108
  termcap, 640

terminating
  processes
    cautions, 544
    kill command, 543-544
    killall command, 544
    user IDs, 543
  programs, 31

test expressions, 333-335

Test Make Tape options,
  516

testing
  Apache Web server, 451
  DNS configuration, 410
  failed verifications (pack-
    ages), 492
  fax service configuration,
    163
  FTP servers, 450
  loopback addresses, 407
  modems, 155
  name resolution (networks),
    410
  network connectivity, 409
  PPP connections, 259
    ifconfig command, 259
  speed (ping command), 260
  PPP interfaces, 417-418
  programs, security, 348
  rvplayer plug-in, 307
  search expressions (find
    command), 511

SLIP interfaces, 417-418
telnet sessions, 313

TeX typesetting system, 80,
  85-86

text
  copying
    pasting, 148
    terminal windows, 206
    X11, 206-208
    xclipboard client, 207-208
    xcutsel client, 206-207
  documents, printing, 92
  editors, 64
    defining default, 74
    emacs, 68-71
    jed, 74
    jmacs, 74
    joe editor, 74
    jpico, 74
    jstar, 74
    pico editor, 72-73
    rjoe, 74
    screen editors, 67-70, 73-74
    sed editor, 75-77
    selecting, 64, 67-70, 73-77
    stream editors, 75
    UNIX, 71-72
    vi, 71-72
    vim, 71-72
  files, 629
    downloading, 289
    editing, 357
    retrieving (Lynx browser),
      298
    utilities, 357
    viewing, 39-42
  formatting, 80, 82, 85
  pasting
    terminal windows, 206
    X11, 206-208
  processing languages, 640
  saving, 207
  search and replace functions,
    75-76
  spell checking, 78-79
  terminals, 590

text-only browsers (Lynx), 296

text-processing systems, 82-86

TFTP (Trivial File Transfer Protocol), 641

time
at command, 403
command settings (crontab files), 397
start times (crontab files), 397-398

timestamps
access, 465

tin utility, 641

title bar (X11 windows), 200-201

Tk scripting language, 590

TKRat mail program, 595

tksysv utility
adding run level services, 444-445
deleting run level services, 444-445
starting, 443
starting/stopping run level services, 446

Token-Ring networks, 595

top command, 617
case-sensitivity, 541
command options, 541
starting, 541
viewing processes, 540-541

top utility, 641

topq command, 95

Torvalds, Linus, 6

touch command, 43, 512

touchpads, 149

tpconfig command, 149-150

translating graphics, 229-233

transport agents, 266

trash, (KDE), 57

trees
directory, compressing, 505
file systems, 472
organization, 473

Trivial File Transfer Protocol (TFTP), 641

troubleshooting
at command, 401-403
backing up hostnames, 410
booting LILO, 353
i386 kernel, 588
modem connections, 251
PPP connections, 261-263
PPP connections (ifconfig command), 259
programs, compiling, 348
sound cards, 240

try_first_pass argument, 384

tsch interface, 640

tutorials (emacs), 69

tuxedo.org Web site, 7

TV (RealPlayer 5.0), 243-246

typesetting, 80
groff system, 82-85
TeX system, 85-86
text-process systems, 82-86

typing variables, 328

U

-u option (fetchmail), 268

\u character, 107

UDP (User Datagram Protocol), 641

UIDs. See User IDs

UIL (User Interface Language), 641

umount command, 617

UMSDOS file system, 590

unalias command, 617

undeleting files, 522-523

uninstalling
packages(rpm), 486-487
software, 482

UNIX, 590
AT&T, 624
Berkeley, 434
BSD, 92, 625
compatibility, 340
fseek function, 630
porting, 340
reserved words, 638
single-user mode, 356
System V, 434
text editors, 71-72

UNIX-to-UNIX copy program (UUCP), 641

unlocking users, 369

unmounting
floppy disks, 471
Zip disk, 134

unzip command, 617

updates
newsgroup, 580

updating
directories (touch command), 43
files
access times, 512
touch command, 43

upgrading
Linux, 595
packages (rpm), 486
software, 482

uptime command, 540

URLs, 641

Usenet
Linux, 580
Lynx browser, 300

User Configurator. See user-cfg tool

User Datagram Protocol (UDP), 641

User Environment Variables, 101

User IDs (UIDs), 362-364, 641
  groups, 362
  processes, 538
    terminating processes, 543

User Interface Language (UIL), 641

user list, 363

user option (mount command), 461

$USER variable, 622

useradd command, 9, 374

usercfg tool, 363
  Archive User window, 368
  groups
    adding, 371-372
    editing, 373
    removing, 373
  Save button, 373
  starting, 363-364
  users
    adding, 365-367
    editing, 367-368
    locking, 368-369
    removing, 370-371
    unlocking, 369
    viewing, 367-368

userdel command, 375, 604

usermod command, 374-375

usermount command, 454-456

username
  creating, 9
  email, 277
  login comparison, 362

users, 362-363
  accounts, creating, 8
    command line, 9
    X11, 9-10
  adding
    to groups, 377
    useradd command, 374
    usercfg tool, 365-367
  agents, 266, 269-276

configuration information, 374
deleting, 370-371, 375
editing
    usercfg tool, 367-368
    usermod command, 374-375
files
    home directory path, 362
    restoring, 479
ftp, 286
information, 362
locking, 368-369
logins, 8
root
    at command, 402
    cautions, 9
    running commands, 11-12
superusers, 640
system administrators, 640
UIDs, 641
unlocking, 369
viewing, 367-368

use_first_pass argument, 384

use_mapped_pass argument, 384

/usr file systems, 472

/usr/local directory, 624

utilities. *See also* commands
  Alien, 500-501
  ar, 624
  autofs, 592
  backup
    mt command, 131
    taper, 513-516
  biff, 625
  bzip2, 592, 625
  compress, 627
  elm, 628
  finger, 629
  gpm, 148-149
  grep, 631
  info, 15-16
  kpackage, 493
    package groups, 493
    removing packages, 495

kppp, 161
ksysv
    adding run level services, 446
    deleting run level services, 447
    starting, 446
linuxconf, 109-110
    creating user accounts, 9-10
    mounting file systems, 126
minicom, 257
ntsysv
    adding run level services, 448
    deleting run level services, 448
    editing run level services, 444
    starting, 448
ps, 542-543
qmail, 594
rpm, 482-483, 486, 492, 496, 500
search (fgrep), 102
tksysv
    adding run level services, 444-445
    deleting run level services, 444-445
    starting, 443
    starting/stopping run level services, 446
xargs, 522

UUCP (UNIX-to-UNIX copy program), 641

uugetty command, 159

V

-v option (fetchmail), 268

value-added resellers of Linux software, 590

/var/spool directory, 624

variables, 327. *See also* strings
  attribute, 641
  bash shell, 103

defining (ksh shell), 103
deleting (tcsh shell), 103
environment, 622, 641
   deleting from command line, 103
   displaying, 100-102
   PATH, 104-108
   setting, 100-105
   temporary, 103
exporting, 102
login shell scripts, editing, 328
PATH, 104-108
persistent
   env command, 327
   export command, 328
referencing, 328
shell scripts, 328-332
substitution, 641
typing, 328
User Environment Variables, 101
value, printing, 100

verifying
packages (rpm), 491-492
software, 482

version file, 540

vfat driver, loading into kernel, 458

vfat file system, 114, 134

vi text editor, 71-72

video
file formats, 245-246
playing, 244
support (Netscape), 306-307

viewing
captures, 210
faxes, 164
fstab, 116
HOWTO documents, 586, 591-592
installed GIMP files, 222
processes
   ps utility, 542-543
   top command, 540-541

screens (xv client), 210-212
space available in storage devices, 117
text files, 39
   cat command, 40-41
   less command, 41-42
   more command, 41-42
users (usercfg tool), 367-368
X11 fonts, 202, 204

vim rpm, installing, 484-485

vim text editor, 71-72

virtual consoles, 12, 172

virtual hosting, 590

virtual memory, 634

VME bus systems, 590

vmlinuz (kernel file), 358

VPNs, 595

W

\w character, 107

wall command, 617

wallpaper (desktop), 182-183

Walnut Creek Web site, 582

WANs, 641

Web servers
Apache
   configuring, 451-452
   enabling, 450-451
   inetd, 450
   testing, 451
   Web site, 450
setting up, 590

Web sites
Adobe Acrobat Reader, 237
Alien (downloading), 500
Amanda (backup software), 468
Apache, 450
Applix Inc, 65
Caldera, 581
Corel, 64
Debian Linux, 582
dict clients, 79

downloading
   Alien, 500
   taper backup utility, 513
   xrpm, 496
   zftape drivers, 513
emacs information, 71
Enlightenment, 192
finding applications, 581
fighting spam, 280
freshmeat.net, 162
FTP server download site, 449
GIMP, 224
GNU, 7
Infomagic, 582
Iomega, 133
KDE, 191, 632
Ken Lee's X and Motif, 582
kernel FTP site, 545
Linux, 581-583
linux conf (downloading), 462
Linux Documentation Project, 133, 531-533, 586
Linux Journal, 583
Linux-supported PC cards Web site, 139
linuxconf homepage, 412
ncftp command information, 292
Netscape, 300
Open Sound System, 240
open source, 7
Plug-and-Play toolset, 534
RealPlayer 5.0, 243
Red Hat Software Inc., 382, 582
software related, 64
Sun Microsystems, 66
Sunsite archive, 357
text file utilities, 357
tuxedo.org, 7
Walnut Creek, 582
WordPerfect for Linux, 65
XFree86 Project, Inc., 583
XFree86 supported graphics cards, 171
xrpm (downloading), 496

web2 dictionary, 77

whatis command, 17

whereis command, 52, 104

which command, 52

while statement, 336

whitespace, 641

who command, 617-618

whoami command, 12

wildcards, 641
  command line, 31-32
  ls command, 38
  patterns, 31
  regular expressions, 31-32

win, 422-425

window dumps, 209

Window Maker, 193-195

window managers, 190
  Enlightenment, 192
  KDE, 191
  selecting
    X11, 190
  starting, 193-195
  use, 190
  Window Maker, 193
  xinitrc, 193

windows
  Archive User window (user-cfg tool), 368
  capturing, 208-213
    portions, 211
    xwd program, 208-209
  closing (X11), 201
  configuring, 186
  maximizing/minimizing, 201
  rxvt terminal windows, 198
  saving dumps (xwd), 209
  sizing
    geometry settings, 198-199
    X11, 200
  terminal
    configuration, 186
    copying text, 206
    pasting text, 206

X11
  capturing, 210
  title bar, 200-201

Windows
  connecting machines to
    Linux system, 424-425
  guide to Linux, 587
  Windows 95 partitions, 118
  Windows NT, comparing to
    Linux, 379
  WinModems, 154

word processors
  Applixware office suite, 65
  commercial, 64
  Star Office, 66

WordPerfect, 64-65, 91-92, 595

write command, 618

writing
  init scripts, 440-441
  man pages, 593
  shell functions, 336-337
  shell scripts, 323
    instrumentation, 325-326
    printdir shell script example, 323-325
    printdir2 shell script example, 325-326
    shell variable example, 328, 330-332
    style, 323
    variables, 328

WWW, 642

WYSIWYG, 642

X

X. *See* X11

x command (mail program), 271

X Window System. *See* X11

X11, 9, 642
  clients (ImageMagick), 225
  configuring mouse, 185
  copying text, 206-208

  customizing, 179-185
  emacs, 68
  Enlightenment, 192
  fonts, 202-205
  GIMP, 217
  graphics conversion programs, 233
  gv command, 234
  help (xman client), 15
  Imakefile, 349
  joysticks, 151
  linuxconf utility, 9-10
  logging on, 173, 176
  Lynx browser, 296
  make xconfig command, 562-570
    Code Maturity Options button, 563
    help, 564
    Loadable Module Support button, 564
  makefile command, 349
  multimedia (xanim), 245
  Netscape Communicator, 303
  pasting text, 206-208
  pdf files (Adobe Acrobat Reader), 237-240
  programs, compiling, 349
  radio, 243
  resource files, 187-188
  screen savers
    passwords, 180
    xlock, 181
    xscreensaver, 180-181
    xset, 179
  selecting window managers, 190
  setting mouse pointer, 184
  shut down, 173
  starting, 170-171, 174-176
  switching to virtual console, 172
  television, 243
  tksysv utility
    adding run level services, 444-445
    deleting run level services, 444-445

starting, 443
starting/stopping run level services, 446
toolkit, 198-200
user account creation, 9-10
virtual consoles, 172
Window Maker, starting, 195
window managers, 190
windows
 capturing, 210
 closing, 201
 maximizing, 201
 minimizing, 201
 moving, 200
 sizing, 200
 title bar, 200-201
xdm, 173
 banner screens, 176-177
 Red Hat Linux, 176
 XF86_VGA16 server, 200
 xinitrc startup script, 178
 xjed editor, 74
 xplaycd command, 242
 xrpm client, installing, 496-497, 500

xanim program, 245-246

xargs utility, 522

xbanner command, 176

xcalc, 23

xclipboard client
 copying text, 207-208
 saving text, 207
 starting, 207

XConfigurator, configuring XFree86, 170

xcutsel client
 copying text, 206-207
 starting, 206

xdm
 banner screens, 177
 configuring, 174-175

xdm command, 173, 176
XDM Mode (run level), 433
Xemacs, 69, 200
xfd client, viewing font character maps, 203-205
xfontsel client, viewing fonts, 203
XFree86, 591
 configuring, 170
 XFree86 Project, Inc. Web site, 583
xhost command, 618
xinit command, 178
.xinitrc system file, 194
xinitrc
 startup script, 178
 window managers, 193
xjed editor, 74
xloadimage client, viewing captures, 210
xloadimage command (desktop wallpaper), 182-183
xlock screen saver client, 181
xlsfonts command, 202-203
xmag client, 212-213
xman client, 15
xmkmf command, 618
xmodmap client (mouse configuration), 186
xplaycd command, 242-243
xrpm client
 installing, 496-497, 500
 installing packages, 498
 listing packages by groups, 498
 querying packages, 497
 removing packages, 497
 starting, 496

xscreensaver screen saver client, 180-181
xset command, 618
xset screen saver client, 179
xsetroot command
 cursor changing, 184
 desktop color, 182
 desktop pattern, 182
xterm terminals, configuring, 186
xv client
 capturing and viewing screens, 210-212
 xwd command, 233
xwd program, capturing windows, 208-209
xwdtopnm command, 233
xwud client, 209

Y - Z

yacc (yet another compiler compiler), 642

zftape drivers, downloading, 513
zgrep command, 62
zip command, 619
Zip drives, 132, 134
 disk capacity, 132
 ejecting disks, 134-135
 installing, 133
 parallel printer support, 133
 protecting, 134
 security, 135
ziptool command, 134
zombie processes, 539
Zoom commands (GIMP), 222

Other Related Titles